Member of the Guild of Motoring Writers

and P G Strasman

**Models covered:**

UK: SAAB 95 Estate, 1498 cc
SAAB 96 Saloon, 1498 cc

USA: SAAB 95 Wagon, 91.4 cu in. and 104 cu in.
SAAB 96 Sedan, 91.4 cu in. and 104 cu in.

**ISBN 978 0 85733 925 6**



ABCDE
FGHIJ
KLMNO
2

**Printed in the UK** *(198–6N3)*

**Haynes Publishing Group**
Sparkford Nr Yeovil
Somerset BA22 7JJ England

**Haynes Publications, Inc**
859 Lawrence Drive
Newbury Park
California 91320 USA

# Acknowledgements

SAAB - SCANIA of America Inc. kindly gave us permission to reproduce certain of their illustrations and also provided technical information.

Our thanks to Brian Horsfall, who not only lent his own SAAB 96 but carried out all of the mechanical work shown in the photographs which illustrate this manual. He also devised many ingenious methods of overcoming the lack of special tools during the dismantling and reassembly of the car.

Thanks are due to everyone at Sparkford who helped with the preparation of this manual: particularly Les Brazier who took the photograhs, Rod Grainger who edited the text and Stanley Randolph who planned the layout of each page.

Castrol Limited provided lubrication details.

# About this manual

## Its aims

This manual shows how to maintain these cars in first class condition and how to carry out repairs when components become worn or break. By doing all maintenance and repair work themselves owners will gain in three ways: they will know the job has been done properly; they will have had the satisfaction of doing the job themselves; and they will have saved garage labour charges. Regular and careful maintenance is essential if maximum reliability and minimum wear are to be achieved.

All the major mechanical and electrical assemblies and most of the minor ones as well have been stripped, overhauled, and rebuilt. Only through working in this way can solutions be found to the sort of problems facing private owners. Other hints and tips are also given which can only be obtained through practical experience.

The step-by-step photographic strip and rebuild sequences shown how each of the major components was removed, taken apart, and rebuilt. In conjunction with the text and exploded illustrations this should make all the work quite clear - even to the novice who has never previously attempted the more complex job.

Although SAAB vehicles are hardwearing and robust, it is inevitable that their reliability and performance will decrease as they become older. Repairs and general reconditioning will become necessary if the car is to remain roadworthy. It is in these circumstances that the manual will prove to be of maximum help, as it is the *only* workshop manual written from practical experience especially for owners of cars covered in this manual (as opposed to service operators and garage proprietors).

Manufacturers' official manuals are usually splendid publications which contain a wealth of technical information. However, because they are issued primarily to help the manufacturers' authorised dealers and distributors they tend to be written in a very technical language, and skip details of certain jobs which are common knowledge to garage mechanics. *Haynes Owner's Workshop Manuals* are different as they are intended primarily to help the owner, and therefore contain details of all sorts of jobs nor normally found in official manuals.

Owners who intend to do their own maintenance and repairs should have a reasonably comprehensive tool kit. Some jobs require special service tools, but in many instances it is possible to get round their use with a little care and ingenuity.

When a component malfunctions garage repairs are becoming more a case of replacing the defective item with an exchange rebuilt unit. This is excellent practice when a component is thoroughly worn out, but is a waste of good money when overall the component is only half worn, and requires the replacement of but a single small item to effect a complete repair. As an example, a non-functioning starter motor can frequently be repaired quite satisfactorily just by fitting new brushes.

A further function of this manual is to show the owner how to examine malfunctioning parts; determine what is wrong; and then how to make the repair.

Given the time, mechanical do-it yourself aptitude, and a reasonable collection of tools, this manual will shown the enthusiastic owner how to maintain and repair his car really economically with minium recourse to professional assistance and expensive tools and equipment.

Threads are UNC throughout with the exception of a few proprietary components. AF sized spanners and sockets are suitable.

## Using the manual

The manual is divided into twelve Chapters. Each Chapter is divided into numbered Sections which are headed in **bold** type between horizontal lines. Each Section comprises serially numbered paragraphs and is referred to in the text as 'Chapter 1, Section 5 . If the Chapter is not mentioned, the Section referred to is in the same Chapter in which the reference occurs.

Whenever the left or right-hand side of a car is mentioned, it is assumed that one is facing forward in the direction of travel.

There are two types of illustration: Figures which are numbered in sequence within each Chapter, eg; Fig 2.7 is the 7th illustration in Chapter 2; and photographs, which are given the same number as the Section and paragraph number where the description occurs, eg; 17.23 belongs to paragraph 23 of Section 17 in that chapter.

Every care has been taken to ensure the accuracy of the information given in this manual but no liability can be accepted by the authors and publishers for any loss, damage or injury caused by any errors in, or omissions from, the information given.

# Contents

SAAB 96 V4

SAAB 95 V4

# Introduction to the SAAB 95 and 96 models

The SAAB 95 Estate car and 96 Saloon were originally introduced to the UK market in October 1960. These models were fitted with three cylinder two stroke engines and three speed gearboxes.

Modifications to both mechanical and body components continued until October 1966 when a Ford Taunus V4 engine and 4 speed gearbox became optionally available on the Saloon only. This option was extended to the Estate car in January 1967 and in January 1968 the two stroke engine and 3 speed gearbox versions were withdrawn from the UK market.

This manual covers V4 engined models produced from October 1966 onwards and includes the Estate (95) the Saloon (96) and the Monte Carlo (Sport) versions. The latter was discontinued at the end of 1968.

# Buying spare parts and vehicle identification numbers

Spare parts are available from many sources, for example SAAB garages, other garages and accessory shops, and motor factors. Our advice regarding spare part sources is as follows:

*Officially appointed SAAB garages* - This is the best source of parts which are peculiar to your car and are otherwise not generally available (eg; complete cylinder heads, internal gearbox components, badges, interior trim etc). It is also the only place at which you should buy parts if your car is still under warranty: non-SAAB components may invalidate the warranty. To be sure of obtaining the correct parts it will always be necessary to give the storeman your car's engine and chassis number, and if possible, to take the 'old' part along for positive identification. Remember that many parts are available on a factory exchange scheme - any parts returned should always be clean! It obviously makes good sense to go straight to the specialists on your car for this type of part for they are best equipped to supply you.

*Other garages and accessory shops* - These are often very good places to buy materials and components needed for the maintenance of your car (eg spark plugs, bulbs, fanbelts, oils and greases, touch-up paint, filler paste, etc). They also sell general accessories, usually have convenient opening hours, charge lower prices and can often be found not far from home.

*Motor factors* - Good factors will stock all of the more important components which wear out relatively quickly (eg clutch components, pistons, valves, exhaust systems, brake cylinders/pipes/hoses/seals/shoes and pads etc). Motor factors will often provide new or reconditioned components on a part exchange basis - this can save a considerable amount of money.

### Vehicle identification numbers

The illustrations clearly show the orientation of all vehicle identification numbers.

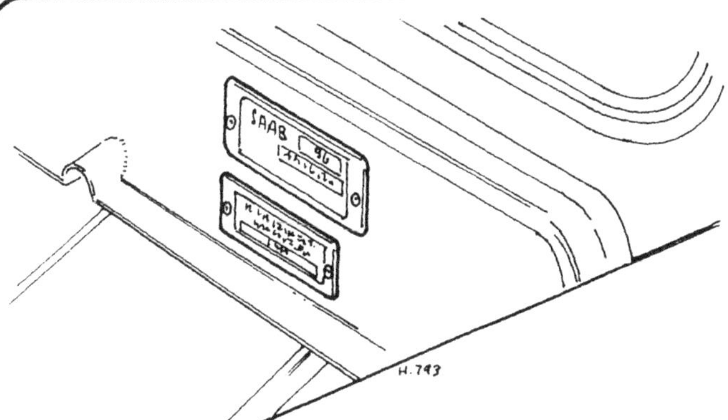

RM10 Location of chassis number (up to 1967) on engine bulkhead

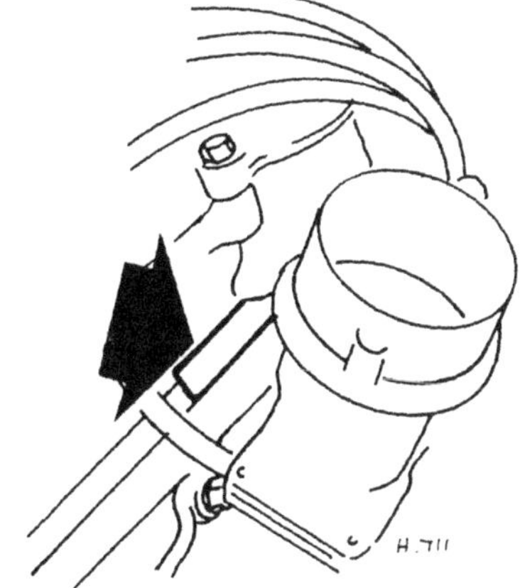

RM11 Location of engine number (up to 1965)

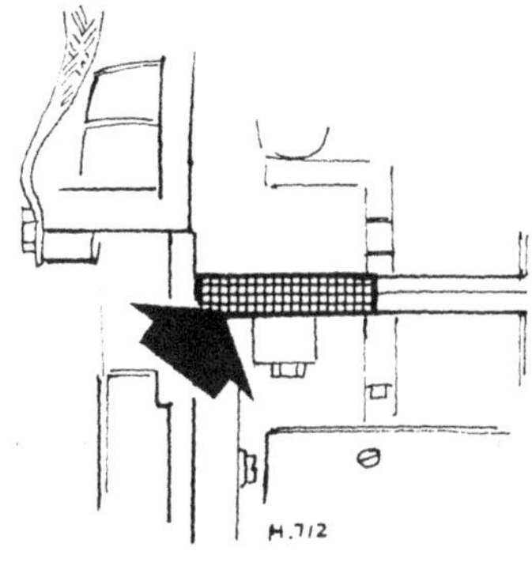

RM12 Location of engine number (1966/67)

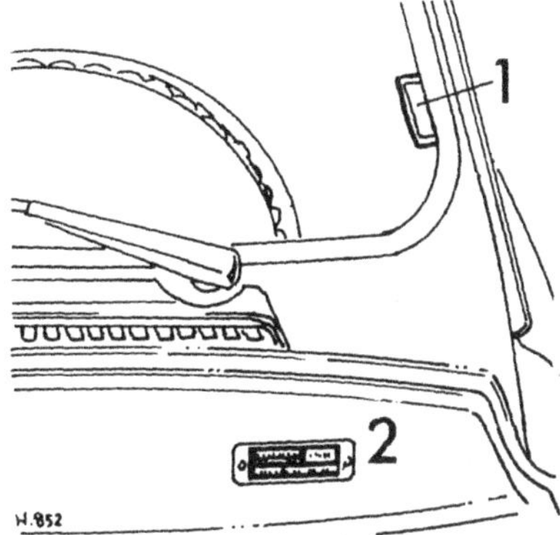


RM14 Location of chassis number (1) and joint colour code (2) of USA cars from 1969 on

**RM13 Location of vehicle identification numbers 1967 onwards**

*Engine number* *Gearbox number* *Colour code and chassis number* *Chassis number imprinted in car body*

# Routine maintenance

The maintenance instructions listed are basically those recommended by the manufacturer. They are supplemented by additional maintenance tasks proven to be necessary.

The additional tasks are indicated by an asterisk (*) and are primarily of a preventative nature in that they will assist in eliminating the unexpected failure of a component due to fair wear and tear.

Maintenance instructions are repeated in certain Chapters where they form part of the repair and servicing procedures.

When a new car is delivered the engine contains sufficient oil for the running-in period. Providing the level is maintained between the low and high marks on the dipstick during this period, topping-up is unnecessary. At the first 'Free service', the running-in oil is drained and the sump replenished to the level of the high mark on the dipstick.

## Every 250 miles (400 km) or at weekly intervals

1 Check the engine oil level and top-up if necessary.
2 Check the coolant level in the cooling system.
3 Check the operation of all lights and direction indicator flashers and renew any faulty bulbs.
4 Check the fluid levels in the clutch and brake hydraulic system reservoirs.
5 Check and inflate the tyres (including the spare) to the

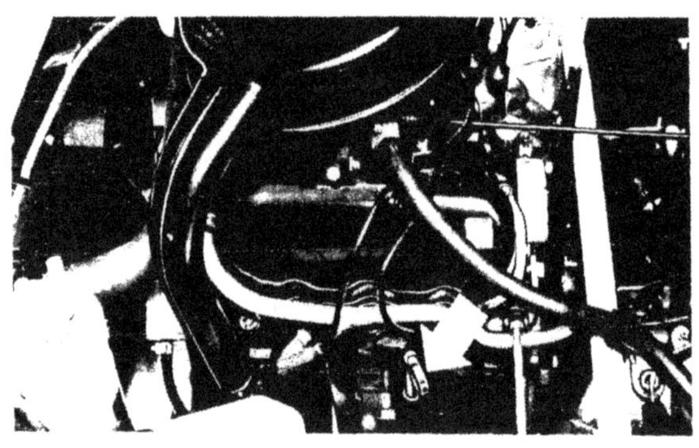

RM1 Location of dipstick

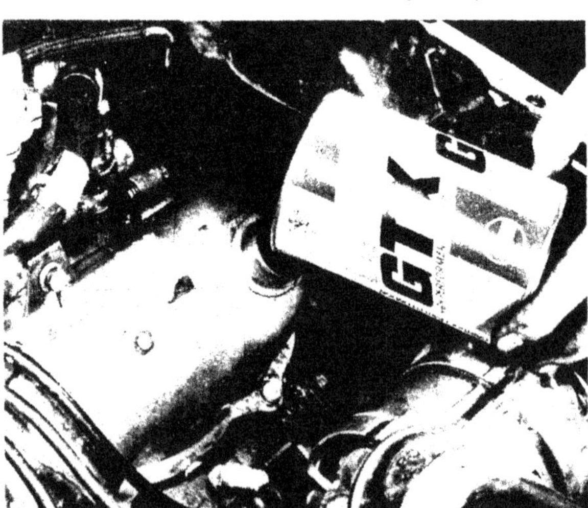

P Topping up engine oil

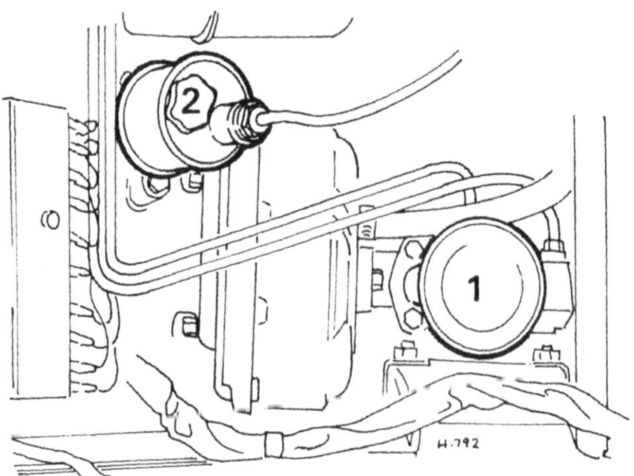


RM2 Brake (1) and clutch (2) fluid reservoirs

P1 Topping up hydraulic reservoir

recommended pressures.
6 Refill the windscreen washer bottle and check that the jets are clear and correctly adjusted.
7 Check the electrolyte level in the battery.
8 Wash the bodywork free from mud and dirt and touch up any chips or scratches to prevent rust setting in.

## At the first 1200 miles (1900 km)

1 Tighten the cylinder head bolts to the specified torque and in the correct sequence.
2 Check and adjust the valve clearances.
3 Check and tighten all accessible nuts and bolts on engine and bodyshell.
4 Change the engine oil.
5 Change the transmission oil and clean the magnetic drain plug.
6 Check the coolant level in the radiator.
7 Check the fluid level in the clutch master cylinder reservoir.
8 Adjust the clutch free-movement if necessary.
9 Check the operation of all lamps, direction indicators, etc.
10 Check, and top-up if necessary, the battery electrolyte level.
11 Check and adjust the alternator drivebelt tension.
12 Check the ignition timing and the contact breaker points setting.
13 Check and top-up if necessary the brake fluid level in the master cylinder reservoir.
14 Adjust the rear brakes.
15 Adjust the handbrake if necessary.
16 Lubricate steering linkage ball joints on early vehicles fitted with grease nipples.
17 Check the front wheel alignment.
18 Adjust the engine idling speed and the mixture.

## Every 6000 miles (9600 km) or at six monthly intervals

1 Change the engine oil and renew the oil filter. It is recommended that you use a 'SAAB' oil filter or a replacement.
The SAAB manufactured filter incorporates a non-return valve which ensures that the lubrication system does not drain completely when the engine is switched off.
2 Adjust the valve clearances.
3 Tighten the manifold bolts.
4 Clean the air cleaner element and move its intake position

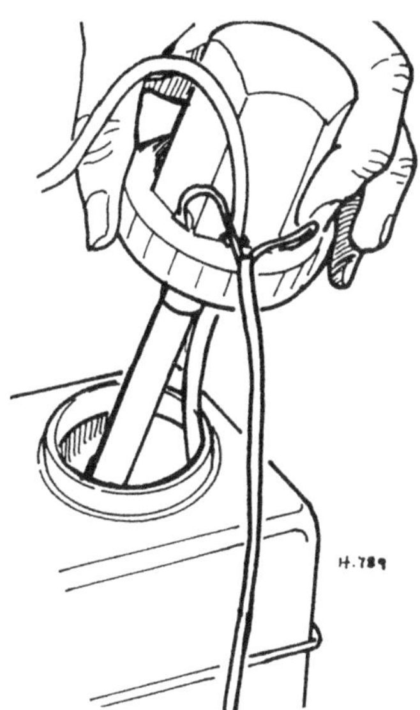


RM3 Windscreen washer reservoir

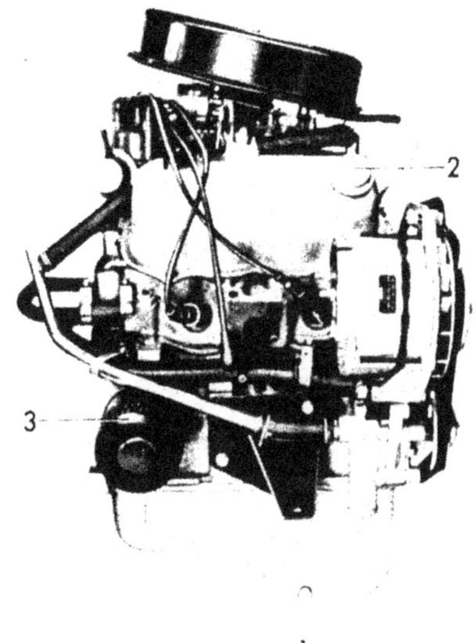


RM4 Engine oil drain plug (1), filler cap (2) and filter (3)

RM5 Transmission oil filler plug (1), level plug (2) and drain plug (3)

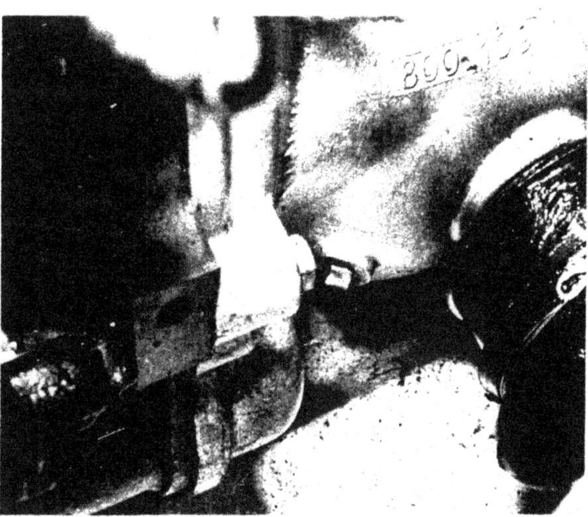

P2 Transmission unit level plug

according to season.
5 Clean the fuel pump filter.
6 Lubricate the throttle linkage.
7 Inspect the exhaust system.
8 Check the carburettor settings and exhaust emission control system adjustment and for security of connections.
9 Check the condition of the coolant hoses and renew as necessary.
10 Check the tension of the alternator drive belt and adjust if necessary. Inspect the condition of the belt and renew if necessary.
11 Check headlamp alignment.
12 Clean and adjust the spark plugs.
13 Service and lubricate the distributor and contact breaker points.
14 Check and top-up the fluid level in the clutch master cylinder reservoir.
15 Check the gearbox oil level and top-up if necessary.
16 Check and top-up if necessary the fluid level in the brake master cylinder.
17 Check the wear of the disc pads and brake linings.
18 Check the caliper units, wheel cylinders and hydraulic lines for leaks.
19 Adjust rear brakes and the handbrake if necessary.
20 Lubricate the steering linkage (early models with grease nipples).
21 Check the front wheel alignment.
22 Check the rubber bellows and dust excluding boots on all steering and suspension and driveshaft components and renew where necessary.
23 Lubricate all door hinges and locks.
24 Check the tyre tread wear.

### Every 12000 miles (19000 km) or at 12 monthly intervals

1 Renew the spark plugs.
2 Change the transmission oil and clean the magnetic drain plug.
3 Renew the fuel filter.
4 Check the steering angles (work for a SAAB dealer).
5 Service and renew if necessary the contact breaker points.
6 On SAAB 95 Estate cars, check and top-up, if necessary, the fluid in the rear shock absorbers.
7 *On models built up until 1970,* the front and rear wheel bearings must be repacked with grease as described in the relevant sections of this manual.
8 Drain and refill the coolant (antifreeze mixture).
9 Renew the air cleaner element.

### Every 24000 miles (38000 km) or at 2 yearly intervals

1 Bleed the brake hydraulic system of all old fluid and replenish with new Castrol Girling Universal Brake and Clutch Fluid which has been stored in an airtight container and has remained unshaken for at least 24 hours.
2 Check for underbody rust or corrosion and de-rust and underseal as necessary.
3 Inspect and renew if necessary the windscreen wiper blades.
4 Rebalance wheels on or off the car to compensate for tyre

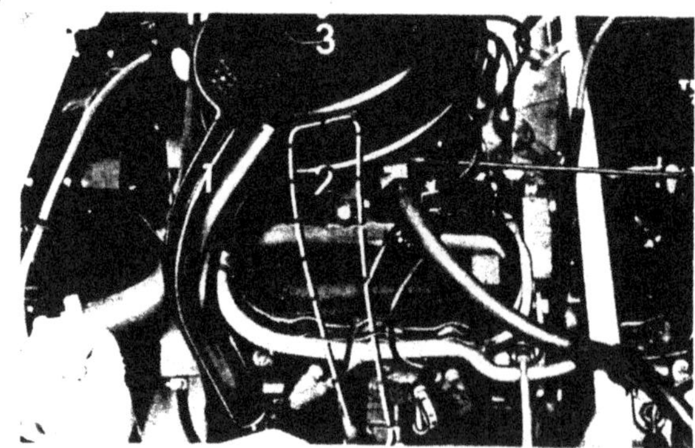


**RM6 Alternative air cleaner positions (winter/summer) - slacken cover nut to adjust**

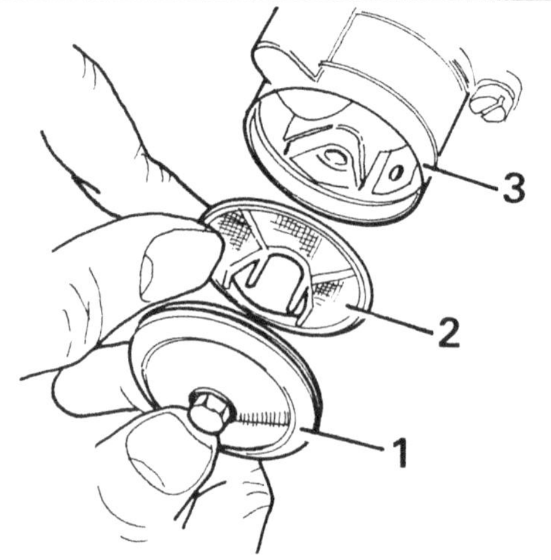


**RM7 Removing fuel pump cover (1) to clean filter (2). Pump body (3)**

**RM8 Adjustment of alternator drive belt**

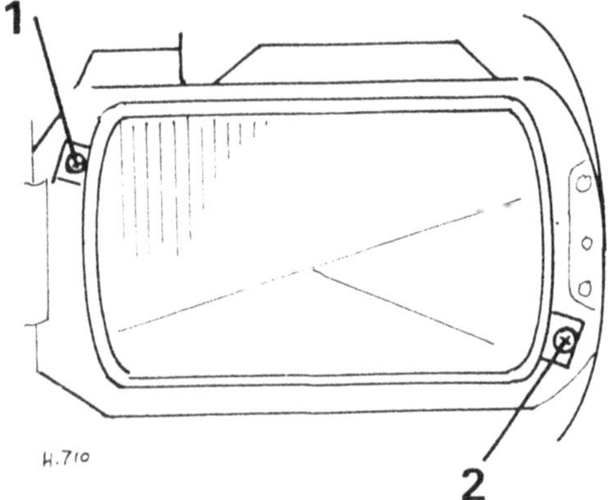


**RM9 Headlight adjustment screws**

P3 Air cleaner element

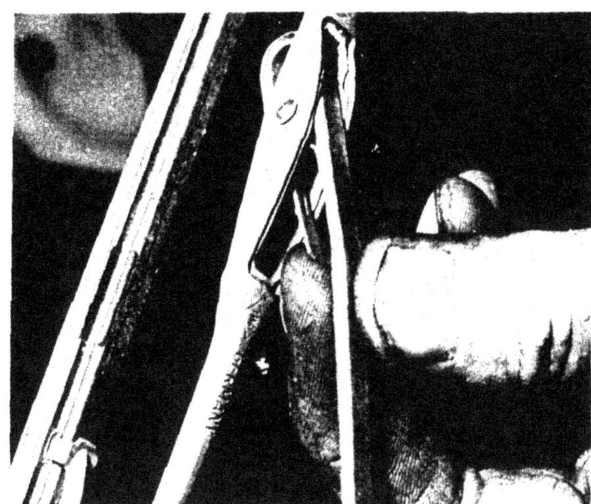
P4 Disconnecting wiper arm from blade

rubber worn away since original balancing.

5 Renew the air filter in the brake vacuum servo unit (lhd vehicles only). To do this, remove the protective shield from the steering column and disconnect the master cylinder pushrod from the brake pedal. Peel off the rubber dust excluder from around the pushrod and withdraw both components from the servo unit. Lever off the new exposed servo filter retainer, renew the filter and tap the retainer back into position. Refit the other components. In very dusty operating conditions, renew the servo air filter more frequently.

*Note: Some components illustrated may vary in design according to* **date of vehicle manufacture but the principle of maintenance remains the same for all models**

# Lubrication chart

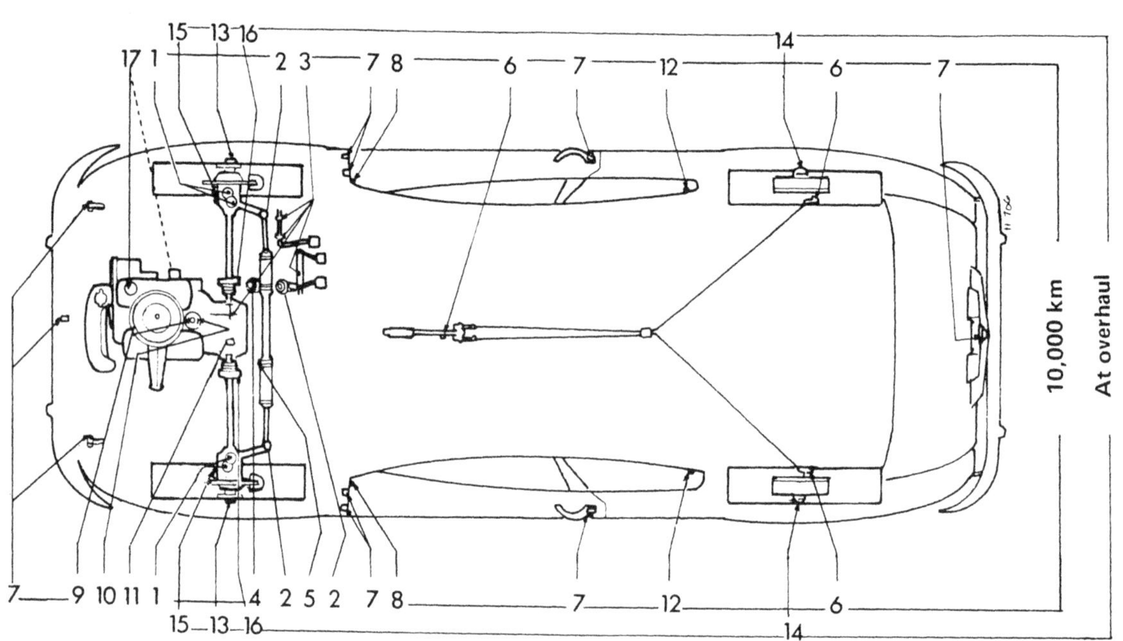


# Recommended lubricants and fluids

| Component/s | Recommended lubricant or fluid |
|---|---|
| 1 Upper and lower ball joints | SAAB Special Chassis Grease* |
| 2 Steering gear and ball joints | SAAB Special Chassis Grease* |
| 3 Throttle and clutch linkage | Castrol GTX |
| 4 Brake fluid | Castrol Girling Universal Brake and Clutch Fluid |
| 5 Clutch fluid (Hydraulic clutch only) | Castrol Girling Universal Brake and Clutch Fluid |
| 6 Handbrake links | Castrol GTX |
| 7 Hinges and locks | Castrol GTX |
| 8 Door check straps | Vaseline |
| 9 Contact breaker cam | Vaseline |
| 10 Distributor (general) | Castrol GTX |
| 11 Gearbox | Castrol Hypoy Light |
| 12 Side window latch (Estate/Wagon) | Vaseline |
| 13 Front wheel bearings† | SAAB Special Chassis Grease* |
| 14 Rear wheel bearings† | SAAB Special Chassis Grease* |
| 15 Driveshaft outer joints† | SAAB Special Chassis Grease* |
| 16 Driveshaft inner joints† | SAAB Special Chassis Grease* |
| 17 Engine | Castrol GTX |

*Do not use any grease other than SAAB Special Chassis Grease, which is specially formulated. Warning this grease is injurious to paintwork

†Repack at overhaul (where applicable)

# Chapter 1 Engine

Contents



## Specifications

*All components are manufactured to metric sizes and tolerances. Imperial equivalents are only shown for adjustment purposes*

### Engine - general

| | |
|---|---|
| Engine type | V4 ohv |
| Maximum bhp | 65 at 4700 rev/min |
| Maximum torque | 85 lb ft (11.7 kg m) at 2500 rev/min |
| Compression ratio | 9.0 : 1 |
| Cylinder bore | 3.54 in (90.0 mm) |
| Stroke | 2.32 in (58.86 mm) |
| Cubic capacity | 91.4 in$^3$ (1498 cc) |
| Firing order | 1 3 4 2 |
| Cylinder numbering sequence: | |
| Right-hand | 1 and 2 |
| Left-hand | 3 and 4 |
| Idling speed | 800 to 900 rev/min |

### Cylinder block

| | |
|---|---|
| Type | One-piece cast iron block and crankcase |
| Number of main bearings | 3 |
| Bore: | |
| Standard | 90.030 to 90.040 mm |
| Oversizes | 0.5 mm and 1.0 mm |

## Crankshaft

| | |
|---|---|
| Main bearing diameter: | |
| Standard (red) | 57.000 to 56.990 mm |
| Standard (blue) | 56.990 to 56.980 mm |
| Undersizes: | |
| 0.05 mm | 56.929 to 56.919 mm |
| 0.25 mm | 56.746 to 56.736 mm |
| 0.50 mm | 56.492 to 56.482 mm |
| 0.75 mm | 56.238 to 56.228 mm |
| 1.00 mm | 55.984 to 55.974 mm |
| Shell bearing to crankpin clearance: | |
| Standard | 0.012 to 0.048 mm |
| Undersize | 0.014 to 0.058 mm |
| Crankshaft endfloat | 0.004 to 0.008 in (0.102 to 0.203 mm) |
| Number of crankshaft gear teeth | 34 |

## Balance shaft

| | |
|---|---|
| Number of bearings | 2 |
| Shaft bearing clearance: | |
| Front | 0.02 to 0.08 mm |
| Rear | 0.03 to 0.07 mm |
| Shaft endfloat | 0.00197 to 0.00591 in (0.05 to 0.15 mm) |
| Bearing (inner diameter): | |
| Front | 50.85 to 50.88 mm |
| Rear | 54.03 to 54.05 mm |
| Shaft journal diameter: | |
| Front | 50.83 to 50.80 mm |
| Rear | 54.00 to 53.98 mm |
| Drive gear backlash limit | 0.01575 in (0.40 mm) |

## Camshaft

| | |
|---|---|
| Number of bearings | 3 |
| Bearing inner diameter: | |
| Front | 41.587 to 41.593 mm |
| Centre | 41.186 to 41.212 mm |
| Rear | 40.805 to 40.831 mm |
| Camshaft journal diameter: | |
| Front | 41.516 to 41.542 mm |
| Centre | 41.135 to 41.161 mm |
| Rear | 40.754 to 40.780 mm |
| Camshaft bearing clearance (all) | 0.077 to 0.0025 mm |
| Endfloat | 0.001 to 0.003 in (0.025 to 0.076 mm) |
| Spacer thickness: | |
| Red | 4.064 to 4.089 mm |
| Blue | 4.089 to 4.114 mm |
| Number of camshaft gear teeth | 68 |
| Backlash wear limit | 0.016 in (0.40 mm) |
| Cam lift | 6.490 mm |

## Pistons

| | |
|---|---|
| Type | Aluminium |
| Diameter: | |
| Standard | 89.978 to 90.002 mm |
| Oversizes | 0.5 mm and 1.0 mm |
| Clearance in bore | 0.001 to 0.002 in (0.03 to 0.06 mm) |
| Maximum weight difference between piston/connecting rod assemblies in same engine | 0.46 oz (13 g) |

## Piston rings

| | |
|---|---|
| Number of rings | 3 (two compression, one oil control) |
| Top compression rings: | |
| Thickness | 1.978 to 1.990 mm |
| Width | 0.15 in (3.76 mm) maximum |
| Clearance in groove | 0.002 to 0.003 in (0.0394 to 0.077 mm) |
| Endgap | 0.010 to 0.020 in (0.250 to 0.500 mm) |
| Lower compression rings: | |
| Thickness | 2.978 to 2.990 mm |
| Width | 0.15 in (3.76 mm) maximum |
| Clearance in groove | 0.002 to 0.003 in (0.394 to 0.077 mm) |
| Endgap | 0.010 to 0.020 in (0.250 to 0.500 mm) |
| Oil control rings: | |
| Thickness | 4.839 to 4.991 mm |
| Width (of rails) | 3.430 to 3.580 mm |

| | |
|---|---|
| Clearance in groove ... | 0.001 to 0.008 in (0.026 to 0.203 mm) |
| Endgap ... | 0.015 to 0.055 in (0.380 to 1.400 mm) |

**Connecting rods**

| | |
|---|---|
| Crankpin diameter: | |
| Standard (blue) ... | 53.99 to 53.98 mm |
| Standard (red) ... | 54.00 to 53.99 mm |
| Undersizes ... | 0.05, 0.25, 0.50, 0.75, 1.0 mm |
| Bearing running clearance: | |
| Standard ... | 0.014 to 0.054 mm |
| Undersize ... | 0.014 to 0.064 mm |

**Valves**

| | |
|---|---|
| Seat angle ... | 45° |
| Seat width ... | 0.059 to 0.070 in (1.5 to 1.7 mm) |
| Stem diameter (inlet valves): | |
| Standard ... | 8.043 to 8.025 mm |
| Oversizes ... | 8.243 to 8.225 mm |
| | 8.443 to 8.425 mm |
| | 8.643 to 8.625 mm |
| | 8.843 to 8.825 mm |
| Stem diameter (exhaust valves): | |
| Standard ... | 8.017 to 7.999 mm |
| Oversizes ... | 8.217 to 8.199 mm |
| | 8.417 to 8.399 mm |
| | 8.617 to 8.599 mm |
| | 8.817 to 8.799 mm |
| Valve guide bore diameter ... | 8.063 to 8.088 mm |
| Stem to guide clearance: | |
| Inlet valves ... | 0.020 to 0.063 mm |
| Exhaust valves ... | 0.046 to 0.089 mm |
| Valve head diameter: | |
| Inlet ... | 1.46 in (37.0 mm) |
| Exhaust ... | 1.26 in (32.0 mm) |
| Valve lift ... | 0.38 in (9.7 mm) |
| Valve clearances (cold): | |
| Inlet ... | 0.014 in (0.35 mm) |
| Exhaust ... | 0.016 in (0.40 mm) |
| Valve spring free length: | |
| Models 95 and 96 ... | 1.78 in (45.2 mm) |
| Monte Carlo ... | 1.85 in (47.0 mm) |

**Tappets (cam followers)**

| | |
|---|---|
| Diameter ... | 22.202 to 22.190 mm |
| Running clearance ... | 0.0009 to 0.0023 in (0.023 to 0.060 mm) |

**Valve timing**

| | |
|---|---|
| Inlet opens ... | 21° BTDC |
| Inlet shuts ... | 82° ABDC |
| Exhaust opens ... | 63° BBDC |
| Exhaust shuts ... | 40° ATDC |

**Lubrication system**

| | |
|---|---|
| Type ... | Camshaft driven, rotor type oil pump; located within sump. Pressure relief valve and full-flow disposable type oil filter |
| Oil pressure at normal operating speeds ... | 47 to 55 lb in$^2$ (3.3 to 3.9 kg cm$^2$) |
| Oil capacity (including filter) ... | 5¾ pints (3.3 litres) |

| **Torque wrench settings** | **lb ft** | **kg m** |
|---|---|---|
| Cylinder head bolts: | | |
| Stage 1 ... | 40 | 5.5 |
| Stage 2 ... | 50 | 7.0 |
| Stage 3 ... | 68 | 9.5 |
| Intermediate plate to cylinder block ... | 15 | 2.0 |
| Engine front-cover ... | 15 | 2.0 |
| Water pump to front-cover ... | 7 | 1.0 |
| Balance shaft pulley bolt ... | 36 | 5.0 |
| Oil pump to crankcase ... | 11 | 1.5 |
| Sump bolts ... | 4 | 0.5 |

| | | |
|---|---|---|
| Rocker cover to cylinder head ... ... ... ... ... | 4 | 0.5 |
| Rocker shaft pillar bolts ... ... ... ... ... ... | 32 | 4.5 |
| Camshaft gear bolt ... ... ... ... ... ... ... | 36 | 5.0 |
| Camshaft thrust plate bolts ... ... ... ... ... | 15 | 2.0 |
| Flywheel bolts ... ... ... ... ... ... ... | 50 | 7.0 |
| Crankshaft gear bolt ... ... ... ... ... ... | 36 | 5.0 |
| Connecting rod (big end) bolts ... ... ... ... ... | 25 | 3.5 |
| Main bearing bolts ... ... ... ... ... ... ... | 72 | 10.0 |
| Inlet manifold: | | |
| Stage 1 ... ... ... ... ... ... ... ... | 5 | 0.7 |
| Stage 2 ... ... ... ... ... ... ... ... | 15 | 2.0 |
| Clutch bellhousing to engine bolts ... ... ... ... | 30 | 4.1 |

## 1 General description

The engine is basically of Ford/Taunus design and manufacture. It is of four cylinder, vee-formation with overhead valves.

The block and cylinder head are of cast iron constuction and the valves operate in guides machined directly into the cylinder head.

The crankshaft is also of cast iron and runs in three main bearings. The camshaft is driven by a fibre gear wheel in mesh with the crankshaft gear. The tappet blocks (cam followers) are accessible after removal of the cylinder heads.

The connecting rods are shrunk onto the gudgeon pins and are supplied as a complete assembly with the piston. The pistons are of aluminium with two compression rings and one oil control.

The lubrication system is of pressure feed type provided by a camshaft-driven rotor design oil pump. A full flow oil filter of disposable cartridge type is screwed into the right-hand side of the crankcase.

Early models have a semi-sealed crankcase ventilation system and later models have a totally enclosed system.

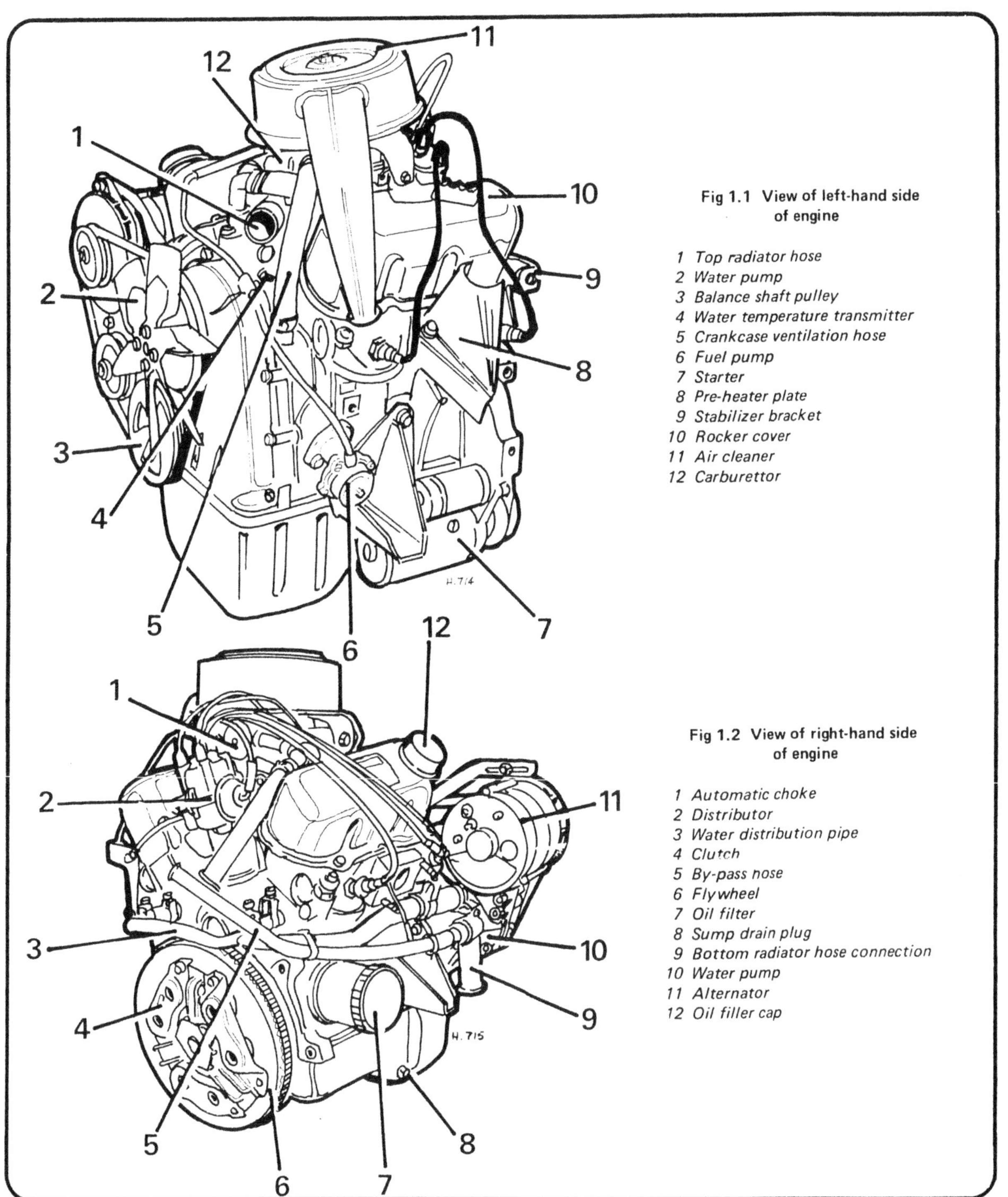


**Fig 1.1 View of left-hand side of engine**

*1 Top radiator hose*
*2 Water pump*
*3 Balance shaft pulley*
*4 Water temperature transmitter*
*5 Crankcase ventilation hose*
*6 Fuel pump*
*7 Starter*
*8 Pre-heater plate*
*9 Stabilizer bracket*
*10 Rocker cover*
*11 Air cleaner*
*12 Carburettor*

**Fig 1.2 View of right-hand side of engine**

*1 Automatic choke*
*2 Distributor*
*3 Water distribution pipe*
*4 Clutch*
*5 By-pass nose*
*6 Flywheel*
*7 Oil filter*
*8 Sump drain plug*
*9 Bottom radiator hose connection*
*10 Water pump*
*11 Alternator*
*12 Oil filler cap*

## 2 Major operations possible with the engine in position

The following operations can be carried out with the engine in position in the bodyframe.

1 Removal of the rocker shaft and valve gear.
2 Removal of the cylinder heads and their replacement.
3 Removal and refitting of the camshaft.
4 Removal and refitting of the tappets (cam followers).
5 Removal and refitting of the distributor, fuel pump and inlet manifold.
6 Removal and refitting of the engine front cover.
7 Removal and refitting of the balance shaft pulley.

## 3 Major operations only possible with engine removed

1 Removal and refitting of sump.
2 Removal and refitting of oil pump.
3 Removal and installation of crankshaft and renewal of main bearing shells.
4 Renewal of piston/connecting rod assemblies and big-end bearing shells.
5 Removal and refitting of flywheel and clutch assembly.

## 4 Method of engine removal

1 The engine may be removed with or without the gearbox as described in the following two Sections.

## 5 Engine removal with transmission unit

1 Disconnect the lead from the battery negative terminal.
2 With the help of an assistant remove the bonnet. This is carried out by opening the bonnet and detaching the hinge locking springs, disconnecting the windscreen washer hose and bending the hinge stay towards the release pin on one side.
3 Open the radiator drain tap and the bleed nipple on the heater matrix, retaining the coolant for further use if it contains antifreeze mixture.
4 *On models produced up to 1968* disconnect the headlamp and direction indicator leads.
5 *On models produced during 1969 and 1970* remove the headlamp bezels and disconnect the headlamp leads. (photo)
6 *On very late models,* disconnect the headlamp washer hoses in addition to the operations described in the preceding paragraph.
7 *On all models,* slacken the four front grille screws and detach the two radiator supports. Detach the radiator upper flexible straps and remove the bonnet lock and control cable. (photo)
8 *On very late models,* disconnect the leads from the headlamp cleaner motor and by slackening the coolant expansion bottle bracket bolt, swivel the cleaner motor to one side.
9 Withdraw the front grille taking care not to damage the paintwork.
10 Disconnect the radiator upper hose from the engine and the lower hose from the radiator.
11 Unscrew and remove the two radiator lower mounting screws and remove the radiator. (photo)
12 Disconnect the heater hoses, all electrical leads and connections from the engine. Mark the leads to facilitate correct reconnection.
13 Remove the air cleaner and cover the carburettor intake to avoid dirt entering.
14 Disconnect the throttle control at the carburettor.
15 Disconnect the engine side stabiliser from its bracket. (photo)
16 Remove the pre-heater plate from the left-hand side of the engine. (photo)
17 Unscrew and remove the flange nuts which attach the exhaust pipes to the cylinder heads. (photo)
18 Disconnect the exhaust pipe clamps at the engine front mounting brackets. (photo)
19 From below the vehicle floor pan, remove the central exhaust pipe rubber supports.
20 Withdraw the spacers which are located between the cylinder heads and exhaust pipes and lower the front silencer box as far as possible. (photo)
21 Remove the alternator and its adjustment strap. (photo)
22 Disconnect the water distributor tube which runs between the water pump and the cylinder block. (photo)
23 Using a suitable hoist and chains or slings round the engine, lift the engine just enough to take its weight.
24 Remove the two engine flexible mountings. (photo)
25 Disconnect the freewheel control at the transmission unit. (photo)
26 Slacken the rear retaining screw on the clutch operating cylinder and withdraw the cylinder and tie it to one side, retaining any shims which are fitted between the cylinder and the transmission unit. There is no need to disconnect the clutch hydraulic system. (photo)
27 Remove the taper pin which connects the gearshift rod to the transmission unit. To do this, unscrew the nut from the taper pin and screw it onto the opposite side of the pin. As the nut is tightened so the pin will be withdrawn. (photo)
28 Disconnect the speedometer cable from the transmission unit.
29 Peel back the front edge of the floor mat and prise out the rubber plug in order to gain access to the rear flexible mounting. Unscrew and remove the rear mounting centre bolt. (photo)
30 Jack-up the front of the vehicle so that the roadwheels are clear of the ground and then support the body side frame members securely on stands or blocks. The engine hoist will have to be raised in conjunction with the jack.
31 Slacken the larger clamps which secure the rubber boots on the driveshaft inner universal joints.
32 Raise the engine about 2 inches (50.0 mm) by means of the hoist and then pull the engine forward to release the engine/transmission rear mounting spigot from its support plate.
33 Rotate the right-hand road wheel until the tee shaped component of the driveshaft inner joint is located horizontally. Now push the engine/transmission to the left as far as possible and disconnect the inner universal joint.
34 Make up suitable temporary clamps which will retain the needle bearings and cups in position and exclude any dirt from the universal joint sections. Plastic bags and two very heavy bands will serve the purpose quite well.
35 Repeat the operations on the opposite universal joint.
36 Hoist the combined engine/transmission unit from the engine compartment taking care not to damage any of the external components in the process. **Note:** If difficulty is experienced in removing the engine/transmission with the starter motor installed, this item can be removed. Refer to Chapter 10 if necessary. (photo).

## 6 Engine - removal without transmission unit.

1 Carry out operations 1 to 24 inclusive as described in the preceding Section and then remove the starter motor.
2 Place a wooden block between the base of the transmission unit and the undershield so that it just supports the transmission and will prevent it from dropping when the engine is withdrawn.
3 Unscrew and remove the clutch housing to engine bolts and then slide the engine forwards until the transmission input shaft clears the clutch mechanism and the engine can be hoisted from the engine compartment. Do not allow the weight of the engine to hang upon the input shaft while it is still engaged with the clutch; also ensure that the wooden support block is secure throughout the engine removal operations.

## 7 Engine/transmission unit - separation after removal

1 Where the engine and transmission have been removed as a combined unit, remove the cover plate from the front of the flywheel.
2 Unscrew the engine to clutch housing bolts and remove them.

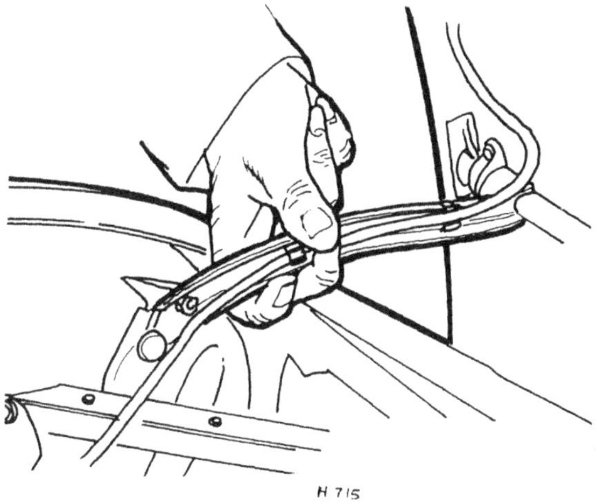

Fig 1.3 Removing the bonnet

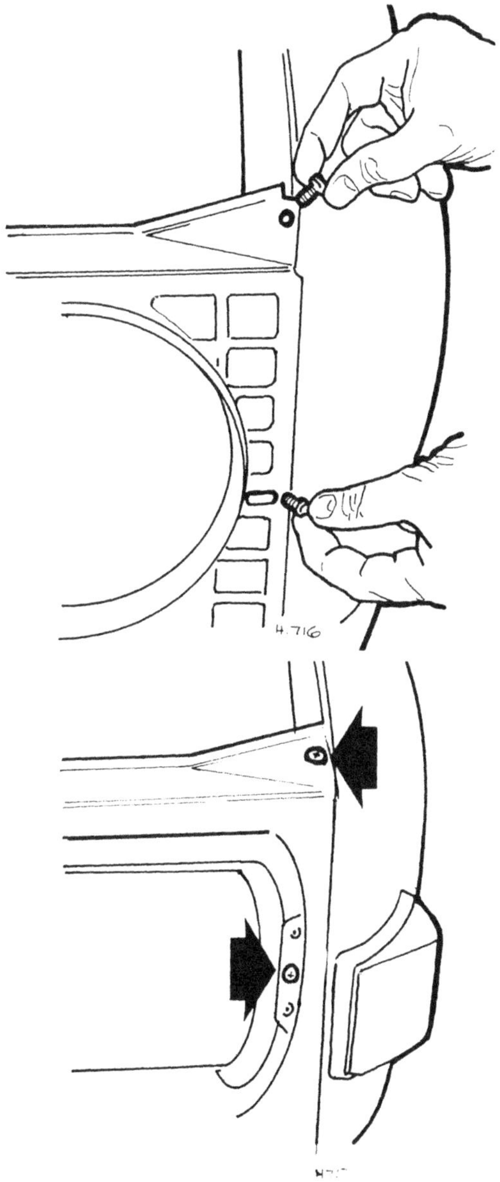

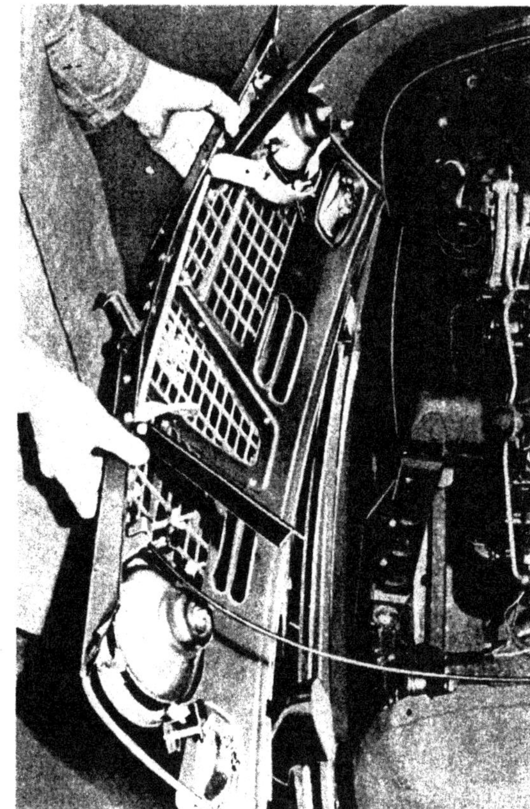

Fig 1.4 Radiator grille screws (top) early models (bottom) late models

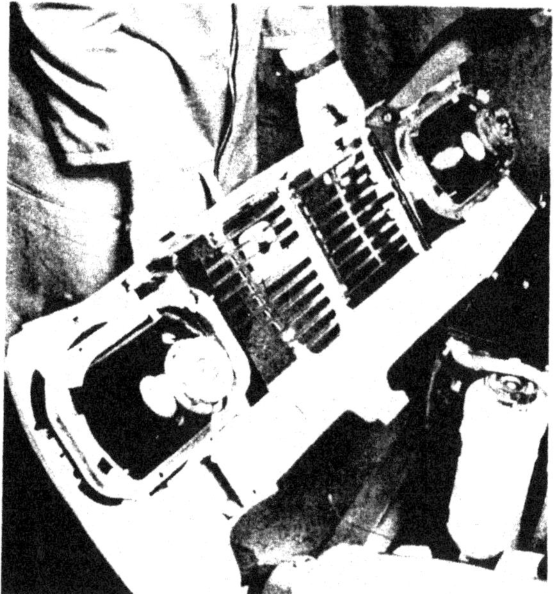

Fig 1.5 Radiator grille removal (top) early models (bottom) late models

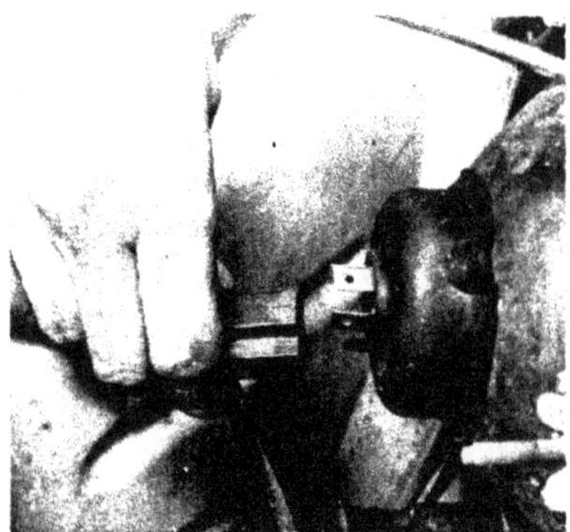
5.5 Disconnecting a headlamp connector plug

5.7 Removing a radiator flexible support strap

5.11 Removing the radiator

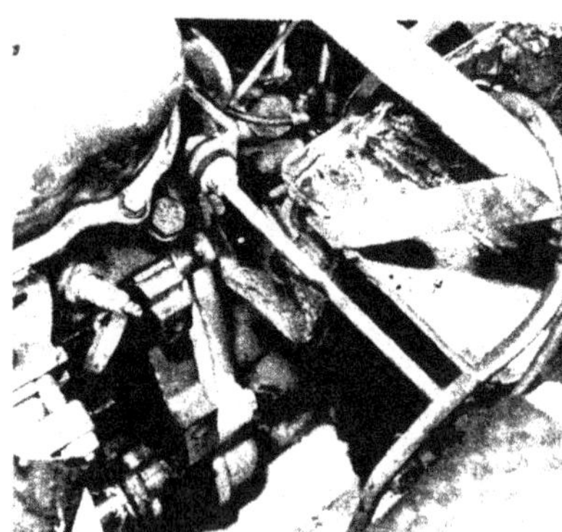
5.15 Location of engine side stabilizer

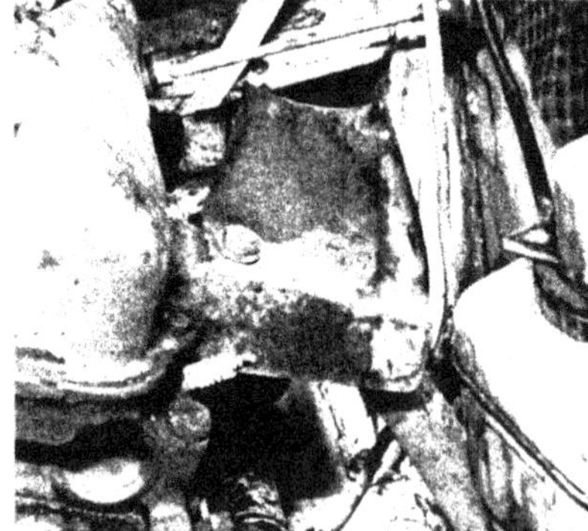
5.16 Location of air intake pre-heater plate

5.17 Unscrewing an exhaust pipe flange nut

5.18 Disconnecting an exhaust down-pipe clamp from its bracket

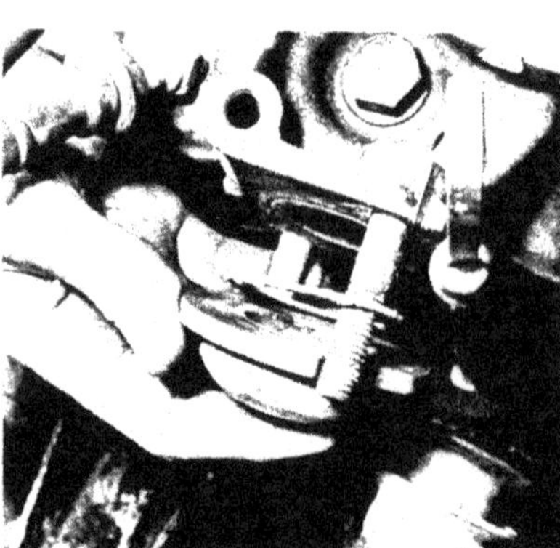
5.20A Exhaust pipe spacer and gasket

5.20B Lowering the front silencer

5.21 Removing the alternator and its adjustment strap

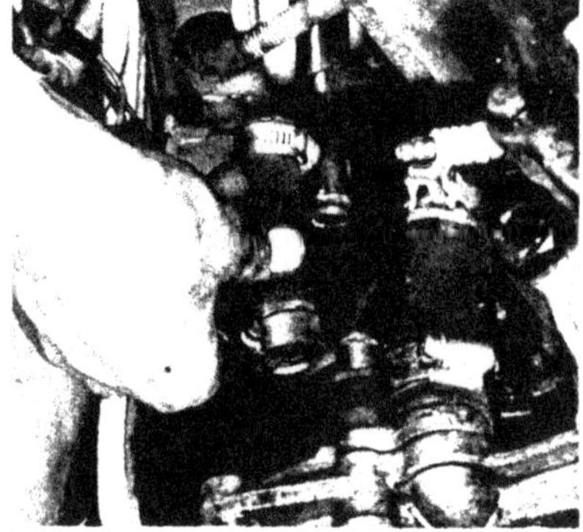
5.22 Disconnecting the water pump from the distribution tube

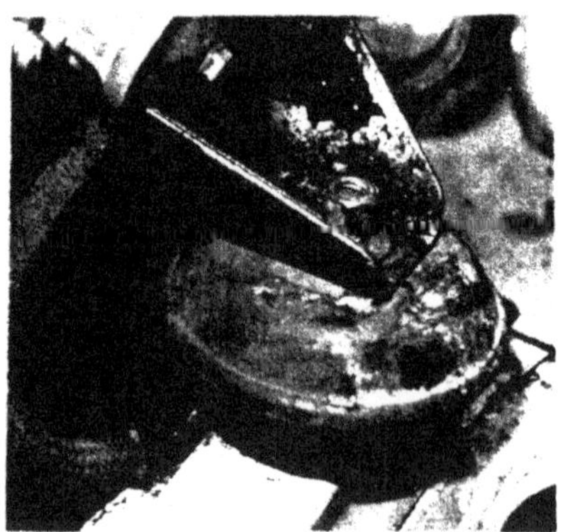
5.24 Removing an engine mounting

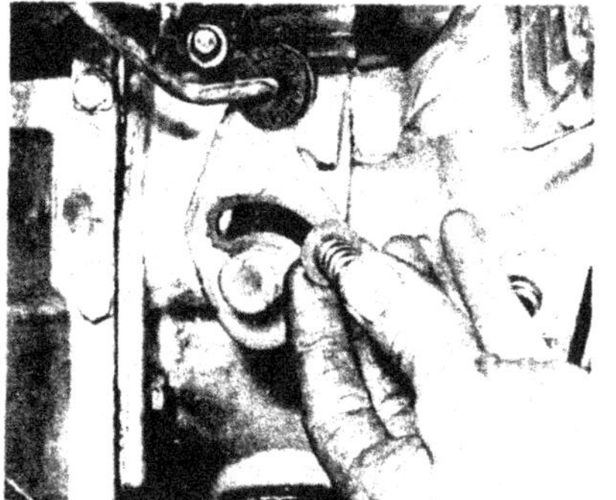
5.25 Disconnecting the freewheel control

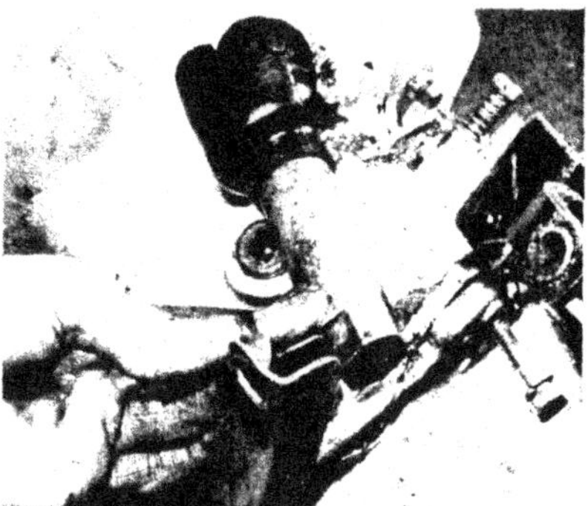
5.26 Disconnecting the clutch operating cylinder from the transmission housing

5.27 Gearchange control joint at transmission unit end

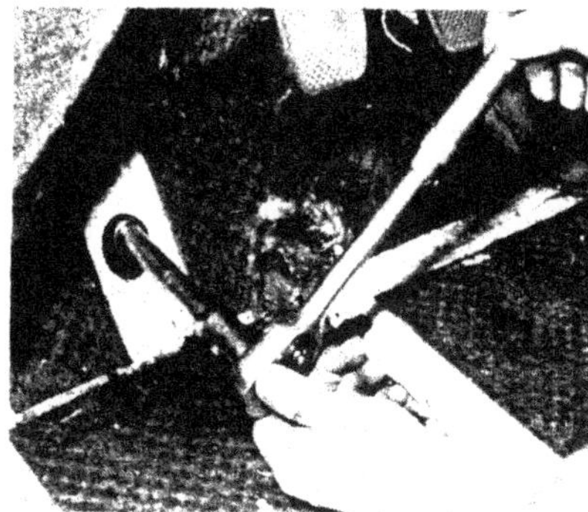
5.29 Unscrewing the transmission unit rear mounting

5.36 Hoisting the engine/transmission unit from the engine compartment

3 Remove the starter motor. Refer to Chapter 10 if necessary.
4 Withdraw the engine from the transmission unit by pulling it in a straight line. Do not allow the weight of the engine to hang upon the input shaft of the transmission unit while the shaft is still engaged with the clutch mechanism.

## 8 Engine - dismantling general

1 It is best to mount the engine on a dismantling stand but if one is not available, then stand the engine on a strong bench so as to be at a comfortable working height.Failing this, the engine can be stripped down on the floor.
2 During the dismantling process the greatest care should be taken to keep the exposed parts free from dirt. As an aid to achieving this, it is a sound scheme to thoroughly clean down the outside of the engine, removing all traces of oil and congealed dirt.
3 Use paraffin or a good grease solvent such as 'Gunk'. The latter compound will make the job much easier, as, after the solvent has been applied and allowed to stand for a time, a vigorous jet of water will wash off the solvent and all the grease and filth. If the dirt is thick and deeply embedded, work the solvent into it with a wire brush.
4 Finally wipe down the exterior of the engine with a rag and only then, when it is quite clean should the dismantling process begin. As the engine is stripped, clean each part in a bath of paraffin or petrol.
5 Never immerse parts with oilways in paraffin, ie the crankshaft, but to clean, wipe down carefully with a petrol dampened rag. Oilways can be cleaned out with wire. If an air line is present all parts can be blown dry and the oilways blown through as an added precaution.
6 Re-use of old engine gaskets is false economy and can give rise to oil and water leaks, if nothing worse. To avoid the possibility or trouble after the engine has been reassembled **always** use new gaskets throughout.
7 Do not throw the old gaskets away as it sometimes happens that an immediate replacement cannot be found and the old gasket is then very useful as a template. Hang up the old gaskets as they are removed on a suitable hook or nail.
8 To strip the engine it is best to work from the top down. The sump provides a firm base on which the engine can be supported in an upright position. When this stage where the sump must be removed is reached, the engine can be turned on its side and all other work carried out with it in this position.
9 Wherever possible, replace nuts, bolts and washers finger-tight from wherever they were removed. This helps avoid later loss and muddle. If they cannot be replaced then lay them out in such a fashion that it is clear from where they came.

## 9 Engine - removal of ancillary components

1 With the engine removed from the vehicle and separated from the transmission unit, ancillary components should be removed before the major task of dismantling begins.
2 Drain the engine oil and discard it.
3 Disconnect the HT leads from the spark plugs and the coil. Disconnect the LT lead from the distributor.
4 Unscrew the distributor clamp screw and remove the distributor. As the distributor is withdrawn, pull off the vacuum tube.
5 Disconnect the fuel inlet pipe from the fuel pump and unscrew the two bolts which secure the pump to the crankcase.
6 Withdraw the fuel pump, operating rod and gasket. Apply a piece of masking tape to the end of the rod which bears against the camshaft to ensure exact replacement.
7 Unscrew and remove the spark plugs.
8 Unscrew and remove the oil filter cartridge. The use of a clamp or chain type wrench will probably be needed for this.

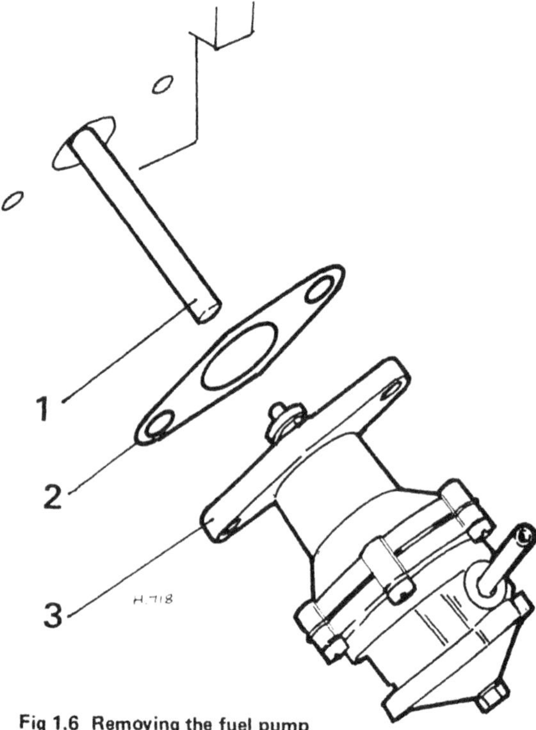


Fig 1.6 Removing the fuel pump

*1 Operating rod*
*2 Gasket*
*3 Pump flange*

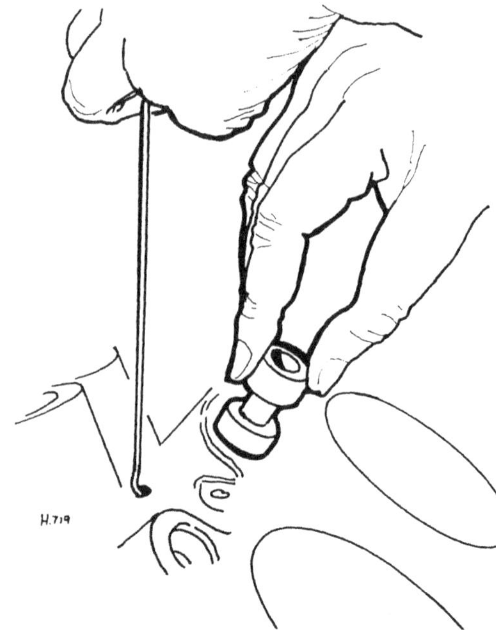


Fig 1.8 Removing a tappet (cam follower)

Fig 1.7 Removing the rocker shaft assembly from one cylinder head

*1 Rocker shaft*
*2 Oil return plate*

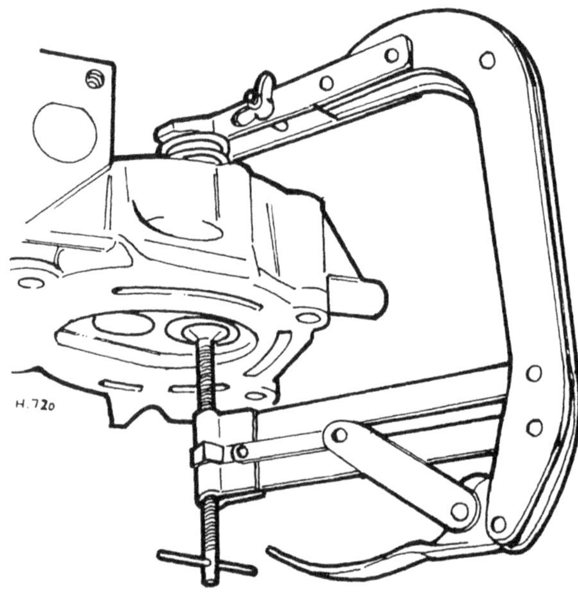


Fig 1.9 Removing a valve

9 Unscrew and remove the oil pressure transmitter switch.

10 Disconnect the water hoses from the automatic choke on the carburettor and unscrew the carburettor flange mounting nuts. Withdraw the carburettor and gasket and the intermediate plate and gasket.

11 Unscrew and remove the inlet manifold nuts and bolts and then tap the manifold loose with a plastic or hide faced mallet. Do not attempt to prise the manifold free or damaged will be caused to the mating faces.

12 Remove the engine side stabiliser bracket.

13 Unscrew and remove the fan securing bolts and detach the fan blade assembly.

14 Remove the clutch assembly from the flywheel (Chapter 5).

**10 Cylinder heads - removal**

1 Unscrew and remove the rocker cover flange bolts and remove the cover from one side of the engine.

2 Unscrew the rocker shaft pillar bolts (evenly a turn at a time) and remove the rocker assembly and the oil return plate.

3 Using a piece of wood with a number of holes punched in it or trays with compartments numbered 1 to 4 right and 5 to 8 left, extract the pushrods and place them in order so that they may be returned to their original locations.

4 Unscrew and remove the cylinder head bolts.
Unscrew them a turn at a time each, starting with the centre

two and then the outer ones in diagonal sequence.
5 Remove the cylinder head. If it is stuck, tap it on its sides using a block of hardwood and a hammer, never attempt to prise it off by inserting a lever in the head joint.
6 Remove the cylinder head gasket.
7 Repeat the foregoing operations on the opposite cylinder head.

## 11 Tappets (cam followers) - removal

1 With the cylinder heads removed, the tappets may be removed using a piece of hooked wire.
2 Place the tappets in strict sequence with reference to left and right-hand sides so that they can be returned to their original locations.

## 12 Valves - removal

1 The valves can be removed from the cylinder head by the following method. Compress each spring in turn with a valve spring compressor until the two halves of the collets can be removed. Release the compressor and remove the spring and spring retainer. (photo)
2 If, when the valve spring compressor is screwed down, the valve spring retaining cap refuses to free to expose the split collet, do not continue to screw down on the compressor as there is a likelihood of damaging it.
3 Gently tap the top of the tool directly over the cap with a light hammer. This will free the cap. To avoid the compressor jumping off the valve spring retaining cap when it is tapped, hold the compressor firmly in position with one hand.
4 Slide the rubber oil control seal off the top of each valve stem and then drop out each valve through the combustion chamber.
5 It is essential that the valves are kept in their correct sequence unless they are so badly worn that they are to be renewed.

## 13 Rocker assemblies - dismantling

1 Using a drift, drive the roll pins from the rocker shaft.
2 Withdraw the spring washers, rocker arms, coil springs and pillars. If the original components are to be refitted, keep them in order.

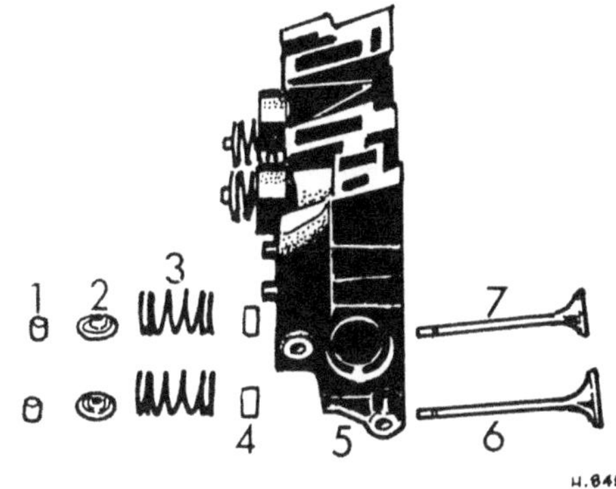


**Fig 1.10 Valve components**

*1 Split collets*
*2 Spring retainer*
*3 Valve spring*
*4 Stem seal*
*5 Cylinder head*
*6 Inlet valve*
*7 Exhaust valve*

12.1 Compressing a valve spring

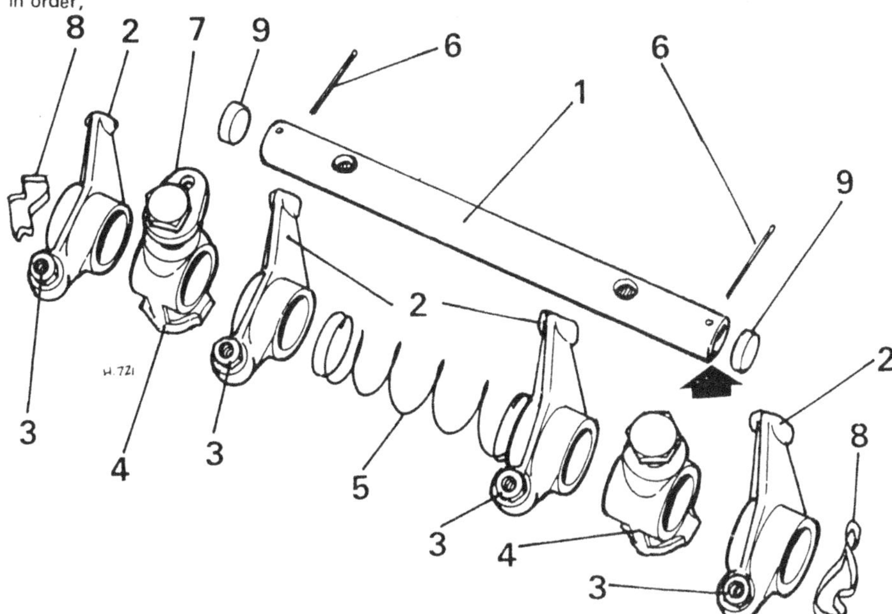


**Fig. 1.11. Rocker gear components**

*1 Shaft*
*2 Arms*
*3 Adjusting screws*
*4 Pillars*
*5 Spring*
*6 Roll pins*
*7 Plate*
*8 Wave washer*
*9 Seal*

*Note: Ground edge of shaft is arrowed; this must be located at bottom*

## 14 Sump - removal

The sump cannot be removed while the engine is still in position in the vehicle.

1 Unscrew the sump flange retaining bolts evenly, a turn, or two, at a time, lower the sump and detach the gasket.

2 If the sump is stuck, do not try to lever it off but cut round the gasket joint using a sharp knife until it is released.

## 15 Oil pump - removal

1 Invert the engine and unscrew and remove the two bolts which secure the oil pump flange to the crankcase.

2 Unscrew the retaining screw from the oil pump gauze intake bracket.

3 Withdraw the oil pump assembly and extract the driveshaft.

## 16 Engine front cover - removal

1 The fan and pulley, also the alternator, having previously been removed unscrew and remove the retaining bolt from the balance shaft pulley. Withdraw the pulley, either by using two levers or an extractor.

2 Disconnect the hoses from the water pump.

3 Unscrew all the bolts which secure the front cover to the front face of the engine block.

4 Tap the rear of the water pump (in a forward direction) in order to loosen the front cover from the engine intermediate plate.

5 The water pump may be removed from the front cover if necessary after withdrawal of the securing bolts.

## 17 Timing gear - removal

1 With the timing gears now exposed after removal of the engine front cover, remove the retaining bolt and pull off the largest gearwheel from the end of the camshaft.

2 Pull off the gearwheel from the end of the balance shaft.

3 Unscrew the (now exposed) intermediate plate retaining bolts and remove the plate and gasket.

## 18 Camshaft - removal

1 Having removed the timing gears as described in the preceding Section, unscrew and remove the camshaft thrust plate bolts.

2 Withdraw the thrust plate key and spacer and pull the camshaft out from the front of the engine. Take particular care that the lobes on the camshaft do not damage the camshaft bearings as they pass through.

## 19 Piston/connecting rod assemblies - removal

1 Before attempting to remove the piston/connecting rod assemblies, remove any carbon or wear ridges from the top of each cylinder bore. Use a bearing scraper for this job and take great care not to mark the lower surfaces of the bores.

2 Examine the connecting rods and their big-end caps. They should be numbered 1 to 4 on both the rod and cap. Number 1 is nearest the front and with the numbers to the left-hand side, the notches in the piston crowns face towards the front of the engine. If no marks are visible, mark the connecting rods and their bearing caps by punch marking or with quick-drying paint.

3 Unscrew and remove the big-end nuts and remove the bearing caps. Push each piston/connecting rod assembly out through the top of the block. (photo)

4 Make sure that the individual shell bearings are in position and temporarily refit the bearing caps.

## 20 Piston rings - removal

1 Each ring should be sprung open only enough to permit it to ride over the lands of the piston.

2 Once a piston ring is out of its groove, the use of three old feeler blades or ¼ in (6.35 mm) wide strips of tin slipped under the ring at equidistant points will facilitate their removal

3 Using a twisting motion, this method of removal will prevent the ring dripping into an empty groove as it is being withdrawn from the piston.

## 21 Flywheel - removal

1 Mark the position of the flywheel in relation to the crankshaft mounting flange.

2 Unscrew and remove the six flywheel securing bolts and pull the flywheel from the flange.

3 If the flywheel rotates when trying to unscrew the bolts, either jam the starter ring gear with a sharp cold chisel or position a block of wood between the inside of the crankcase and a crankshaft web.

## 22 Balance shaft - removal

1 Using a plastic or hide faced mallet, drive the balance shaft out from the rear of the cylinder block.

2 The sealing plug will emerge first and then the balance shaft can be withdrawn taking care not to damage the shaft bearings.

## 23 Crankshaft and main bearings - removal

1 Note that the arrows on the three main bearing caps face towards the front of the engine. Check that the caps are numbered 1,2 and 3 for correct refitting. (photo)

2 Unscrew and remove the bolts from each of the main bearing caps.

3 Withdraw the main bearing caps and lift the crankshaft from the crankcase.

4 The shell bearings may be detached from the crankcase and the bearing caps if necessary but keep them in strict order.

5 Withdraw the oil seal from the crankshaft.

6 If necessary, remove the gearwheel from the front of the crankshaft using a suitable extractor.

## 24 Oil pump - servicing

1 The oil pump should only require servicing after a very high mileage has been covered or in the event of low oil pressure being recorded when all other engine components are known to be in first class order.

2 Unscrew the intake pipe from the oil pump body.

3 Unscrew the cover bolts and remove the cover.

4 Withdraw the inner and outer rotors from the oil pump body.

5 Punch a hole in the relief valve cover plate using a sharpened drift.

6 Screw in a self-tapping screw and using this as a leverage point, extract the cover plate.

7 Extract the spring and relief valve.

8 Obtain a new inner and outer rotor and insert them into the pump body. Using a straight edge and a feeler gauge, check the clearance between the face of the body and the faces of the rotors. This should be 0.004 in (0.1 mm). Where the clearance is incorrect, grind the faces of the pump body or rotors as necessary by rubbing on emery cloth placed on a piece of plate glass.

9 Again using feeler gauges, check the clearance between the

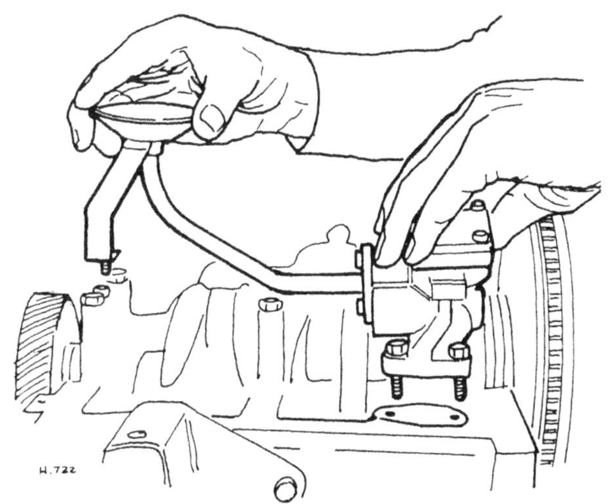


Fig 1.12 Removing the oil pump

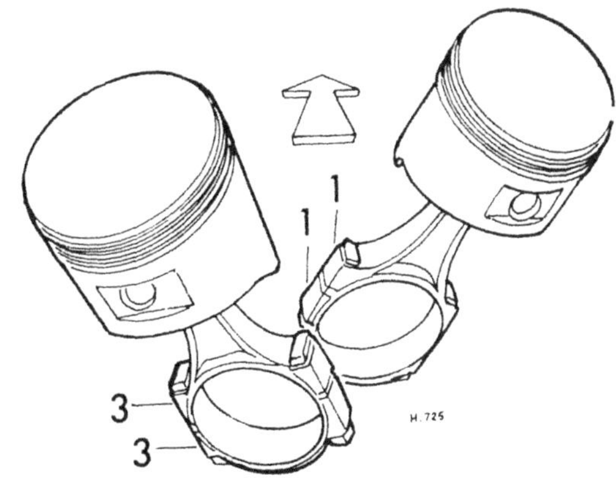


Fig 1.15 Method of marking connecting rods and big-end caps

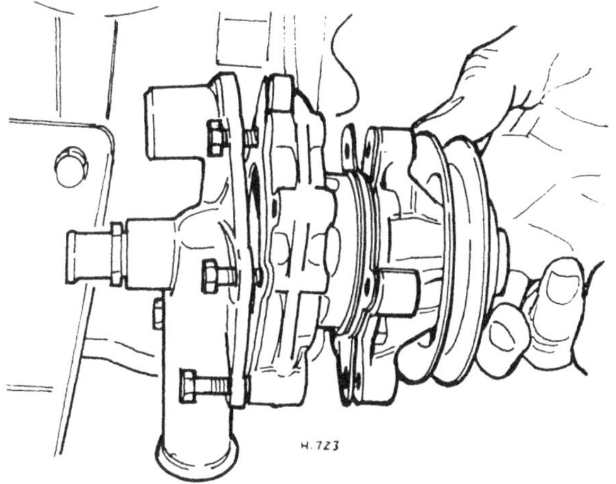


Fig 1.13 Removing the water pump

19.3 Removing a piston/connecting rod assembly through the top of the block

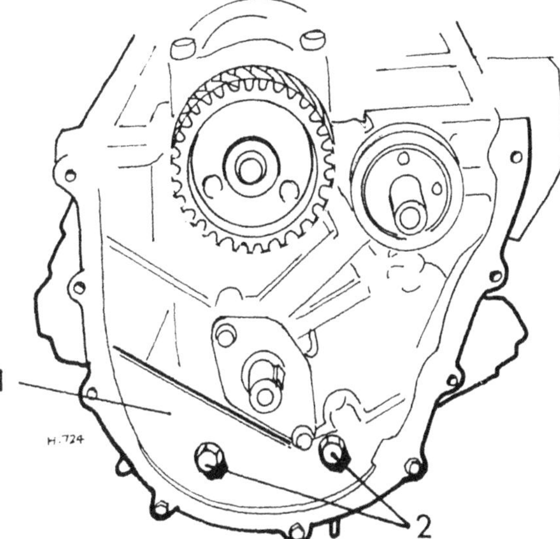


Fig 1.14 Removing the intermediate plate

*1 Intermediate plate* *2 Retaining bolts*

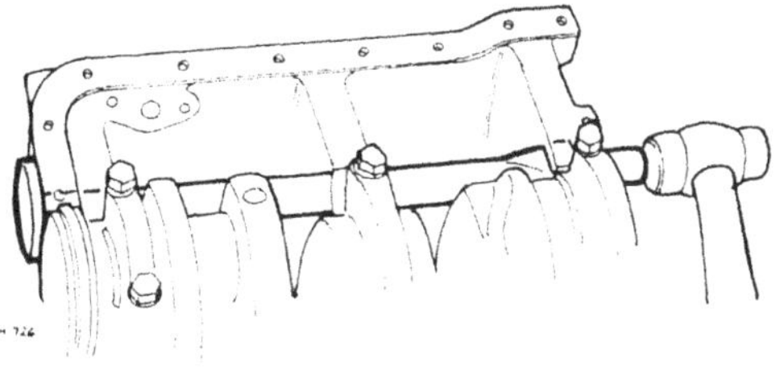

Fig 1.16 Removing the balance shaft

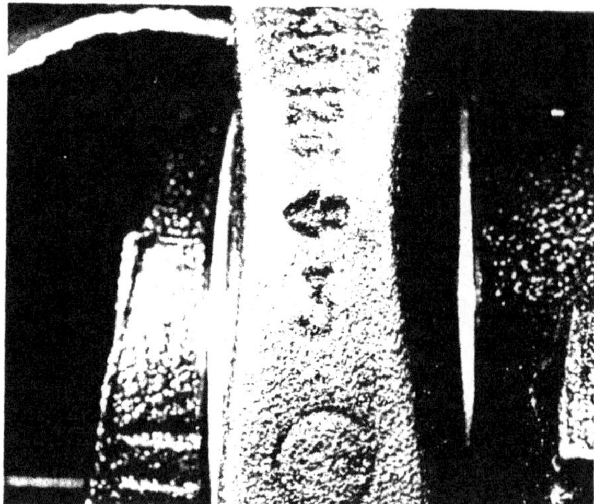
23.1 Main bearing cap markings

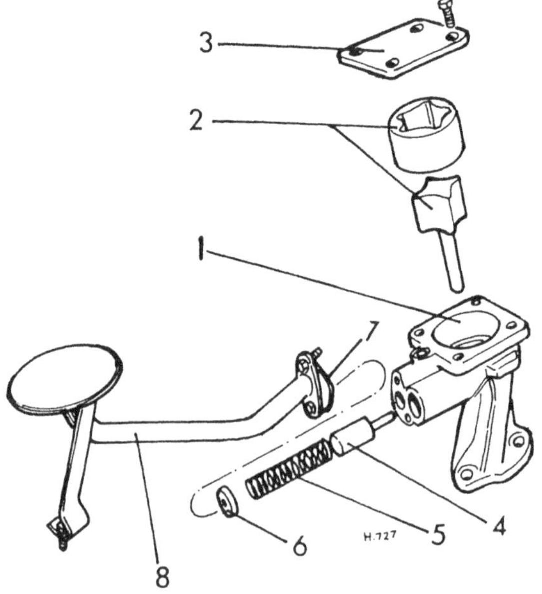

Fig 1.17 Oil pump components

| | |
|---|---|
| *1 Body* | *5 Spring* |
| *2 Rotors* | *6 Valve cover plate* |
| *3 Cover* | *7 Gasket* |
| *4 Pressure relief valve* | *8 Intake pipe* |

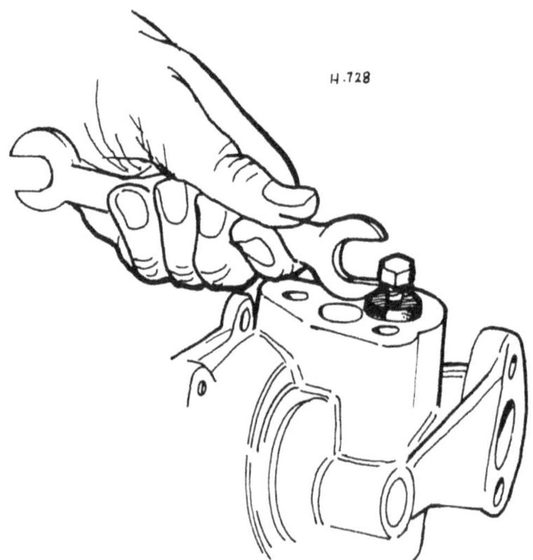

Fig 1.18 Levering out the oil pump relief valve cover plate

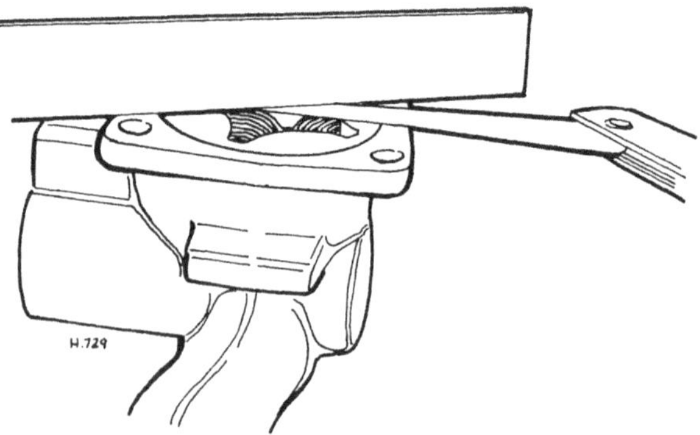

Fig 1.19 Checking oil pump rotor endfloat

outer rotor and the oil pump body. If the clearance is greater than 0.012 in (0.3 mm) then a new pump body will be required.
10 Wash all components free from grinding dust in paraffin.
11 Install the relief valve and spring and apply engine oil to them.
12 Press in a new cover plate until it bottoms against its stop.
13 Drift in the centre of the cover plate using a ¼ in (6.35 mm) diameter rod until it is fully home.
14 Reassemble the oil pump, liberally applying engine oil to the rotors. Use a new gasket between the intake pipe and the pump body and tighten the cover bolts evenly to a torque of 11 lb/ft (1.5 kg/m).

## 25 Crankcase ventilation systems

1 Two types of system may be encountered, the semi-enclosed type installed on engines up to number "16100" and the totally enclosed type fitted from engine number "16101".
2 No maintenance is normally required to either system except to check the security and condition of the hoses.

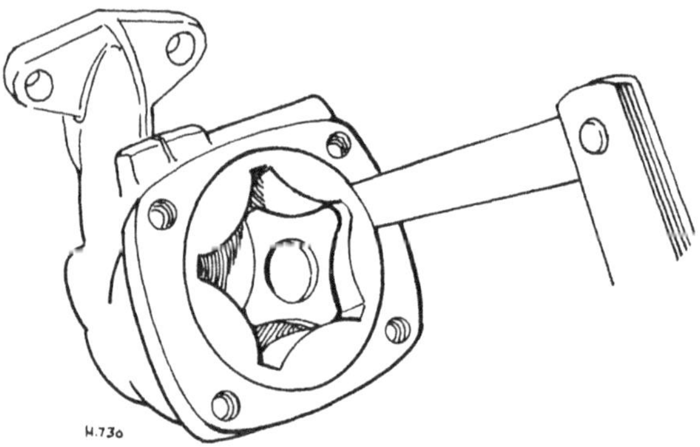

Fig 1.20 Checking oil pump rotor to body clearance

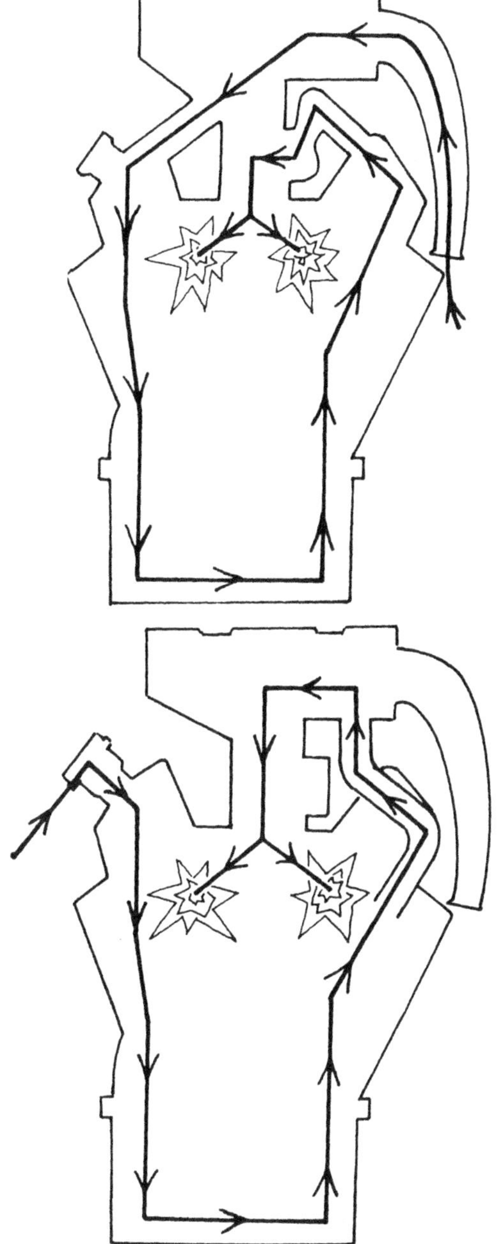

Fig 1.21 Types of crankcase ventilation system

*(top) semi-enclosed (bottom) totally enclosed*

3 On the totally enclosed system, any malfunction may be caused by clogging of the flame trap or regulator valve in the carburettor intermediate flange. In either case, remove the component, wash thoroughly in paraffin and dry with air from a tyre pump.

## 26 Engine components - examination for wear

When the engine has been stripped down and all parts properly cleaned, decisions have to be made as to what needs renewal and the following sections tell the examiner what to look for. In any border line case it is always best to decide in favour of a new part. Even if a part may still be serviceable its life will have been reduced by wear and the degree of trouble needed to replace it in the future must be taken into consideration. However, these things are relative and it depends on whether a quick 'survival' job is being done or whether the car as a whole is being regarded as having many thousands of miles of useful and economical life remaining.

## 27 Crankshaft - examination and renovation

1 Look at the three main bearing journals and the four crankpins and if there are any scratches or score marks then the shaft will need regrinding. Such conditions will nearly always be accompanied by similar deterioration in the matching bearing shells.
2 Each bearing journal should also be round and can be checked with a micrometer or caliper gauge around the periphery at several points. If there is more than 0.001 in (0.0254 mm) of ovality regrinding is necessary.
3 A main SAAB agent or motor engineering specialist will be able to decide to what extent regrinding is necessary and also supply the special undersize shell bearings to match whatever may need grinding off.
4 Before taking the crankshaft for regrinding check also the cylinder bores and pistons as it may be advantageous to have the whole engine done together.

## 28 Crankshaft main bearings and big end connecting rod bearings - examination and renovation

1 With careful servicing and regular oil and filter changes bearings will last for a very long time but they can still fail for unforeseen reasons. With big end bearings the indications are regular rhythmic knocking from the crankcase, the frequency depending on engine speed. It is particularly noticeable when the engine is under load. This symptom is accompanied by a fall in oil pressure although this is not normally noticeable unless an oil pressure gauge is fitted. Main bearing failure is usually indicated by serious vibration, particularly at higher engine revolutions, accompanied by a more significant drop in oil pressure and a 'rumbling' noise.
2 Bearing shells in good condition have bearing surfaces with a smooth, even, matt silver/grey colour all over. Worn bearings will show patches of a different colour where the bearing metal has worn away and exposed the underlay. Damaged bearings will be pitted or scored. It is nearly always well worthwhile fitting new shells as their cost is relatively low. If the crankshaft is in good condition it is merely a question of obtaining another set of standard size. A reground crankshaft will need new bearing shells as a matter of course.

## 29 Cylinder bores - examination and renovation

1 A new cylinder is perfectly round and the walls parallel throughout its length. The action of the piston tends to wear the walls at right angles to the gudgeon pin due to side thrust. This wear takes place principally on that section of the cylinder swept by the piston rings.
2 It is possible to get an indication of bore wear by removing the cylinder heads with the engine still in the car. With the piston down in the bore first signs of wear can be seen and felt just below the top of the bore where the top piston ring reaches and there will be a noticeable lip. If there is no lip it is fairly reasonable to expect that bore wear is not severe and any lack of compression or excessive oil consumption is due to worn or broken piston rings or pistons (see next Section).
3 If it is possible to obtain a bore measuring micrometer measure the bore in the thrust plane below the lip and again at the bottom of the cylinder in the same plane. If the difference is more than 0.003 in (0.0762 mm) then a rebore is necessary. Similarly, a difference of 0.003 in (0.0762 mm) or more across the bore diameter is a sign of ovality calling for a rebore.
4 Any bore which is significantly scratched or scored will need reboring. This symptom usually indicates that the piston or rings

are damaged also in that cylinder. In the event of only one cylinder being in need of reboring it will still be necessary for all four to be bored and fitted with new oversize pistons and rings.
5 Your SAAB agent or local motor engineering specialist will be able to rebore and obtain the necessary matched pistons. If the crankshaft is undergoing regrinding also it is a good idea to let the same firm renovate and reassemble the crankshaft and pistons to the block. A reputable firm normally gives a guarantee for such work. In cases where engines have been rebored already to their maximum, new cylinder liners are available which may be fitted. In such cases the same reboring precesses have to be followed and the services of a specialist engineering firm are required.

## 30 Pistons and piston rings - examination and renovation

1 Worn pistons and rings can usually be diagnosed when the symptoms of excessive oil consumption and low compression occur and are sometimes, though not always, associated with worn cylinder bores. Compression testers that fit into the spark plug holes are available and these can indicate where low compression is occurring. Wear usually accelerates the more it is left so when the symptoms occur early action can possibly save the expense of a rebore.
2 Another symptom of piston wear is piston slap - a knocking noise from the crankcase not to be confused with big end bearing failure. It can be heard clearly at low engine speed when there is no load (idling for example) and is much less audible when the engine speed increases. Piston wear usually occurs in the skirt or lower end of the piston and is indicated by vertical streaks in the worn area which is always on the thrust side. It can also be seen where the skirt thickness differs.
3 Piston ring wear can be checked by first removing the rings from the pistons. Then place the rings in the cylinder bores from the top, pushing them down about 1½ inches (38.1 mm) with the head of a piston (from which the rings have been removed) so that they rest square in the cylinder. Then measure the gap at the ends of the ring with a feeler gauge. If it exceeds 0.020 in (0.5080 mm) for the two top compression rings, 0.059 in (1.40 mm) for the oil control ring then they need renewal.
4 The groove in which the rings locate in the piston can also become enlarged in use. The clearance between ring and piston, in the groove, should not exceed 0.003 in (0.762 mm) for the top two compression rings and 0.008 in (0.203 mm) for the lower oil control ring.
5 However, it is rare that a piston is only worn in the ring grooves and the need to replace them for this fault alone is hardly ever encountered. Wherever pistons are renewed the weight of the four piston/connecting rod assemblies should be kept within the limit variation of 0.46 oz (13 g) to maintain engine balance.

## 31 Connecting rods and gudgeon pins - examination and renovation

1 Any wear or distortion found in the gudgeon pin, small end or connecting rod will mean fitting a complete piston/connecting rod assembly as the individual components cannot be dismantled.
2 Connecting rods are not subject to wear but in extreme circumstances such as engine seizure they could be distorted. Such conditions may be visually apparent but where doubt exists they should be changed. The bearing caps should also be examined for indications of filing down which may have been attempted in the mistaken idea that bearing slackness could be remedied in this way. If there are such signs then the connecting rods should be replaced.

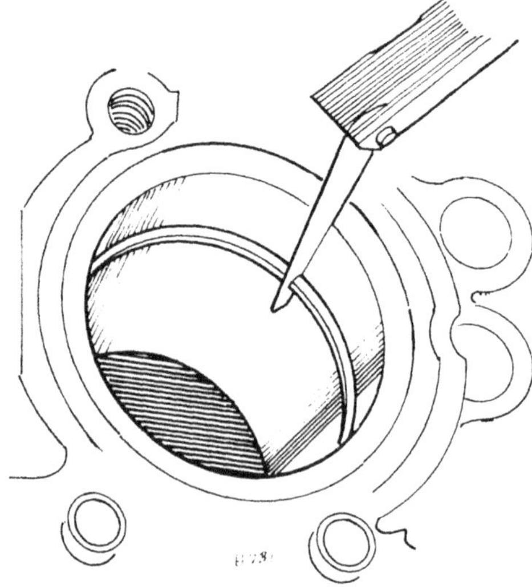

Fig 1.22 Measuring a piston ring end gap

## 32 Camshaft and camshaft bearings - examination and renovation

1 The camshaft bearing bushes should be examined for signs of scoring and pitting. If they need renewal they will have to be dealt with professionally as although it may be relatively easy to remove the old bushes, the correct fitting of new ones requires special tools. If they are not fitted evenly and square from the very start they can be distorted thus causing localized wear in a very short time. See your SAAB dealer or local engineering specialist for this work.
2 The camshaft itself may show signs of wear on the bearing journals, cam lobes or the skew gear. The main decision to take is what degree of wear justifies replacement, which is costly. Any signs of scoring or damage to the bearing journals must be rectified and as undersize bearing bushes are not supplied the journals cannot be reground. Renewal of the whole camshaft is the only solution. Similarly, excessive wear on the skew gear which can be seen where the distributor driveshaft teeth mesh will mean renewal of the whole camshaft.
3 The cam lobes themselves may show signs of ridging or pitting on the high points. If the ridging is light then it may be possible to smooth it out with fine emery. The cam lobes, however, are surface hardened and once this is penetrated wear will be very rapid thereafter. The cams are also offset and tapered to cause the tappets to rotate - thus ensuring that wear is even - so do not mistake this condition for wear.

## 3 Balance shaft and bearings - examination and renovation

1 Check the balance shaft journals for scoring or wear. Where this is evident renew the balance shaft.
2 Examine the two balance shaft bearings. If these are worn or scored, then they must be renewed.

This is a job for your SAAB dealer having the necessary removal and fitting tools.

## 34 Tappets - examination and renovation

1 The faces of the tappets which bear on the camshaft should show no signs of pitting, scoring or other forms of wear. They should also not be a loose fit in their housing. Wear is only normally encountered at very high mileages or in cases of neglected engine lubrication. Renew if necessary.

## 35 Valves and valve seats - examination and renovation

1 With the valves removed from the cylinder heads examine the heads for signs of cracking, burning away and pitting of the edge where it seats in the port. The seats of the valves in the cylinder head should also be examined for the same signs. Usually it is the valve that deteriorates first but if a bad valve is not rectified the seat will suffer and this is more difficult to repair.
2 Provided there are no obvious signs of serious pitting the valve should be ground with its seat. This may be done by placing a smear of carborundum paste on the edge of the valve and using a suction type valve holder, grinding the valve in situ. This is done with a semi-rotary action, twirling the handle of the valve holder between the hands and lifting it occasionally to re-distribute the traces of paste. Use a coarse paste to start with. As soon as a matt grey unbroken line appears on both the valve and seat the valve is 'ground in'. All traces of carbon should also be cleaned from the head and neck of the valve stem. A wire brush mounted in a power drill is a quick and effective way of doing this.
3 If the valve requires renewal it should be ground into the seat in the same way as an old valve.
4 Another form of valve wear can occur on the stem where it runs in the guide in the cylinder head. This can be detected by trying to rock the valve from side to side. If there is any movement at all it is an indication that the valve stem or guide is worn. Check the stem first with a micrometer at points all along and around its length and if they are not within the specified size new valves will probably solve the problem. If the guides are worn, however, they will need reboring for oversize valves. The valve seats will also need recutting to ensure they are concentric with the stems.
5 When all valve grinding is completed it is essential that every trace of grinding paste is removed from the valves and ports in the cylinder head. This should be done with thorough washing in petrol or paraffin and blowing out with a jet of air. If particles of carborundum should work their way into the engine they would cause havoc with bearings or cylinder walls.

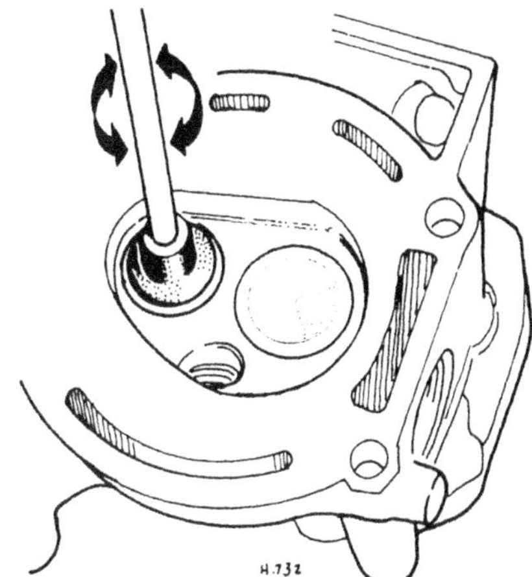

Fig 1.23 Grinding in a valve

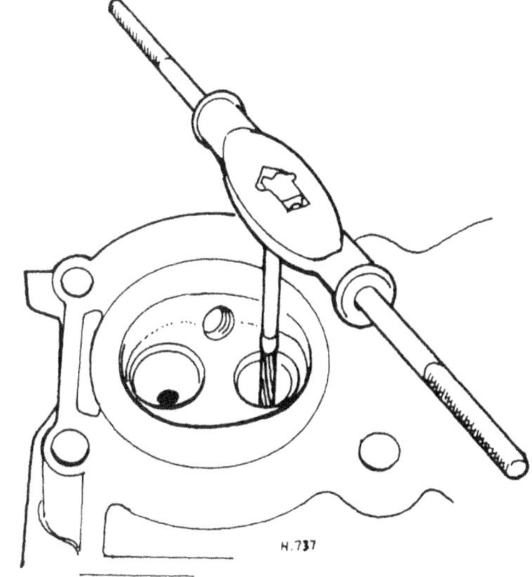

Fig 1.24 Reaming a worn valve guide

## 36 Timing gears - examination and renovation

1 Any wear which takes place in the timing mechanism will be on the teeth of the fibre gear which is driven from the crankshaft gear. The backlash, which can be measured with a feeler gauge between the gear teeth, should not exceed 0.016 in (0.40 mm). The balance shaft gear backlash should be the same but this is not so critical. If the crankshaft gear to camshaft gear backlash is excessive the fibre gear wheel should be renewed.

## 37 Flywheel and ring gear - examination and renovation

1 Drill two holes, each on opposite sides of the ring gear. Use a 0.28 or 0.32 in (7.0 or 8.0 mm) diameter drill located between the root of the two teeth and the edge of the flywheel . Take care that the drill does not touch the flywheel.
2 If the ring gear does not split during the drilling process, knock it off with a cold chisel.
3 Place the new ring gear on a metal plate and heat it from below with a blow torch, testing its expansion frequently, until by offering it to the flywheel, it drops into position(chamfered edge towards shoulder).
4 An alternative method of heating is in a domestic oven at a temperature between 400 and 450°F (204 to 232°C). Do not exceed the recommended temperature levels or the induction hardness of the ring gear will be lost.
5 Allow the ring gear to cool naturally without quenching.
6 A badly scored flywheel should be renewed. If the central spigot bush is worn extract it by first filling it with grease and tapping in a close fitting rod. The hydraulic pressure will remove the bush and enable a new one to be pressed in.

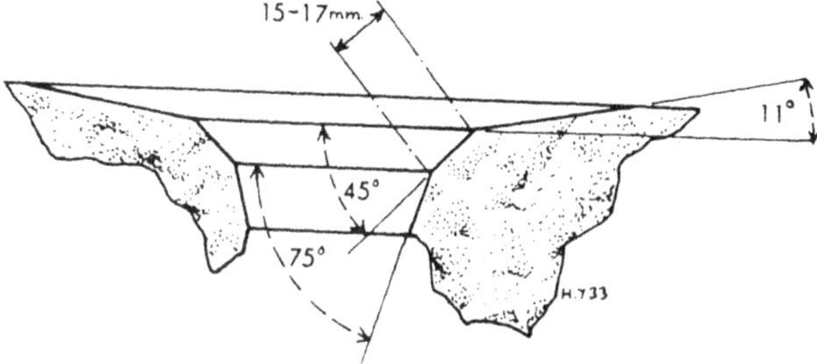

Fig 1.25 Valve seat recutting diagram

*Seat width for all valves after recutting should be between 0.059 and 0.070 in (1.5 and 1.7 mm)*

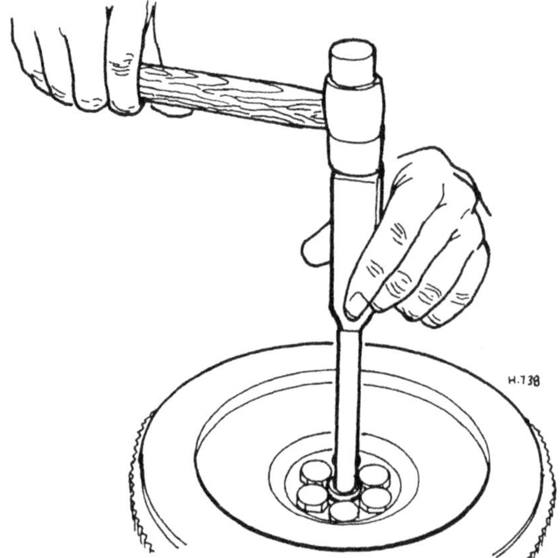


Fig 1.26 Removing a worn flywheel spigot bush

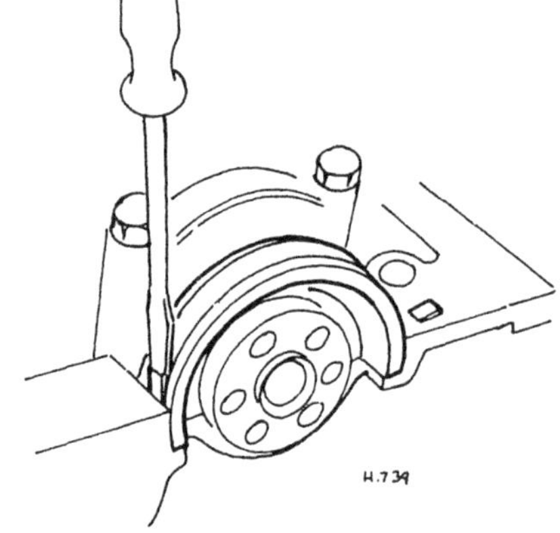


Fig 1.27 Installing rear main bearing wedge seals

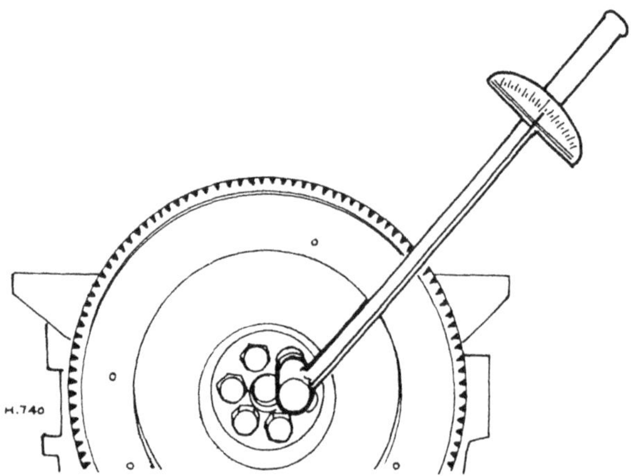


Fig 1.28 Fitting the flywheel

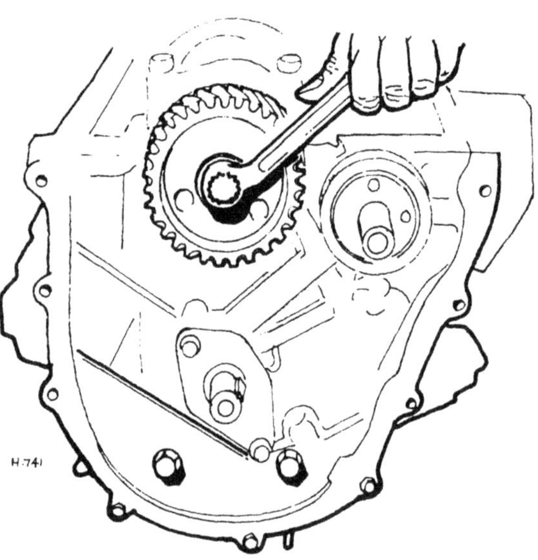


Fig 1.29 Fitting the crankshaft gear

## 38 Cylinder heads and piston crowns - decarbonising

1 When cylinder heads are removed either in the course of an overhaul or for inspection of bores or valve condition when the engine is in the car it is normal to remove all carbon deposits from the piston crowns and heads.
2 This is best done with a cup shaped wire brush and an electric drill and is fairly straightforward when the engine is dismantled and the pistons removed. Sometimes hard spots of carbon are not easily removed except by a scraper. When cleaning the pistons with a scraper take care not to damage the surface of the piston in any way.
3 When the engine is in the car certain precautions must be taken when decarbonising the piston crowns in order to prevent dislodged pieces of carbon falling into the interior of the engine which could cause damage to cylinder bores, pistons and rings - or if allowed into the water passages damage to the water pump. Turn the engine, therefore, so that the piston being worked on is at the top of its stroke and then mask off the adjacent cylinder bore and all surrounding water jacket orifices with paper and adhesive tape. Press grease into the gap all round the piston to keep carbon particles out and then scrape all carbon away by hand carefully. Do not use a power drill and wire brush when the engine is in the car as it will be virtually impossible to keep all the carbon dust clear of the engine. When completed carefully clear out the grease round the rim of the piston with a matchstick or something similar - bringing any carbon particles with it. Repeat the process on the other three piston crowns. It is not recommended that a ring of carbon is left round the edge of the piston on the theory that it will aid oil consumption. This was valid in the earlier days of long stroke low revving engines but modern engines, fuels and lubricants cause less carbon deposits any way and any left behind tends merely to cause hot-spots.

## 39 Rocker gear - examination and renovation

1 Examine the rocker shafts for distortion, rolling them on a piece of plate glass will reveal this if present.
2 If the shafts are distorted, scored or grooved, renew them.
3 Check the bearing surfaces of the rocker arms. If these are deeply scored or recessed they must be renewed. Very shallow marks can be removed by rubbing them on an oilstone but ensure that the original contour is maintained.
4 Ensure that all oil holes and drillings are clear.

## 40 Engine reassembly - general

1 All components of the engine must be cleaned of oil sludge and oil gaskets and the working area should also be cleared and

clean. In addition to the normal range of good quality socket spanners and general tools which are essential, the following must be available before reassembly begins:

Complete set of new gaskets.
Supply of clean rags.
Clean oil can full of clean engine oil.
Torque spanner.
All new spare parts as necessary.

**41 Engine reassembly - crankshaft, main bearings and balance shaft**

1 Fit the shell bearings into the main webs of the crankcase and oil them liberally.
2 Lower the crankshaft carefully into position and fit the correct main bearing caps complete with shells (liberally oiled). Smear the rear face of the rear bearing cap with gasket cement. (photos)
3 Tighten the front and rear main bearing cap bolts to a torque of 72 lb/ft (10.0 kg/m) but tighten the centre cap bolts with the fingers only at this stage.
4 Press the crankshaft forward and at the same time lever the centre main bearing cap to the rear. Holding the two components in this attitude, tighten the bolts in a similar manner to those on the front and rear caps. (photo)
5 Smear gasket cement to the outer periphery of a new crankshaft rear oil seal and oil the inner lips of the seal and drive it into position with a piece of tubing. (photos)
6 Oil the balance shaft journals and bearings liberally and insert the shaft into position from the rear of the cylinder block. (photo)
7 Smear the new balance shaft sealing plug with gasket cement and drive it into position in the block so that its flat side faces outwards.
8 Coat two new wedged shaped seals with gasket cement and press them into position on either side of the rear main bearing cap.
9 Refit the flywheel to the crankshaft, ensuring that the marks made before removal are in alignment and tighten new bolts to a torque of 50 lb/ft (7.0 kg/m). (photo)
10 Fit the Woodruff key to the crankshaft and press the gear on using hand pressure only. Screw in the retaining bolt and washer to pull the gear into position on the crankshaft. Finally tighten the bolt to a torque of 36 lb/ft (5.0 kg/m). (photo)

**42 Engine reassembly - pistons, connecting rods, camshaft, timing gear and front cover**

1 Fit the piston rings to each piston so that in a sectional view they will appear as shown in Fig. 1.30.
2 With the mark on the piston crown facing forward, twist the rings and their spring components so that the end gaps take up the positions indicated.
3 Apply oil liberally to the piston rings and piston surfaces and fit a piston ring compressor. Checking that the mark on the piston crown faces the front of the engine, insert the connecting rod/piston assembly into the cylinder bore until the compressor rests on the top face of the block. Using the stock of the hammer press the piston into the bore (photo).
4 Insert the bearing shells into the recesses in the connecting rod and matching cap and assemble to the crankshaft journal after liberally applying oil. Use new bolts and tighten the big-end nuts to a torque of 25 lb/ft (3.5 kg/m) (photos).
5 Repeat the operations on the remaining three piston/connecting rod assemblies, ensuring that all components are installed in their original sequence. Connect the big-ends with the crankshaft journal at the lowest point of its 'throw'.
6 Apply engine oil to the camshaft bearings in the crankcase and install the camshaft (photo).
7 Fit the spacer (countersunk side towards camshaft) and the

41.2A Lowering the crankshaft into the crankcase

41.2B Fitting the rear main bearing cap

41.4 Neutralising crankshaft endfloat

41.5A Smearing gasket cement to the crankshaft rear oil seal

41.5B The crankshaft rear oil seal installed

41.6 Inserting the balance shaft

41.9 Refitting the flywheel

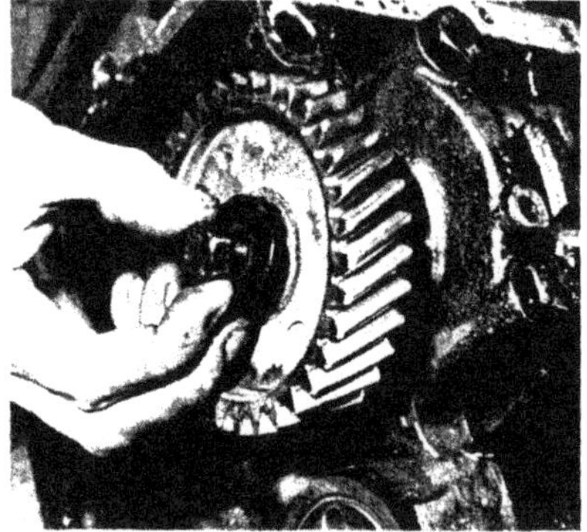
41.10 Fitting the crankshaft drive gear

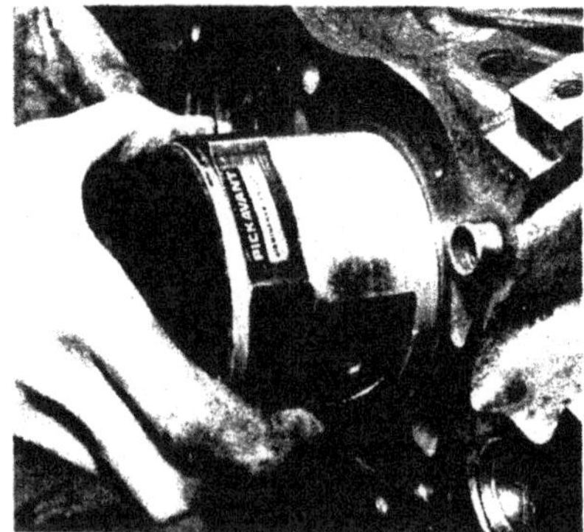
42.3 Preparing to install piston/connecting rod assembly

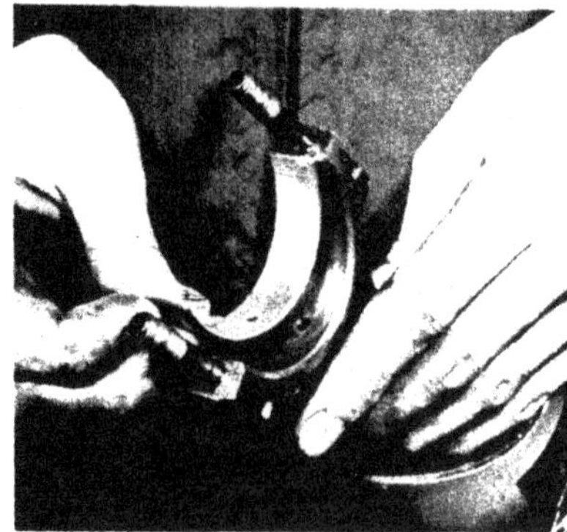
42.4A Fitting a shell bearing to a connecting rod

42.4B Fitting a big-end bearing cap

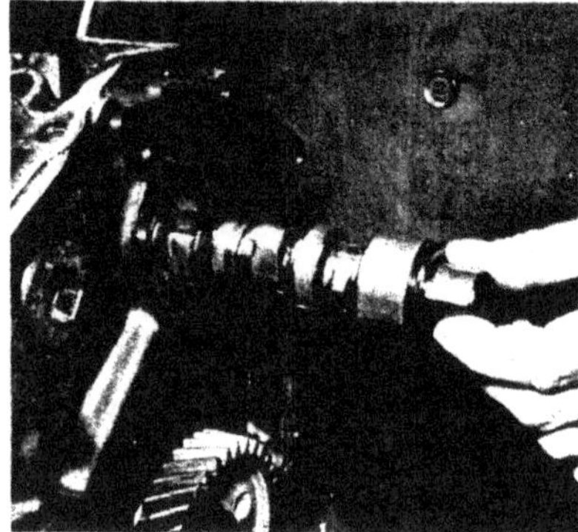
42.6 Installing the camshaft

42.8 Fitting the camshaft thrust plate

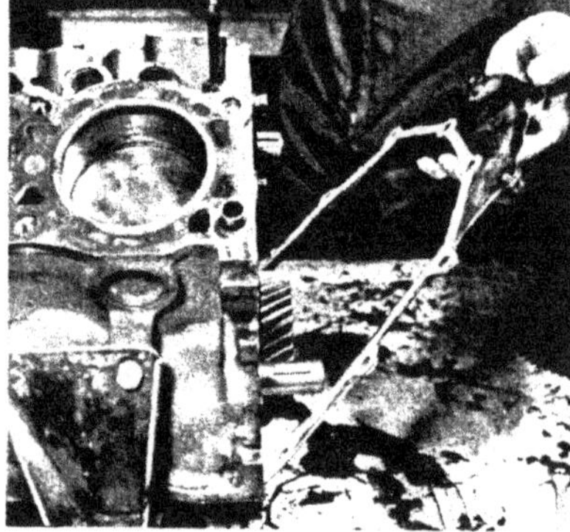
42.9 Locating a gasket to the front of the cylinder block

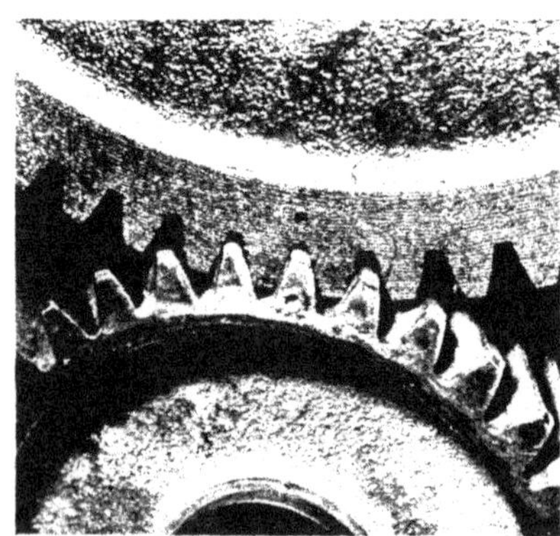
42.11 Crankshaft and camshaft timing gear marks

42.12 Crankshaft and balance shaft timing gear marks

42.18 Fitting the engine front cover

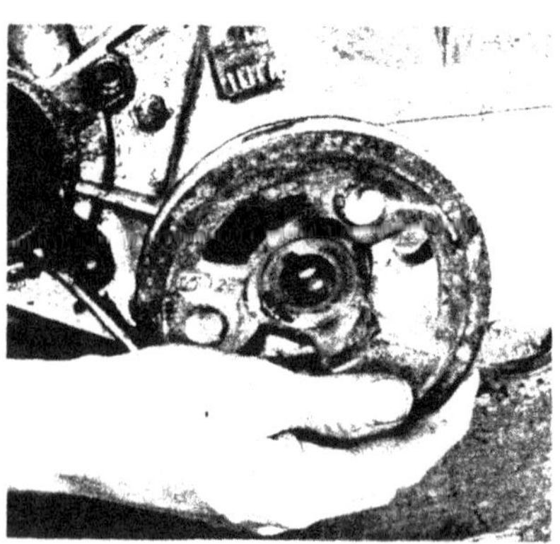
42.19 Fitting the balance shaft pulley

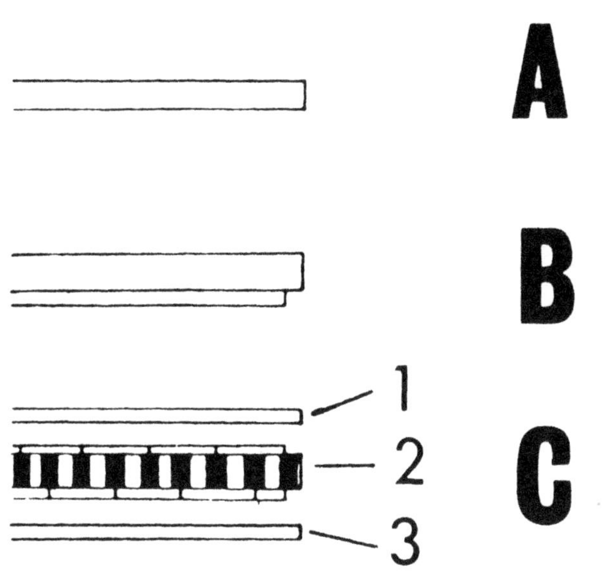


Fig 1.30 Sectional fitting diagram for piston rings

*A Top compression ring (chrome plated)*
*B Lower compression ring*
*C Oil control ring 1 and 3 Rails 2 Spring*

Woodruff key.

8 Fit the thrust plate to the front of the camshaft in such a way that the oil gallery hole is masked. To be correct camshaft endfloat must not exceed 0.0030 in (0.076 mm). Two spaces are available to adjust the endfloat (marked red and blue). Dismantle and refit the alternative one if it is necessary to correct the endfloat (photo).

9 Smear gasket cement to the front face of the cylinder block and locate a new gasket (photo).

10 Smear the rear face of the intermediate plate with gasket cement and position it against the gasket. Fit the two upper retaining bolts, finger tight and then screw in the two lower bolts a few turns as dowels. Check that the lower edge of the intermediate plate is flush with the crankcase side flanges and tighten the two upper bolts. Remove the two lower bolts.

11 Turn the crankshaft until the mark on the crankshaft gear is towards, and in line with, the camshaft. Fit the fibre camshaft gear so that its mark is towards and in alignment with, the mark on the crankshaft gear. Fit the camshaft gear securing bolt and washer (photo).

12 Fit the gear wheel to the balance shaft so that its mark is in line with the second mark on the crankshaft gear (photo).

13 When correctly fitted lines joining the centres of each gear wheel bolt will pass through the centre of the alignment marks.

14 Drift out the balance shaft pulley oil seal and press a new one into the engine front cover.

15 If the fan pulley bearing is worn, now is the time to renew it by pressing on the centre shaft so that the bearing is ejected to the rear and the fan blade mounting flange is extracted at the same time. Press the new bearing into position from the rear of the cover and then supporting the bearing on a block, press the mounting flange onto the shaft from the front.

16 Fit the water pump to the front cover using new gaskets.

17 Locate a new gasket to the front face of the intermediate plate, coating both sides with gasket cement.

18 Fit the engine front cover and finger tighten only at this stage the nine securing bolts (photo).

19 Oil the seal contact area of the balance shaft pulley and insert it through the oil seal in the engine front cover so that it engages with its key (photo).

20 Move the engine front cover to left or right until it is centralised about the balance shaft pulley. Tighten the front cover bolts to their specified torque.

21 Tighten the balance shaft pulley bolt and washer.

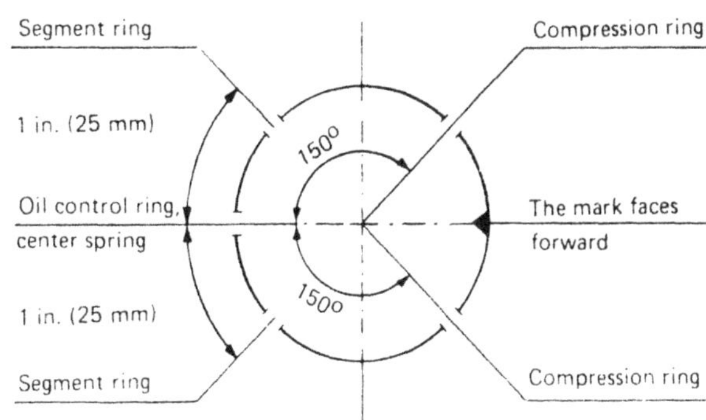


Fig 1.31 Piston ring end gap fitting diagram

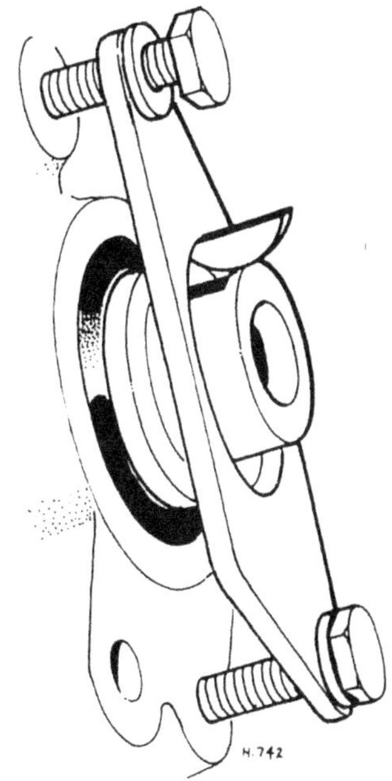


Fig 1.32 Correct fitting of camshaft thrust plate

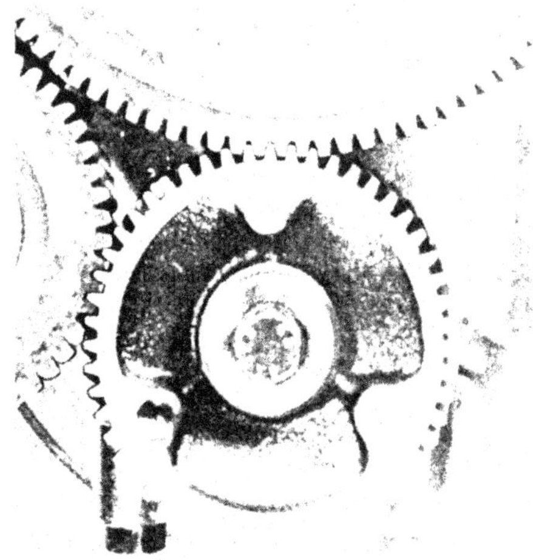

Fig 1.33 Timing gears correctly aligned

43.1 Fitting the oil pump driveshaft

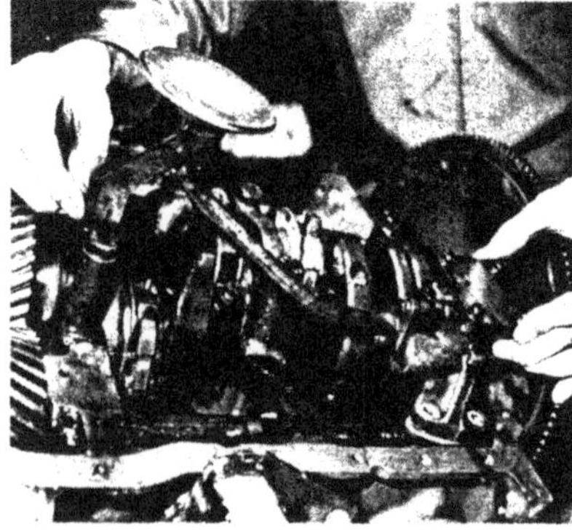
43.2 Fitting the oil pump

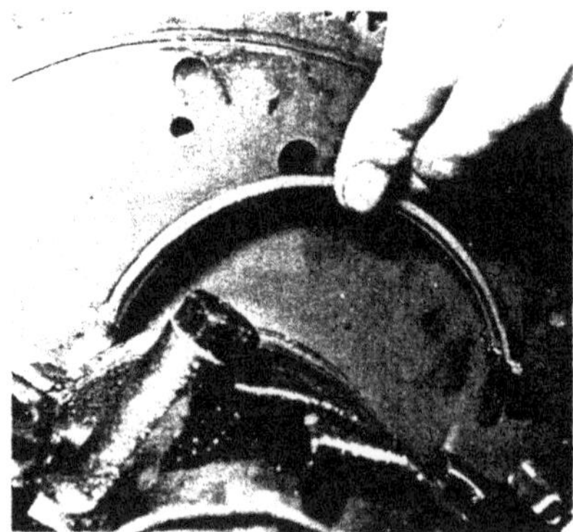
43.3 Fitting rubber seal to rear main bearing cap groove

43.5 Fitting the sump

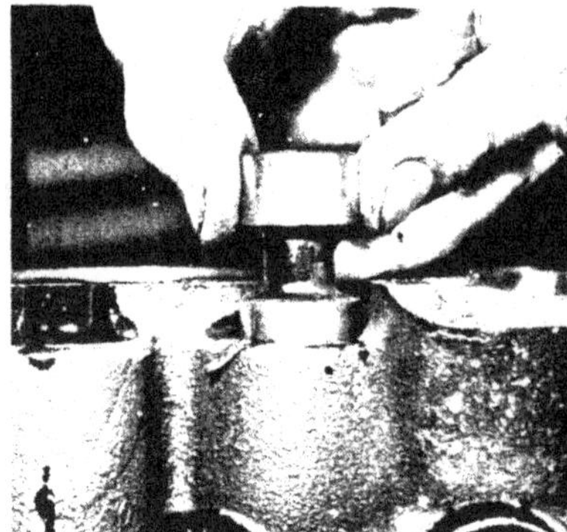
43.6 Inserting a tappet (cam follower) into the cylinder block

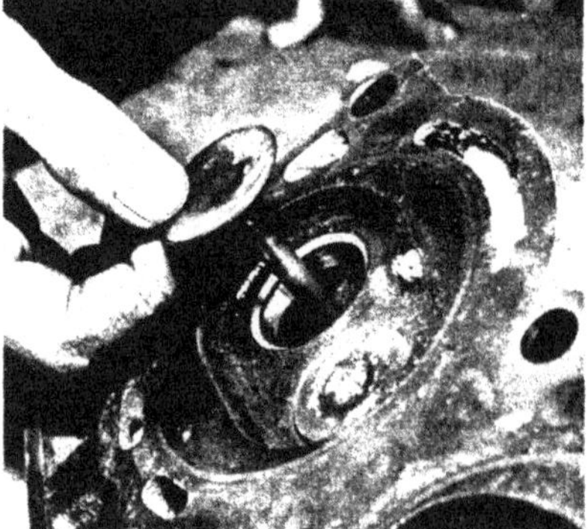
43.7A Installing a valve in the cylinder head

43.7B Fitting a valve stem oil seal

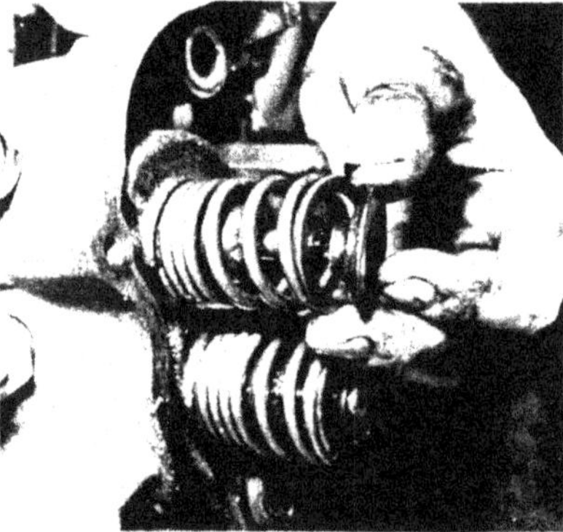
43.7C Valve springs correctly installed

43.9 Installation of a cylinder head gasket

43.10A Lowering a cylinder head into position

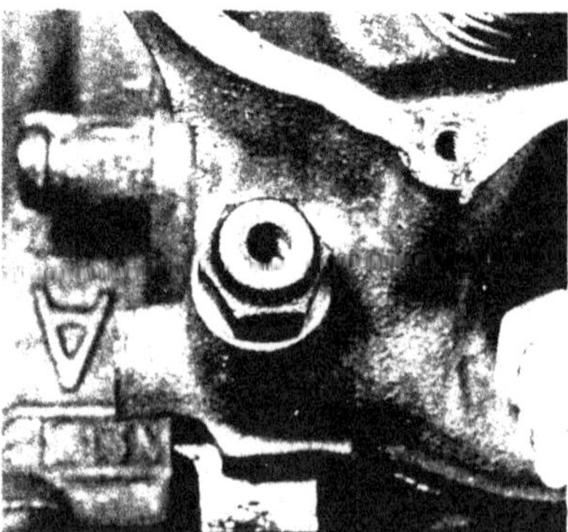
43.10B Cylinder head bolt for earth strap connection

43.12 Cylinder head and inlet manifold gasket interlocked

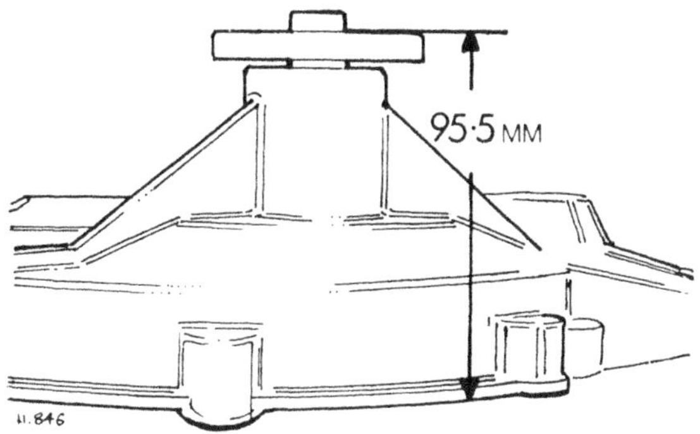


Fig 1.34 Correct positioning of fan mounting flange on its shaft

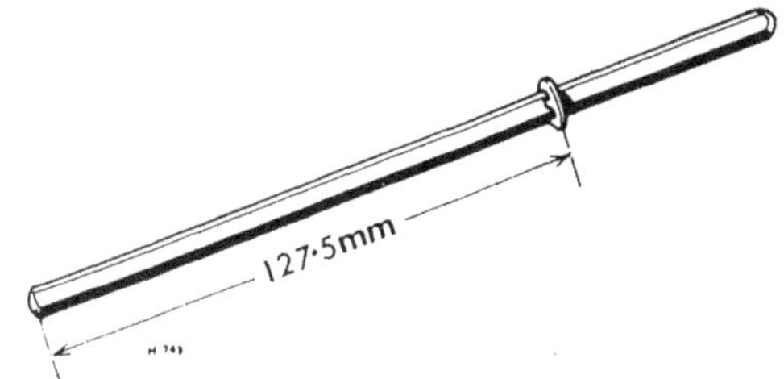


Fig 1.35 Correct location of oil pump driveshaft stop plate

## 43 Engine reassembly - oil pump, sump, tappets, valves, cylinder heads and inlet manifold

1 Insert the oil pump driveshaft (pointed-end first) into the cylinder block. Check that the stop plate is located as shown (photo).

2 Fit the oil pump complete with new joint gasket. Tighten the oil pump flange bolts first, followed by the intake tube bracket bolt (photo).

3 Fit a new rubber seal into the groove in the rear main bearing cap (photo).

4 Apply gasket cement to the corners of the crankcase to sump flange where the front cover, intermediate plate and sump meet. Smear the crankcase flanges with gasket cement and stick the sump gaskets in position. **Ensure that the gasket end tabs locate beneath the ends of the rear main bearing rubber seal.**

5 Fit the sump and tighten the bolts evenly, noting that the two bolts with the rubber washers are located adjacent to the balance shaft rear bearing (photo).

6 Invert the engine and having oiled the tappets, return them to their original locations (photo).

7 Refit the valves to their original cylinder head positions. Use new valve stem oil seals and if the engine has covered more than 20000 miles (32000 km) fit new valve springs as well. The three close coils of each valve spring should be located at the bottom. Reassembly of the valve components is a reversal of dismantling. The use of a little thick grease will help to retain the split cotters in position while the spring compressor is being released (photos).

8 Ensure the faces of both cylinder heads and block are scrupulously clean and free from old gasket fragments, scale and carbon.

9 Locate a new cylinder head gasket on the left and right-hand positioning dowels. The two gaskets are not interchangeable and are marked "FRONT TOP". Do not use gasket cement when fitting them (photo).

10 Lower each cylinder head into position on its positioning dowel and insert the cylinder head bolts finger tight noting that on the right-hand cylinder head the rear outer bolt secures the engine earth strap (photos).

11 Tighten each set of cylinder head bolts in the sequence shown and progressively in three stages. Set the torque wrench initially to 40 lb/ft (5.5 kg/m) and tighten all bolts. Reset the torque wrench to 50 lb/ft (7.0 kg/m) and go round the bolts again. Finally, reset the torque wrench to 68 lb/ft (9.5 kg/m) and tighten the bolts for the last time.

12 Smear the inlet manifold mating surfaces of the cylinder heads with gasket cement and fit a new gasket, **ensuring that the projection on the right-hand cylinder head gasket enters the cut-out in the inlet manifold gasket** (photo).

13 Locate the inlet manifold and insert the securing bolts. Tighten in the sequence shown in Fig. 1.40 first to a torque of 5 lb/ft (0.7 kg/m) for nuts and bolts and then to 15 lb/ft (2.0 kg/m) (photo).

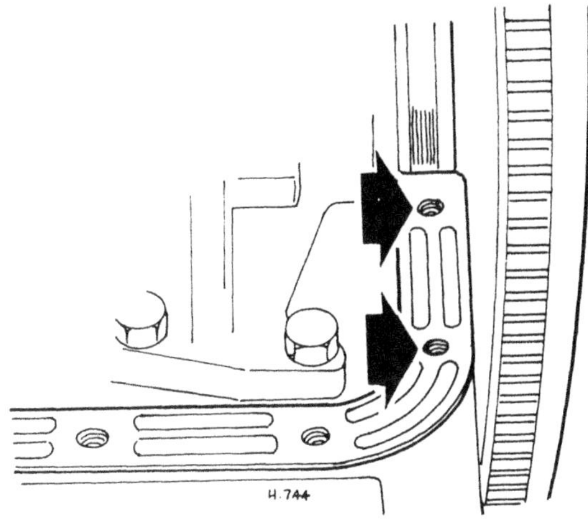


Fig 1.36 Location of the two sump bolts which have rubber sealing washers

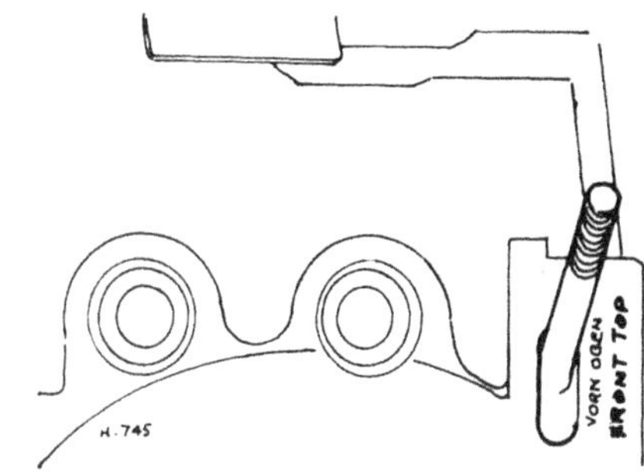


Fig 1.37 A cylinder head gasket correctly located

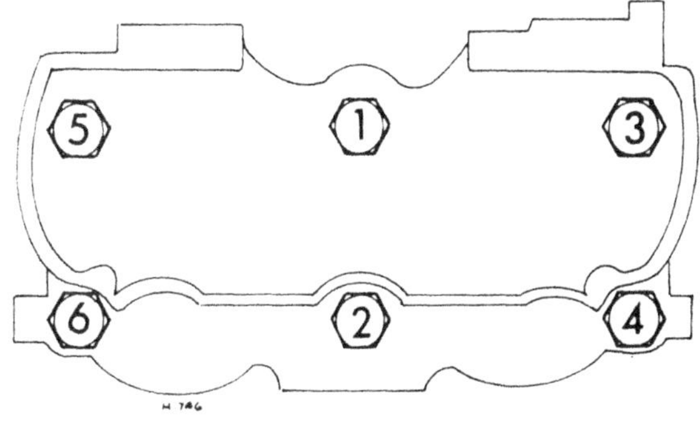


Fig 1.38 Cylinder head bolt tightening sequence

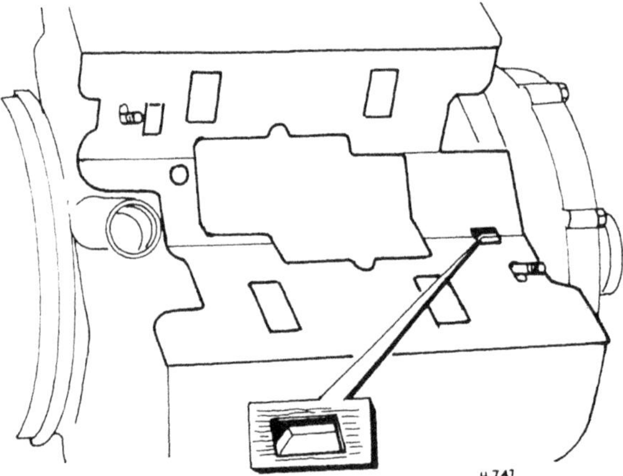


Fig 1.39 Installation of inlet manifold gasket

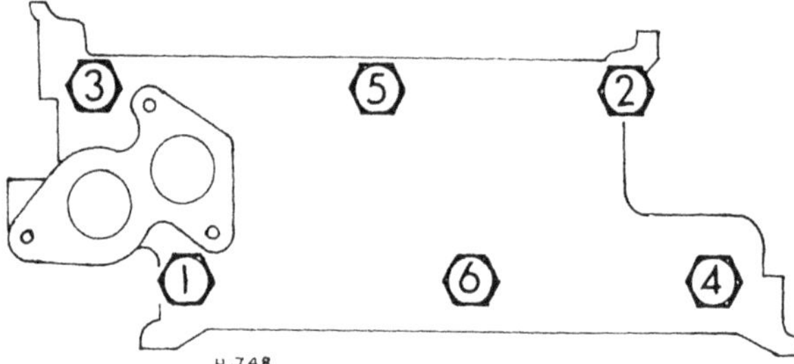


Fig 1.40 Inlet manifold bolt tightening sequence

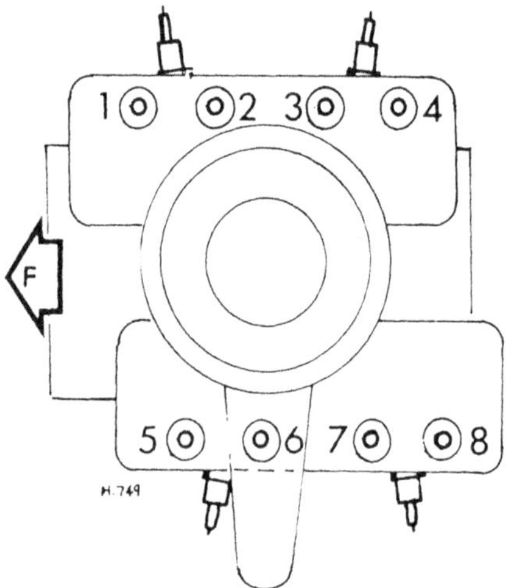


Fig 1.41 Cylinder and valve sequence diagram

*Valves 2–3–6–7 are exhaust*
*Valves 1–4–5–8 are inlet*

## 44 Engine reassembly - rocker gear and valve adjustment

1 Dip the end of each pushrod in engine oil and push it into engagement with its tappet (cam follower) (photo).
2 If the rocker gear has been dismantled ensure that the rocker shaft oil holes face downwards (ground-edge to bottom).
3 First insert a roll pin into the shaft and install the various components in their correct order. The pillars with the oil outlets must be located at the rear on the right-hand side of the engine and at the front on the left-hand side of the engine.
4 Fit the oil return plates and the rocker shaft assemblies, engaging the pushrods under the rocker arms before the pillar bolts are tightened alternatively a turn at a time (photos).
5 Adjust the valve clearances. To do this, turn the balance shaft pulley until its notch is opposite the tdc mark on the engine front cover (see Chapter 4). Move the pulley back-and-forth just enough to check whether the rocker arms on cylinders 1 or 4 are rocking and are depressing the valve stems.

If the rocker arms on no.1 cylinder are rocking then number 4 piston is at tdc on its compression stroke and the following valve clearances can be adjusted:

3 exhaust
5 inlet
7 exhaust
8 inlet

If the rocker arms on no. 4 cylinder are rocking then number 1 piston is at tdc on its compression stroke and the following valve clearances can be adjusted.

1 inlet
2 exhaust
4 inlet
6 exhaust

The valve clearances are inlet 0.014 in (0.35 mm) exhaust 0.016 in (0.40 mm) both set **Cold**.
6 The rocker arm adjusters are of interference thread type and are self-locking without the use of a locknut. Adjust the valve clearances so that the feeler gauge is a stiff sliding fit between the heel of the rocker arm and the end-face of the valve stem. (photo).
7 When valve adjustment is complete, fit new rocker cover gaskets and tighten the rocker cover bolts just sufficiently to grip, but not overcompress, the gasket. Always fit the cover with the oil filler to the right-hand cylinder head (photos).

## 45 Ancillary components - refitting before engine installation

1 This is a reversal of the removal procedure given in Section 9. Where more detailed descriptions are needed refer to the appropriate Chapters of this manual, (for example: carburettor refitting and adjustment Chapter 3; timing the ignition, Chapter 4).
2 Fit the clutch assembly to the flywheel and centralise the driven plate using a dowel or an old input shaft (photo).
3 Refit the fan assembly (photo).
4 Install the carburettor, intermediate plate and the two pressed steel gaskets, (both marked "TOP") (photos).
5 Screw in a new oil filter cartridge (hand-tight only). The nut on the casing is for removal purposes not tightening (photo).
6 Screw the oil pressure transmitter switch into the cylinder block (photo).
7 Refit the fuel pump and its operating rod, using a new joint gasket (photos).
8 Install the distributor. To do this, turn the engine until number 1 piston is at tdc on its compression stroke (feel the compression by placing a finger over number 1 plug hole). Continue turning until the notch on the balance shaft pulley is opposite the 6° mark on the engine front cover (photos).

Turn the rotor about 35° clockwise from the body alignment mark and then insert the distributor into its recess. As the distributor drive gears mesh, the rotor will turn anticlockwise and its alignment mark will coincide with the *line* on the distributor body. On some distributors there is a 35° *dot* on the distributor body to facilitate installation. To obtain perfect alignment after installation of the distributor, rotate the body slightly and then fit the clamp plate and bolt and connect the vacuum tube.
9 If the thermostat housing has been removed or dismantled, refit it using new gaskets (photo).
10 Screw in the spark plugs, correctly gapped. Use a new set if they have been in service for 10000 miles (16000 km) or more.
11 Fit the distributor cap and leads to the plugs and coil.

43.13 Lowering the inlet manifold into position

44.1 Installing the pushrods

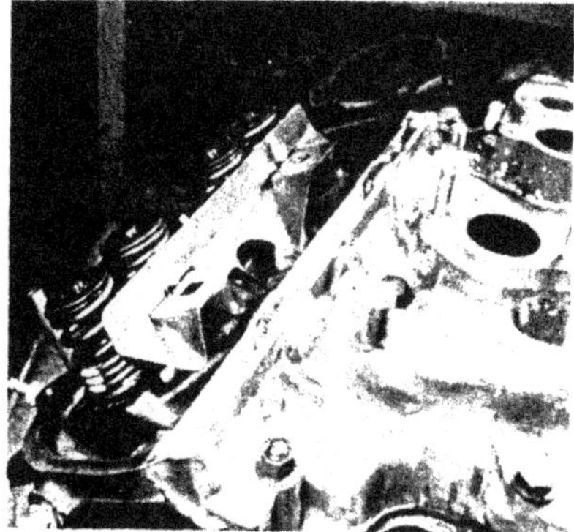
44.4A Correct location of oil return plate

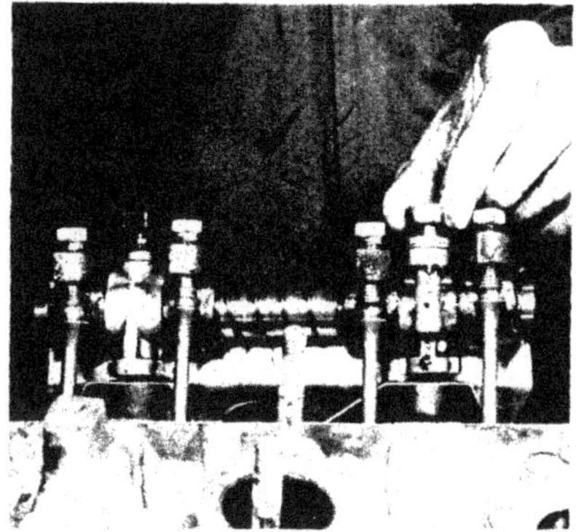
44.4B Installing a rocker shaft assembly and pillar bolts

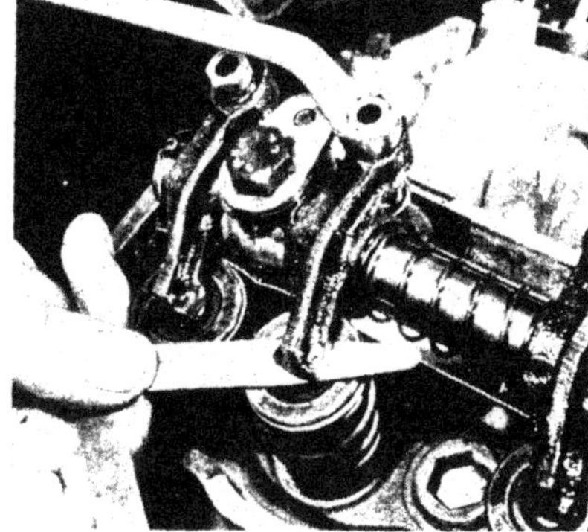
44.6 Adjusting a valve clearance

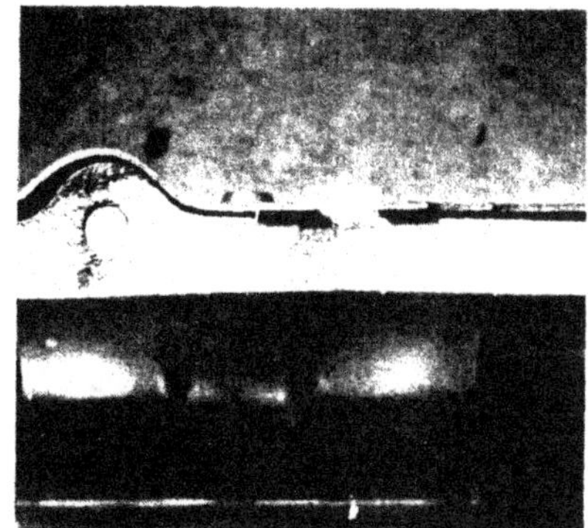
44.7A Rocker cover gasket retaining tab

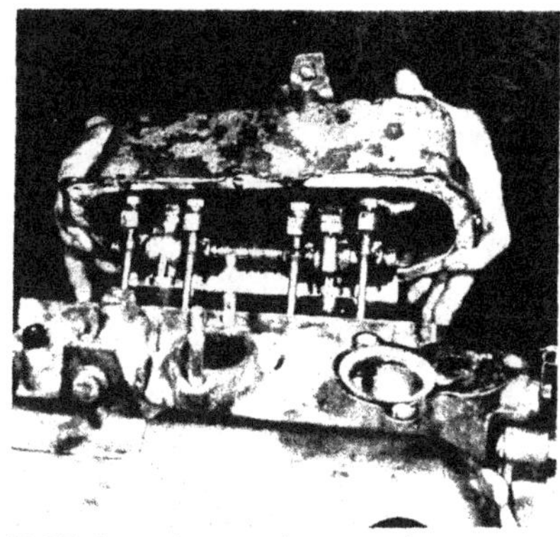
44.7B Lowering a rocker cover into position

45.2 Installing the clutch assembly with driven plate ready for centring

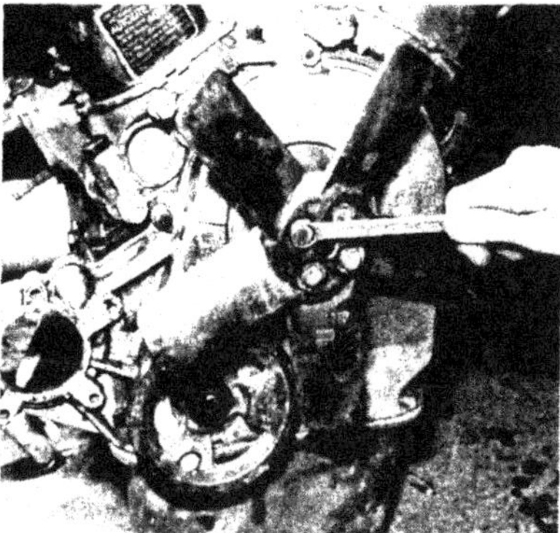
45.3 Tightening a fan securing bolt

45.4A Fitting the carburettor intermediate plate and gaskets

45.4B Fit the carburettor

45.5 Screwing in the oil filter cartridge

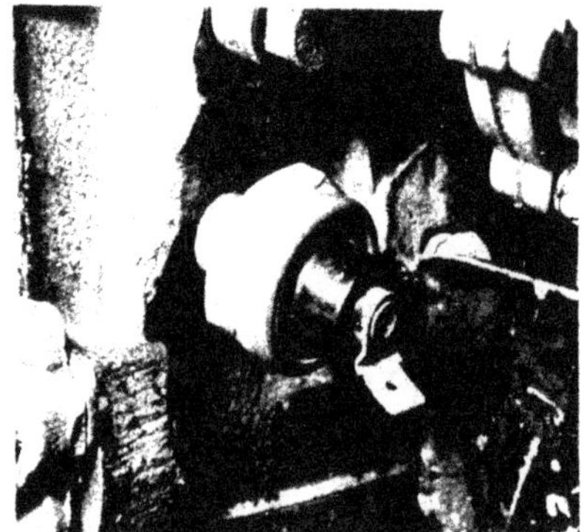
45.6 Location of oil pressure switch

45.7A Fuel pump operating rod

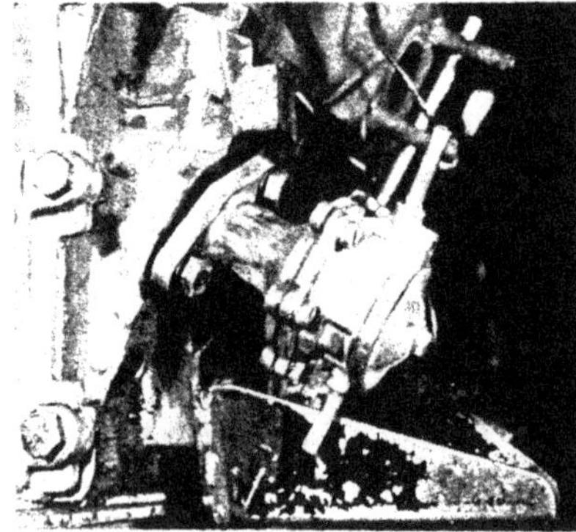
45.7B Installing the fuel pump

45.8A Ignition timing marks

45.8B Inserting the distributor into its recess

45.8C Distributor clamp plate and bolt

45.9 Refitting the thermostat housing

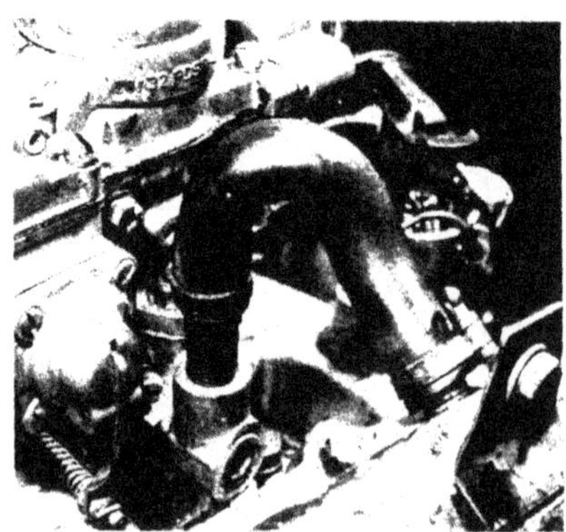
45.12A Rocker box breather pipe

45.12B Crankcase breather non-return valve

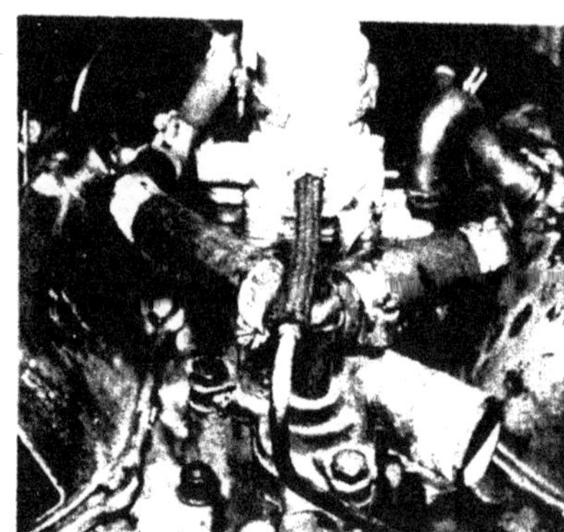
45.13 Fuel pump to carburettor flexible connection

45.14 Water connections to carburettor automatic choke

48.5 Engaging driveshaft inner joint components

12 Connect the breather pipe between the left-hand rocker box cover and the non-return valve which is screwed into the carburettor intermediate plate (photos).
13 Connect the fuel line between the fuel pump and the carburettor (photo).
14 Connect the water pipes to the carburettor automatic choke housing (photo).

## 46 Engine installation - general

1 Although the engine can be replaced by one man using a suitable winch, it is easier if two are present, one to lower the engine into the engine compartment and the other to guide the engine into position and to ensure it does not foul anything.
2 At this stage one or two tips may come in useful. Ensure all loose leads, cables, etc. are tucked out of the way. If not it is easy to trap one and so cause much additional work after the engine is replaced.
3 Two pairs of hands are better than one when refitting the bonnet. Do not tighten the bonnet securing bolts fully until it is ascertained that the bonnet is on straight.

## 47 Engine installation with transmission in-situ

1 The engine must be positioned suitably so that the sling used to remove it can be easily refitted and the lifting tackle hooked on. Position the engine the right way round in front of the car and then raise it so that it may be brought into position over the car or the car rolled into position underneath it.
2 The transmission unit should be raised to its approximately normal position using a wooden block.
3 Lower the engine steadily into the engine compartment, keeping all ancillary wires, pipes and the cables well clear of the sides. It is best to have a second person guiding the engine while it is being lowered.
4 The tricky part is finally mating the engine to the transmission unit, which involves locating the gearbox input shaft into the clutch housing and flywheel. Provided that the clutch friction plate has been centred correctly as described in Chapter 5, there should be little difficulty. Grease lightly the splines of the gearbox input shaft first. It may be necessary to rock the engine from side to side in order to get the engine fully home. Under no circumstances let any strain be imparted onto the gearbox input shaft. This could occur if the shaft was not fully located and the engine was raised or lowered more than the amount required for very slight adjustment of position.
5 As soon as the engine is fully up to the gearbox bellhousing replace the bolts holding the two together.
6 The final positioning of the engine brackets onto the mountings requires some attention because the positioning bolts on the mounting are angled inwards and therefore do not exactly line up with the holes in the brackets. However, they are flexibly mounted so provided two people are doing the work they may be levered into position whilst the engine is lowered.
7 Replace all electrical connections and the generator, the fuel lines and carburettor linkages, cooling system hoses and radiator in the reverse order as described in Section 6 or detailed in the next Section.
8 Reconnect the exhaust pipes to the manifolds.
9 Refill the engine with new oil and replace the coolant liquid.

## 48 Engine/transmission unit - installation

1 This is essentially a reversal of the removal procedure described in Section 5 but observe the following sequence of operations.
2 Mate the engine to the transmission in a similar manner to that described in the preceding Section.
3 Check that the inner universal joints are fitted with the correct type of grease.
4 Lower the combined unit into the engine compartment until the engine mounting brackets are about 2 in (5.8 mm) above the mounting pads (photo).
5 Insert the tee-pieces of the driveshafts into the inner universal joints. To do this, locate one horizontally and one vertically and push the engine first to one side and then the other. Engage the horizontal one first and then the vertical one. The cups of the vertically positioned tee-piece must be carefully held in position - to prevent the needle rollers being displaced.
6 Fit the engine stabiliser but tighten it only when the engine has been finally installed on its mountings (photo).
7 Lower the engine onto its mounting pads and tighten the securing bolts.
8 Lower the vehicle onto its roadwheels.
9 Fit new clamps round the inner universal joints.
10 Connect the rear mounting bracket assembly, ensuring that the travel limit washer is correctly located otherwise when the vehicle is in operation it is possible for the power unit to move forward on its flexible mountings and cause the fan to touch the radiator.
11 Inside the vehicle, refit the rubber plug and roll the floor mat into position.
12 Reconnect the speedometer cable and freewheel control to the transmission unit also the gearshift rod (note the reversing lamp switch and adjustable operating plate) (photo).
13 Refit the clutch operating cylinder and adjust the clutch as described in Chapter 5.
14 Use new gaskets when connecting the exhaust pipes to the cylinder heads (photo).
15 Connect the exhaust pipe clips under the vehicle.
16 Refit the alternator and adjust the drive belt (Chapter 2) and reconnect all leads, controls and cables to the engine, connect the fuel pipe to the fuel pump (photo).
17 Refit the radiator and connect all hoses.
18 Install the front grille panel and radiator straps and stays, noting the rubber faced clips at the grille lower mounting points (photo).

48.6 Tighten the engine stabilizer rod locknut

48.12 Gearchange rod at transmission unit end

48.14 Exhaust pipe to manifold flange joint

48.16 Refitting the alternator

48.18 Front grille lower mounting clips

19 Reconnect the headlamp and direction indicator leads.
20 Refill the cooling system as described in Chapter 2.
21 Fill the engine with the correct grade and quantity of oil.
22 Top-up the transmission unit oil level if necessary.
23 Reconnect the lead to the battery negative terminal.
24 With the help of an assistant, refit the bonnet.

## 49 Engine - initial start up after major overhaul

1 Make sure that the battery is fully charged and that all lubricants, coolants and fuel are replenished.

2 If the fuel system has been dismantled it will require several revolutions of the engine on the starter motor to get the petrol up to the carburettor.

3 As soon as the engine fires and runs keep it going at a fast tickover only (no faster) and bring it up to normal working temperature.

4 As the engine warms up there will be odd smells and some smoke from parts getting hot and burning off oil deposits. The signs to look for are leaks of oil or water which will be obvious if serious. Check also the clamp connections of the exhaust pipes to the manifolds as these do not always 'find' their exact gas tight position until the warmth and vibration have acted on them and it is almost certain that they will need tightening further. This should be done of course with the engine stopped.

5 When running temperature has been reached adjust the idling speed as described in Chapter 3.

6 Stop the engine and wait a few minutes to see if any lubricant or coolant is dripping out when the engine is stationary.

7 Road test the car to check that the timing is correct and giving the necessary smoothness and power. Do not race the engine - if new bearings and/or pistons and rings have been fitted it should be treated as a new engine and run in at reduced revolutions for 500 miles (800 km).

8 After a mileage of about 1200 miles (1900 km) check the torque setting of the cylinder head bolts and adjust the valve clearances (both with the engine cold) also check the security of all engine and transmission nuts and bolts.

9 After removal and refitting of the front grille panel, check the alignment of the headlamps.

## 50 Fault diagnosis - engine

| Symptom | Reason/s | Remedy |
|---|---|---|
| Engine will not turn over when starter switch is operated | Flat battery<br>Bad battery connections<br>Bad connections at solenoid switch and/or starter motor | Check that battery is fully charged and that all connections are clean and tight. |
| | Defective solenoid | Bridge the main terminals of the solenoid switch with a piece of heavy duty cable in order to operate the starter. |
| | Starter motor defective | Remove and overhaul starter motor. |
| Engine turns over normally but fails to fire and run | No spark at plugs | Check ignition system according to procedures given in Chapter 4. |
| | No fuel reaching engine | Check fuel system according to procedures given in Chapter 3. |
| | Too much fuel reaching the engine (flooding) | Check the fuel system as above. |
| Engine starts but runs unevenly and misfires | Ignition and/or fuel system faults | Check the ignition and fuel systems as though the engine had failed to start. |
| | Incorrect valve clearances | Check and reset clearances. |
| | Burnt out valves<br>Blown cylinder head gasket/s | Remove cylinder heads and examine and overhaul as necessary. |
| | Worn out piston rings<br>Worn cylinder bores | Remove cylinder heads and examine pistons and cylinder bores. Overhaul as necessary. |
| Lack of power | Ignition and/or fuel system faults | Check the ignition and fuel systems for correct ignition timing and carburettor settings. |
| | Incorrect valve clearances | Check and reset the clearances. |
| | Burnt out valves<br>Blown cylinder head gasket/s | Remove cylinder heads and examine and overhaul as necessary. |
| | Worn out piston rings<br>Worn cylinder bores | Remove cylinder heads and examine pistons and cylinder bores. Overhaul as necessary. |
| Excessive oil consumption | Oil leaks from crankshaft rear oil seal, timing cover gasket and oil seal, rocker cover gasket, oil filter gasket, sump gasket, sump plug washer | Identify source of leak and renew seal as appropriate. |
| | Worn piston rings or cylinder bores resulting in oil being burnt by engine. Smoky exhaust is an indication | Fit new rings or rebore cylinders and fit new pistons, depending on degree of wear. |
| | Worn valve guides and/or defective valve stem seals. Smoke blowing out from the rocker cover vents is an indication | Remove cylinder heads and recondition valve stem bores and valves and seals as necessary. |
| Excessive mechanical noise from engine | Wrong valve to rocker clearances | Adjust valve clearances. |
| | Worn crankshaft bearings<br>Worn cylinders (piston slap)<br>Worn timing gears | Inspect and overhaul where necessary. |

*Note: When investigating starting and uneven running faults do not be tempted into snap diagnosis. Start from the beginning of the check procedure and follow it through. It will take less time in the long run. Poor performance from an engine in terms of power and economy is not normally diagnosed quickly. In any event the ignition and fuel systems must be checked first before assuming any further investigation needs to be made.*

# Chapter 2 Cooling system

**Contents**



**Specifications**

| | |
|---|---|
| **Type** ... ... ... ... ... ... ... ... ... | Pressurised with pump and fan |
| **Capacity (including heater)** | |
| 1967–68 models ... ... ... ... ... ... ... | 13.2 pints (7.5 litres) |
| 1969 onwards models ... ... ... ... ... ... | 11.9 pints (6.8 litres) |
| 1969 (North American) models ... ... ... ... ... | 12.5 pints (7.1 litres) |
| **Thermostat opening range** | |
| Early type opens ... ... ... ... ... ... ... | 189°F (87°C) |
| Later type opens ... ... ... ... ... ... ... | 181°F (83°C) |
| **Radiator pressure cap rating (opens)** ... ... ... ... | 2.2 to 4.3 lb in$^2$ (0.25 to 0.30 kg cm$^2$) |
| **Fan belt deflection** ... ... ... ... ... ... ... | 5/16 in (7.6 mm) |

## 1 General description

The cooling system is of positive circulation, pressurized type incorporating an impeller type pump driven by a belt from the balance shaft pulley. This belt also drives the fan which is mounted on a bearing pressed into the engine front cover.

A thermostat, water temperature transmitter and radiator and cylinder block drain plugs are fitted.

The vehicle interior heater and the automatic choke operate by connections to the engine cooling system.

There are certain differences in detail and water circulation layouts of models according to date of manufacture, the main difference being that before 1969 an expansion bottle was not included in the system.

## 2 Cooling system - draining

1 On all models remove the radiator filler cap and on 1969 models onwards remove the cap from the expansion bottle as well.

2 Unscrew the radiator drain tap and collect the coolant in a suitable container. When coolant has ceased to run out, the two cylinder block drain plugs should be unscrewed. This operation need not be carried out if only the radiator is being removed.

3 To drain the expansion bottle, disconnect it from its bracket and raise it so that its contents will drain through its connecting tube and out through the radiator drain tap.

4 The system cannot be fully drained unless the vehicle heater control is placed in the fully on position.

## 3 Cooling system - flushing

1 With time, the radiator and the jacketing waterways in the engine may become restricted or even blocked with scale and sediment deposits so reducing the efficiency of the cooling system. This is when flushing is necessary.

2 With the system drained and taps removed run water from a hose through it for several minutes to clear loose deposits. It may be necessary to probe the drain outlet while this is going on.

3 Close the drain taps and refill the system with water and a proprietary chemical radiator cleaner. Replace the filler cap and run the engine for ten to fifteen minutes. Then drain out and flush thoroughly with clean water. If the scale deposits are particularly heavy a second treatment may be necessary. Under no circumstances, however, should the cleaning compound be left in the system.

4 In severe cases of clogging, remove the radiator and reverse flush it. This is done by inverting the radiator and forcing water against the normal direction of flow by inserting the hose in the bottom hose connection.

## 4 Cooling system - filling

1 Check that the radiator drain tap is closed, also the two cylinder block drain plugs.

2 Place the heater control to the fully on position and open the heater bleed nipple.

3 Pour coolant into the expansion bottle until it reaches the

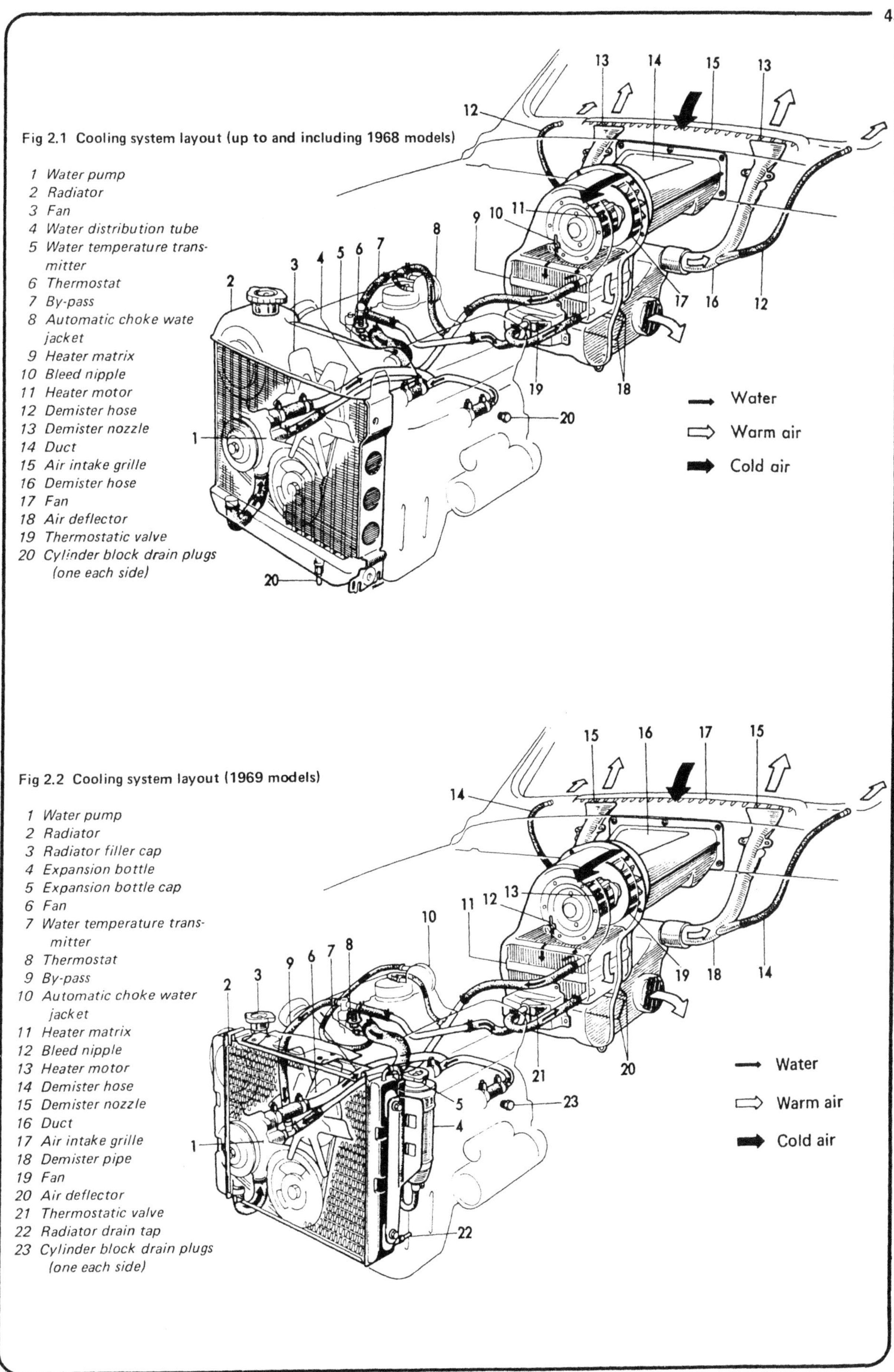


Fig 2.1 Cooling system layout (up to and including 1968 models)

*1 Water pump*
*2 Radiator*
*3 Fan*
*4 Water distribution tube*
*5 Water temperature transmitter*
*6 Thermostat*
*7 By-pass*
*8 Automatic choke wate jacket*
*9 Heater matrix*
*10 Bleed nipple*
*11 Heater motor*
*12 Demister hose*
*13 Demister nozzle*
*14 Duct*
*15 Air intake grille*
*16 Demister hose*
*17 Fan*
*18 Air deflector*
*19 Thermostatic valve*
*20 Cylinder block drain plugs (one each side)*

Fig 2.2 Cooling system layout (1969 models)

*1 Water pump*
*2 Radiator*
*3 Radiator filler cap*
*4 Expansion bottle*
*5 Expansion bottle cap*
*6 Fan*
*7 Water temperature transmitter*
*8 Thermostat*
*9 By-pass*
*10 Automatic choke water jacket*
*11 Heater matrix*
*12 Bleed nipple*
*13 Heater motor*
*14 Demister hose*
*15 Demister nozzle*
*16 Duct*
*17 Air intake grille*
*18 Demister pipe*
*19 Fan*
*20 Air deflector*
*21 Thermostatic valve*
*22 Radiator drain tap*
*23 Cylinder block drain plugs (one each side)*

**Fig 2.3 Cooling system layout (1970 models onwards)**

*1 Water pump*
*2 Radiator*
*3 Radiator filler cap*
*4 Expansion bottle*
*5 Expansion bottle cap*
*6 Fan*
*7 Water temperature gauge*
*8 Thermostat*
*9 Bypass*
*10 Automatic choke water jacket*
*11 Heat exchanger*
*12 Bleed nipple*
*13 Heater motor*
*14 Demister hose*
*15 Demister nozzle*
*16 Duct*
*17 Air intake grille*
*18 Demister pipe*
*19 Fan*
*20 Air deflector*
*21 Thermostatic valve*
*22 Radiator drain tap*
*23 Cylinder drain plugs (one each side*

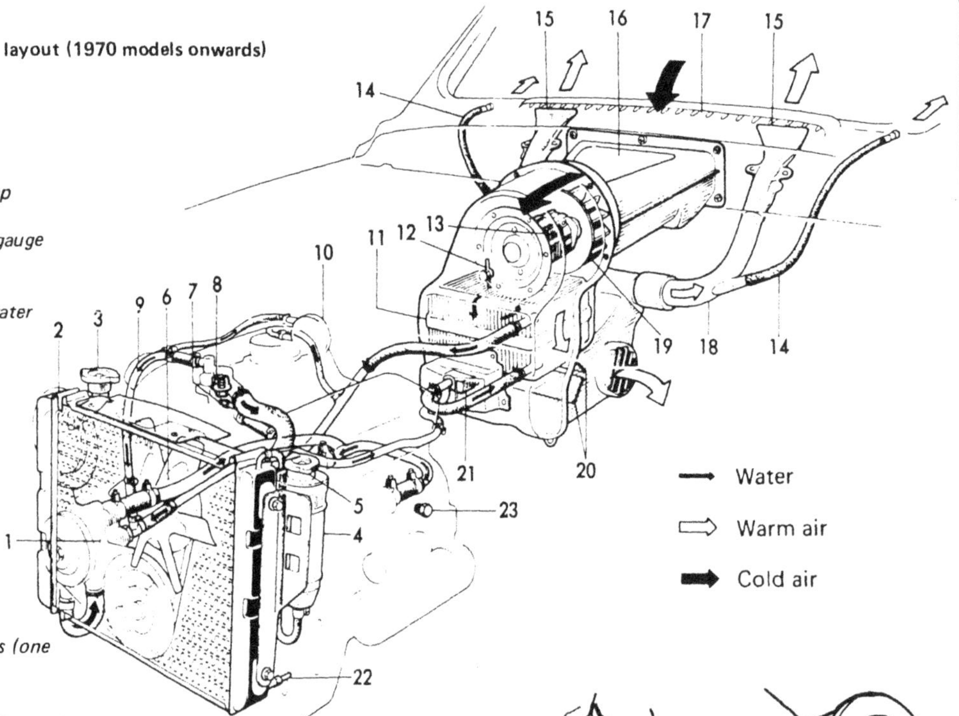

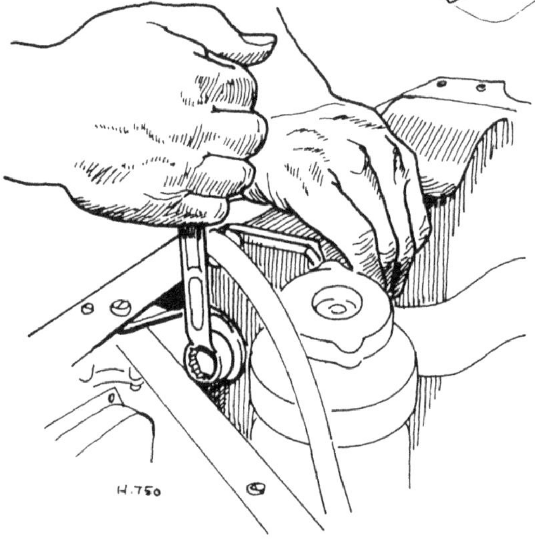

**Fig 2.4 Removing a radiator upper securing bolt**

**Fig 2.5 Removing the thermostat housing cover**

*1 Thermostat housing cover*
*2 Thermostat*
*3 Gasket*

6.4 A radiator lower mounting

7.4 Thermostat housing hose branch connection

7.6 Thermostat and seating

maximum level mark.

4 Fill the radiator to within one inch (25.4 mm) of the filler neck.

5 Start the engine and run it at varying speeds until coolant emerges from the heater bleed nipple, then close the nipple.

6 Top-up the radiator and refit both the radiator and expansion bottle caps.

7 Check and top-up, if necessary, the coolant level in the expansion bottle during the first few days running as trapped air will be vented during this period and cause a drop in the expansion bottle fluid level.

8 Never add cold water to a hot engine and where large quantities of topping-up liquid are required, always add antifreeze to it in order to maintain the strength of the mixture.

## 5 Antifreeze mixture

1 In climatic conditions where the ambient temperature is likely to drop below freezing point the use of antifreeze is essential. If the coolant is permitted to freeze in the car serious damage can result.

2 A good proprietary brand (such as Castrol Antifreeze) should be used and may be left in the cooling system for at least a year. All antifreeze solutions contain corrosion inhibitors which will keep the system in good condition whatever the climatic conditions.

3 The quantity of antifreeze which should be used for various levels of protection is given in the table below, expressed as a percentage of the cooling system capacity.

| Antifreeze volume | Protection to: | Spec. gravity |
|---|---|---|
| 10% | -8°C (17°F) | 1.017 |
| 15% | -13°C (7°F) | 1.024 |
| 20% | -19°C (-3°F) | 1.032 |

4 Always be guided by the antifreeze manufacturers instructions however, as variations in strength do occur between products of different makes.

## 6 Radiator - removal, inspection and refitting

1 Drain the cooling system as described in Section 2.

2 Remove the bonnet as described in Chapter 1.

3 Disconnect the radiator top and bottom hoses.

4 Unscrew and remove the radiator upper and lower retaining bolts and lift the radiator out of the engine compartment. Where an expansion bottle is fitted, disconnect the tube from the radiator as the latter is withdrawn (photo).

5 Refitting is a reversal of removal. Refill the system as described in Section 4.

## 7 Thermostat - removal, testing and refitting

1 A faulty thermostat can cause overheating or failure of the engine to warm up quickly in cold weather. It will also affect the performance of the heater.

2 Drain the coolant through the radiator drain tap into a suitable container.

3 Remove the air cleaner and the carburettor.

4 Disconnect the water hoses from the thermostat housing (photo).

5 Unscrew and remove the bolts which secure the thermostat cover and remove the cover.

6 Peel off the gasket and lift out the thermostat. If the thermostat is stuck in its seating, cut carefully round its edge with a sharp pointed knife to release it. On no account attempt to prise or lever it out by its bridge piece (photo).

7 To test whether the thermostat functions as it should, suspend it in a pan of water with a piece of string. Then, with a thermometer in the water (not touching the pan) note at what temperature it starts to open. This should be 189°F (87°C) for early type units and 181 °F (83°) for later units. Check that the thermostat closes once again (after cooling naturally). Should it fail on any of these checks it must be renewed. Note that the operation of the thermostat is not instantaneous so allow sufficient time when testing it. Should the thermostat have stuck open it would have been apparent when the housing cover was removed.

8 Replacement of the thermostat is a reversal of the removal precedure. Ensure that the mating faces of the two flanges are clean and use a new gasket. It is a sensible insurance to use a sealing compound also such as 'Hermetite'. If the housing is very deeply corroded it should be renewed.

## 8 Water pump - removal and refitting

1 Drain the coolant through the radiator drain tap into a suitable container.

2 Remove the alternator and its mounting bracket and detach the drivebelt (photo).

3 Unscrew the bolts at the rear of the engine front cover which will then enable the water pump front and rear sections to be drawn off. If the bolts are not completely withdrawn, the rear

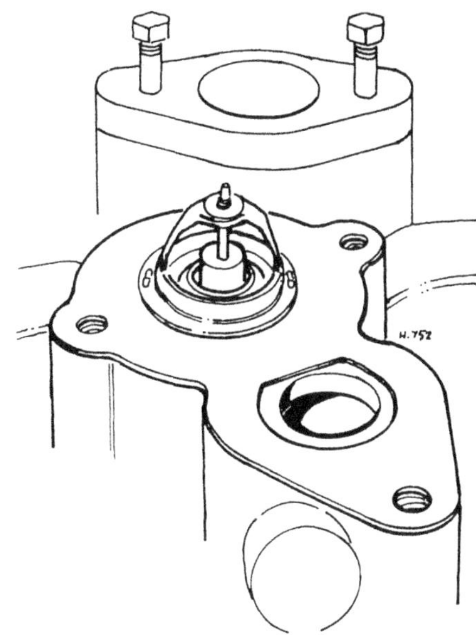


Fig 2.6 Correct orientation of thermostat in housing

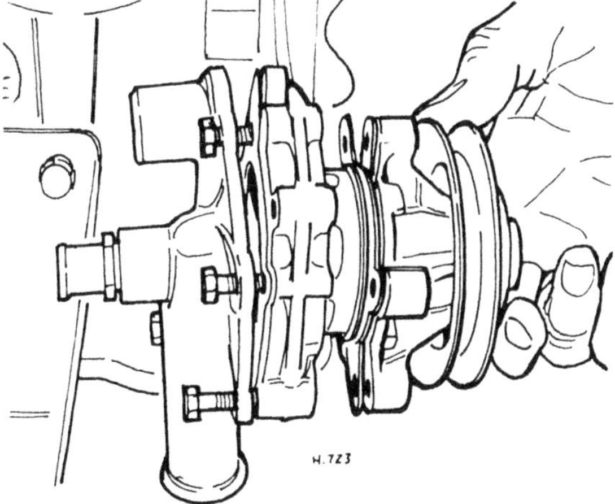


Fig 2.7 Removing water pump front housing and impeller

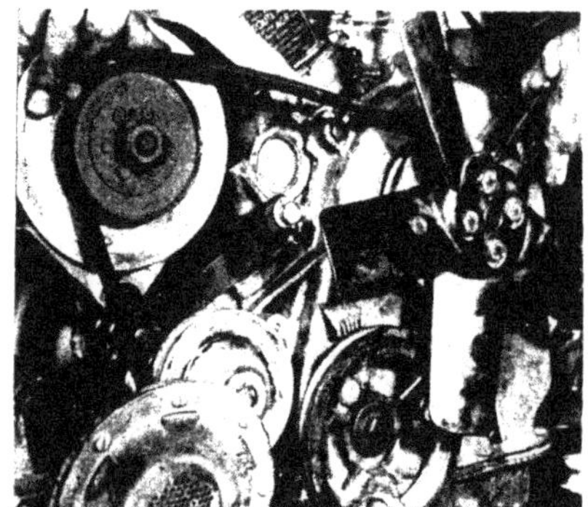

8.2 Slipping off the alternator/water pump drive belt

8.3A Removing the impeller section of the water pump

8.3B Removing the water pump rear housing

9.6 Locating the water pump seal

9.7 Preparing to press on the water pump impeller

11.1 Checking drive belt deflection

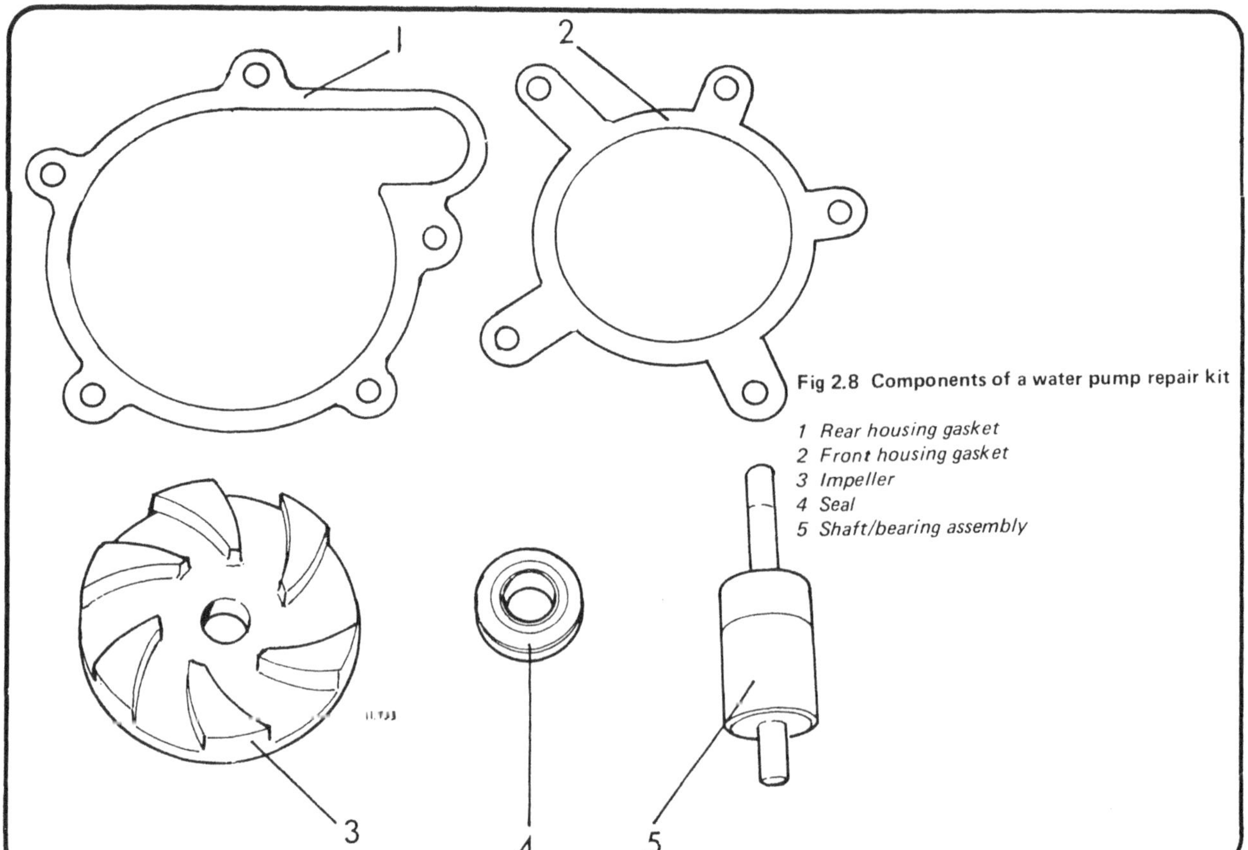

**Fig 2.8 Components of a water pump repair kit**

*1 Rear housing gasket*
*2 Front housing gasket*
*3 Impeller*
*4 Seal*
*5 Shaft/bearing assembly*

section of the water pump and its gasket can remain undisturbed (photos).

4 Installation is a reversal of removal but use a new gasket and check that the mating surfaces are quite clean.

5 Adjust the drivebelt tension as described in Section 11.

## 9 Water pump - servicing

1 In the event of leakage from the water pump seal or other malfunction it is recommended that an exchange pump be purchased, as in all probability the bearing will have worn and other components will have corroded.

2 Where suitable presses are available however, obtain a repair kit and proceed in the following manner.

3 Support the rear face of the water pump front housing on a tubular distance piece and press out the combined shaft/bearing/impeller assembly simultaneously from the pulley and housing. One way to do this is to support the housing with a short piece cut from a cast-iron rainpipe and then placing the whole assembly in the vice jaws and pressing on the nose of the shaft. When the shaft is flush with the housing obtain a suitable piece of rod slightly smaller than the shaft in diameter and use this to press it right through.

4 No further dismantling is necessary as all the components of the shaft and bearing come together as a repair kit.

5 Commence reassembly by pressing the shaft/bearing assembly (longer shaft leading) into the front face of the water pump housing. Coat the outer surface of the bearing with Loctite before pressing in and only apply pressure to the bearing outer track.

6 Invert the housing and from the rear press on the seal with its carbon face away from the bearing (photo).

7 Now press on the impeller while supporting the shaft and bearing assembly at the front of the housing. When correctly located there should be a clearance of between 0.025 and 0.030 in (0.6350 and 0.7620 mm) between the faces of housing and impeller (photo).

8 Support the front face of the water pump pulley on a tubular distance piece and press the shaft into it from the rear. Do not let the press impinge upon the impeller during this operation. When correctly fitted, the shaft should protrude through the pulley by between 0.03 and 0.08 in (0.8 and 2.0 mm).

## 10 Fan bearing - renewal

1 To renew the fan bearing which is pressed into the engine front cover, refer to Chapter 1, Section 42.

## 11 Fanbelt - adjustment and renewal

1 To adjust the fanbelt, slacken the alternator mounting pivot bolts, also the two adjustment link bolts. Pull the alternator away from the engine and retighten the link bolt to provide a downward deflection of 5/16 in (7.6 mm) at the centre of the top run of the belt (photo).

2 Fully tighten the link and pivot bolts.

3 If a new belt is to be fitted, loosen the alternator link and pivot bolts and push the alternator in towards the engine as far as possible. Lift the driving belt over the rim of the alternator pulley and then remove it from the other three pulleys.

4 Refitting is a reversal of removal. Adjust the new belt as described earlier in this Section.

## 12 Water temperature gauge and transmitter - testing and renewal

1 In the event of non-operation of the temperature gauge first check the security of the connections at the gauge and the transmitter.

2 Disconnect the lead from the transmitter unit which is located just below the thermostat housing. With the ignition switched on, the gauge should register "L" (cold). Earth the lead when the gauge should register "H" (hot). If the test is positive then the gauge is serviceable otherwise renew the gauge as described under instrument removal in Chapter 11 (photo).

3 If the gauge and the wiring are in good order then it is the transmitter unit which is at fault and it should be renewed.

4 Drain coolant from the radiator and cylinder block until by carefully unscrewing the transmitter unit it can be observed that the coolant level is below that of the unit.

5 Tighten the radiator and cylinder block taps, coat the threads of the new transmitter unit with gasket cement and screw it into position.

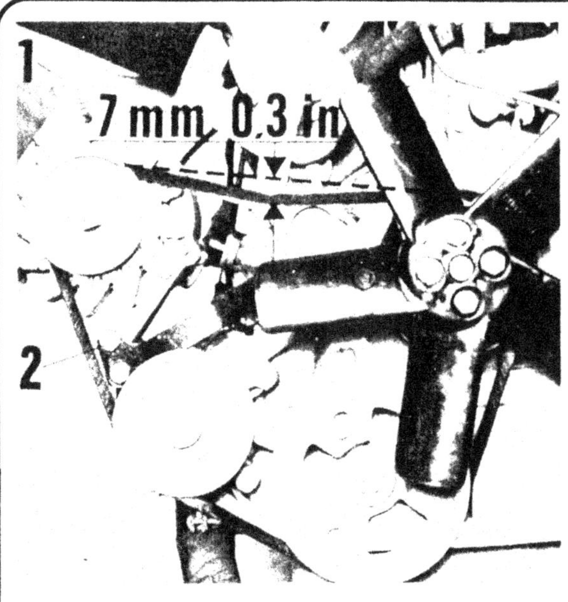


Fig 2.9 Fan belt adjustment diagram

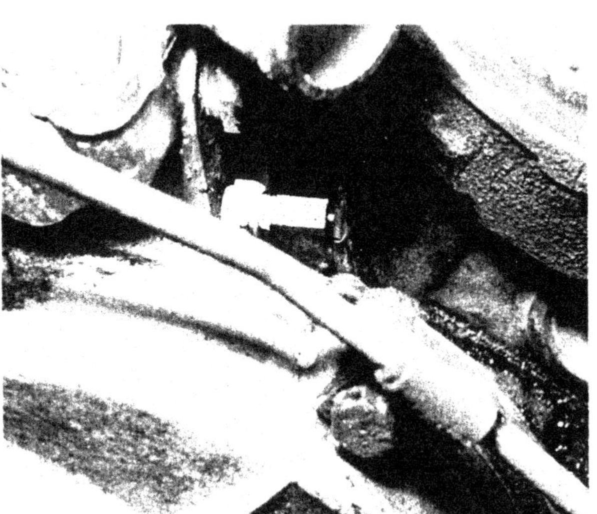

12.2 Location of water temperature transmitter

## 13 Fault diagnosis - cooling system

| Symptom | Reason/s | Remedy |
|---|---|---|
| Loss of coolant | Leak in system | Examine all hoses, hose connections, drain taps and the radiator and heater for signs of leakage when the engine is cold, then when hot and under pressure. Tighten clips, renew hoses and repair radiator. Examine gasket between inlet manifold and thermostat housing elbow for signs of leaks. |
| | Defective radiator pressure cap | Examine cap for defective seal or spring and renew if necessary. |
| | Overheating causing rapid evaporation due to excessive pressure in system forcing vapour past radiator cap | Check reasons for overheating. |
| | Blown cylinder head gasket, causing excess pressure in cooling system forcing coolant past radiator cap | Remove suspect cylinder head (or heads) and renew gasket. |
| | Cracked block or head or inlet manifold due to freezing or careless reassembly | Strip engine and examine. Repair as required. |
| Overheating | Insufficient coolant in system | Top up. |
| | Water pump not turning properly due to slack fan belt | Tighten fan belt. |
| | Kinked or collapsed water hoses causing restriction to circulation of coolant. | Renew hose as required. |
| | Faulty thermostat (not opening properly) | Fit new thermostat. |
| | Engine out of tune | Check ignition setting and carburettor adjustments. |
| | Blocked radiator either internally or externally | Flush out cooling system and clean out cooling fins. |
| | Cylinder head gasket blown, forcing coolant out of system | Remove head (or heads) and renew gasket. |
| | New engine not run-in | Adjust engine speed until run-in. |
| | Binding brakes causing excessive power load on engine | Check and adjust brakes. |
| | Blocked or restricted exhaust system | Examine exhaust system for kinks, dents or blockage. |
| Engine running too cool | Missing, faulty or wrong type of thermostat | Fit new thermostat. |

# Chapter 3

# Carburation, fuel and exhaust systems

Contents



Specifications

## Fuel pump

| | |
|---|---|
| Type ... | Mechanical, operated by pushrod from eccentric on camshaft |
| Pressure ... | 3.4 to 4.3 lb in$^2$ (0.24 to 0.30 kg cm$^2$) at 4000 rev/min (crankshaft) |

## Fuel tank

| | Up to 1970 | 1970 onwards |
|---|---|---|
| Capacity: | | |
| Saab 95 ... | 9.5 gals (43.0 litres) | 9.2 gals (42.0 litres) |
| Saab 96 and Monte Carlo ... | 8.8 gals (40.0 litres) | 8.4 gals (38.0 litres) |

## Carburettors

| | |
|---|---|
| 1967–68 vehicles (up to chassis No 46137 for Saab 95 and No 434173 for Saab 96 and Monte Carlo ... | Solex downdraught type 28-32 PDSIT-7 (automatic choke) |
| 1967–68 vehicles (from chassis No 46138 for Saab 95 and No 434174 for Saab 96 and Monte Carlo) ... | Solex downdraught type 32-PDSIT-4 (automatic choke) |

| Solex carburettors - specifications: | 28-32PDSIT-7 | 32-PDSIT-4 | With exhaust emission control |
|---|---|---|---|
| Main jet ... | 125 | 127.5 | 127.5 |
| Choke tube ... | 25.5 | 25.5 | 25.5 |
| Emulsion jet ... | 110 | 95 | 100 |
| Idling jet (fuel) ... | 50 | 50 | 42.5 |
| Idling jet (air) ... | 1.5 | 1.5 | 1.5 |
| Fuel inlet valve ... | 1.5 | 1.5 | 1.5 |
| Accelerator pump jet ... | 50 | 50 | 50 |
| Accelerator pump capacity (10 strokes) ... | 0.6 in$^3$ (10 cm$^3$) | 0.6 in$^3$ (10 cm$^3$) | 0.6 in$^3$ (10 cm$^3$) |
| Idling speed ... | 800 to 900 rev/min | 800 to 900 rev/min | 800 to 900 rev/min |
| Fast idling: | | | |
| Stage 1 ... | 1100 to 1300 rev/min | 1100 to 1300 rev/min | 1100 to 1300 rev/min |
| Stage 2 ... | 1700 to 1900 rev/min | 1700 to 1900 rev/min | 1700 to 1900 rev/min |
| Stage 3 ... | 2700 to 2900 rev/min | 2700 to 2900 rev/min | 2700 to 2900 rev/min |

| | |
|---|---|
| 1969 vehicles – Ford downdraught type ... ... ... ... | C8GH-9510-G or C8GH-9510-H (with exhaust emission control) |
| 1970 vehicles – Ford downdraught type ... ... ... ... | C8GH-9510G or 70TW-9510-AA (with exhaust emission control) |
| 1971 models (from chassis No 96-600233 for Saab 95 and No 95-95060 for Saab 96) ... ... ... ... ... | Ford downdraught type 71TW-9510-JB-JC or 71TW-9510-LA (with exhaust emission control) |

*All Ford carburettors have automatic choke*

**Ford carburettor specifications (all models)**

| | |
|---|---|
| Main jet * ... ... ... ... ... ... ... ... | 135 |
| Fuel inlet valve ... ... ... ... ... ... ... | 2.0 |
| Accelerator pump capacity (10 strokes) ... ... ... ... | 0.33 to 0.45 $in^3$ (5.5 to 7.5 $cm^3$) |
| Idling speed ... ... ... ... ... ... ... ... | 800 to 900 rev/min |
| (With exhaust emission control) ... ... ... ... ... | 900 rev/min |
| Fast idling speed (third step of cam) ... ... ... ... | 1800 to 2000 rev/min |
| (With exhaust emission control) ... ... ... ... ... | 1900 tc 2100 rev/min |

| | | |
|---|---|---|
| * *Carburettor types* | *71TW-9510-JB-JC* | *main jet 125* |
| | *71TW-9510-LA* | *main jet 137* |
| *(if fitted)* | *71TW-9510-JA* | *main jet 132* |

## 1 General description

The fuel system incorporates a rear mounted fuel tank from which fuel is drawn by a mechanically-operated pump actuated by the camshaft.

Various types of carburettor are fitted according to date of manufacture and reference should be made to Specifications Section for details and applications.

From 1970 all models are fitted with a filter in the fuel line between the fuel pump and carburettor.

From 1971 all models are fitted with a modified fuel tank to permit internal expansion of the fuel. As from the same date, vehicles destined for operation in North America are fitted with a fuel evaporative control system (see Section 8) also an emission control deceleration valve (Section 23) and a temperature - controlled air cleaner (Section 3).

Fig 3.1 Removing the air cleaner element

## 2 Air cleaner - removal, servicing and refitting

1 The air cleaner is of circular type, mounted on top of the engine and serves a dual purpose of filtration and silencing of the air intake.

2 The air cleaner element is of paper (disposable) type and it should be serviced as described in the 'Routine Maintenance' Section of this manual.

3 A feature of the air cleaner is that its intake nozzle may be turned, in cold conditions, to draw air from the area of a pre-heater plate. This is necessary to prevent icing of the carburettor and to reduce engine internal condensation.

4 To gain access to the filter element, unscrew and remove the cover centre bolt which secures the air cleaner assembly to the bridge of the carburettor intake.

5 Remove the element and wipe the air cleaner cover and base clean before fitting the new element.

6 The air cleaner base is secured by brackets fitted to the rocker covers (photo).

2.6 Removing the air cleaner base

## 3 Air cleaner (North America 1970 onwards).

1 This modified type of air cleaner is designed to maintain the air entering the carburettor at a temperature above 90°F (32°C) in the interest of reduced exhaust pollution.

2 The operating principle is that air is drawn from the region of the exhaust pipe and is mixed with cold air by means of a

regulator flap controlled by a thermostatic bulb.
3 Suspected failure of the mechanism may by verified by carrying out the following tests.
4 Disconnect the front hose and provided the engine is cold and the temperature within the engine compartment is below 85°F (29°C) the flap valve should be in its forward attitude closing the cold air intake.
5 Start the engine and run it at a fast idle for a few minutes noting that as the engine and engine compartment temperature rise, the valve plate should move to the rear position.
6 If the flap valve does not move as indicated, remove the three screws and check for wear or breaks in the linkage.
7 An alternative method of testing is to remove the flap valve and check the operation of the thermostat in hot and cold water.
8 If the unit is defective, renew it.

## 4 Fuel pump - testing in position

1 The fuel pump is located on the left-hand side of the crankcase.
2 Disconnect the coil HT lead from the centre of the distributor cap or from the coil itself.
3 Disconnect the pump to carburettor pipe at the pump outlet.
4 Spin the engine on the starter and observe the open pump outlet nozzle. A good spurt of fuel should be ejected every second revolution of the engine.

## 5 Fuel pump - removal and refitting

1 Disconnect the fuel inlet and outlet pipes from the pump and plug the inlet pipe.
2 Unscrew and remove the nuts and lockwashers which secure the pump flange to the crankcase and withdraw the pump, gasket and pushrod. Mark the end of the pushrod which contacts the camshaft with a piece of masking tape so that it can be refitted in its original position.
3 Refitting is a reversal of removal but always use a new gasket.

## 6 Fuel pump - servicing

1 Clean the pump filter periodically as described in the 'Routine Maintenance' Section.
2 A repair kit can be obtained for use when overhauling a faulty pump but if there is wear in the sleeves or body of the pump then it will probably be more economical to renew the pump on an exchange reconditioned basis.
3 Commence dismantling by unscrewing and removing the cover bolt and cover and extracting the filter gauge.
4 Scratch or file a mark across the edges of the upper and lower body flanges so that they can be refitted in their original positions.
5 Unscrew and remove the flange securing screws and separate the upper and lower body sections.
6 The upper body section incorporates valves which cannot be dismantled.
7 Stand the lower body on its flange and resting on a flat surface. Depress the spring retaining ring and withdraw the semi-circular lock washer from the groove in the operating rod. Withdraw the spring retaining ring and immediately refit the lock-washer to prevent the operating rod groove passing through the small seal in the pump body and tearing its lips. This seal cannot be renewed.
8 Hold the pump body in the left hand and depress the flexible diaphragm with the right. Detach the lockwasher for the second time from the operating rod and then release the diaphragm only enough to permit the diaphragm to operating-rod pin to be pushed out.
9 Withdraw the operating-rod away from the diaphragm so that the lockwasher groove does not pass through the seal in the pump body. Remove the diaphragm and spring.
10 Commence reassembly by smearing the diaphragm rod with a little grease and connecting it to the diaphragm with its pin.
11 Further reassembly is then a reversal of dismantling. Ensure that the upper and lower pump bodies are fitted with their flange marks in alignment and only tighten the flange screws when the pushrod is depressed and the diaphragm is not under tension.

## 7 Fuel tank (1971 models onwards) - description

This type of fuel tank permits internal expansion of the fuel. When the tank is filled, an air space is left above the surface of the fuel. This space is maintained by the action of a spring-loaded valve in the venting tube located in the filler neck. With the filler cap removed the valve is shut and the trapped air prevents the fuel rising above a pre-determined level.

When the filler cap is refitted, the valve is opened to provide an exit for the air and fuel vapours when the fuel expands and conversely to draw in air when the fuel contracts.

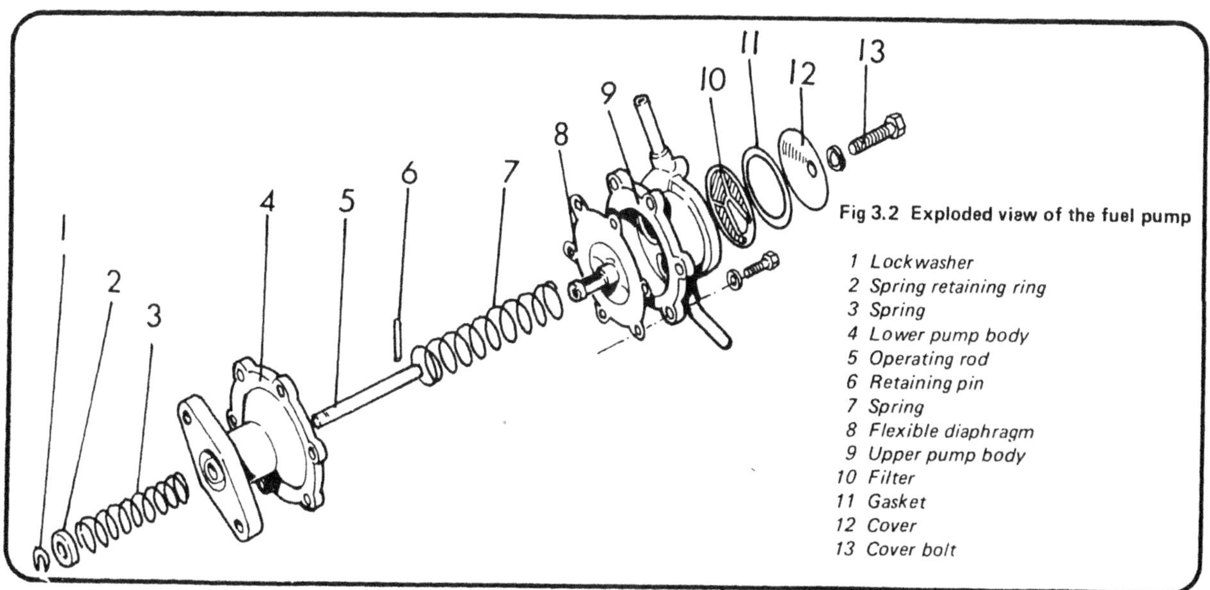


Fig 3.2 Exploded view of the fuel pump

*1 Lockwasher*
*2 Spring retaining ring*
*3 Spring*
*4 Lower pump body*
*5 Operating rod*
*6 Retaining pin*
*7 Spring*
*8 Flexible diaphragm*
*9 Upper pump body*
*10 Filter*
*11 Gasket*
*12 Cover*
*13 Cover bolt*

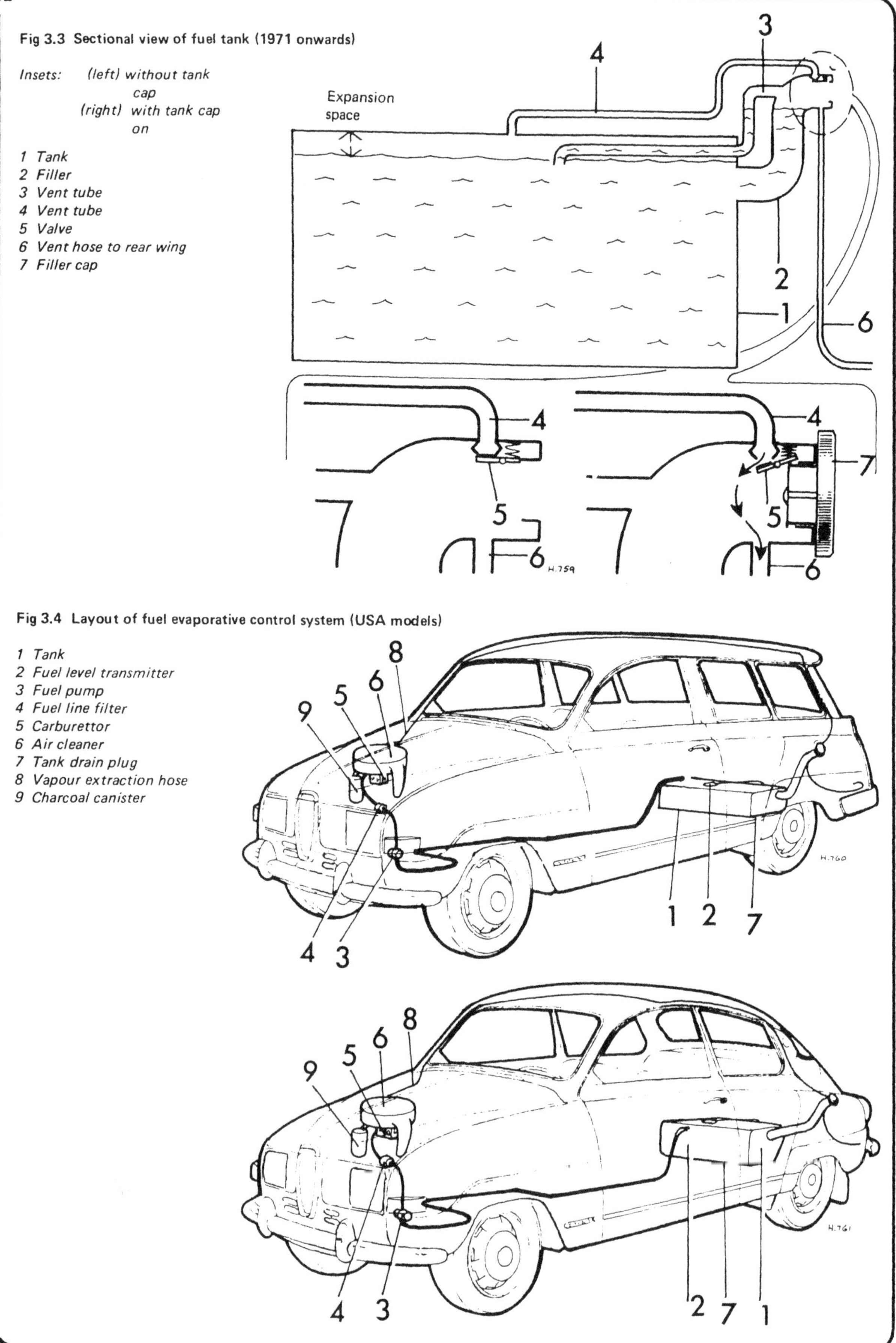


**Fig 3.3 Sectional view of fuel tank (1971 onwards)**

*Insets: (left) without tank cap*
*(right) with tank cap on*

*1 Tank*
*2 Filler*
*3 Vent tube*
*4 Vent tube*
*5 Valve*
*6 Vent hose to rear wing*
*7 Filler cap*

**Fig 3.4 Layout of fuel evaporative control system (USA models)**

*1 Tank*
*2 Fuel level transmitter*
*3 Fuel pump*
*4 Fuel line filter*
*5 Carburettor*
*6 Air cleaner*
*7 Tank drain plug*
*8 Vapour extraction hose*
*9 Charcoal canister*

## 8 Fuel evaporative control (North American vehicles)

In order to prevent the emission to atmosphere of fumes from the fuel tank, vehicles built for operation in North America from 1971 onwards incorporate a charcoal canister in a closed fume extraction system.

The fumes absorbed by the charcoal are continuously and automatically extracted through the carburettor and burned within the engine all the time that the engine is running.

Servicing is limited to periodically checking the security of the connecting hoses and renewing the charcoal canister every 24000 miles (38000 km).

## 9 Fuel tank - removal and installation

1 Remove the drain plug from the base of the tank and drain the contents into a suitable receptacle.
2 Inside the vehicle remove the rear seat cushion and backrest.
3 On Saloon models, lift out the spare wheel and remove the front part of the luggage boot floor.
4 On Estate versions, remove the shield which covers the tank by disconnecting the two spiral fasteners.
5 Disconnect the leads from the fuel gauge transmitter unit and the earth lead from the body.
6 Disconnect the fuel lines from the tank outlet nozzle.
7 Disconnect the two tank securing straps. On the saloon, the strap nuts are accessible through holes in the rear sloping panel.
8 Jack-up the rear of the vehicle, securely, and unscrew the clips on the vent and filler tubes located under the rear wing. Take care that road dirt and mud does not enter the open tank or vent tubes.
9 Raise the right-hand side of the tank and withdraw if from the vehicle in an upward direction towards the rear.
10 Installation of the fuel tank is a reversal of removal but ensure that the filler neck rubber grommet is correctly located and that the vent pipes (1970 onwards) are not kinked or trapped.

## 10 Fuel tank - servicing and repair

1 If the tank contains a lot of sediment or sludge, shake it vigorously using two or three changes of paraffin and then allow it to drain thoroughly.
2 Should a leak develop in the fuel tank do not be tempted to solder over the hole. Fuel tank repair is a specialist job and unless lengthy safety precautions are observed can be a very dangerous procedure. It is probably as cheap these days to buy a new tank rather than have the faulty one repaired.
3 Occasionally drain the tank when there is very little fuel left in it so that any accumulated water or sediment will be flushed out and discarded. This action will safeguard the tank against corrosion and help to prevent clogging of the fuel line filter.

## 11 Solex carburettors (1967 - 68 models) - general description

These carburettors are of downdraught type, the fuel supply being regulated by fixed jets mounted in the carburettor body. An automatic choke is fitted, an accelerator pump and an econostat device.

The two types of carburettor fitted are similar but the 28-32 PDSIT-7 has an internally vented float chamber whilst the 32 PDSIT-4 is vented through a valve (open when the throttle valve is closed) to atmosphere.

The choke comprises a strangler (closed when the engine is cold) and a bimetallic spring which opens the strangler in proportion to the increased temperature of the coolant in the engine cooling system.

With the engine idling, the throttle plate will be almost closed but held open in accordance with the position of the throttle stop screw. Under idling conditions, the vacuum in the idling passage below the throttle plate will be very high and cause the fuel to be drawn through the main jet to the idling jet. Once through the idling jet, air is mixed with the fuel and this mixture is regulated by the volume control screw to provide the correct engine requirements.

In order to facilitate the transfer from idling conditions to normal driving, a low speed system is incorporated which supplies a fuel/air mixture through two drillings in the carburettor throat located just above the throttle plate.

When the engine is operating at higher speeds or with heavier loading the fuel is continuously metered through the main jet. Thereafter it passes through the emulsion tube and is mixed with air to form a mixture of predetermined fuel/air ratio.

The econostat device is basically a booster to ensure the supply of sufficient fuel at high speeds. It is fed directly from the float chamber and relies upon vacuum to draw up fuel and eject it into the carburettor throat.

When the throttle plate is opened quickly during periods of rapid acceleration, the fuel/air mixture tends to become lean. To compensate for this, an accelerator pump is fitted on the right-hand side of the float chamber which is interconnected with the throttle plate. By the inclusion of a ball type valve, the required additional injection of fuel during conditions of acceleration is made through a tube and jet into the carburettor throat.

## 12 Solex carburettors - slow running adjustment

1 Run the engine until its normal operating temperature is reached.
2 Turn the throttle stop screw until the engine is running at a slightly faster than normal idling speed.
3 Turn the volume control screw slowly inwards until the engine begins to run lumpily and then unscrew the screw until this condition disappears and the engine idles smoothly.
4 Readjust the throttle stop screw to provide the recommended idling speed level (800 to 900 rev/min).
5 Alternative and more precise methods of slow-running adjustment can be made using 'Colortune' or a vacuum gauge connected to the inlet manifold.

## 13 Solex carburettors - removal and installation

1 Drain about 4 pints (2.3 litres) from the cooling system through the radiator drain tap.
2 Remove the air filter.
3 Disconnect the water hoses from the automatic choke.
4 Disconnect the throttle control linkage at the carburettor.
5 Disconnect the vacuum pipe at the carburettor nozzle.
6 Disconnect the fuel inlet pipe.
7 Unscrew and remove the two carburettor flange securing nuts and lift the carburettor from the inlet manifold.
8 On 32 PDSIT -4 type carburettors, the hose may be detached from the crankcase emission control valve and the intermediate flange withdrawn.
9 Installation is a reversal of removal but always fit new gaskets and bleed the cooling system as described in Chapter 2.

## 14 Solex carburettors - dismantling and examination

1 Disconnect the control rod link which runs between the automatic choke and the throttle butterfly plate arm. This is carried out by removing the circlip from the end of the rod.
2 Unscrew and remove the screw from the float chamber cover. Lift off the cover and the gasket.
3 Unscrew the needle (inlet) valve from the float chamber cover.
4 Remove the float from the float chamber and then unscrew

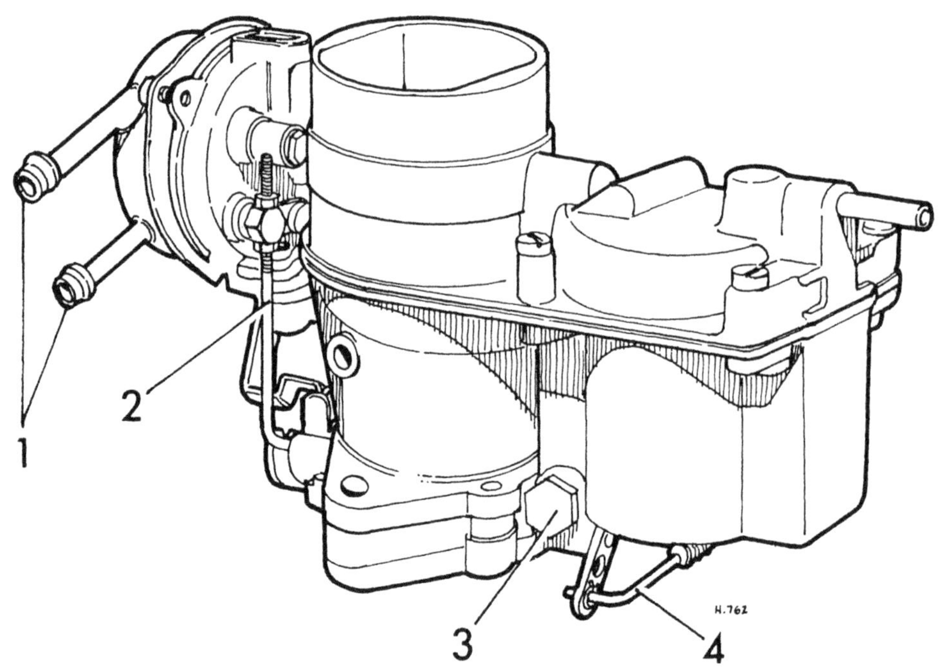


**Fig 3.5 View of right-hand side of Solex type 28-32 PDSIT-7 carburettor**

*1 Water connections to automatic choke*
*2 Fast idling link*
*3 Main jet plug*
*4 Accelerator pump link*

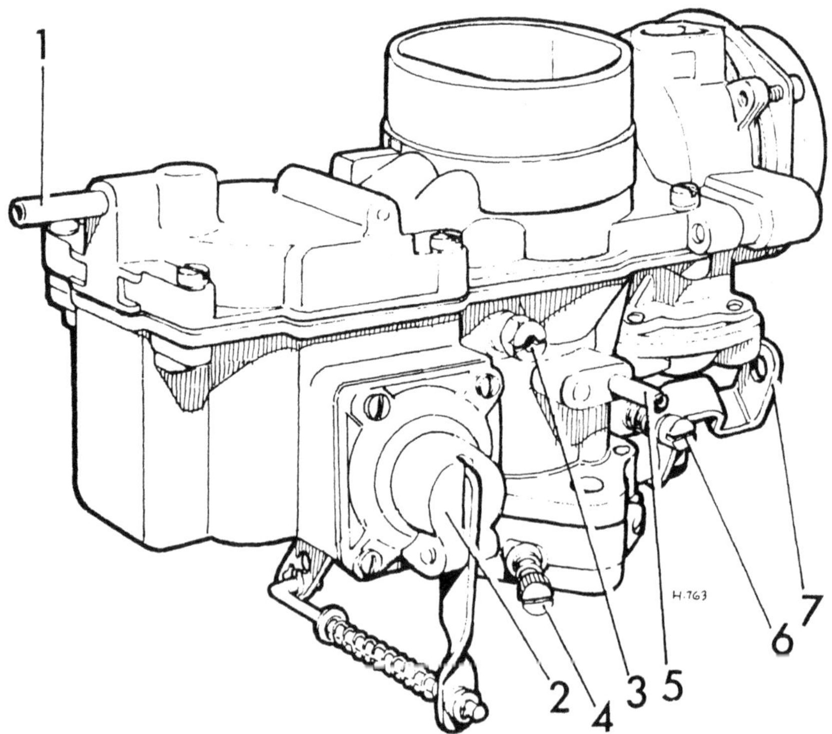


**Fig 3.6 View of left-hand side of Solex type 28-32 PDSIT-7 carburettor**

*1 Fuel inlet*
*2 Accelerator pump*
*3 Idling (fuel) jet*
*4 Volume control screw*
*5 Vacuum connection for distributor*
*6 Throttle stop screw*
*7 Throttle control lever*

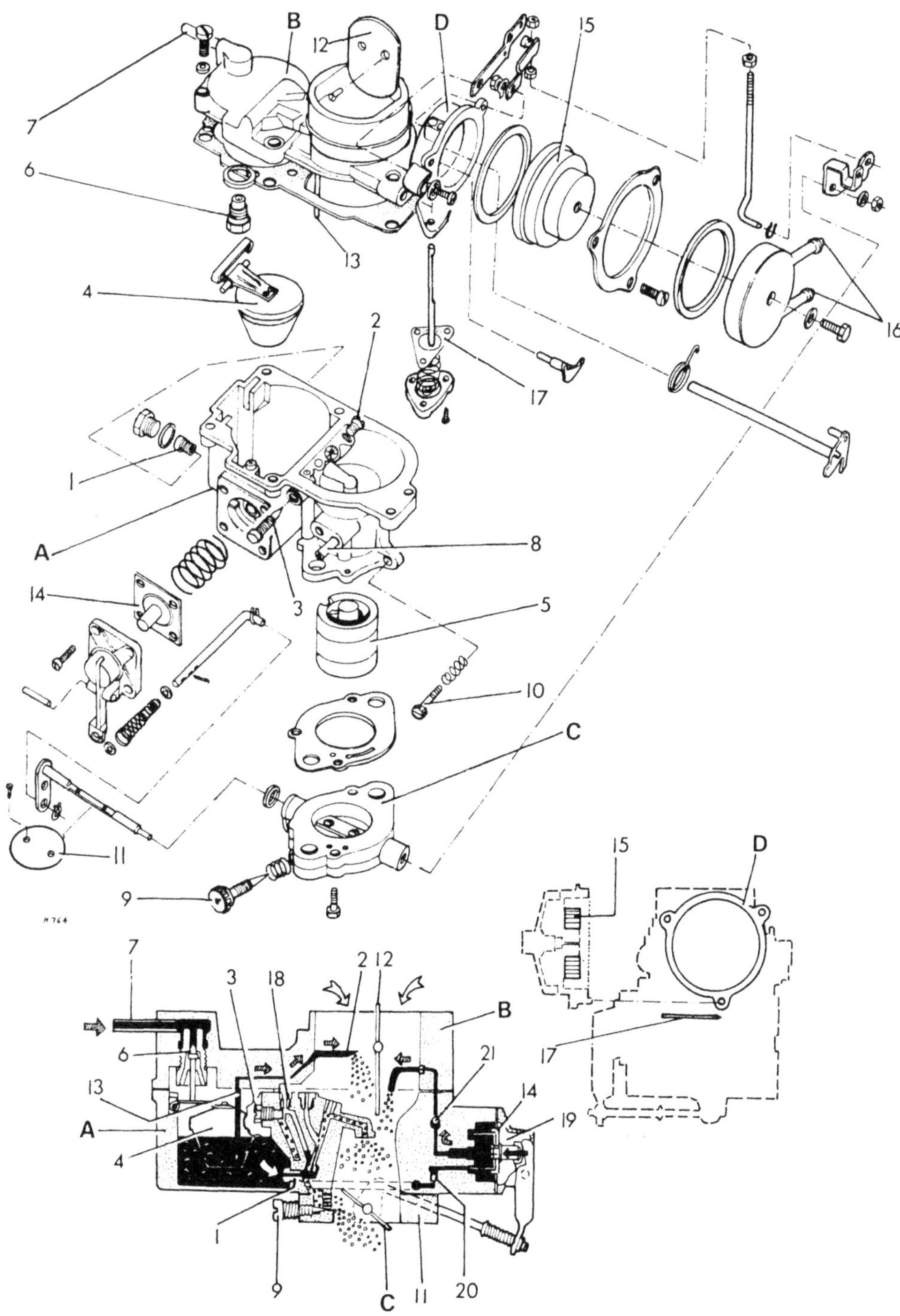


**Fig 3.7 Exploded view of Solex type 28-32 PDSIT-7 carburettor**

*1 Main jet*
*2 Emulsion jet*
*3 Idling (fuel) jet*
*4 Float*
*5 Choke tube*
*6 Fuel inlet needle valve*
*7 Fuel inlet*
*8 Vacuum connection for distributor*
*9 Volume control screw*
*10 Throttle stop screw*
*11 Throttle valve plate*
*12 Choke valve plate*
*13 Econostat tube*
*14 Accelerator pump diaphragm*
*15 Thermostatic (bimetallic) spring for automatic choke*
*16 Water connections to automatic choke*
*17 Vacuum diaphragm for automatic choke*
*18 Idling (air) jet*
*19 Accelerator pump*
*20 Accelerator pump inlet valve*
*21 Accelerator pump outlet valve*
*A Float chamber*
*B Float chamber cover*
*C Throttle body*
*D Automatic choke housing*

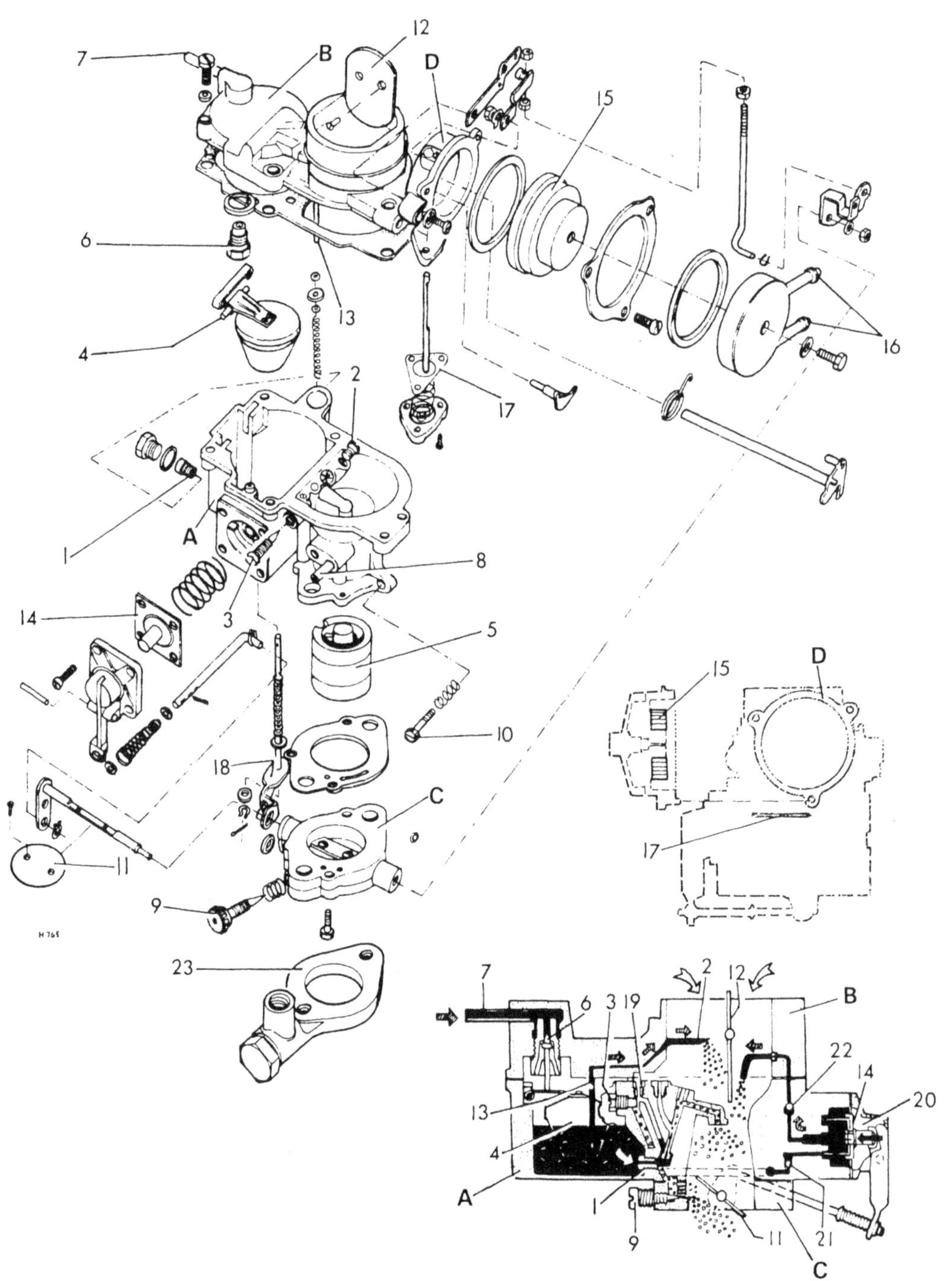


**Fig 3.8 Exploded view of Solex type 32 PDSIT-4 carburettor**

*1 Main jet*
*2 Emulsion jet*
*3 Idling (fuel) jet*
*4 Float*
*5 Choke tube*
*6 Fuel inlet needle valve*
*7 Fuel inlet*
*8 Vacuum connection for distributor*
*9 Volume control screw*
*10 Throttle stop screw*
*11 Throttle valve plate*
*12 Choke valve plate*
*13 Econostat tube*
*14 Accelerator pump diaphragm*
*15 Thermostatic (bimetallic) spring for automatic choke*
*16 Water connections to automatic choke*
*17 Vacuum diaphragm for automatic choke*
*18 Float chamber vent regulator*
*19 Idling (air) jet*
*20 Accelerator pump*
*21 Accelerator pump inlet valve*
*22 Accelerator pump outlet valve*
*23 Intermediate flange*
*A Float chamber*
*B Float chamber cover*
*C Throttle body assembly*
*D Automatic choke housing*

the plug from the float chamber and unscrew the main jet (photo).

5 Extract the accelerator pump jet and then unscrew the idling jet, the emulsion tube jet, the accelerator pump cover and diaphragm.

6 Examine all components for wear and blow through the jets with air from a tyre pump; never attempt to probe them with wire or their calibration will be ruined.

7 If wear is observed in the throttle or choke plate spindles, renew the carburettor complete, on an exchange basis.

8 Obtain a repair kit for the particular model caburettor and use all the components supplied on reassembly.

## 15 Solex carburettors - reassembly and adjustment

1 Reassembly is a reversal of dismantling but check the following points when assembly is complete.

2 Set the throttle plate arm partially open and then close the choke strangler plate fully. With the choke plate fully closed the throttle plate should just be open showing a clearance of 0.032 in (0.8 mm) between its edge and the carburettor rod.

3 The setting of the automatic choke allows for the choke strangler plate to be wide open at a temperature of between 140 and 149$^{o}$F (60 and 65$^{o}$C). The correct setting is obtained when the mark on the rotatable section of the automatic choke housing is in alignment with the centre peak of the five pointers on the fixed section of the automatic choke housing.

4 If the rotatable housing is turned clockwise (after slackening the securing screws) the choke will open fully at a higher temperature and if turned in an anticlockwise direction it will open at a lower temperature. This arrangment provides a suitable adjustment range for extremes of climate.

5 After the carburettor has been dismantled and reassembled, the automatic choke spring should be hooked onto the driver cam spring retainer and the housing turned until the marks are in alignment. Ensure that the choke strangler plate is free to move towards the closed position.

6 Checking the float level cannot be carried out without a special tool which is basically a graduated glass right angular tube screwed into the hole from which the main jet plug has been removed. With the engine idling, the fuel level in the tube will be the same as that within the float chamber which should be 0.59 in (15.0 mm) from the top of the float chamber bowl.

## 16 Ford carburettors - general description

The carburettors fitted from the 1969 model onwards differ in detail from the Solex types previously fitted although the operating principle is essentially similar.

Only the main jet is removable and all other linkage adjustments are preset in production. A water heated automatic choke is fitted. A modified type of carburettor is fitted where exhaust emission control equipment is installed.

As from 1971, a carburettor built to closer tolerances is fitted to provide a purpose-built unit for the more exacting emission control requirements applicable in most operating territories. The servicing and overhaul of this type of carburettor is similar to the other models of Ford manufacture.

## 17 Ford carburettors - slow-running adjustment

1 Run the engine until normal operating temperature is reached.

2 Adjust the throttle stop screw until the engine is idling as slowly as possible without stalling.

3 Screw the volume control screw in or out until the engine runs smoothly without any tendency to 'hunt'.

4 Screw in the throttle stop screw until the normal idling speed is resumed (800 to 900 rev/min).

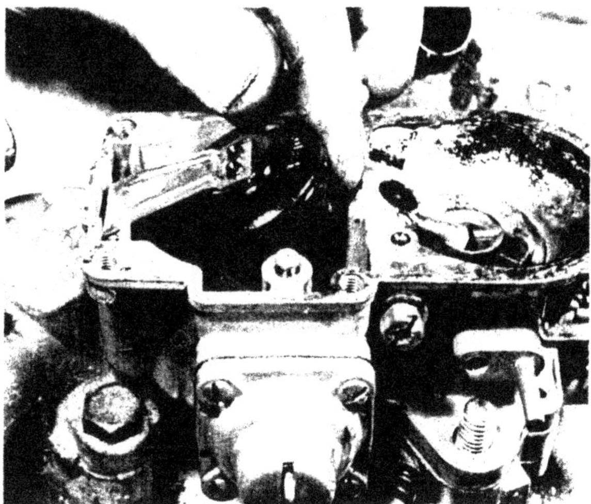

14.4 Removing the carburettor float

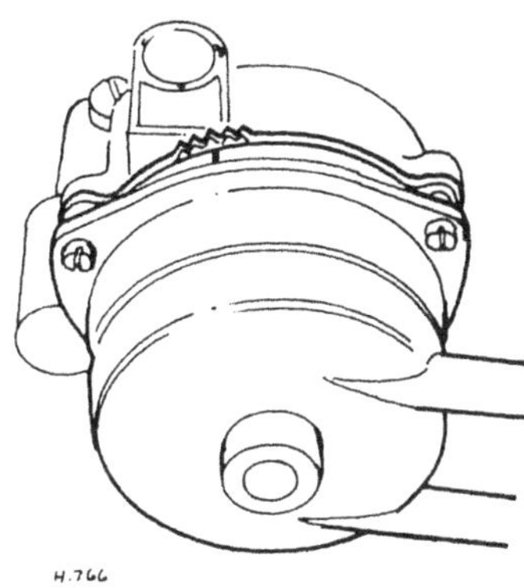


Fig 3.9 Automatic choke setting marks (Solex carburettors)

5 Alternative and more precise methods of slow-running adjustment can be made using 'Colortune' or a vacuum gauge connected to the inlet manifold.

## 18 Ford carburettors - removal and installation

1 The procedure is similar to that described in paragraphs 1 to 7 of Section 13 for Solex models.

2 When installing the carburettor and intermediate flange, ensure that a new gasket is located under each component so that the mark 'OBEN' is visible when looking down from above. Fill and bleed the cooling system.

## 19 Ford carburettors - dismantling and examination

1 Unscrew the three securing screws and remove the rotatable section of the automatic choke housing.

2 Unscrew the stepped cam from the throttle body.

3 Unscrew and remove the float chamber cover screws and lift off the cover, retaining the spring.

4 Peel off the cover gasket and then invert the float chamber and extract the ball and weight from the accelerator pump fuel orifice.

5 Unscrew and remove the accelerator pump cover, diaphragm and spring.

6 Remove the accelerator pump rod and lever from the throttle

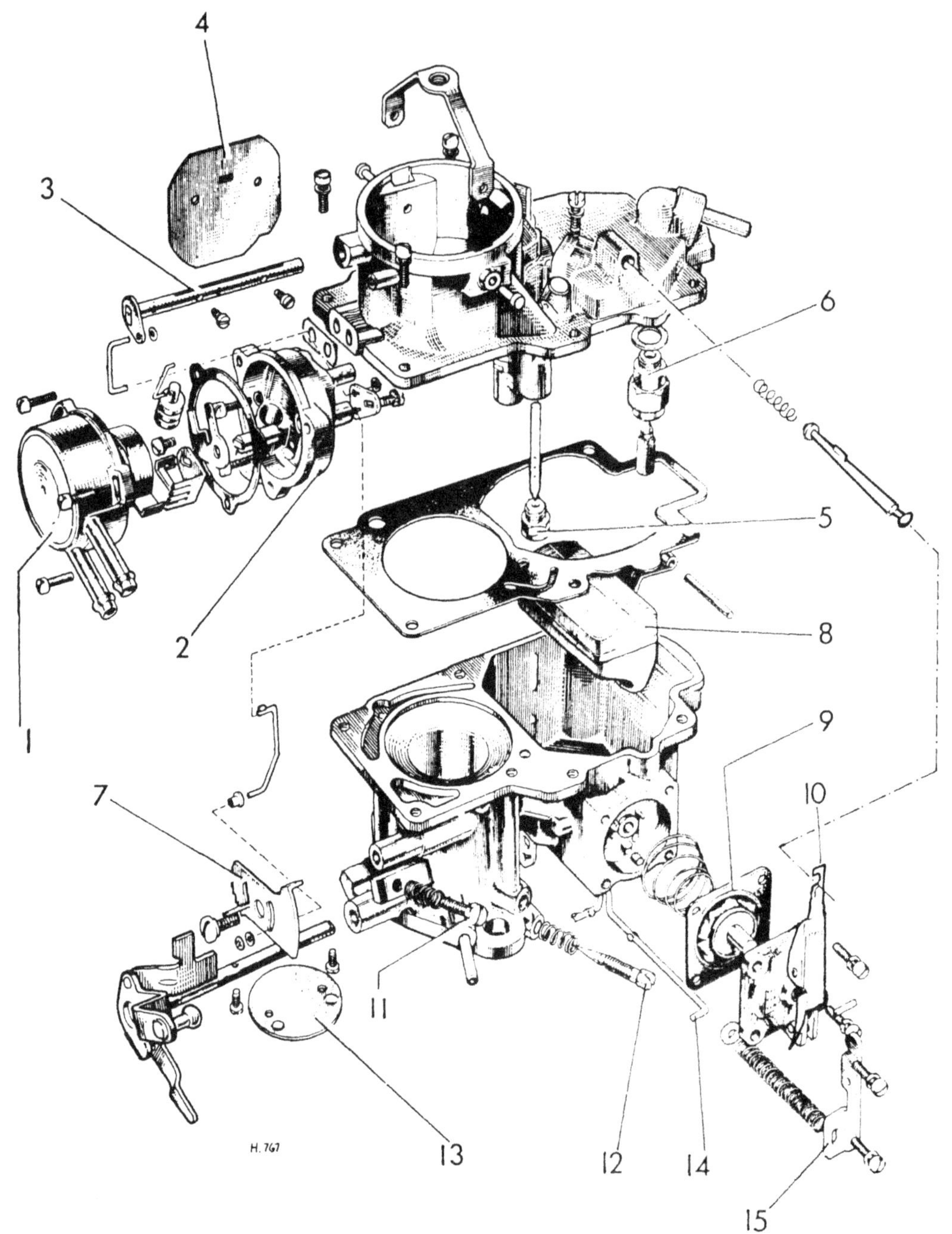


Fig 3.10 Exploded view of Ford type carburettor (1969–70)

*1 Thermostatic spring housing (automatic choke)*
*2 Automatic choke housing (fixed section)*
*3 Choke valve plate spindle*
*4 Choke valve plate*
*5 Main jet*
*6 Fuel inlet needle valve*
*7 Stepped cam*
*8 Float*
*9 Accelerator pump diaphragm*
*10 Vent actuating lever*
*11 Throttle stop screw*
*12 Volume control screw*
*13 Throttle valve plate*
*14 Accelerator pump rod*
*15 Accelerator pump lever*

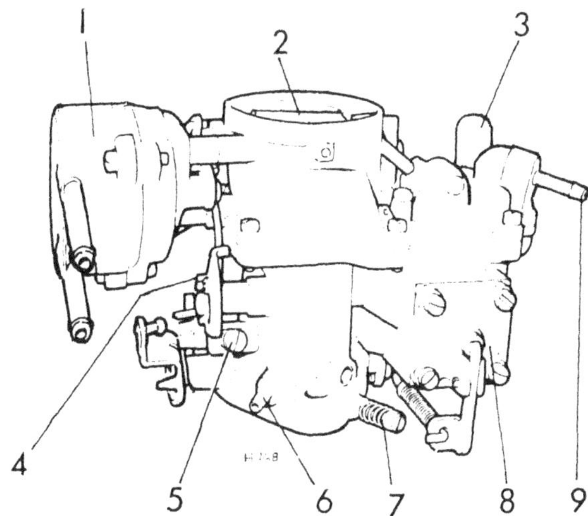


Fig 3.11 Ford type carburettor (1971 onwards)

1 *Automatic choke housing*
2 *Choke valve plate*
3 *Float chamber vent connection*
4 *Stepped cam*
5 *Throttle stop screw*
6 *Vacuum connection for distributor*
7 *Volume control screw*
8 *Accelerator pump*
9 *Fuel inlet*

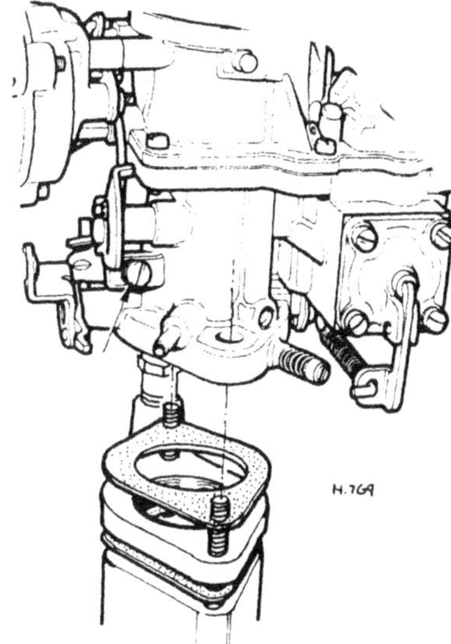

Fig 3.12 Correct location of carburettor flange and intermediate plate gaskets (Ford carburettors)

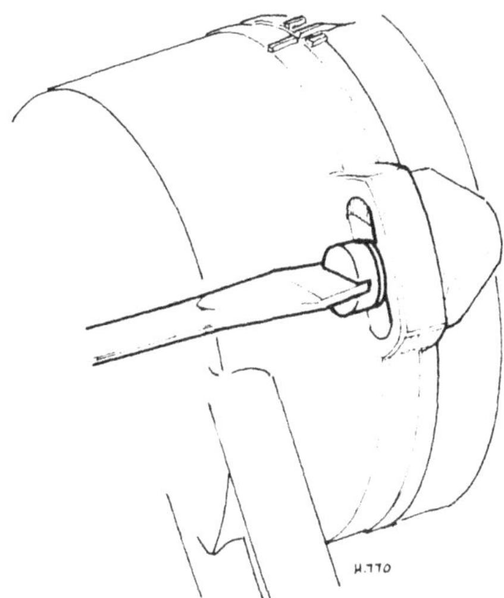

Fig 3.13 Removing an automatic choke rotatable housing section screw (Ford carburettors)

Fig 3.14 Ball and weight located in accelerator pump fuel orifice (Ford carburettors)

butterfly valve plate spindle.
7 If necessary remove the throttle stop and volume control screws and their springs.
8 If essential, remove the throttle butterfly plate and withdraw the spindle.
9 Remove the float and unscrew the float needle (inlet) valve.
10 Unscrew the main jet.
11 Unscrew the automatic choke fixed housing and then remove the pins which secure the air cleaner mounting bridge on the top of the carburettor intake.
12 If essential, remove the choke butterfly plate and withdraw the spindle.
13 Examine all components for wear and blow through the jets with air from a tyre pump, never attempt to probe them with wire or their calibration will be ruined.
14 If wear is observed in the throttle or choke plate spindles, renew the carburettor complete, on an exchange basis.
15 Obtain a repair kit for the particular model carburettor and use all the components supplied, on reassembly.

## 20 Ford carburettors - reassembly and adjustment

1 Insert the throttle valve spindle into the carburettor body.
2 Locate the accelerator pump lever on the spindle so that the side marked "O" is facing upward.
3 Fit the throttle valve plate to the spindle so that the punch marks are facing downwards when the throttle is closed. Before tightening the throttle plate retaining screws check that the plate is centralised and the spindle rotates freely.
4 Refit the throttle stop and volume control screws.
5 Locate the accelerator pump rod between the operating levers of the pump and throttle valve.
6 Fit the accelerator pump diaphragm and spring (small end

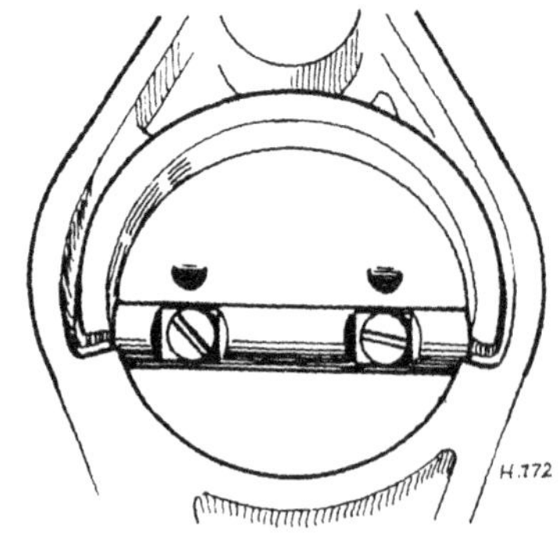


Fig 3.15 A correctly fitted throttle valve plate (Ford carburettors)

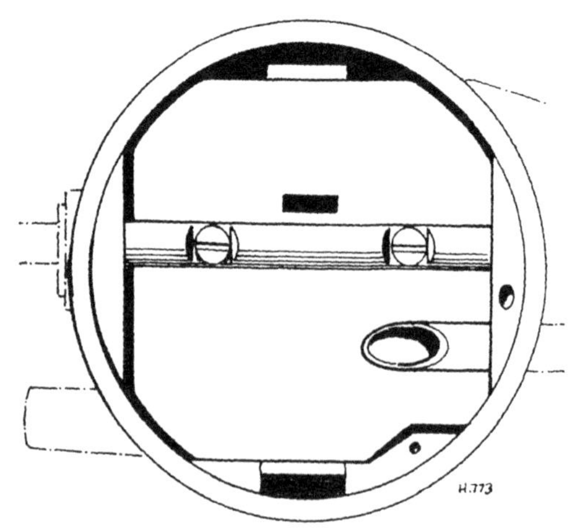


Fig 3.16 A correctly fitted choke valve plate (Ford carburettors)

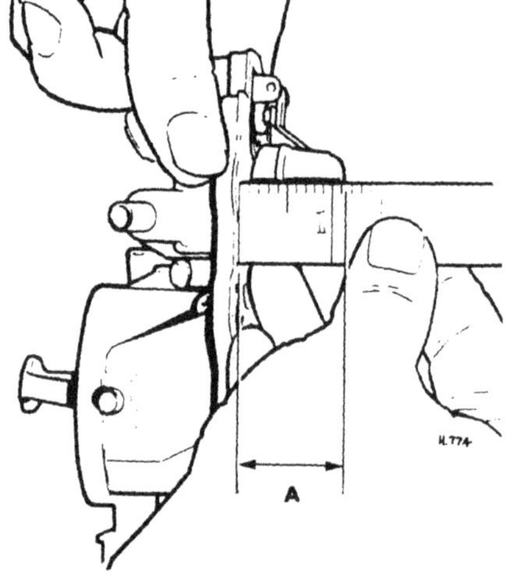


Fig 3.17 Float adjustment diagram (Ford carburettors)

*A 1.08 in (27.5 mm)*

*B 1.34 in (34.0 mm)*

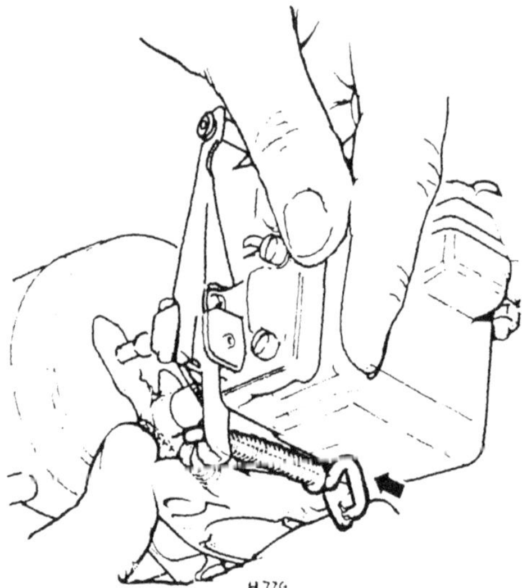


Fig 3.18 Accelerator pump connecting rod (Ford carburettors)

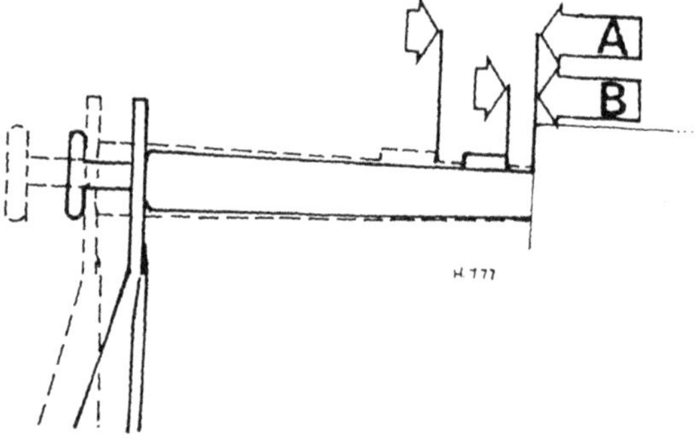


Fig 3.19 Float chamber vent valve setting diagram (Ford carburettors)

*A 0.32 to 0.40 in (8.0 to 10.0 mm) throttle wide open*

*B 0.008 to 0.012 in (0.2 to 0.3 mm) throttle fully closed*

facing cover) and the cover.

7 Fit the choke valve plate in a manner similar to that for the throttle (paragraph 3).

8 Fit the air cleaner support bridge using new pins.

9 Fit the fixed section of the automatic choke housing using a new gasket.

10 Connect the accelerator pump rod to the choke valve plate spindle.

11 Screw in the main jet and the inlet needle valve.

12 Fit the float and check its adjustment. If the dimensions illustrated vary from those specified, bend the float arm or stop as necessary.

13 Insert the ball followed by the weight into the accelerator pump fuel orifice.

14 Fit the float chamber valve spring into the top cover and fit the cover and then insert the float chamber valve pushrod and tighten the cover screws.

15 Screw on the stepped cam and fit the rotatable section of the automatic choke thermostatic spring housing.

16 Provided the carburettor has been handled gently during dismantling and reassembly the following adjustments are unlikely to be required.

17 The specified discharge of the accelerator pump can only be checked by fully opening the throttle valve (throttle stop screw fully unscrewed) ten times and catching the ejected fuel in a measuring glass. Compare the volume discharged with that shown for the particular carburettor in Specifications. To increase the volume of fuel discharged, slightly compress the swan neck on the connecting rod. To reduce the volume of fuel discharged, slightly straighten the swan neck.

18 Check the setting of the float chamber vent valve by taking the measurements illustrated in Fig. 3.19 first with the throttle fully open and then with it fully closed. Bend the lever at the pushrod end if necessary.

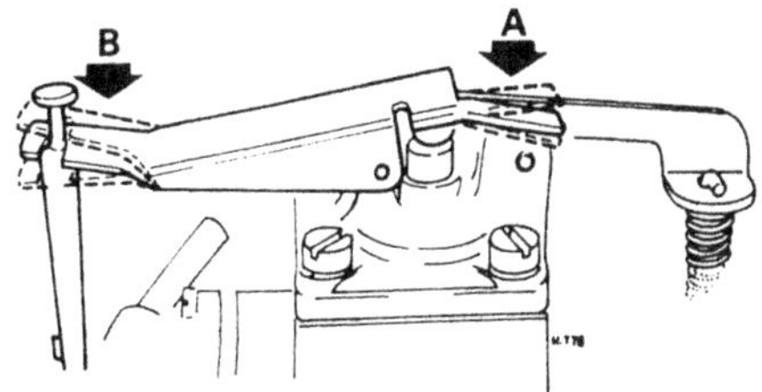


**Fig 3.20 Float chamber vent valve lever adjustment points (Ford carburettors)**

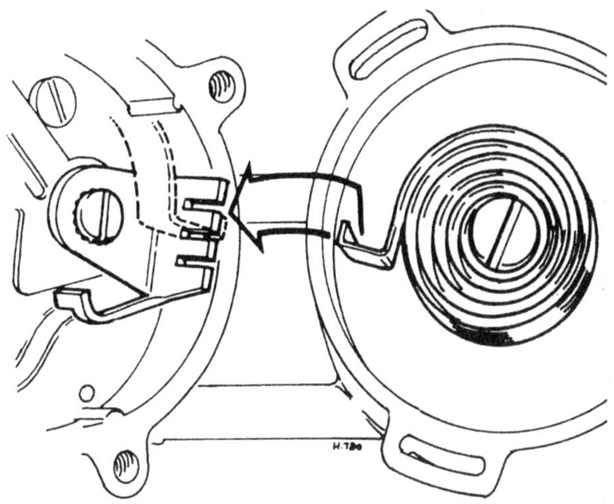

**Fig 3.21 Automatic choke thermostatic spring and retaining lever (Ford carburettors)**

## 21 Ford carburettors - automatic choke setting and adjustment

### *(a) Carburettor removed*

1 Normally the automatic choke assembly should not be altered from its standard setting which is for the end of the thermostatic spring to be engaged in the centre slot of the spring retaining lever and the mark on the rotatable section of the automatic choke housing to be in alignment with the centre mark on the fixed section of the housing.

2 Where the automatic choke mechanism has been dismantled or new components fitted, then check and adjust the unit in the following manner.

3 Remove the rotatable section of the housing and spring and depress the vacuum piston fully. Move the choke valve plate towards the closed position until the tongue of the spring retaining lever makes contact with the vacuum piston lever. The choke valve plate should now be open sufficiently to permit the passage of a twist drill, 0.17 to 0.19 in (4.2 to 4.7 mm) in diameter. If necessary bend the tongue on the spring retaining lever to adjust the choke plate opening.

4 The position of the stepped cam should be checked while the choke valve plate is being tested for correct opening position. The mark on the stepped cam should be exactly opposite the corner of the throttle stop lever otherwise adjust the setting by bending the linkrod.

5 Now open the throttle valve plate fully so that the choke spindle arm is in contact with the stop on the stepped cam. The choke valve plate should now be open enough to permit the passage of a twist drill 0.19 to 0.23 in (4.8 to 5.8 mm) in diameter between the edge of the valve plate and the carburettor body. If adjustment is required, bend the stop on the stepped cam.

### *(b) Carburettor in position in vehicle*

6 Checking the setting and operation of the automatic choke when the carburettor is in position in the vehicle is preferably carried out with the engine cold. If it is warm or hot remove the

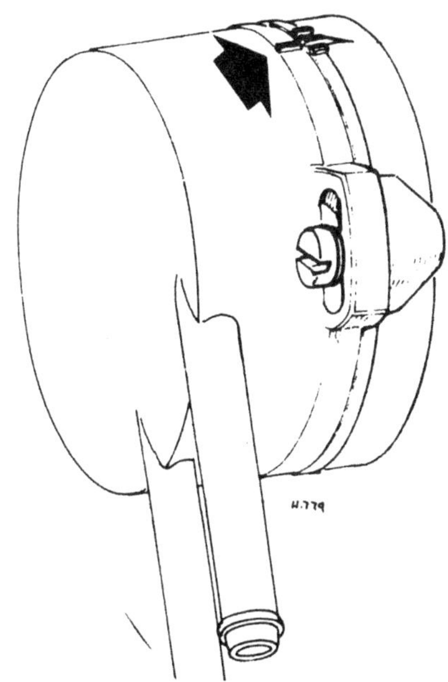

**Fig. 3.22. Automatic choke setting in temperate climates (Ford carburettors) (Sec. 21)**

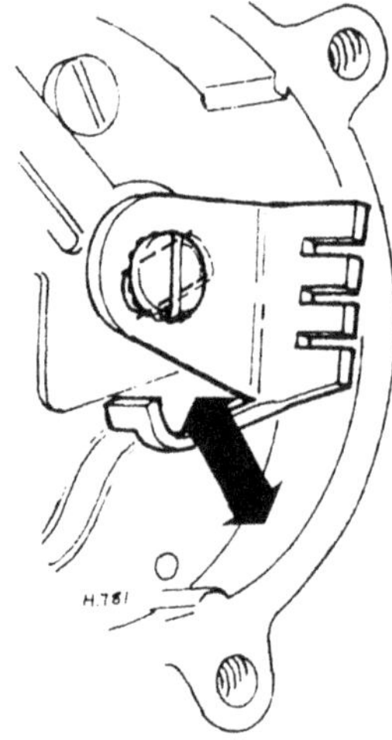

Fig 3.23 Adjusting automatic choke spring retainer tongue to provide correct choke valve plate opening (Ford carburettors)

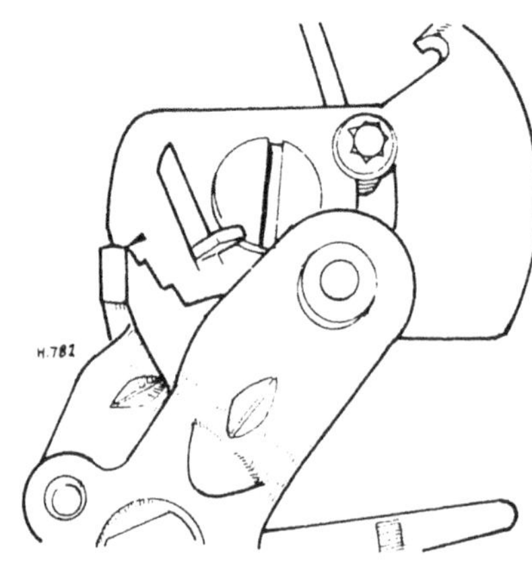

Fig 3.24 Checking stepped cam setting in relation to throttle stop lever (Ford carburettors)

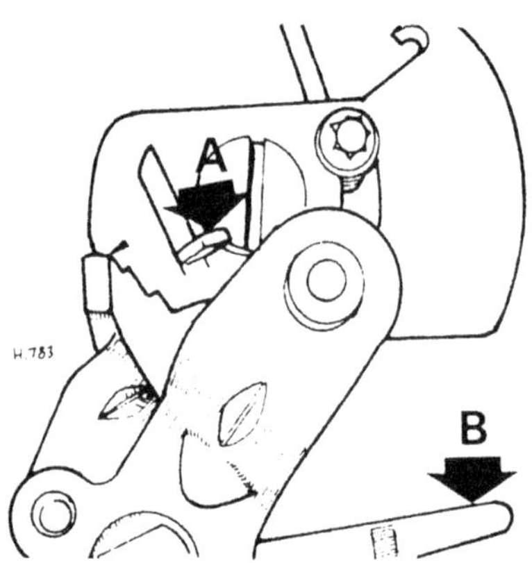


Fig 3.25 Choke spindle arm (b) and stepped cam stop (a) (Ford carburettors)

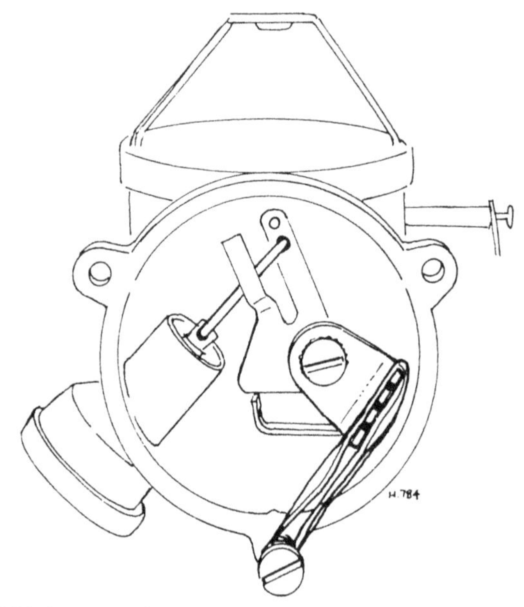

Fig 3.26 Location of rubber band used to hold spring retainer in 'COLD' position during automatic choke adjustment (Ford carburettors)

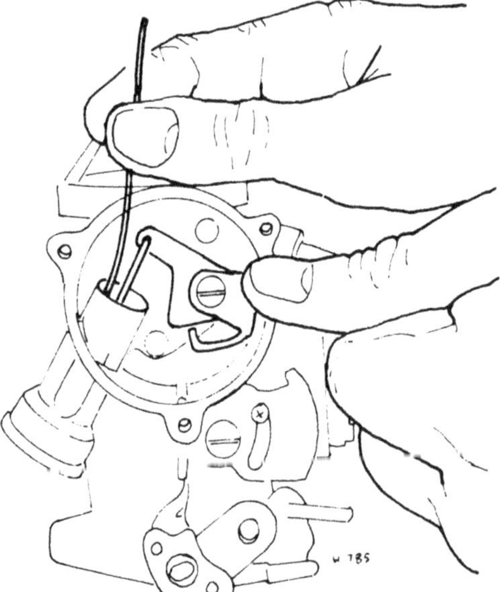

Fig 3.27 Setting the automatic choke (USA 1970 onwards - Ford carburettors)

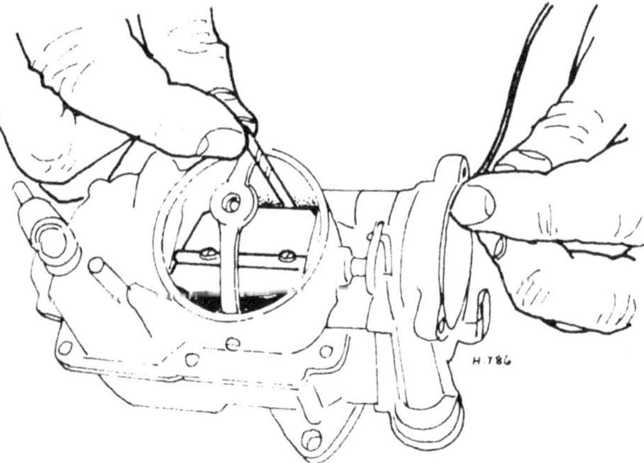

Fig 3.28 Checking the choke valve plate opening (USA 1970 onwards - Ford carburettors)

rotatable section of the housing and the thermostatically controlled spring and then replace the cover housing screw. Now stretch a rubber band between this screw and the spring retaining lever to cause the thermostatic spring retainer to assume its normal attitude as though the engine were cold.
7 Remove the air cleaner and depress the accelerator pedal. Observe that the choke valve plate closes and that the stepped cam is engaged at the highest point.
8 Start the engine and check that the choke valve plate opens enough to permit passage of an 0.18 to 0.20 in (4.5 to 5.0 mm) diameter twist drill. Close the choke valve plate with the fingers and then release it and check that it returns to its former position. Failure to return to its correct position may be due to leakage at the bottom of the vacuum piston or between the choke housing and the carburettor. If necessary adjust the tongue of the spring retaining lever.
9 Depress the accelerator pedal and the engine speed will slow down as the stepped cam moves to the third catch. The mark on the third catch should be in alignment with the corner of the throttle stop lever otherwise adjust by bending the linkrod.
10 Switch off the engine and depress the accelerator fully and check that the choke valve plate opens enough to permit passage of an 0.19 to 0.23 in (4.8 to5.8 mm) diameter twist drill. If necessary, bend the stop on the cam disc.
11 Remove the rubber band, refit the choke housing and spring and then adjust the engine slow running.

## 22 Automatic choke adjustment (North American models - 1970 on)

1 Remove the rotatable section of the automatic choke housing and withdraw the thermostatic spring.
2 Insert a piece of wire 0.040 in (1.02 mm) in diameter into the inner air bleed slot in the vacuum piston bore. Hold the vacuum piston lever with the finger to retain the wire in the slot and the vacuum piston in contact with the lower end of the wire.
3 Now check the opening of the choke valve plate. This should allow the passage of a rod or twist drill between 0.080 and 0.100 in (2.0320 and 2.54 mm) in diameter. If adjustment is required, bend the tongue of the spring retaining lever.

## 23 Emission control system (North American models - 1970 on)

1 These vehicles are fitted with a sophisticated exhaust emission control system which includes a modified carburettor and distributor, an air cleaner which incorporates a thermostatically controlled mixer valve (see Section 3) and a deceleration valve.
2 The deceleration valve is connected to the inlet manifold through the medium of the carburettor intermediate plate. During deceleration, the vacuum in the inlet manifold causes the deceleration valve to be lifted from its seat and draws a metered quantity of fuel/air mixture from the carburettor fuel pick-up tube and air bleed into the manifold. This arrangement improves the combustion within the cylinders and so reduces considerably the fume emission from the exhaust system.
3 Adjustment of the slow-running is critical and should be checked in the following manner. Run the engine until normal operating temperature is attained and then set the throttle stop screw so that the engine runs at 900 rev/min when checked against a tachometer connected to it. Failure to achieve the required slow-running speed may indicate a faulty deceleration valve.
4 Using a CO analyser, adjust the volume control screw until the exhaust gas reading is between 1.5 and 2%.
5 Every 6000 miles (9600 km) check and adjust the deceleration valve in the following manner. Run the engine to normal operating temperature and disconnect the hose which runs between the valve and the carburettor. If the valve is off its seat (indicated by suction at the end of the disconnected tube) then the valve must be adjusted as follows:

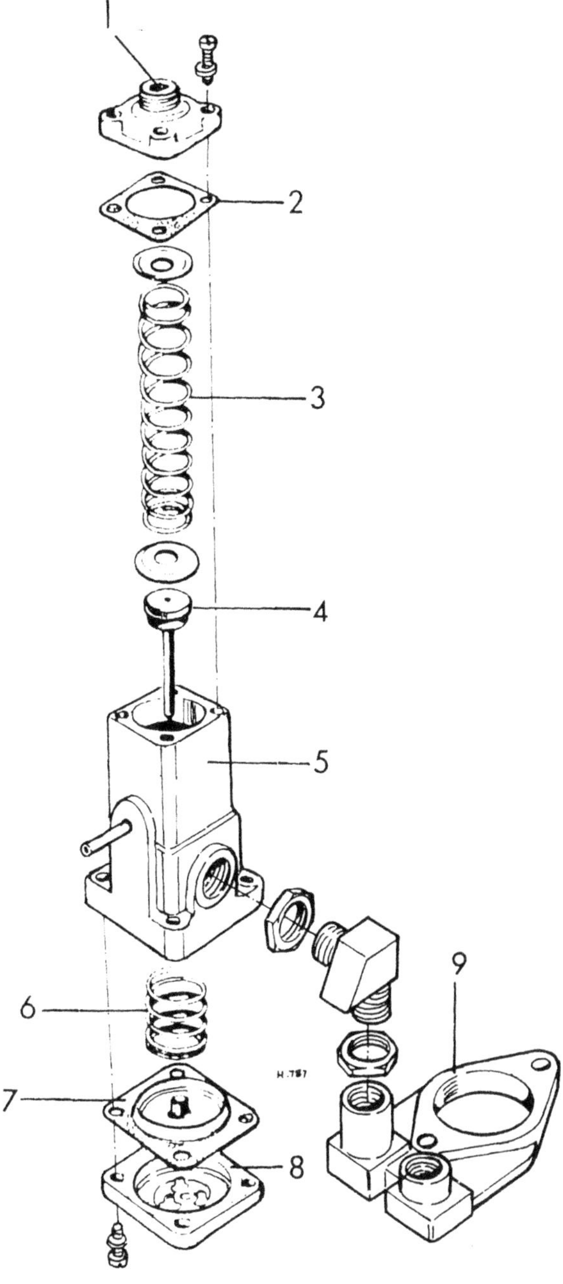


**Fig 3.29 Exploded view of the deceleration valve (USA 1970 onwards)**

*1 Adjusting screw*
*2 Gasket*
*3 Spring*
*4 Valve*
*5 Valve body*
*6 Spring*
*7 Diaphragm*
*8 Bottom cover*
*9 Intermediate plate*

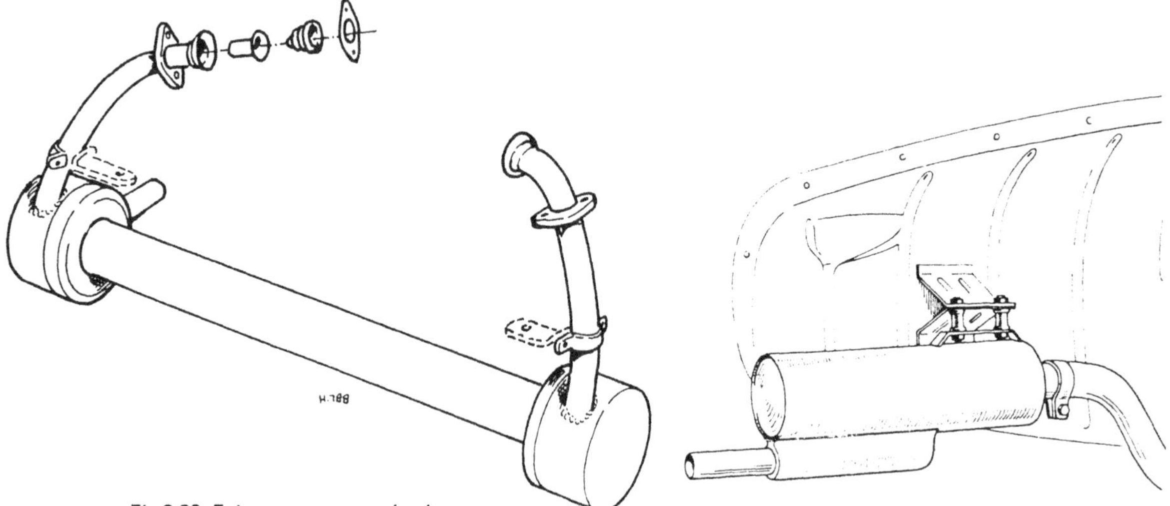

Fig 3.30 Exhaust port expansion box

Fig 3.31 Exhaust rear silencer

6 Remove the air cleaner and screw the deceleration valve adjusting screw either in or out until with the engine running at 3000 rev/min and thethrottle suddenly released the engine drops to idling (900 rev/min) in 7 to 8 seconds. Screw in the adjusting screw to reduce the time taken for engine speed to drop or unscrew it to increase the time.
7 Refit the air cleaner and recheck the speed drop test, readjust if necessary.
8 If stalling or irregular idling is evident check the valve for a ruptured diaphragm. To do this, cover the bleed hole in the deceleration bottom cover with the finger, if stalling is eliminated and smooth idling restored, dismantle the valve and renew the diaphragm .

## 24 Exhaust system - inspection and renewal

1 Examination of the exhaust pipe and silencers at regular intervals is worthwhile as small defects may be repairable when, if left they will almost certainly require renewal of one of the sections of the system. Also, any leaks, apart from the noise factor, may cause poisonous exhaust gases to get inside the car which can be unpleasant, to say the least, even in mild concentrations. Prolonged inhalation could cause sickness and giddiness.
2 To remove the front expansion box, jack-up the front end of the vehicle, disconnect the battery negative lead and the starter motor cable.
3 Remove the starter motor.
4 Disconnect both exhaust downpipes from the engine also the pipe support brackets at the engine mountings.
5 Slacken the clamp which secures the exhaust pipe to the expansion box outlet. Apply releasing fluid to this joint and pull the expansion box out of engagement with the exhaust pipe.
6 Withdraw the expansion box by first lowering it and then pulling the right-hand engine connecting pipe out through the hole in the engine compartment bottom shield. Turn this pipe so that it is positioned between the radiator grille and the front bumper. This will enable the left-hand pipe connection to be withdrawn and then the complete expansion box to be removed.
7 The rear silencer box can be removed by jacking-up the right-hand side of the vehicle and removing the rear road wheel. Disconnect the silencer to exhaust pipe clamp and apply releasing fluid to the connection.
8 Disconnect the silencer from its mounting bracket and then twist the silencer off the end of the exhaust pipe.
9 If the exhaust pipe section is to be removed or renewed on its own, it can be withdrawn together with the rear silencer by slackening the clamp which secures the exhaust pipe to the front expansion box and withdrawing the pipe and silencer to the rear, leaving the front expansion box in position (photo).
10 Refitting is a reversal of removal but always use new gaskets at the engine connections and check and renew if necessary the system rubber mountings. Ensure that all three exhaust system components are in correct alignment before finally tightening the clamp bolts.

## 25 Fuel gauge transmitter unit - fault finding

1 If the fuel gauge does not operate correctly, the fault is either in the fuel tank transmitter unit, the gauge or the wiring.
2 To check the transmitter unit, disconnect the electrical supply lead from the unit and switch on the ignition. The gauge should read "FULL". Now connect this lead to earth when the gauge should read "EMPTY". If these tests prove in order then the fault is in the transmitter.
3 If the gauge does not read "FULL" with the lead disconnected from the transmitter then disconnect the lead from the gauge. If the gauge reads "FULL" under these conditions then the fault lies in the interconnecting wiring. If the gauge indicates anything other than "FULL" then it is faulty.
4 If the lead is disconnected from the transmitter unit and earthed and the gauge shows anything other than "EMPTY" then check the wiring and connections for security.

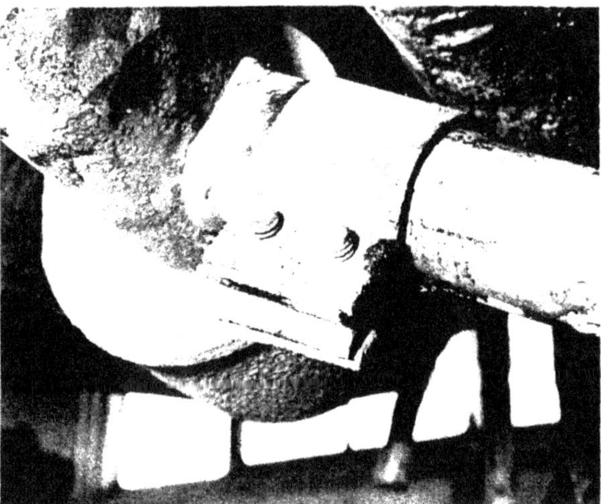

24.9 Exhaust pipe to front expansion box clamp

## 26 Fault diagnosis - carburation, fuel and exhaust systems

| Symptom | Reason/s | Remedy |
|---|---|---|
| Excessive fuel consumption | Air cleaner choked and dirty giving rich mixture | Remove, clean and replace air cleaner. |
| | Fuel leaking from carburettor, fuel pumps, or fuel lines | Check for and eliminate all fuel leaks. Tighten fuel line union nuts. |
| | Float chamber flooding | Check and adjust float level. |
| | Generally worn carburettor | Remove, overhaul and replace. |
| | Distributor condenser faulty | Remove, and fit new unit. |
| | Balance weights or vacuum advance mechanism in distributor faulty | Remove and overhaul distributor. |
| | Carburettor incorrectly adjusted, mixture too rich | Tune and adjust carburettor. |
| | Idling speed too high | Adjust idling speed. |
| | Contact breaker gap incorrect | Check and reset gap. |
| | Valve clearances incorrect | Check rocker arm to valve stem clearances and adjust as necessary. |
| | Incorrectly set spark plugs | Remove, clean and regap. |
| | Tyres under-inflated | Check tyre pressures and inflate if necessary. |
| | Wrong spark plugs fitted | Remove and replace with correct units. |
| | Brakes dragging | Check and adjust brakes. |
| Insufficient fuel delivery or weak mixture | Fuel tank air vent restricted | Clean out air vent. |
| | Partially clogged filters in pump and fuel line | Remove and clean filters. |
| | Dirt lodged in float chamber needle housing | Remove and clean out float chamber and needle valve assembly. |
| | Incorrectly seating valves in fuel pump | Remove, dismantle, and clean out fuel pump |
| | Fuel pump diaphragm leaking or damaged | Remove and overhaul fuel pump. |
| | Gasket in fuel pump damaged | Remove and overhaul fuel pump. |
| | Fuel pump valves sticking due to petrol gumming | Remove and thoroughly clean fuel pump. |
| | Too little fuel in fuel tank (prevalent when climbing steep hills) | Refill fuel tank. |
| | Union joints on pipe connections loose | Tighten joints and check for air leaks. |
| | Split in fuel pipe on suction side of fuel pump | Examine, locate and repair. |
| | Inlet manifold to block or inlet manifold to carburettor or intermediate plate leaking | Test by pouring oil along joints - bubbles indicate leak. Renew gasket as appropriate. |
| Difficult cold starting | Clogged jets | Clear. |
| | Loose main jet plug | Tighten. |
| | Choke flap not closing | Check mechanism. |
| | Weak mixture | Adjust slow-running. |
| Difficult starting when engine hot | Incorrect float level | Adjust or renew defective float. |
| | Flooded carburettor | Check needle valve. |
| Erratic idling | Clogged idling jet | Clear. |
| | Incorrect float level | Check level, also tightness of needle valve. |
| | Incorrectly set slow-running | Adjust. |
| | Leak in vacuum connection to distributor | Rectify. |
| 'Pinking' | Use of fuel with too low an octane rating | Fill tank with correct grade. |
| | Incorrect carburettor jets (mixture too weak) | Compare with Specifications. |
| | Carbon deposits in combustion chamber | Decarbonise. |
| | Displaced or deformed cylinder head gasket causing pre-ignition particularly on overrun | Remove head and renew gasket. |
| | Incorrect type spark plugs | Renew. |
| Misfiring or lack of power | Water in fuel | Drain tank. |
| | Clogged fuel line | Clear. |
| | Faulty fuel pump | Overhaul |
| | Clogged filters or air cleaner | Clean or renew. |
| | Carburettor icing | Move air cleaner intake to winter position. |
| | Incorrect slow-running | Adjust. |

# Chapter 4 Ignition system

**Contents**



**Specifications**

## Distributor

| | Distributor | Vacuum unit |
|---|---|---|
| Make ... | Bosch | |
| Identification: † | | |
| *Up to and including* | | |
| **Chassis No 46-137 (model 95)** * ... | 0-231-146-044 | 1-237-121-215 |
| Chassis No 434-173 (model 96) * ... | 0-231-146-024 | 1-237-121-215 |
| *From* | | |
| Chassis No 46-138 (model 95) ... | 0-231-146-033 | 1-237-121-261 |
| Chassis No 434-174 (model 96) ... | 0-231-146-033 | 1-237-121-261 |
| Chassis No 47-504 (model 95) ... | 0-231-146-072 | 1-237-121-261 |
| Chassis No 444-942 (model 96) ... | 0-231-146-072 | 1-237-121-261 |
| Chassis No 49-093 (model 95) ... | 0-231-146-073 | 1-237-121-261 |
| Chassis No 453-130 (model 96) ... | 0-231-146-073 | 1-237-121-261 |
| Chassis No 65-001 (model 95) ... | 0-231-146-084 | 1-237-121-335 |
| Chassis No 520-001 (model 96) ... | 0-231-146-084 | 1-237-121-335 |
| North American vehicles (1971 on) ... | 0-231-167-039 | 1-237-121-849 |

* *Distributors marked are fitted in conjunction with semi-enclosed crankcase ventilation system, all other types are used in conjunction with fully enclosed crankcase ventilation systems.*

*† It is essential to replace a worn or defective distributor with one of the same serial number*

| | |
|---|---|
| Static ignition setting (test lamp) ... | 6° BTDC |
| Ignition setting with stroboscope ... | 6° BTDC at 800 rev/min (vacuum pipe disconnected and plugged) |
| North American models (exhaust emission control system) ... | 3° BTDC at 800 rev/min (both vacuum pipes disconnected and plugged) |
| Dwell angle ... | 50° ± 2° |
| Contact breaker gap ... | 0.016 in (0.4 mm) |
| Direction of rotor rotation ... | Clockwise (half crankshaft speed) |
| Firing order ... | 1 3 4 2 |

## Ignition coil

| | |
|---|---|
| Type ... | Bosch K 12 |

## Spark plugs

| *Up to chassis number* | Autolite | Bosch | Champion | NGK |
|---|---|---|---|---|
| 55-766 (model 95) ) ... | AE 22 | W225 T35 | L82Y | B-7H |
| 487-638 (model 96) ) ... | AER 22 | | | |
| *From chassis number* | | | | |
| 55-767 (model 95) ) 487-639 (model 96) ) ... | AG 22 | W200 T30 | N9Y | BP7E |
| North American vehicles (1971 onwards) ... | AG 32 | W145 T30 | N-11Y | BP6E |

| | |
|---|---|
| Spark plug gap ... | 0.024 to 0.028 in (0.6 to 0.7 mm) |

## Torque wrench setting

| | lb ft | kg m |
|---|---|---|
| Spark plugs ... | 22 to 29 | 3.0 to 4.0 |

## 1 General description

In order that the engine can run correctly it is necessary for an electrical spark to ignite the fuel/air mixture in the combustion chamber at exactly the right moment in relation to engine speed and load. The ignition system is based on feeding low tension (LT) voltage from the battery to the coil where it is converted to high tension (HT) voltage. The high tension voltage is powerful enough to jump the spark plug gap in the cylinders many times a second under high compression pressures, providing that the system is in good condition and that all adjustments are correct.

The ignition system is divided into two circuits. The low tension circuit and the high tension circuit.

The low tension (sometimes known as the primary) circuit consists of the battery, the lead to the control box, the lead to the ignition switch, the lead from the ignition switch to the low tension or primary coil windings (terminal SW), and the lead from the low tension coil windings (coil terminal CB) to the contact breaker points and condenser on the distributor.

The high tension circuit consists of the high tension or secondary coil windings, the heavy ignition lead from the centre of the coil windings, the heavy ignition lead from the centre of the coil to the centre of the distributor cap, the rotor arm, and the spark plug leads and spark plugs.

The system functions in the following manner. Low tension voltage is changed in the coil into high tension voltage by the opening and closing of the contact breaker points in the low tension circuit. High tension voltage is then fed via the carbon brush in the centre of the distributor cap to the rotor arm of the distributor cap, and each time it comes in line with one of the four metal segments in the cap, which are connected to the spark plug leads, the opening and closing of the contact breaker points causes the high tension voltage to build up, jump the gap from the rotor arm to the appropriate metal segment and so, via the spark plug lead, to the spark plug; where it finally jumps the spark plug gap before going to earth.

The ignition is advanced and retarded automatically, to ensure the spark occurs at just the right instant for the particular load at the prevailing engine speed.

The ignition advance is controlled both mechanically and by a vacuum operated system. The mechanical governor mechanism comprises two weights, which move out from the distributor shaft as the engine speed rises due to centrifugal force. As they move outwards they rotate the cam relative to the distributor shaft, and so advance the spark. The weights are held in position by two light springs and it is the tension of the springs which is largely responsible for correct spark advancement.

The vacuum control consists of a diaphragm, one side of which is connected, via a small bore tube, to the carburettor, and the other side to the contact breaker plate. Depression in the inlet manifold and carburettor, which varies with engine speed and throttle opening, causes the diaphragm to move, so moving the contact breaker plate, and advancing or retarding the spark.

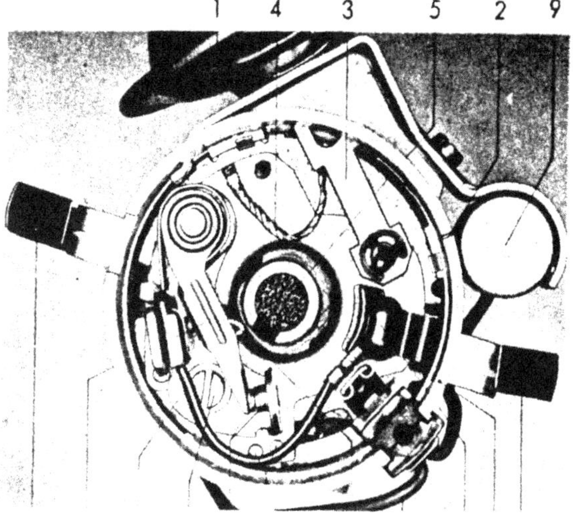


Fig 4.1 Distributor (cap removed) viewed from above

1 *Vacuum unit*
2 *Rotor alignment mark (after installation of distributor)*
3 *Vacuum unit connecting rod*
4 *Earth lead*
5 *Lubrication pad*
6 *Rotor setting dot (prior to installation of distributor)*
7 *Cap securing spring*
8 *Moveable baseplate bearing*
9 *Condenser*
10 *LT lead*
11 *Fibre heel of contact breaker arm*
12 *Screwdriver pivots for contact breaker arm adjustment*
13 *Contact breaker points*
14 *Fixed contact breaker arm securing screw*
15 *Fixed breaker arm*
16 *Moveable breaker arm*

## 2 Contact breaker - adjustment

1 To adjust the contact breaker points to the correct gap, first pull off the two clips securing the distributor cap to the distributor body, and lift away the cap. Clean the cap inside and out with a dry cloth. It is unlikely that the four segments will be badly burned or scored, but if they are the cap will have to be renewed.

2 Inspect the carbon brush located in the top of the cap- see that it is unbroken and stands proud of the plastic surface.

3 Gently prise the contact breaker points open to examine the condition of their faces. If they are rough, pitted or dirty, it will be necessary to remove them for resurfacing, or for replacement points to be fitted.

4 Presuming the points are satisfactory, or that they have been cleaned and replaced, measure the gap between the points by turning the engine over until the heel of the breaker arm is on the highest point of the cam.

5 A 0.016 in (0.4 mm) feeler gauge should now just fit between the points (photo).

6 If the gap varies from this amount slacken the contact plate securing screw (photo).

7 Adjust the contact gap by inserting a screwdriver in the notched hole, in the breaker plate. Turn clockwise to increase and anticlockwise to decrease the gap. When the gap is correct tighten the securing screw and check the gap again.

8 Making sure the rotor is in position replace the distributor cap and clip the spring blade cap retainers into position.

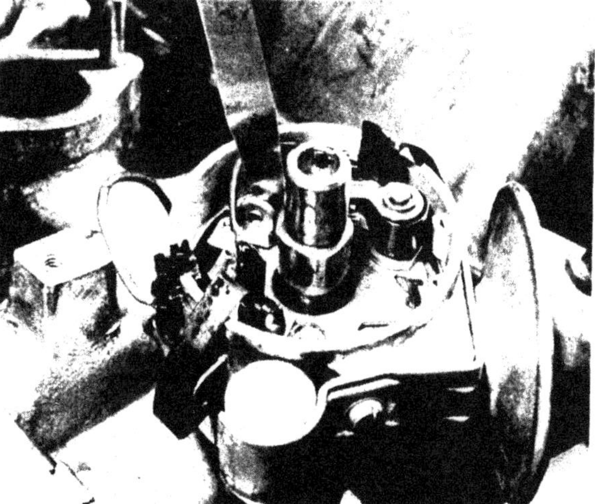

2.5 Checking the contact breaker points gap with a feeler gauge

9 A more precise method of setting the contact breaker gap to conform with the requirements of individual engines can be obtained with the use of a dwell angle tester. Any variation in the points gap (and in turn the dwell angle) will affect the timing. The correct dwell angle is 50° ± 2°.

### 3 Contact breaker points - renewal

1 Slip back the spring clips which secure the distributor cap in position. Remove the distributor cap and lay it to one side, only removing one or two of the HT leads from the plugs if necessary to provide greater movement of the cap.
2 Pull the rotor from the distributor shaft.
3 Disconnect the lead which runs from the moveable spring type contact breaker arm to the LT connecting clip (photo).
4 On certain types of distributor a retaining clip and washers must be removed from the top of the contact breaker pivot post.
5 Press the spring arm of the moveable contact breaker from its support and withdraw the contact breaker arm.
6 Unscrew and remove the fixed contact breaker arm from the distributor baseplate.
7 Inspect the faces of the contact points. If they are only lightly burned or pitted then they may be ground square on an oilstone or by rubbing a carborundum strip between them. Where the points are found to be severely burned or pitted, then they must be renewed and at the same time the cause of the erosion of the points established. This is most likely to be due to poor earth connections from the battery negative lead to body earth or the engine strap. Remove the connecting bolts at these points, scrape the surfaces free from rust and corrosion, and tighten the bolts using a star type lock washer. Other screws to check for security are: the baseplate to distributor body securing screws, the condenser securing screw and the distributor body to lockplate bolt. Looseness in any of these could contribute to a poor earth connection. Check the condenser (Section 4).
8 Refitting is a reversal of removal but some distributors include shims at the spring contact arm anchorage to ensure correct alignment of the contact point faces. Apply a trace of engine oil to the breaker pivot post and to the felt pad at the top of the distributor shaft. Smear the high points of the cam with petroleum jelly.
9 Reset the contact breaker gap as described in Section 2.

### 4 Condenser (capacitor) - removal, testing and refitting

1 The condenser ensures that with the contact breaker points open, the sparking between them is not excessive to cause severe pitting. The condenser is fitted in parallel and its failure will automatically cause failure of the ignition system as the points will be prevented from interrupting the low tension circuit.
2 Testing for an unserviceable condenser may be effected by switching on the ignition and separating the contact points by hand. If this action is accompanied by a blue flash then condenser failure is indicated. Difficult starting, missing of the engine after several miles running or badly pitted points are other indications of a faulty condenser.
3 The surest test is by substitution of a new unit.
4 Removal and refitting of the externally mounted condenser is by means of a single securing screw.

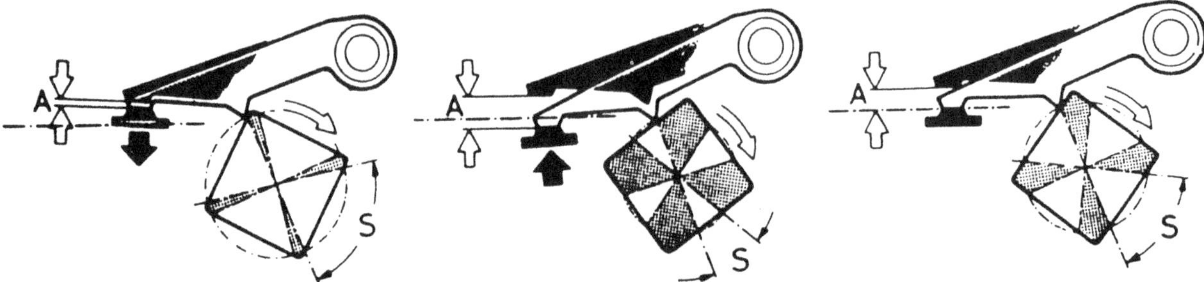


**Fig 4.2 Diagram showing effect of points gap upon dwell angle**

*A – Breaker point gap* *S – Dwell angle*

*Gap too narrow, Angle too wide* — *Gap too wide, Angle too narrow* — *Gap correct, Angle correct*

2.6 Slackening the fixed contact breaker arm screw

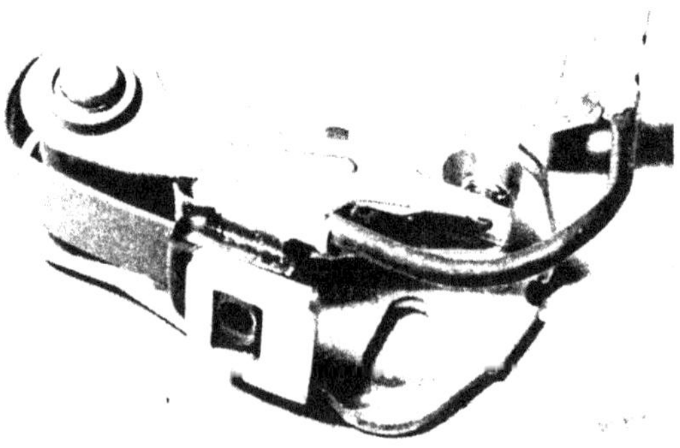

3.3 The contact breaker assembly

## 5 Distributor - removal and refitting

1 The distributor is mounted at the rear of the engine between the two rocker covers.
2 Pull the HT cables from the spark plugs.
3 Prise off the retaining spring clips and remove the distributor cap.
4 Disconnect the distributor LT cable.
5 Pull off the vacuum pipe.
6 Turn the engine until the marks on the distributor rotor and the distributor body are in alignment.
7 Unscrew the distributor clamp bolt and remove the clamp and then withdraw the distributor from its location.
8 Provided the engine has not been turned, refitting the distributor is a reversal of removal making sure that the rotor/body marks are in perfect alignment **after the gears have meshed between distributor drive and oil pump drive and the camshaft.**
9 If the engine has been turned while the distributor has been removed, then proceed in the following manner.
10 Turn the engine so that with number 1 piston on its compression stroke, the mark on the balance shaft pulley is opposite the $6^o$ btdc mark on the front engine cover index (remove a spark plug to feel the compression being generated in number 1 cylinder).
11 Turn the distributor rotor so that its mark is in alignment with the distributor body dot and then insert the distributor into its recess ensuring that its drive gear meshes correctly with the camshaft and oil pump driveshaft. Turn the balance shaft pulley slightly if necessary to engage the gears fully. Check that the rotor mark now aligns with the line on the distributor body. If not, turn the body until it does.
12 Tighten the distributor clamp bolt so that the distributor can still be turned.
13 Reconnect the LT cable and then check the ignition timing in the manner described in the following Section.

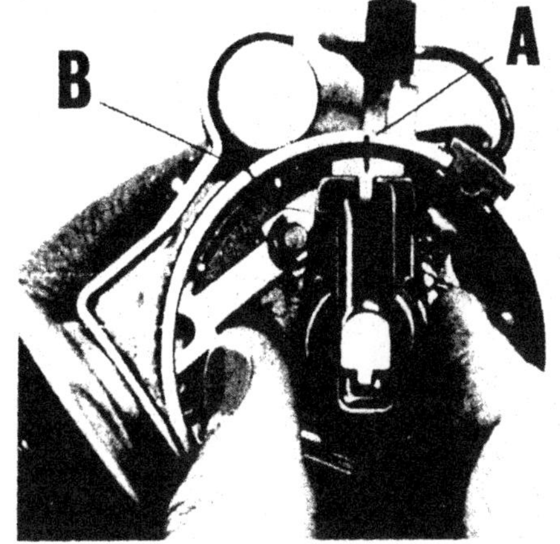


**Fig 4.4 Alignment of rotor and body marks prior to installation of distributor**

*A pre-installation DOT*
*B Alignment LINE after installation*

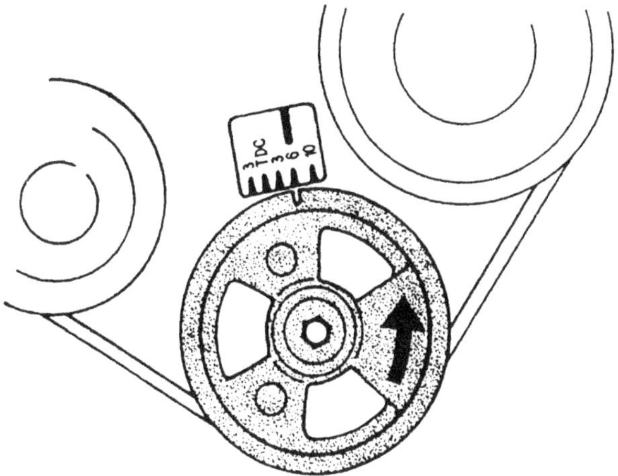


Fig 4.5 Ignition timing marks

## 6 Timing the ignition

1 To set the basic ignition timing, turn the balance shaft pulley until the notch on the pulley is opposite the $6^o$ mark on the engine front cover index (number 1 piston must be on its compression stroke). The balance shaft may most easily be turned by pushing the vehicle forward with the freewheel control locked and third gear engaged. Note that the balance shaft rotates in an anticlockwise direction (opposite to the rotational direction of the crankshaft).
2 Connect a test lamp between the LT terminal inside the distributor and earth and switch on the ignition.
3 Slacken the distributor clamp bolt and turn the distributor

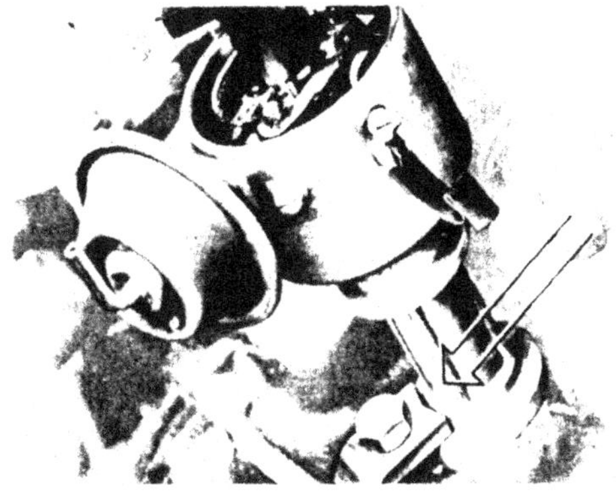

Fig 4.3 Location of distributor clamp and clamp bolt

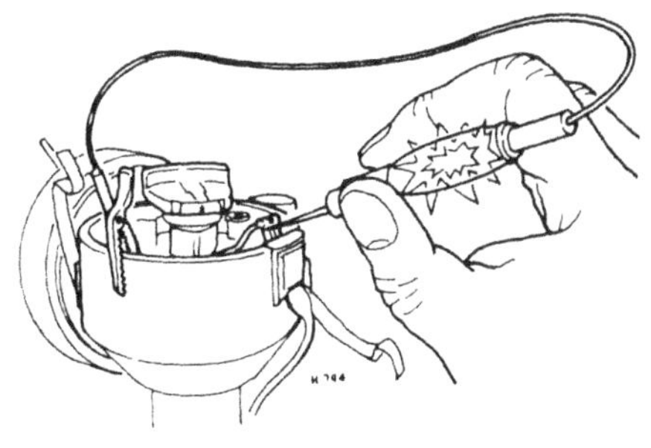

Fig 4.6 Basic timing using a test lamp

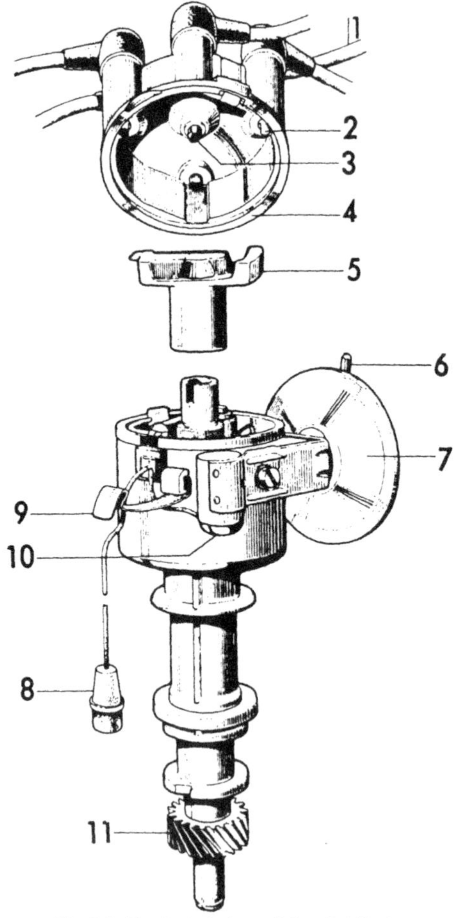


Fig 4.7 Exploded view of the distributor

*1 HT lead*
*2 Contact segment*
*3 Carbon brush*
*4 Cap*
*5 Rotor*
*6 Vacuum pipe connection*
*7 Vacuum unit*
*8 LT lead and connector*
*9 Cap securing spring*
*10 Condenser*
*11 Drive gear*

until the position is established where slight finger pressure on the rotor in a clockwise direction will cause the test lamp to light (points just open). As soon as the finger is removed, the test lamp should go out.

4 Tighten the distributor clamp bolt, remove the test lamp and switch off the ignition.

5 For further precision adjustment, the use of a stroboscope, tachometer and dwell angle tester are required to indicate the settings given in Specifications and this is probably best left to your SAAB dealer.

## 7 Distributor - dismantling, servicing and reassembly

1 Remove the rotor.

2 Disconnect the LT lead from the terminal clip within the distributor.

3 Remove the capacitor and its lead.

4 Remove the circlip from the top of the vacuum unit control rod pivot post.

5 Unscrew and remove the two screws which secure the vacuum unit to the distributor body and withdraw the unit.

6 Unscrew and remove the two screws which serve to hold the distributor cap retaining screws and also the fixed baseplate. On some model distributors these screws are not fitted and the baseplate cannot be detached from the distributor body.

7 Remove the contact breaker arm assembly.

8 From the lower end of the distributor shaft, drive out the tension pin which secures the gear to the shaft and then remove the gear using a suitable extractor.

9 Withdraw the distributor shaft complete with counterweights and springs through the top of the distributor.

10 Pick out the lubricating felt and remove the circlip and washer from the recess in the top of the distributor shaft. Note: On distributors which do not have removable baseplates, the operations described in the preceding paragraphs 9 and 10 cannot be carried out and the unit cannot be serviced to the same extent as other types of distributor. Check for wear in the moveable baseplate.

11 The mechanical advance mechanism may be dismantled and weak or worn springs or other components renewed as necessary.

12 If the shaft bearing in the distributor body is worn, drift it out by driving it into the interior of the distributor. Soak the new bearing in hot engine oil prior to fitting and press it into position until its lower edge is flush with the distributor body.

13 Reassembly is a reversal of dismantling.

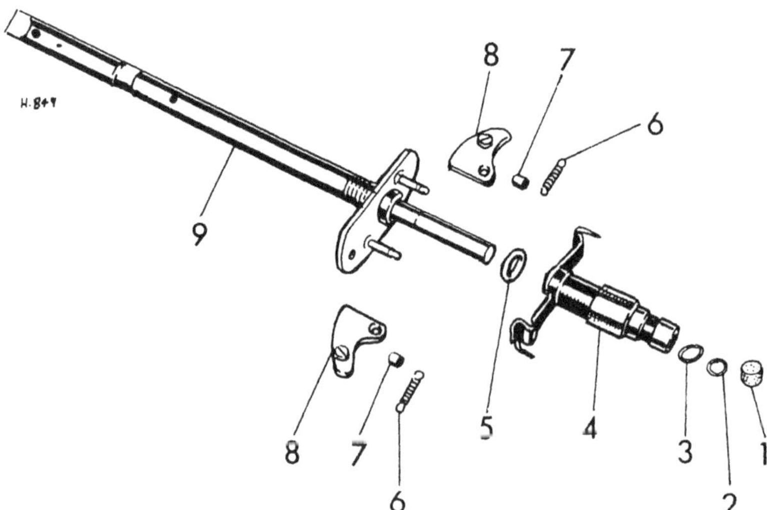


Fig 4.8 Exploded view of the distributor mechanical advance mechanism

*1 Lubrication felt*
*2 Circlip*
*3 Thrust washer*
*4 Cam*
*5 Spacer*
*6 Counterweight return springs*
*7 Retaining ring*
*8 Counterweights*
*9 Distributor shaft*

## 8 Distributor - modified type for North American emission control system

1 A modified type of distributor is fitted to vehicles operating in North America which have full emission control systems.
2 The distributor is similar to standard models with the exception of the vacuum unit which is of double acting type and has an additional connection to the manifold intermediate flange.

## 9 Coil polarity

1 High tension (HT) current should be negative at the spark plug terminals. This will be the case if the LT leads to the coil primary terminals have been correctly connected.
2 Incorrect connection of these leads will cause up to 60% loss of spark efficiency at the spark plug electrodes, and may cause rough idling and misfiring at speed.
3 Ensure that the LT lead from the distributor connects to the negative (-) or CB terminal of the coil.

## 10 Spark plugs and HT leads

1 The correct functioning of the spark plugs is vital for the correct running and efficiency of the engine.
2 At intervals of 6,000 miles (9600 km), the plugs should be removed, examined, cleaned, and if worn excessively, replaced. The condition of the spark plugs will also tell much about the overall condition of the engine.
3 If the insulator nose of the spark plug is clean and white with no deposits, this is indicative of a weak mixture, or too hot a plug (a hot plug transfers heat away from the electrode slowly - a cold plug transfers it away quickly).
4 The plugs fitted as standard are as listed in Specifications at the head of this Chapter. If the tip and insulator nose are covered with hard black looking deposits, then this is indicative that the mixture is too rich. Should the plug be black and oily, then it is likely that the engine is fairly worn, as well as the mixture being too rich.
5 If the insulator nose is covered with light tan to greyish brown deposits, then the mixture is correct and it is likely that the engine is in good condition.
6 If there are any traces of long brown tapering stains on the outside of the white portion of the plug, then the plug will have to be renewed, as this shows that there is a faulty joint between the plug body and the insulator, and compression is being allowed to leak away.
7 Plugs should be cleaned by a sand blasting machine which will free them from carbon more thoroughly than cleaning by hand. The machine will also test the condition of the plugs under compression. Any plug that fails to spark at the recommended pressure should be renewed.
8 The spark plug gap is of considerable importance, as, if it is too large or too small, the size of the spark and its efficiency will be seriously impaired. The spark plug gap should be set to the figure given in Specifications at the beginning of this Chapter.
9 To set it, measure the gap with a feeler gauge, and then bend open, or close, the outer plug electrode until the correct gap is achieved. The centre electrode should never be bent as this may crack the insulation and cause plug failure if nothing worse.
10 When replacing the plugs, refit the leads from the distributor in the correct firing order, which is 1 3 4 2, No 1 cylinder being the one nearest the radiator and on the right-hand side.
11 The plug leads require no routine attention other than being kept clean and wiped over regularly.
12 At intervals of 3,000 miles (5,000 Km) or 3 months, however, pull the leads off the plugs and distributor one at a time and make sure no water has found its way onto the connections. Remove any corrosion from the brass ends, wipe the collars on top of the distributor and refit the leads.

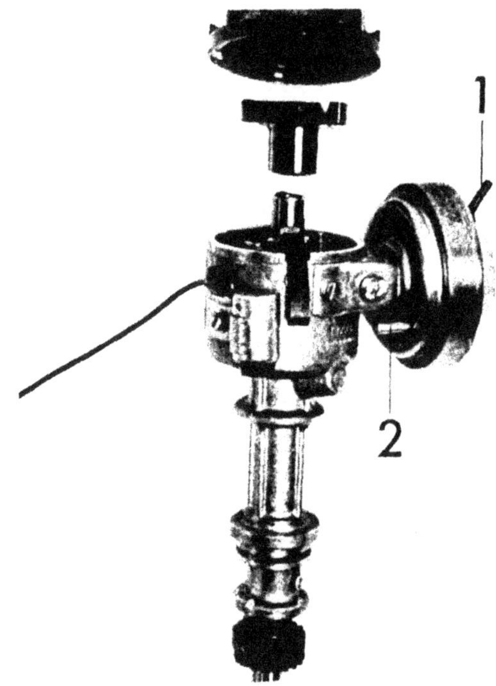


**Fig 4.9 Distributor fitted to USA models (1971 onwards)**

*1 Vacuum pipe connection from carburettor*
*2 Hose connection from intermediate flange*

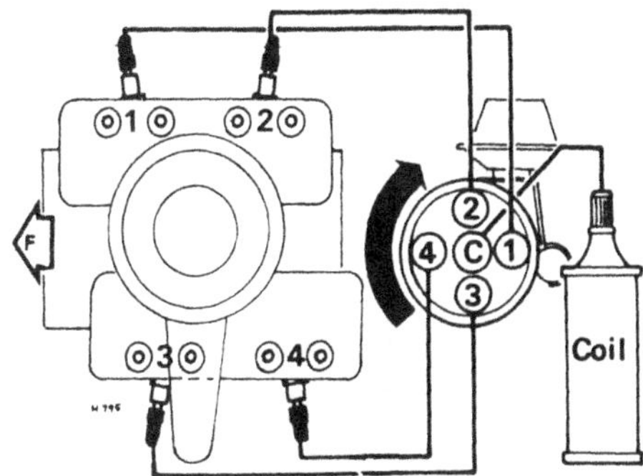


**Fig 4.10 Diagram showing cylinder numbering sequence and HT lead connections to spark plugs**

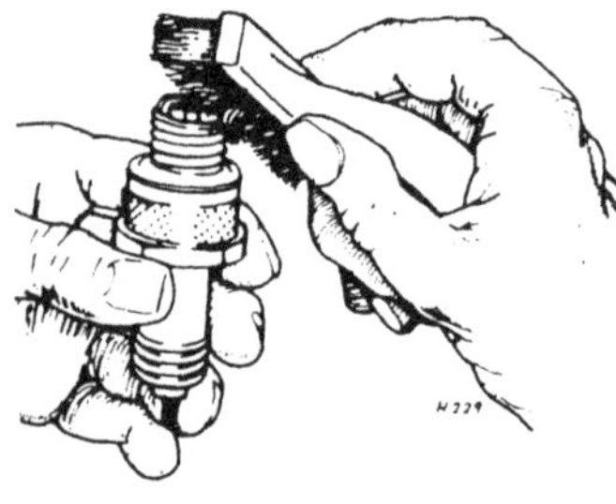

*Cleaning deposits from electrodes and surrounding area using a fine wire brush.*

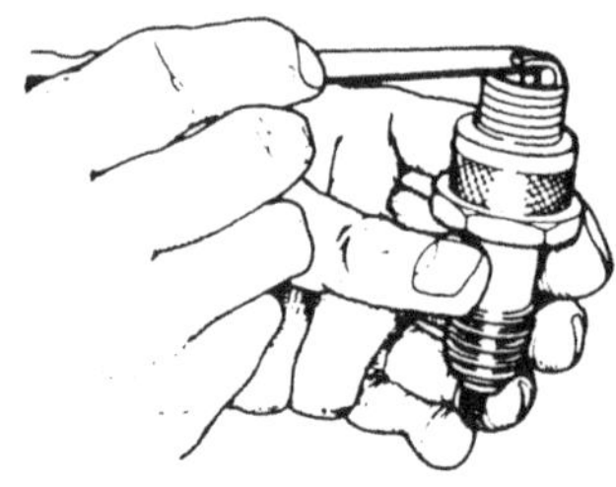

*Checking plug gap with feeler gauges*

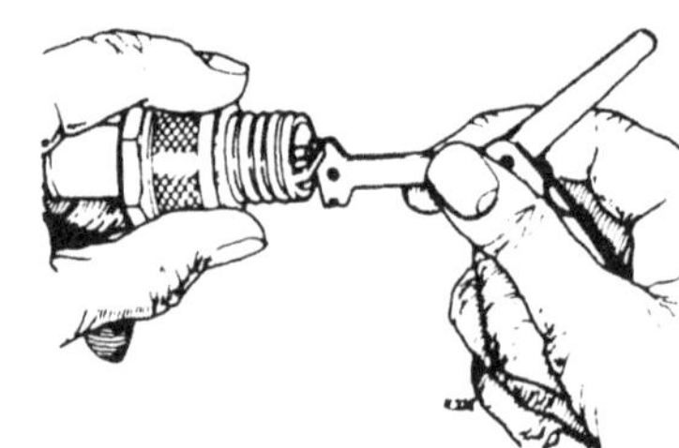

*Altering the plug gap. Note use of correct tool.*

**Spark plug maintenance**

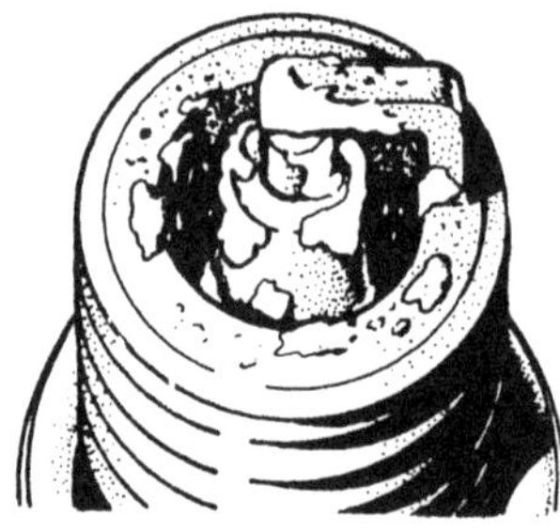

*White deposits and damaged porcelain insulation indicating overheating*

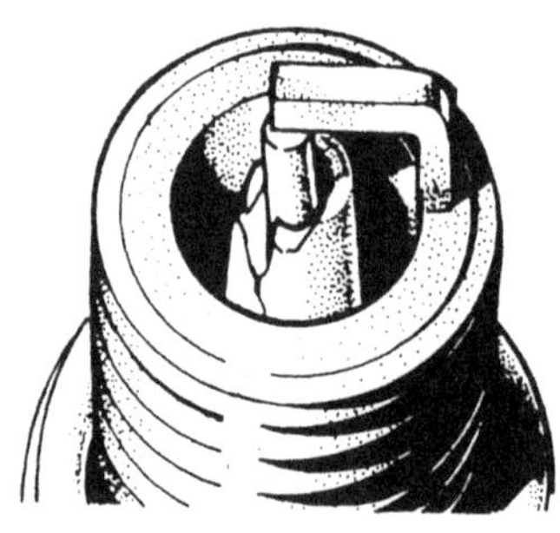

*Broken porcelain insulation due to bent central electrode*

*Electrodes burnt away due to wrong heat value or chronic pre-ignition (pinking)*

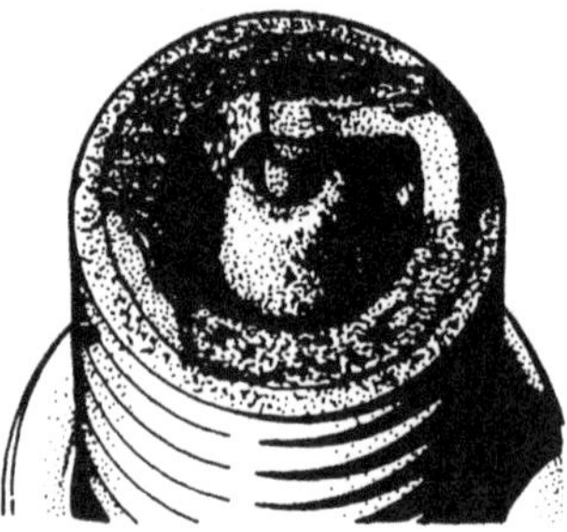

*Excessive black deposits caused by over-rich mixture or wrong heat value*

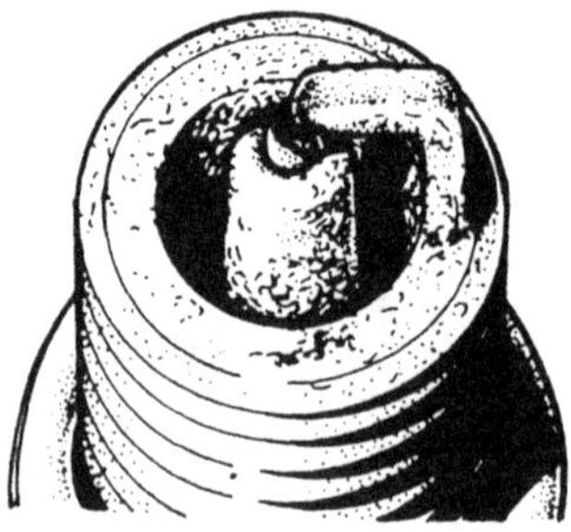

*Mild white deposits and electrode burnt indicating too weak a fuel mixture*

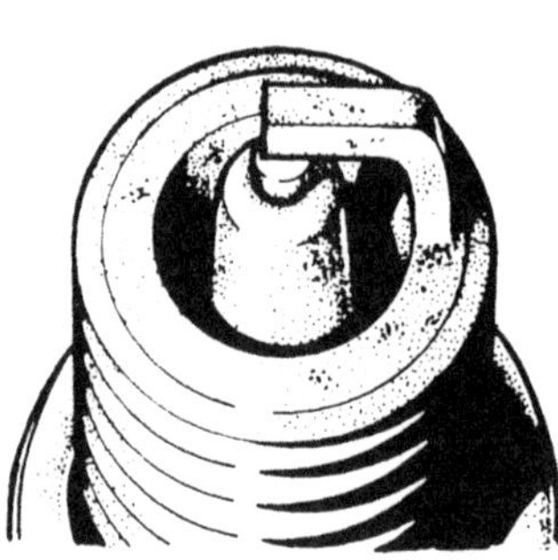

*Plug in sound condition with light greyish brown deposits*

**Spark plug electrode conditions**

## 11 Ignition system - fault symptoms

There are two general symptoms of ignition faults. Either the engine will not fire, or the engine is difficult to start and misfires. If the engine will not fire, or the engine is difficult to start and misfires, if it is a regular misfire, i.e. the engine is only running on two or three cylinders, the fault is almost sure to be in the high tension circuit. If the misfiring is intermittent, the fault could be in either the high or low tension circuits. If the engine stops suddenly, or will not start at all, it is likely that the fault is in the low tension circuit. Loss of power and overheating, apart from faulty carburettor settings, are normally due to faults in the distributor, or incorrect ignition timing.

## 12 Fault diagnosis - engine fails to start

1 If the engine fails to start and it was running normally when it was last used, first check that there is fuel in the petrol tank. If the engine turns over normally on the starter motor and the battery is evidently well charged, then the fault may be in either the high or low tension circuits. First check the HT circuit. **Note:** If the battery is known to be fully charged, the ignition comes on, and the starter motor fails to turn the engine, **check the tightness of the leads on the battery terminals** and also the secureness of the earth lead to the **connection to the body.** It is quite common for the leads to have worked loose even if they look and feel secure. If one of the battery terminal posts gets very hot when trying to operate the starter motor this is a sure indication of a faulty connection to that terminal.
2 One of the commonest reasons for bad starting is wet or damp spark plug leads and distributor. Remove the distributor cap. If the condensation is visible, internally dry the cap with a rag and also wipe over the leads. Replace the cap.
3 If the engine still fails to start, check that current is reaching the plugs by disconnecting each plug lead in turn at the spark plug ends and holding the end of the cable about 3/16 inch (4.726 mm) away from the cylinder block. Spin the engine on the starter motor.
4 Sparking between the end of the cable and the block should be fairly strong with a regular blue spark (hold the lead with rubber to avoid electric shocks), if current is reaching the spark plugs. Remove them and clean and regap them to 0.024 - 0.028 inch (0.6604 to 0.7112 mm). The engine should now start.
5 Spin the engine as before, when a rapid succession of blue sparks between the end of the lead and the block indicates that the coil is in order, and that either the distributor cap is cracked, the carbon brush is stuck or worn, the rotor arm is faulty, or the contact points are burnt, pitted or dirty. If the parts are in bad shape, clean and reset them.
6 If there are no sparks from the end of the lead from the coil, then check the connections of the lead to the coil and distributor cap, and if they are in order, check out the low tension circuit, starting with the battery.
7 Switch on the ignition and turn the balance shaft pulley so that the contact breaker points have fully opened. Then with either a 20 volt voltmeter or bulb and length of wire, check that current from the battery is reaching the starter solenoid switch. No reading indicates that there is a fault in the cable to the switch or in the connections at the switch or at the battery terminals. Alternatively, the battery earth lead may not be properly earthed to the body.
8 Check the switch terminal on the coil (it is marked + and the lead from the switch is connected to it). No reading indicates loose connections or a broken wire from the A3 terminal on the fuse unit. If this proves to be at fault, remedy and re-start the car.
9 Check the contact breaker terminal on the coil (it is marked - and the lead to the distributor is connected to it). If no reading is recorded on the voltmeter then the coil is broken and must be replaced. The car should start when a new coil has been fitted.
10 If a reading is obtained at the - terminal then check the wire from the coil for loose connections etc. The final check on the low tension circuit is across the contact breaker points. No reading indicates a broken condenser, which when replaced will enable the car to finally start.

## 13 Fault diagnosis - engine misfires

1 If the engine misfires regularly, run it at a fast idling speed, and short out each of the spark plugs in turn by placing an insulated screwdriver across the plug terminal to the cylinder block.
2 No difference in engine running will be noticed when the plug in the defective cylinder is short circuited. Short circuiting the working plugs will accentuate the misfire.
3 Remove the plug leads from the end of the defective plug and hold it about 3/16 in (4.76 mm) away from the block. Restart the engine. If sparking is fairly strong and regular the fault must lie in the spark plug.
4 The plug may be loose, the insulation may be cracked or the elctrodes may have burnt away giving too wide a gap for the spark to jump across. Worse still, the earth electrode may have broken off. Either renew the plug, or clean it, reset the gap and then test it.
5 If there is no spark at the end of the plug lead, or if it is weak and intermittent, check the ignition lead from the distributor to the plug. If the insulation is cracked or damaged, renew the lead. Check the connections at the distributor cap.
6 If there is still no spark, examine the distributor cap carefully for signs of tracking. This can be recognised by a very thin black line running between two or more segments, or between a segment and some other part of the distributor. These lines are paths which now conduct electricity across the cap thus letting it run to earth. The only answer is to fit a new distributor cap.
7 Apart from the ignition timing being incorrect, other causes of misfiring have already been dealt with under the section dealing with failure of the engine to start.
8 If the ignition timing is too far retarded, it should be noted that the engine will tend to overheat, and there will be quite a noticeable drop in power. If the engine is overheating and power is down, and the ignition is correct, then the carburettor should be checked as it is likely that this is where the fault lies.

# Chapter 5 Clutch

Contents



Specifications

| | | |
|---|---|---|
| **Type** ... ... ... ... ... ... ... ... ... | Single dry plate, coil spring pressure plate with hydraulic actuation | |
| **Free movement (slave cylinder pushrod to release fork arm)** ... ... ... ... ... ... ... ... | 0.16 in (4.0 mm) | |
| **Friction lining internal diameter** ... ... ... ... ... ... | 5 in (127.0 mm) | |
| **Friction lining external diameter** ... ... ... ... | 7.5 in (190.5 mm) | |
| **Friction lining thickness** ... ... ... ... ... ... | 0.33 in (8.4 mm) | |
| **Master cylinder** | Up to 1969 | After 1969 |
| Type ... ... ... ... ... ... ... ... ... | Girling | Lockheed |
| Cylinder diameter ... ... ... ... ... ... ... ... | 5/8 in | 5/8 in |
| Stroke ... ... ... ... ... ... ... ... ... | 1.38 in (35.0 mm) | 1.22 in (31.0 mm) |
| Fluid line connection ... ... ... ... ... ... | 3/8 in UNF 24 | 7/16 in 20 UNF-2B |
| Maximum pedal stroke ... ... ... ... ... ... | 6.3 in (160.0 mm) | 5.1 in (130.0 mm) |
| **Slave cylinder (fitted in conjunection with both types of master cylinder)** | | |
| Cylinder diameter ... ... ... ... ... ... ... ... | ¾ in | |

| **Torque wrench settings** | lb ft | kg m |
|---|---|---|
| Pressure plate cover bolts ... ... ... ... ... ... | 20 | 2.8 |
| Clutch bellhousing to engine bolts ... ... ... ... | 30 | 4.1 |

## 1 General description

The clutch is of single dry plate design and incorporates a driven plate, a pressure plate assembly of coil spring type and a ball bearing release bearing.

Clutch operation is hydraulic by means of a foot pedal-operated master cylinder and a slave cylinder.

Maintenance consists of maintaining the clutch-pedal free movement and keeping the master cylinder reservoir topped-up to the correct level.

## 2 Clutch - adjustment

1 To compensate for wear to the clutch friction linings which causes a decrease in the clearance between the faces of the release bearing and pressure plate, the clutch pedal free movement must be checked and adjusted at the frequencies indicated in 'Routine Maintenance'.

2 To adjust the clutch, slacken the locknut on the adjusting screw which is located on the left-hand side of the clutch bellhousing and turn the adjusting screw.

**Fig 5.1 Clutch major components**

*1 Pressure plate assembly*
*2 Driven plate*
*3 Flywheel*

3 The adjustment is correct when by pushing the slave cylinder operating rod to release fork connection in a forward direction, there is a free movement (before the release fork and bearing contacts the clutch pressure plate) of 0.16 in. (4.0 mm).
4 When adjustment is correct, tighten the adjusting screw locknut and check that the clutch pedal has to be released by approximately 1 3/8 in. (35.0 mm) before the clutch is fully engaged.

## 3 Clutch pedal - removal and refitting

1 The difference in type of master cylinder fitted to models built before and after 1969 should be observed.
2 On late models remove the protective cover from the steering column.
3 On all models remove the split pin and clevis pin from the pedal arm.
4 On late models, the operating rod may now be pulled out of the end of the vertically mounted master cylinder.
5 Remove the pedal return spring and then remove the circlip from the pedal cross-shaft and withdraw the clutch pedal.
6 Refitting is a reversal of removal but grease the cross-shaft bearings and fit a new split pin to the pedal arm clevis.
7 Check the free movement as described in the preceding Section.

## 4 Clutch - removal, servicing and installation

1 Remove the engine from the vehicle, leaving the transmission unit in position as described in Chapter 1.
2 Mark the position of the pressure plate in relation to the flywheel and then unscrew each of the six bolts which hold the clutch assembly to the rear face of the flywheel. Unscrew these bolts only a turn at a time in diametrically opposite sequence until the pressure of the coil springs which are located within the pressure plate cover has been relieved.
3 Withdraw the pressure plate and catch the driven plate (friction disc) as it drops from its location (photo).
4 A clutch will wear according to the way in which it is used. Much intentional slipping of the clutch while driving - rather than the correct selection of gears - will accelerate wear. It is best to assume, however, that the friction disc will need renewal every 35,000 miles (56000 km) at least and that it will be *worth* replacing it after 25,000 miles (40000 km). The maintenance history of the car is obviously very useful in such cases.
5 Examine the surfaces of the pressure plate and flywheel for signs of scoring. If this is only light it may be left, but if very deep the pressure plate unit will have to be renewed. If the

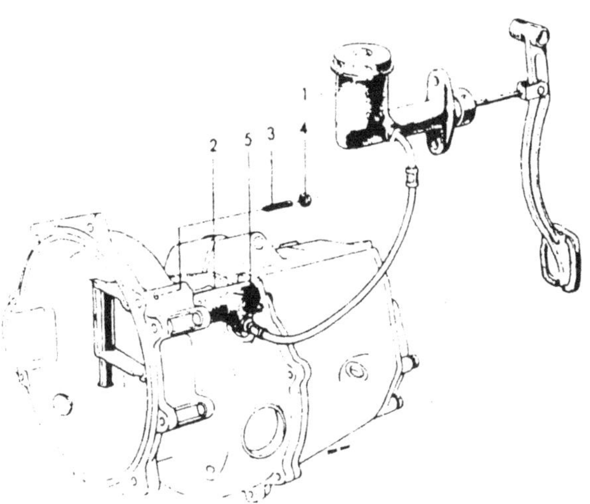


**Fig 5.2 Clutch hydraulic system with early type master cylinder**

*1 Master cylinder*
*2 Slave cylinder*
*3 Adjustment screw*
*4 Locknut*
*5 Bleed nipple*

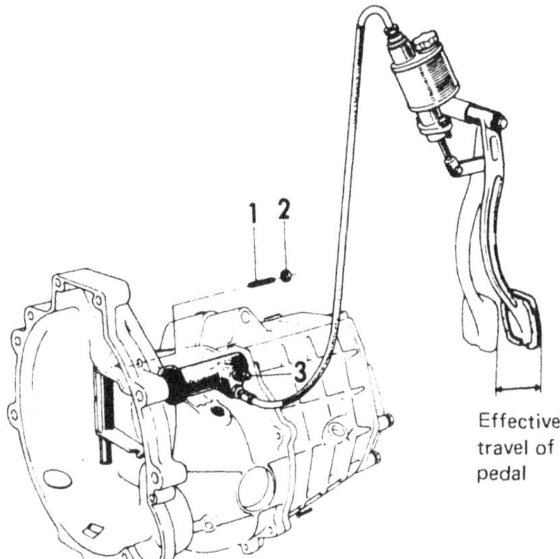


**Fig 5.3 Clutch hydraulic system with late type master cylinder**

*1 Adjusting screw*
*2 Locknut*
*3 Bleed nipple*

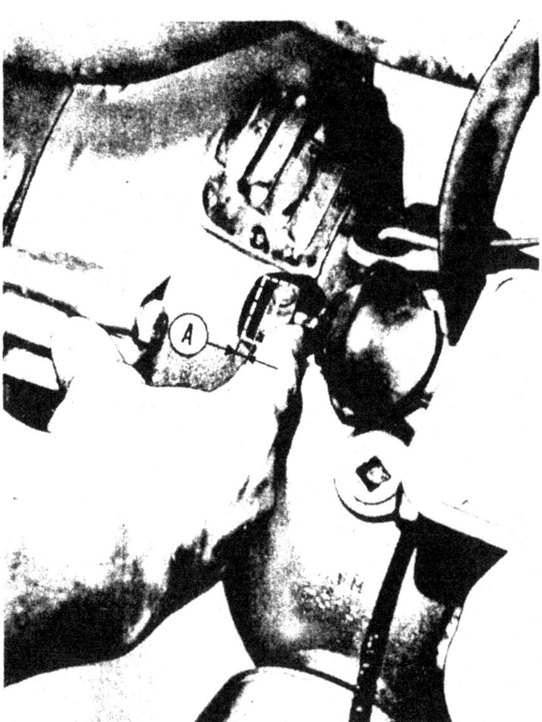


**Fig 5.4 Checking clutch free-movement (note inspection hole rubber cover peeled back) A = 0.16 in (4.0 mm)**

flywheel is deeply scored it should be taken off and advice sought from an engineering firm. Provided it may be machined completely across the face the overall balance of engine and flywheel should not be too severely upset. If renewal of the flywheel is necessary the new one will have to be balanced to match the original.

6 The friction plate lining surfaces should be at least 1/32 in. (0.8 mm) above the rivets, otherwise the disc is not worth putting back. If the lining material shows signs of breaking up or black areas where oil contamination has occurred it should also be renewed. If facilities are readily available for obtaining and fitting new friction pads to the existing disc this may be done but the saving is relatively small compared with obtaining a complete new disc assembly which ensures that the shock absorbing springs and the splined hub are renewed also. The same applies to the pressure plate assembly which cannot be readily dismantled and put back together without specialised tools and balancing equipment. An allowance is usually given for exchange units.

7 If the original pressure plate assembly is being refitted, align the locating marks made before it was removed from the flywheel. Hold the driven plate against the face of the flywheel so that its longer splined hub will face towards the gearbox. Then locate the pressure plate and insert the securing bolts evenly but only finger tight so that the driven plate is just held in position, sandwiched between the pressure plate and flywheel.

8 It is necessary to position the driven plate centrally and accurately, in relation to the pressure plate assembly so that the gearbox input shaft can locate right through the clutch into the spigot bearing recess in the flywheel when the transmission and engine are put together.

9 Centralise the driven plate either by using a dowel rod or an old clutch shaft and inserting it through the splined hub of the driven plate until its end engages squarely in the spigot bush in the centre of the flywheel.

10 Retaining the rod or shaft in this position, tighten the pressure plate cover bolts to a torque of 20 lb/ft (2.8 kg/m) a turn at a time, in diametrically opposite sequence.

11 Withdraw the rod or shaft used as a guide and then install the engine as described in Chapter 1.

12 Check and adjust if necessary the clutch pedal free movement.

## 5 Clutch release bearing - renewal

1 The release bearing is accessible after removal of the engine and will normally be serviced at the same time as the clutch mechanism is overhauled.

2 The release bearing is of ball type, grease sealed for life and if

4.3 Removing clutch assembly from the flywheel

5.2 Clutch release bearing and arm

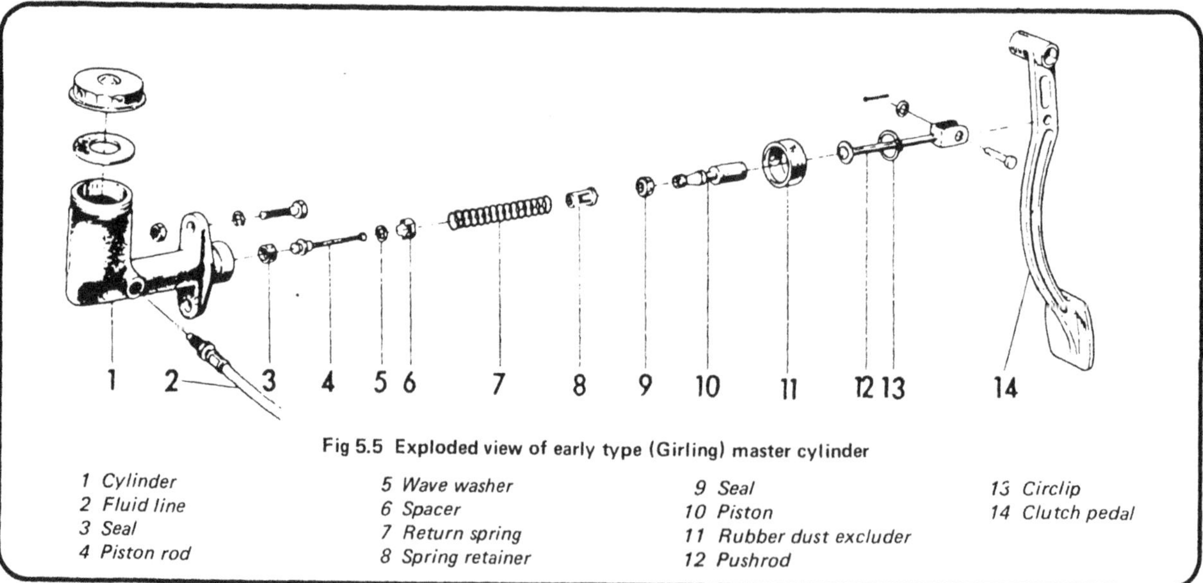


Fig 5.5 Exploded view of early type (Girling) master cylinder

*1 Cylinder*
*2 Fluid line*
*3 Seal*
*4 Piston rod*
*5 Wave washer*
*6 Spacer*
*7 Return spring*
*8 Spring retainer*
*9 Seal*
*10 Piston*
*11 Rubber dust excluder*
*12 Pushrod*
*13 Circlip*
*14 Clutch pedal*

on inspection it is found to be noisy or slack in operation (having turned it by hand) it must be renewed complete (photo).

3 Pull the clutch release fork forward and remove the two spring clips which retain the bearing in the cut-outs in the release fork arms.

4 The pressure face of the release bearing may have an integral graphite ring or it may be Teflon coated to provide a low friction surface. When renewing the release bearing, ensure that one of the same type is obtained.

5 Installation of the new release bearing is a reversal of removal but ensure that the retaining spring clips are correctly engaged.

6 Check the clutch pedal free movement after the engine has been coupled to the transmission.

## 6 Master cylinder (early type) - removal, servicing, refitting

1 Disconnect the fluid pipe from the clutch slave cylinder and depress the clutch pedal several times until all the hydraulic fluid is ejected into a clean vessel.

2 Disconnect the operating pushrod from the clutch pedal by removing the split pin and cotter pin.

3 Unscrew and remove the two flange securing bolts and remove the master cylinder from the engine rear bulkhead.

4 Peel the rubber dust cap from the end of the master cylinder and extract the circlip. Withdraw the pushrod.

5 The piston assembly will now be ejected. Carefully prise up the tongue of the spring retainer and dismantle the piston components.

6 Discard all rubber seals.

7 By compressing the piston return spring, the valve spindle can then be slipped through the keyhole shaped hole in the spring retainer and separated.

8 Wash all components in methylated spirit or clean hydraulic fluid and examine for wear. If any 'bright' wear areas are evident on the surfaces of the piston or cylinder bore, renew the complete master cylinder.

9 Obtain a repair kit and refit all the parts supplied making sure that the new seals are manipulated into position using the fingers only and that their lips and chamfers are correctly located. (Fig. 5.6).

10 Reassembly and refitting are a reversal of removal and dismantling.

11 Refill the master cylinder reservoir with clean fluid which has been stored in an airtight container and has remained unshaken for the previous 24 hours.

12 Bleed the clutch hydraulic system as described in Section 9.

13 Check the clutch pedal free movement and adjust if necessary.

## 7 Master cylinder (late type) - removal, servicing, refitting

1 Carry out the operations described in paragraphs 1 to 4 in the preceding Section.

2 The piston assembly and spring will now be ejected.

3 Discard all rubber seals.

4 Carry out the operations described in paragraphs 8 to 13 of the preceding Section but note that the washer (2) located between the end of the piston and the seal (3) must have its convex face towards the piston. (Fig. 5.8).

## 8 Slave cylinder - removal, servicing and refitting

1 Disconnect the fluid line from the slave cylinder and plug the line to prevent loss of fluid.

2 Unscrew and remove the slave cylinder securing bolt and then withdraw the slave cylinder leaving the push-rod attached to the upper arm of the clutch release fork. On some models a packing washer may be located between the slave cylinder and clutch bellhousing.

3 Peel back the dust cover from the end of the cylinder and extract the circlip.

4 Withdraw the piston/seal assembly and return spring.

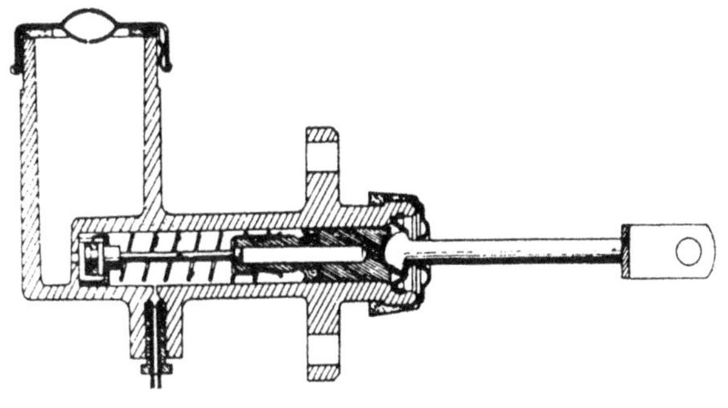

Fig 5.6 Sectional view of early type (Girling) master cylinder

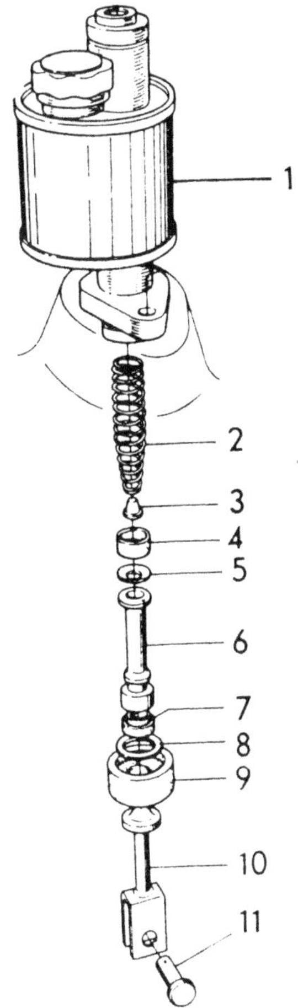


Fig 5.7 Exploded view of later type (Lockheed) master cylinder

*1 Reservoir and cylinder assembly*
*2 Return spring*
*3 Spring retainer*
*4 Seal*
*5 Washer*
*6 Piston*
*7 Seal*
*8 Circlip*
*9 Dust excluder*
*10 Pushrod*
*11 Clevis pin*

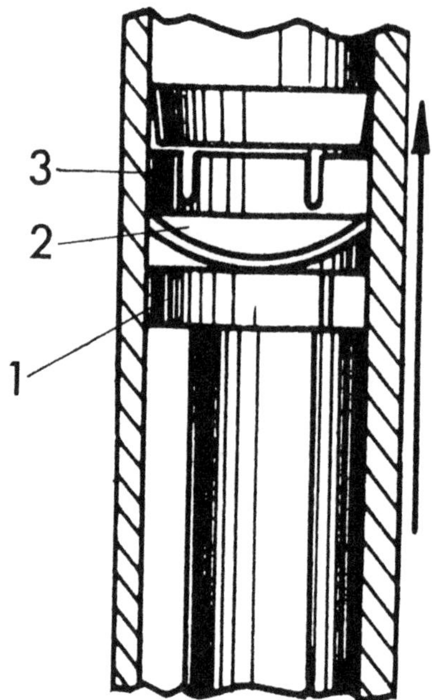


Fig 5.8 Section of later type (Lockheed) master cylinder showing correct location of cupped washer

*1 Piston*
*2 Washer*
*3 Seal*

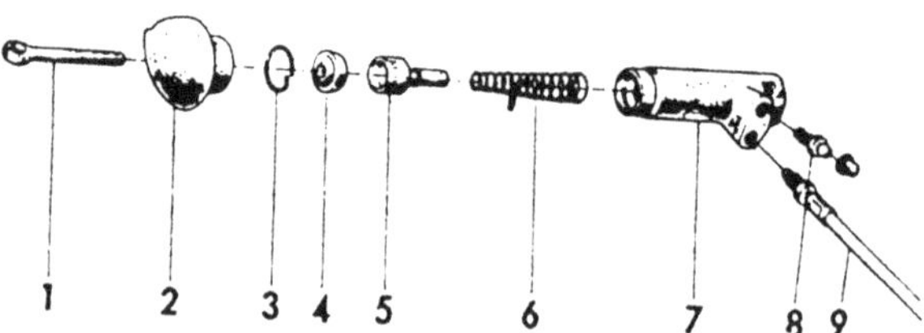


Fig 5.9 Exploded view of clutch slave cylinder

*1 Pushrod*
*2 Rubber dust excluding cover*
*3 Circlip*
*4 Seal*
*5 Piston*
*6 Return spring*
*7 Cylinder*
*8 Bleed nipple*
*9 Fluid line*

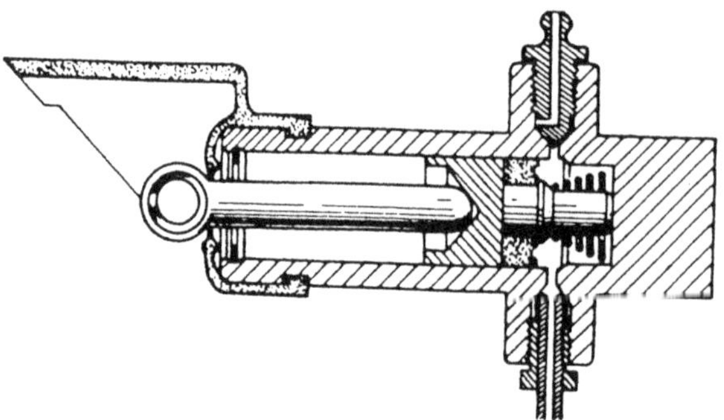

Fig 5.10 Sectional view of clutch slave cylinder

5 Wash all components in methylated spirit or clean hydraulic fluid and examine the surfaces of the piston and cylinder bore for scoring or 'bright wear areas'. If any are evident, renew the cylinder complete.

6 Discard the seal and fit a new one, manipulating it into position using the fingers only.

7 Refit the piston to the cylinder having first dipped it in clean hydraulic fluid.

8 Fit the circlip and then pack the dust cover with rubber grease and locate it over the end of the cylinder.

9 Refit the slave cylinder to the clutch bellhousing by first passing the pushrod through the rubber dust cover (refit packing washer if applicable). Reconnect the fluid line.

10 Bleed the clutch hydraulic system as described in the following Section and then check the clutch pedal free-movement and adjust if necessary (Section 2).

## 9 Clutch hydraulic system - bleeding

1 Attach a plastic or rubber bleed tube to the nipple on the slave cylinder.

2 Place the open end of the bleed tube in a jar which has been filled to a depth of about 1½ in. (38 mm) with hydraulic fluid. Ensure that the end of the tube is kept below the surface of the fluid throughout the bleeding operation.

3 Unscrew the bleed nipple half a turn and have an assistant depress the clutch pedal to the full extent of its travel and then remove the foot quickly so that the pedal returns unimpeded. Repeat this operation until air bubbles cease to be expelled from the end of the bleed tube.

4 Tighten the bleed nipple while the pedal is in its fully depressed position, using a spanner of short length.

5 The master cylinder reservoir must be kept topped-up throughout the bleeding operation with hydraulic fluid which has been stored in an airtight container and remained unshaken for at least 24 hours. Failure to keep the reservoir topped-up will cause air to be drawn into the system and the bleeding process will have to start all over again.

## 10 Clutch faults - diagnosis and rectification

1 Provided the clutch is not intentionally slipped excessively, or the pedal used as a footrest, which may possibly keep the release bearing spinning due to permanent contact with the diaphragm spring, the only malfunction of the clutch one may expect would be due to wear of the friction plate. This normal wear will become obvious when the clutch starts to slip, that is the engine turns normally but the car fails to accelerate properly or it slows down on hills. In such cases the clutch must be examined and repaired immediately. Delay could be costly. For this job the engine will need to be removed.

2 Squealing noises from the clutch (and make sure the squeals *are* from the clutch and not the fan belt or water pump) are most likely to come from a worn out clutch release bearing. The actual efficiency of the clutch may not be immediately affected but if the bearing is not repaired in good time the wear will increase. This will lead to excessive and uneven wear of the clutch disc. Another cause of squealing could be due to the friction plate being worn out or contaminated. In either case the inspection and repair will involve removal of the engine.

3 Clutch spin, or failure to disengage completely when the pedal is fully depressed, can be caused by one or more of several reasons. The symptoms are that it is either impossible, or the gearbox makes a very noisy 'crunch' when trying to engage bottom gear in the usual manner. First of all check the hydraulic system operation and condition to ensure that the clutch release lever is moving as necessary. If this is satisfactory then the clutch disc is sticking to the pressure plate or flywheel, or the release bearing is so badly worn that it is incapable of moving the diaphragm spring evenly or adequately. This will almost invariably be indicated by squeals and noises when the clutch

pedal is operated. Check by stopping the engine, engaging a gear, depressing the clutch and putting on the handbrake. Then try starting the engine. If it refuses to turn, the clutch is stuck solid and should be removed and examined. If the engine is started without difficulty try using the clutch in the normal manner. If the drive continues to 'creep' a little when the pedal is fully depressed carry on slipping the clutch for a few moments to try and rub off whatever may have been on the friction surfaces as a temporary measure. If no improvement of any kind results there must be a serious internal defect which will require engine removal and examination of the clutch.

4 The other fault which is associated with the clutch but not necessarily caused by a clutch defect is judder, particularly noticeable when moving away from rest. First check the security and condition of the engine mountings and the transmission rear mounting. Examine the driveshaft joints for wear and service them as described in Chapter 7.

5 If diagnosis indicates that the judder is due to a clutch fault it will be caused by 'snatching' between the friction surfaces - and possibly associated with concurring problems of clutch spin or clutch slip. In this case the engine will need removal for further inspection of the clutch.

6 Faulty clutch operation can sometimes be caused by flexing of the master cylinder when the clutch pedal is depressed. This is caused by cracking due to metal fatigue of the bulkhead mounting directly behind the master cylinder flange. If inspection proves this to be the case, weld the cracks or fit a reinforcing plate (photo).

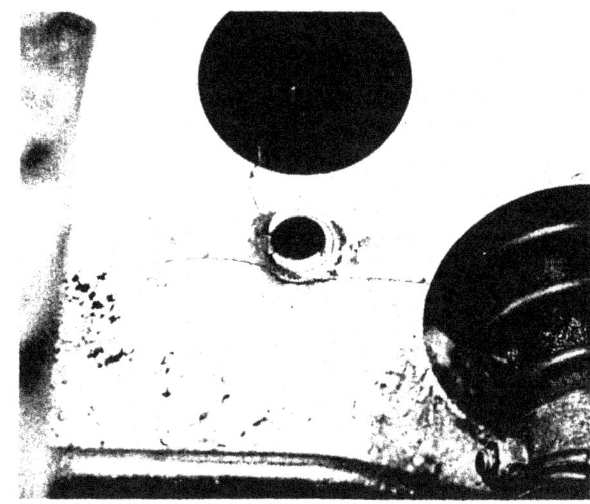

10.6 Cracked bulkhead at clutch master cylinder mounting

# Chapter 6 Transmission

**Contents**



**Specifications**

| | |
|---|---|
| **Type** | Integral unit gearbox and final drive to front wheels. Four forward speeds and one reverse. Synchromesh on all forward speeds. |
| **Gear ratios (overall)** | |
| 1st | 17.0 : 1 |
| 2nd | 10.2 : 1 |
| 3rd | 6.3 : 1 |
| 4th | 4.1 : 1 |
| Reverse | 15.5 :1 |
| **Differential ratio (pinion to crownwheel)** | 4.88 : 1 |
| **Number of pinion teeth** | 8 |
| **Number of crownwheel teeth** | 39 |
| **Oil capacity** | 2½ pints (1.4 litres) |

| **Torque wrench settings** | **lb ft** | **kg m** |
|---|---|---|
| Transmission end casing bolts | 18 | 2.5 |
| Crownwheel bolts | 18 | 2.5 |
| Primary shaft nut | 36 | 5.0 |
| Countershaft nut | 60 | 8.3 |
| Pinion shaft nut: | | |
| 1st stage | 90 | 12.5 |
| 2nd stage | 45 | 6.2 |
| Differential bearing cap nuts | 29 | 4.0 |

## 1 General description

The transmission unit is located immediately to the rear of the engine and incorporates the gearbox, freewheel and differential/final drive in one assembly.

The transmission has four forward speeds (all with synchromesh) and one reverse.

The main transmission shafts are carried on ball or roller races and the gears on needle rollers or directly splined to the shafts. (Fig 6.1)

The clutch bellhousing and differential housing are of light alloy construction and form one unit at the front end of the transmission assembly.

Gear selection is by means of a steering column gearchange mechanism which is of rod and universal joint design.

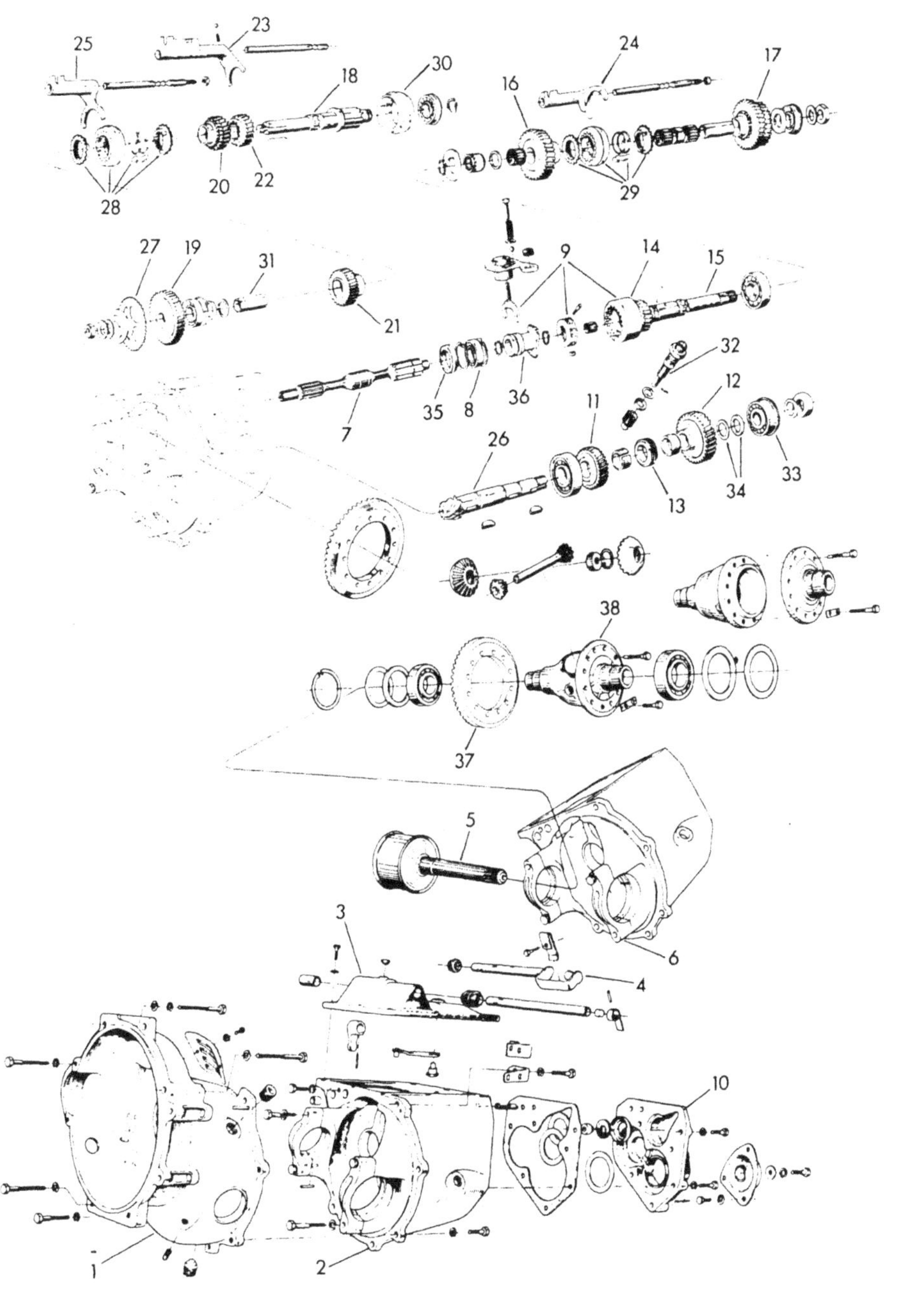


**Fig 6.1 Exploded view of transmission unit**

*1 Clutch bellhousing*
*2 Transmission casing*
*3 Top cover*
*4 Gearchange shaft*
*5 Inner driveshaft splined stub*
*6 Differential main bearing cap*
*7 Input shaft*
*8 Input shaft bearing*
*9 Freewheel assembly*
*10 End-cover*
*11 4th gear on pinion shaft*
*12 3rd gear on pinion shaft*
*13 Speedometer drive gear on pinion shaft*
*14 Countershaft drive gearwheel*
*15 Primary shaft*
*16 4th gear on primary shaft*
*17 3rd gear on primary shaft*
*18 Countershaft*
*19 Countershaft driven gear (from primary shaft)*
*20 1st gear on countershaft*
*21 2nd gear on countershaft*
*22 Reverse gear*
*23 Reverse gear selector fork*
*24 3rd/4th selector fork*
*25 1st/2nd selector fork*
*26 Pinion shaft*
*27 Friction brake on countershaft*
*28 1st/2nd synchronizer*
*29 3rd/4th synchronizer*
*30 Countershaft bearing seat*
*31 Countershaft bearing spacer*
*32 Speedometer driven gear*
*33 Pinion rear bearing*
*34 Pinion rear bearing spacer and shim*
*35 Input shaft oil seal*
*36 Freewheel locking device*
*37 Crownwheel*
*38 Differential carrier*

## 2 Transmission unit - removal and installation

1 The transmission is removed as a combined unit with the engine. Removal and installation is fully described in Chapter 1 as is also the separation of the engine from the transmission unit (Section 7).

## 3 Transmission - removal of clutch bellhousing, selector forks and shafts, differential, pinion rear bearing and countershaft

1 With the transmission unit removed, drain the oil and clean the exterior with paraffin or a grease solvent such as 'Gunk'.
2 Having disconnected the inner universal joints at the time of removing the engine/transmission, the inner driveshaft stubs will be projecting from each side of the differential housing. These driveshaft stubs are splined and retained in position by a spring ring engaging in a groove in the splined section of the stub and to remove them from the differential they must be tapped outwards from behind their joints flanges.
3 Unscrew and remove the bolts which secure the clutch bell-housing to the tranmission casing and then withdraw the bell-housing, complete with release fork and bearing and the splined input shaft. The input shaft will have to be turned slightly during this operation to ensure that it clears the differential assembly. (photo).
4 Remove the top cover and gearchange shaft from transmission casing. (photo)
5 Unscrew and remove the bolts from the two differential main bearing caps and lift out the differential assembly. Carefully retain the spacers and shims from each side for refitting (provided no new components are installed) (photo).
6 Partially extract the hub from the (now exposed) freewheel sleeve and then locate a heavy rubber band round the projecting rollers to retain them. Withdraw the hub in an anticlockwise direction and extract the centre needle roller bearing assembly. Unscrew and remove the speedometer drivegear. (Fig. 6.3) (photos).
7 Unbolt the end cover and drift it from the casing complete with the two centre shafts (1st/2nd and 3rd/4th). Support the forks as the cover and shafts are withdrawn and retain any shims. Extract the detent balls and springs. An alternative method of removing the selector shafts is to slacken the locknuts and unscrew the shafts from the end-cover. (Figs. 6.4/6.5) (photo).
8 If the pinion shaft rear bearing only is to be renewed, now is the time to do it. Engage two gears (reverse and third).
9 Flatten the tab washer and unscrew the nut at the rear end of the pinion shaft. **This nut is left-hand threaded.** Using a two legged puller located behind the bearing outer track snap ring, draw the bearing off the threaded end of the pinion shaft.
10 As from transmission "F 39522", the pinion shaft rear bearing has a split inner track which is removable in two sections (photo).
11 Drive the reverse selector shaft forwards using a brass drift, retaining the detent ball and spring from the selector fork, also the plug from the end of the shaft. All three gear selector forks may now be withdrawn from the transmission casing (photos).
12 Engage reverse and third gear again simultaneously so that the nut on the front end of the countershaft can be unscrewed, also the nut on the end of the primary shaft. As from transmission number "108911" an oil catcher is fitted to improve the lubrication of the countershaft bearings and this must be removed before the nut is unscrewed.
13 Move the 1st/2nd synchronizer sleeve to the neutral position and then position a semi-circular distance piece between the rear face of the 1st speed gear and the rear inside wall of the transmission casing. Using a suitable support frame and a length of studding, press the countershaft out of the rear of the casing. This will release the countershaft gear. Remove the spacer and Woodruff key.
14 If required, remove the circlip, draw off the bearing and its seat and withdraw the reverse gear.
15 The front bearing which supports the countershaft can be removed or refitted without first withdrawing the primary shaft (see next Section), although it will be easier if the primary shaft is first removed.

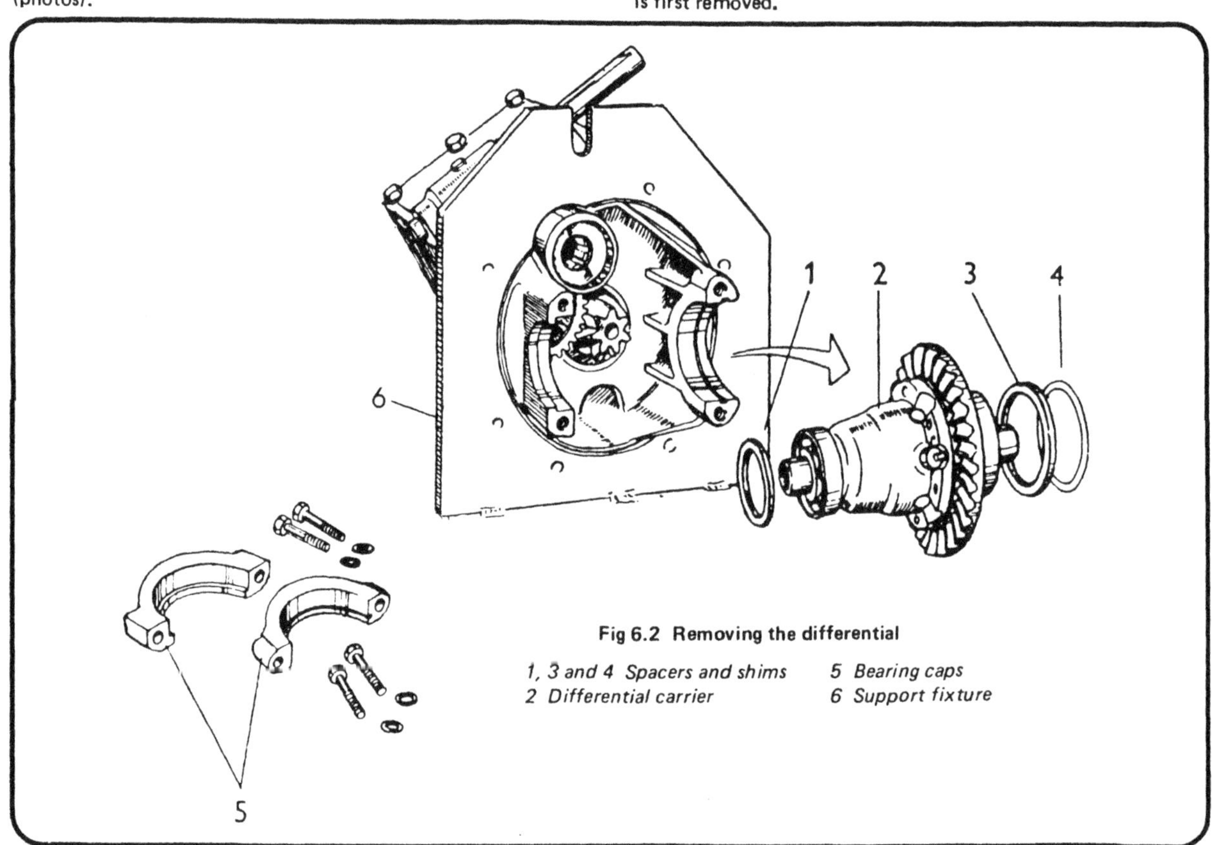


**Fig 6.2 Removing the differential**

*1, 3 and 4 Spacers and shims* *2 Differential carrier* *5 Bearing caps* *6 Support fixture*

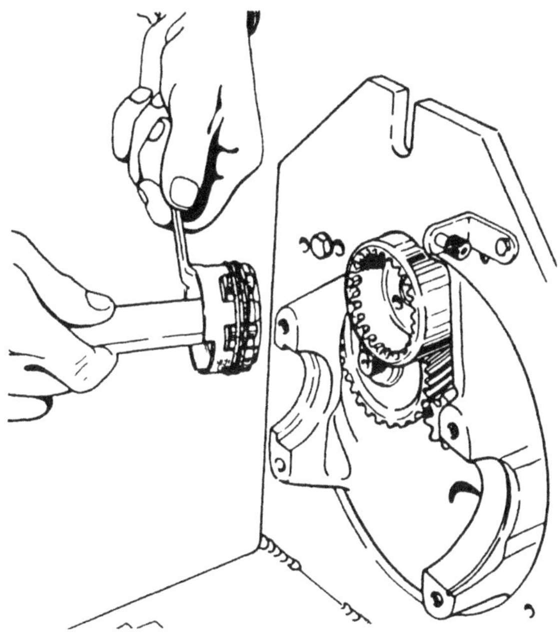

Fig 6.3 Removing the freewheel hub

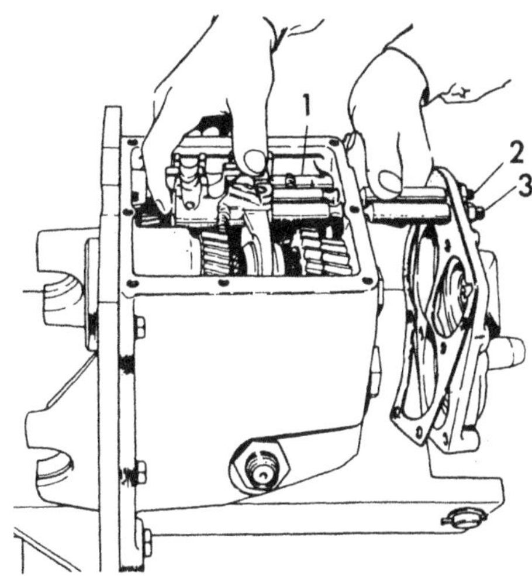


Fig 6.5 Withdrawing the end-cover with selector shafts attached

*1 Reverse* *2 1st/2nd* *3 3rd/4th*

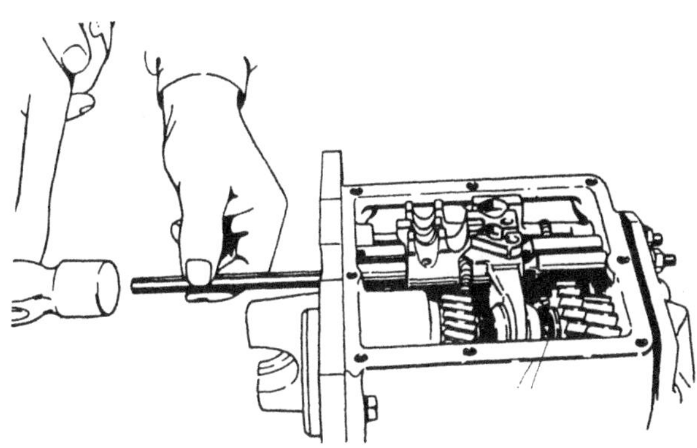

Fig 6.4 Using a rod to drive out a selector shaft and to loosen the end cover

Fig 6.6 Preparing to drive out the countershaft

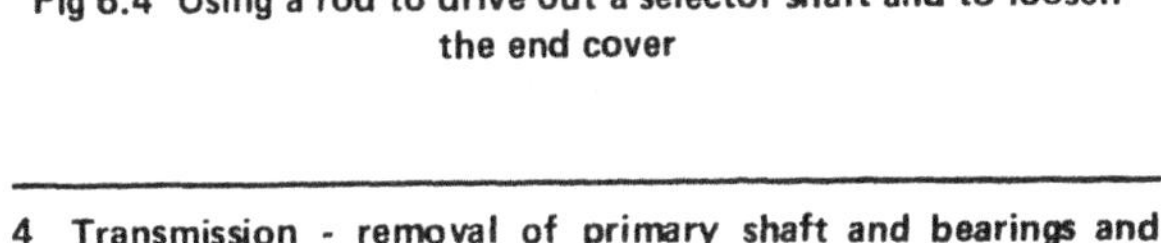

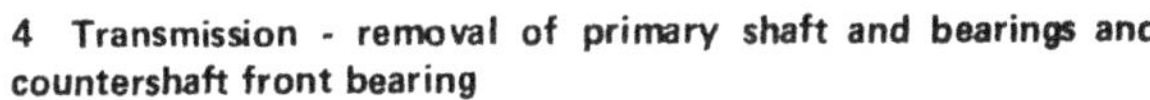

### 4 Transmission - removal of primary shaft and bearings and countershaft front bearing

1 Flatten the tab washer and unscrew the nut from the end of the primary shaft.

2 Press the primary shaft out towards the front of the transmission casing. This can be done by making up a suitable frame and using studding or a long bolt as a pressure tool or alternatively carefully driving it out with a soft faced mallet (photo).

3 With the primary shaft removed complete with gears and synchronizer unit, the countershaft front bearing can be removed by tapping it out towards the differential with a hide or plastic faced mallet.

4 Drive out the rear primary shaft bearing using a piece of tubing as a drift.

5 Remove the thrust washer and locking pin and the circlip from the primary shaft and extract the front bearing. If necessary, remove the oil catcher from the transmission casing (photo).

### 5 Transmission - removal and dismantling of pinion shaft and bearings

1 The pinion shaft rear bearing can be removed without disturbing the primary shaft or the countershaft as described in Section 3 (paragraph 8,9 and 10). Where the front bearing and shaft are to receive attention then proceed as follows.

2 Remove the speedometer drive gear and then unscrew the left-hand threaded nut from the end of the pinion shaft.

3 Pull off the rear bearing from the shaft using a suitable extractor. Retain the spacer and shims from inside the bearing. As from transmission no. "F 39522" a new type bearing is used having a split inner track. This type of bearing should be removed in two sections.

4 Press the pinion shaft out towards the differential, extracting third gear as it is withdrawn. The shaft may be driven out with a soft faced mallet provided 3rd gear os supported. (Fig 6.7) (photo)

5 If the pinion shaft must be dismantled, first extract the roller retaining ring from the front bearing but do not dismantle the bearing. Simply press the shaft from the bearing inner track and

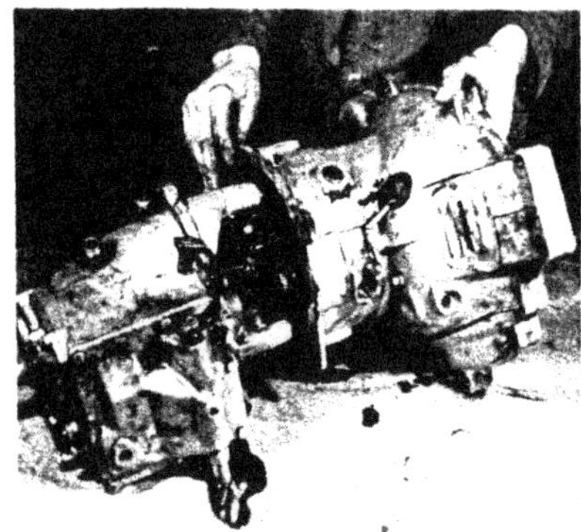
3.3 Withdrawing the clutch bellhousing from the transmission unit

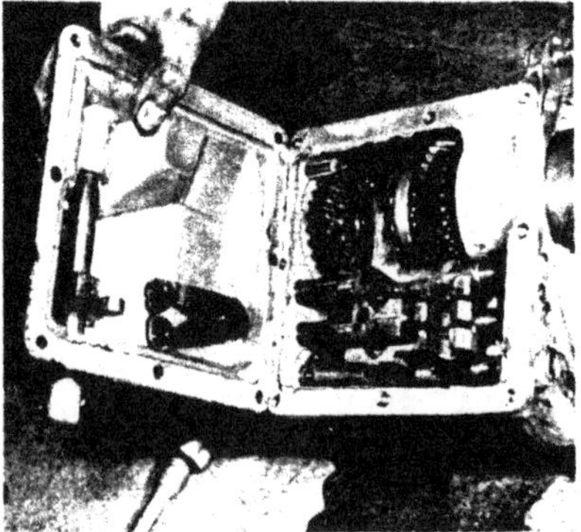
3.4 Removing the top cover

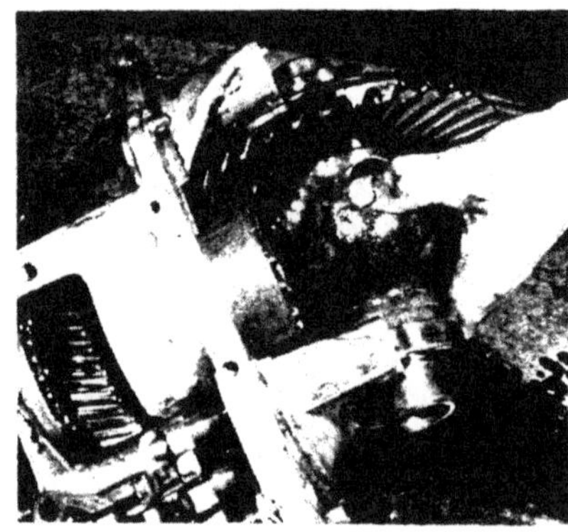
3.5 Lifting out the differential assembly

3.6A Extracting the freewheel hub

3.6B Retaining freewheel hub rollers with an elastic band

3.6C Extracting the freewheel needle roller bearing

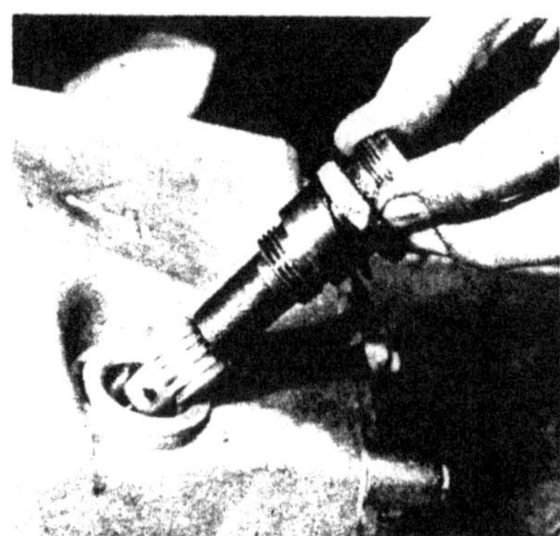
3.6D Removing the speedometer driven gear

3.7 Withdrawing a selector shaft

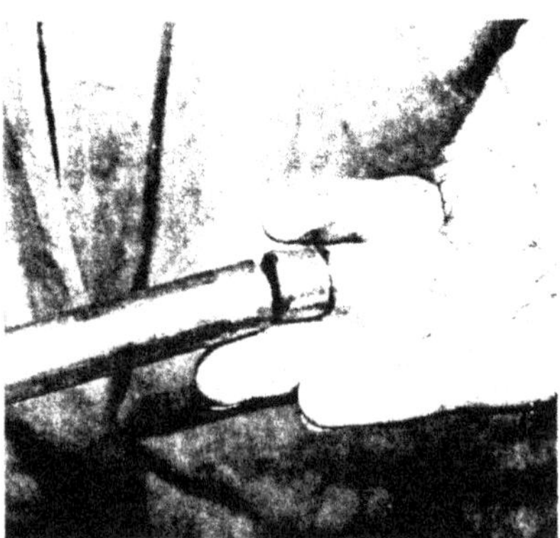
3.11A Reverse selector shaft and end-plug

3.11B Withdrawing the selector shafts

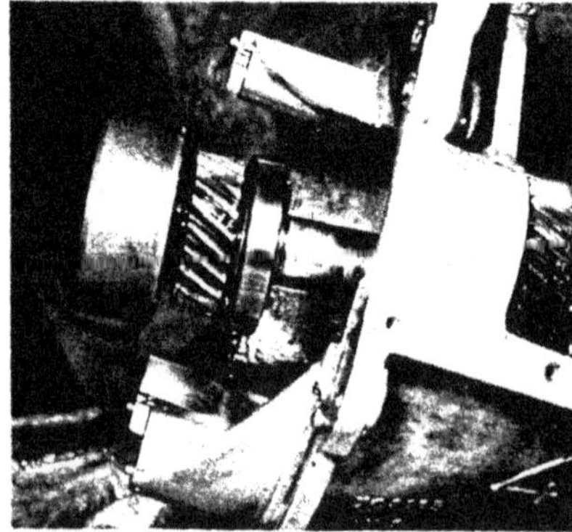
4.2 Removing the primary shaft

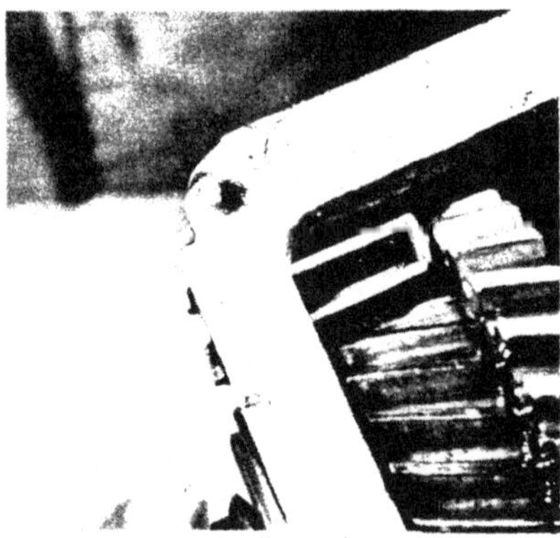
4.5 Primary shaft oil supply catcher

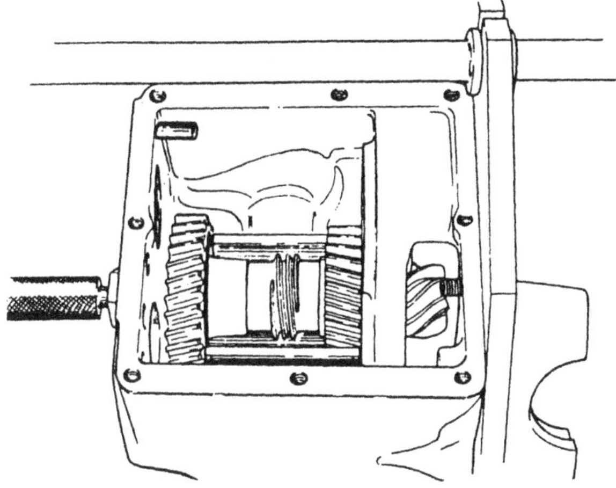

Fig 6.7 Pressing out the pinion shaft

5.4 Removing the pinion shaft with 3rd gear supported

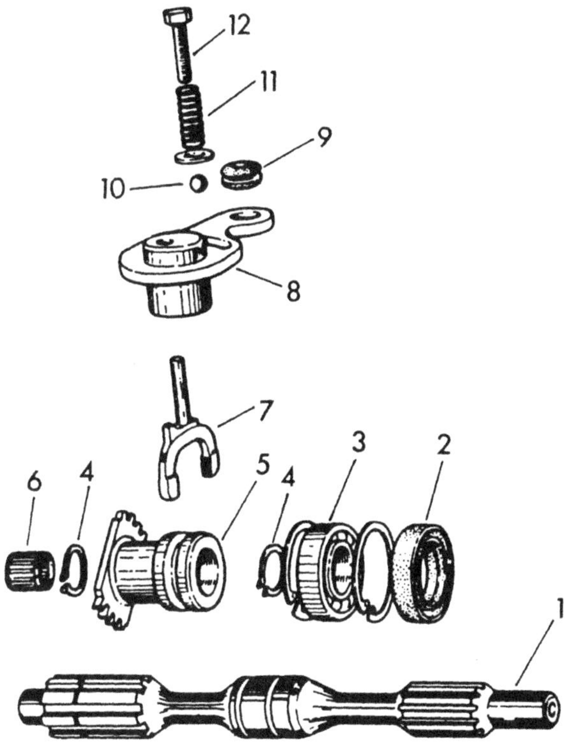


Fig 6.8 Clutch input shaft and freewheel components

| | |
|---|---|
| *1 Input shaft* | *7 Operating fork* |
| *2 Oil seal* | *8 Operating lever* |
| *3 Bearing* | *9 Grommet* |
| *4 Circlip* | *10 Ball* |
| *5 Locking sleeve* | *11 Spring* |
| *6 Needle roller bearing* | *12 Operating lever lock bolt* |

then refit the retaining ring.

## 6 Transmission assemblies and components - examination and renovation general

1 With the transmission unit now dismantled into major components, all parts should be washed in paraffin and examined for wear, distortion, chipping of teeth and scoring.

2 Drive out and discard all oil seals as a matter of course and purchase new ones.

3 Do not attempt to remove bearings and other components unless the necessary pullers and extractors are available. Similarly unless the necessary gauges and tools are available for reassembly and setting up, take the unit to your SAAB dealer.

## 7 Clutch input shaft, bearing and oil seal - servicing

1 The input shaft is supported by a bearing in the clutch bellhousing. Located against the front face of the bearing is an oil seal. Remove the clutch bellhousing.

2 Prise out the oil seal and then extract the bearing retaining circlip, the shaft front circlip and the freewheel device circlip located at the rear.

3 Pull the input shaft forward and catch the freewheel locking device and operating fork which will be released and then pull the bearing from the input shaft. (Fig 6.8)

4 Commence refitting by locating the bearing (numbers visible) in the bellhousing seat. (photo).

5 Insert the bearing retaining circlip. (photo)

6 Insert the input shaft through the bearing from the release fork side. (photo)

7 At the same time, hold the freewheel locking device and fork in position, also the shaft rear circlip, so that the input shaft may pass through them.(photo)

8 Fit the input shaft circlips at the front face of the bearing and at the rear (photo)

9 Fit the freewheel locking device travel limit circlip to the splined section of the input shaft at the rear end . (photo)

10 Slide a new oil seal carefully over the front of the input shaft and drive it into its recess with a tubular drift. Fill the space between the lips of the seal with grease. (Fig 6.9) (photo).

7.4 Input shaft bearing

7.5 Fitting the input shaft bearing circlip

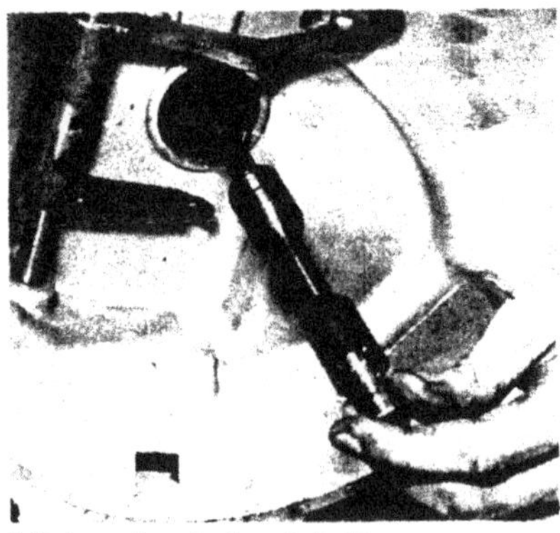
7.6 Inserting the input shaft

7.7 Holding the freewheel locking device and fork ready to receive the input shaft

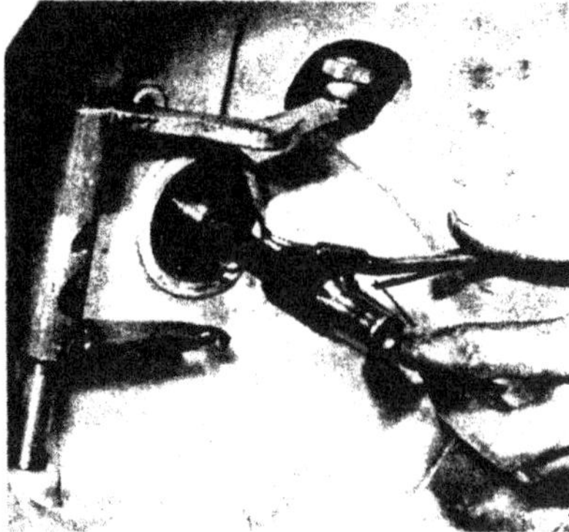
7.8 Fitting the input shaft front circlip

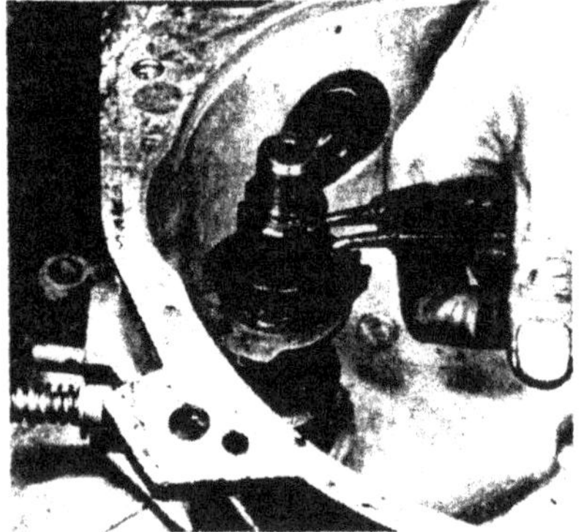
7.9 Fitting the freewheel locking device travel limit circlip

7.10 Fitting the input shaft oil seal

8.6 Using a small clamp to retain the freewheel hub rollers

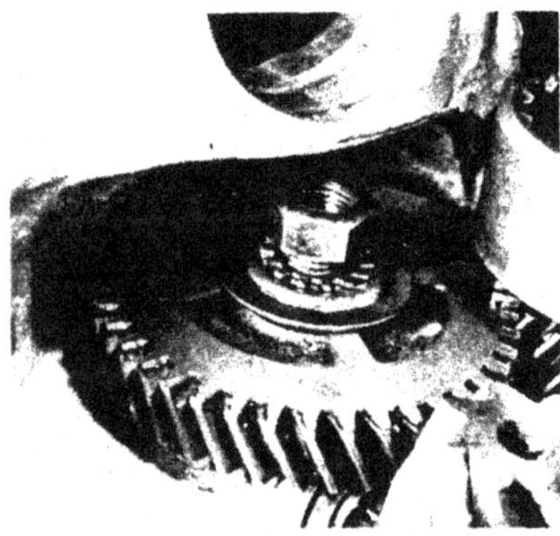
9.1A Countershaft friction brake with thrust and lockwashers and nut

9.1B Removing the friction brake

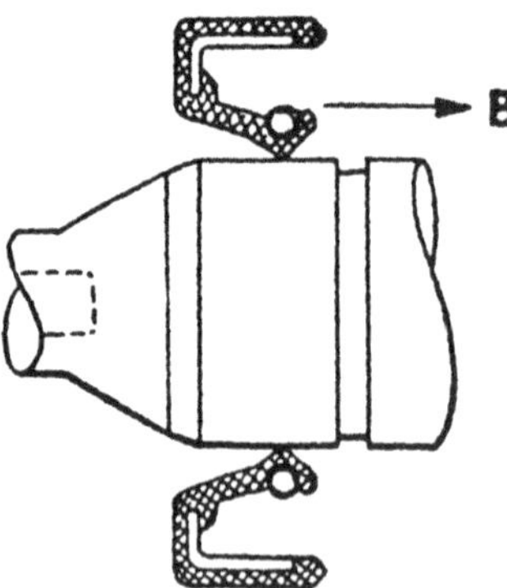


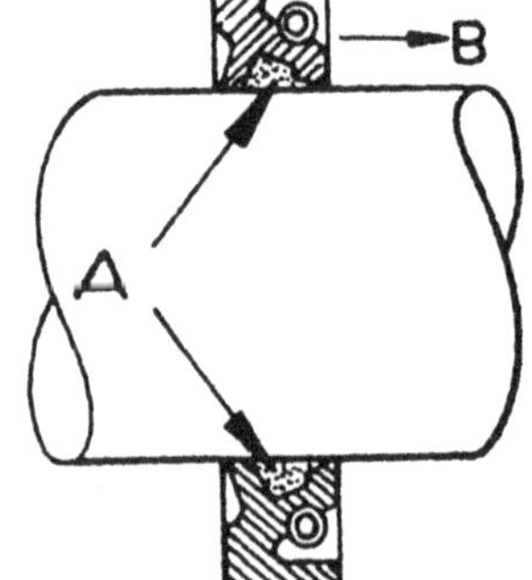


Fig 6.9 Sectional view of single and dual lipped type input shaft oil seals A grease packing B towards transmission casing

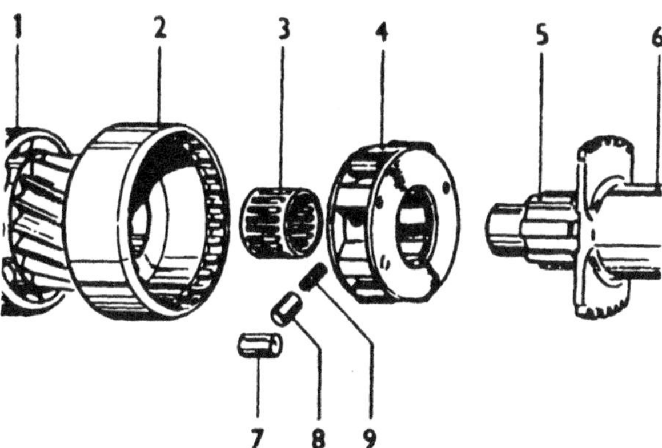


Fig 6.10 Exploded view of the freewheel

*1 Bearing*
*2 Freewheel sleeve (attached to primary shaft)*
*3 Needle roller bearing*
*4 Freewheel hub*
*5 Input shaft*
*6 Locking sleeve*
*7 Roller*
*8 Plunger*
*9 Spring*

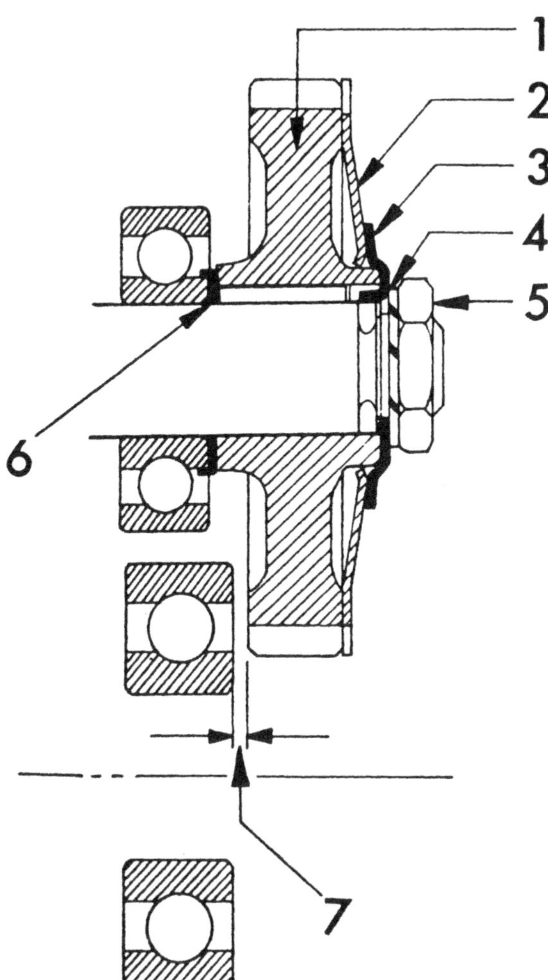


Fig 6.11 Sectional view of the countershaft friction brake

*1 Countershaft driven gear*
*2 Friction wheel*
*3 Friction washer*
*4 Lockwasher*
*5 Nut*
*6 Shim*
*7 Clearance (countershaft gear to primary shaft bearing), minimum 0.02 in (0.5 mm)*

## 8 Freewheel - servicing

1 Remove the clutch input shaft as described in the preceding Section.

2 Unscrew the operating lever lock-bolt and extract the ball and spring.

3 Extract the freewheel hub from its sleeve as described in Section 3.

4 A spring loaded plunger is located under each roller and these should be checked for wear and spring tension. (Fig 6.10)

5 In cases where the hub is worn, fit a new hub assembly complete with rollers; never use the old rollers. If the sleeve is also worn then the complete primary shaft/sleeve assembly will be required as a unit.

6 If the hub, rollers and plungers are sticking, then they should be dismantled and washed in paraffin. Note that on reassembly, the hub should be inserted into the sleeve turning it in an anti-clockwise direction and ensuring that the figures stamped on the rim of the hub are facing outwards, and are visible. A small piston ring clamp is useful to compress the rollers and springs prior to insertion. (photo)

7 Reassembly and refitting are reversals of removal and dismantling but check that the freewheel engages positively when the hub is turned clockwise.

## 9 Countershaft friction brake - renewal

1 The countershaft driven gear is fitted with a friction brake device to eliminate backlash between the countershaft driven gear and the primary shaft drive gear. It is essentially a spring loaded sprocket having one less tooth than the countershaft driven gear. If may be removed after unscrewing the countershaft nut, having one larger cut-out for this purpose (photos).

2 When fitting a new friction brake, check that the spring tongues lie within the specified distance from the contact surface.

3 Ensure that the countershaft gear has its machined surface towards the friction brake.

4 Using feeler gauges, check that there is a clearance between the rear of the countershaft gear and the front face of the primary shaft bearing of at least 0.02 in (0.5 mm) otherwise a shim will have to be fitted to increase the gap.

5 In order not to flatten or distort the spring tongues of the friction brake, tighten the nut on the end of the countershaft to a torque of 60 lb/ft (8.3 kg/m) only.

## 10 Synchronizer units - servicing

1 Wear in the synchronizer assemblies can normally be ascertained during normal driving when the gear change is noisy or can easily be 'beaten'.

2 Having removed the unit from its shaft, check that the synchronizer rings fit squarely on the cones. If they rock about, try lapping the components by applying fine valve grinding paste and rotating the ring about the cone in both directions.

3 When lapping is completed, the clearances between the synchronizer ring and the dog ring must be at least 0.04 in (1.0 mm) ro allow for subsequent wear.

4 If new synchronizer units are to be installed always fit them as matched assemblies (as supplied).

5 In order to provide easier selection of 1st gear when the engine is idling, gearboxes from number "139984" are fitted with a modified synchronizer unit having three fewer teeth than previous units. Springs of higher rating are also included in later 1st/2nd speed units and it is recommended that these are fitted when older type gearboxes are being overhauled.

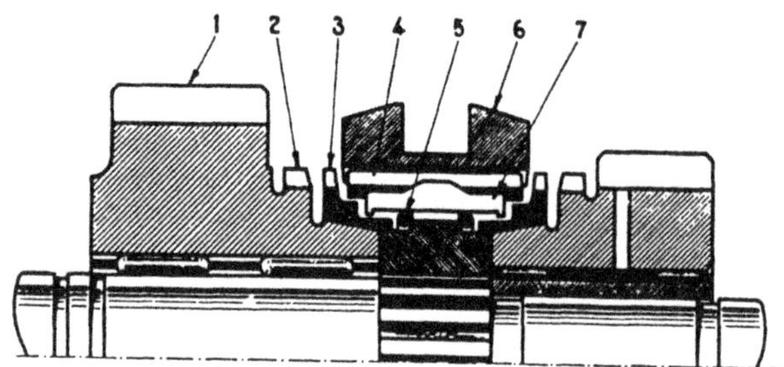


Fig 6.12 Part section view of synchronizer unit

*1 Gearwheel*
*2 Dog teeth*
*3 Synchronizer ring*
*4 Synchronizer hub*
*5 Spring*
*6 Synchronizer sleeve*
*7 Blocker bar*

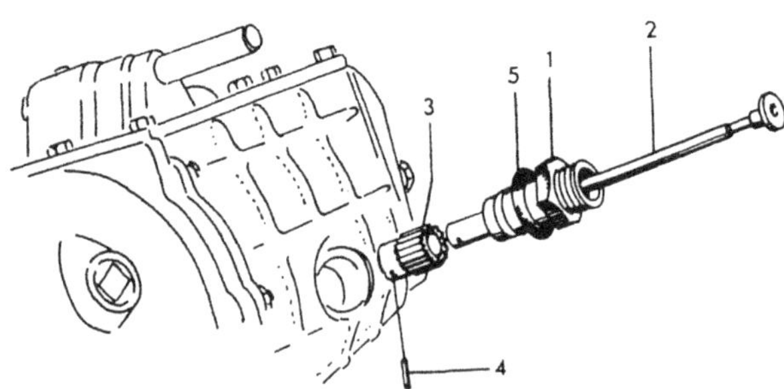


Fig 6.13 Speedometer driven gear components

*1 Bearing sleeve*
*2 Spindle*
*3 Gear*
*4 Tension pin*
*5 Gasket*

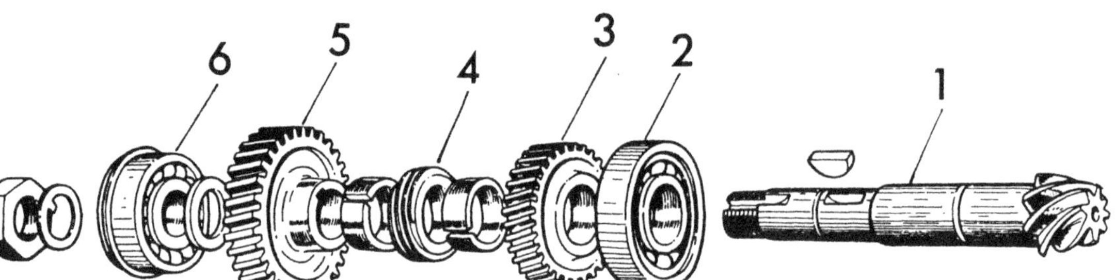


Fig 6.14 Pinion shaft and gear train up to chassis numbers "470,000" and "52,000"

*1 Pinion shaft*
*2 Front bearing*
*3 4th gear*
*4 Speedometer drive gear*
*5 3rd gear*
*6 Rear bearing*

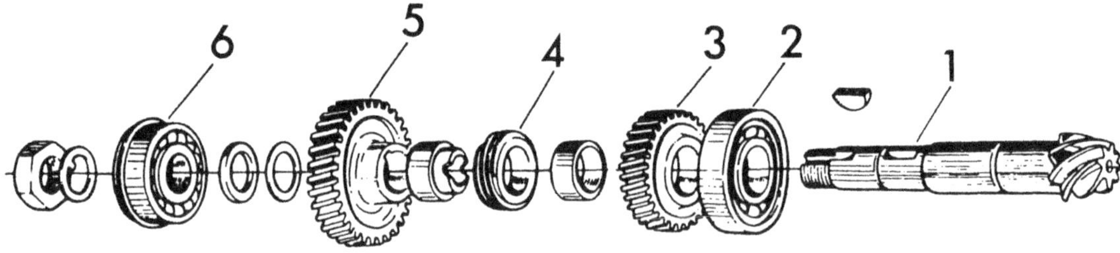


Fig 6.15 Pinion shaft and gear train from chassis numbers "470,000" and "52,001"

*1 Pinion shaft*
*2 Front bearing*
*3 4th gear*
*4 Speedometer drive gear*
*5 3rd gear*
*6 Rear bearing*

**11 Speedometer driven gear - adjustment**

1 The speedometer driven gear may be dismantled and worn components renewed in the following manner.

2 Unscrew the knurled ring and disconnect the speedometer cable (transmission still in vehicle).

3 Unscrew and remove the bearing sleeve, spindle and gear. Detach the gasket.

4 Drive out the tension pin which secures the gear to the spindle.

5 Renew worn components and reassemble.

6 In order to prevent oil leakage, shims are available in thicknesses of 0.008 and 0.02 in (0.2 and 0.5 mm) for insertion between the gear and bearing sleeve to provide a spindle endfloat of between 0.002 and 0.008 in (0.05 and 0.2 mm). Always use a new gasket.

**12 Transmission - reassembly of pinion and primary shaft and countershaft**

1 Check that all small components have been removed from the transmission interior and that the transmission casing is thoroughly clean both inside and out.

2 Check that new components and gaskets are to hand. Should the 3rd or 4th gears have to be renewed then they must be renewed as matching pairs.

3 If the pinion shaft has been dismantled, press on the roller bearing until its inner track is in contact with the pinion gear shoulder. (Figs 6.14/6.15)

4 Press on the 4th gearwheel noting that on early assemblies the numbers engraved on the gearwheel must face the same way as those on the 4th speed gearwheel on the primary shaft. On later assemblies, there are no numbers but an "X" is marked on

the gearwheel which must face towards the gear end of the pinion shaft.

5 Fit the first spacer, the speedometer drive gear and the second spacer to the pinion shaft. (photo)

6 Pass the pinion shaft into the transmission casing from the differential end and then fit the 3rd gearwheel to the shaft. The third gear must be positioned at the front end of the transmission casing during this operation to avoid the projecting speedometer drive gear boss. Locate the Woodruff key in the pinion shaft and then press the shaft fully home making sure that as the shaft passes through the third gear, the key and keyway are in alignment (photos).

7 If the pinion rear bearing centre track is of one piece type, fit a 0.14 in (3.6 mm) thick thrust washer and then press on the bearing to the shaft. if the pinion rear bearing centre track is of three piece construction, the spacer/shim pack must be fitted so that the spacer (1.4 in - 36.0 mm in diameter) is located next to the bearing.

8 Press the front ballrace complete with outer circlip onto the pinion shaft. With bearings having three section construction, fit the inner track first followed by the remainder of the assembly (photos)

9 Fit a new tab washer and screw on the left-hand threaded nut only finger tight at this stage (photo).

10 On transmission units up to number "276503" fit the front bearing, the circlip and the thrust washer and 4th speed needle roller bearing to the primary shaft. Ensure that the circlip prevents the thrust washer from rotating. On later transmission units, an oil thrower is located in front of the bearing and the circlip is no longer fitted. (Fig 6.16) (photo).

11 At this point, the countershaft front bearing must be pressed into position from the front of the transmission casing (photo).

12 Assemble the primary shaft gear train comprising 3rd and 4th speed gearwheel, synchronizer sleeve and rings. Lower the gear train into the transmission casing and locate them in position, with a dummy shaft or rod (photo).

12.5 Pinion shaft with bearing, 4th speed gear, two spacers and speedometer drive gear

12.6A Inserting pinion shaft into transmission casing

12.6B Location of 3rd speed gear to permit installation of pinion shaft

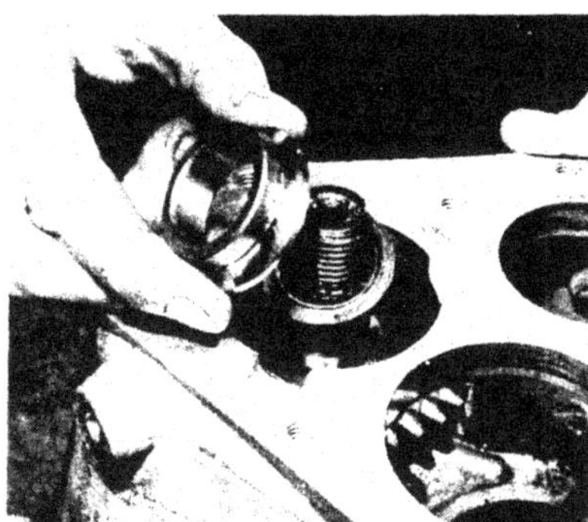
12.8A Fitting thrust washer and bearing inner track to pinion shaft

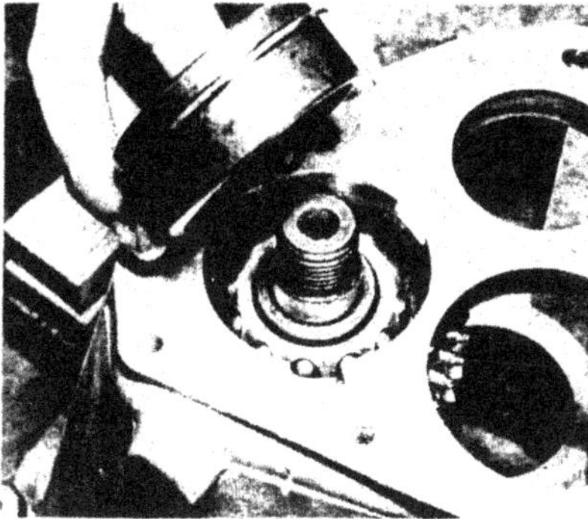
12.8B Fitting ball cage and bearing outer track to pinion shaft

12.9 Screwing on pinion shaft nut with lock plate located below it

12.10 Primary shaft thrust washer and circlip engaged in thrust washer cutout

12.11 Countershaft front bearing

12.12 Primary shaft gear train

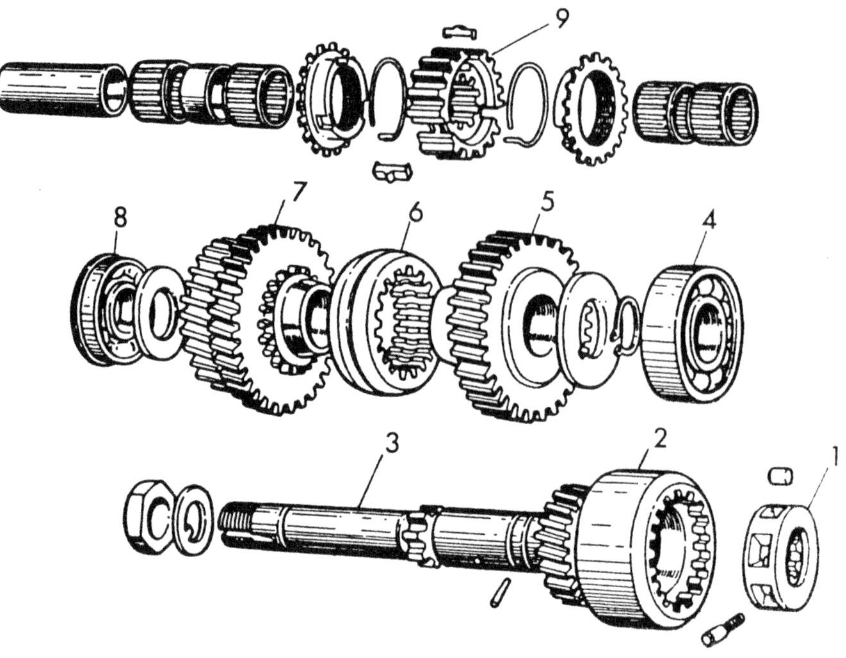


Fig 6.16 Primary shaft gear train

*1 Freewheel hub*
*2 Freewheel sleeve*
*3 Primary shaft*
*4 Front bearing*
*5 4th gear*
*6 3rd/4th synchronizer sleeve*
*7 3rd gear*
*8 Rear bearing*
*9 Synchronizer hub*

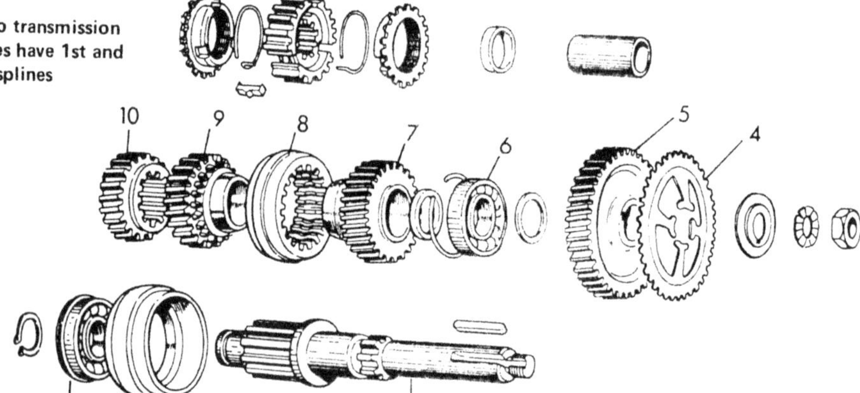


**Fig 6.17 Countershaft gear train up to transmission number "F 108910" – later assemblies have 1st and 2nd speed gears directly mounted on splines**

*1 Countershaft*
*2 Rear bearing seat*
*3 Rear bearing*
*4 Friction wheel*
*5 Driven gear*
*6 Front bearing*
*7 2nd gear*
*8 1st/2nd synchronizer sleeve*
*9 1st gear*
*10 Reverse gear*
*11 Synchronizer hub*

13 Pass the primary shaft into the transmission casing from the front end until its splines enter the synchronizer hub (photo).

14 Using the interior of the freewheel sleeve (needle bearings removed) as a pressure point, press the primary shaft fully home so that the 3rd speed gear is hard against the rear end of the transmission casing.

15 Fit the needle roller bearing, spacer and bush for the 3rd speed gear (inserted inside the gear hub) onto the primary shaft.

16 Fit the spacer washer (bevelled side towards threaded end of shaft) and the rear bearing and press the bearing onto the primary shaft. Fit a new tab washer and tighten the shaft nut (fingers only) (photo).

17 If the countershaft rear bearing, seat and reverse gear have been removed, refit them to the larger diameter splined end of the countershaft.

18 Hold the driven gear of the countershaft so that the machined face of this gearwheel will be towards the clutch bell-housing end of the transmission and then position the second gear wheel (complete with needle roller bearing, spacer and bush) the first gearwheel and the synchronizer unit. (Fig 6.17)

19 Lower the countershaft gear train into the transmission casing and pass the countershaft (complete with first speed needle bearing) through the geartrain from the rear end of the transmission casing noting that a spacer must be fitted between the front bearing and second gear (photos).

20 Just as the end of the countershaft becomes visible through the bearing aperture at the differential end of the transmission casing, the countershaft driven gear must be offered up to the countershaft. If the countershaft is driven further towards the differential than this then the countershaft driven gear cannot be fitted to the shaft as it will impinge on the freewheel hub and the pinion teeth.

21 Press the countershaft fully home, ensuring that the shaft splines engage with the synchronizer unit. On later transmission units (from number "108911") first and second gearwheels are spline mounted.

22 Check that the rear bearing outer circlip is in position.

23 Engage two gears simultaneously (second and fourth) and rotate third gear so that the countershaft driven gearwheel keyway aligns with the keyway in the countershaft and drive home the key (photo).

24 Fit the friction wheel using a new friction washer and lockwasher.
25 Tighten the countershaft end-nut to a torque of 60 lb/ft (8.3 kg/m).
26 Now tighten the pinion shaft nut (left-hand thread) to 90 lb/ft (12.5 kg/m) unscrew it and finally tighten to 45 lb/ft (6.2 kg/m).
27 Tighten the primary shaft to a torque of 36 lb/ft (5.0 kg/m).
28 Check the clearance between the friction wheel and the primary shaft bearing face (as described in Section 8).
29 Bend up the lockwasher tab to secure the shaft nut on the primary shaft but leave the one on the pinion shaft until adjustment has been carried out (see Section 13).

## 13 Gear selector shafts, forks, clutch housing, input and output shafts - reassembly

1 Set the first/second synchronizer unit and reverse gear in the neutral position.
2 Locate the detent balls and their springs in the reverse selector fork. To do this and retain the balls in position pending insertion of the selector shafts, make up a metal or wooden rod to act as a dummy shaft. Insert the spring and ball in the hole in the fork, press them down with a thin bar and then slide the dummy rod over them to retain them in the depressed position (photo).

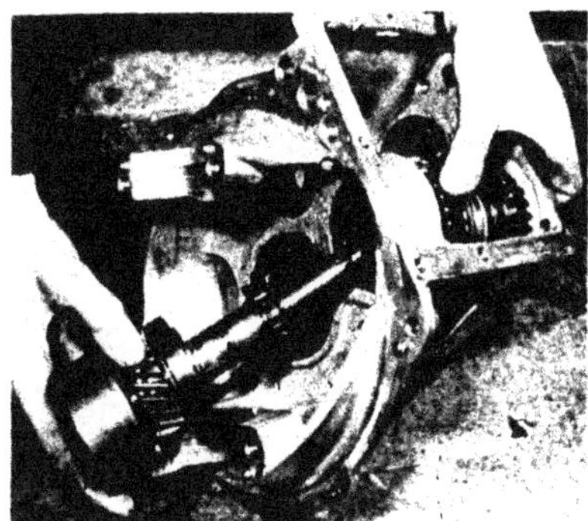
12.13 Inserting the primary shaft into the gear train

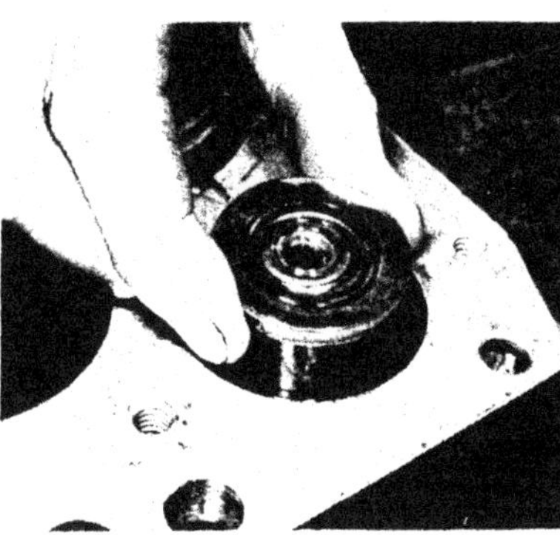
12.16A Fitting primary shaft rear bearing spacer

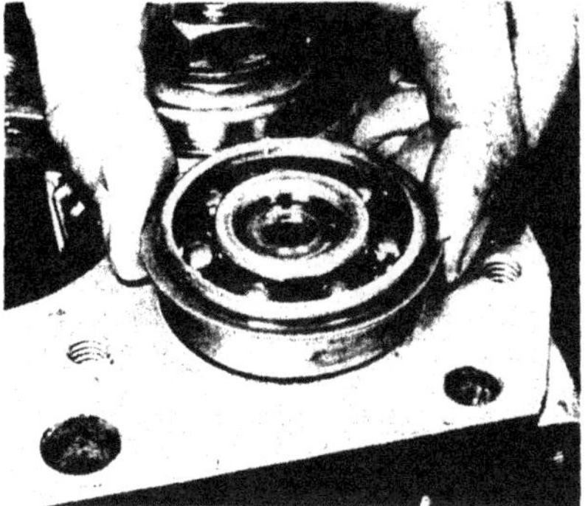
12.16B Fitting primary shaft rear bearing

12.16C Primary shaft nut and locking plate

12.19A Countershaft gear train

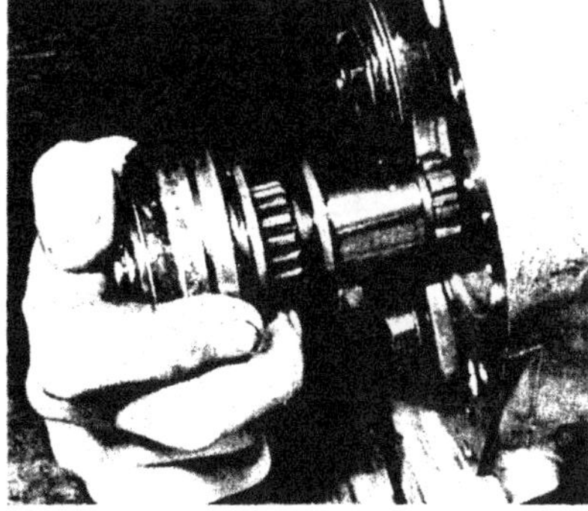
12.19B Inserting the countershaft into the gear train

12.23 Countershaft driven gear and key

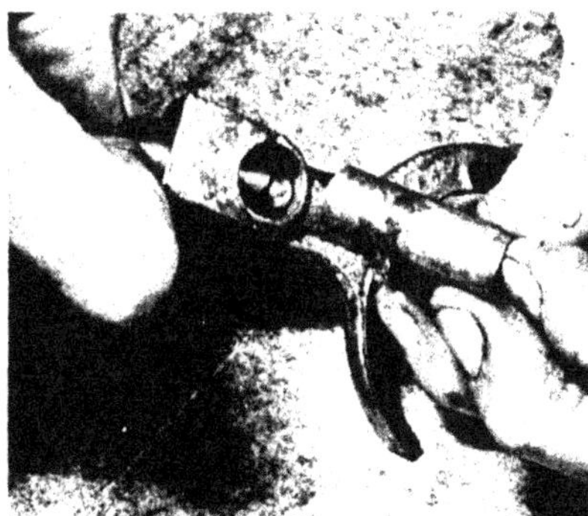
13.2 Method of fitting detent ball and spring to reverse selector fork

13.3A Inserting reverse selector shaft

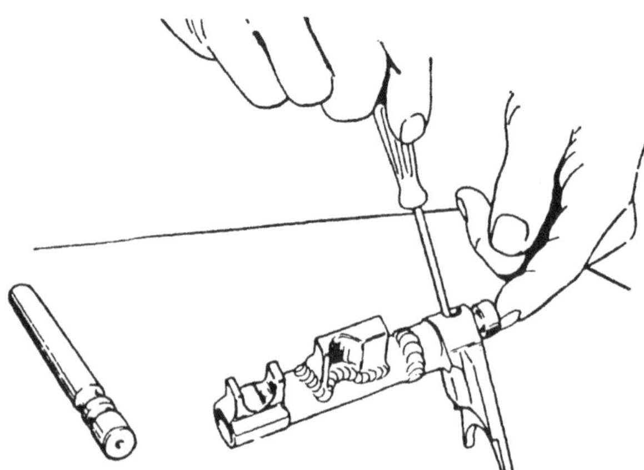
Fig 6.18 Locating detent ball in reverse selector fork

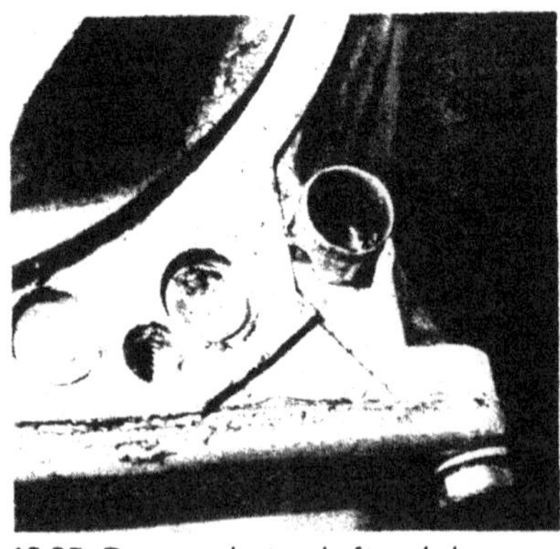
13.3B Reverse selector shaft end plug

13.4A Fitting 1st/2nd selector shaft

13.4B Fitting 3rd/4th selector fork

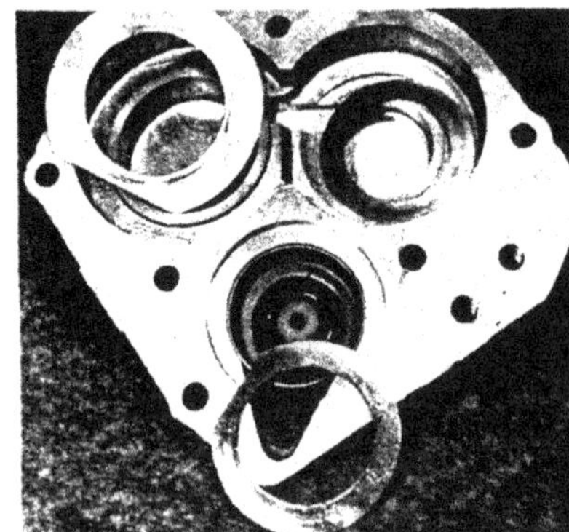
13.5A End-cover shims

13.5B Fitting the end-cover

13.11 Preparing to fit the transmission top-cover

13.15 Installing the differential

13.16 Fitting the differential bearing caps

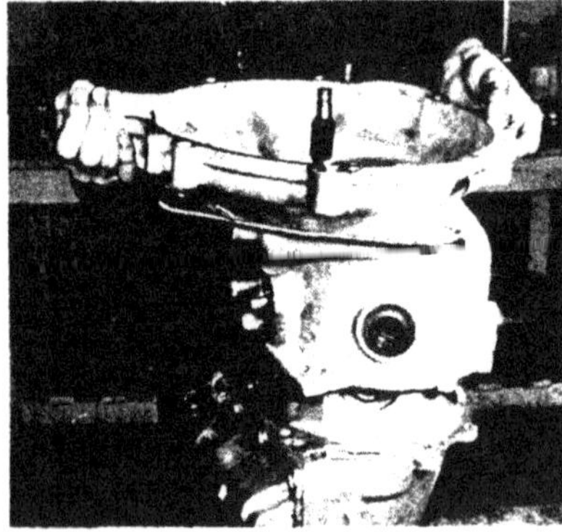
13.18 Fitting the bellhousing to the transmission unit

13.19 Fitting the inner driveshafts

3 Engage the reverse fork with the reverse gearwheel and then insert the reverse selector shaft from the rear end of the transmission casing into the fork so that it pushes the dummy shaft out of its location end yet does not allow the detent balls and springs to be displaced. Drive in the blanking plug at the reverse selector shaft end recess (photos).

4 Repeat the fitting procedure for the first/second and third/fourth selector forks and shafts (photos).

5 Where none of the three rear bearings in the transmission casing have been renewed then the end-cover may now be refitted complete with the original end bearing outer track shims. Use a new cover gasket (dry without jointing compound) and tighten the securing bolts to a torque of 18 lb/ft (2.5 kg/m). When locating the cover, make sure that the rubber washer presses the plastic plug against the end of the primary shaft and that the oil passage in the components is not clogged. Also check that one of the longer bolts is not incorrectly located opposite the reverse gear selector fork which could cause it to jam (photo).

**If new shaft bearings have been installed, then the adjustments described in the following section must first be carried out before fitting the end-cover.**

6 Once the end-cover is fitted, adjust the gear selector shafts. To do this, move the selector forks, in turn, to each gear position and check that the fork is not under pressure to overide the correct detent position. There should also be a similar gap between the synchronizer sleeve and the adjacent gearwheel in all gear positions. Where these conditions are not satisfactory, screw the selector shafts in, or out, by means of the screwdriver slot in the end face of the shaft and finally tighten the locknuts.

7 Refit the speedometer driven gear.

8 Smear jointing compound on the top cover mating face of the transmission casing.

9 Set the gear selector forks in the neutral position.

10 Set the dogs and catch in the top cover also in the neutral position (Fig 6.20)

11 Locate the top cover on the transmission casing, ensuring that the dogs engage in the cut outs of the selector forks, not the detent spring holes (photo).

12 Tighten the top cover securing bolts evenly.

13 Check the operation of the gearchange rod on the transmission.

14 Check the operation of the freewheel hub which should engage firmly when rotated in a clockwise direction.

15 Provided no dismantling has been carried out to the differential unit, it can be refitted to its bearing seats with the shim and spacer packs located as originally installed on each side of the bearing. (photo).

16 Locate the bearing caps and tighten the securing bolts to 29 lb/ft (4.0 kg/m) torque. (photo)

17 If the differential has been dismantled or new bearings or components installed then the adjustments and setting procedure described in Section 15 must first be carried out.

18 Smear jointing compound onto the front face of the transmission casing and bolt on the clutch bellhousing. The clutch input shaft will have to be turned slightly during this operation so that it clears the differential. Smear the input shaft splines with graphite grease (photo)

19 Fit the inner driveshaft stubs, ensuring that the seals are renewed as described in Chapter 7 and that the shafts engage with their retaining springs (photo).

20 Refill the unit with the correct grade and quantity of oil.

## 14 Transmission - adjustments after overhaul

1 A special tool (784237) is available for establishing the end-cover bearing shim packs but if one cannot be borrowed then an alternative method can be used.

2 Using a smear of grease, locate a new gasket to the endface of the transmission casing.

3 Locate shims in the countershaft rear bearing recess of the end-cover so that when the end-cover is offered up to the transmission casing and reasonable hand pressure applied, a feeler

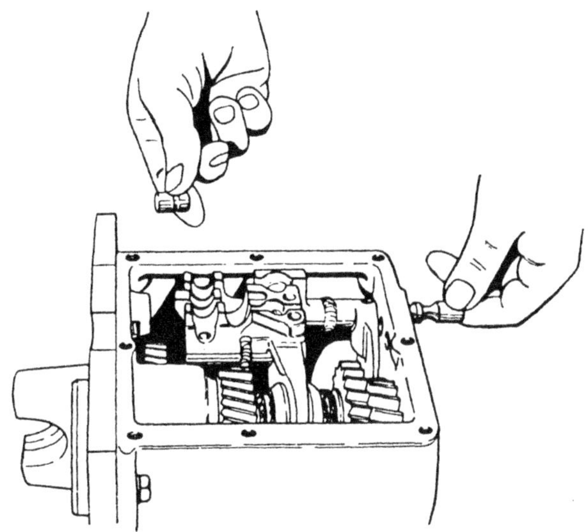

Fig 6.19 Removing detent ball locating tool as reverse selector shaft is inserted into fork

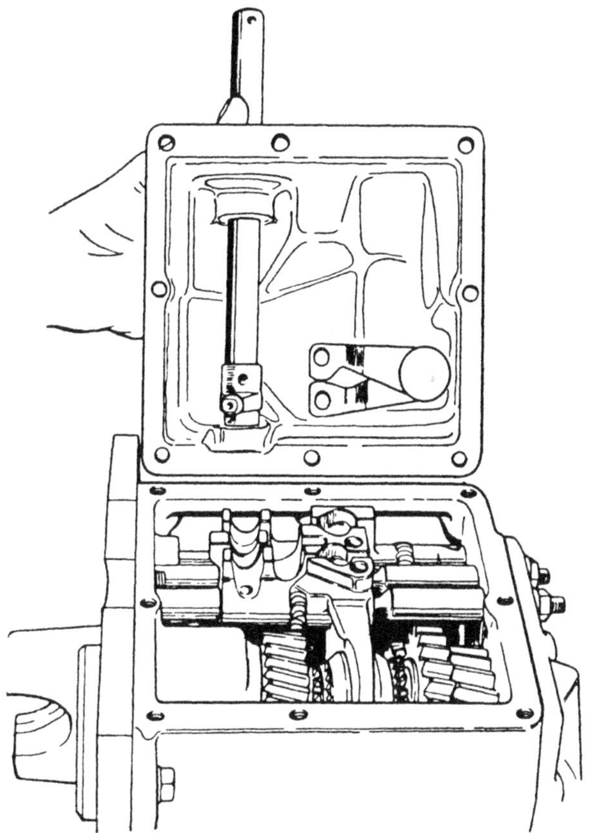

Fig 6.20 Fitting the transmission top cover

gauge (not exceeding 0.002 in 0.05 mm) will be a sliding fit between the end-cover and the gasket. Keep the end-cover square during the checking and insert the feeler gauge adjacent to the bearing recess.

4 Repeat the procedure for the pinion and primary shaft bearings. Keep the selected shim packs identified for final fitting to their respective recesses. Shims are available in thicknesses of 0.004 in (0.10 mm), 0.006 in (0.15 mm) and 0.012 in (0.30 mm).

5 With the end-cover bolts fitted and tightened to a torque of 18lb/ft (2.5 kg/m) the pinion adjustment should be checked. The pinion endface carries a crownwheel matching set number and the pinion adjustment tolerance. A special measuring tool (784146) must be used to check the pinion projection which should not deviate from the figure marked on it by more than ± 0.002 in (0.05 mm) otherwise the spacer/shim pack which is located between the pinion bearing and third gear will have to be altered. Spacers are available in thicknesses 0.112 in (3.1 mm) and 0.142 in (3.6 mm) and shims 0.004 in (0.1 mm), 0.006 in (0.15 mm) and 0.012 in (0.3 mm). Any combination must include not more than one spacer and three shims. On early type transmission units, the spacer fits next to the gear and the shims next to the bearing. On later type units with the rear bearing having a two piece centre track then the spacer should be fitted next to the bearing and the shims next to the gearwheel.

6 If adjustment is to be carried out then the end-cover must be unbolted and the pinion nut removed (left-hand thread). Provided the front of the pinion is secured, the rear bearing can then be withdrawn using a two legged puller and the spacer/shim pack adjusted as required.

7 When reassembling, again tighten the pinion shaft end nut in two stages: first, to 90 lb/ft (12.5 kg/m) ; then unscrew, and tighten again, to 45 lb/ft (6.2 kg/m). Re-check the pinion projection and then bend-up the tab of the lockwasher,.

## 15 Differential - dismantling, reassembly and adjustment

1 With the differential bearing caps removed (and the spacers retained) and the differential assembly removed from the transmission unit, the bearings should be drawn or drifted from their locations but only if they are to be renewed otherwise removal will destroy them.

2 Unscrew each of the crownwheel bolts and remove the crownwheel.

3 Drive out the differential pinion shaft and after removal of the circlips or retaining rings remove the pinions and gearwheels. The pinion shaft and internal components of the differential

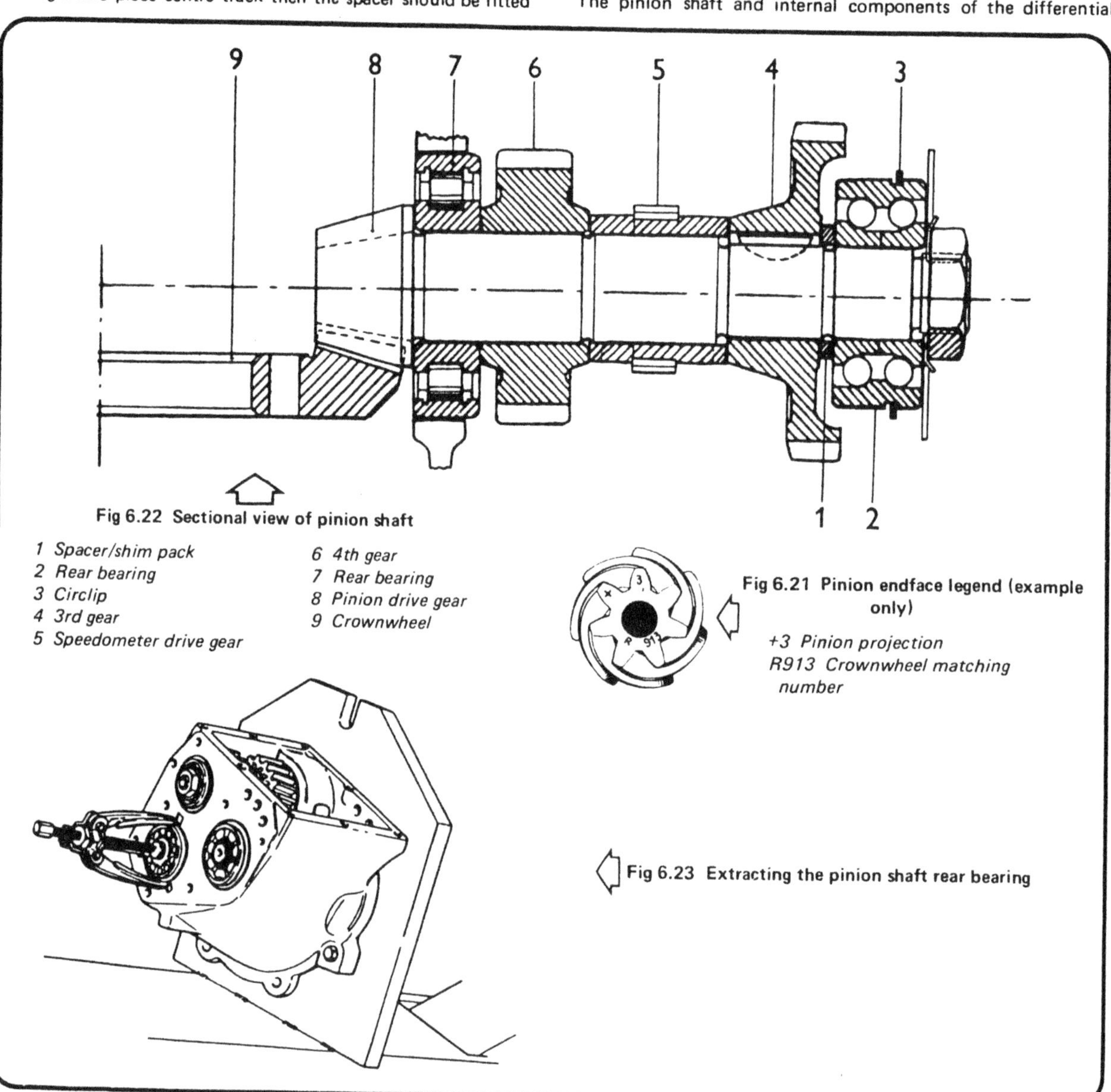


Fig 6.22 Sectional view of pinion shaft

1 Spacer/shim pack
2 Rear bearing
3 Circlip
4 3rd gear
5 Speedometer drive gear
6 4th gear
7 Rear bearing
8 Pinion drive gear
9 Crownwheel

Fig 6.21 Pinion endface legend (example only)

+3 Pinion projection
R913 Crownwheel matching number

Fig 6.23 Extracting the pinion shaft rear bearing

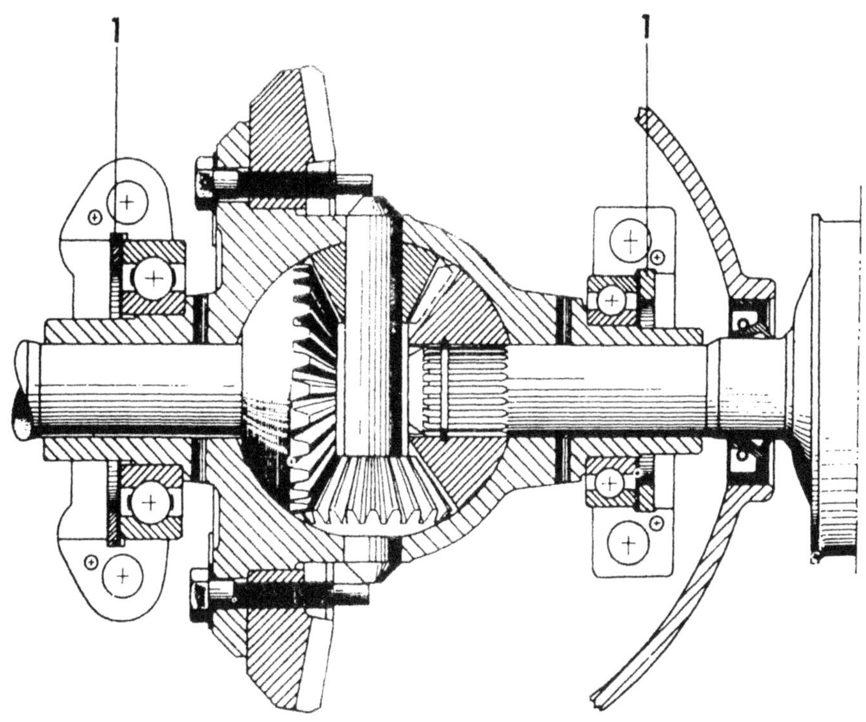


Fig 6.24 Location of differential spacers and shims

carrier can be removed without detaching the crownwheel by unscrewing and removing the two longer crownwheel securing bolts.

4 If the crownwheel is to be renewed then the pinion shaft must also be renewed, as they are supplied as a matching pair. From transmission number "F.68929" components differ from earlier units.

5 Reassembly is a reversal of dismantling: tighten the crownwheel bolts to a torque of 18 lb/ft (2.5 kg/m).

6 If any components, other than those contained within the differential carrier have been renewed, then the backlash must be checked and adjusted in the following manner.

7 Locate the differential assembly in its bearing seats with a spacer and shims at each side (shims nearer bearing) so that there is no movement of the differential between the bearings, neither are the bearings being forced outwards. When correctly estimated, the spacers should be able to be easily pushed into their recesses using thrust pressure.

8 Fit the bearing caps (not interchangeable) and tighten the securing nuts to a torque of 29 lb/ft (4.0 kg/m).

9 Lock the pinion shaft by inserting a screwdriver, or similar, into the speedometer drive gear aperture in the transmission casing and then checking the backlash of the crownwheel by turning it back-and-forth using hand pressure. With a dial-gauge mounted so that its point is at right-angles to the flank of the tooth at the periphery of the crownwheel, first zero the dial gauge when hand pressure is applied in a forward direction to the crownwheel and then with pressure applied in a rearward direction read off the backlash. The reading should agree with the figure engraved on the crownwheel (0.006 in - 0.15 mm). Check the backlash at four different points on the crownwheel and ensure that the four readings do not differ by more than ± 0.002 in (0.05 mm) otherwise both crownwheel and pinion must be renewed as a matched pair.

10 If the backlash does not conform with that specified, remove the bearing caps and adjust the thickness of the spacer/shim packs. Shims may be moved from one side to the other or new shims substituted, these are available in the following thicknesses: spacers 0.13 in (3.4 mm), 0.15 in (3.9 mm) and shims 0.004 in (0.1 mm) 0.006 in (0.15 mm) 0.012 in (0.3 mm).

11 Changing the position of a 0.004 in (0.1 mm) thick shim from one side to the other will result in a change of backlash of 0.002 in (0.05 mm).

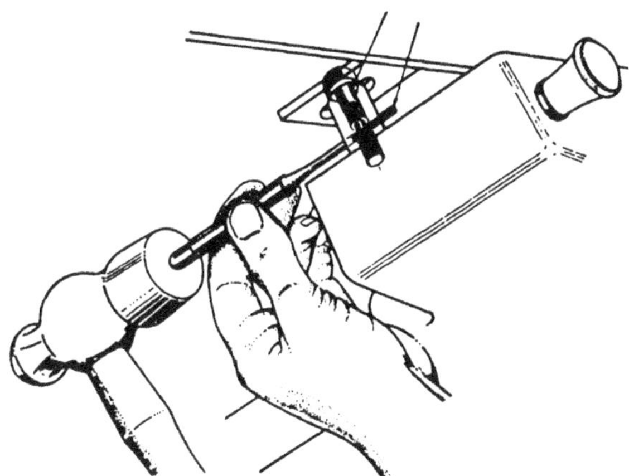

Fig 6.25 Removing locking pins from steering column support shroud screws

## 16 Steering column gearchange mechanism - adjustments

1 Whenever faulty operation of the gearchange linkage occurs or the combined steering column/gearchange lever lock functions incorrectly, the following adjustments should be carried out in the order described. The adjustments must also be carried out if the gearchange mechanism has been dismantled and reassembled.

### *(a) Steering column position adjustment*

2 As the gearchange lever and the steering column are both supported by the same bracket under the facia panel, the setting of the bracket screws is critical to the correct operation of the gearchange linkage.

3 Engage top gear and push the lever towards the facia panel and then pull it away. The total movement of the gearchange lever knob should be between 0.3 and 0.5 in (8.0 to 12.0 mm).

4 If the movement is incorrect, lossen the screws under the facia panel and adjust the position of the steering column

shroud. The tension pins need only be driven out if the screws are to be removed.

*(b) Twist stop adjustment*

5 Engage reverse gear and push the twist stop up the gearchange rod and at the same time turn the ignition key to "L" checking that the ignition lock plunger locates in the twist stop. (Fig. 6.26).

6 With the twist stop now hanging on the lockplunger, move the twist stop up the rod by a distance of approximately 0.08 in (2.0 mm) and then gently tighten the stop screw (Fig. 6.27).

7 Turn the ignition key to "G" and engage first gear. Gently tighten the two clamp screws on the twist stop.

8 Engage reverse gear and slacken the stop screw then re-engage first gear and fully tighten the clamp screws.

9 Finally engage reverse gear for the last time and tighten the stop screw just enough to stop it from working loose.

**17 Steering column gearchange mechanism (rhd) - dismantling and reassembly**

1 The gearchange mechanism can be removed separately or together with the steering column (see Chapter 8).

2 To remove the mechanism, leaving the steering column in position, disconnect the gearchange rod universal joint and carefully retain the return spring (see Section 19) (Fig. 6.28).

3 Remove the steering wheel (Chapter 8) and the direction indicator switch.

4 Unscrew and remove the gearshift lever pivot bolt and remove the lever.

5 Unscrew the three screws which secure the twist stop of the gearchange lever lock. The screws are accessible through the holes in the steering column support shroud (ignition key in "G" and first gear engaged).

6 Drive out the pin which secures the reverse catch carrier sleeve to the gearchange rod.

7 Use a piece of tubing about 10 in (254.0 mm) long which will slide up the reverse catch casing as the gearchange rod is withdrawn to prevent displacement of the spring.

8 Withdraw the gearchange rod from the steering column support shroud.

9 Unscrew the forked nut and remove the washer, spring and felt ring all of which are accessible within the shroud.

10 If required, the reverse catch casing can now be removed, the spring compressed and the temporary piece of tubing withdrawn downwards and the upper washer extracted sideways. Carefully release the tension of the spring and remove the plastic and metal washers which are located underneath it.

11 Renew all worn or damaged components including the felt ring which should be well greased.

12 Commence reassembly by locating the spring and washer on the forked nut. Screw in the nut until there is a clearance of 0.04 in (1.0 mm) between the flange of the nut and the edge of the support shroud.

13 Insert the gearchange rod into the support shroud and at the same time locate the twist stop for the gearchange lever lock so that its marking is towards the steering wheel. Turn the ignition key to "L" so that the lock plunger slides into the twist stop.

14 Refit the gearchange lever, checking to see that the three leaf springs are correctly located and that the pivot bolt is not overtightened to prevent free movement of the lever.

15 Refit the direction indicator switch.

16 Refit the steering wheel and reconnect the gearchange rod universal joint.

17 Carry out the adjustments described in Section 16.

**18 Steering column gearchange mechanism (lhd) - dismantling and reassembly**

1 To remove the gearchange mechanism leaving the steering column in position in the vehicle, disconnect the gearchange rod universal joint (see Section 19).

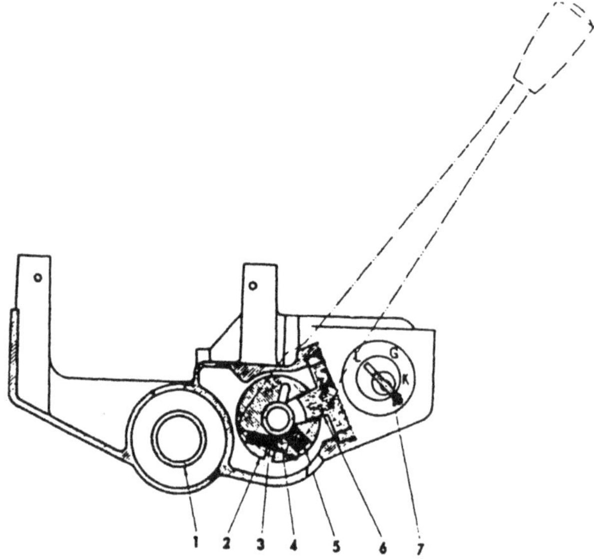


**Fig 6.26 Gear lever lock**

*1 Steering column*
*2 Twist stop*
*3 Clamp screw*
*4 Gearchange rod*
*5 Stop screw*
*6 Lock plunger*
*7 Lock cylinder and key*

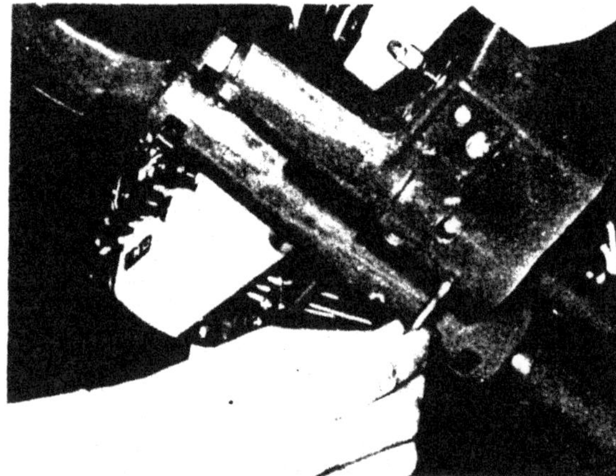

**Fig 6.27 Tightening a twist stop adjustment screw with an Allen key**

2 Pass a rod through the square aperture located on the rear of the gearchange lever housing and hold the turn stop from rotating.

3 Press in the gearchange lever and turn it through 90°.

4 Pull the gearchange rod downwards sufficiently far so that it can be withdrawn through the square aperture.

5 Unscrew the gearchange lever knob, remove the lever and collect the plastic ball, spring and turn stop. Retain the plastic bearing from the end of the lever.

6 Unscrew and remove the stop screw on the bottom of the steering column support shroud and then unscrew the chrome nut. The gearchange lever housing can now be withdrawn and the fibre washer and rubber grommet extracted.

7 If necessary, the chrome nut, fibre washer and shims can be completely removed after removal of the circlip.

8 Drive out the pin from the lower end of the gearchange rod and then withdraw the rod downwards so that the turn stop can be removed from the gearlever lock. Retain the return spring and its holder.

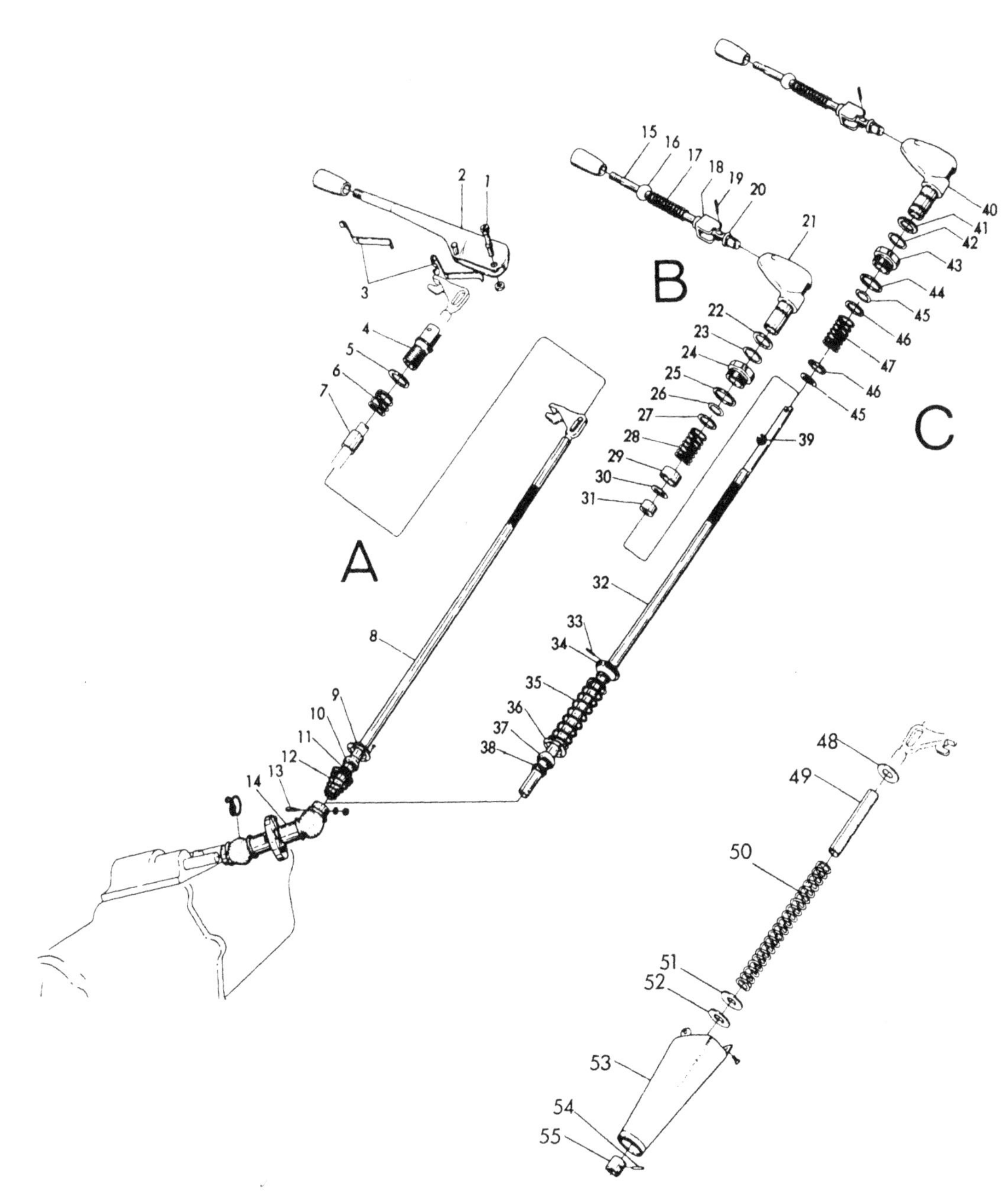


**Fig 6.28 Exploded view of gearchange mechanism**

*A Rhd vehicles*
*B Lhd vehicles (early)*
*C Lhd vehicles (later)*
*D Reverse catch assembly (rhd vehicles)*
*1 Pivot bolt*
*2 Gearchange lever*
*3 Springs*
*4 Forked nut*
*5 Washer*
*6 Spring*
*7 Felt ring*
*8 Gearchange rod*
*9 Retainer*
*10 Bush*
*11 Bush*
*12 Return spring*
*13 Tapered pin*
*14 Universal joint*
*15 Gearchange lever*
*16 Ball*
*17 Spring*
*18 Turn stop*
*19 Pin*
*20 Plastic bearing*
*21 Gearchange lever housing*
*22 and 23 Washers*
*24 Chrome nut*
*25 Fibre washer*
*26 Circlip*
*27 Washer*
*28 Spring*
*29 Bush*
*30 Washer*
*31 Felt ring*
*32 Gearchange rod*
*33 Pin*
*34 Spring retainer*
*35 Spring*
*36 Retainer*
*37 Rubber bush*
*38 Bush*
*39 Rubber ball*
*40 Gearchange lever housing*
*41 and 42 Washers*
*43 Chrome nut*
*44 Fibre washer*
*45 Circlip*
*46 Washer*
*47 Spring*
*48 Washer*
*49 Plastic sleeve*
*50 Spring*
*51 Plastic washer*
*52 Washer*
*53 Casing*
*54 Pin*
*55 Carrier sleeve*

9 Remove the washers, bush and felt ring from the steering column shroud.
10 Renew all worn or damaged components and renew the felt ring which should be well greased.
11 Commence reassembly by fitting the felt ring, washers, bush and spring to the steering column shroud.
12 Locate the return spring and its holder onto the gearchange rod, also the twist stop with its marking towards the steering wheel and then slide the rod into the support shroud from below.
13 Drive in the pin above the spring holder.
14 Fit the fibre washer and nut to the gearchange lever housing and locate the retaining ring in its groove. The number of shims fitted should provide no clearance at the nut but in fact make it slightly stiff to turn. Apply a little grease to the fibre washer and bearing surfaces of the nut.
15 Refit the gearchange lever housing into the support shroud turning the gearchange rod so that its angled hole is correctly orientated. (Fig. 6.29).
16 Lower the gearchange lever housing towards the shroud and fit the rubber grommet between the gearchange rod and the housing on the same side as the gearchange lever.
17 Tighten the chrome nut and its stop screw.
18 Check that the plastic bearing, plastic ring and tension pin are all correctly located on the gearchange lever and then fit the turn stop, spring and plastic ball.
19 Press the gearchange rod downwards and insert the gearchange lever through the square aperture in its housing. Screw on the knob.
20 Pull the gearchange lever outwards, align the plastic bearing located at the end of the lever with the hole in the rod and then release the lever.
21 Insert a rod to hold the turn stop while the gearchange lever is turned through 90° to lock it in position.
22 Reconnect the gearchange rod universal joint and finally carry out the adjustments described in Section 16.

## 19 Gearchange rod universal joint - servicing

1 The only maintenance required is to periodically peel back the rubber dust-cover and apply some lithium based grease. Renew the dust-covers if they are split or perished, also the flexible disc.
2 Removal of the universal joint is carried out by extracting the tapered pins which secure it to the gearchange rod upper and lower sections. These tapered pins have threads at both ends and the nut should be removed from one end and screwed onto the opposite end when, as it is tightened, the pin will be extracted. (Figs. 6.30/6.31).
3 Refitting is a reversal of removal.

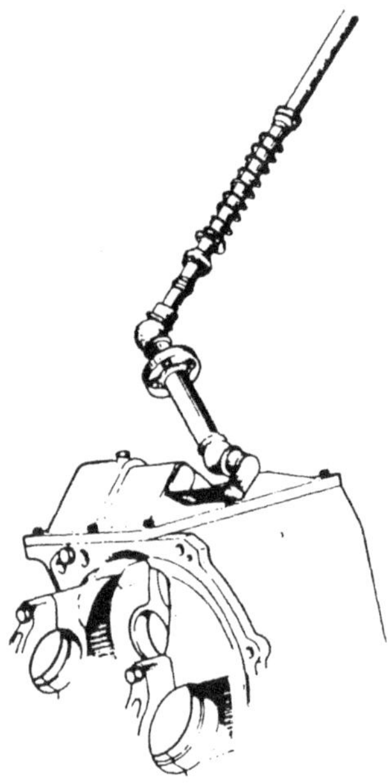

Fig 6.30 Gearchange rod universal joint (rhd vehicles)

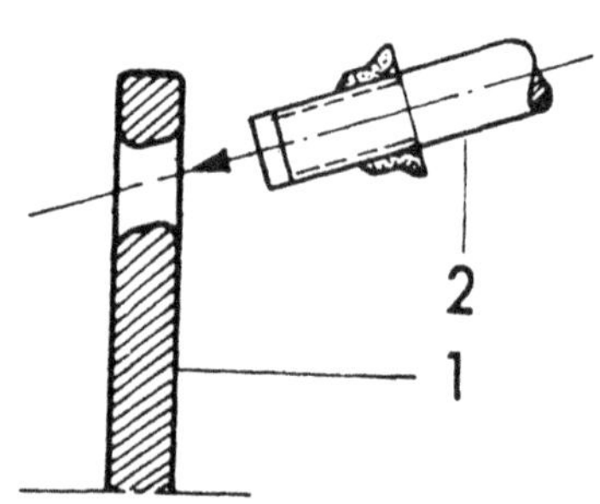


Fig 6.29 Correct orientation of hole in gearchange rod (lhd)

*1 Gearchange rod* *2 Gearchange lever*

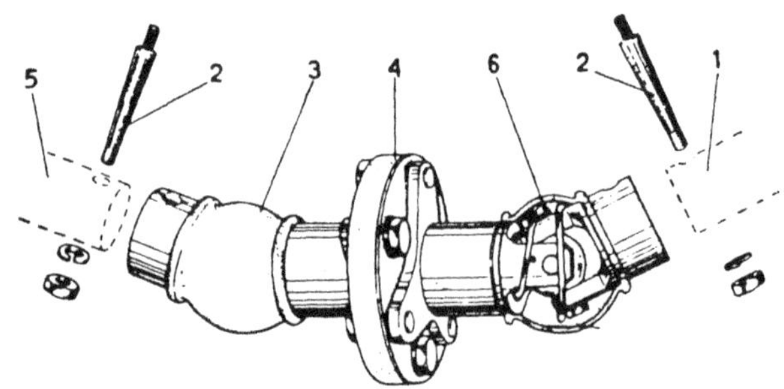


Fig 6.31 Gearchange rod universal joint (lhd vehicles)

*1 Gearchange rod*
*2 Tapered pin*
*3 Dust excluder*
*4 Flexible disc*
*5 Operating shaft*
*6 Spring*

## 20 Fault finding chart

| Symptom | Reason/s | Remedy |
|---|---|---|
| Weak or ineffective synchromesh | Synchronising cones worn, split or damaged | Dismantle and overhaul transmission. Fit new gear wheels and synchronising cones. |
| | Baulk ring synchromesh dogs worn, or damaged | Dismantle and overhaul. Fit new baulk ring synchromesh |
| Jumps out of gear | Broken gearchange fork rod spring | Dismantle and replace spring |
| | Gearbox coupling dogs badly worn | Dismantle gearbox. Fit new coupling dogs |
| | Selector fork rod groove badly worn | Fit new selector fork rod |
| Excessive noise | Incorrect grade of oil in transmission or oil level too low | Drain, refill or top up transmission with correct grade of oil |
| | Bush or needle roller bearings worn or damaged | Dismantle and overhaul transmission. Renew bearings |
| | Gear teeth excessively worn or damaged | Dismantle, overhaul transmission. Renew gearwheels |
| Excessive difficulty in engaging gear | Clutch pedal adjustment incorrect | Adjust clutch pedal correctly |

# Chapter 7 Driveshafts and front suspension

## Contents



## Specifications

### Driveshafts

**Type** ... Three section, with two universal joints:
Inner joint, needle bearing type;
Outer joint, ball and dome type

### Front suspension

**Type** ... Upper and lower wishbones, coil springs and double acting hydraulic shock absorbers

| **Coil springs:** | **1967** | **1968-1970** | **1971** | **1971 (export)** |
|---|---|---|---|---|
| Number of coils ... | 9.5 | 10.5 | 10.5 | 9.75 |
| Free length ... | 15.4 in (391.0 mm) | 16.0 in (405.0 mm) | 16.4 in (416.0 mm) | 14.5 in (368.0 mm) |
| Colour identification ... | Yellow | Green | Blue | White |

**Shock absorbers**
Length:
Closed ... 9¾ in (250.0 mm)
Extended ... 15 3/8 in (390.0 mm)
Stroke (fitted to vehicle) ... 3¼ in (82.0 mm)

### Road wheels and tyres

**Wheel size** ... 4J x 15 in

**Tyres (model 95)**
Size ... 5.60 x 15 (crossply) or 155SR15 (radial)
Pressures:
Light load:
Front ... 24 lb in$^2$ (1.7 kg cm$^2$)
Rear ... 24 lb in$^2$ (1.7 kg cm$^2$)
Full load:
Front ... 27 lb in$^2$ (1.9 kg cm$^2$)
Rear ... 30 lb in$^2$ (2.1 kg cm$^2$)

**Tyres (model 96)**
Size ... 5.20 x 15 or 5.60 x 15 (crossply) or 155SR15 (radial)
Pressures:
Light load:
Front ... 24 lb in$^2$ (1.7 kg cm$^2$)
Rear ... 24 lb in$^2$ (1.7 kg cm$^2$)
Full load:
Front ... 27 lb in$^2$ (1.9 kg cm$^2$)
Rear ... 27 lb in$^2$ (1.9 kg cm$^2$)

**Tyres (Monte Carlo)**

| | |
|---|---|
| Size ... | 155 x 15 (tubed) |
| Pressures: | |
| Light load: | |
| Front ... | 21 lb in$^2$ (1.5 kg cm$^2$) |
| Rear ... | 20 lb in$^2$ (1.4 kg cm$^2$) |
| Full load: | |
| Front ... | 24 lb in$^2$ (1.7 kg cm$^2$) |
| Rear ... | 24 lb in$^2$ (1.7 kg cm$^2$) |

| **Torque wrench settings** | **lb ft** | **kg m** |
|---|---|---|
| Outer driveshaft nut ... | 130 | 18.0 |
| Roadwheel nuts ... | 58 to 72 | 8.0 to 9.9 |
| Shock absorber mounting bolts ... | 30 | 4.1 |

Fig 7.1 Layout of front suspension

## 1 General description

The driveshafts are of three section design and incorporate inner and outer universal joints. The inner universal joint is splined to the differential side gears and retained in position by a spring locking ring which locates in matching grooves in the end of the inner driveshaft and the differential side gear. The inner driveshaft joint terminates in an internally recessed cup and that of the centre driveshaft in a tee, supported in needle roller bearings and cups. The centre driveshaft terminates at the outer universal joint in a splined section which is retained in the dome of the universal joint by means of a spring locking ring. Power is transmitted from the inner to outer domes of the outer universal joint through six large steel balls. The outer driveshaft (stub axle) is an integral part of the joint outer dome and it is to the outer driveshaft that the road wheel hub is splined and upon which the outer driveshaft carrier is supported on a double row ball-race. For replacement purposes, the outer driveshaft, hub and outer universal joint are supplied as an assembly matched and balanced and cannot be renewed as separate components. Both the inner and outer universal joints are packed with grease and fitted with rubber dust excluders. These do not require any maintenance unless the dust excluders are renewed in which case

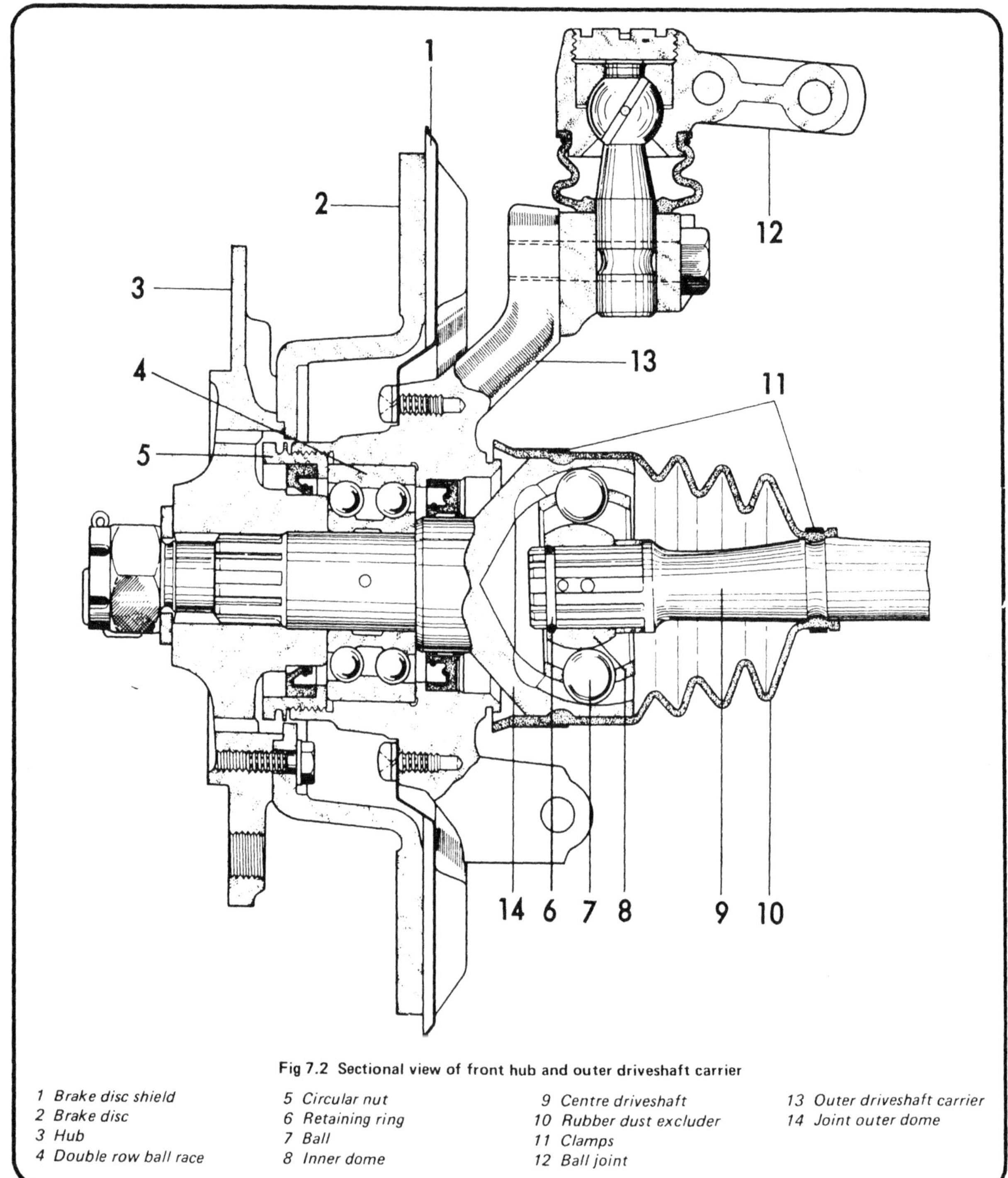


Fig 7.2 Sectional view of front hub and outer driveshaft carrier

*1 Brake disc shield*
*2 Brake disc*
*3 Hub*
*4 Double row ball race*
*5 Circular nut*
*6 Retaining ring*
*7 Ball*
*8 Inner dome*
*9 Centre driveshaft*
*10 Rubber dust excluder*
*11 Clamps*
*12 Ball joint*
*13 Outer driveshaft carrier*
*14 Joint outer dome*

the joints should be repacked with recommended grease.

The front suspension is of independent type incorporating coil springs, double acting telescopic type hydraulic shock absorbers and a stabilizer bar. The outer driveshaft carrier swivels at top and bottom by means of balljoints which are positively located by an upper and lower control arm of wishbone formation.

### 2 Centre and outer driveshaft assemblies - removal and refitting

1 Remove the hub cap from the roadwheel. As the shaft nut is very tight it is preferable at this stage to remove the split pin and unscrew the nut half a turn. Jack-up the front of the vehicle and remove the roadwheel.

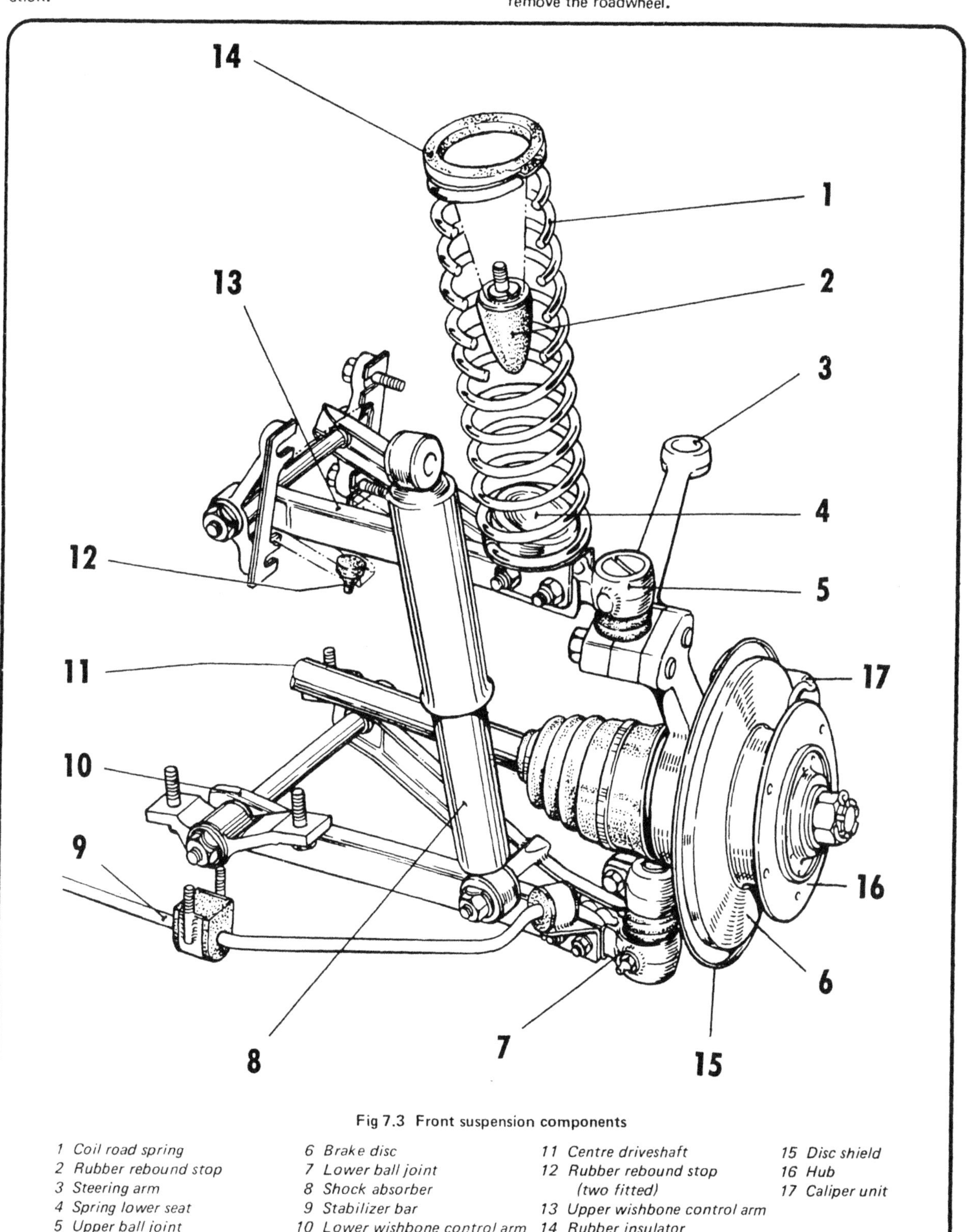


Fig 7.3 Front suspension components

1 *Coil road spring*
2 *Rubber rebound stop*
3 *Steering arm*
4 *Spring lower seat*
5 *Upper ball joint*
6 *Brake disc*
7 *Lower ball joint*
8 *Shock absorber*
9 *Stabilizer bar*
10 *Lower wishbone control arm*
11 *Centre driveshaft*
12 *Rubber rebound stop (two fitted)*
13 *Upper wishbone control arm*
14 *Rubber insulator*
15 *Disc shield*
16 *Hub*
17 *Caliper unit*

2 Remove the two bolts which secure the brake caliper to the outer driveshaft carrier. Slide the caliper complete with pads from the disc and tie it up under the wing so that no strain is placed upon the flexible hose. There is no need to disconnect the hydraulic pipe.

3 Remove the shaft nut (previously loosened) and washer and using a suitable extractor, pull the hub/disc assembly from the splined end of the outer driveshaft (photos).

4 Every 12,000 miles (19000 km) the front hub bearings should be repacked with grease when the stage of dismantling so far described, has been reached.

5 Remove the large clip which secures the rubber boot in position on the inner universal joint. (Fig. 7.4)

6 Disconnect the upper balljoint from the outer driveshaft carrier (two cotter bolts) - see Section 6 (photo).

7 Disconnect the lower balljoint from the carrier in a similar manner (one cotter bolt) (photo).

8 Open the inner universal joint and fit temporary covers to both exposed parts of the joint to retain the needle rollers and to exclude dirt. Plastic bags and heavy rubber bands are quite suitable if they are securely fastened with tape or wire.

9 Withdraw the centre driveshaft complete with outer driveshaft, outer driveshaft carrier and outer universal joint. (Fig. 7.5)

10 Commence refitting by filling the needle bearing grooves in the inner universal joint with recommended grease.

11 With the temporary covers still fitted pass the complete centre and outer driveshaft assembly under the wing and through the driveshaft cutout. Remove the covers and insert the shaft and needle bearings into engagement with the section of joint which is part of the inner driveshaft.

12 Refit the inner joint rubber boot and clip.

13 Reconnect the upper and lower balljoints to the outer driveshaft carrier and then refit the brake disc and hub. Tighten the shaft nut as much as possible and then refit the caliper and roadwheel and lower the jack.

14 Fully tighten the shaft nut to 130 lb/ft (18 kg/m) and insert a new split pin once the jack has been removed (photo).

## 3 Inner driveshaft - removal, refitting and oil seal renewal

1 If the object of removing the driveshaft assembly is to renew the oil seal located in the transmission casing then the complete driveshaft (three sections) should be removed as one unit without disconnecting the universal joints.

2 Jack-up the front of the vehicle and remove the roadwheel.

3 Disconnect the upper and lower balljoints from the outer driveshaft carrier and then support the carrier to prevent strain on the brake caliper flexible hose.

4 With a drift located behind the flange of the inner driveshaft,

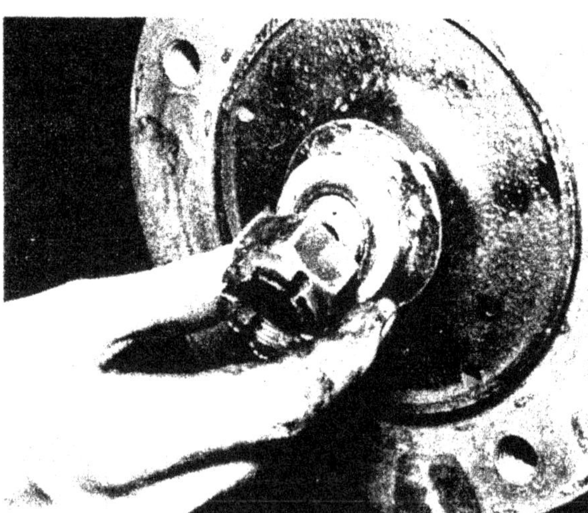

2.3A Removing an outer driveshaft hub nut

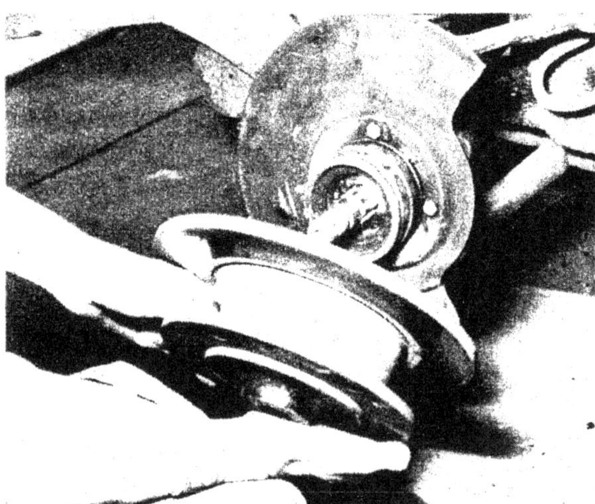

2.3B Withdrawing a front hub/disc assembly

2.6 Removing upper ball joint cotter bolt

2.7 Removing lower ball joint cotter bolt

drive it out of engagement with the differential side-gear. The inner driveshaft is retained by a spring ring located in grooves machined into the outer surface of the shaft and the bore of the side-gear. Only drive the inner driveshaft out sufficiently to gain access to the oil seal in the transmission casing otherwise the flexible brake hose will be strained. Do not disconnect the inner universal joint by pulling it during the foregoing operations.

5 Prise the oil seal from the transmission casing and drift in a new one squarely, ensuring that the lips with the spring behind them face inwards and that the outer face of the oil seal is 0.1 in. (2.5 mm) below the surface of the transmission casing (Figs. 7.6/7.7).

6 Refitting is a reversal of removal but ensure that the splines of the inner driveshaft do not cut the lips of the new seal as the shaft is inserted into the transmission casing.

7 Should one of the inner driveshafts shear at any time, the broken section may be removed from the differential side-gear by first removing the opposite shaft assembly, and inserting a forked drift which will pass the differential shaft. This method will avoid the necessity of stripping the transmission unit. (Fig. 7.8)

2.14 Fitting a new split pin to outer driveshaft castellated nut

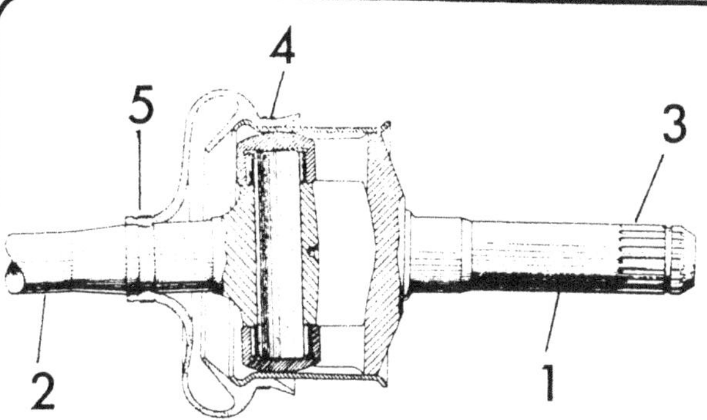


Fig 7.4 Sectional view of inner universal joint

*1 Inner driveshaft*
*2 Centre driveshaft*
*3 Retaining ring groove*
*4 Large dust excluder clip*
*5 Small dust excluder clip*

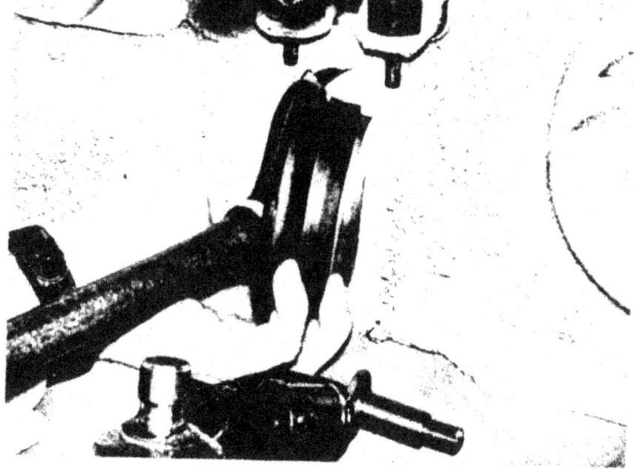

Fig 7.5 Withdrawal of driveshaft assembly (protective cover fitted)

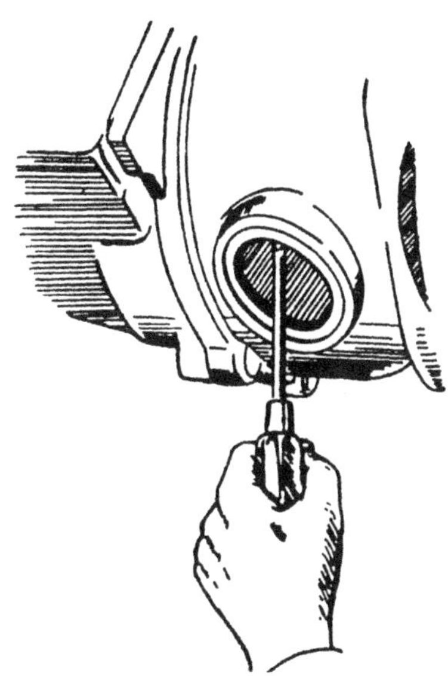

Fig 7.6 Prising out the inner driveshaft oil seal from the transmission casing

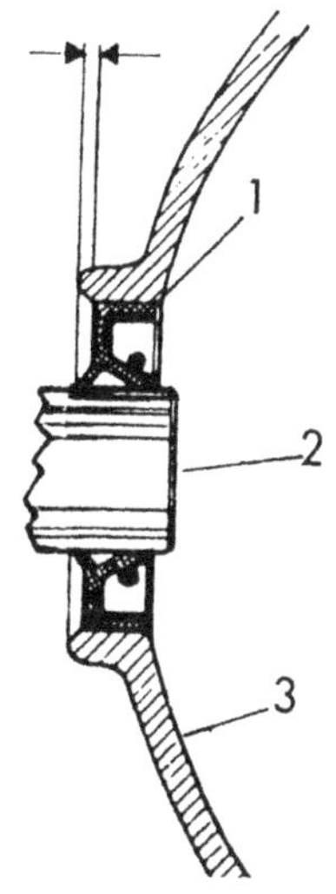


Fig 7.7 Inner driveshaft oil seal installation diagram

*1 Oil seal*
*2 Inner driveshaft*
*3 Transmission casing*

## 4 Inner universal joint - servicing

1 The most likely failure of the inner or outer joints will be tearing or deterioration of the rubber dust excluding boots. Renewal of the boots can only be carried out after dismantling of the outer universal joint, (see next Section) so that the boots can be slid from the centre shaft.

2 If the needle rollers are worn they must be renewed (photo).

3 If the bearing cups are worn, withdraw them and refit them again after turning them through 90° to present new bearing surfaces to the needle rollers. If the bearing cup grooves are severely ridged, then the complete driveshaft assembly must be renewed (photo).

## 5 Outer universal joint - servicing

1 Remove the driveshaft assembly as described in Section 2, paragraphs 1 to 9.

2 Thoroughly clean the outer driveshaft and carrier assembly in paraffin.

3 Withdraw the carrier from the outer driveshaft using a press or puller (photo).

4 Prise up the tab which locks the circular nut to the carrier and unscrew it with a 'C' spanner or by careful use of a cold chisel. (Fig. 7.9) (photo).

5 Renew the oil seal in the circular nut (photo).

6 Drift the double ball race and oil seal from the carrier.

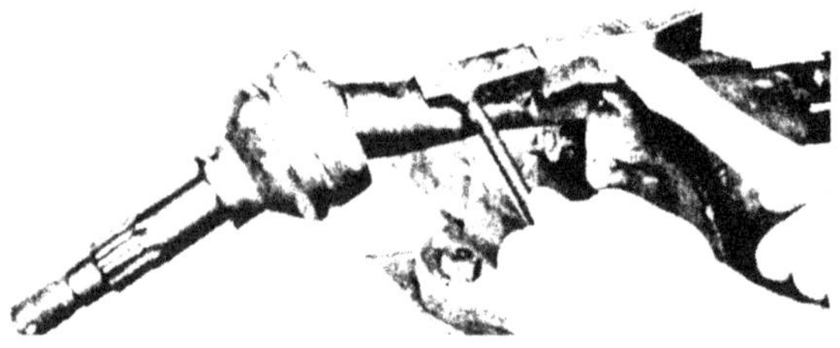

Fig 7.10 Tapping off the outer driveshaft and universal joint from the centre driveshaft

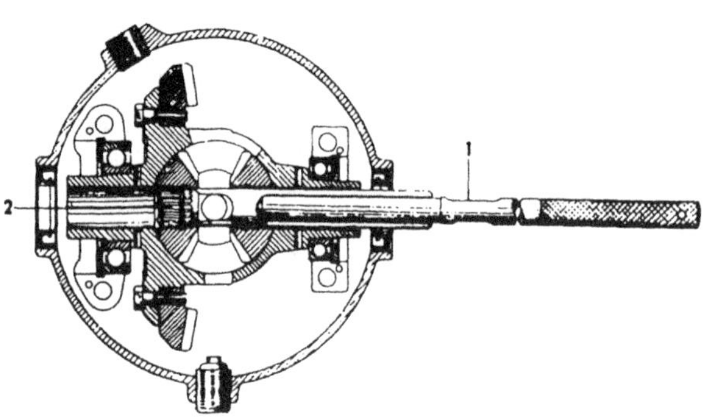


Fig 7.8 Removing a sheared inner driveshaft

*1 Forked drift* *2 Broken section of inner driveshaft*

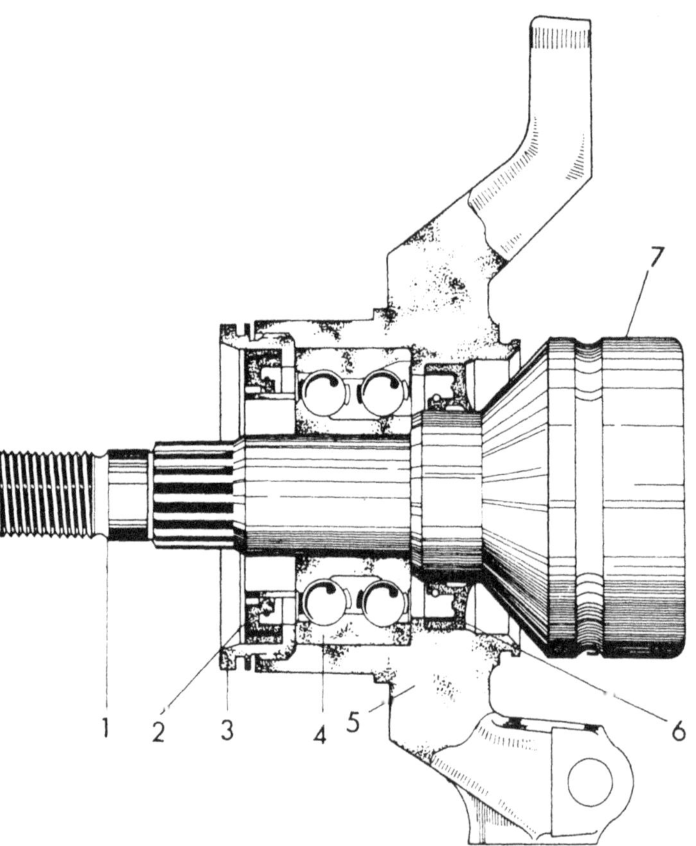


Fig 7.9 Sectional view of outer driveshaft and carrier

*1 Outer driveshaft*
*2 Outer oil seal*
*3 Circular nut*
*4 Double row ball race*
*5 Outer driveshaft carrier*
*6 Inner oil seal*
*7 Universal joint outer dome*

7 Press a new oil seal into the carrier (photo).
8 Install a new ballrace to the carrier ensuring that the reference numbers on the bearing face outwards (towards the shaft nut). (photo)
9 Drive in the bearing by applying pressure to its outer track only (photo).
10 Apply grease to the oil seal lips and to the bearing, screw the circular nut into the carrier, tightening it to 130 lb/ft (18.0 kg/m). The carrier will probably have to be bolted to the bench during this operation.
11 Bend down the tabs of the circular nut lockplate (photo).
12 Secure the centre driveshaft in a vice fitted with jaw protectors and then drift the outer driveshaft complete with universal joint from the centre driveshaft. (Fig. 7.10).
13 It is not recommended that the outer universal joint should be dismantled as wear will almost certainly have taken place in the outer dome ball tracks and it is therefore preferable to renew the outer driveshaft/universal joint assembly complete. The joint will come apart if the inner dome is turned through 90°.
14 At this stage, new rubber boots can be fitted to the centre driveshaft for positioning over either the inner or outer universal joints as required.
15 Locate a new spring retaining ring on the splined section of the centre driveshaft and using a pair of pipe grips or similar pliers, compress the ring into its groove. With the ring compressed, insert the shaft into the inner dome of the outer universal joint and tap the other end of the shaft smartly so that the ring (still in its compressed state) will press into the bore of the dome. Remove the pliers and push the driveshaft fully home so that the retaining ring engages in the groove in the bore of the inner dome. (Fig. 7.12)

16 Fit new clamps to the inner and outer necks of the universal joint rubber boot.

17 Carry out the operations described in paragraphs 13 and 14 of Section 2.

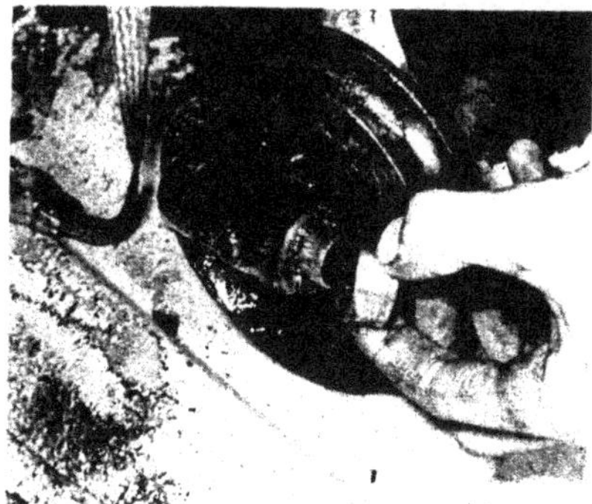
4.2 Drivehsaft tee joint needle bearings and cup

4.3 Inner driveshaft bearing cup grooves

5.3 Withdrawing outer driveshaft carrier

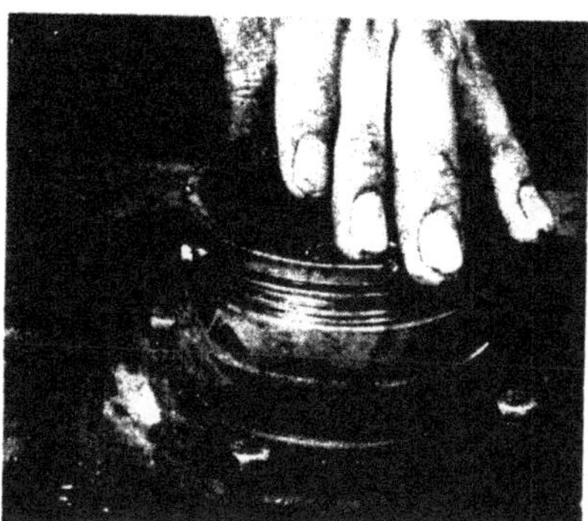
5.4 Unscrewing circular nut from outer driveshaft carrier

5.5 Oil seal located in circular nut

5.7 Oil seal located in outer driveshaft carrier

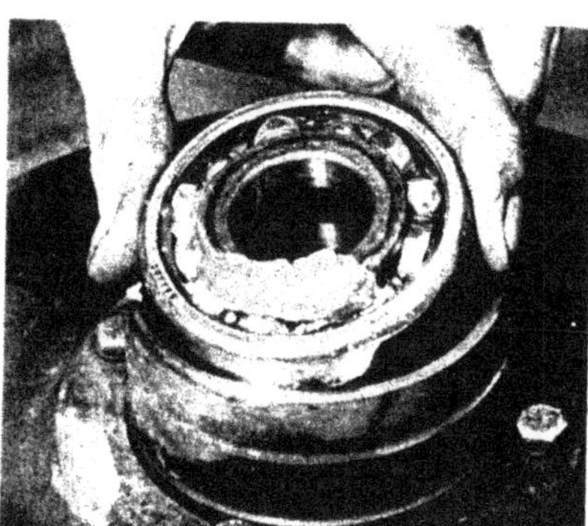
5.8 Double row ball bearing being fitted to outer driveshaft carrier

5.9 Driving in the outer driveshaft carrier bearing

5.11 Securing the tab on the circular nut locking plate

Fig 7.11 Locating a retaining ring on the centre driveshaft

Fig 7.12 Compressing the centre driveshaft retaining ring prior to inserting the shaft into the outer universal joint

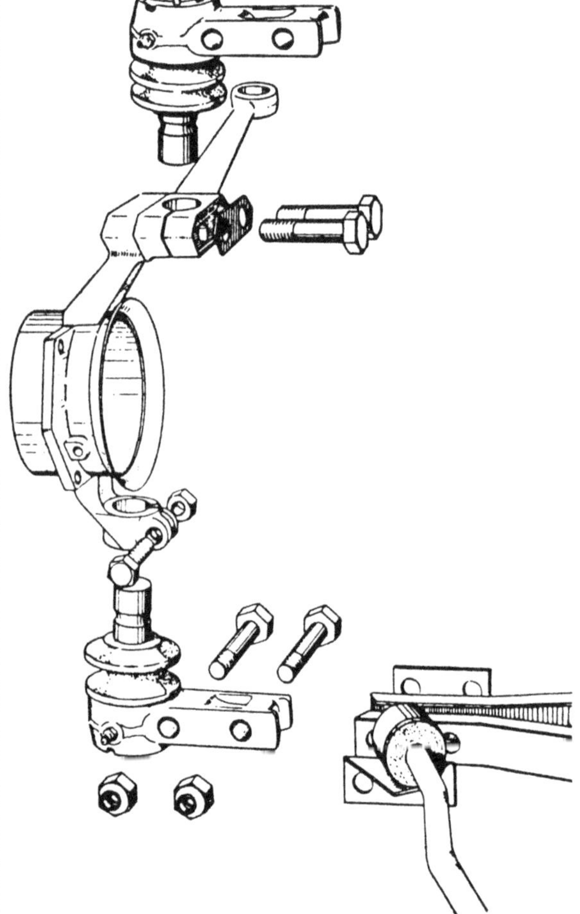

Fig 7.13 Outer driveshaft carrier and upper and lower ball joints

Fig 7.14 Road spring compressed prior to removal of upper ball joint

## 6 Outer driveshaft carrier balljoints - removal and refitting

1 Jack-up the front of the vehicle and remove the road wheel.
2 If the lower balljoint is to be removed, unscrew and remove the single cotter bolt which secures it to the outer driveshaft carrier and the two bolts which retain it to the lower suspension wishbone. (Fig. 7.13)
3 If the upper balljoint is to be removed then clamp type spring compressors must be fitted to the front coil road spring. (Fig 7.14)
4 Unscrew and remove the two cotter bolts which secure the balljoint and the steering arm to the outer driveshaft carrier and the two bolts which secure the balljoint to the upper suspension wishbone.
5 Always renew the balljoint dust excluding boots if they are split or perished.
6 Refitting is a reversal of removal but always fit new lockplates under the bolts and bend up the tabs.

## 7 Outer driveshaft carrier balljoints - adjustment for wear

1 If by gripping the upper or lower wishbones, they can be made to move in relation to the outer driveshaft carrier then the balljoints must be adjusted.
2 To do this, disconnect the balljoint from the carrier by removing the cotter bolts.
3 Remove the dust excluding boot and then release the staking which secures the grooved disc in position.
4 Turn the disc until the balljoint stud is stiff to move but still can be moved in all directions of travel by hand pressure alone.
5 Re-stake the disc by using a sharp cold chisel to bend the flange metal into the disc groove.
6 Refit the dust excluder (use a new one if the original has deteriorated) and reconnect the balljoint to the outer driveshaft carrier.

## 8 Front shock absorbers - removal, testing and refitting

1 The front shock absorbers have rubber bushed eye type mountings at top and bottom. To remove the unit simply withdraw the anchor bolts.
2 Secure the lower mounting in a vice and with the shock absorber held in a vertical attitude, push and pull the upper section ten or twelve times to the full extent of its travel. Unless there is a definite resistance in both directions the unit is faulty and must be renewed as an assembly. If a new unit is being fitted then it must be held in the vertical position and given several full strokes and then installed immediately without laying it down in order to exclude air from the internal valve system.
3 Periodically check the rubber bushes at the shock absorber mountings and renew them if their centre holes have become elongated, or if the bushes have deteriotated through oil contamination.
4 Tighten the upper and lower mounting bolts to a torque of 30 lb/ft (4.1 kg/m).

## 9 Suspension upper wishbone - removal and refitting

1 Jack-up the front of the vehicle and remove the roadwheel.
2 Remove the shock absorber.
3 Compress the road coil spring using suitable clamps.

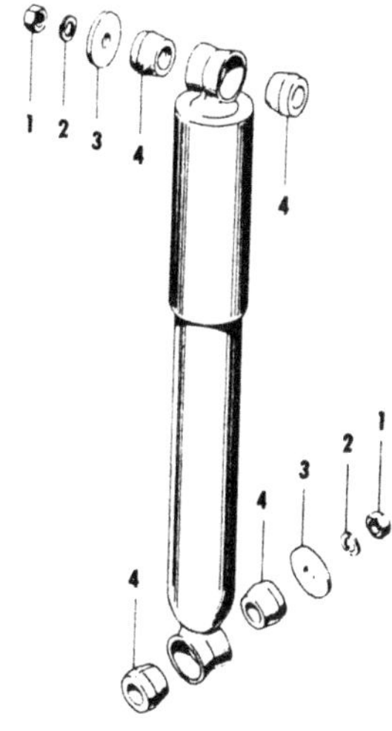


**Fig 7.15 A front shock absorber and mountings**

*1 Nut*
*2 Lockwasher*
*3 Plain washer*
*4 Rubber bushes*

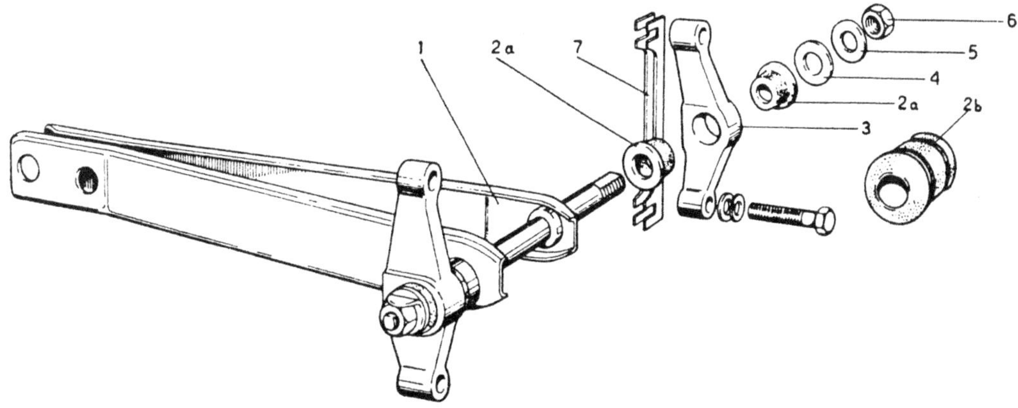


Fig 7.16 **Upper suspension wishbone and mountings**

*1 Wishbone control arm*
*2a Split type rubber bushes*
*2b Single piece rubber bush (alternative)*
*3 Bearing bracket*
*4 Plain washer*
*5 Tab washer*
*6 Nut*
*7 Shims (camber adjustment)*

4 Unscrew and remove the two bolts which secure the balljoint and coil spring seat to the upper wishbone.
5 Unscrew the bolts which secure the pivot bearing brackets but do not disconnect them completely. (Fig. 7.16)
6 Remove the coil spring complete with its clamps.
7 Now withdraw the wishbone and bearing brackets, retaining any shims which are located beneath the brackets.
8 If the rubber pivot bushes are to be renewed, bend up the tabwashers and unscrew the nuts at both ends of the pivot shaft. Draw off the bearing brackets and remove the split type or single section rubber bushes according to pattern.
9 If the rubber bushes are of single section type they should be driven into the bearing bracket using a suitable drift. If necessary, smear them with brake fluid to facilitate their entry; never use oil or grease. (Fig. 7.17).
10 Always use new tab washers and before tightening the pivot nuts, set the brackets to the correct fitting angle otherwise the rubber bushes will be distorted when the brackets are bolted into position.
11 Check that the spring seat contains the rubber and metal washers and that the rubber rebound stop is in good condition and correctly located under the wishbone.
12 Locate the coil spring and reconnect the balljoint.
13 Insert the original shims behind the bearing brackets and bolt up the brackets. The shims set the camber angle.
14 Carefully release the coil spring clamps and remove them.
15 Refit the shock absorber and the road wheel and lower the vehicle.
16 Check the steering angles and wheel alignment (Chapter 8).

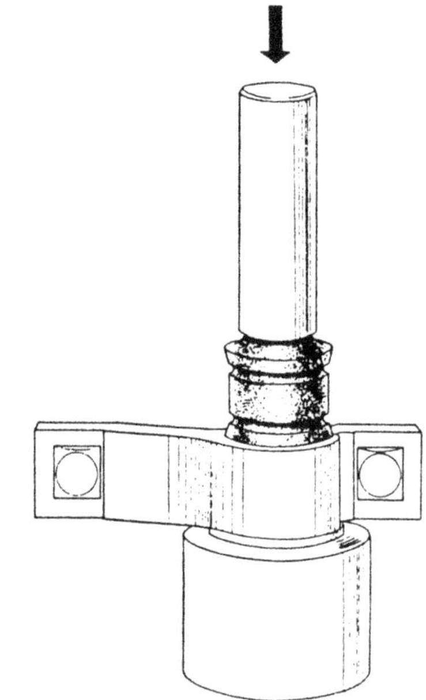

Fig 7.17 Fitting a new single section type rubber bush to an upper suspension wishbone bearing bracket

## 10 Suspension lower wishbone - removal and refitting

1 The procedure for the removal, rebushing and refitting of the suspension lower wishbone is similar to that described for the upper wishbone in the preceding Section, except for the following points. (Fig. 7.19).
2 Releasing the lower balljoint also releases the stabilizer bar end bearing.
3 The suspension wishbone bearing brackets are bolted to the floor pan without insertion of shims.
4 If new bushes have been installed, check the alignment of the bearing brackets in relation to the wishbone before tightening the pivot nuts and bending over new tabwashers to avoid distortion of the bushes when the bearing brackets are bolted into position.

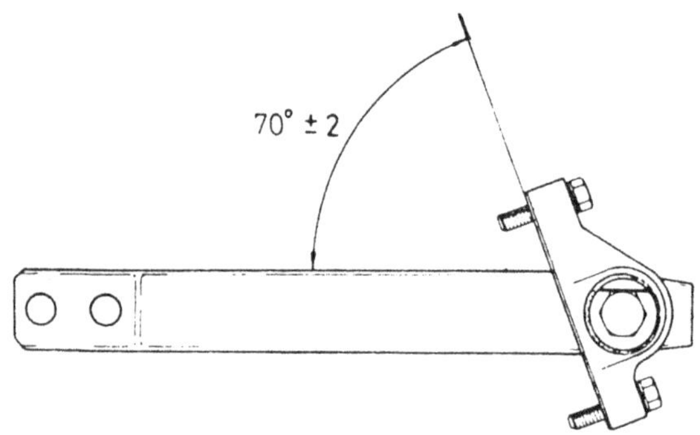


Fig 7.18 Upper suspension wishbone bearing bracket alignment diagram

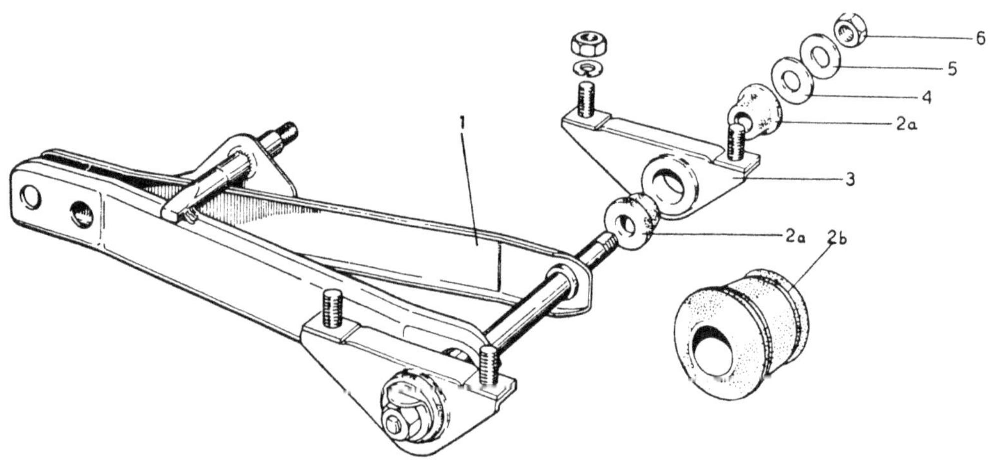


Fig 7.19 Suspension lower wishbone and mountings

*1 Wishbone control arm*
*2a Split type rubber bushes*
*2b Single section type rubber bush*
*3 Pivot bearing bracket*
*4 Plain washer*
*5 Tab washer*
*6 Nut*

## 11 Front coil spring - removal and refitting

1 Jack-up the front of the vehicle and remove the road wheel.
2 Using a pair of pipegrips or a similar tool, unscrew the rubber rebound stop from within the coil spring and let it drop down inside the coils. If it is difficult to unscrew, an alternative method to provide clearance for coil spring removal is to remove the two rubber stops from the travel limit brackets below the arms of the upper wishbone.
3 Remove the shock absorber and then compress the spring with suitable clamps.
4 Unscrew and remove the two bolts which secure the upper balljoint to the upper wishbone and detach the spring seat.
5 Withdraw the coil spring (still secured in the clamps).
6 If a new coil spring is to be fitted then both front springs should be renewed as a pair, paying particular attention to the spring types and application as given in the 'Specifications' Section. The spring clamps will have to be removed from the old spring and fitted to the new one and dependent upon their lengths it may mean that a threaded rod type compressor will have to be employed to enable the clamps to be removed and installed.
7 Refitting is a reversal of removal but check that the rubber and metal washers in the upper spring seat are in good condition, otherwise renew them. Also check the condition of, and renew if necessary, the rebound stops.

## 12 Stabilizer bar - removal and refitting

1 Jack-up the front of the vehicle and remove both front wheels.
2 From inside the engine compartment unscrew the nuts from the mounting brackets and then unbolt the end-brackets.
3 Withdraw the complete stabilizer bar assembly towards the right-hand side of the car.

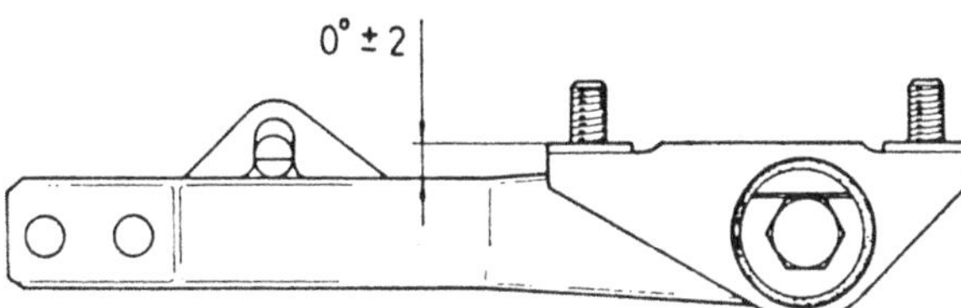


Fig 7.20 Lower suspension wishbone bearing bracket alignment diagram

4 Where either of the mounting bracket bushes require renewal then it is recommended that they are renewed, one at a time, with the stabilizer bar in position on the vehicle.
5 To renew the end-bracket bushes, disconnect both brackets from the lower suspension wishbones and twist the stabilizer bar downwards.

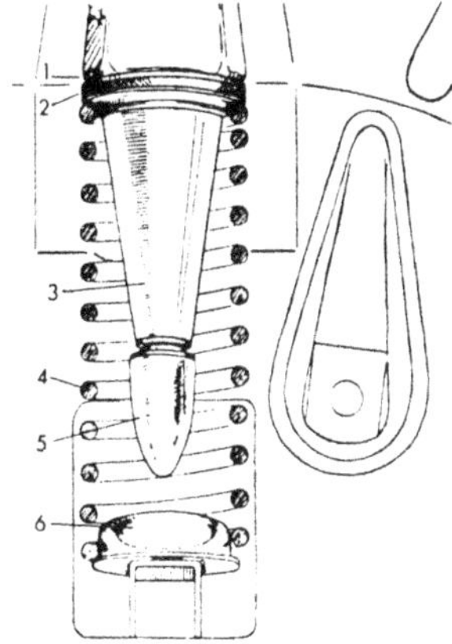


Fig 7.21 Front road spring mounting detail

*1 Metal ring*
*2 Rubber insulator*
*3 Rebound stop support cone*
*4 Coil spring*
*5 Rubber rebound stop*
*6 Spring seat*

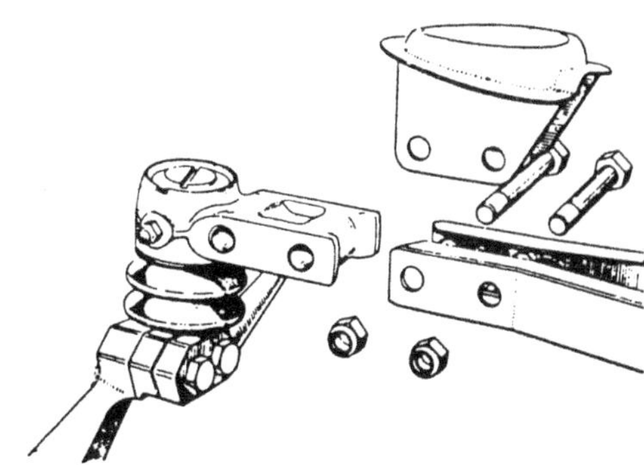

Fig 7.22 Attachment of spring seat and ball joint to upper wishbone arm

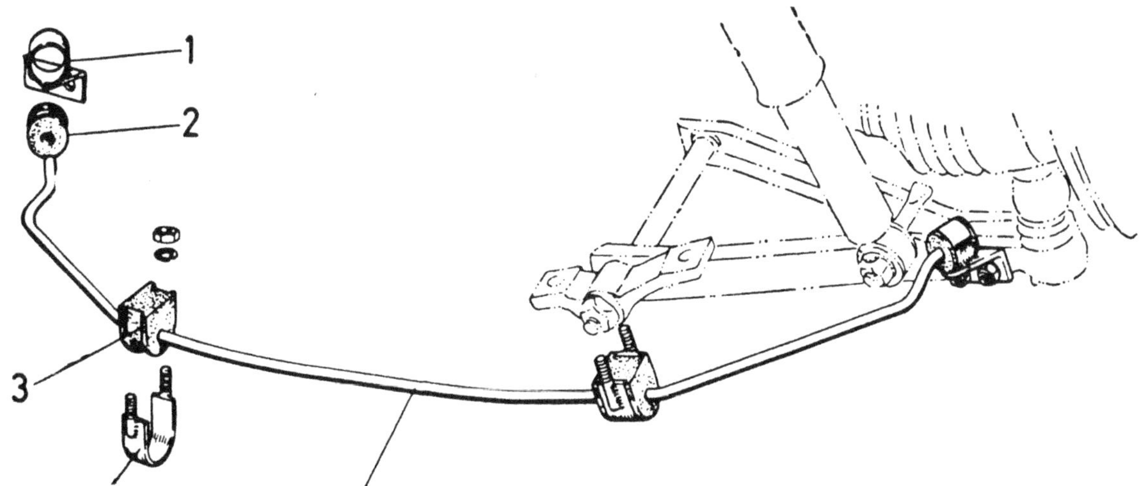


Fig 7.23 Stabilizer bar and bearings

*1 End bracket*
*2 Rubber bush*
*3 Centre bracket bush*
*4 Centre bracket*
*5 Stabilizer bar*

## 13 Fault diagnosis - driveshafts and front suspension

| Symptom | Cause | Remedy |
|---|---|---|
| Steering vague, vehicle wanders | Uneven tyre pressures | Inflate tyres. |
| | Faulty shock absorbers | Renew. |
| | Broken coil spring | Renew (as pair). |
| | Worn balljoints | Adjust or renew. |
| Stiff or heavy steering | Low tyre pressures | Inflate. |
| | Balljoints dry | Lubricate. |
| Wheel wobble and vibration | Wheel nuts loose | Tighten. |
| | Wheels out of balance | Re-balance. |
| | Weak coil springs | Renew (as pair). |
| | Faulty shock absorbers | Renew. |
| | Worn bearings in outer driveshaft carrier | Renew (also oil seals). |

*See also 'Fault diagnosis' – Chapter 8.*

# Chapter 8 Steering

Contents



Specifications

**Steering type** ... Rack and pinion

**Ratio**

| | |
|---|---|
| Up to 1968 ... | 14 : 1 |
| From 1969 ... | 15.5 : 1 |

**Number of turns of steering wheel lock-to-lock**

| | |
|---|---|
| Up to 1968 ... | 2¼ |
| From 1969 ... | 2.7 |

**Pinion end clearance**

| | |
|---|---|
| Up to and including 1968 models ... | 0.004 to 0.008 in (0.1 to 0.2 mm) |
| From 1969 models ... | 0.005 in (0.12 mm) maximum |

**Rack radial play**

| | |
|---|---|
| Up to and including 1968 models ... | 0.012 in (0.3 mm) maximum |
| From 1969 models ... | 0.01 in (0.25 mm) maximum |

**Front wheel alignment**

| | |
|---|---|
| Camber ... | $\frac{3}{4}^{o} \pm \frac{1}{4}^{o}$ |
| Castor ... | $2^{o} \pm \frac{1}{2}^{o}$ |
| Steering axis inclination ... | $7^{o} \pm 1^{o}$ |
| Toe-in ... | $0.08 \pm 0.04$ in ($2.0 \pm 1.0$ mm) |

**Torque wrench setting**

| | lb ft | kg m |
|---|---|---|
| Trackrod end locknut ... | 25 to 36 | 3.5 to 5.0 |

## 1 General description

The steering gear is of rack and pinion type, the gear being left or right-handed according to requirement. Movement is transmitted through a two spoked steering wheel splined to the steering column and then through a flexible joint to the pinion of the steering gear. The rack is connected to the steering arms of the outer driveshaft carriers by means of adjustable length trackrods and balljointed trackrod-ends.

Attached to the steering column is the gearchange mechanism (see Chapter 6). A combined gearlever/ignition lock is fitted, servicing of which is described both in Chapter 6 and in Section 12 of this Chapter.

## 2 Steering gear - adjustments with assembly in vehicle

1 Adjustments and lubrication are not normally to be considered routine maintenance but after a considerable mileage it may be necessary to take up wear which has taken place in the rack and pinion components. The addition of grease to the internal mechanism should only be required if, due to deterioration, the rubber dust excluding bellows have been renewed.

2 *To adjust the pinion endfloat,* (the need for which may be indicated by knocking, particularly when traversing uneven road surfaces), jack-up the front of the vehicle so that both road wheels are off the ground.

3 Unscrew the locknut (12) (Fig. 8.2) and the adjusting screw (11) until all tension of the coil spring (10) has been released.

4 Unbolt and remove the bearing cover (8) together with the shims (7).

5 Adjust the thickness of the shim pack until the pinion endfloat for models up to and including 1967 is between 0.004 and 0.008 in. (0.1 and 0.2 mm). Shims are available in thicknesses of 0.004 and 0.012 in. (0.1 and 0.3 mm). For vehicles built from 1968 onwards, the endfloat should be 0.005 in. (0.12 mm) and

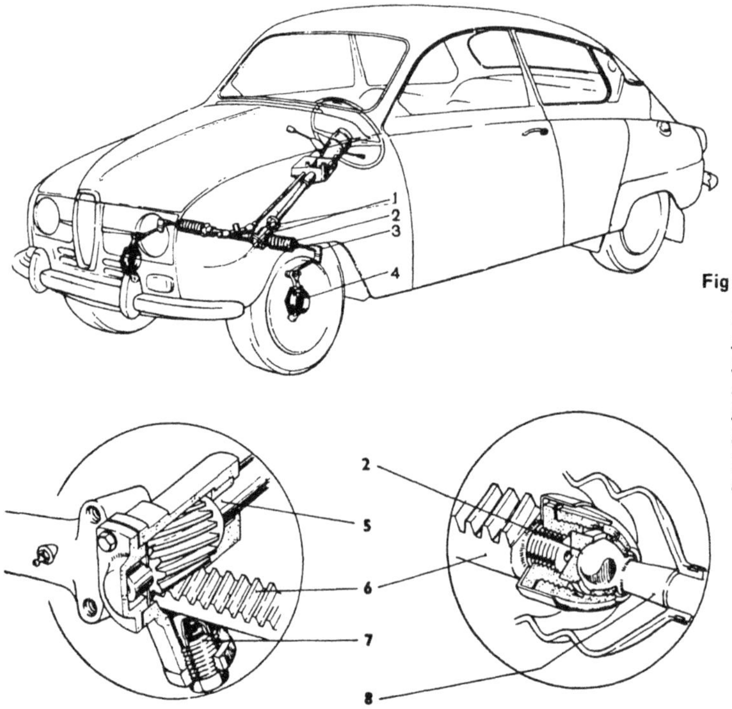

**Fig 8.1 Layout and cutaway view of steering gear**

*1 Rack and pinion assembly*
*2 Trackrod ball*
*3 Trackrod-end*
*4 Outer driveshaft carrier/steering arm*
*5 Pinion*
*6 Rack*
*7 Rack adjusting screw*
*8 Trackrod*

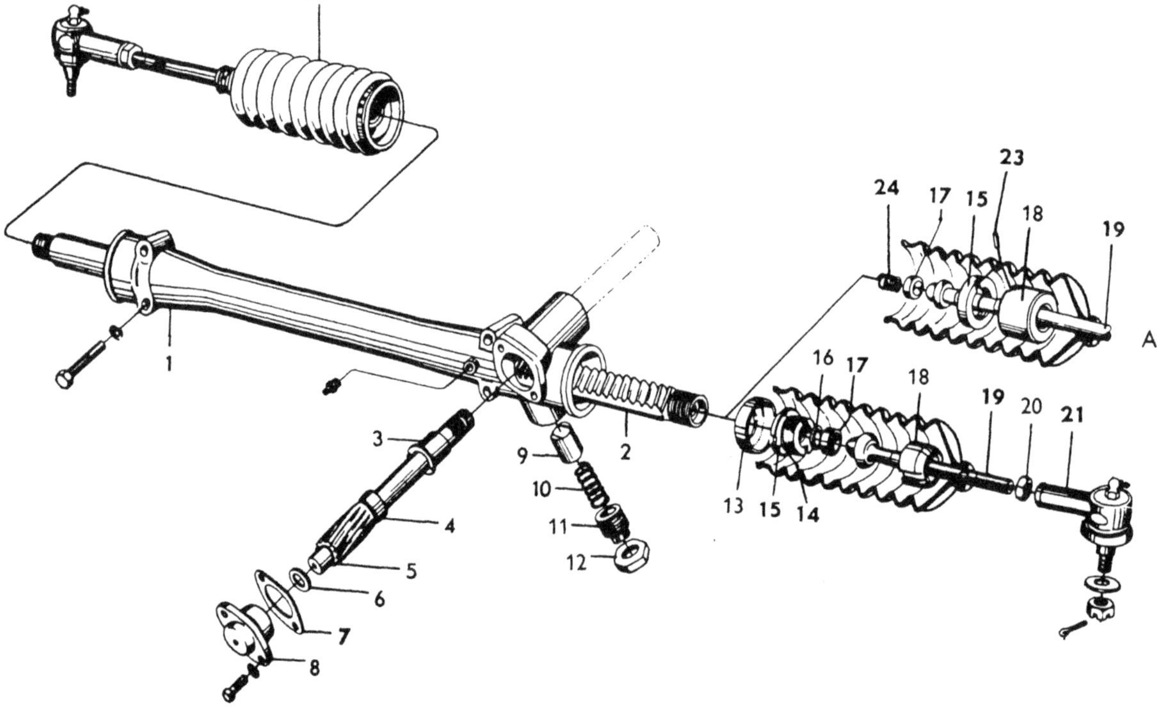

**Fig 8.2 Exploded view of steering gear (lhd)**

*1 Housing*
*2 Rack*
*3 Bush*
*4 Spacer*
*5 Pinion*
*6 Washer*
*7 Shim*
*8 Bearing/cover*
*9 Plunger*
*10 Spring*
*11 Rack adjusting screw*
*12 Locknut*
*13 Cupped locking sleeve*
*14 Shim*
*15 Nut*
*16 Spring washer*
*17 Ball inner seat*
*18 Ball outer seat*
*19 Trackrod*
*20 Locknut*
*21 Trackrod-end*
*22 Bellows*
*A Later design*
*23 Locking pin*
*24 Spring*

shims are available in thicknesses of 0.0276 in. (0.07 mm), 0.004 in. (0.1 mm), 0.012 in. (0.3 mm) and 0.028 in. (0.7 mm).
6 When adjustment is correct, apply a little grease to the end of the pinion and refit the bearing cover.
7 *The adjustment of the steering rack radial play* must now be carried out. With the adjusting screw (11) and locknut (12) previously slackened, tighten the adjusting screw until the rack becomes stiff when the steering is moved.
8 Unscrew the adjusting screw just enough to remove any stiffness in the rack when it is moved from lock-to-lock. Tighten the locknut and recheck for free movement of the rack.

## 3 Trackrod-ends - removal and refitting

1 Jack-up the front of the vehicle and remove the road wheel.
2 Slacken the locknut which secures the trackrod to the trackrod-end.
3 Remove the split pin, nut and washer from the trackrod-end balljoint stud and using a suitable extractor, separate the balljoint from the steering arm. (Fig. 8.5).
4 Unscrew the trackrod-end from the trackrod.
5 Before refitting, check the condition of the rubber dust excluder on the balljoint and renew if necessary.
6 Always use a new split pin and check and adjust the wheel alignment as described in Section 13.

## 4 Steering gear rubber bellows - renewal with gear in vehicle

1 Where the dust excluding bellows have split or perished, then they must be renewed immediately. This operation can be carried out without removing the steering gear from the vehicle.
2 Jack-up the front of the vehicle and remove the road wheels.
3 Remove the trackrod-ends as described in the preceding Section.
4 Unscrew the large and small clamps from each bellows and withdraw the bellows over the trackrod.
5 Move the steering to full lock and grease the exposed portion of the rack and the inner balljoint. Fit the new bellows and tighten the clamps.
6 Move the steering to the full opposite lock and grease that end of the rack assembly. Fit the remaining bellows and clamps.
7 Connect the trackrod-ends, fit the roadwheels and lower the jack.
8 Check and adjust the wheel alignment as described in Section 13.

## 5 Steering gear - removal and installation

1 Remove the bonnet lid and disconnect the battery negative lead.
2 Jack-up the front of the vehicle so that both roadwheels are clear of the ground and then remove them.
3 Disconnect the trackrod-ends from the steering arms as described in Section 3 (photo).
4 On lhd vehicles remove the left-hand trackrod-end and on rhd vehicles remove the right-hand one.
5 Remove the lower taper pin from the gearchange shaft universal joint and disconnect the joint from the transmission unit (Chapter 6).
6 Disconnect the free wheel control from the transmission unit.
7 Unbolt the clutch slave cylinder from the clutch bellhousing and tie it up, out of the way.
8 Release the throttle return spring and tie the throttle spindle so that it is fully deflected.
9 Disconnect the speedometer cable from the transmission unit.
10 On lhd vehicles turn the steering wheel to full left-lock and on rhd vehicles to full right-lock. Unscrew the pinch bolt which secures the steering column flexible coupling to the splined section of the pinion. Lift the steering wheel enough to

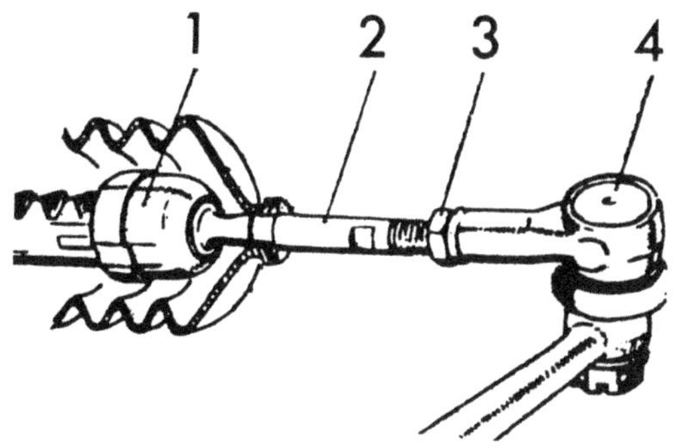


Fig 8.3 Trackrod and trackrod-end

*1 Inner ball joint*
*2 Trackrod*
*3 Locknut*
*4 Trackrod-end*

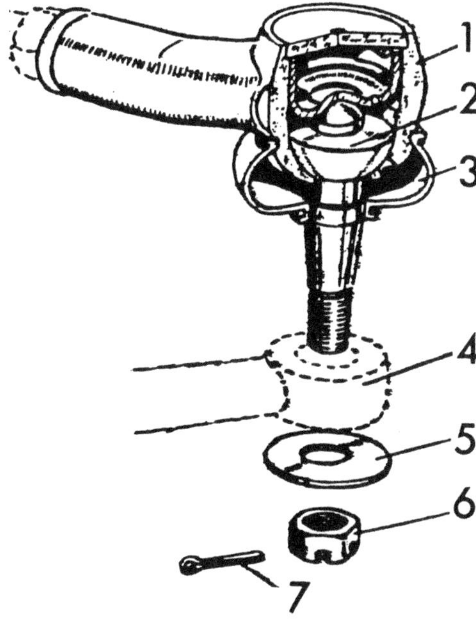


Fig 8.4 Cutaway view of a trackrod-end ball joint

*1 Casing*
*2 Ball*
*3 Rubber boot*
*5 Washer*
*6 Castellated nut*
*7 Split pin*

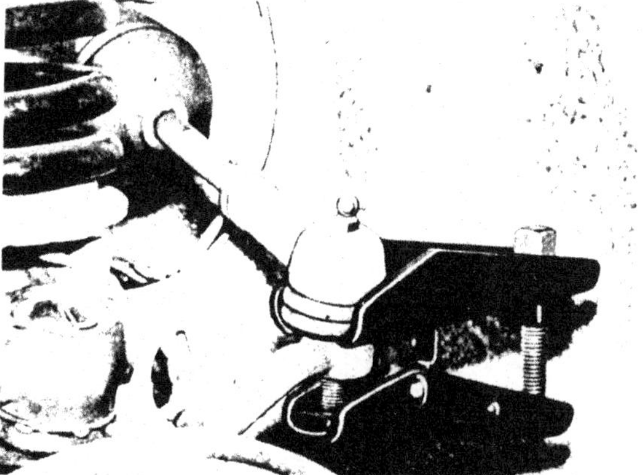

Fig 8.5 Separating a trackrod-end ball joint from the steering arm

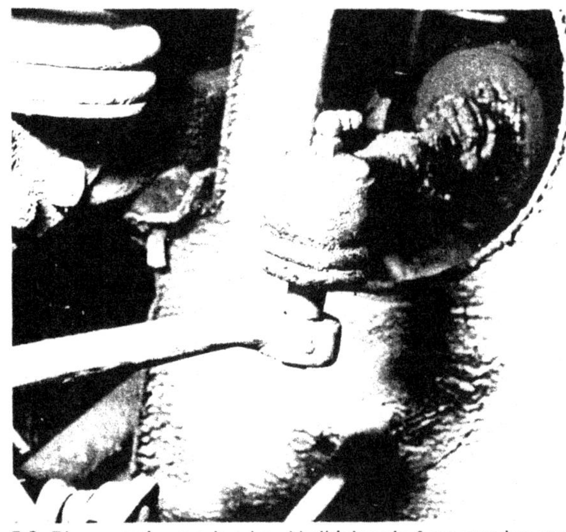
5.3 Disconnecting trackrod-end ball joint pin from steering arm

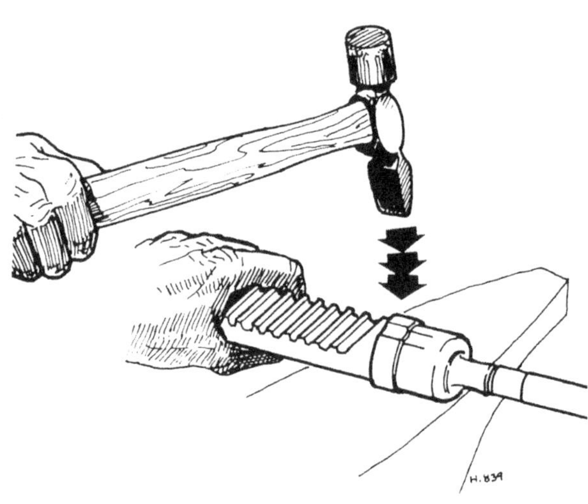

Fig 8.8 Securing an early type ball joint with a locking sleeve tab

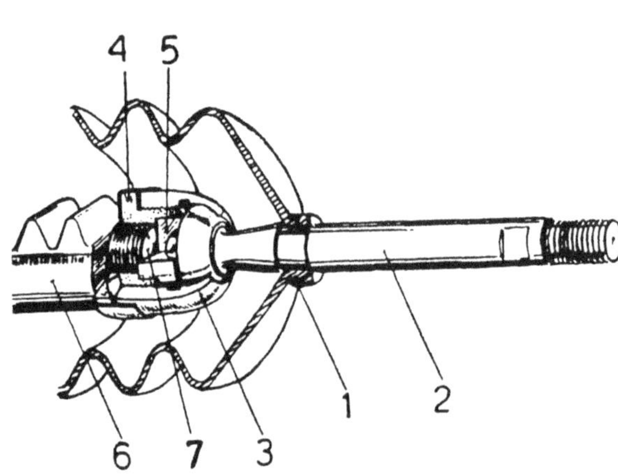

Fig 8.6 Cutaway view of early type ball joint

*1 Bellows clamp*
*2 Trackrod*
*3 Ball outer seat*
*4 Nut*
*5 Ball inner seat*
*6 Rack*
*7 Washer*

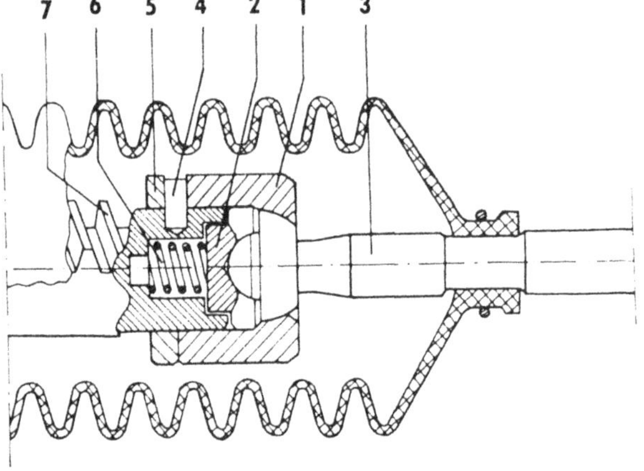

Fig 8.9 Sectional view of later type ball joint

*1 Ball outer seat*
*2 Ball inner seat*
*3 Trackrod*
*4 Locking pin*
*5 Locknut*
*6 Spring*
*7 Rack*

Fig 8.7 Removing an early type ball joint nut

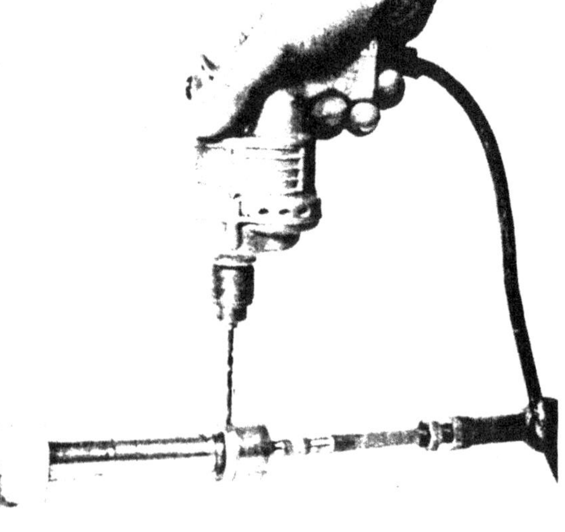
Fig 8.10 Drilling out a locking pin from a later type ball joint

disengage the flexible coupling clamp from the pinion splines.
11 Remove the panel which surrounds the steering gear pinion housing aperture on the engine rear bulkhead.
12 Unscrew and remove the four bolts which secure the steering gear in position.
13 Remove the rubber grommet from the engine rear bulkhead and on lhd vehicles lift the left-hand side of the steering gear forwards over the gearshift fork shaft until the pinion and pinion housing are clear of the bulkhead. On rhd vehicles the procedure is similar but lift the right-hand side forward.
14 The steering gear may now be passed out to the left or right (according to drive) between the wing and its support stay cross bar.
15 Installation is a reversal of removal but the following points must be observed.
16 Set the spokes of the steering wheel so that they are horizontal.
17 Set the rack at the centre of its travel and then offer the steering gear into position so that the splines of the pinion engage with the steering column clamp without disturbing the setting of the steering wheel or the rack.
18 Once the securing bolts on the steering gear have been tightened adjust the lengths of the trackrods so that the trackrod-end balljoints will just drop into the eyes of the steering arms (roadwheels in the 'straight-ahead' position). The lengths of the two trackrods should now be approximately equal.
19 Check that the steering wheel spokes are still horizontal and tighten the clamp pinch bolt on the steering column.
20 Check and adjust the wheel alignment (see Section 13).

### 6 Steering gear (early models) - servicing

1 Slacken the trackrod-end locknuts and remove the trackrod-ends. Some trackrods have flats milled into them so that a spanner can be used to hold them still or to rotate them during wheel alignment setting.
2 Release the clamps and remove the rubber bellows.
3 Withdraw the rack from one side of the housing until the inner balljoint assembly is exposed.
4 Bend up the tabs on the retaining cupped lockwasher and then unscrew the balljoint outer seat from the rack. A 'C' spanner will be required for this.
5 Dismantle the balljoint and retain the shims, inner balljoint seat and spring washer.
6 Repeat the dismantling procedure on the remaining balljoint at the opposite end of the rack.
7 Unscrew the locknut from the rack adjuster screw and remove the adjuster screw, spring and plunger.
8 Unscrew and remove the pinion bearing cover, shims and washer and withdraw the pinion.
9 The rack may now be withdrawn from the steering gear housing. If necessary the balljoint nuts may be unscrewed from each end of the rack by engaging a flat bar in their end slots. (Fig. 8.7)
10 The pinion spacer may only be removed from the housing after the rack has been withdrawn.
11 If the pinion or rack bushes require renewal they may be driven from the housing using a suitable drift. On some models, the rack bushes are retained with a pin.
12 Clean all components and check for wear and broken or chipped teeth. If the pinion teeth are worn, the pinion may be rotated through 180° (to present the unworn teeth to the rack) when reassembling it into the housing.
13 Reassembly is a reversal of dismantling but the following points must be observed. Lubricate all components with grease during reassembly. The pinion spacer must be fitted before the rack is inserted into its housing.
14 Adjust the pinion endfloat and rack radial play as described in Section 2.
15 Assemble and adjust each of the balljoints located at the rack-ends by inserting shims and tightening the outer seat complete with a new locking washer. When correctly shimmed, the balljoint should have no end play but should move in all directions freely when moved by hand pressure. A good test is to hold the steering gear vertically with the balljoint, trackrod and trackrod-end all fitted and at the top. At whatever angle the balljoint is set it should not move under the weight of the trackrod and trackrod-end which it supports.
16 When adjustment is correct, drive the locking tabs into the grooves of the balljoint nut and outer seat.
17 Refit the rubber bellows and clamps, leaving the smaller clamps slack pending checking the wheel alignment after installation.

### 7 Steering gear (later models) - servicing

1 Slacken the trackrod-end locknuts and remove the trackrod-ends.
2 Release the clamps and remove the rubber bellows. (Fig. 8.9)
3 Centre punch the lockpins which secure the balljoint outer seats and drill them out very carefully. (Fig. 8.10)
4 Unscrew and remove the outer seat using two 'C' spanners - one, to retain the locknut. (Fig. 8.11)
5 The remainder of the dismantling procedure is as described in the preceding Section (paragraphs 7 to 12).
6 The rack balljoint should be adjusted in a similar manner to that described in the preceding Section (paragraph 15) except that with the later joint, shims are not used.
7 When adjustment is correct and the locknut tightened, new holes must be drilled to accommodate new lock pins. These holes must be 3/16 in. (4.75 mm) diameter and 0.47 in. (12.0 mm) depth and located at least 45° from the spanner cut-out in the locknut.
8 Finally stake the lockpin in position at four equidistant points. (Fig. 8.12)

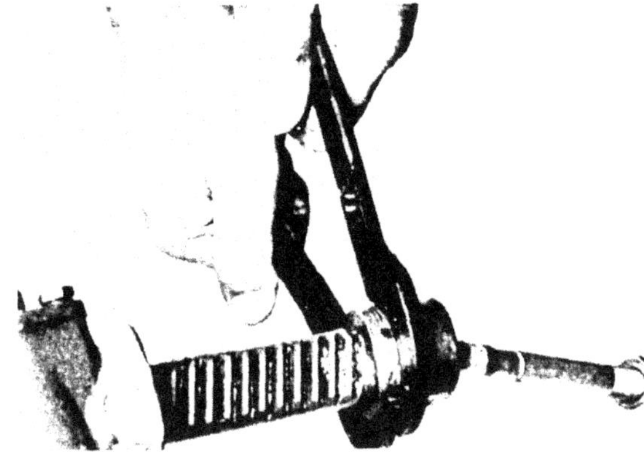

Fig 8.11 Unscrewing the ball outer seat from a later type ball joint (Sec 7)

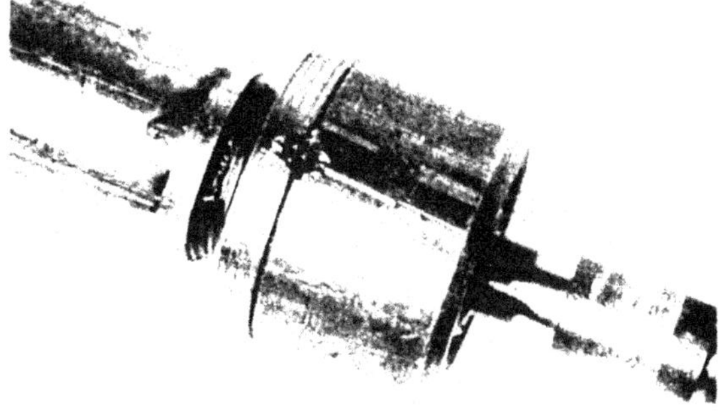

Fig 8.12 Locking pin correctly staked on a later type ball joint

9 Take particular care that all swarf from drilling is carefully removed and then refit the rubber bellows and clamps. Leave the smaller clip slack pending checking the wheel alignment (Section 13).

## 8 Steering wheel (up to and including 1967) - removal and refitting

1 Disconnect the horn switch lead at the connector under the facia panel.
2 Remove the horn button from the centre of the steering wheel by prising it with a knife blade.
3 Disconnect the horn lead fron the contact plate.
4 Unscrew the steering wheel retaining nut and remove it and the spring type lockwasher.
5 Pull the steering wheel from its splines. If it is stuck tight a puller must be used but take care not to damage the surface of the wheel during the operation.
6 Withdraw the direction indicator cancelling cam and washer from the steering shaft.
7 Refitting is a reversal of removal but check the clearance between the cancelling cam and the projection on the direction indicator switch. With the switch in neutral, the correct clearance should be 0.008 to 0.024 in. (0.2 to 0.6 mm). Adjust if necessary by inserting shims between the switch and the support shroud. The cancelling cam must be fitted so that its centre axis is in alignment with the centre axis of the switch housing with the roadwheels in the 'straight-ahead' position.

Fig 8.13 Prising out the horn button (up to and including 1967 models)

## 9 Steering wheel (1968 to 1970) - removal and refitting

1 Remove the safety-pad from the centre of the steering wheel by rotating the pad anticlockwise.
2 The remainder of the removal operations are as described in the preceding Section except that a horn button is not fitted.
3 Refitting is as described in the preceding Section except that the safety-pad underside should be smeared with grease before screwing it down. Screw it down until it becomes stiff to turn and then screw it down further until the cut-outs in the pad engage securely with the spokes of the steering wheel.

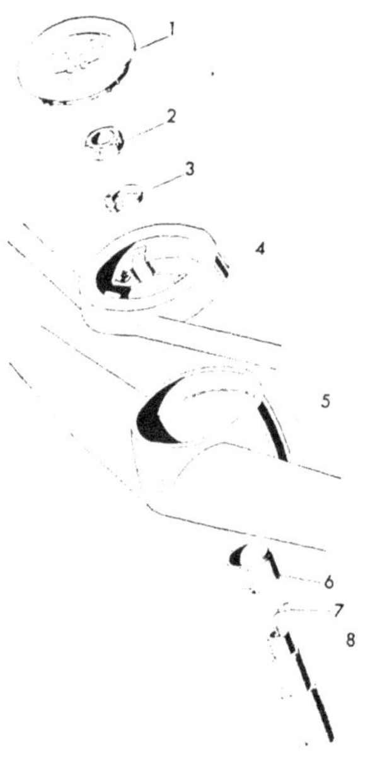


Fig. 8.14. Steering wheel and horn button (up to and including 1967 models)

*1 Horn button*
*2 Nut*
*3 Spring lockwasher*
*4 Horn ring*
*5 Steering wheel*
*6 Direction indicator cancelling cam*
*7 Horn switch lead*
*8 Steering column*

## 10 Steering wheel (1970 onwards) - removal and refitting

1 Remove the safety pad and horn contact from the steering wheel by unscrewing the four crosshead screws from the rear of the spokes.
2 Removal and refitting the steering wheel is then as described for earlier types in Section 8.

## 11 Steering column - removal and refitting

1 Remove the steering wheel, according to type as described in either Section 8, 9 or 10.
2 Unscrew and remove the pinch bolt from the clamp which secures the steering shaft to the pinion of the steering gear. (Fig. 8.17).
3 Unscrew and remove the nut from the upper end of the gearchange shaft universal joint and remove the taper pin.
4 Drive out the two locking pins from the screws which secure the steering column support shroud. The steering column, gearchange mechanism and support shroud can now be removed from the vehicle once the screws are released.
5 Draw the steering shaft out of its bushes which are in turn secured within rubber bushes located in the support shroud. These bushes, the cardboard spacer between them and the electrical leads may be removed if required.
6 Reassembly and refitting are reversals of dismantling and removal, but note that the rubber bushes in the support shroud are not interchangeable. The thinner bush is located at the top

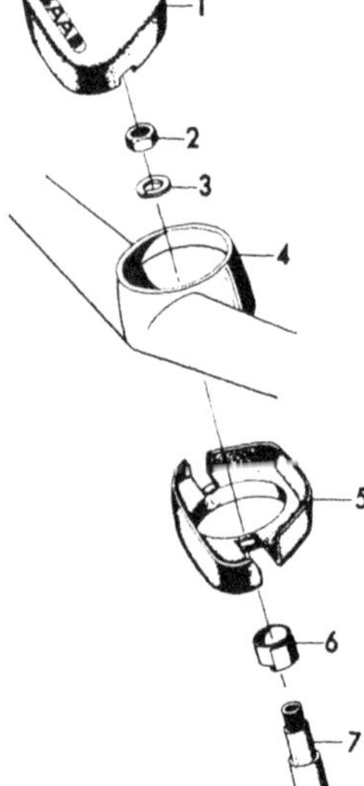


Fig. 8.15. Steering wheel and safety pad (1968 to 1970 models)

*1 Pad*
*2 Nut*
*3 Spring lockwasher*
*4 Steering wheel*
*5 Cover*
*6 Indicator cancelling cam*
*7 Steering column*

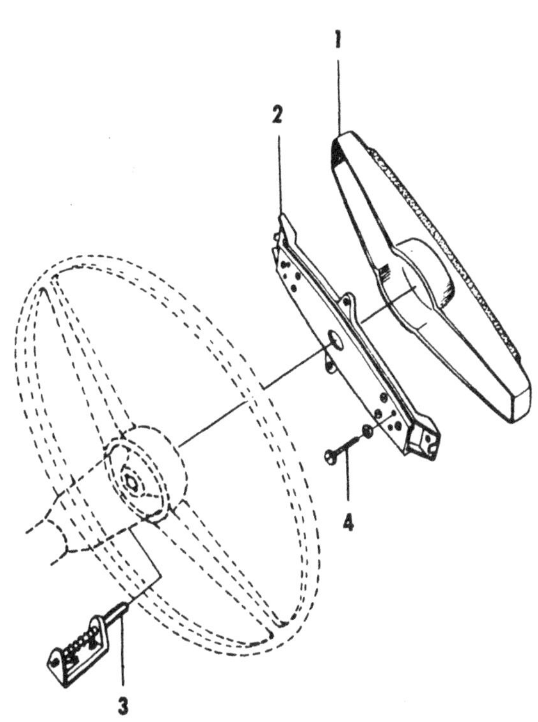


Fig 8.16 Steering wheel (1970 models onward)

*1 Safety pad and cover*
*2 Horn contact bar*
*3 Sliding contact*
*4 Retaining screws (four)*

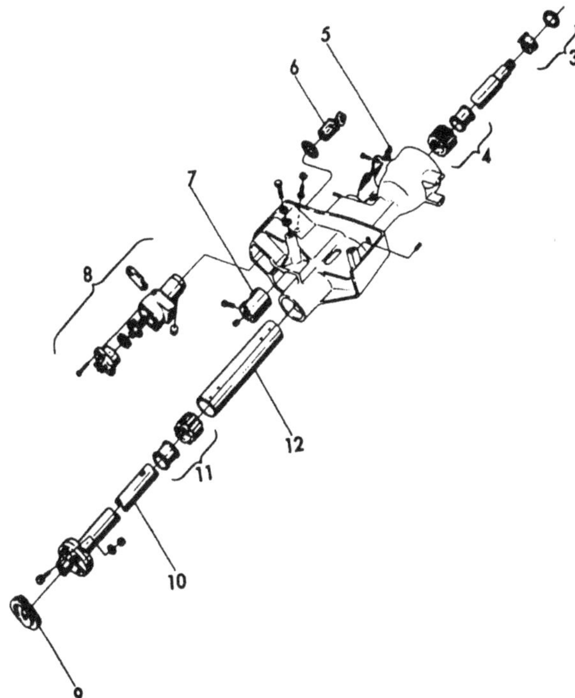


Fig 8.17 Exploded view of the steering column (lhd)

*3 Direction indicator cancelling cam*
*4 Upper bush assembly*
*5 Support shroud and cover*
*6 Ignition lock cylinder*
*7 Twist stop*
*8 Gear lever lock*
*9 Rubber grommet*
*10 Steering shaft*
*11 Lower bush assembly*
*12 Sleeve*

Fig 8.19 Collapsible type steering column fitted to late models

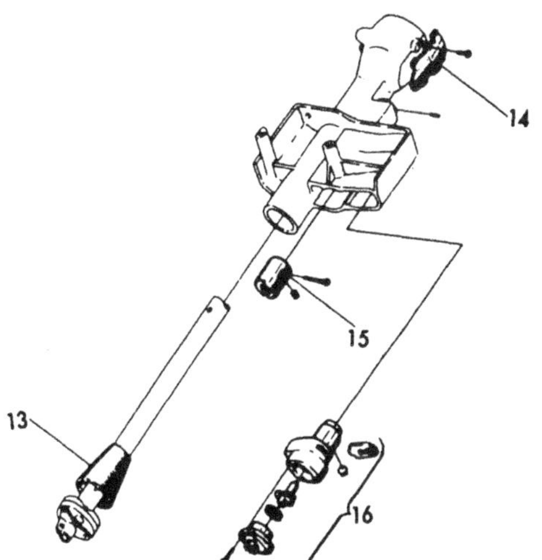


Fig 8.18 Component variations on rhd steering column

*13 Cone*
*14 Support shroud and cover*
*15 Twist stop*
*16 Gear lever lock*

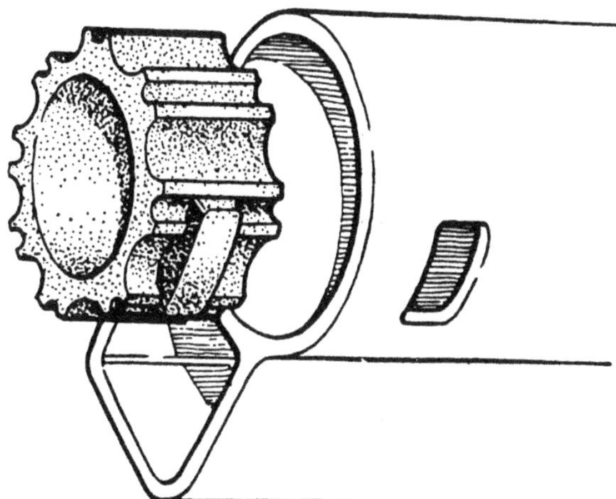

Fig 8.20 Steering column lower rubber bush

and both bushes are tapered and marked with an arrow on their positioning lugs which must point towards the steering wheel. (Fig.8.20)

7 For complete dismantling details for the gearchange mechanism and for adjustment procedure when the support shroud and gearchange linkage are reconnected, refer to Chapter 6.

8 Before refitting the steering wheel (spokes horizontal) check that the roadwheels are in the 'straight-ahead' position and that the direction indicator cancelling cam is correctly aligned with the switch in its neutral mode.

## 12 Combined gear lever/ignition lock - dismantling and reassembly

1 The removal, refitting and adjustment of the reverse gear twist stop is described in Chapter 6, Sections 16 and 17.

2 To remove the ignition lock, insert the key and turn it until it just passes the right-hand end of the "ASSA" mark. (Fig. 8.21)

3 With the key in this position, depress the lock catch-pin using a bent rod inserted through the underside of the steering column support shroud. (Figs. 8.22 and 8.23)

4 Withdraw the lock cylinder through the cylinder aperture.

5 Remove the single retaining screw and remove the gearlever lock.

6 With the cylinder removed, it is possible for the locking-pins inside to become displaced so that the key cannot be turned. If this happens, tap the key and cylinder (held with retaining plunger upwards) on a piece of wood.

7 If the lock has to be removed because the ignition key has been lost then the lock cylinder face will have to be drilled before the catch pin can be depressed. A hole 0.12 (3.0 mm) in diameter and 0.4 in. (10.0 mm) deep should be drilled as shown. (Fig. 8.24)

8 To reassemble, slide the lock plunger into the gearlever lock and then fit the lock into the steering column support shroud. (Fig. 8.25)

9 Insert the retaining screw and tighten it gently and then fit the lock plug.

10 Using a pair of flat-nosed pliers, turn the pin within the lock until it enters the groove in the end of the cylinder. Position the ignition key at the right-hand end of the "ASSA" mark and then depress the catch-pin. Fit the index plate so that it holds the catch pin depressed.

11 Now fit and locate the lock index plate against the retaining lug on the outside of the cylinder. Insert the cylinder/index plate assembly into the gearlever lock and tighten the gearlever lock retaining screw fully.

## 13 Front wheel alignment

1 Correct front wheel alignment is essential to ensure good steering and slow tyre wear. Before checking any of the steering suspension angles, make sure that the tyres are correctly inflated, that the front roadwheels are not buckled and that the steering linkage is in good order with no wear in the balljoints.

2 Wheel alignment includes the following angles:

*Camber,* which is the angle at which the front road wheels are set from the vertical when viewed from the front of the vehicle. Camber is regarded as positive when the roadwheel is tilted outwards at its top (Fig. 8.26).

*Castor,* is the angle between the steering axis and a vertical line when viewed from the sides of the vehicle. Castor is regarded as positive when the steering axis (a line drawn through the outer driveshaft carrier upper and lower balljoint centres) is inclined to the rear at the top (Fig. 8.27).

*Steering axis (or king-pin) inclination,* is the angle when viewed from the front of the vehicle, between vertical and an imaginary line drawn between the upper and lower suspension balljoints. (Fig. 8.28)

*Toe-in,* is the amount by which the distance between the front

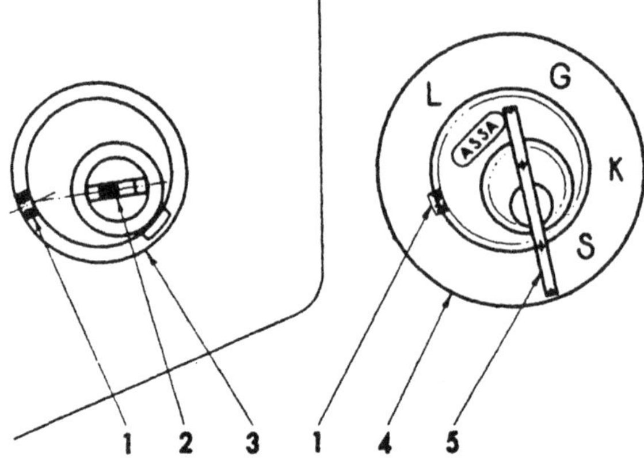


Fig 8.21 Position of key to permit removal or refitting of ignition lock

*1 Plunger*
*2 Position of locking pin*
*3 Gear lever lock*
*4 Index plate*
*5 Ignition key*

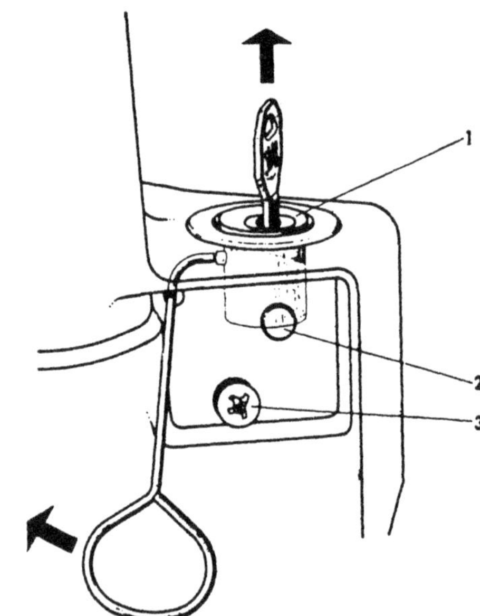


Fig 8.22 Removing ignition lock cylinder

*1 Cylinder*
*2 Lock-plug*
*3 Retaining screw*

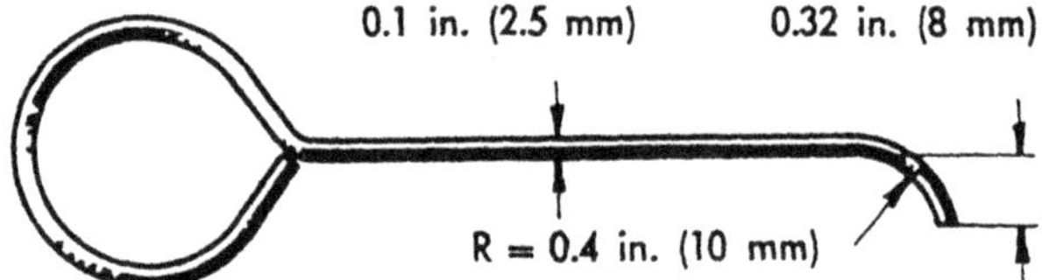


Fig 8.23 Dimensional diagram for lock plunger release tool

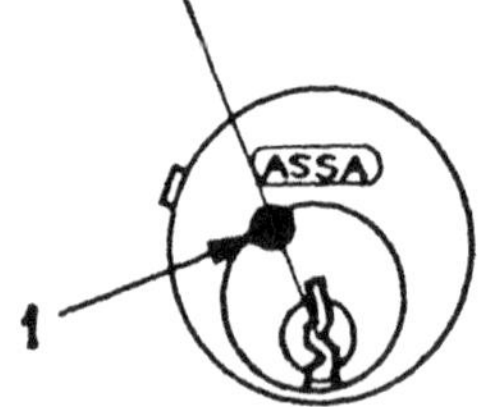


Fig 8.24 Drilling diagram for lock cylinder removal (key lost)

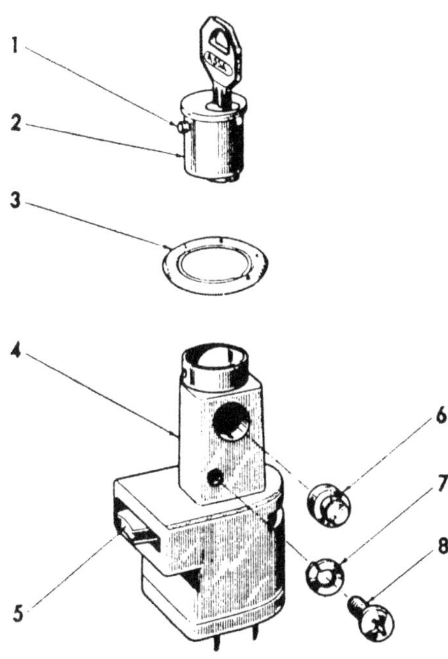


Fig 8.25 Components of gear lever/ignition lock

| | |
|---|---|
| *1 Plunger* | *5 Lock plunger* |
| *2 Cylinder* | *6 Lock plug* |
| *3 Index plate* | *7 Spring lock washer* |
| *4 Gear lever lock* | *8 Crosshead screw* |

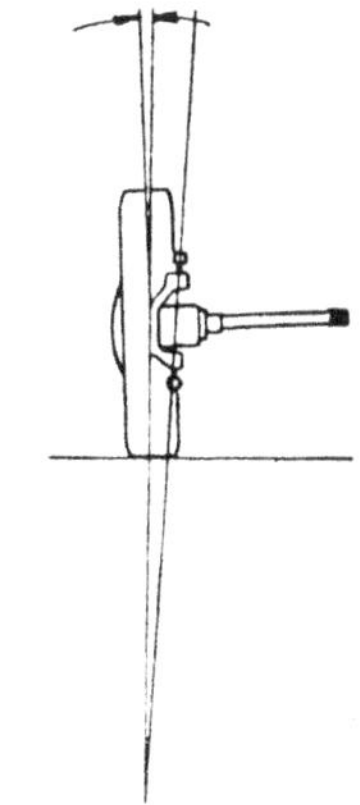

Fig 8.26 Camber angle (positive)

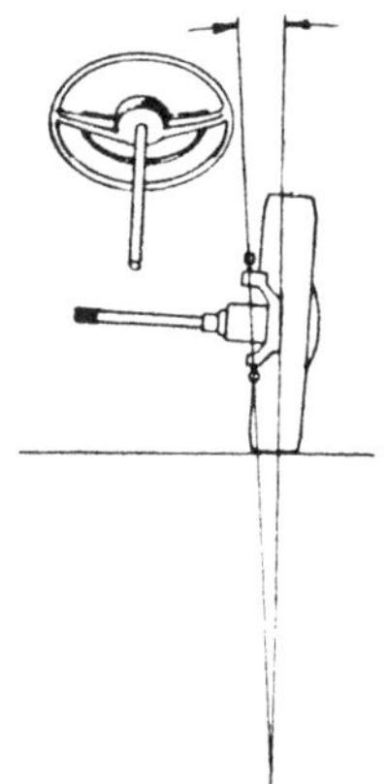

Fig 8.28 Steering axis inclination (king pin)

inside edges of the roadwheels (measured at hub height) is less than the distance measured in a similar manner between the rear inside edges of the wheels (Fig. 8.29).

3 It is preferable to have the steering angles checked on up-to-date setting equipment at a service station but the following adjustments can be carried out satisfactorily by the home mechanic.

4 The camber angle is varied by adding or removing shims at the rear of the suspension upper wishbone bearing brackets. The same number and thickness of shims must be fitted behind each bearing bracket on each side of the vehicle. The correct camber angle is three-quarters of a degree $\pm$ quarter of a degree and a very accurate plumb line cum protractor will have to be made up and located against the wheel rims to check this satisfactorily.

5 Variation of the camber angle also varies the steering axis inclination and provided the camber angle is correctly set, any deviation from the specified figure of $7^o \pm 1^o$ for steering axis inclination must be due to a distorted outer driveshaft carrier and it will have to be renewed.

6 The castor angle may be altered by removing or adding a shim from the rear of one of the suspension upper wishbone bearing brackets and adding or removing a shim of identical thickness at the opposite bearing bracket (on the same side of the vehicle). The correct castor angle is $2^o \pm \frac{1}{2}^o$ positive.

7 To check and adjust the toe-in, place the vehicle on level ground with the roadwheels in the 'straight-ahead' position. The vehicle should not be loaded or contain passengers.

8 Obtain or make up a tracking gauge. One may be easily made from a bar or tube, cranked to clear the sump and transmission unit, having a locknut and setscrew at one end.

9 With the gauge measure the distance between the two inner wheel rims at hub height at the fronts of the roadwheels.

10 Make a mark on the tyre wall and push or pull the vehicle so that the roadwheel moves through $180^o$ (half a turn). Measure the distance between the inner wheel rims at hub height at the rear of the roadwheels. This last measurement should be greater by between 0.0 and 0.08 in. (1.0 and 2.0 mm) to provide the correct front wheel toe-in.

11 If the toe-in is incorrect, slacken the locknuts on the trackrod-ends and also the smaller clamps on the steering gear rubber bellows and turn each trackrod an equal amount. If the steering gear, linkage or trackrod-ends have been removed or

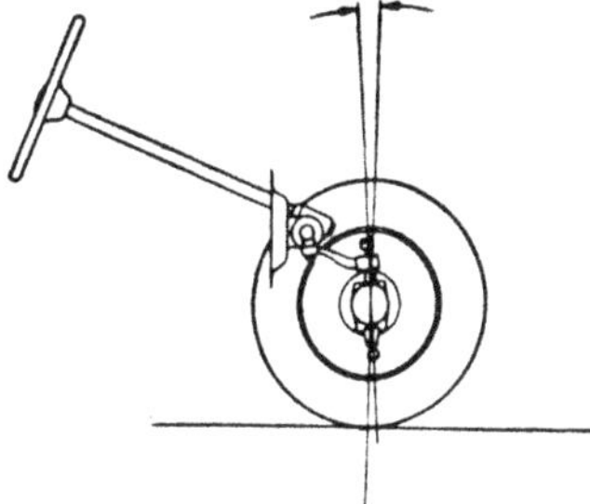

Fig 8.27 Castor angle (positive)

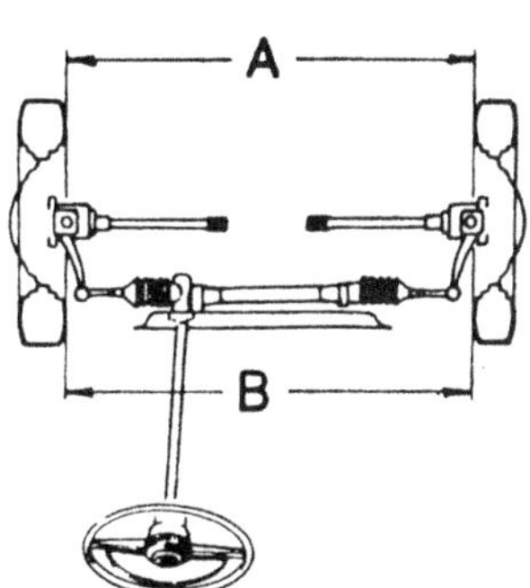


Fig 8.29 Front wheel toe-in diagram. Dimension A is less than B

Fig 8.30 Altering the length of a trackrod to adjust the toe-in

*1 Locknut* *2 Bellows small clamp*

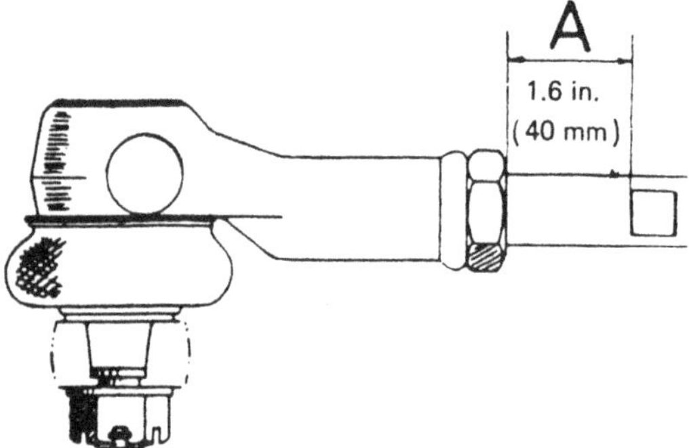


Fig 8.31 Trackrod setting diagram (early type)

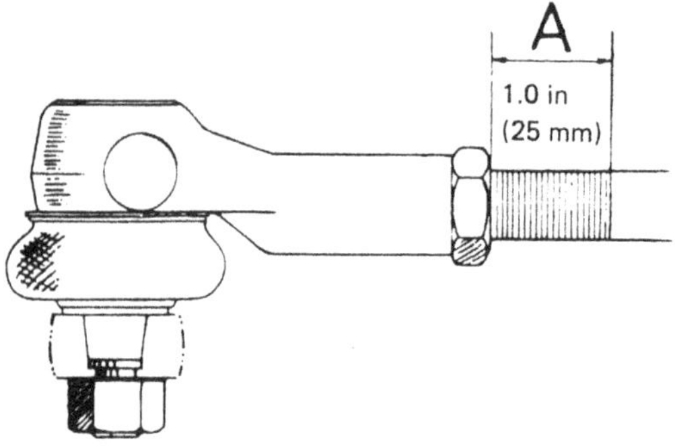


Fig 8.32 Trackrod setting diagram (later type)

dismantled and refitted or reassembled prior to checking the toe-in it is important that the two trackrods are set initially to equal lengths. This can be done by measuring the length of exposed thread on late type rods or, on early type rods, the distance between the spanner flat and the trackrod-end locknut. A pair of pipegrips will normally be needed to rotate the trackrod. (Figs. 8.31 and 8.32)

12 When the toe-in has been correctly adjusted, check that the length of exposed threads (or spanner flat to locknut) does not exceed that indicated neither does it vary between one trackrod and the other by more than 0.08 in. (2.0 mm), otherwise the steering components or gear are probably damaged or severely worn.

13 Finally tighten the locknuts holding the trackrod-ends in the centre of their arcs of travel. Tighten the bellows clamps.

14 Never attempt to check wheel alignment with the front roadwheels jacked-up or immediately after the vehicle has been lowered unless it has been driven a short distance to settle the suspension.

## 14 Fault diagnosis - steering

*Before diagnosing faults from this chart, check that any irregularities are not caused by:*

*1 Binding brakes*
*2 Incorrect 'mix' of radial or crossply tyres*
*3 Incorrect tyre pressures*
*4 Misalignment of bodyframe*

*Refer also to 'Fault diagnosis' – Chapter 7*

| Symptom | Reason/s | Remedy |
|---|---|---|
| Steering vague, car wanders | Steering angles incorrect | Check and adjust. |
| | Steering wheel free play excessive | Adjust or renew linkage and gear. |
| Steering stiff and heavy | Lack of lubrication in steering gear or suspension swivels | Grease. |
| | Front wheel toe-in incorrect | Check and adjust. |
| | Steering angles incorrect | Check and adjust. |
| | Steering gear pinion or rack adjustments too tight | Release and re-adjust. |
| | Steering column bent | Renew. |
| Wheel wobble and vibration | Excessive free play in steering gear or linkage | Adjust or renew as necessary. |

# Chapter 9 Rear suspension and hubs

Contents



Specifications

## Rear coil springs

| | |
|---|---|
| Number of coils ... ... ... ... ... ... ... ... | 9 |
| Free length ... ... ... ... ... ... ... ... | 13.5 in (342.0 mm) |
| Wire diameter: | |
| Saab 95 ... ... ... ... ... ... ... | 0.45 in (11.4 mm) |
| Saab 96 and Monte Carlo ... ... ... ... ... | 0.43 in (11.0 mm) |
| Identification: | |
| Saab 95 ... ... ... ... ... ... ... | White |
| Saab 96 and Monte Carlo ... ... ... ... ... | Yellow |

## Shock absorbers

| | |
|---|---|
| Type: | |
| Saab 95 ... ... ... ... ... ... ... | Hydraulic, lever |
| Saab 96 and Monte Carlo ... ... ... ... ... | Hydraulic telescopic |
| Stroke ... ... ... ... ... ... ... ... | 4¼ in (106.0 mm) |

## Wheels and tyres

These specifications are combined with those for the front wheels in Chapter 7.

## Torque wrench setting

| | lb ft | kg m |
|---|---|---|
| Rear hub nut ... ... ... ... ... ... ... | 65 | 9.0 |

## 1 General description

The rear suspension comprises a tubular axle attached to the bodyshell by three rubber bushed type bearings, coil type road springs and double acting hydraulic shock absorbers. The axle tube is also retained at its outer ends by rubber bushed links. At the extremities of the axle are located the stub axles upon which the combined hub/brake drums are supported on inner and outer ballraces.

The SAAB 95 Estate car is fitted with lever type shock absorbers whereas the SAAB 96 Saloon is fitted with telescopic type units, otherwise the suspension layout is identical. (Fig.9.1).

## 2 Rear hub/drum - removal, servicing and refitting

1 Jack-up the rear of the vehicle and support it securely on blocks or axle stands. Remove the road wheel.
2 With a screwdriver lever off the dust cap and remove the split pin, castellated nut and thrust washer. (Fig. 9.2) (photo).
3 Release the handbrake fully and then using a suitable puller remove the hub/drum assembly. (Fig. 9.3) (photo).
4 Prise out the oil seal from the hub inner recess and extract the inner bearing circlip.
5 If the bearings are to be renewed, extract the inner circlip

2.2 Removing dust cap from rear hub

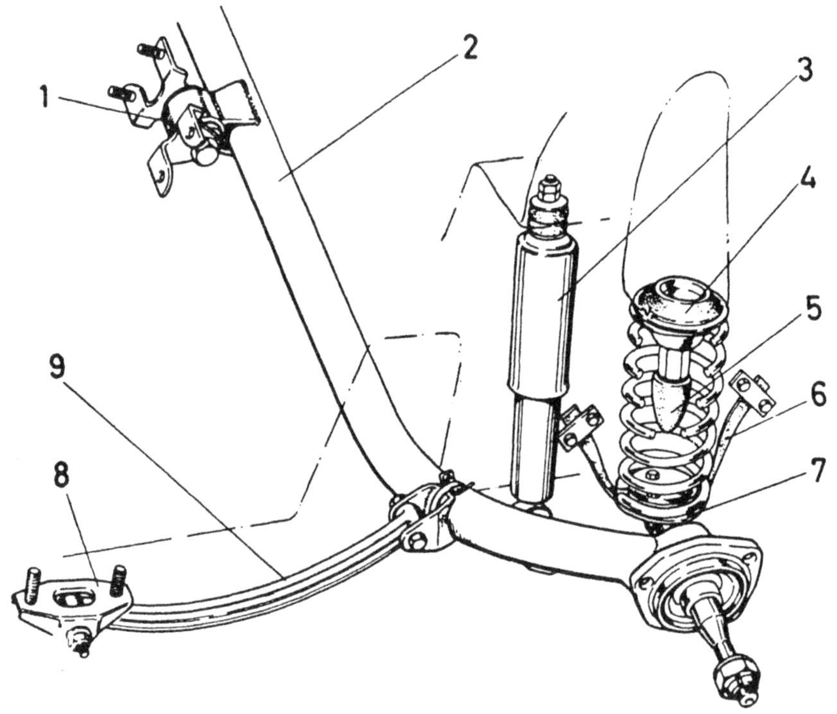


Fig 9.1 Rear suspension layout of SAAB 96 Saloon

*1 Centre bearing*
*2 Rear axle tube*
*3 Shock absorber*
*4 Spring upper seat*
*5 Rebound stop*
*6 Check strap*
*7 Spring lower seat*
*8 Side link body bracket*
*9 Side link*

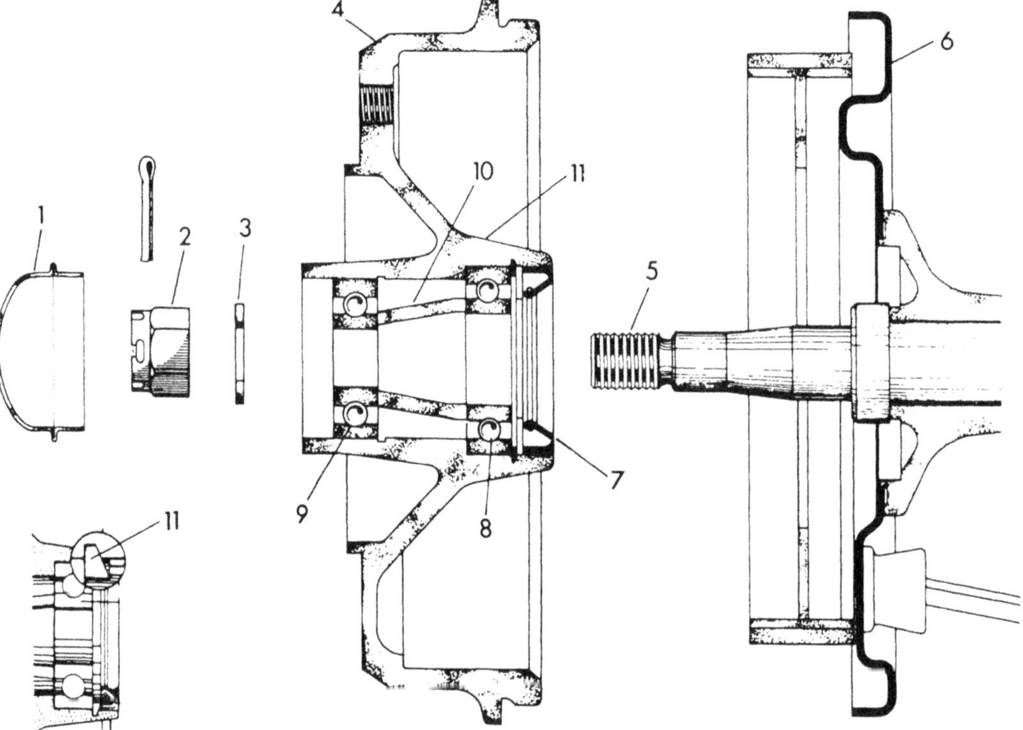


Fig 9.2 Sectional view of a rear hub

*1 Dust cap*
*2 Hub nut*
*3 Thrust washer*
*4 Hub/drum assembly*
*5 Stub axle*
*6 Brake backplate*
*7 Oil seal*
*8 Inner bearing*
*9 Outer bearing*
*10 Spacer sleeve*
*11 Bearing circlip (see inset for correct installation of circlip)*

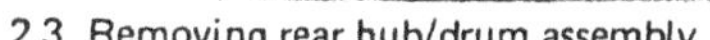

2.3 Removing rear hub/drum assembly

2.5 Rear hub bearing spacer/sleeve

2.9 Tightening a rear hub nut

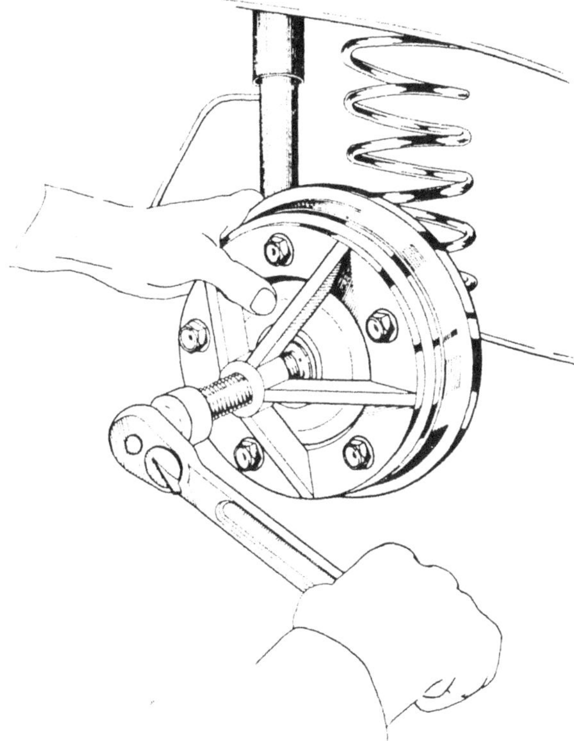

Fig 9.3 Using an extractor to remove a rear hub/drum assembly

and oil seal and drift the bearings from their seats. Extract the spacer/sleeve. Press, or drive in, the new ones with a piece of tubing which must locate on the bearing outer tracks only. Ensure the spacer is correctly located between the bearings (photo).

6 Half fill the space between the inner and outer bearings with wheel bearing grease, fit the circlip (chamfer towards oil seal) and then carefully tap in a new oil seal.

7 Examine the seal rubbing surface of the stub axle and if it is scored or rough, clean it up with very fine emery cloth.

8 Lightly grease the lips of the oil seal and then refit the hub/drum assembly taking care not to catch the lips of the oil seal on the stub axle screw threads.

9 Refit the thrust washer and tighten the castellated nut to a torque of 65 lb/ft (9.0 kg/m). Insert a new split pin. (photo)

10 Refit the dust cap and the road wheel and lower the jack.

11 Whenever the brake drums are removed to check or renew the linings, it is a good idea to wipe out the old grease from between the inner or outer races and repack half-full with fresh grease. On vehicles built up to 1970, repacking the rear wheel bearings must be carried out at 12000 miles (19000 km) intervals and this can of course be carried out without removing the oil seal from the hub.

## 3 Rear shock absorber (telescopic type) - removal, testing, refitting

1 Jack-up the rear of the vehicle and remove the roadwheel.

2 From inside the luggage boot unscrew the locknut and securing nut and remove the shock absorber mounting components. (Fig. 9.4).

3 Disconnect the shock absorber lower mounting from the rear axle tube and lift away the unit.

4 Grip the shock absrober vertically in a vice by means of its lower mounting eye and extend and compress the unit to the full extent of its travel about ten or twelve times. Unless stiff resistance is felt in both directions on every stroke, the shock absorber must be renewed.

5 Refitting is a reversal of removal but renew the rubber mounting components if they are compressed or the conical bushes have elongated holes. Do not overtighten the upper mounting nuts but tighten them so that about 1/8 in (3.2 mm) of thread is showing above the locknut.

## 4 Rear shock absorber (lever type)- removal, testing, refitting

1 Jack-up the rear of the vehicle and remove the roadwheel.

2 The shock absorber is accessible from below the wing and can be removed after disconnecting it from the axle tube and from its body mounting plate. (Fig. 9.5).

3 If necessary, the mounting plate can be unbolted from the body noting its insulating rubber bushes and spacers.

4 Testing the shock absorber should be carried out in a similar manner to that described for telescopic units in the preceding Section except that the lever will be operated.

5 As described in 'Routine Mantenance' the lever type shock absorber must be checked and the fluid lever topped up if necessary, every 12000 miles (19000 km). Brush all dirt and mud from around the filler plug before unscrewing it.

6 Refitting is a reversal of removal but renew any rubber bushes which may have worn or deteriorated.

## 5 Rear road spring - removal and refitting

1 Jack-up one side of the vehicle and support the body under the rear end of the sill.

2 Remove the roadwheel.

3 On SAAB 95 Estate car models, disconnect the shock absorber link from the axle tube.

4 Disconnect the check strap at its rear bracket and lower the

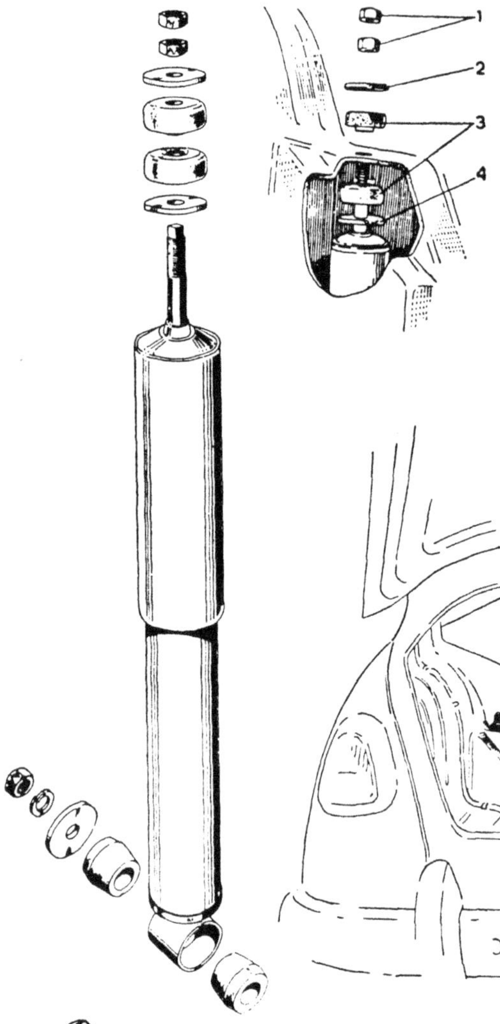

Fig 9.4 SAAB 96 shock absorber and mountings

*1 Securing nut and locknut*
*2 Washer*
*3 Rubber bushes*
*4 Washer*

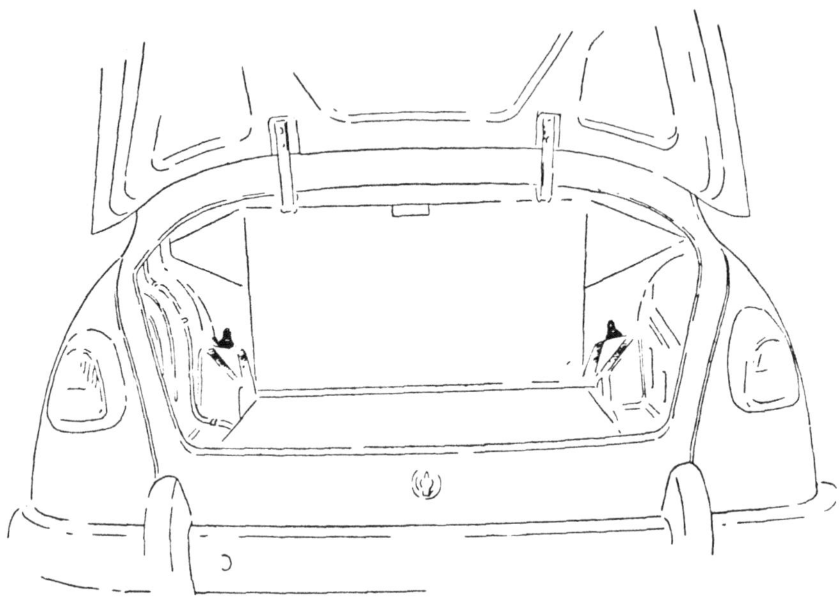

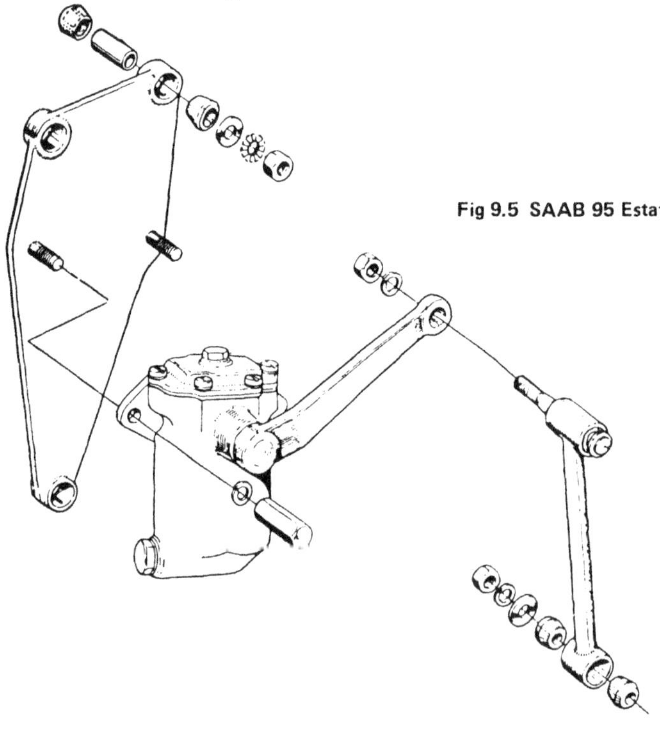

Fig 9.5 SAAB 95 Estate lever type shock absorber and mounting plate

rear axle assembly.

5 The coil spring may now be removed from its seats.

6 With the spring removed, the rubber rebound stop may be unscrewed if it requires renewal.

7 Check the condition of the check strap and renew it if it is showing signs of deterioration.

8 Commence refitting by screwing in the rebound stop complete with metal seating washer.

9 Locate the coil spring in its seat (unground end facing downwards and correctly positioned).

10 Refit the check strap so that each of its ends project 0.6 in (15.0 mm) beyond the securing brackets. (Fig. 9.7).

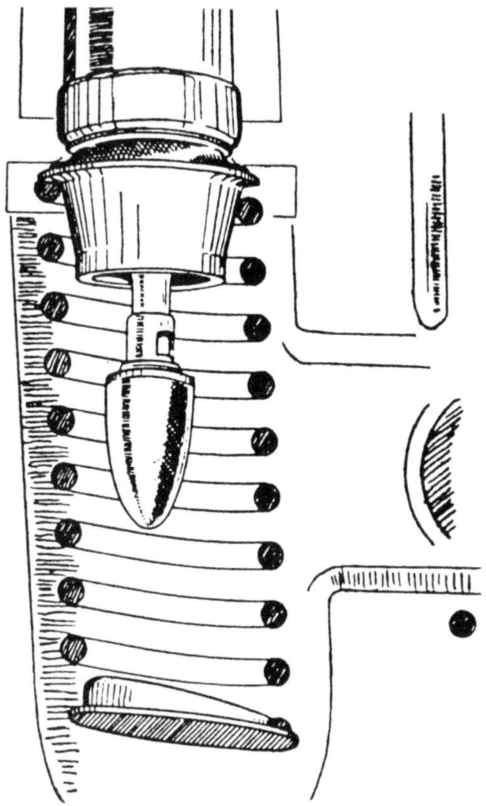

Fig 9.6 Sectional view of rear coil spring and seats and rebound stop

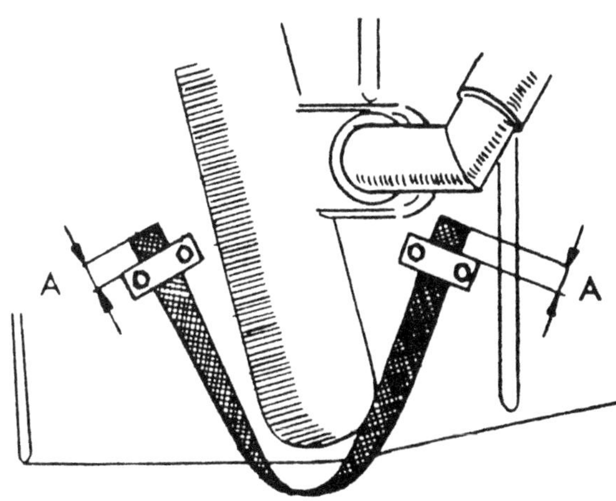


Fig 9.7 Check strap setting diagram

*A = 0.6 in (15.0 mm)*

## 6 Rear axle centre bearing bushes - renewal

1 Although it is easier to carry out this operation with the axle removed (see Section 8) it can be achieved with the axle still in position in the vehicle.

2 Jack-up the rear of the vehicle and support securely.

3 Disconnect the exhaust pipe and rear silencer bracket.

4 Unscrew and remove the bolt from the rear axle centre bearing. Disconnect the side links from the axle.

5 Pull the axle tube downwards and retain it in this position to provide access to the bearing by inserting two rods or bars between the axle and the floor pan to bridge the axle tunnel.

6 Using a long bolt with washers and tubular distance piece, extract the rubber bush. (Fig. 9.8).

7 Refit the new bush by the same method, applying a little brake fluid if necessary to facilitate the entry of the bush into the bearing housing.

8 Remove the temporary rods or bars and return the axle to its normal position. Reconnect the side links.

9 Refit the centre bearing bolt but do not tighten it at this stage.

10 Reconnect the exhaust pipe and silencer brackets.

11 Lower the vehicle to the ground and then tighten the centre bearing bolt fully.

## 7 Side link bushes - renewal

1 The bonded type rubber bushes are very tight in the bearing sleeves of the side links and it will probably be better to exchange the complete assemblies for new ones already bushed.

2 Where a press is available however, the sleeves at both ends of the side link should be heated and the bushes pressed out after the vehicle has been jacked-up and the side links removed (brackets accessible under rear seat) (Fig. 9.9).

3 Insert the new bushes by the same method.

4 The body brackets must be fitted to the side links so that

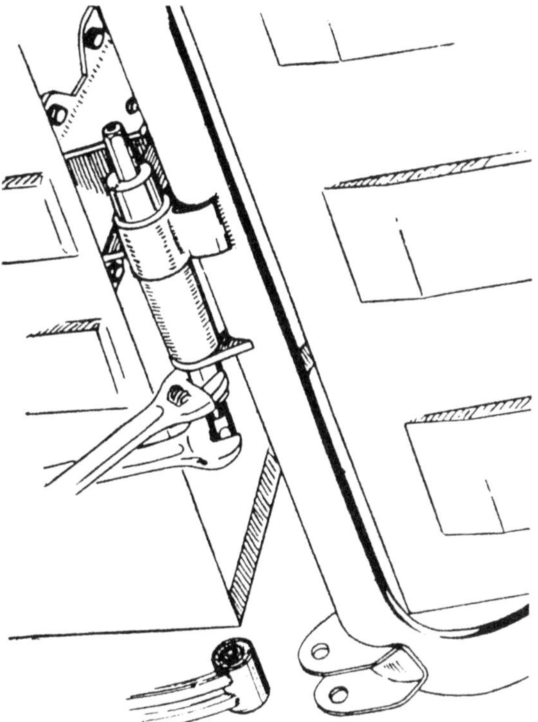

Fig 9.8 Drawing out the rubber bush from the rear axle centre bearing

when the bracket to link securing bolts are tightened, the correct bracket to link alignment is obtained (Fig. 9.10).

5 Bolt the side link brackets to the body and connect (but do not tighten at this stage) the links to the rear axle. Ensure that the connecting bolts enter from the outside in the direction of the centre bearing.

6 Lower the vehicle and fully tighten the side link to rear axle connecting bolts.

## 8 Rear axle assembly - removal and installation

1 Jack-up the rear of the vehicle and remove the roadwheels.

2 Disconnect the exhaust pipe and rear silencer brackets.

3 Disconnect the brake hoses at the body bracket unions (see Chapter 9). Disconnect the shock absorber lower mountings.

4 Remove the coil road springs as described in Section 5.

5 Support the axle tube on blocks or stands and disconnect the brake cable clamps from the axle also the cable clevises from the levers on the brake backplates.

6 Unbolt (4 bolts) the axle centre bearing bracket from the floor pan. (Fig 9.11)

7 Unbolt the side link brackets from the body floor pan, the nuts being accessible after removal of the rear seat cushion.

8 The rear axle assembly complete with hubs may now be removed from the vehicle.

9 Installation is a reversal of removal but reference must be made to the procedure for tightening the side link bolts (Section 7) also for fitting the check straps (Section 5).

10 When installation is complete, bleed the brakes as described in Chapter 9.

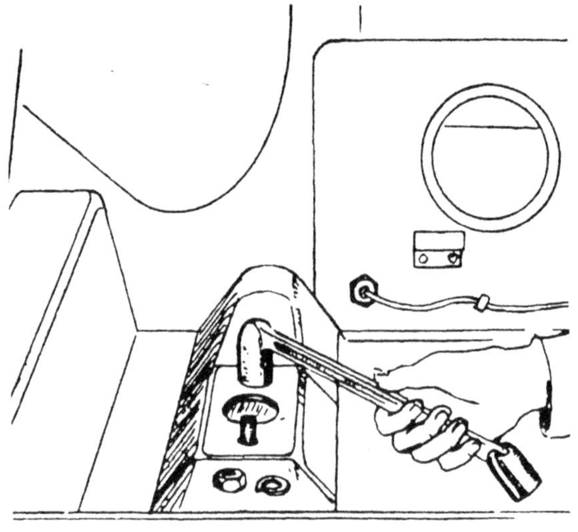

Fig 9.9 Unscrewing a side link mounting bracket from under the rear seat cushion

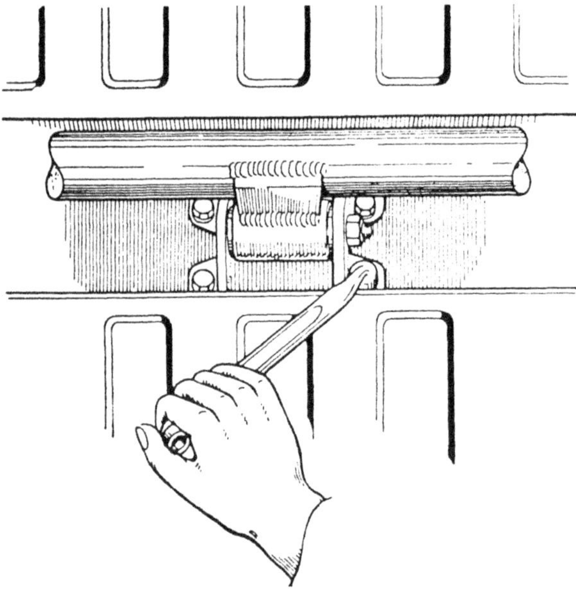

Fig 9.11 Unbolting the rear axle centre bearing bracket

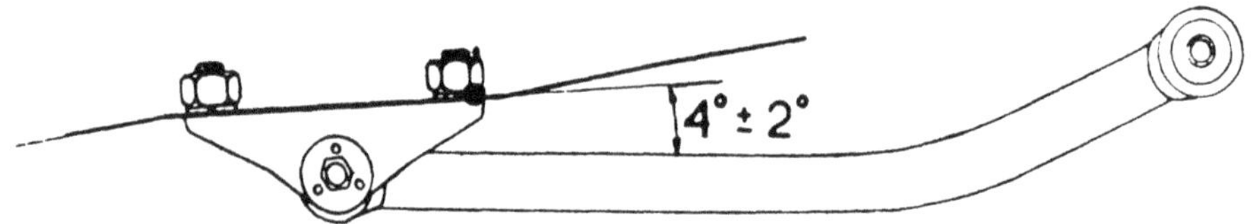


Fig 9.10 Side link to bracket alignment diagram

## 9 Fault diagnosis - rear suspension and hubs

| Symptom | Reason/s | Remedy |
|---|---|---|
| Vibration or knocking | Worn rear hub bearings | Renew. |
| | Loose hub nuts | Tighten to torque. |
| | Worn shock absorber bushes | Renew. |
| | Worn axle mounting bushes | Renew. |
| Uneven tyre wear on rear wheels | Worn hub bearings | Renew. |
| | Worn or loose axle mountings | Renew or tighten. |
| Rolling on corners or pitching | Weak road spring | Renew. |
| | Faulty shock absorber | Renew. |

# Chapter 10 Braking system

**Contents**



**Specifications**

| | |
|---|---|
| **System type** | Four wheel hydraulic, dual circuit disc front, drum rear. Servo assistance after 1969. Mechanically operated handbrake on rear wheels. |
| **Disc brakes** | |
| Disc diameter | 10½ in (266.70 mm) |
| Caliper piston diameter | 2 in (50.8 mm) |
| Minimum disc thickness (after regrinding) | 0.355 in (9.0 mm) |
| Maximum disc run-out | 0.08 in (0.2 mm) |
| **Drum brakes** | |
| Drum diameter | 8 in (203.2 mm) |
| Wheel cylinder diameter: | |
| Saab 96 and Monte Carlo | 5/8 in (15.9 mm) |
| Saab 95 (up to and including 1969) | ¾ in (19.1 mm) |
| Saab 95 (from 1970) | 5/8 in (15.9 mm) |
| Brake shoe dimensions | 8 in x 1½ in (203.2 x 38.1 mm) |
| Maximum drum internal diameter (after grinding) | 8.06 in (204.7 mm) |
| **Vacuum servo unit (lhd only)** | |
| 1969 to 70 | Lockheed 4258-193 |
| 1971 onwards | ATE T51-734 |

| **Torque wrench settings** | **lb ft** | **kg m** |
|---|---|---|
| Master cylinder non-return valves | 28 | 3.8 |
| Reservoir cover bolts | 6 | 0.7 |
| Rigid pipeline unions | 28 | 3.8 |

## 1 General description

The braking system is of four wheel type and comprises a dual hydraulic circuit, disc brakes on the front wheels and drum brakes on the rear. Lhd vehicles built after 1969 incorporate vacuum servo assistance. (Figs. 10.1/10.2).

The hydraulic circuits are somewhat unusual in that the individual circuit comprises a front brake and a diagonally opposite rear brake.

The handbrake is of cable type and operates on the two rear wheels only.

A brake warning switch and indicator lamp are fitted to advise the driver in the event of a leak in the hydraulic circuit.

The disc caliper units are of single piston, swing type incorporating wedge shaped friction pads.

## 2 Brakes - adjustment

1 The front disc brakes are self-adjusting and require no attention but the rear drum brake shoes must be adjusted

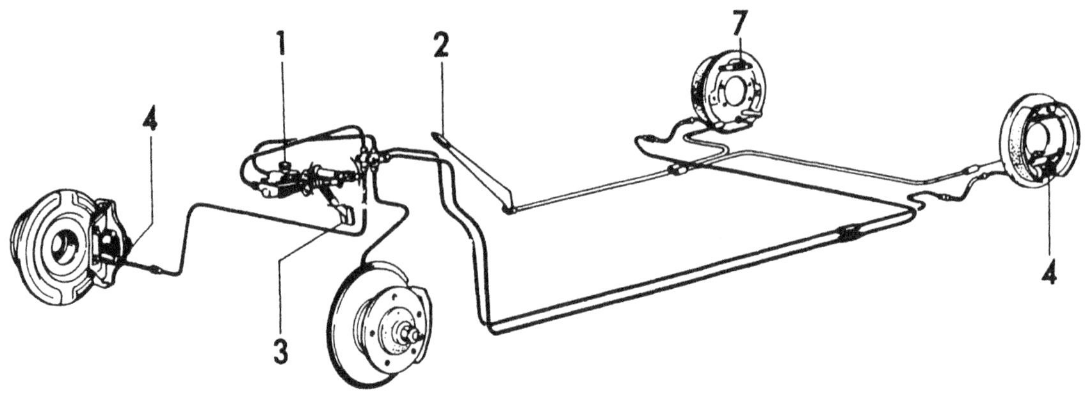


Fig 10.1 Dual hydraulic circuits (up to and including 1968)

*1 Master cylinder/reservoir*
*2 Handbrake lever*
*3 Brake pedal*
*4 Caliper unit*
*7 Rear shoe adjuster*

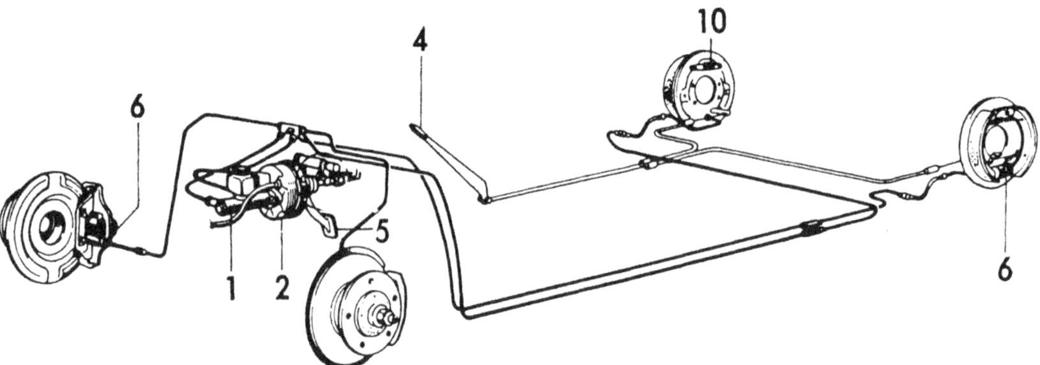


Fig 10.2 Dual hydraulic circuits (from 1969)

*1 Master cylinder/reservoir*
*2 Vacuum servo unit*
*4 Handbrake lever*
*5 Brake pedal*
*6 Caliper unit*
*10 Rear shoe adjuster*

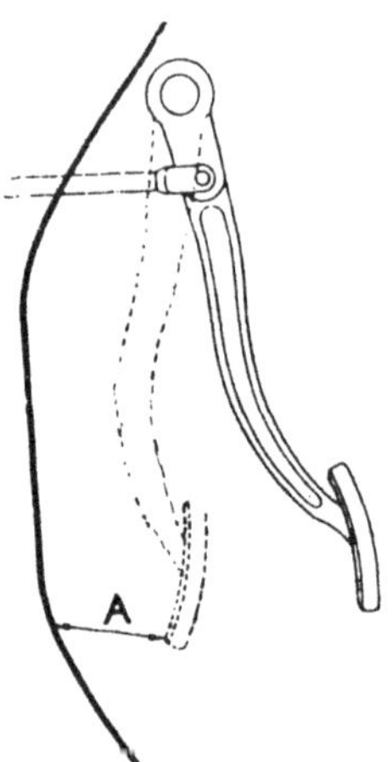


**Fig 10.3 Minimum pedal to toe-board dimension (up to and including 1968 models)**

*A = 2.6 in (65.0 mm) with pedal depressed*

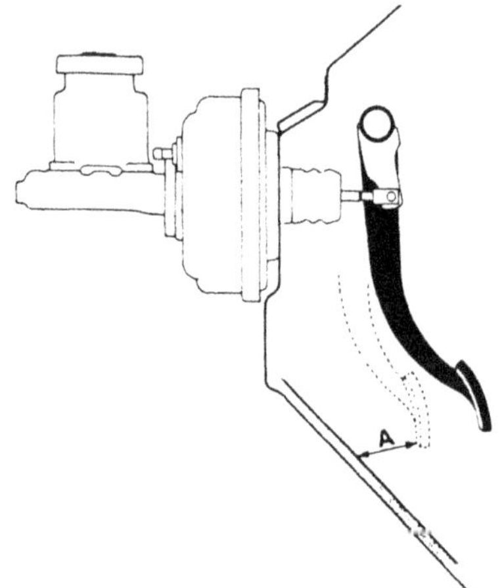


Fig 10.4 Minimum pedal to toe-board dimension (1969 onwards)

*A = 2.3 in (58.4 mm) with pedal depressed*

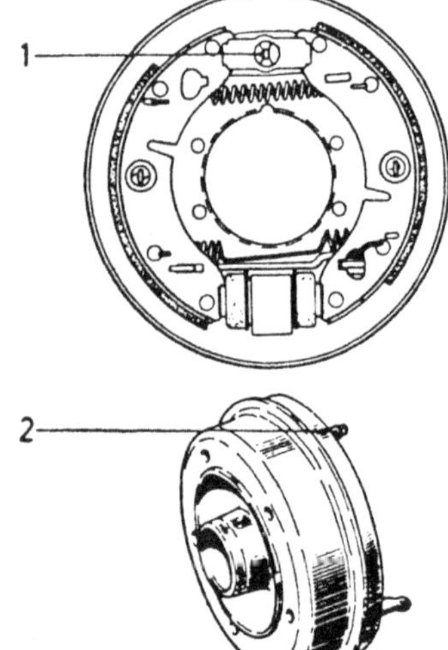


Fig 10.5 Rear brake adjuster (2) and adjuster wedge (1)

regularly and in any event when the brake pedal can be depressed further than the specified minimum distance from the toe-board. In the case of vehicles built after 1969 and equipped with vacuum servo, the pedal measurement must be carried out with the engine idling.

2 To adjust the brakes, jack-up the rear of the vehicle so that the roadwheels are clear of the ground.

3 Release the handbrake fully and depress the brake pedal hard, several times, to centralise the brake shoes.

4 Turn the square-headed adjuster on each of the rear brake backplates until the wheel is locked and then unscrew the adjuster one or two 'clicks' until the wheel rotates freely. (Fig 10.5).

5 When adjustment is complete, depress the brake pedal and then check that the rear wheels rotate freely. Failure to do so may indicate air in the hydraulic system (bleed as described in Section 12), a seized wheel cylinder or lack of free-movement at the brake pedal.

6 Free movement at the pedal should be between 0.12 and 0.24 in (3 to 6 mm) and can be adjusted by releasing the lock

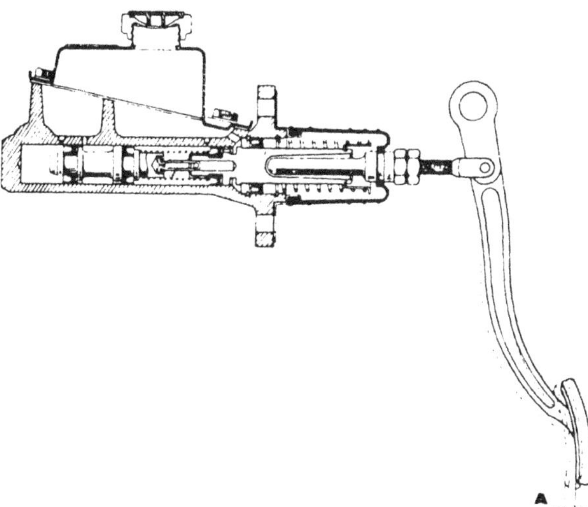


Fig 10.6 Brake pedal free movement adjustment diagram (master cylinders up to and including 1968)

*A = 0.012 to 0.24 in (3.0 to 6.0 mm)*

3.2 Disc pad cotter pins and spring clip

(this adjustment not applicable to 1969 onwards models) (Fig. 10.6).

7 Lower the vehicle and apply the handbrake.

## 3 Front disc brakes - inspection, removal and refitting of pads

1 Every 6000 miles (9600 km), jack-up the front of the vehicle, remove the roadwheels and inspect the thickness of the friction pads. When the pads have worn down to a minimum thickness of 0.06 in (1.5 mm) excluding the backing plate they must be renewed. Always renew the pads on both front wheels at the same time.

2 To remove the pads, flatten the ends of the cotter pins and withdraw them. (photo)

3 Detach the spring retaining clips and pull out the two friction pads from the caliper using a pair of pliers if necessary to grip them with. Retain the anti-squeak shims which are located at the rear of each pad. (photo)

4 Insert a flat bar into the caliper opening and press the piston fully into the housing, keeping the piston perfectly square in the cylinder during the process. This operation will cause the fluid level to rise in the master cylinder reservoir and some fluid should be syphoned out to prevent it overflowing.

5 Fit the new pads complete with shims correctly located, the spring clip and the new split pins supplied. In order to engage the lower split pin in the inner caliper hole the spring clip will have to be prised upwards with a screwdriver. Bend over the ends of the split pins.

6 Repeat the renewal operations on the opposite caliper and then depress the foot brake pedal several times to bring the new pads into contact with the disc.

7 Check and if necessary top-up the fluid level in the master cylinder reservoir.

## 4 Rear drum brakes - inspection, removal and refitting of shoes

1 Jack-up the rear of the vehicle and remove the roadwheel.

2 Using a bright torch or pencil light examine the thickness of the shoe linings through the inspection hole provided in the drum. If the friction material is thinner than 1/10 in (2.5 mm) the shoes must be renewed. Always renew the shoes in both rear brakes at the same time and exchange the shoes for factory reconditioned ones; do not reline them yourself as this is unlikely to prove satisfactory. (Fig. 10.8).

3 To remove the shoes, release the handbrake fully and unscrew the adjuster on the backplate as far as it will go.

4 Remove the hub/drum assembly as described in the preceding

3.3 Withdrawing a friction pad

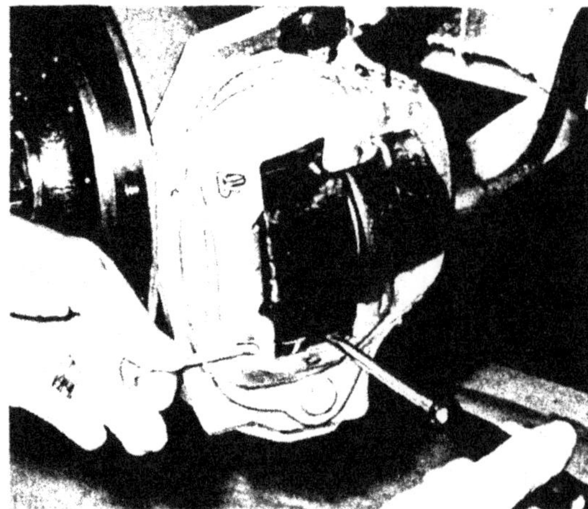

Fig 10.7 Fitting a disc pad cotter pin

Fig 10.8 Brake shoe inspection hole (1)

4.5 Rear brake assembly showing correct location of components

Chapter.

5 Before removing the shoes note carefully the position of the leading and trailing edges (lining does not extend to end of shoe at both ends), also mark the holes in which the return springs engage in the shoe web (photo).

6 Remove the shoe steady springs by gripping the cupped retainer with a pair of pliers and first depressing it and then turning it through 90° to release it. (Fig. 10.9).

7 Prise the tops of the brake shoes outwards against the action of the return spring and disengage the shoes from the slots in the

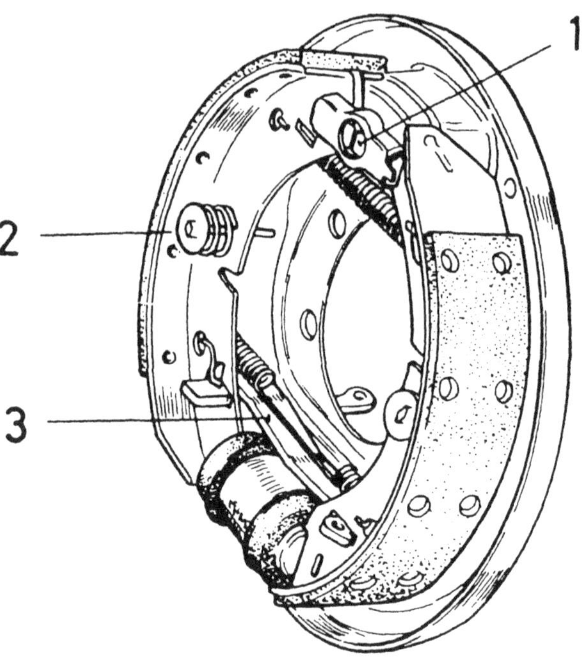


Fig 10.9 Rear brake components

*1 Adjuster wedge*
*2 Shoe steady*
*3 Handbrake link*

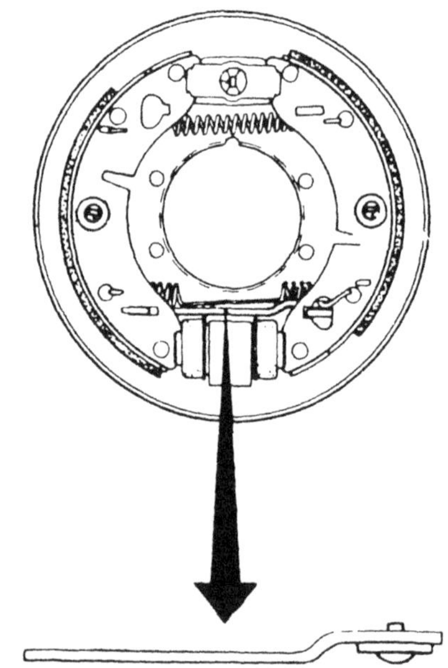

Fig 10.10 Correct location of lower shoe return spring and handbrake link (arrowed)

adjuster cams.

8 Prise the bottom ends of the shoes from the slots in the wheel cylinder pistons at the same time disengaging the shoes from the handbrake lever.

9 Place the brake shoe assembly on the bench and remove the return springs and handbrake lever and its spring.

10 An elastic band or a piece of wire should be placed round the wheel cylinder to retain the pistons in position while the brake shoes are removed. **Do not touch the brake pedal while the drum is off.**

11 Apply a trace of brake grease to the slots in which the ends of the shoes engage, also to the shoe sliding surfaces on the backplate.

12 To refit the shoes, lay them out on the bench so that their leading and trailing ends are correctly positioned.

13 Engage the shoe return springs in their correct holes.

14 Maintaining slight outwards pressure on the shoes to hold the return springs in position, locate the shoe (nearer the front of the vehicle) in the adjuster and piston slots, having first removed the rubber band or wire. Engage the handbrake lever in the rectangular slot in the shoe web.

15 Engage the handbrake lever in the hole in the opposing shoe making sure that the return spring is correctly located to exert downwards pressure on the lever. (Fig 10.10)

16 Prise the shoe into the slots in the adjuster cam and wheel cylinder piston.

17 Refit the hub/drum assembly and adjust the brakes as described in Section 2.

18 Fit the roadwheel and lower the jack.

## 5 Master cylinder (up to and including 1968 models) - removal, servicing and refitting

1 The master cylinder is of tandem type and should be dismantled and reassembled for the following causes: (Fig 10.11).

(a) leakage of fluid
(b) faulty operation (see Fault Diagnosis - Section 22)
(c) at three yearly intervals (35000 miles - 56000 km) for the renewal of rubber seals.

2 Disconnect the fluid outlet pipes at the master cylinder unions. Plug the fluid lines to prevent ingress of dirt.

3 Disconnect the pushrod from the clevis fork on the brake pedal.

4 Unscrew the master cylinder flange securing nut which is accessible from within the engine compartment and the upper

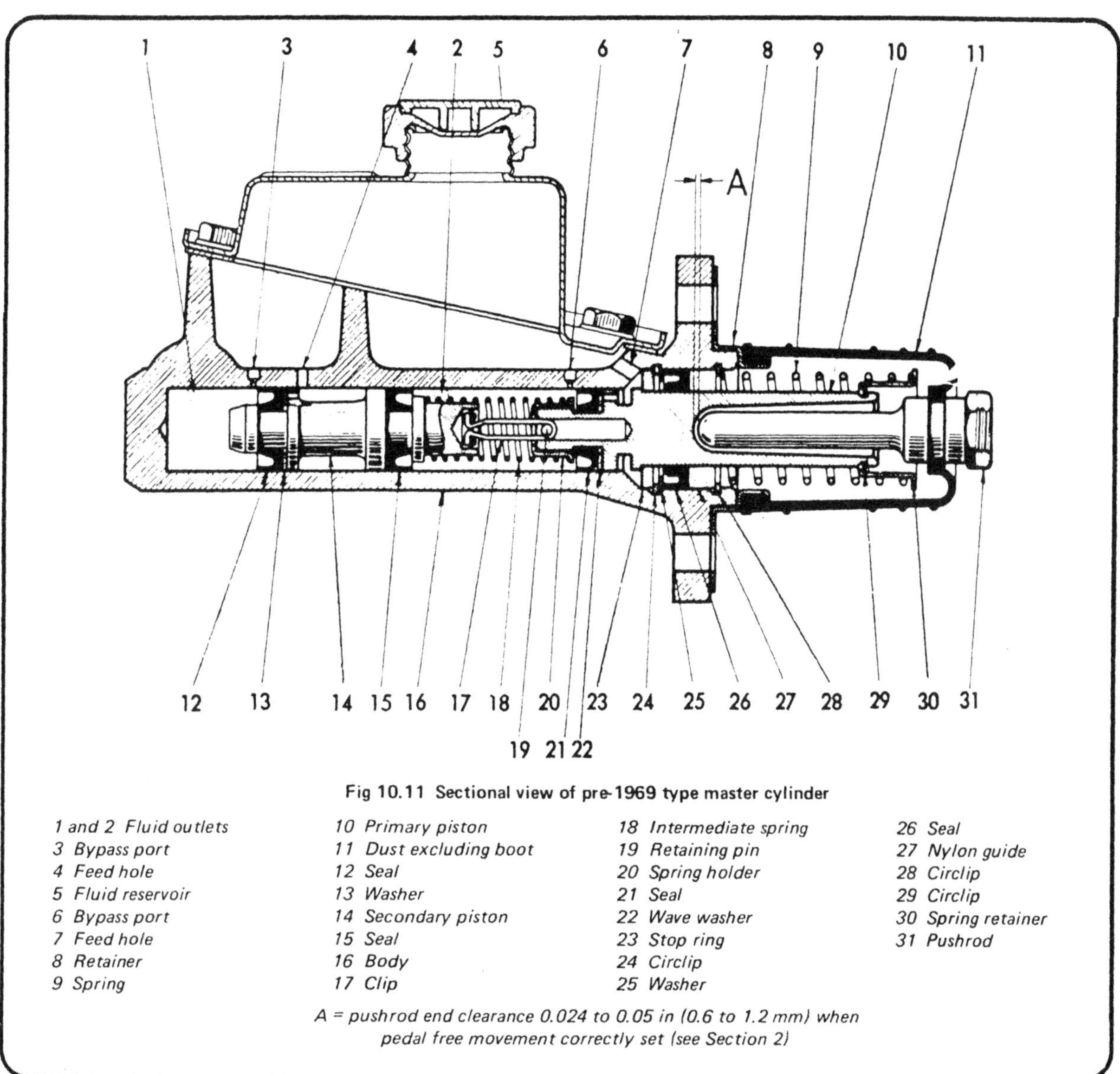


Fig 10.11 Sectional view of pre-1969 type master cylinder

*1 and 2 Fluid outlets*
*3 Bypass port*
*4 Feed hole*
*5 Fluid reservoir*
*6 Bypass port*
*7 Feed hole*
*8 Retainer*
*9 Spring*
*10 Primary piston*
*11 Dust excluding boot*
*12 Seal*
*13 Washer*
*14 Secondary piston*
*15 Seal*
*16 Body*
*17 Clip*
*18 Intermediate spring*
*19 Retaining pin*
*20 Spring holder*
*21 Seal*
*22 Wave washer*
*23 Stop ring*
*24 Circlip*
*25 Washer*
*26 Seal*
*27 Nylon guide*
*28 Circlip*
*29 Circlip*
*30 Spring retainer*
*31 Pushrod*

*A = pushrod end clearance 0.024 to 0.05 in (0.6 to 1.2 mm) when pedal free movement correctly set (see Section 2)*

bolt which is accessible from within the vehicle. Withdraw the master cylinder.
5 Clean the exterior of the unit and then pull off the rubber bellows (11) (Fig. 10.11) and retainer (8) and withdraw the pushrod (31).
6 Depress the spring retainer (30) and using a small screwdriver, extract the clip (29).
7 Remove the circlip (28) the nylon bearing (27) the seal (26) and washer (25)
8 Remove the circlip (24).
9 Compress the intermediate spring (18) together with its holder (20) and drive out the retaining pin (19) using a suitable drift. The pistons (10 and 14) will now be released to permit their withdrawal after removal of the spring and holder. The clip (17) on the secondary piston cannot be detached.
10 Extract the non-return valves, making sure that the spring clip (44) is not distorted when removing it from the valve body. (Fig 10.12).
11 Remove the brake fluid reservoir cover (6 bolts) and peel off the gasket.
12 With the master cylinder now completely dismantled wash all components in methylated spirit or clean brake fluid. Examine the surfaces of the pistons or cylinder bores for scoring or

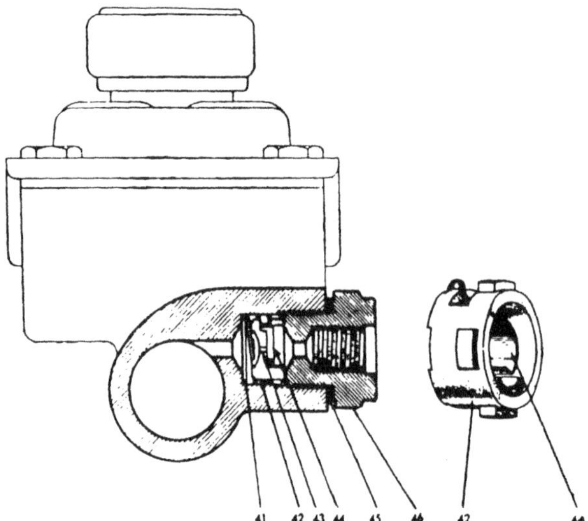


Fig 10.12 Non-return valve (master cylinder pre-1969)

*41 Spring*
*42 Valve body*
*43 Equalizing hole*
*44 Spring clip*
*45 Gasket*
*46 Union nut*

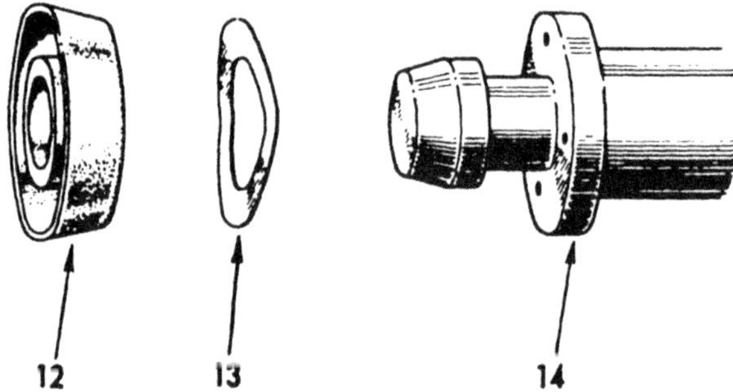


Fig 10.13 Fitting diagram for secondary piston components (master cylinder pre-1969)

*12 Seal*
*13 Wave washer*
*14 Secondary piston*

'bright' wear areas. Where these are evident, renew the master cylinder complete.
13 Obtain a repair kit which will contain all the necessary components and seals.
14 Reassembly is a reversal of dismantling but dip each component in clean hydraulic fluid before fitting. Use the fingers only to manipulate the new seals into position and check that their lips and chamfers are correctly orientated. (Fig 10.13)
15 Grease the rounded end of the pushrod with silicone grease before inserting it into the primary piston.
16 Tighten the non-return valves to a torque of 28 lb/ft (3.8 kg/m).
17 Use a new gasket and tighten the reservoir cover bolts to a torque of 6 lb/ft (0.7 kg/m).
18 Install the master cylinder and connect the pushrod to the brake pedal.
19 Connect the fluid lines to the master cylinder outlets and tighten the unions to a torque of 28 lb/ft (3.8 kg/m).
20 Refill the fluid reservoir with clean hydraulic fluid which has been stored in an airtight container and has remained unshaken for at least 24 hours.
21 Bleed the hydraulic system (see Section 12).

## 6 Master cylinder (1969 to 1970 models) - removal, servicing, and refitting

1 Refer to paragraph one of the preceding Section.
2 Remove the protective shield from the steering column and disconnect the pushrod from the brake pedal.
3 Unscrew the unions at the fluid outlet pipes on the master cylinder body.
4 Unscrew and remove the two nuts which secure the master cylinder to the vacuum servo unit and withdraw the master cylinder leaving the servo unit in position.
5 If the complete master cylinder/vacuum servo unit is to be removed as one assembly, do not remove the master cylinder retaining nuts but disconnect the vacuum hose and unscrew the four servo unit securing nuts which are accessible from within the vehicle interior.
6 Dismantling, inspection and reassembly is very similar to the procedures described in the preceding Section except for detail differences in component design.
7 Refitting is a reversal of removal. On completion of installation, bleed the hydraulic system (Section 12).

## 7 Master cylinder (1971 models onwards) - removal, servicing and refitting

1 The removal procedure is the same as described in paragraphs 2 to 5 of Section 6. Also remove the air cleaner.
2 Commence dismantling by removing the circlip (10) (Fig. 10.17) and then unscrew the stop screw (13).
3 Pull out the primary piston (12) and spring(5) and seal.
4 Pull out the secondary piston (4) with spring and seal.
5 To remove and refit the seal (6) on the primary piston, the screw (9) must be unscrewed and the spring, spring retainer, spacer and washer removed.
6 Carry out the operations described in paragraphs 12 to 15 of Section 5.
7 Refit the unit to the vehicle, connect the fluid pipes, the vacuum hose and fit the air cleaner. Bleed the hydraulic system as described in Section 12.

## 8 Caliper unit - removal, servicing and refitting

1 Remove the friction pads as described in Section 3.
2 Bend back the tab washers and unscrew and remove the two bolts which secure the caliper unit to the outer driveshaft carrier. Draw the caliper unit off the brake disc (photo).
3 Unscrew the flexible hose ¼ of a turn at its connection with

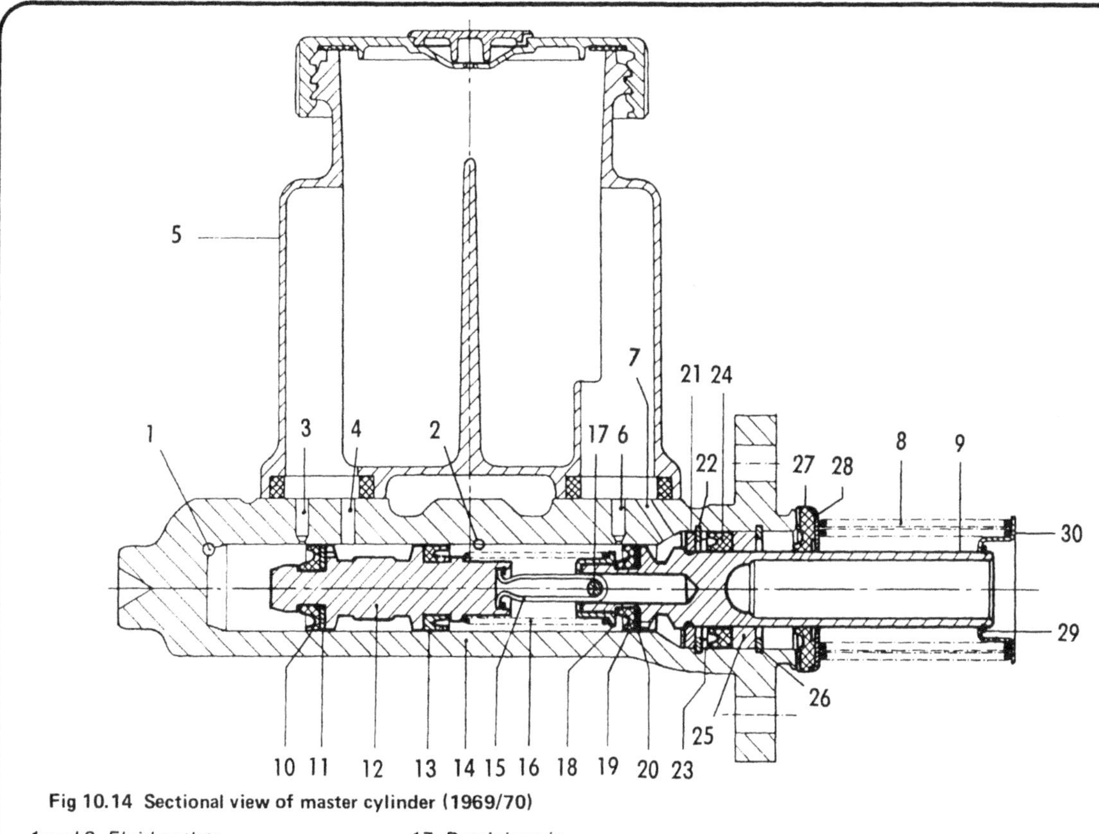


**Fig 10.14 Sectional view of master cylinder (1969/70)**

*1 and 2 Fluid outlets*
*3 Bypass port*
*4 Feed hole*
*5 Fluid reservoir*
*6 Bypass port*
*7 Feed hole*
*8 Spring*
*9 Primary piston*
*10 Seal*
*11 Washer*
*12 Secondary piston*
*13 Seal*
*14 Body*
*15 Clip*
*16 Spring*
*17 Retaining pin*
*18 Spring holder*
*19 Seal*
*20 Washer*
*21 Stop ring*
*22 Circlip*
*23 Washer*
*24 Seal*
*25 Nylon guide*
*26 Circlip*
*27 Gasket*
*28 Washer*
*29 Circlip*
*30 Spring retainer*

**Fig 10.15 Exploded view of master cylinder (1969/70)**

*1 Reservoir*
*2 Non-return valve*
*3 Body*
*4 Seal*
*5 Washer*
*6 Secondary piston*
*7 Clip*
*8 Retaining pin*
*9 Seal*
*10 Spring*
*11 Spring holder*
*12 Seal*
*13 Washer*
*14 Stop ring*
*15 Circlip*
*16 Washer*
*17 Seal*
*18 Nylon guide*
*19 Circlip*
*20 Gasket*
*21 Washer*
*22 Primary piston*
*23 Spring*
*24 Spring*
*25 Spring holder*
*26 Clip*

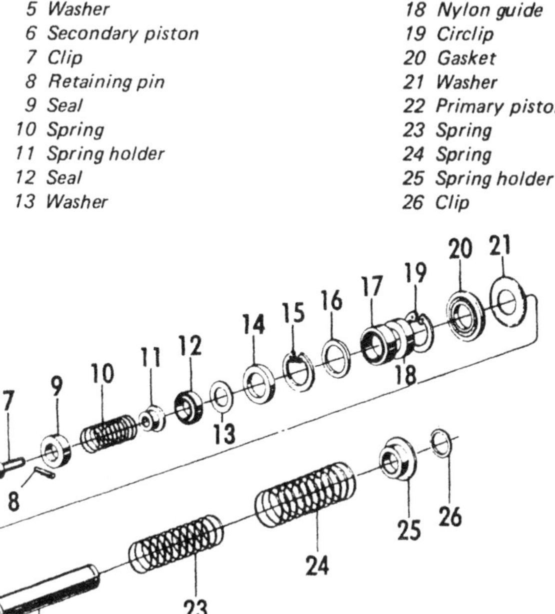

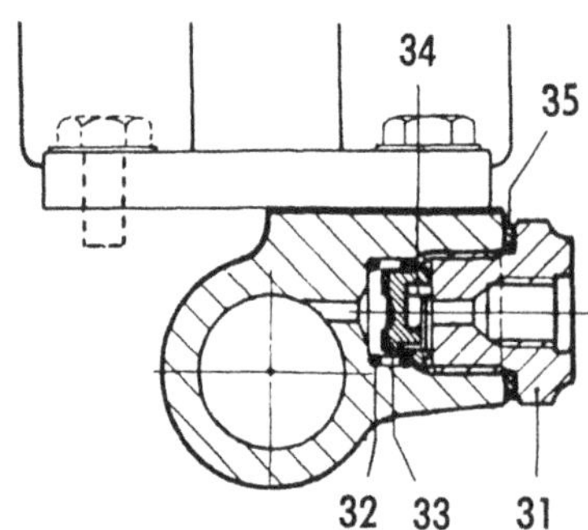


**Fig 10.16 Non-return valve (master cylinder 1969/70)**

*31 Union*
*32 Spring*
*33 Body*
*34 Spring*
*35 Gasket*

the caliper unit and then disconnect it completely *by unscrewing the caliper from the hose* so that the hose is not twisted. Plug the hose to prevent loss of fluid and the ingress of dirt.

4 Detach the two springs which hold the caliper cylinder housing to the caliper body and remove the cylinder housing.

5 Clean the exterior of the assembly taking care that dirt does not enter the flexible hose port.

6 Examine the hinge pin and springs for wear and corrosion and renew as necessary. The caliper body may be separated from the support bracket by compressing the spring on the hinge pin and removing the lockwasher and circlip.

7 Expel the piston from the cylinder by applying air pressure components in methylated spirit or clean hydraulic fluid.

8 Examine the surfaces of the piston and cylinder for scoring or 'bright' wear areas. If these are evident, renew the cylinder housing complete.

9 If the piston and cylinder are not worn, obtain a repair kit and remove the piston and wiper seals.

10 Manipulate a new piston seal into its groove using the fingers only. Apply some clean hydraulic fluid to the seal and cylinder

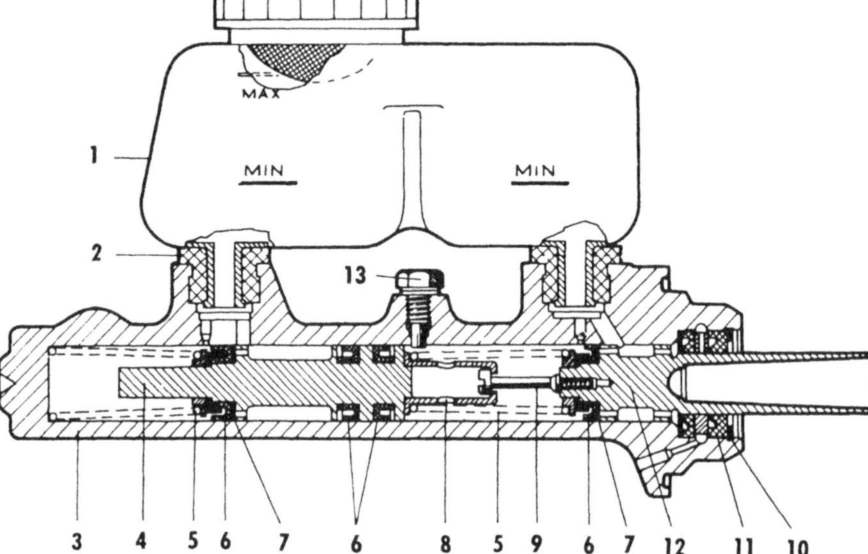


**Fig 10.17 Sectional view of master cylinder (1971 onwards)**

*1 Fluid reservoir*
*2 Rubber gasket*
*3 Body*
*4 Secondary piston*
*5 Spring*
*6 Seals*
*7 Washer*
*8 Sleeve*
*9 Screw*
*10 Circlip*
*11 Gasket*
*12 Primary piston*
*13 Stop screw*

8.2 Removing a caliper unit

bore and insert the piston squarely into it. Do not press the piston fully home but leave about 3/8 in (9.5 mm) projecting. Fit the wiper seal (groove towards piston) in its retainer and press them into position using a piece of suitable tubing to bear upon the retainer (Fig. 10.19).

11 Reassembly of the cylinder housing to the caliper body and the attachment of the support bracket is a reversal of dismantling as is the refitting of the caliper unit to the outer driveshaft carrier but use a new lockplate under the two securing bolts and bend-up the tabs when the bolts have been fully tightened.

12 When refitting is complete bleed the hydraulic system as described in Section 12.

## 9 Wheel cylinder - removal, servicing and refitting

1 Remove the roadwheel, pull off the hub/drum assembly and remove the brake shoes as previously described.

2 Disconnect the handbrake cable from the lever on the backplate.

3 Unscrew the union at the fluid inlet on the back plate and disconnect the pipe. Plug the pipe to prevent loss of fluid and ingress of dirt.

4 Unscrew the bleed nipple from the wheel cylinder at the

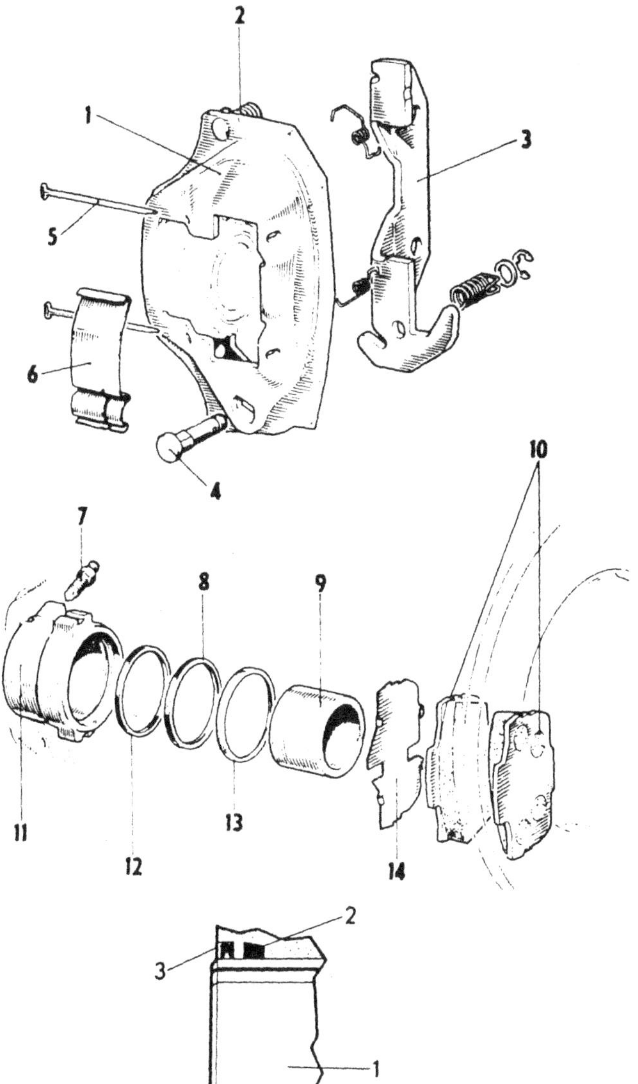


Fig 10.18 Exploded view of a disc caliper unit

1 Caliper body
2 Steady pin and spring
3 Support bracket
4 Hinge pin
5 Split pins
6 Spring clip
7 Bleed nipple
8 Wiper seal
9 Piston
10 Friction pad
11 Cylinder
12 Piston seal
13 Wiper seal retainer
14 Anti-squeak shim

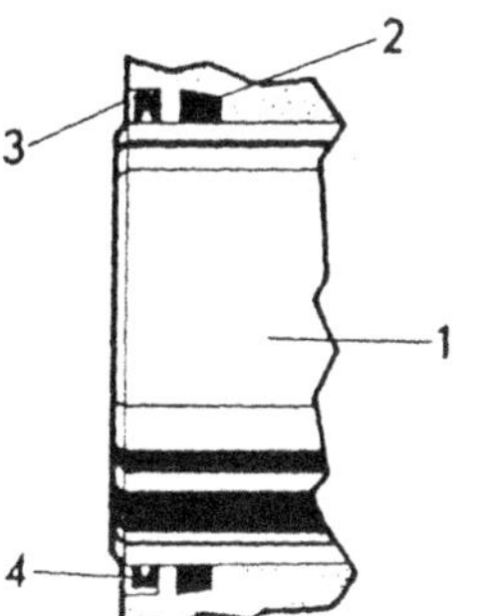


Fig 10.19 Caliper wiper seal fitting diagram

1 Piston
2 Piston seal
3 Wiper seal retainer
4 Wiper seal

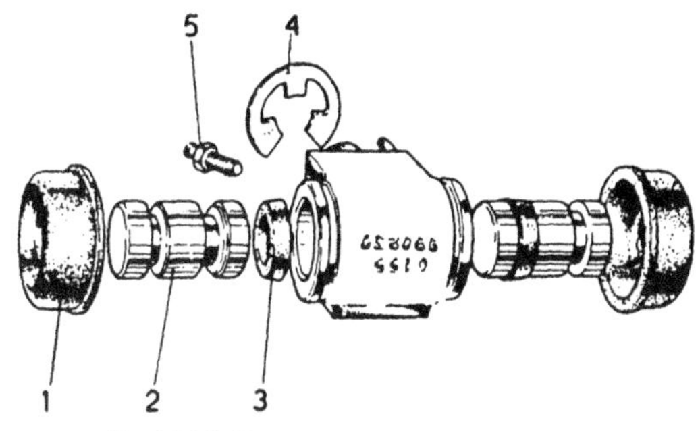


Fig 10.20 Exploded view of a rear brake wheel cylinder

1 Dust excluding boot
2 Piston
3 Piston seal
4 Circlip
5 Bleed nipple

backplate.(Fig 10.20)

5 Withdraw the retaining circlip and remove the wheel cylinder from the backplate.

6 Peel off the dust excluding boots and withdraw the pistons.

7 Wash all components in methylated spirit or clean hydraulic fluid and inspect the piston and cylinder surfaces for scoring or 'bright' wear areas. If these are evident, renew the wheel cylinder complete.

8 If the pistons and cylinder are in good order, discard the seals and obtain a repair kit.

9 Manipulate the new seals into position using the fingers only and then fit the pistons after having dipped them in clean hydraulic fluid. Take care not to nip or trap the lips of the seals during the reassembly operations.

10 Fit the wheel cylinder to the backplate noting the positioning dowel. Screw in the bleed nipple. (Fig. 10.21).

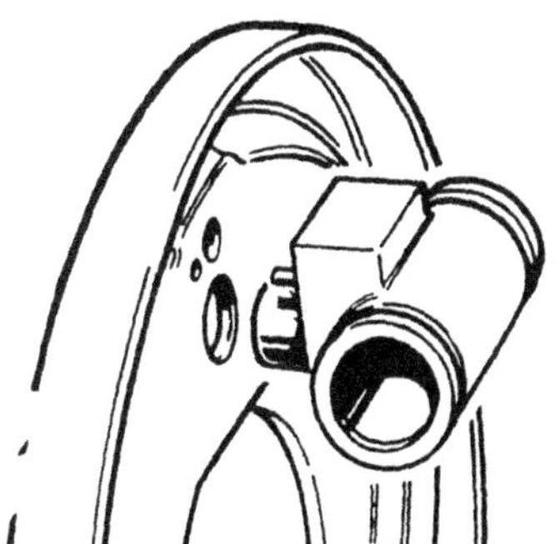

Fig 10.21 Wheel cylinder locating dowel and backplate hole

11 Refit the brake shoes and hub/drum assembly and reconnect the handbrake cable.
12 Reconnect the fluid inlet pipe and bleed the hydraulic system (Section 12).
13 Adjust the rear brake shoes (Section 2).

## 10 Flexible hoses - inspection and renewal

1 Inspect the condition of the flexible hydraulic hoses leading to each of the front disc brake calipers and also the two at the front of the rear axle. If they are swollen, damaged or chafed, they must be renewed.
2 Wipe the top of the brake master cylinder reservoir and unscrew the cap. Place a piece of polythene sheet over the top of the reservoir and refit the cap. This is to stop hydraulic fluid syphoning out during subsequent operations.
3 To remove a front flexible hose, wipe the union and brackets free of dust and undo the union nuts from the metal pipe ends.
4 Undo and remove the locknuts and plain washers securing each flexible hose end to the bracket and lift away the flexible hose.
5 To remove a rear flexible hose follow the instructions for the front flexible hose.
6 Refitting in both cases is the reverse sequence to removal. It will be necessary to bleed the brake hydraulic system as described in Section 12. If one hose has been removed it is only necessary to bleed at the cylinder nearest the hose and at the diagonally opposite one.

## 11 Rigid brake lines - inspection and renewal

1 At six monthly intervals, inspect the condition of the rigid brake lines. If there are signs of corrosion or the pipe has been bent by stones or chafed by rubbing against an adjacent component, it must be renewed.
2 Remove the damaged section and take it to a service station who will use it to make up a new pipe to the original pattern complete with compression nuts and flanged ends.
3 After fitting the new pipe, bleed the system (Section 12)

## 12 Hydraulic system - bleeding

1 Removal of all the air from the hydraulic system is essential to the correct working of the braking system, and before undertaking this, examine the fluid reservoir cap to ensure that the vent hole is clear. Check the level of fluid in the reservoir and top-up if required.
2 Check all brake line unions and connections for possible seepage, and at the same time check the condition of the rubber hoses which may be provided.
3 If the condition of the caliper or wheel cylinders is in doubt, check for possible signs of fluid leakage.
4 If there is any possibility that incorrect fluid has been used in the system, drain all the fluid out and flush through with methylated spirits. Renew all piston seals and cups since they will be affected and could possibly fail under pressure.
5 Gather together a clean jam jar, a 12 inch (300 mm) length of tubing which fits tightly over the bleed screws and a tin of the correct brake fluid.
6 To bleed the system, clean the area round the bleed nipples and fit the bleed tube to the left front caliper. (Fig 10.22)
7 If the vehicle has vacuum servo assistance, depress the brake pedal several times to destroy the vacuum.
8 Place the end of the tube in the clean jar which should contain sufficient fluid to keep the end of the tube underneath during the operation.
9 Open the bleed screw ¼ turn with a spanner and depress the brake pedal. After slowly releasing the pedal, pause for a moment to allow the fluid to recoup in the master cylinder and then depress it again. This will force air from the system. Continue until no more air bubbles can be seen coming from the tube. At intervals make certain that the reservoir is kept topped up, otherwise air will enter at this point again.
10 Finally press the pedal down fully and hold it there whilst the bleed screw is tightened.
11 Repeat the operation on the right rear brake wheel cylinder and then the front right and left rear. (Fig 10.23)
12 When completed check the level of the fluid in the reservoir and then check the feel of the brake pedal, which should be firm and free from any 'sponginess', which is normally associated with air in the system.
13 Use only new fluid (which has been stored in an airtight container and remained unshaken for 24 hours) for topping-up and discard the fluid in the bleed jar unless it is wished to retain it for use in the jar at future bleeding operations. **Never be tempted to use the expelled fluid for topping-up the reservoir.**

## 13 Vacuum servo unit - description, removal and refitting

1 On lhd vehicles built after 1969, a vacuum servo unit is fitted into the brake hydraulic circuit in series with the master cylinder, to provide assistance to the driver when the brake pedal is depressed. This reduces the effort required by the driver to operate the brake under all braking conditions.
2 The unit operates by vacuum obtained from the induction manifold and comprises basically a booster diaphragm and check valve. The servo unit and hydraulic master cylinder are connected together so that the servo unit piston rod acts as the master cylinder pushrod. The driver's braking effort is transmitted through another pushrod to the servo unit piston and its built in control system. The servo unit piston does not fit tightly into the cylinder, but has a strong diaphragm to keep its edges in constant contact with the cylinder wall. so assuring an air tight seal between the two parts. The forward chamber is held under vacuum conditions created in the inlet manifold of the engine and, during periods when the brake pedal is not in use, the controls open a passage to the rear chamber so placing it under vacuum conditions as well. When the brake pedal is depressed, the vacuum passage to the rear chamber is cut off and the chamber opened to atmospheric pressure. The consequent rush of air pushes the servo piston forward in the vacuum chamber and operates the main pushrod to the master cylinder.
3 The controls are designed so that assistance is given under all conditions and, when the brakes are not required, vacuum in the rear chamber is established when the brake pedal is released. All air from the atmosphere entering the rear chamber is passed through a small air filter.
4 Under normal operating conditions the vacuum servo unit is very reliable and does not require overhaul except at very high mileages.
5 When a fault occurs, replace the unit on a factory exchange basis; do not attempt to dismantle it.
6 The vacuum servo unit may be removed either in conjunction with the master cylinder for later separation or the hydraulic master cylinder removed first and then the servo unit removed separately from the bulkhead. Both methods are described in Section 6.

## 14 Handbrake - adjustment

1 Adjustment of the handbrake is normally automatic and any slackness is taken up when the rear brakes are adjusted. However, after a high mileage the cable may stretch or after dismantling or reassembly of the linkage additional adjustment may be required as described in the following operations.
2 Jack-up the rear of the vehicle so that the roadwheels are clear of the ground.
3 Remove the right-hand front seat and release the handbrake lever fully.
4 Tighten the left-hand adjusting nut until the rear left brake shoes are locked. Slacken the nut until the wheel rotates freely

Fig 10.22 Bleeding a front disc caliper

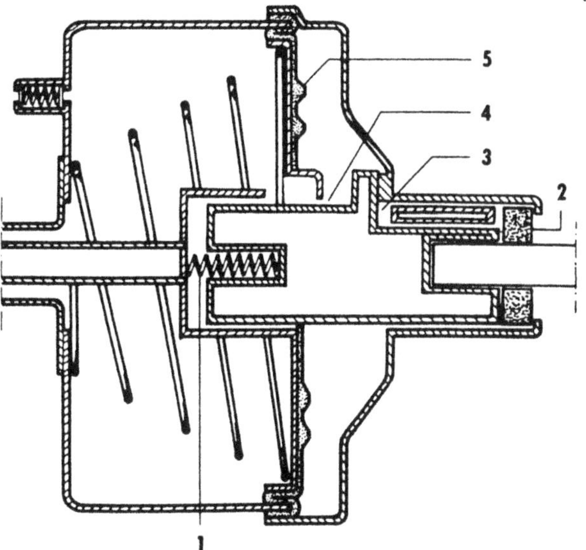


Fig 10.24 Sectional view of vacuum servo unit (brake pedal released)

*1 Return spring*
*2 Air filter*
*3 Air entry*
*4 Vacuum channel*
*5 Diaphragm*

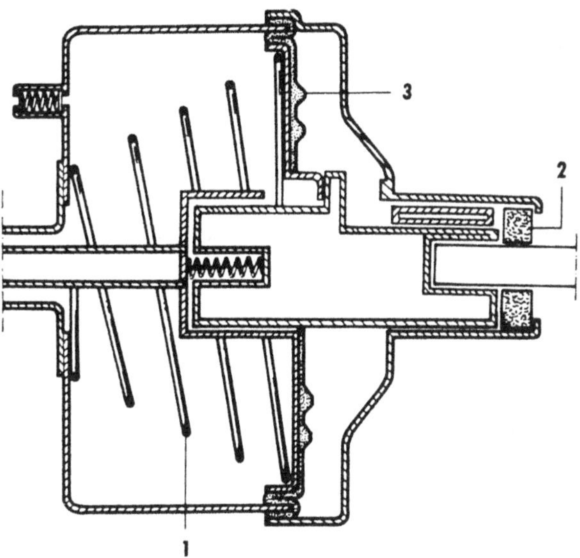


Fig 10.25 Sectional view of vacuum servo unit (brake pedal depressed)

*1 Diaphragm spring*
*2 Air filter*
*3 Diaphragm*

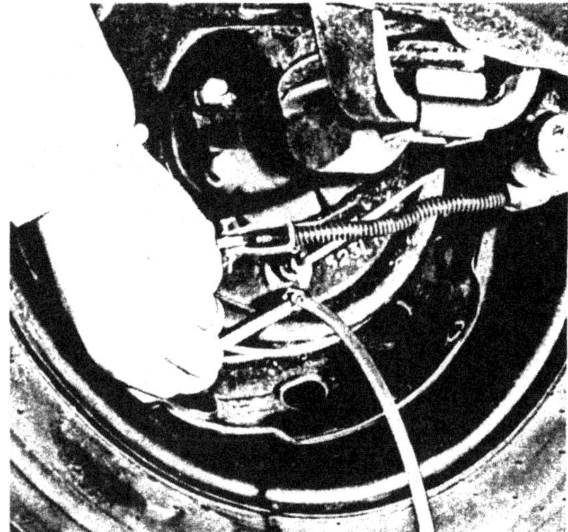

Fig 10.23 Bleeding a rear drum brake

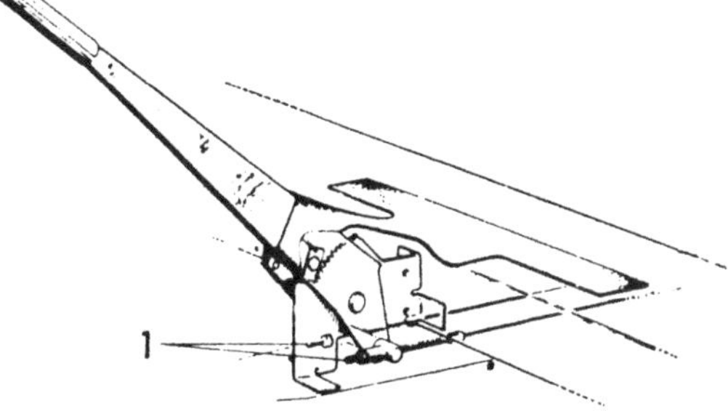


Fig 10.26 Location of handbrake adjusting nuts (1)

and then unscrew the nut one complete turn.

5 Repeat the adjustment procedure on the right-hand nut in conjunction with the rear right-hand brake.

6 Check the operation of the handbrake lever which should lock the rear wheels after pulling it into the third step of the ratchet.

7 Lower the vehicle to the ground.

## 15 Handbrake cable - renewal

1 Remove one of the front seats and the rear seat cushions.

2 Jack-up the rear of the vehicle and remove the roadwheel from the side on which the cable is to be withdrawn.

3 Unscrew and remove the respective adjusting nut under the handbrake lever.

4 Withdraw the cable assembly from the sleeve under the rear seat cushion.

5 Remove the clamps used to hold the cable to the rear axle.

6 Remove the split pin from the clevis pin at the back plate lever and disconnect the clevis from the lever.

7 Prise the grommet from the inclined panel of the rear axle tunnel.

8 Withdraw the cable assembly to the rear and remove it.

9 Installation of the new cable is a reversal of removal but remember to fit the grommet to it before installing it.

10 When installation is complete, adjust the cable as described in the preceding Section.

## 16 Handbrake lever (up to and including 1970) - removal, dismantling, reassembly and refitting

1 Push back the front seats or remove one of them to provide better accessibility.

2 Peel back the rubber boot from the base of the lever and unscrew and remove the adjusting nuts.

3 Remove the circlip and withdraw the pivot pin.

4 Withdraw the handbrake lever and retain the spacers.

5 Remove the split pin and clevis pin from the ratchet pawl and withdraw the pawl.

6 The pawl-rod may now be moved towards the handgrip which will expose the locknut, release button, spring and washer, all of which may be removed.

7 Reassembly and refitting are reversals of removal and dismantling but set the pawl-rod locknut so that the release button projects about 0.4 in (10.0 mm) when the pawl is engaged with the ratchet.

## 17 Handbrake lever (1971 onwards) - removal, dismantling, reassembly and refitting

1 All procedures are similar to those described in the preceding Section except that the release button is removed by unscrewing it *after* the pawl has been disconnected from the handbrake lever.

2 When reassembling, screw on the release button until it reaches the bottom of the threads on the pawl-rod. Adjust its position (not more than one turn) so that it will be correctly aligned to enter the end of the handbrake lever.

3 After reassembly, check that the lower face of the release button projects by 0.32 in (8.0 mm). (Fig 10.29)

## 18 Brake pedal (up to and including 1968 models) - removal and refitting

1 The brake and clutch pedals are of pendant type and use a common cross-shaft. The shaft bearings are of self-lubricating type.

2 Remove the steering column and the gearchange shaft as described in Chapter 8.

3 Disconnect the clutch operating pushrod from the clutch pedal.

4 Remove the split pins from both ends of the cross-shaft and then draw the clutch pedal off the cross-shaft to the left.

5 Disconnect the brake pedal operating pushrod at the adjusting nut and then withdraw the cross-shaft to the left and remove the brake pedal in a downward direction. (Fig 10.30)

6 Check the shaft bearings for wear and renew them if they are worn by driving out the old and pressing in the new.

7 Refitting is a reversal of removal but always use new split pins on the cross-shaft and adjust the pedal free movement as described in Section 2.

## 19 Brake pedal (1969 onwards) - removal and refitting

1 The operations are similar to those described in the preceding Section except that the steering column and gearchange shaft do not have to be removed, only the column protective shield.

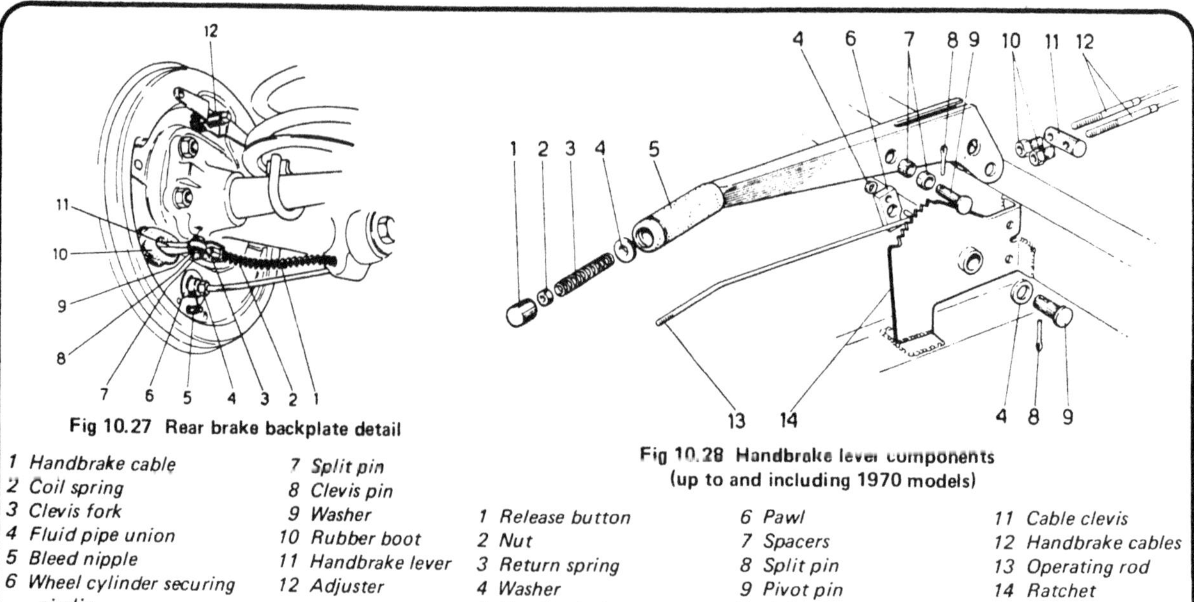

Fig 10.27 Rear brake backplate detail

1 *Handbrake cable*
2 *Coil spring*
3 *Clevis fork*
4 *Fluid pipe union*
5 *Bleed nipple*
6 *Wheel cylinder securing circlip*
7 *Split pin*
8 *Clevis pin*
9 *Washer*
10 *Rubber boot*
11 *Handbrake lever*
12 *Adjuster*

Fig 10.28 Handbrake lever components (up to and including 1970 models)

1 *Release button*
2 *Nut*
3 *Return spring*
4 *Washer*
5 *Handbrake lever*
6 *Pawl*
7 *Spacers*
8 *Split pin*
9 *Pivot pin*
10 *Adjusting nuts*
11 *Cable clevis*
12 *Handbrake cables*
13 *Operating rod*
14 *Ratchet*

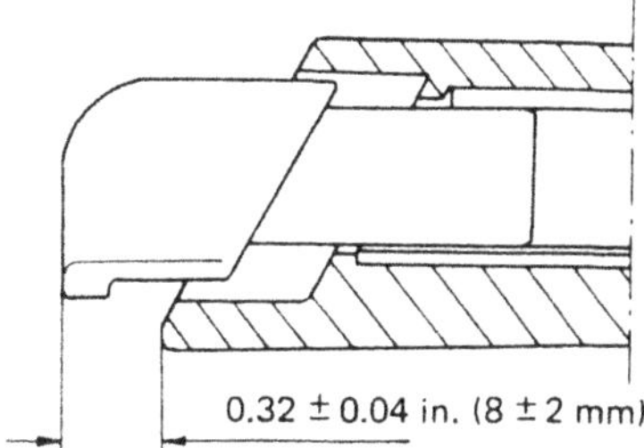


Fig 10.29 Handbrake lever (1971 onwards) release button adjustment diagram

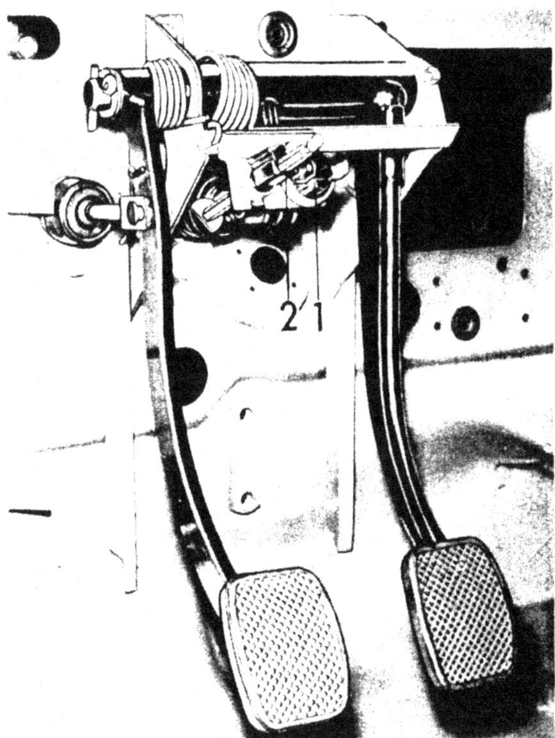


**Fig 10.30 Pedal arrangement (up to and including 1968 models)**

*1 Stop lamp switch* *2 Excess brake pedal travel switch*

2 Remove the bracket on which the stop lamp switch and brake warning switch are mounted. (Fig 10.31)
3 Remove the split pin from the right-hand end of the cross-shaft, withdraw the cross-shaft to the left and remove the brake pedal in a downward direction. (Fig 10.32)
4 Refitting is a reversal of removal, no adjustment for brake pedal free movement being required or provided for.

## 20 Stop lamp and excess pedal travel switches - adjustment

1 Both switches are mounted on a bracket and are actuated by the movement of a short lever at the left-hand end of the brake pedal cross-tube. The method of connection to the lever varies according to date of vehicle production but the principle of operation is identical. (Fig 10.33/10.34)
2 The stop lamp switch should be adjusted so that the stop lamps (ignition on) will illuminate during the initial 1/32 in (0.8 mm) projection of the switch plunger when the foot brake pedal is depressed.
3 The excess pedal switch should only illuminate the brake

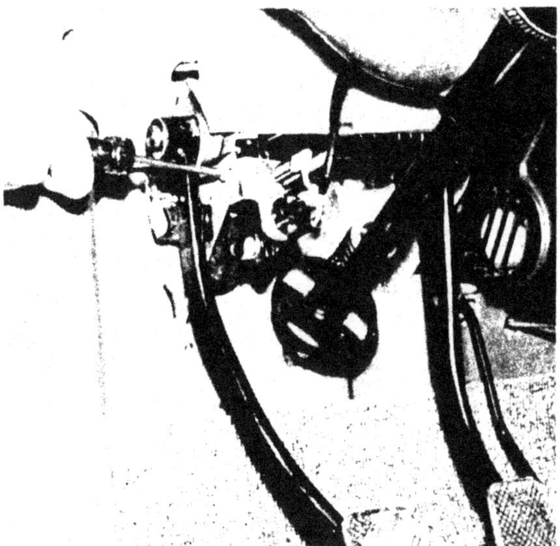

Fig 10.31 Removing brake pedal switch bracket (1969 onwards)

Fig 10.32 Withdrawing a split pin from the pedal cross-shaft (1969 onwards)

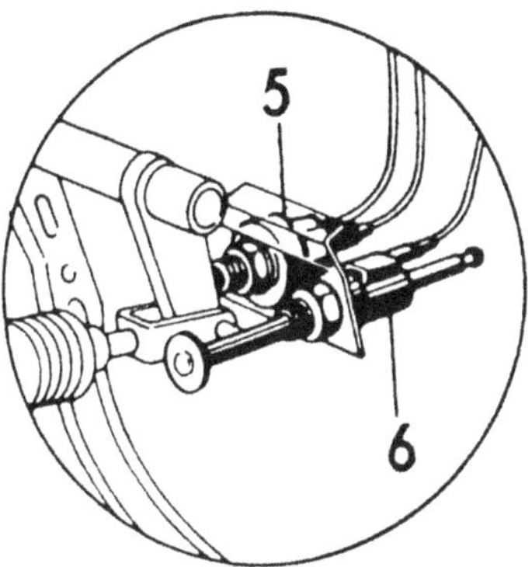


Fig 10.33 Brake pedal switches (up to and including 1968 models)

*5 Stop lamp switch* *6 Excess brake pedal travel switch*

warning lamp when the brake pedal passes the specified pedal to toe-board measurement as described in Section 2. As this can never happen with a braking system in good condition, the adjustment of the switch will have to be made by disconnecting the pushrod from the brake pedal and then holding the pedal 3/8 in (9.5 mm) nearer the toe-board then specified. Set the switch to close the circuit at this position and then reconnect the master cylinder pushrod and re-check the operation.
4 Remember that if the warning lamp comes on, this can indicate either a leak in one of the hydraulic circuits or that the rear brake shoes are in need of adjustment or require renewal.

## 21 Discs and drums - inspection and renovation

1 Whenever the friction pads or linings are checked for wear, examine the surfaces of the discs and drums.
2 Light, even scoring is normal but deep grooves in a disc will necessitate its renewal by removing the front hub assembly (see Chapter 7) or regrinding. (minimum thickness 0.355 in - 9.0 mm).
3 Similar grooves in the brake drums may be removed by skimming at an engineering works provided the new maximum internal diameter does not exceed 8.06 in (204.7 mm), otherwise the drum will have to be renewed.

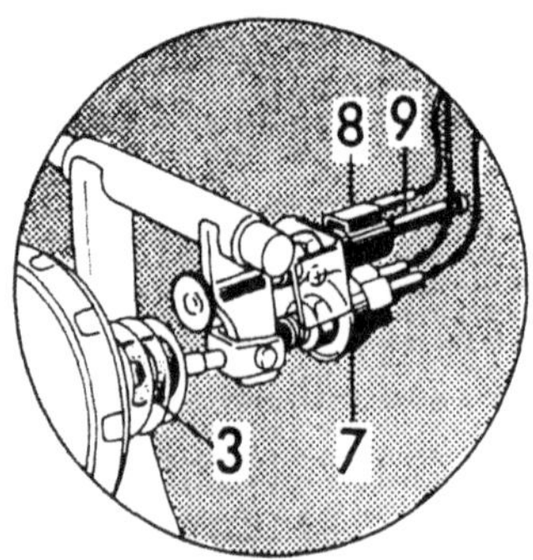


**Fig 10.34 Brake pedal switches (1969 onwards)**

*3 Vacuum servo unit air filter*
*7 Stop lamp switch*
*8 Excess pedal travel switch*
*9 Switch plunger*

4 Jerky brake pedal action can be caused by a distorted disc or out-of-round brake drum in which case, renew the disc and skim or renew the drum.

## 22 Fault diagnosis - braking system

| Symptom | Reason/s | Remedy |
|---|---|---|
| Pedal travels almost to floorboards before brakes operate | Brake fluid level too low | Top up master cylinder reservoir. Check for leaks. |
| | Caliper leaking | Dismantle caliper, clean, fit new rubbers and bleed brakes. |
| | Master cylinder leaking (bubbles in master cylinder fluid) | Dismantle master cylinder, clean and fit new rubbers. Bleed brakes. |
| | Brake flexible hose leaking | Examine and fit new hose if old hose leaking Bleed brakes. |
| | Brake line fractured | Replace with new brake pipe. Bleed brakes. |
| | Brake system unions loose | Check all unions in brake system and tighten as necessary. Bleed brakes. |
| | Pad or shoe linings over 75% worn | Fit replacement pads or shoes. |
| | Brakes badly out of adjustment | Jack up car and adjust brakes. |
| Pedal travel normal after second or third rapid application | Air in system | Bleed brakes. |
| Brake pedal feels springy | New linings not yet bedded-in | Use brakes gently until springy pedal feeling leaves. |
| | Brake discs or drums badly worn or cracked | Fit new brake discs or drums. |
| | Master cylinder securing nuts loose | Tighten master cylinder securing nuts. Ensure spring washers are fitted. |
| Brake pedal feels spongy and soggy | Caliper or wheel cylinder leaking | Dismantle caliper or wheel cylinder, clean, fit new rubbers and bleed brakes. |
| | Master cylinder leaking (bubbles in master cylinder reservoir) | Dismantle master cylinder, clean and fit new rubbers and bleed brakes. Replace cylinder if internal walls scored. |
| | Brake pipe line or flexible hose leaking | Fit new pipeline or hose. |
| | Unions in brake system loose | Examine for leaks, tighten as necessary. |
| | Air in system | Bleed brakes. |
| Excessive effort required to brake car | Pad or shoe linings badly worn | Fit replacement brake shoes and linings. |
| | New pads or shoes recently fitted - not yet bedded-in | Use brakes gently until braking effort normal |
| | Harder linings fitted than standard causing increase in pedal pressure | Remove pads or shoes and replace with normal units. |
| | Linings and brake drums contaminated with oil, grease or hydraulic fluid | Rectify source of leak, clean brake drums, fit new linings. |
| | Servo vacuum pipe leaking | Renew. |
| | Servo air filter clogged | Renew (see Routine Maintenance). |
| | Servo unit faulty | Remove and exchange. |
| Brakes uneven and pulling to one side | Linings and discs or drums contaminated with oil, grease or hydraulic fluid | Ascertain and rectify source of leak, clean discs or drums, fit new pads or shoes. |
| | Tyre pressures unequal | Check and inflate as necessary. |
| | Radial ply tyres fitted at one end of the car only | Fit radial ply tyres of the same make to all four wheels. |
| | Brake caliper loose | Tighten securing nuts and bolts. |
| | Brake pads or shoes fitted incorrectly | Remove and fit correct way round. |
| | Different type of linings fitted at each wheel | Fit the pads or shoes specified by the manufacturer all round. |
| | Anchorages for front suspension or rear suspension loose | Tighten front and rear suspension pick-up points including spring anchorage. |
| | Brake discs or drums badly worn, cracked or distorted | Fit new brake discs or drums. |
| Brakes tend to bind, drag or lock-on | Brake shoes adjusted too tightly | Slacken off brake shoe adjusters. |
| | Air in system | Bleed brakes. |
| | Seized caliper or wheel cylinder | Overhaul or renew. |

# Chapter 11 Electrical system

**Contents**



**Specifications**

**System type** ... 12 volt negative earth

**Battery capacity** ... 44 amp/hr
Lhd models from 1971 onwards ... 60 amp/hr

**Alternator**

| | |
|---|---|
| Make and type ... | Bosch K1 |
| Rated voltage ... | 14 |
| Rated rev/min ... | 2000 |
| Maximum permissible continuous load ... | 35 amp |
| Minimum brush length (wear limit) ... | 0.34 in (9.0 mm) |

**Voltage regulator**

Type ... Bosch AD1 14V

**Starter motor**

| | **1967 to 68 models** | **1969 models onwards** |
|---|---|---|
| Make ... | Bosch | Bosch |
| Type ... | EF12V 0.8PS/0001208029 | GF12V1.0PS/0001311024 |
| Output ... | 0.8 hp | 1.0 hp |
| Number of pinion teeth ... | 9 | 9 |
| Number of ring gear teeth ... | 138 | 138 |
| Armature endfloat ... | 0.002 to 0.012 in (0.05 to 0.3 mm) | |

**Windscreen wiper motor**

Type:
Up to and including 1969 ... Lucas DL 3A
From 1970 models ... Lucas 15 W

**Bulb types (up to 1968)**

| | **Wattage** |
|---|---|
| Headlamp (sealed beam) ... | 50/40 |
| Headlamp (bulb) ... | 45/40 |
| Front parking and direction indicator ... | 21/5 |
| Rear stop and direction indicator ... | 21 |
| Tail ... | 5 |

| | |
|---|---|
| Number plate ... ... ... ... ... ... ... | 5 |
| Reversing (Monte Carlo) ... ... ... ... ... ... | 21 |
| Fog and spot (Monte Carlo) ... ... ... ... ... | 45 |
| Instrument lamps ... ... ... ... ... ... ... | 2 |
| Luggage boot ... ... ... ... ... ... ... | 4 |
| Clock (Monte Carlo) ... ... ... ... ... ... | 4 |
| Side repeater (North America) ... ... ... ... ... | 4 |
| Tachometer (North America) ... ... ... ... ... | 2 |
| Interior lamp ... ... ... ... ... ... ... | 5 |

## Bulb types (from 1969)

| | Wattage |
|---|---|
| Headlights, sealed beam ... ... ... ... ... ... | 50/40 |
| Headlights, asymmetric up to and including model 1972 ... | 45/40 |
| Headlights, asymmetric as from model 1973 ... ... ... | 60/55 |
| Parking light, front ... ... ... ... ... ... ... | 5 |
| Direction indicator light, front ... ... ... ... ... | 21 |
| Parking and direction indicator lights, front (USA) ... ... | 5/21 |
| Direction indicator light, rear ... ... ... ... ... | 21 |
| Tail light ... ... ... ... ... ... ... ... | 5 |
| Stop light ... ... ... ... ... ... ... ... | 21 |
| Number plate light ... ... ... ... ... ... ... | 5 |
| Control and instrument lamps ... ... ... ... ... | 1, 2 |
| Control lamp, hazard warning signal ... ... ... ... | 2 |
| Dome light ... ... ... ... ... ... ... ... | 5 |
| Trunk light ... ... ... ... ... ... ... ... | 4 |
| Back-up light ... ... ... ... ... ... ... | 21 |
| Side position light (USA) ... ... ... ... ... ... | 4 |
| Lighting tachometer (USA) ... ... ... ... ... | 2 |

## Torque wrench setting

| | lb ft | kg m |
|---|---|---|
| Headlamp wiper arm bolt ... ... ... ... ... ... | 8.0 | 1.1 |

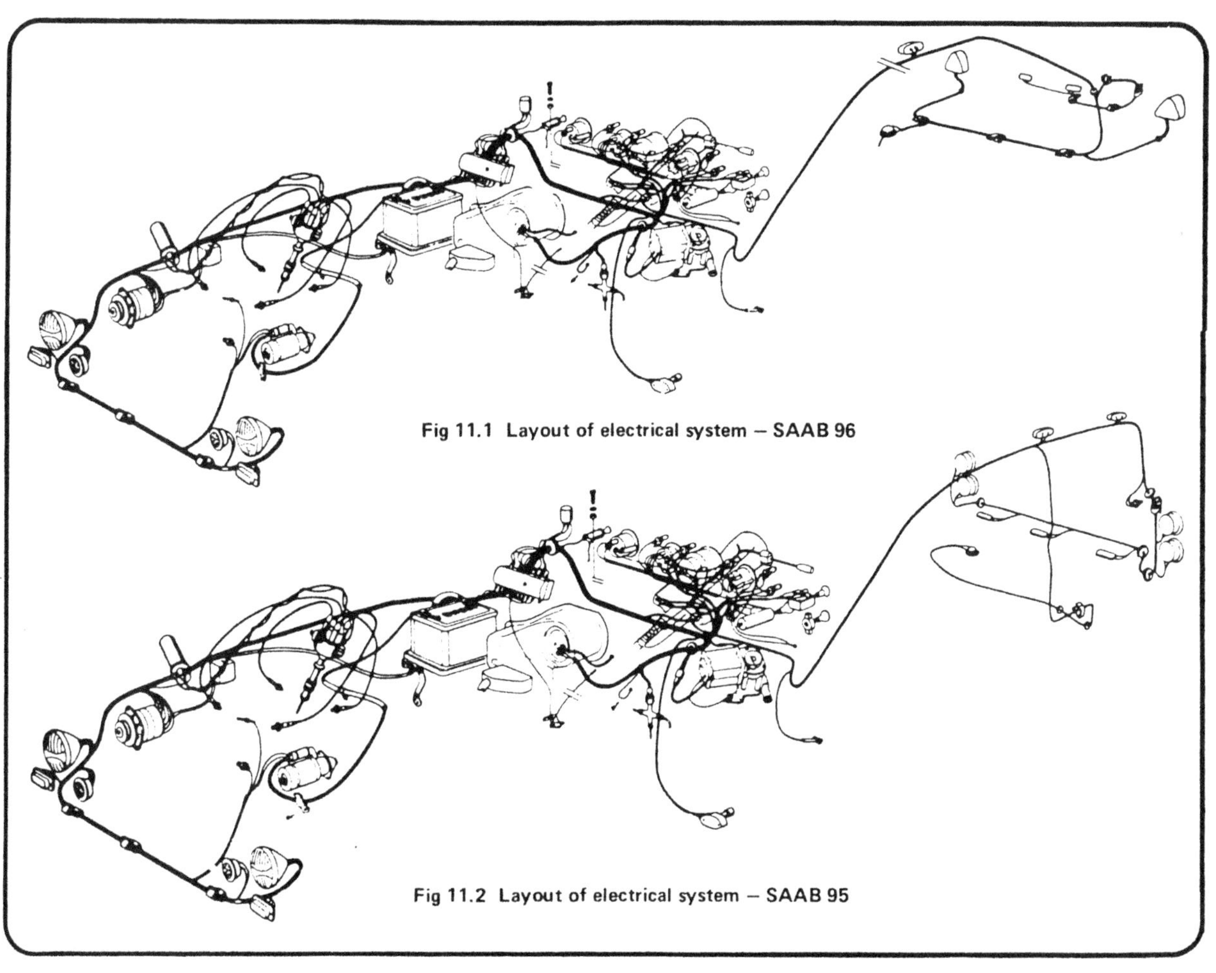

Fig 11.1 Layout of electrical system – SAAB 96

Fig 11.2 Layout of electrical system – SAAB 95

## 1 General description

The electrical system is of 12 volt, negative earth type and includes an alternator and voltage regulator, a pre-engaged starter motor and a range of conventional lights and accessories.

Certain models from 1971 onwards incorporate a washer/wiper device for cleaning the headlamp lenses. The Monte Carlo version is fitted with auxiliary driving lights and reversing lights.

All models have their electrical circuits protected by fuses.

## 2 Battery - removal and refitting

1 The battery is located within the engine compartment on the right-hand side.

2 Disconnect the negative lead and then the positive lead from the battery terminals (in that order).

3 Unscrew the wing nuts from the battery holding bolts and lift the battery from its location.

4 Refitting is a reversal of removal; securely tighten the terminal bolts and smear the terminals with petroleum jelly to prevent subsequent corrosion.

## 3 Battery - maintenance and inspection

1 Normal weekly battery maintenance consists of checking the electrolyte level of each cell to ensure that the separators are covered by ¼ inch (6 mm) of electrolyte. If the level has fallen, top up the battery using distilled water only. Do not overfill. If a battery is overfilled or any electrolyte spilled, immediately wipe away the excess as electrolyte attacks and corrodes any metal it comes into contact with very rapidly.

2 If the battery has the 'Auto-fil' device, a special topping up sequence is required. The balls in the 'Auto-fil' battery are part of the automatic topping up device which ensures correct electrolyte level. The vent chamber should remain in position at all times except when topping up or taking specific gravity readings. If the electrolyte level in any of the cells is below the bottom of the filling tube top up as follows:

a) Lift off the vent chamber cover.
b) With the battery level, pour distilled water into the trough until all the filling tubes and trough are full.
c) Immediately replace the cover to allow the water in the trough and tubes to flow into the cells. Each cell will automatically receive the correct amount of water.

3 As well as keeping the terminals clean and covered with petroleum jelly, the top of the battery, and especially the top of the cells, should be kept clean and dry. This helps prevent corrosion and ensures that the battery does not become partially discharged by leakage through dampness and dirt.

4 Once every three months remove the battery and inspect the battery securing bolts, the battery clamp plate, tray and battery leads for corrosion (white fluffy deposits on the metal which are brittle to touch). If any corrosion is found clean off the deposit with ammonia and paint over the clean metal with an anti-rust anti-acid paint.

5 At the same time inspect the battery case for cracks. If a crack is found, clean and plug it with one of the proprietary compounds marketed by such firms as Holts for this purpose. If leakage through the crack has been excessive then it will be necessary to refill the appropriate cell with fresh electrolyte as detailed later. Cracks are frequently caused to the top of the battery case by pouring in distilled water in the middle of winter *after* instead of *before* a run. This gives the water no chance to mix with the electrolyte and so the former freezes and splits the battery case.

6 If topping up the battery becomes excessive and the case has been inspected for cracks that could cause leakage, but none are found, the battery is being overcharged and the voltage regulator will have to be checked and reset.

7 With the battery on the bench at the three monthly interval check, measure the specific gravity with a hydrometer to determine the state of charge and condition of the electrolyte. There should be very little variation between the different cells and, if a variation in excess of 0.025 is present it will be due to either:

a) Loss of electrolyte from the battery at some time caused by spillage or a leak, resulting in a drop in the specific gravity of the electrolyte when the deficiency was replaced with distilled water instead of fresh electrolyte.
b) An internal short circuit caused by buckling of the plates or similar malady pointing to the likelihood of total battery failure in the near future.

8 The specific gravity of the electrolyte for fully charged conditions, at the electrolyte temperature indicated, is listed in Table A. The specific gravity of a fully discharged battery at different temperatures of the electrolyte is given in Table B.

*Table A – Specific gravity - battery fully charged*

| | | |
|---|---|---|
| 1.268 at | 100°F or 38°C | electrolyte temperature |
| 1.272 at | 90°F or 32°C | " " |
| 1.276 at | 80°F or 27°C | " " |
| 1.280 at | 70°F or 21°C | " " |
| 1.284 at | 60°F or 16°C | " " |
| 1.288 at | 50°F or 10°C | " " |
| 1.292 at | 40°F or 4°C | " " |
| 1.296 at | 30°F or -1.5°C | " " |

*Table B – Specific gravity - battery fully discharged*

| | | |
|---|---|---|
| 1.098 at | 100°F or 38°C | electrolyte temperature |
| 1.102 at | 90°F or 32°C | " " |
| 1.106 at | 80°F or 27°C | " " |
| 1.110 at | 70°F or 21°C | " " |
| 1.114 at | 60°F or 16°C | " " |
| 1.118 at | 50°F or 10°C | " " |
| 1.122 at | 40°F or 4°C | " " |
| 1.126 at | 30°F or -1.5°C | " " |

## 4 Battery - electrolyte replenishment

1 If the battery is in a fully charged state and one of the cells maintains a specific gravity reading which is 0.025 or more lower than the others and a check of each cell has been made with a voltage meter to check for short circuits (a four to seven second test should give a steady reading of between 1.2 and 1.8 volts), then it is likely that electrolyte has been lost from the cell with the low reading at some time.

2 Top the cell up with a solution of 1 part sulphuric acid to 2.5 parts of water. If the cell is already fully topped up draw some electrolyte out of it with a pipette.

3 When mixing the sulphuric acid and water **never add water to sulphuric acid** – always pour the acid slowly onto the water in a glass container. **If water is added to sulphuric acid it will explode.**

4 Continue to top up the cell with the freshly made electrolyte and then recharge the battery and check the hydrometer readings.

## 5 Battery charging and precautions when charging or starting from an external source

1 In order to protect the alternator, it is essential to observe the following whenever the electrical system is being attended to, or the battery charged from an external source, or the engine started by means of a stand-by battery and 'jump' leads.

2 Always make sure that the negative terminal of the battery is

earthed. If the terminal connections are accidentally reversed or if the battery has been reverse charged the alternator diodes will burn out.
3 The output terminal on the alternator marked "B+" must never be earthed but should always be connected directly to the positive terminal of the battery.
4 Whenever the alternator is to be removed or when disconnecting the terminals of the alternator circuit always disconnect the battery earth terminal first.
5 The alternator must never be operated without the battery to alternator cable connected.
6 If the battery is to be charged by external means always disconnect both battery cables before the external charge is connected.
7 Should it be necessary to use a booster charger or booster battery to start the engine always double check that the negative cable is connected to negative terminal and the positive cable to positive terminal.
8 In winter time when heavy demand is placed upon the battery, such as when starting from cold and much electrical equipment is continually in use, it is a good idea to occasionally have the battery fully charged from an external source at the rate of 3.5 to 4 amps.
9 Continue to charge the battery at this rate until no further rise in specific gravity is noted over a four hour period.
10 Alternatively, a trickle charger charging at the rate of 1.5 amps can be safely used overnight.
11 Specially rapid 'boost' charges which are claimed to restore the power of the battery in 1 to 2 hours are most dangerous as they can cause serious damage to the battery plates through overheating.
12 While charging the battery note that the temperature of the electrolyte should never exceed 100°F (37.8°C).

## 6 Alternator - general description

1 The alternator is of Bosch manufacture and varies slightly in design according to date of vehicle manufacture but the operating principle is the same.
2 The advantage of the alternator over other types of generator is that it provides a charge at much lower revolutions even at engine idling speed.
3 No maintenance is required other than keeping the driving belt correctly tensioned.

## 7 Alternator - removal and refitting

1 Carefully mark the leads which connect to the terminals on the rear plate of the alternator and then disconnect them. The later type alternator has a plug-in connection for the three lower leads.
2 Slacken the mounting and adjustment bolts and push the alternator in towards the engine so that the drive belt can be slipped off the pulley (photo).
3 Remove the mounting and adjustment bolts and lift the alternator from the engine compartment (photo).
4 Refitting is a reversal of removal but ensure that the leads are correctly connected and that the drive belt is correctly tensioned (Chapter 2).

## 8 Alternator (up to chassis numbers 95/47295 and 96/443386) - servicing

1 It is not recommended that the unit is tested, or dismantled beyond the operations described in this Section. Due to the sensitive nature of the alternator internal diodes, it is better to have the unit tested by an auto-electrician having the necessary equipment rather than risk damage by the use of make-shift testing circuits.
2 Unscrew the nut from the alternator driving pulley. To prevent the pulley turning during this operation, locate an old belt in the groove of the pulley and grip it in a vice as near to the pulley wheel as possible. Do not grip the pulley itself either in a vice or with a Stilson type wrench or the pulley will be distorted or damaged, which will cause subsequent failure of the driving belt.
3 To renew the carbon brushes, mark the relative positions (to each other) of the drive end bracket, the bush end housing and rear protective ring and then remove the rear protective ring (three screws).
4 Unscrew and withdraw the brush holder plate.
5 If the brushes have worn to the minimum specified length of 0.34 in. (9.0 mm), unsolder their leads and fit new brushes. When soldering the new brush leads, localise the heat and make sure that the solder does not run into the cable covering. (Fig. 11.7).
6 Refitting is a reversal of removal.
7 To renew the rotor bearings, proceed as for carbon brush

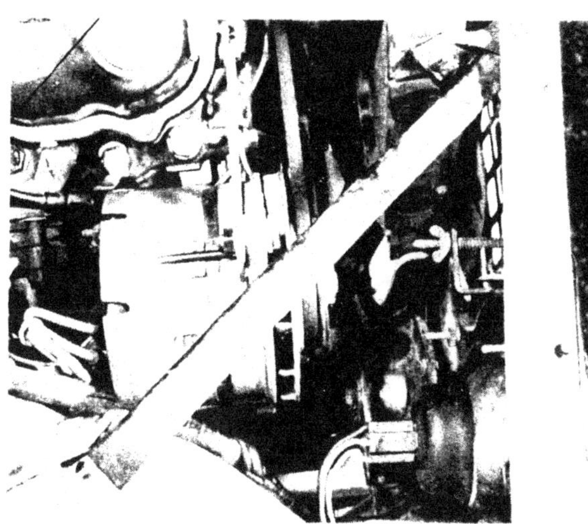
7.2 Alternator adjustment strap and drive belt

7.3 Alternator mounting cradle

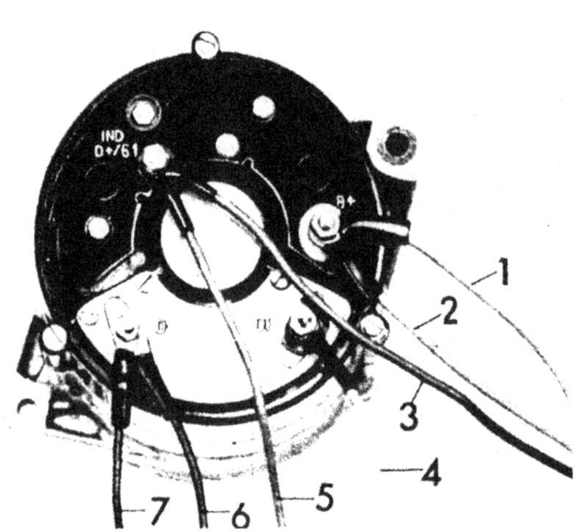


**Fig 11.3 Alternator rear plate terminals and leads (up to chassis numbers 95/47295 and 96/443386)**

*1 Grey (85) to B+*
*2 Grey (74) to B+*
*3 Red (72) to D+/61*
*4 Yellow (73) to DF*
*5 Red (61) to D+/61*
*6 Black (49) to D–*
*7 Black (47) to D–*

**Fig 11.4 Alternator rear plate terminals and leads (from chassis numbers 95/47296 and 96/443387)**

*1 Grey (85) to B+*
*2 Grey (74) to B+*
*3 Black to earth (1970 model only)*
*4 Yellow (73) to DF*
*5 Red (72 e) to D+*
*6 Black (49) to D–*

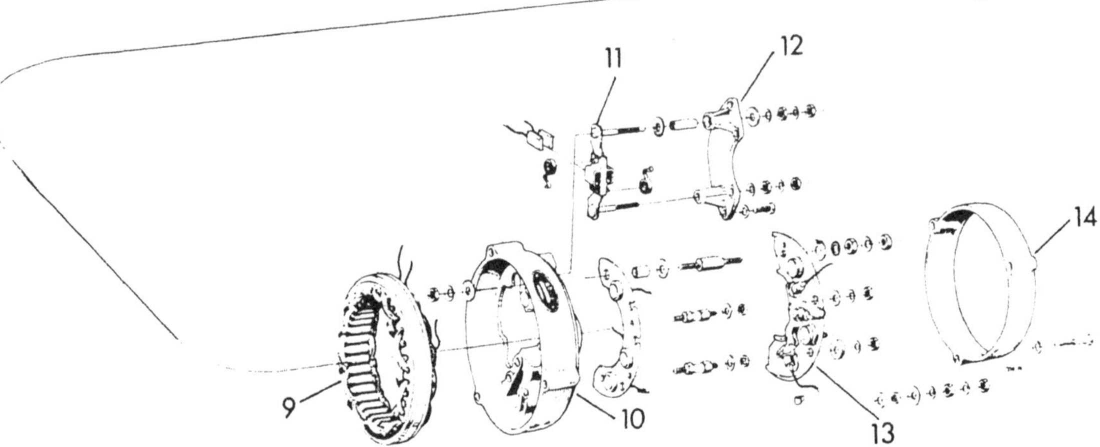


**Fig 11.5 Exploded view of early type alternator**

*1 Driving pulley*
*2 Fan*
*3 Drive end bracket*
*4 Drive end bracket bearing*
*5 Drive end bracket bearing retaining plate*
*6 Rotor*
*7 Slip rings*
*8 Rear bearing*
*9 Stator*
*10 Brush end housing*
*11 Brush holder*
*12 Brush holder plate*
*13 Diode support*
*14 Rear protective ring*

renewal and then unscrew the drive end bracket bolts and withdraw the drive end bracket, stator and rotor. (Fig. 11.8).
8 Support the drive end bracket and carefully press out the rotor from it.
9 Remove the ball race at the slip ring end using a two or three-legged puller.
10 To remove the front bearing, press the rotor from the drive end bracket and then unscrew and remove the bearing retaining plate.
11 Check the condition of the slip rings; they should be clean and smooth otherwise polish them with fine glass paper.
12 Reassembly is a reversal of dismantling but pack the bearings with recommended grease and ensure that the bearing which is pressed into the drive end bracket has its sealed side towards the driving pulley.
13 Align the marks made on the drive end bracket, brush end housing and rear protective cover, fit the securing bolts and then locate the driving pulley and tighten the securing nut to a torque of 28 lb/ft (3.9 kg/m).

## 9 Alternator (from chassis numbers 95/47.296 and 96/443.387) - servicing

1 The servicing of this type of alternator is very similar to the operations described in the preceding Section except that differences in detail of components should be noted.

## 10 Voltage regulator - fault testing

1 If the ignition warning lamp comes on and does not go out when engine speed increases, first check that the alternator drive belt is not slack and slipping and also that the cable connections are secure.
2 Pull out the plug from the voltage regulator and bridge the "D+" and "DF" tags of the plug. (Fig. 11.14).
3 Start the engine and run it up to 2000 rev/min. If the ignition warning lamp goes out immediately, the voltage regulator is

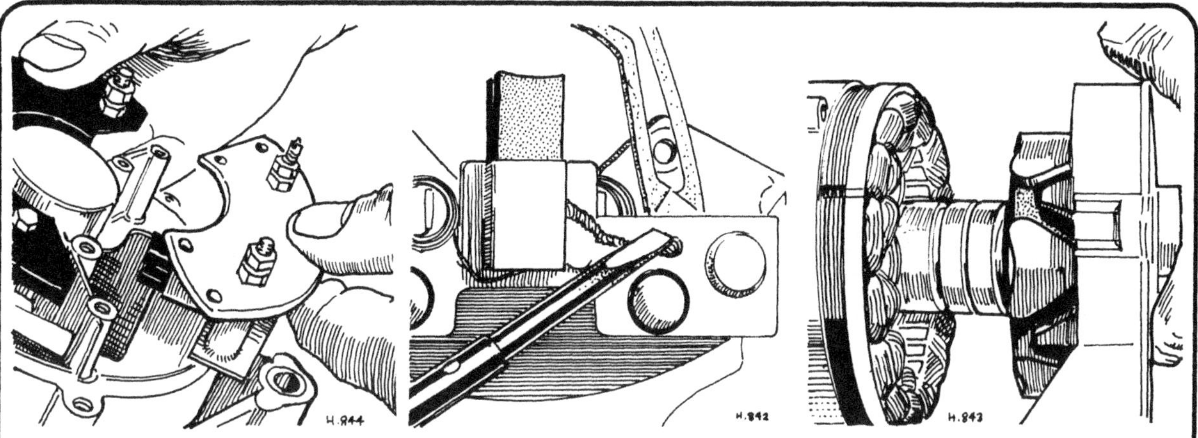

Fig. 11.6. Removing the brush holder plate from an early type alternator (Sec. 8)

Fig. 11.7. Soldering alternator brush leads (Sec. 8)

Fig. 11.8. Removing the drive end bracket, stator and rotor from an early type alternator (Sec. 8)

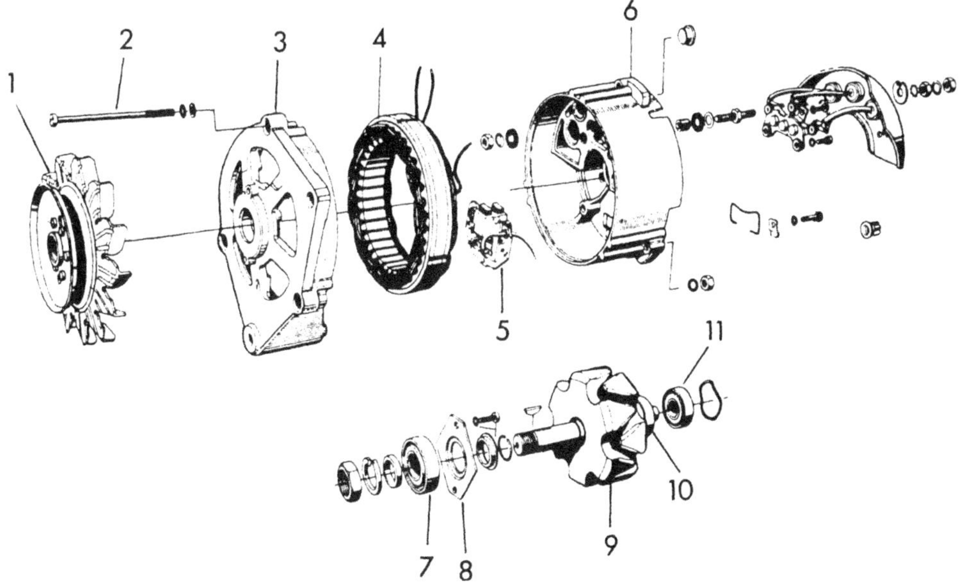


Fig. 11.9. Exploded view of later type alternator (Sec. 9)

*1 Fan*
*2 Tie bolt*
*3 Drive end bracket*
*4 Stator*
*5 Brush holder*
*6 Brush end housing*
*7 Drive end bracket bearing*
*8 Bearing retaining plate*
*9 Rotor*
*10 Slip rings*
*11 Rear bearing*

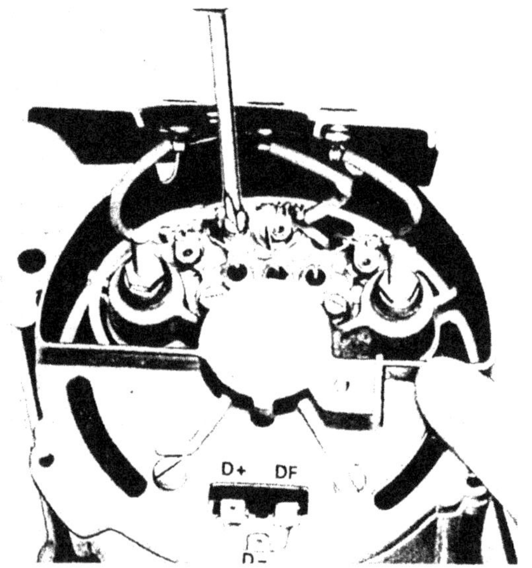

Fig 11.10 Removing brush holder plate connecting cable (later type alternator)

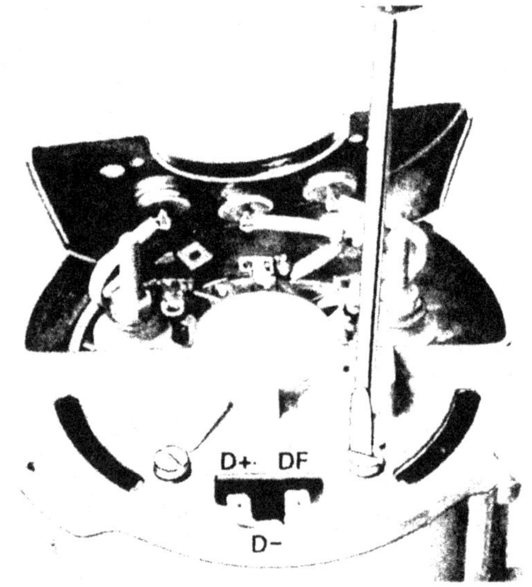

Fig 11.11 Removing brush holder plate securing screws (later type alternator)

Fig 11.12 Removing the brush holder plate (later type alternator)

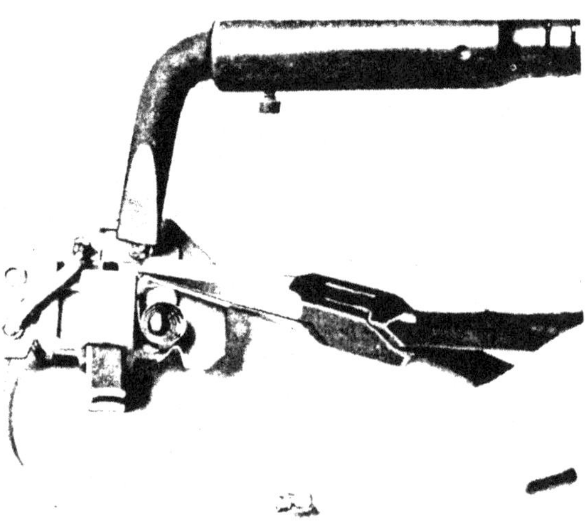
Fig 11.13 Unsoldering a brush lead (later type alternator)

defective and must be renewed. Do not run the engine at a speed higher than 2000 rev/min with the plug leads bridged or the electrical accessories may be damaged due to current being produced with too high a voltage.

4 If the warning lamp stays on or flashes on and off then it is the alternator which is defective and should be repaired or renewed.

## 11 Starter motor - general description

The starter motor is of the pre-engaged type. When the ignition key is turned, the solenoid is energised and moves the forked engagement lever, which in turn, meshes the pinion assembly with the ring gear of the flywheel. It is then that the main starter motor contacts close and the flywheel is rotated to start the engine.

Incorporated in the pinion assembly is a clutch device which ensures that the drive pinion is disengaged from the flywheel ring

Fig. 11.14 Bridging the voltage regulator connecting plug tags to test the alternator output

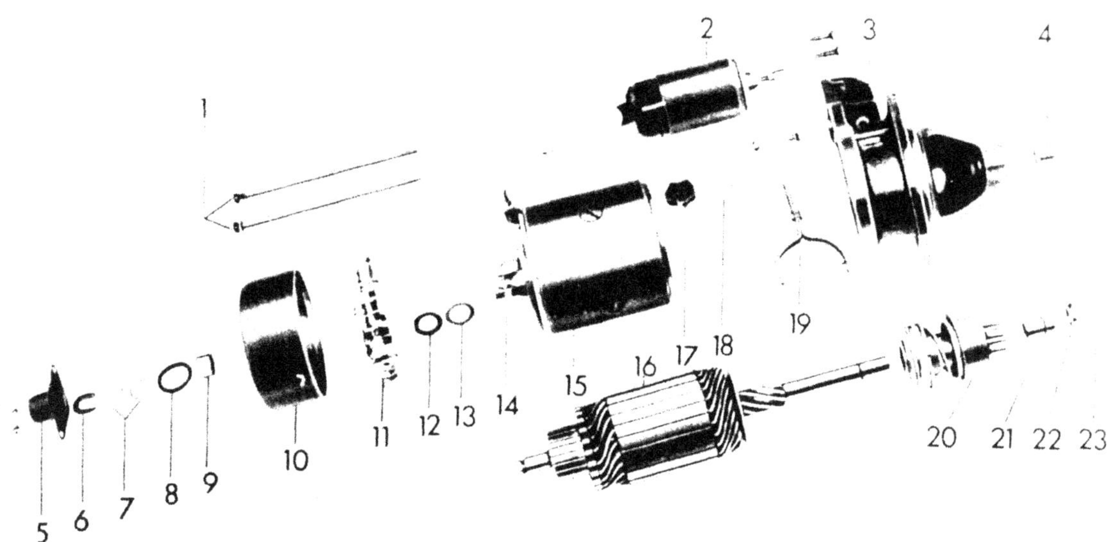


Fig 11.15 Exploded view of the starter motor

*1 Tie bolts*
*2 Solenoid switch*
*3 Drive end bracket*
*4 Bearing bush*
*5 Protective cap*
*6 'U' washer*
*7 Shims*
*8 Rubber washer*
*9 Bearing bush*
*10 Commutator end cover*
*11 Brush plate assembly*
*12 Fibre washer*
*13 Steel washer*
*14 Field coils*
*15 Starter yoke*
*16 Armature*
*17 Rubber plug*
*18 Steel washer*
*19 Drive pinion engagement lever*
*20 Starter drive pinion*
*21 Starter pinion bearing bush*
*22 Stop washer*
*23 Circlip*

gear as soon as the engine fires and the engine speed exceeds that of the starter motor.

## 12 Starter motor - testing in position

1 If the starter motor fails to operate then check the condition of the battery by turning on the headlamps. If they glow brightly for several seconds and then gradually dim the battery is in an uncharged condition.

2 If the headlights glow brightly and it is obvious that the battery is in good condition, then check the tightness of the battery wiring connections (and in particular the earth lead from the battery terminal to its connection on the body frame). If the positive terminal on the battery becomes hot when an attempt is made to work the starter this is a sure sign of a poor connection on the battery terminal. To rectify, remove the terminal, clean the mating faces thoroughly and reconnect. Check the connections on the rear of the starter solenoid. Check the wiring with a voltmeter or test lamp for breaks or shorts.

3 Test the continuity of the solenoid windings by connecting a test lamp (low wattage) and 12 volt battery between the solenoid main terminal nut nearest the starter motor and the solenoid body. If the two windings are in order, the lamp will light. Now connect the test lamp (high wattage bulb) between the two main terminals of the solenoid. Energise the solenoid by applying a 12 volt supply between the terminal "3" and the solenoid body. The solenoid should be heard to operate and the test bulb will illuminate. (Fig. 11.16).

4 If the battery is fully charged, the wiring in order, and the starter/ignition switch working and the starter motor still fails to operate then it will have to be removed from the car for examination. Before this is done ensure that the starter motor pinion has not jammed in mesh with the flywheel by engaging a gear and rocking the car to and fro. This should free the pinion if it is stuck in mesh with the flywheel teeth.

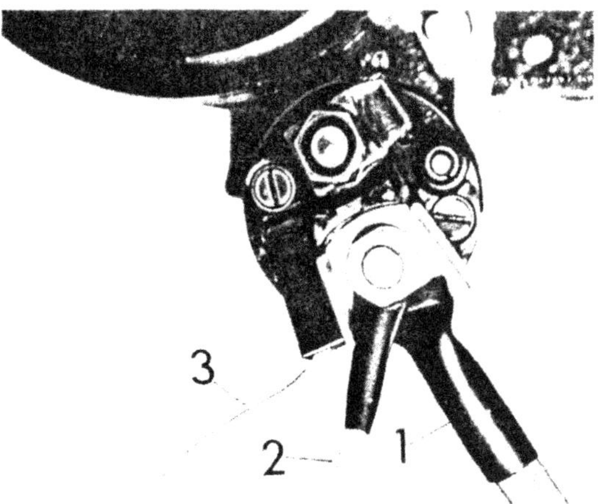


Fig 11.16 Starter solenoid cable connections

*1 Red cable from battery +* *2 Grey (85) from alternator*
*3 Yellow (84) from ignition switch*

### 13 Starter motor - removal and installation

1 Disconnect the lead from the battery negative terminal.
2 Disconnect the cables from the solenoid and starter terminals (photo).
3 Unscrew the two starter securing bolts and withdraw the starter motor (photo).
4 Installation is a reversal of removal.

### 14 Starter motor - dismantling, inspection and reassembly

1 Disconnect the lead from the motor field windings at the solenoid lower terminal nut.
2 Unscrew and remove the two screws which secure the solenoid to the drive end bracket.
3 Unhook the solenoid plunger from the pinion engagement lever and withdraw the solenoid switch.
4 From the commutator end, unscrew and remove the protective cap and extract the 'U' washer, the shims and rubber washer.
5 Unscrew the two tie-bolts and remove the commutator end cover.
6 Using a piece of bent wire, pull back the brush springs so that the brushes can be withdrawn from their holders.
7 Remove the brush holder plate, fibre and steel washers. If the brushes are worn, their leads should be disconnected from the brush holder plate and the field winding terminal tags by using a soldering iron. Refit the new brushes, taking care to localise the heat, particularly in the case of the field winding leads. (Fig. 11.17).
8 Separate the starter yoke from the drive end bracket and then unscrew the pinion engagement lever pivot bolt.
9 Extract the rubber plug and steel washer from the drive end bracket.
10 Withdraw the armature complete with drive pinion and engagement lever from the drive end bracket. Detach the engagement lever from the drive pinion assembly.
11 Examine the condition of the commutator at the end of the armature. If it is burned or blackened it should be polished with very fine glass paper (not emery). Do not undercut the mica separators between the commutator segments.
12 If the drive pinion is sticky in operation, wash it thoroughly in paraffin and apply a trace of light oil to the spiral threads on the commutator shaft. If the drive pinion must be dismantled for renewal of a component, drive the stop washer down the shaft to expose the circlips, using a piece of tubing. Extract the circlip and pull off the stop washer and drive pinion assembly.
13 Refitting the pinion assembly is a reversal of removal but use a new stop washer and circlip. Having driven the new stop washer down the shaft to enable the circlip to be located in its groove, the stop washer may be drawn back into position by using a two legged extractor.
14 Reassembly is a reversal of dismantling but the commutator

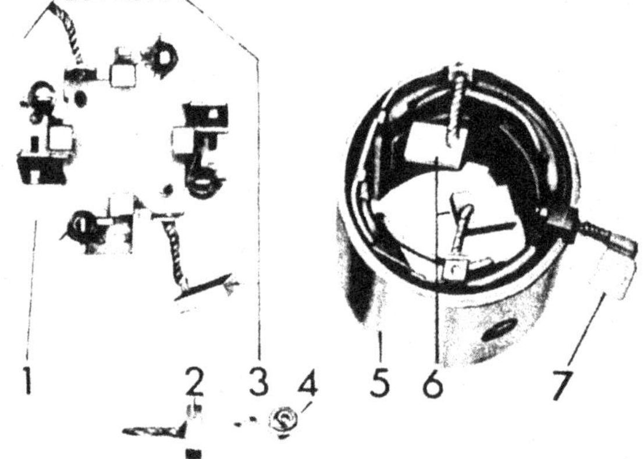


**Fig 11.17 Starter motor brush holder plate and field coils**

*1 Brush holder plate*
*2 Brush*
*3 Negative brush*
*4 Brush tension spring*
*5 Starter yoke*
*6 Positive brush*
*7 Field coil lead*

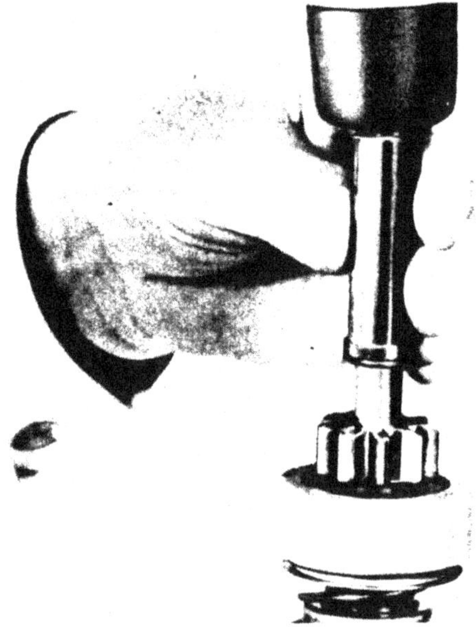

**Fig 11.18 Driving the starter drive stop washer down to expose the circlip**

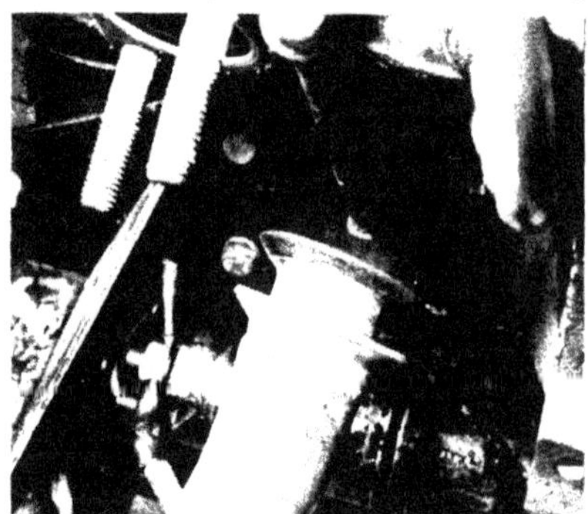

13.2 Starter motor and leads located below exhaust downpipe

13.3 Withdrawing the starter motor

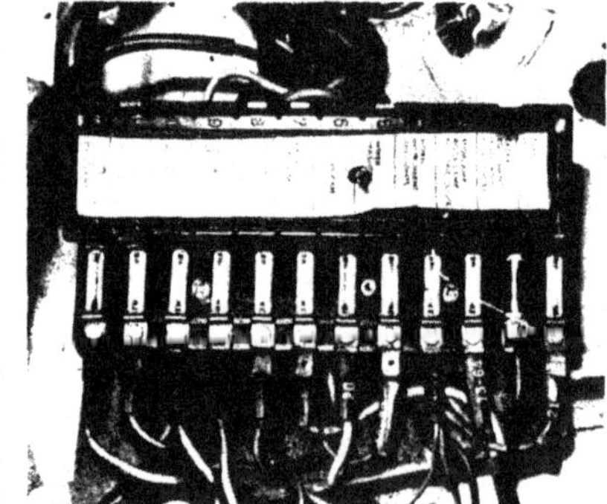

15.1 Fuse location on engine bulkhead

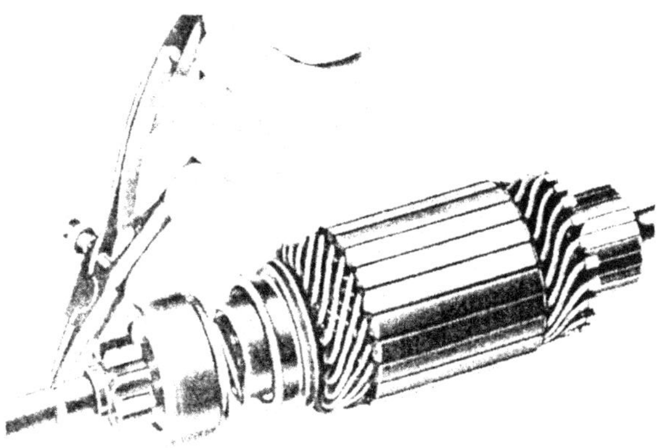

Fig 11.19 Extracting the starter pinion retaining circlip

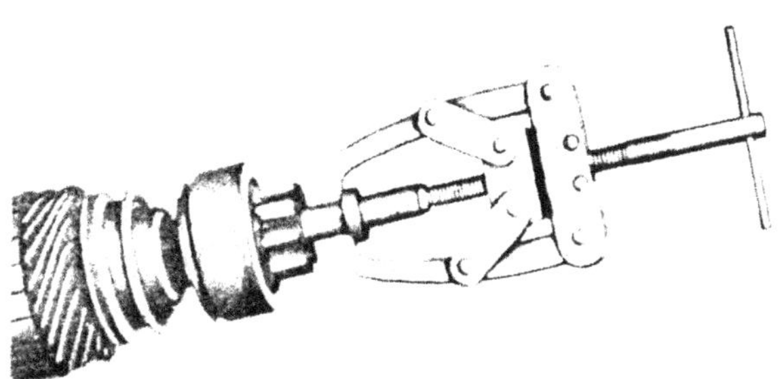

Fig 11.20 Method of drawing stop washer over circlip on starter armature shaft

endfloat must be between 0.002 and 0.012 in. (0.05 and 0.3 mm). If it is outside this tolerance then the shim pack within the commutator protective cap should be adjusted.

## 15 Fuses

1 A bank of twelve 8 amp fuses is located on the right-hand side of the engine compartment rear bulkhead. In addition, there is a separate 2.5 amp fuse to protect the headlamp lens cleaning device (Section 25) (photo).
2 Always renew a fuse with one of the same rating and if the same fuse blows twice in succession, thoroughly check the circuit for shorting, also the electrical accessories which are served by it.

## 16 Headlamps and switches - general description

1 According to the operating territory for which they are destined, vehicles may be equipped with bulb type headlamps or sealed beam units of circular design (up to and including 1968 models). The sealed beam units are only fitted to lhd vehicles. (Figs. 11.22 and 11.23).
2 Vehicles built from 1969 onwards may be fitted with bulb type headlamps of rectangular design or alternatively have circular sealed beam units (lhd vehicles only). (Figs. 11.24 and 11.25).

## 17 Headlamp (circular type) - bulb renewal

1 Raise the bonnet and peel the rubber grommet from the rear of the headlamp (photo).
2 Release the retaining spring and withdraw the bulb holder. (Fig. 11.26).
3 Change the bulb using a cloth to prevent finger marks and ensure that the bulb locating lug is correctly engaged. Refit the bulb holder and grommet (photo).

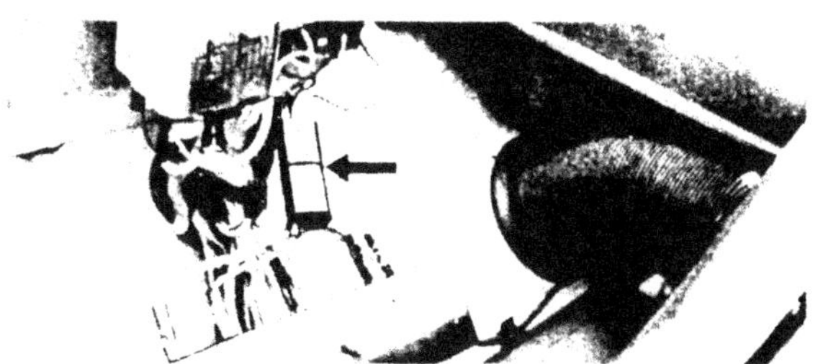

Fig 11.21 The fuse box with headlamp cleaning device separately located (arrowed)

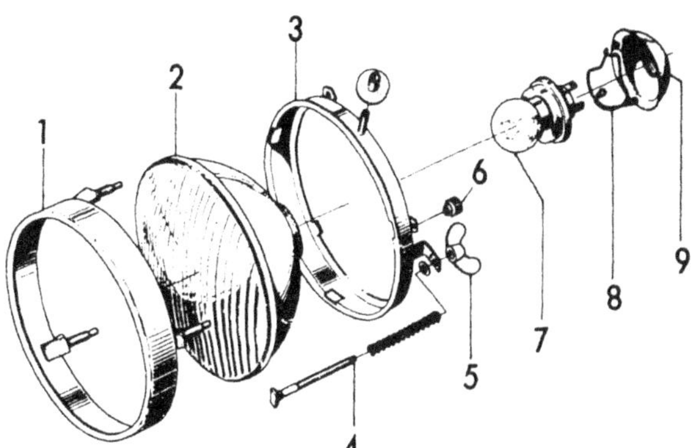


Fig 11.22 Exploded view of circular design, bulb type headlamp

*1 Bezel*
*2 Lamp unit*
*3 Support ring*
*4 Adjusting screw*
*5 Wing nut*
*6 Mounting nut*
*7 Bulb*
*8 Holder spring*
*9 Rubber seal*

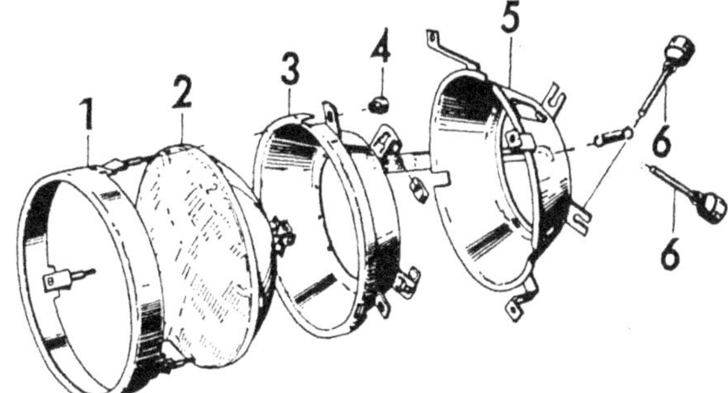


Fig 11.23 Exploded view of sealed beam headlamp (up to 1968, lhd only)

*1 Bezel*
*2 Sealed beam unit*
*3 Support ring*
*4 Nut*
*5 Lamp shell*
*6 Adjusting screw*

## 18 Headlamp (rectangular type) - bulb renewal

1 Raise the bonnet and peel back the rubber seal behind the headlamp.
2 Pull off the wiring connector.
3 Press in the bulb holder securing ring and turn it anti-clockwise. Release the ring together with the spring and bulb holder.
4 Change the bulb using a cloth to avoid finger marks and then fit the bulb holder so that its locating lug is at the bottom. Refit the securing ring and the rubber seal with its draining lip at the bottom.

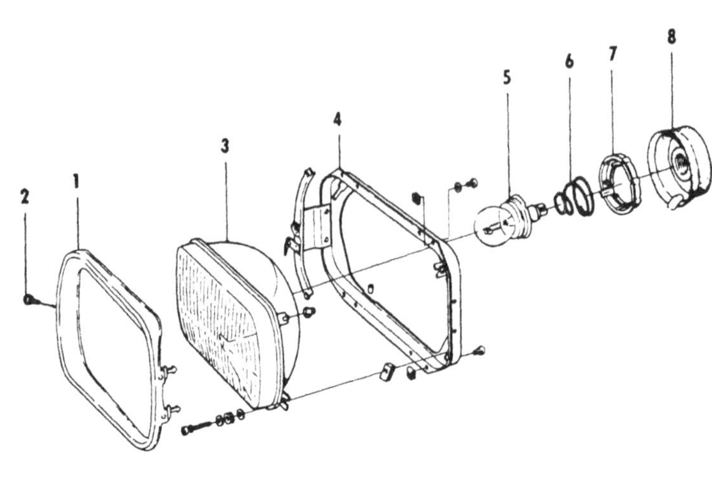


Fig 11.24 Exploded view of rectangular design, bulb type headlamp

*1 Bezel*
*2 Securing screw*
*3 Lamp unit*
*4 Support plate*
*5 Bulb*
*6 Coil spring*
*7 Bulb holder retaining ring*
*8 Rubber seal*

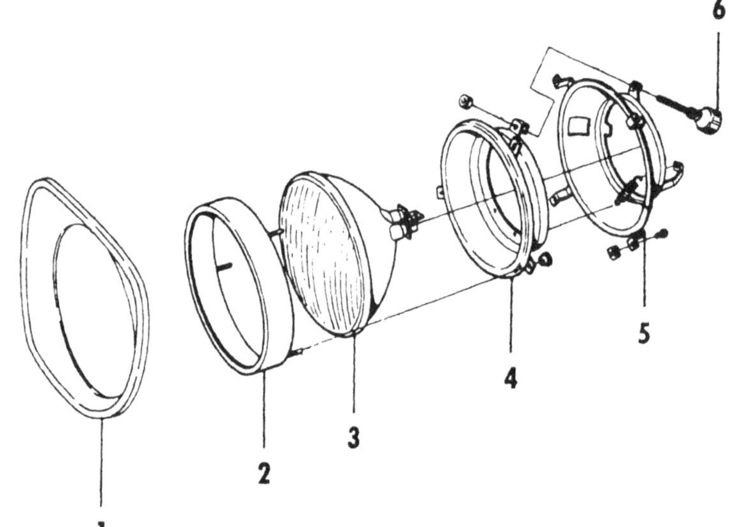


Fig 11.25 Exploded view of headlamp sealed beam unit (1969 onwards lhd only)

*1 Decor surround*
*2 Bezel*
*3 Sealed beam unit*
*4 Support ring*
*5 Shell*
*6 Adjusting screw*

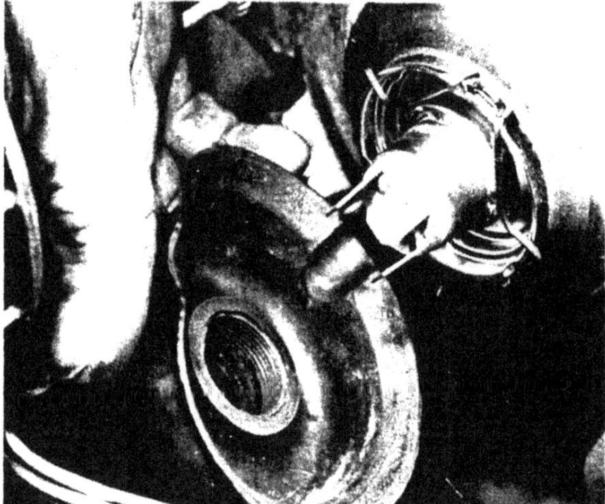

17.1 Headlamp rear sealing grommet

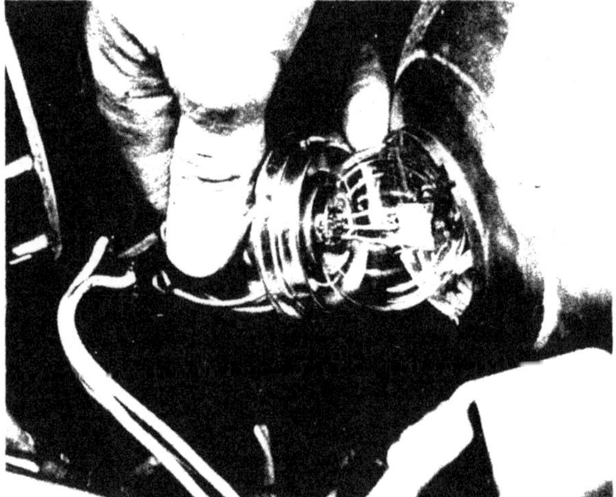

17.3 Headlamp bulb holder

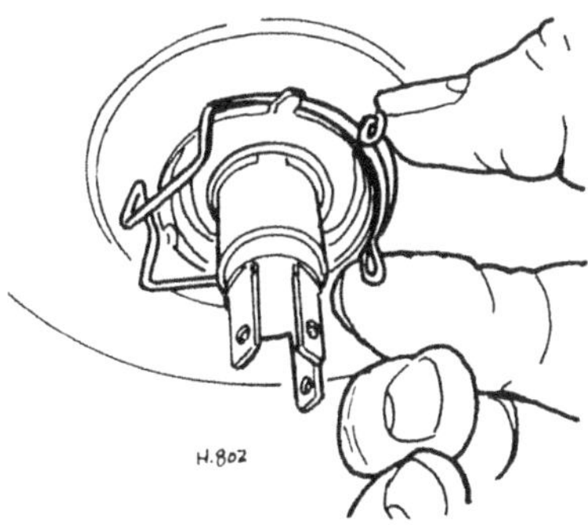


Fig 11.26 Removing a bulb holder from a circular type headlamp

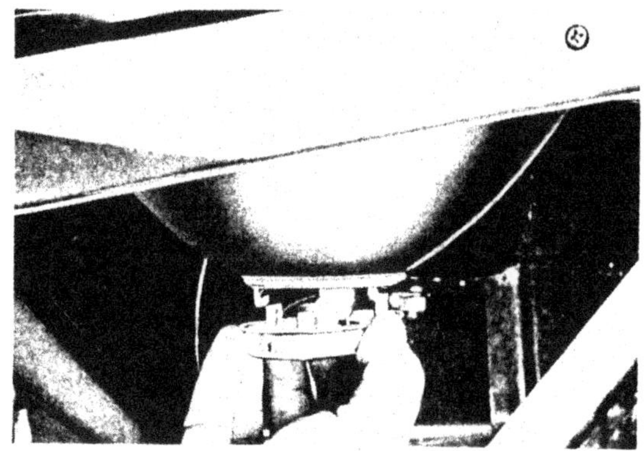

Fig 11.27 Removing a bulb holder from a rectangular headlamp

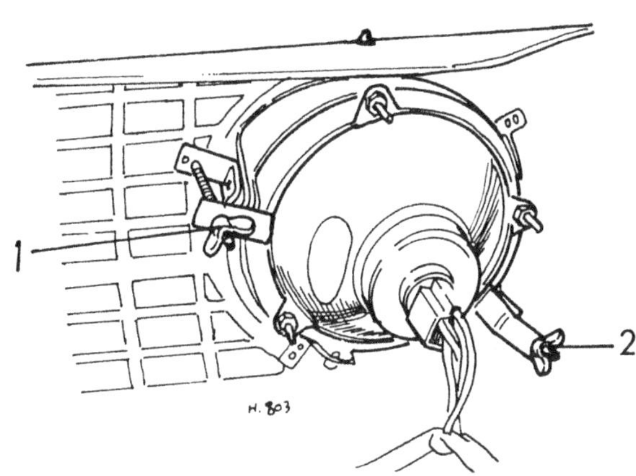


Fig 11.28 Location of circular (bulb type) adjusting screws

*1 Horizontal adjustment 2 Vertical adjustment*

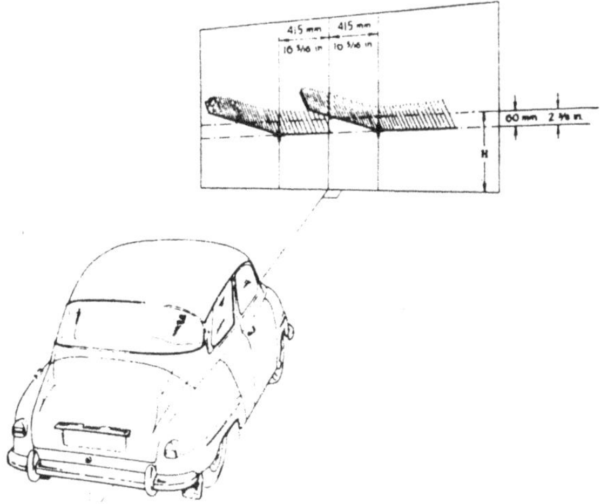


Fig 11.29 Headlamp alignment diagram (circular bulb type - rhd)

## 19 Headlamp sealed beam unit - renewal

1 Withdraw the cable connecting plug from the rear of the headlamp unit.
2 Unscrew and remove the three nuts which secure the chrome bezel and withdraw it. Lift out the sealed beam unit.
3 Locate the new headlamp unit ensuring that it locates correctly into the recesses of the headlamp shell.
4 Reconnect the plug and bezel.

## 20 Headlamps (circular - bulb type - rhd vehicles) - alignment

1 Although it is recommended that headlamp alignment is carried out by a service station using up-to-date optical beam setting equipment, the descriptions given in this and the following two Sections will provide a satisfactory alternative.
2 Inflate the tyres to the specified pressures and position the vehicle (unladen) on a flat surface so that the distance from the front bumper to a wall or screen is 16.5 ft (5.0 metres).
3 Mark the screen with a horizontal line at the height of the lamp centres (H) and two vertical lines, one each side of and at a distance of 16 5/16 in. (415.0 mm) from the centre line of the vehicle.
4 Adjust the two wing nuts at the rear of the headlamp until the bottom centre point of the Vee shaped light beam is 2 3/8 in. (60.3 mm) below the intersection of the horizontal and vertical lines on the screen. (Fig. 11.29).
5 Mask the correctly aligned headlamp and repeat the operations on the opposite one. Finally check both lamps unmasked.

## 21 Headlamps (circular - bulb type - lhd vehicles) - alignment

1 Refer to the preceding Section but although the adjustment procedure is identical, the light pattern will be sloping upwards to the right as shown. (Fig. 11.30).

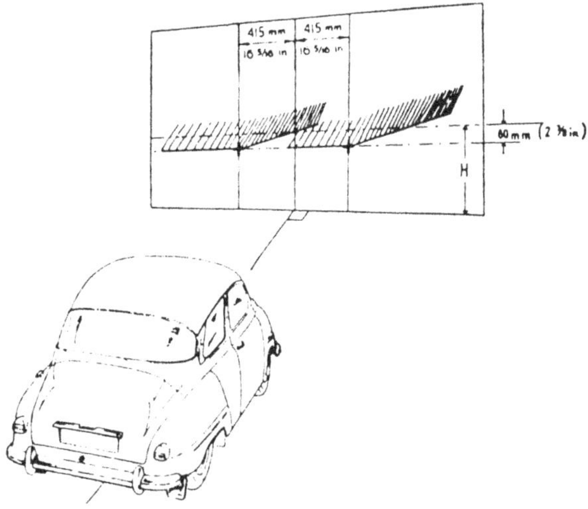


Fig 11.30 Headlamp alignment diagram (circular bulb type - lhd)

## 22 Headlamps (rectangular - bulb type - lhd vehicles) - alignment

1 The procedure is similar to that described in Section 20 but the difference in marking on the screen must be observed.
2 Each lamp is aligned individually on dipped beam and the adjusting screws are accessible from the front after removal of the decor surround (one screw). (Fig. 11.32).

## 23 Headlamps (rectangular - bulb type - lhd vehicles) - alignment

1 Refer to the preceding Section but although the adjustment procedure is identical, the light pattern will be sloping upwards to the right as shown. (Fig. 11.33).

## 24 Headlamp sealed beam units - alignment

1 This type of headlamp unit is normally only fitted to lhd vehicles.
2 Place the vehicle, unladen, with correctly inflated tyres on a level surface so that the front of the vehicle is 24.6 ft (7.5 metres) from a screen or wall.
3 Mark the screen with a horizontal line at the same height as that of the headlight centres.
4 Make a vertical line one each side of and at a distance of 16.3 in. (415.0 mm) from the centre line of the vehicle.
5 Switch on to main beam and mask one lamp. Adjust the adjusting screws (accessible from the front after removal of the decor surround) until the light pattern is as shown with its centre 6 in. (152.4 mm) on either side of the vertical centre line and its upper edge level with the horizontal line (Fig. 11.34).
6 Mask the lamp just adjusted and then repeat the operations on the other headlamp.

## 25 Headlamp cleaning device - description, adjustment, servicing

1 A mechanically operated headlamp lens wiper and washer arrangement is fitted to vehicles produced from 1971 onwards. The wiper linkage is driven from an electric motor mounted below the left-hand headlamp. (Fig. 11.35).
2 A multi-position switch which operates in conjunction with the windscreen wiper motor provides flexible control of the windscreen and headlamp wiper devices.
3 Adjustment of the wiper blade travel is carried out by removing the decor surrounds from the headlamps and detaching

Fig 11.31 Headlamp alignment diagram (rectangular bulb type - rhd)

Fig 11.33 Headlamp alignment diagram (rectangular bulb type lhd)

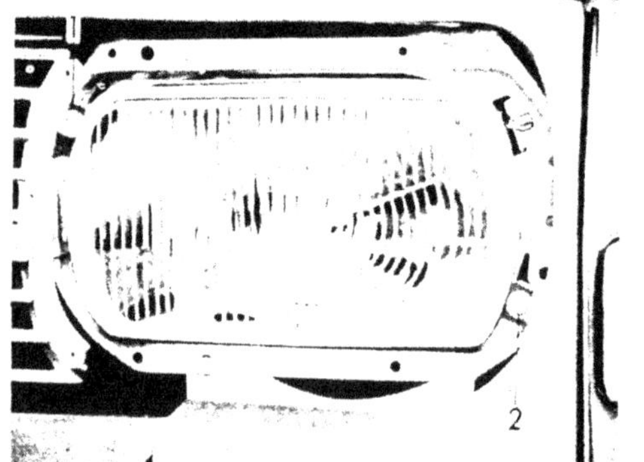


Fig 11.32 Location of adjustment screws (rectangular bulb type headlamps)

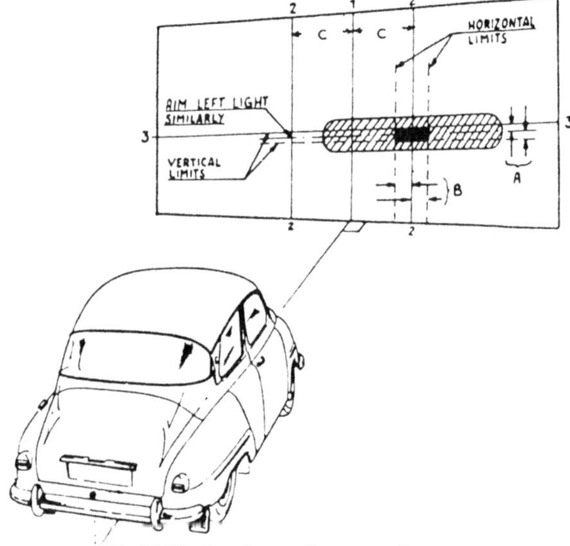


Fig 11.34 Headlamp alignment diagram (sealed beam units - lhd)

*1 Vehicle centre line* — *A = 2 in (50.8 mm)*
*2-2 Centre line of headlamps (vertical)* — *B = 6 in (152.4 mm)*
*3-3 Horizontal centre line of headlamps* — *C = 16.3 in (415.0 mm)*

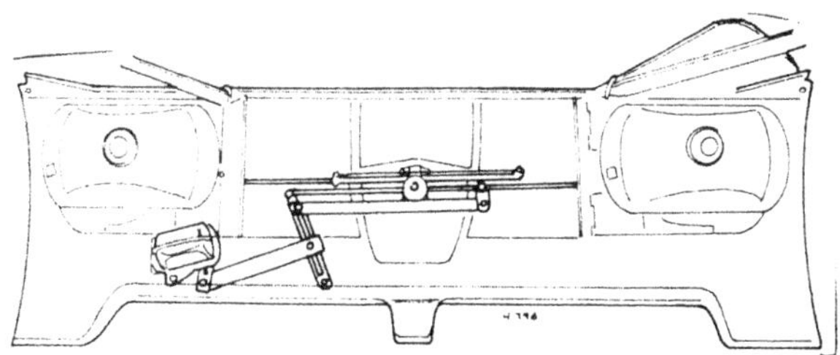

Fig 11.35 Headlamp cleaning device

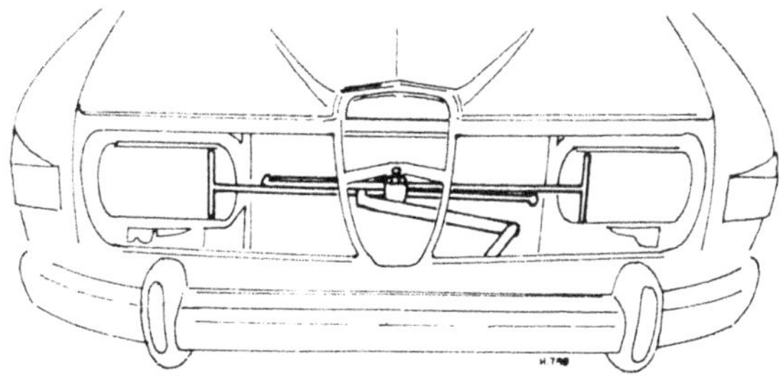

Fig 11.36 Headlamp wiper/washer device with radiator grille removed

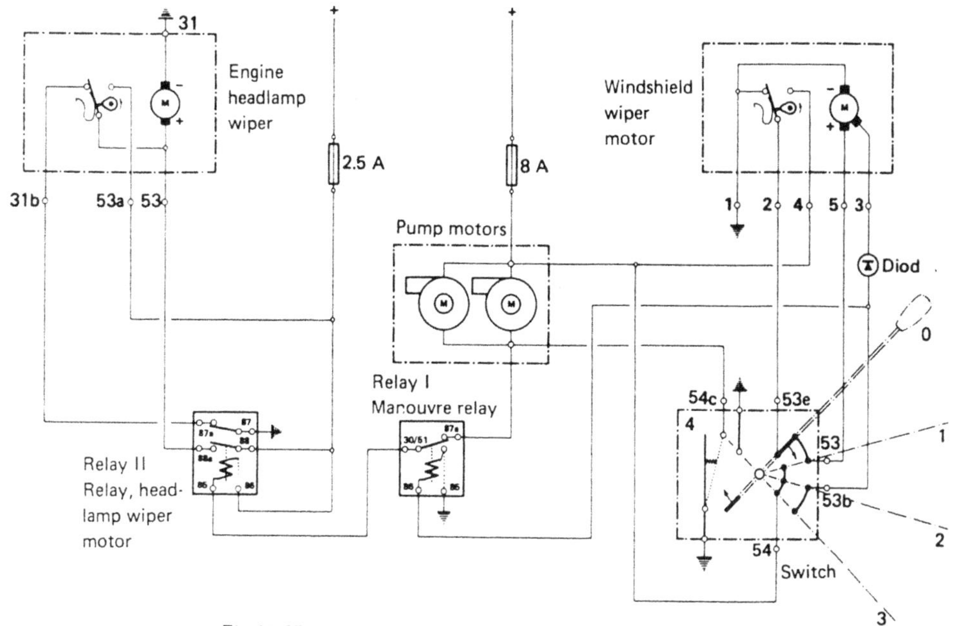


Fig 11.37 Headlamp cleaning device circuit diagram

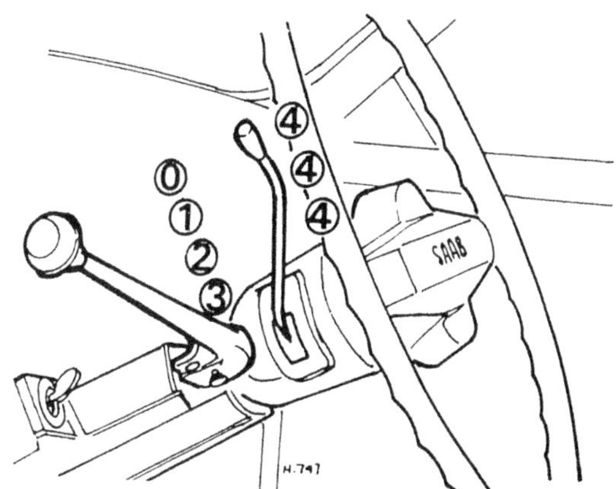


Fig 11.38 Wiper/washer switch attached to the steering column

*0 – Off*
*1 Windscreen wipers, low speed*
*2 Windscreen wipers, full speed plus headlamp wipers*
*3 Windscreen wipers, full speed plus headlamp wipers plus screen and headlamp washers*
*4 (Control depressed towards steering wheel in all selection positions) provides washing of screen and lamps*

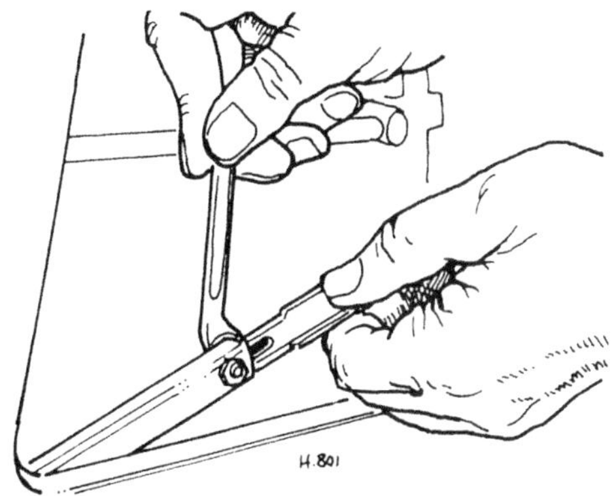

Fig 11.39 Adjusting length of pushrod to vary headlamp wiper blade parking position

the three sections of the radiator grille.

4 Adjustment of the wiper blade parking position may be made by altering the length of the short pushrod. (Fig. 11.39).

5 The nylon cords must be tensioned so that the individual wiping lengths of the two wipers are equal and there is no slackness in the cords. To achieve this, slacken the locking screw in the cord clamps and move the clamps as required. (Fig. 11.40).

6 Occasionally apply a little grease to the bushes through which the operating rods pass.

7 If a new wiper blade has to be fitted, detach the circlip from the wiper operating rod and pull off the wiper blade.
8 Where the complete headlamp wiper assembly has to be removed for repair or renewal, detach the decor surrounds from the headlamps and disconnect the hoses from the washer jets.
9 Remove the three sections of the radiator grille.
10 Detach the two springs at the wiper operating rod bushes.
11 Unscrew and remove the bolt which secures the crank to the spindle of the headlamp wiper motor. (Fig. 11.41).
12 Remove the long crank arm from its bearing in the front

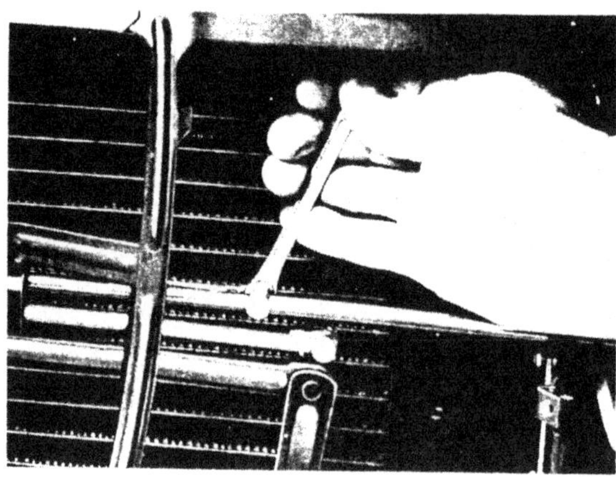

Fig 11.40 Adjusting the headlamp wiper blade nylon cords

Fig 11.41 Headlamp wiper motor spindle/crank bolt

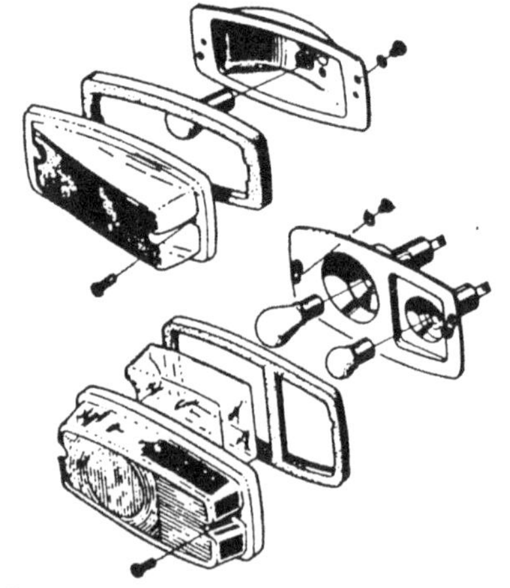

Fig 11.42 Front parking and direction indicator lamp unit (up to and including 1968)

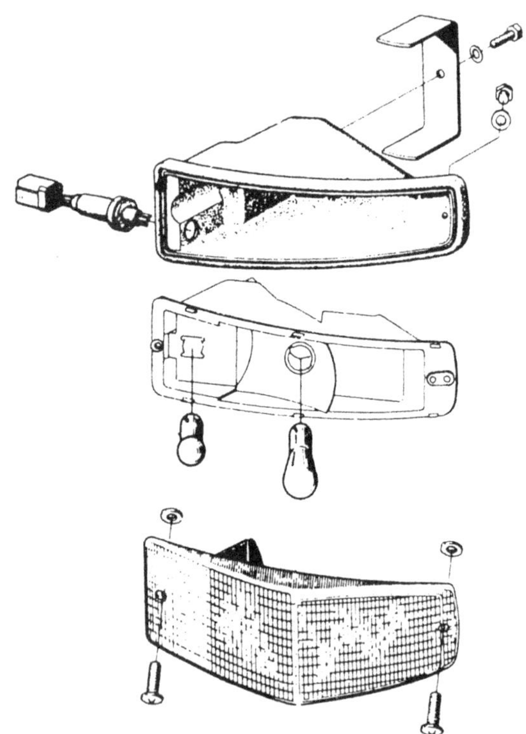

Fig 11.43 Front parking and direction indicator lamp unit (1969 onwards)

26.1 Front lamp unit lens and bulbs

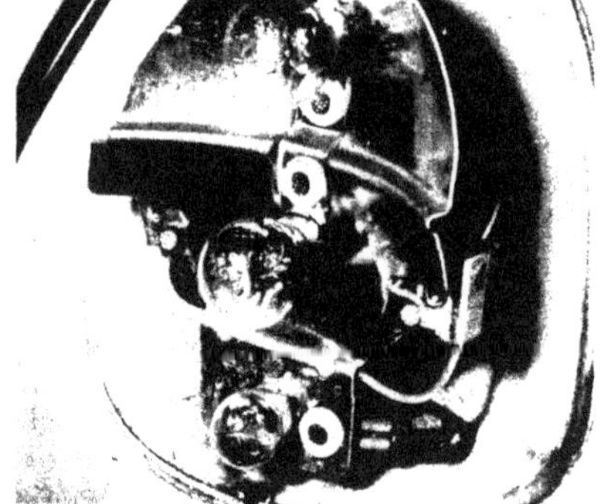

27.1A Rear lamp unit bulbs

27.1B Reversing lamp

body panel, also the wiper operating rod bush.
13 Remove the crank arms and operating rods sideways from behind the centre air grille struts.
14 Disconnect the lead from the wiper motor and then remove the motor by unscrewing its two support screws and the spindle nut.
15 Refitting is a reversal of removal but tighten the crank arm bolt on the wiper motor spindle to a torque of 8 lb/ft (1.1 kg/m) having applied Loctite to the threads.

## 26 Front parking and direction indicator lamps - bulb renewal

1 The design of these lamps differs according to date of vehicle manufacture but both types use two independent bayonet fitting bulbs which are accessible after removal of the front lens (two screws). (Figs. 11.42/43 (photo).

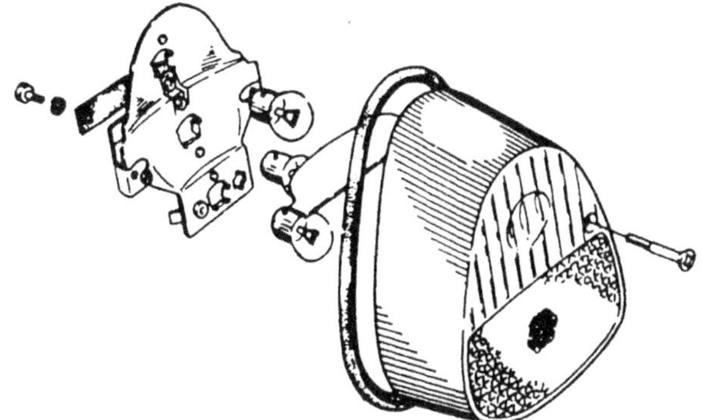

Fig 11.44 Rear stop, tail and direction indicator lamp unit (SAAB 96 and Monte Carlo)

## 27 Rear stop, tail, direction indicator and reversing lamp - bulb renewal

1 The design of these lamps varies between the particular vehicle models and date of manufacture. Bulbs are of bayonet fitting type and are accessible after removal of the lamp lenses and their securing screws. (Figs. 11.44, 11.45 and 11.46) (photos).

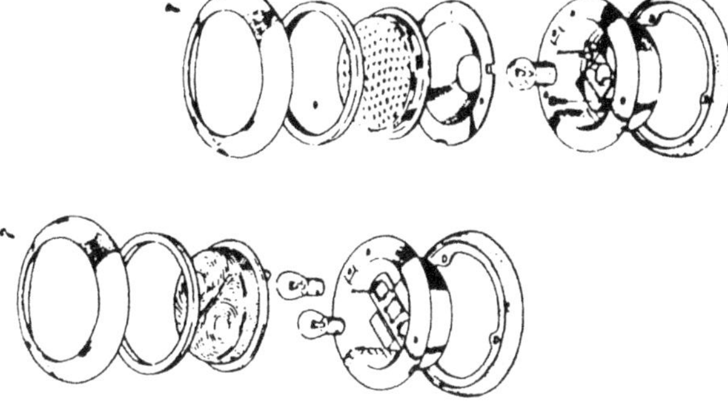

Fig 11.45 Rear stop, tail and direction indicator lamp unit (SAAB up to and including 1968)

## 28 Direction indicators (flashers) - servicing

1 The flasher unit is mounted under the instrument panel in conjunction with a relay which indicates through the medium of two warning lamps that the direction indicators are working correctly.
2 If one of the front or rear flashers ceases to operate then the warning lamp will not come on and the opposing lamp of the pair will flash more rapidly.
3 Provided all the bulbs are in good condition and the connecting wiring is secure and in order, then any fault must lie in the flasher unit itself which should therefore be renewed complete, no repair being possible.
4 As from 1966 onwards, North American models are fitted with a different type of flasher unit which also controls the operation of the hazard warning flashers.
5 As previously mentioned in Chapter 8, a clearance must be maintained between the indicator cancelling cam and the projection of the switch on the steering column. This clearance should be between 0.008 and 0.024 in. (0.2 to 0.6 mm) with the switch in the neutral mode. If adjustment is required, fit shims between the switch and the steering column support shroud.

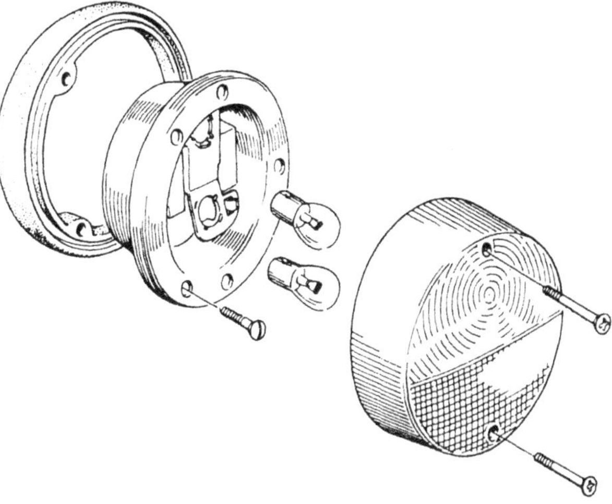

Fig 11.46 Rear stop, tail, direction indicator and reversing lamp unit (SAAB 95, 1969 onwards)

## 29 Horns - maintenance and adjustment

1 The horns are fitted inside the front panel of the engine compartment and comprise a matched pair, one high and one low note.
2 Occasionally check the security of the horn mountings and the wiring and connections.
3 Adjustment of horn note is rarely required but should it be, turn the screw (marked with red paint) on the rear of the horn until an acceptable note is obtained.

## 30 Windscreen wipers - description, maintenance and adjustment

1 The wiper mechanism comprises an electric motor mounted on the engine compartment rear bulkhead driving mechanical linkage through a crank secured to the wiper motor spindle. (Fig. 11.48)
2 The wiper motor differs in type according to date of vehicle manufacture.
3 Maintenance is minimal as the motor bearings and gears are grease packed in production. Occasionally check the security of the connecting wiring.
4 Every two years, or earlier if they fail to wipe clean, renew the wiper blades.
5 Should the wiper blade parking position require adjustment, slacken the gear housing cover screws which will enable the fixed contact to be moved one way or the other until the parking position is correct.

## 31 Windscreen wiper motor and linkage - removal and refitting

1 Remove the circlip from the motor crank to linkage connection. This is rather inaccessible being located below the motor mounting plate and it may be easier to remove the mounting plate bolts and turn the wiper motor to bring the crank arm into view.
2 Carefully retain the mounting plate rubber insulators.
3 Mark the electrical leads to the wiper motor and disconnect them at their snap connectors. Lift the motor away.
4 Refitting is a reversal of removal.
5 If it is required to remove the linkage, first unbolt the wiper arms from their driving spindles (photo).
6 Unscrew and remove the spindle housing nuts, washers and distance pieces from the front of the scuttle and then remove the linkage complete from the rear of the scuttle.
7 When refitting the linkage, check that the spindles project equally by adjusting the backnuts and do not overtighten the spindle securing nuts, but sufficiently to reasonably compress the seals which should be in good condition.

## 32 Windscreen wiper motor - repair and overhaul

1 Servicing of the wiper motor should be restricted to renewal of the brushes. Smaller components are not generally available as spares and in any event it will be more economical to exchange the motor for a factory reconditioned unit when wear develops in the gears and other major components.
2 Unscrew and remove the gearbox cover plate bolts and lift off the cover.

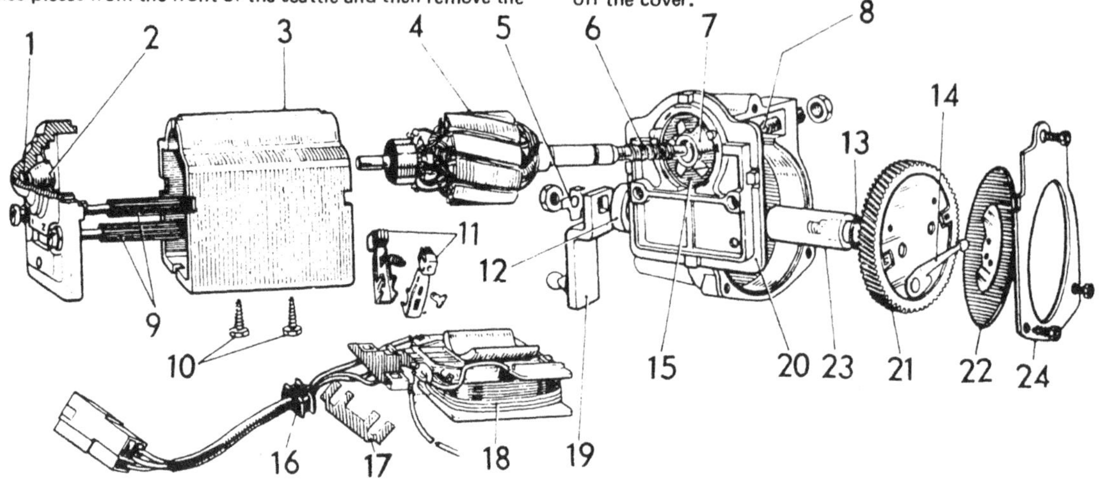


Fig 11.47 Exploded view of windscreen wiper motor fitted up to and including 1969 models

*1 Thrust pad*
*2 Spherical bearing*
*3 Yoke*
*4 Armature*
*5 Tab washer*
*6 Worm gear*
*7 Spherical bearing*
*8 Endfloat adjuster and thrust pad*
*9 Tie bolts and insulating sleeves*
*10 Pole piece securing screws*
*11 Brush gear*
*12 Bush*
*13 Washer*
*14 Limit switch moving contact*
*15 Bearing retainer*
*16 Grommet*
*17 Brush arm retainer*
*18 Field coil*
*19 Crank arm*
*20 Drive end bracket*
*21 Gearwheel*
*22 Limit switch fixed contact plate*
*23 Porous bronze bush*
*24 Gearbox cover plate*

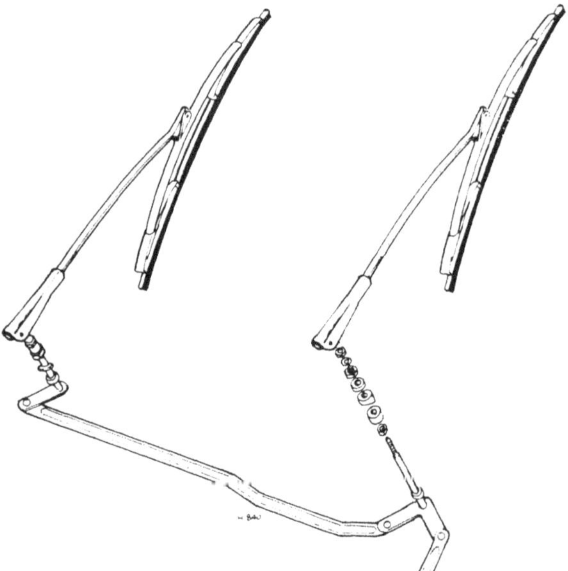

Fig 11.48 Windscreen wiper motor linkage

31.5 Windscreen wiper arm to driving spindle pinch bolt

3 Carefully note the position of the crank arm in relation to the shaft and gear so that it may be refitted correctly.
4 Secure the crank arm in the jaws of a vice and then unscrew the arm to shaft retaining nut and remove the crank arm and washer.
5 Withdraw the shaft and gear assembly from the gearbox.
6 Withdraw the yoke tie-bolts and remove the yoke and armature from the gearbox.
7 Detach the brush gear from the armature commutator; if the brushes are badly worn, renew the brush gear as an assembly.
8 Ensure that the new brushes move freely in their boxes and clean the commutator with a fuel soaked rag.
9 Reassembly is a reversal of dismantling but apply engine oil sparingly to the armature shaft bearings and bushes and grease the gear teeth liberally.
10 Set the armature endfloat by tightening the thrust screw until it just touches the end of the armature shaft and then unscrew it a ¼ of a turn and lock it.

## 33 Instruments - removal and refitting

1 The instruments vary slightly in layout and position dependent upon the date of vehicle manufacture but each instrument may be removed individually from the instrument panel and they are accessible from behind it.
2 To remove the speedometer, disconnect the electrical leads from the instrument to the earthing screw.
3 Withdraw the panel lampholders with their leads.
4 Unscrew the knurled ring which secures the speedometer drive cable to the speedometer head. As from 1970, the speedometer drive cable connection is of bayonet fitting type.
5 Unscrew the one or two instrument strap securing nuts (according to vehicle model) and withdraw the speedometer through the front of the instrument panel.
6 The fuel and temperature gauges (up to and including the 1969 models) may be removed individually in a similar manner to that described in the preceding paragraphs. These instruments on later model vehicles form a single cluster and this should be removed as a unit for later separation of the two instruments.

## 34 Speedometer drive cable - removal and refitting

1 Disconnect the lower end of the cable from the transmission unit as described in Chapter 6, Section 11.
2 Disconnect the upper end of the cable from the speedometer head by unscrewing the knurled ring or releasing the bayonet fitting according to type.
3 Withdraw the cable assembly into the engine compartment through the aperture in the bulkhead.
4 Install the new cable by passing it into the vehicle interior through the engine rear bulkhead aperture. Remember to fit the grommet to the cable and secure the nut at the upper end with a piece of masking tape to prevent the nut from sliding down during installation.
5 Make sure that the cable has no sharp bends and will not rub against any components or body projections likely to damage it.

## 35 Tachometer - installation

1 The Monte Carlo version is fitted with a tachometer as standard equipment and this instrument can be fitted to the other models in the range if desired.
2 The instrument is of electrically operated type connected to the ignition primary (LT) circuit.
3 Connect the instrument wiring as indicated, taking particular

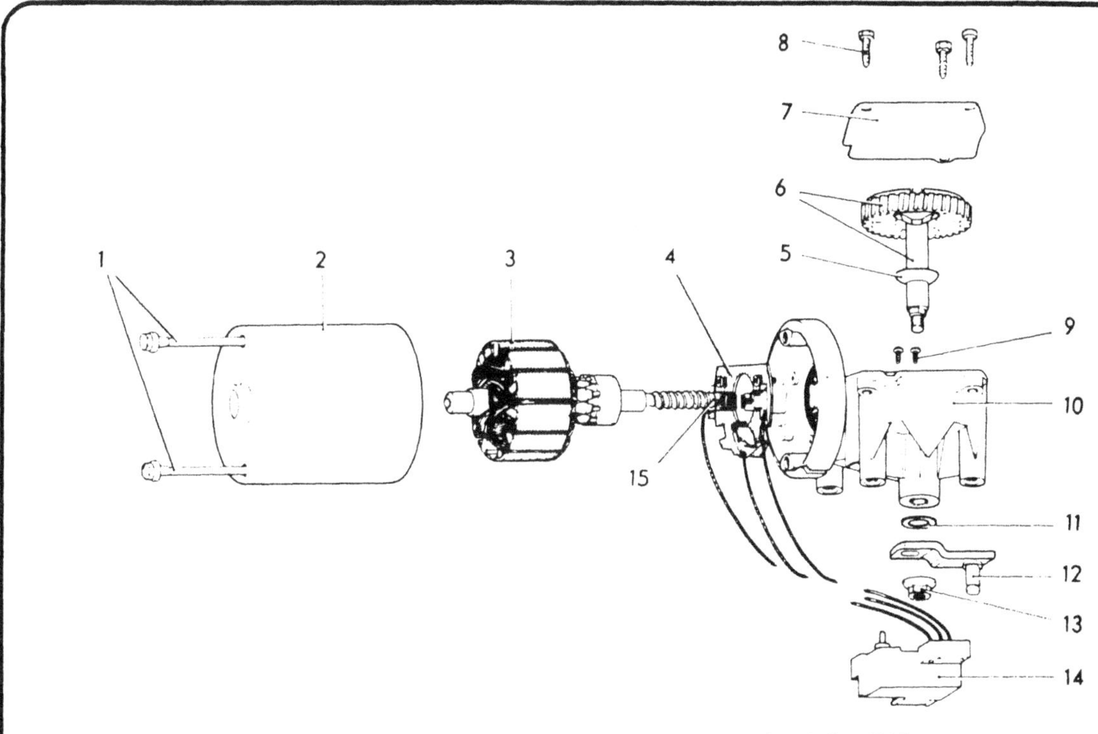


Fig 11.49 Exploded view of windscreen wiper motor fitted after 1969

*1 Tie bolts*
*2 Yoke*
*3 Armature*
*4 Brush gear*
*5 Cupped washer*
*6 Shaft/gear assembly*
*7 Gearbox cover plate*
*8 Cover screws*
*9 Parking contact screws*
*10 Gearbox*
*11 Flat washer*
*12 Crank arm*
*13 Securing nut*
*14 Parking contact*

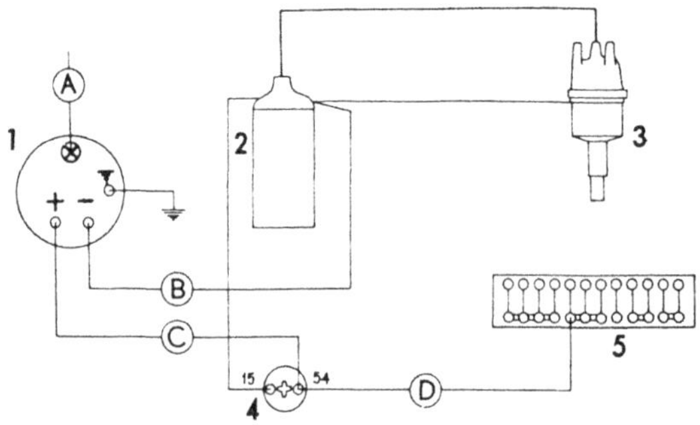


Fig 11.50 Tachometer wiring diagram

*1 Tachometer*
*2 Ignition coil*
*3 Distributor*
*4 Ignition switch*
*5 Fuse block*
*A Instrument lighting lead*
*B Lead from ignition coil to negative terminal on tachometer*
*C Lead from terminal (54) on ignition switch to positive lead on tachometer*
*D Lead from ignition switch to fuse block*

Fig 11.51 Radio location in lhd vehicle

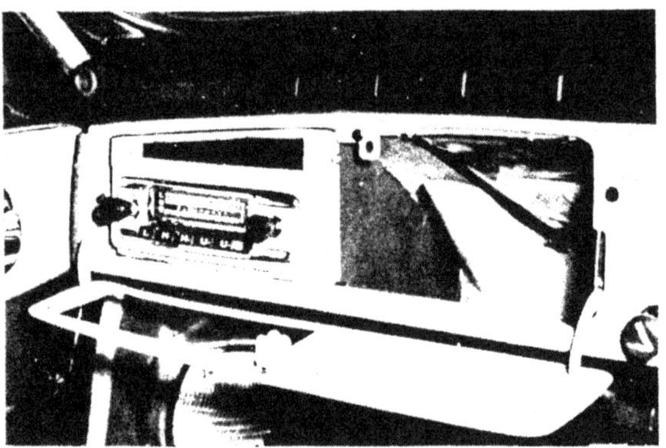

Fig 11.52 Radio location in rhd vehicle

Fig 11.53 Recommended siting of radio aerial

care that the positive and negative leads are correctly attached to the instrument terminals.

## 36 Radio - guide to installation

1 Installation of a car radio is really a job for a professional but where the fitting is being undertaken by the home mechanic, then the following guide lines should be borne in mind.
2 The receiver should be located in the instrument panel or glove compartment according to whether the vehicle is left or right-hand drive.
3 The recommended position for the aerial is on the left-hand front wing, as remote as possible from the ignition coil.
4 Connect the receiver to the ignition switch or the spare terminal of the fuse block.
5 Always include a cartridge type fuse in the feed line to the receiver.
6 Check that the receiver is of negative earth type or is suitable for conversion to this polarity.
7 Ensure that the ignition system is adequately suppressed and be prepared to add suppressors to the windscreen wiper and headlamp wiper motors if they cause interference once the radio receiver is installed.

## 37 Auxiliary lamps - guide to fitting

1 The Monte Carlo is already equipped with a fog and spot lamp but if such lamps are to be fitted to the other models in the range then the following guide lines should be observed.
2 Choose lamps which have brackets designed for the vehicle or are of universal fitting pattern.
3 Locate the operating switches conveniently to hand where they will not be masked by other controls or the steering wheel.
4 Connect the supply cable through the fuse box and ensure that all electrical leads are of suitable diameter to carry the required current.
5 Remember UK regulations demand that lamps are fitted as a pair and mounted so that their centres are at least 24 in. (61.1 cm) but not more than 42 in. (106.7 cm) from the ground and not more than 16 in. (40.6 cm) from the outer extremities of the vehicle. Failure to observe the mounting conditions means that the lamps can only be used in fog or falling snow.

## 38 Fault diagnosis - electrical system

| Symptom | Reason/s | Remedy |
|---|---|---|
| Starter motor fails to turn engine | Battery discharged | Charge battery. |
| | Battery defective internally | Fit new battery. |
| | Battery terminal leads loose or earth lead not securely attached to body | Check and tighten leads. |
| | Loose or broken connections in starter motor circuit | Check all connections and tighten any that are loose. |
| | Starter motor switch or solenoid faulty | Test and replace faulty components with new. |
| | Starter brushes badly worn, sticking, or brush wires loose | Examine brushes, replace as necessary, tighten down brush wires. |
| | Commutator dirty, worn or burnt | Clean commutator, recut if badly burnt. |
| | Starter motor armature faulty | Overhaul starter motor, fit new armature. |
| | Field coils earthed | Overhaul starter motor. |
| Starter motor turns engine very slowly | Battery in discharged condition | Charge battery. |
| | Starter brushes badly worn, sticking, or brush wires loose | Examine brushes, replace as necessary, tighten down brush wires. |
| | Loose wires in starter motor circuit | Check wiring and tighten as necessary. |
| Starter motor operates without turning engine | Starter motor pinion sticking on the screwed sleeve | Remove starter motor, clean starter motor drive. |
| | Pinion or flywheel gear teeth broken or worn | Fit new gear ring to flywheel, and new pinion to starter motor drive. |
| Starter motor noisy or excessively rough engagement | Pinion or flywheel gear teeth broken or worn | Fit new gear teeth to flywheel, or new pinion to starter motor drive. |
| | Starter motor retaining bolts loose | Tighten starter motor securing bolts. Fit new spring washer if necessary. |
| Battery will not hold charge for more than a few days | Battery defective internally | Remove and fit new battery. |
| | Electrolyte level too low or electrolyte too weak due to leakage | Top up electrolyte level to just above plates. |
| | Plate separators no longer fully effective | Remove and fit new battery. |
| | Battery plates severely sulphated | Remove and fit new battery. |
| | Fan/alternator belt slipping | Check belt for wear, renew if necessary, and tighten. |
| | Battery terminal connections loose or corroded | Check terminals for tightness, and remove all corrosion. |
| | Alternator not charging properly | Take car to auto-electrician. |
| | Short in lighting circuit causing continual battery drain | Trace and rectify. |
| | Regulator unit not working correctly | Take car to auto-electrician. |
| Ignition light fails to go out, battery runs flat in a few days | Fan belt loose and slipping or broken | Check, replace and tighten as necessary. |
| | Alternator faulty | Take car to auto-electrician. |

**Failure of individual electrical equipment to function correctly is dealt with alphabetically, item by item, under the headings listed below.**

| Symptom | Reason/s | Remedy |
|---|---|---|
| Fuel gauge gives no reading (see also Chapter 3) | Fuel tank empty! | Fill fuel tank. |
| | Electric cable between tank sender unit and gauge earthed or loose | Check cable for earthing and joints for tightness. |
| | Fuel gauge case not earthed | Ensure case is well earthed. |
| | Fuel gauge supply cable interrupted | Check and replace cable if necessary. |
| | Fuel gauge unit broken | Renew fuel gauge. |
| Fuel gauge registers full all the time (see also Chapter 3) | Electric cable between tank unit and gauge broken or disconnected | Check over cable and repair as necessary. |
| Horn operates all the time | Horn push either earthed or stuck down | Disconnect battery earth. Check and rectify source of trouble. |
| | Horn cable to horn push earthed | Disconnect battery earth. Check and rectify source of trouble. |
| Horn fails to operate | Blown fuse | Check and renew if broken. Ascertain cause. |
| | Cable or cable connection loose, broken or disconnected | Check all connections for tightness and cables for breaks. |
| | Horn has an internal fault | Remove and overhaul horn. |

| Symptom | Reason/s | Remedy |
|---|---|---|
| Horn emits intermittent or unsatisfactory noise | Cable connections loose | Check and tighten all connections. |
| | Horn incorrectly adjusted | Adjust horn until best note obtained. |
| Lights do not come on | If engine not running, battery discharged | Push-start car, charge battery. |
| | Light bulb filament burnt out or bulbs broken | Test bulbs in live bulb holder. |
| | Wire connections loose, disconnected or broken | Check all connections for tightness and wire cable for breaks. |
| | Light switch shorting or otherwise faulty | By-pass light switch to ascertain if fault is in switch and fit new switch as appropriate. |
| Lights come on but fade out | If engine not running, battery discharged | Push-start car and charge battery. |
| Lights give very poor illumination | Lamp glasses dirty | Clean glasses. |
| | Reflector tarnished or dirty | Fit new reflectors. |
| | Lamps badly out of adjustment | Adjust lamps correctly. |
| | Incorrect bulb with too low wattage fitted | Remove bulb and replace with correct grade. |
| | Existing bulbs old and badly discoloured | Renew bulb units. |
| Lights work erratically - flashing on and off, especially over bumps | Battery terminals or earth connections loose | Tighten battery terminals and earth connection. |
| | Lights not earthing properly | Examine and rectify. |
| | Contacts in light switch faulty | By-pass light switch to ascertain if fault is in switch and fit new switch as appropriate. |
| Wiper motor fails to work | Blown fuse | Check and replace fuse if necessary. |
| | Wire connections loose, disconnected or broken | Check wiper wiring. Tighten loose connections. |
| | Brushes badly worn | Remove and fit new brushes. |
| | Armature worn or faulty | If electricity at wiper motor, remove and fit replacement. |
| | Field coils faulty | Purchase reconditioned wiper motor. |
| Wiper motor works very slowly and takes excessive current | Commutator dirty, greasy or burnt | Clean commutator thoroughly. |
| | Drive to spindles bent or unlubricated | Examine drive and straighten. Lubricate. |
| | Wiper arm spindle binding or damaged | Remove, fit replacement. |
| | Armature bearings dry | Replace with new bearings. |
| | Armature badly worn or faulty | Remove, fit replacement motor. |
| Wiper motor works slowly and takes little current | Brushes badly worn | Remove and fit new brushes. |
| | Commutator dirty, greasy or burnt | Clean commutator thoroughly. |
| | Armature badly worn or faulty | Remove and fit replacement motor. |
| Wiper motor works but wiper blades remain static | Driving linkage disengaged or faulty | Examine and if faulty renew. |
| | Wiper arm spindle damaged or worn | Examine and if faulty renew. |
| | Wiper motor gearbox parts badly worn | Renew unit. |

**Wiring diagram Monte Carlo rhd model 1967**

*The range of the electrical system is shown by the wiring system below. To simplify the identification, the wires have been covered with insulation of different shades, as follows:*

| | |
|---|---|
| *Black* | *7, 7b, 18, 45, 46, 47, 49, 71, 80, 105, 106, 107, 108, 109, 123e, 124, 135, 138, 139, 140* |
| *Red* | *5, 21, 28, 28e, 28f, 32, 39, 61, 63, 65, 67, 68, 72, 83, 86, 86e, 126, 129* |
| *Green* | *16, 22, 50, 51, 52, 53, 54, 55, 56, 57, 58, 60, 82, 101, 102, 103, 104, 110, 119, 121, 133, 143* |
| *Grey* | *4, 25b, 25be, 29, 29e, 35, 44a, 62a, 64, 69, 70, 74, 75, 85, 89, 113, 117, 142, 144* |
| *White* | *20, 23b, 24b, 40, 42b, 66, 95, 97, 98, 118, 122, 122e, 128a, 131* |
| *Yellow* | *17, 23a, 24a, 33, 43, 44b, 62b, 73, 81, 84, 99, 100, 100e, 112, 112e, 128b, 130* |
| *Brown* | *14, 14c, 15, 30, 30e, 137, 141* |
| *Blue* | *13, 25a, 25ae, 41, 42a, 145* |

**Key to numbers in the figure**

1 *Direction indicators and side lights*
2 *Headlights*
3 *Horn*
4 *Foglight and spotlight*
5 *Ignition coil*
6 *Spark plugs*
7 *Distributor*
8 *Voltage regulator*
9 *Alternator*
10 *Starter*
11 *Battery*
12 *Fuse box*
13 *Temperature meter*
14 *Oil gauge*
15 *Back-up light switch*
16 *Stop light switch*
17 *Heater fan motor*
18 *Windshield-washer pump*
19 *Wiper motor*
20 *Direction indicator repeater lights*
21 *Charge indicator light*
22 *Indicator light, oil pressure*
23 *High beam indicator light*
24 *Indicator light, fuel*
25 *Flasher*
26 *Tachometer*
27 *Temperature gauge*
28 *Fuel gauge*
29 *Speedometer, odometer and trip meter*
30 *Electric clock*
31 *Ignition and starter switch*
32 *Manoeuvre relay, light*
33 *Dimming relay*
34 *Spotlight switch*
35 *Headlight switch and instrument illumination rheostat*
36 *Fog light switch*
37 *Heater fan switch*
38 *Windshield wiper and washer switch*
39 *Cigarette lighter*
40 *Courtesy light switch*
41 *Courtesy light with switch*
42 *Horn button*
43 *Direction indicator switch with headlight flasher and dimmer switch*
44 *Fuel tank gauge*
45 *Back-up lights*
46 *Stop lights, direction indicators and tail lights*
47 *Number plate lights*
48 *Trunk light*

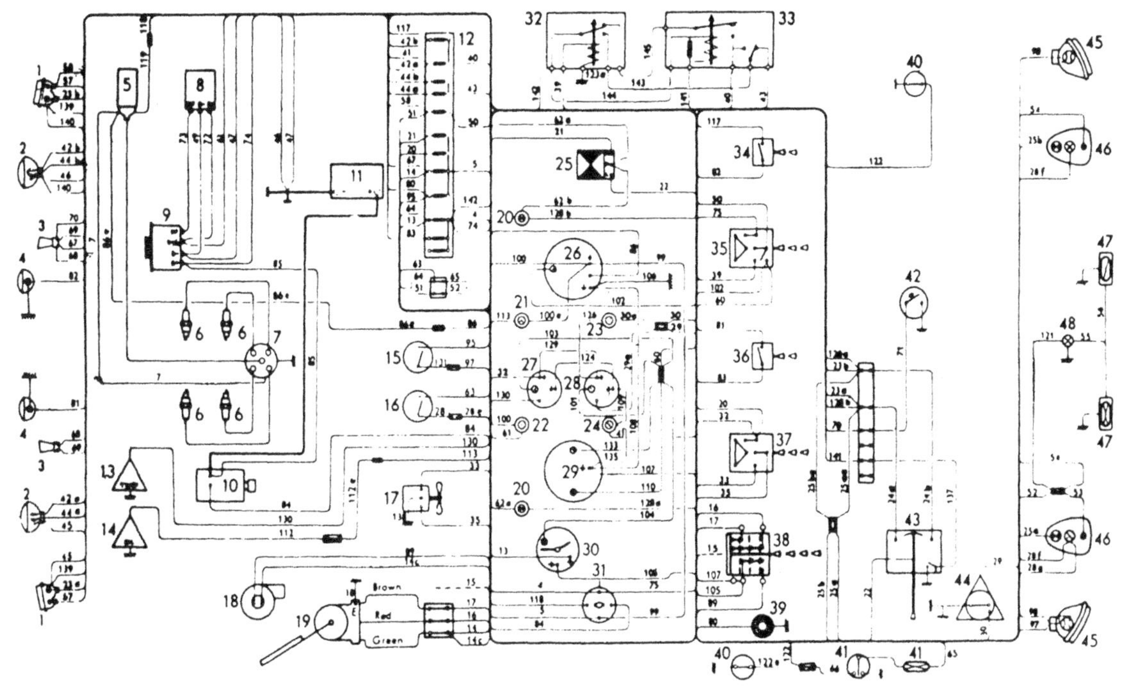

**Wiring diagram Monte Carlo USA model 1967**

*The range of the electrical system is shown by the wiring system below. To simplify the identification, the wires have been covered with insulation of different shades, as follows:*

| | |
|---|---|
| *Black* | *7, 7b, 18, 19, 45, 46, 47, 49, 71, 80, 105, 106, 107, 108, 109, 123e, 124, 135, 138, 139, 140* |
| *Red* | *5, 21, 28, 28e, 28f, 32, 39, 61, 63, 65, 67, 68, 72, 83, 86, 86e, 126, 129* |
| *Green* | *16, 22, 22e, 22f, 50, 51, 52, 53, 54, 55, 56, 57, 58, 60, 82, 101, 102, 103, 104, 110, 119, 121, 133, 146, 147* |
| *Grey* | *4, 25b, 29, 35, 44a, 62a, 62b, 64, 69, 70, 74, 75, 85, 89, 113, 117, 142, 144* |
| *White* | *20, 23b, 24b, 24be, 24bf, 40, 42b, 66, 95, 97, 98, 118, 122, 122e, 128a, 131* |
| *Yellow* | *17, 23a, 24a, 24ae, 24af, 33, 43, 44b, 62b, 73, 81, 84, 99, 100, 100e, 112, 112e, 128b, 130* |
| *Brown* | *14, 14c, 15, 30, 137, 141, 141e* |
| *Blue* | *13, 25a, 41, 42a* |

**Key to numbers in the figure**

1 *Direction indicators and side lights*
2 *Headlights*
3 *Horn*
4 *Foglight and spotlight*
5 *Ignition coil*
6 *Spark plugs*
7 *Distributor*
8 *Voltage regulator*
9 *Alternator*
10 *Starter*
11 *Battery*
12 *Fuse box*
13 *Temperature meter*
14 *Oil gauge*
15 *Back-up light switch*
16 *Stop light switch*
17 *Heater fan motor*
18 *Windshield-washer pump*
19 *Wiper motor*
20 *Direction indicator repeater lights*
21 *Charge indicator light*
22 *Indicator light, oil pressure*
23 *High beam indicator light*
24 *Indicator light, fuel*
25 *Ignition and starter switch*
26 *Electric clock*
27 *Speedometer, odometer and trip meter*
28 *Temperature gauge*
29 *Fuel gauge*
30 *Tachometer*
31 *Flasher*
32 *Manoeuvre relay, light*
33 *Dimming relay*
34 *Dimming switch*
35 *Cigarette lighter*
36 *Spotlight switch*
37 *Fog light switch*
38 *Headlight switch and instrument illumination rheostat*
39 *Warning flasher switch*
40 *Heater fan switch*
41 *Windshield wiper and washer switch*
42 *Courtesy light switch*
43 *Courtesy light and switch*
44 *Horn button*
45 *Direction indicator switch*
46 *Fuel tank gauge*
47 *Back-up lights*
48 *Stop lights, direction indicators and tail lights*
49 *Number plate lights*
50 *Trunk light*

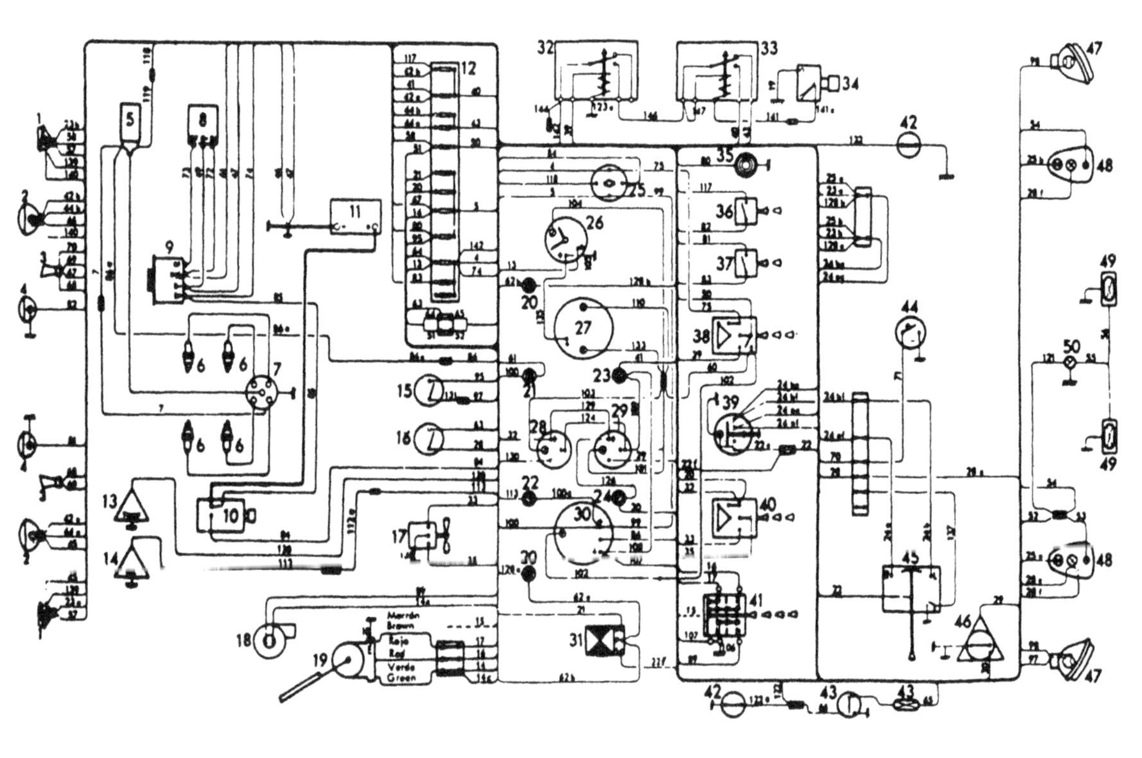

**Wiring diagram De Luxe USA model 1968**

*The range of the electrical system is shown by the wiring system below. To simplify the identification, the wires have been covered with insulation of different shades, as follows:*

| | |
|---|---|
| *Black* | *7, 23a, 45, 46, 47, 49, 71, 80, 88, 88e, 105, 107, 108, 109, 124, 135, 138, 139, 140* |
| *Red* | *5, 21, 28, 28e, 28f, 32, 39, 61, 63, 65, 67, 68, 72, 72e, 86, 86e, 111, 113, 116, 126, 129* |
| *Green* | *22, 22e, 22f, 50, 51, 52, 53, 54, 55, 56, 57, 58, 59, 101, 102, 103, 104, 110, 121, 133* |
| *Grey* | *4, 16, 16e, 25b, 29, 35, 44a, 62a, 64, 69, 70, 74, 75, 85* |
| *White* | *20, 23b, 24b, 24be, 24bf, 40, 42b, 66, 95, 97, 98, 99, 118, 122, 122e, 128a, 131* |
| *Yellow* | *24a, 24ae, 24af, 33, 43, 44b, 73, 84, 115, 128b* |
| *Brown* | *14, 30, 89, 130, 137, 137c* |
| *Blue* | *13, 17, 17e, 25a, 41, 42a, 112* |

**Key to numbers in the figure**

*1 Direction indicators and side lights*
*2 Headlights*
*3 Horn*
*4 Ignition coil*
*5 Spark plugs*
*6 Distributor*
*7 Voltage regulator*
*8 Alternator*
*9 Starter*
*10 Battery*
*11 Fuse box*
*12 Temperature gauge, sending unit*
*13 Oil pressure switch*
*14 Back-up light switch*
*15 Stop light switch*
*16 Brake warning contact*
*17 Heater fan motor*
*18 Windshield-washer pump*
*19 Wiper motor*
*20 Direction indicator repeater light*
*21 Brake warning light*
*22 Charge indicator light*
*23 Indicator light, oil pressure*
*24 High beam indicator light*
*25 Indicator light, fuel*
*26 Ignition and starter switch*
*27 Electric clock*
*28 Speedometer, odometer and trip meter*
*29 Temperature gauge*
*30 Fuel gauge*
*31 Tachometer*
*32 Dimmer switch*
*33 Flasher*
*34 Cigarette lighter*
*35 Switches for extra equipment*
*36 Headlight switch*
*37 Instrument illumination rheostat*
*38 Heater fan switch*
*39 Warning flasher switch*
*41 Courtesy light with switch*
*42 Switch for windshield wiper, washer and signal horn*
*43 Direction indicator switch with headlight flasher and dimmer switch*
*44 Fuel tank gauge*
*45 Back-up lights*
*46 Stop lights, direction indicators and tail lights*
*47 Number plate light*
*48 Trunk light*

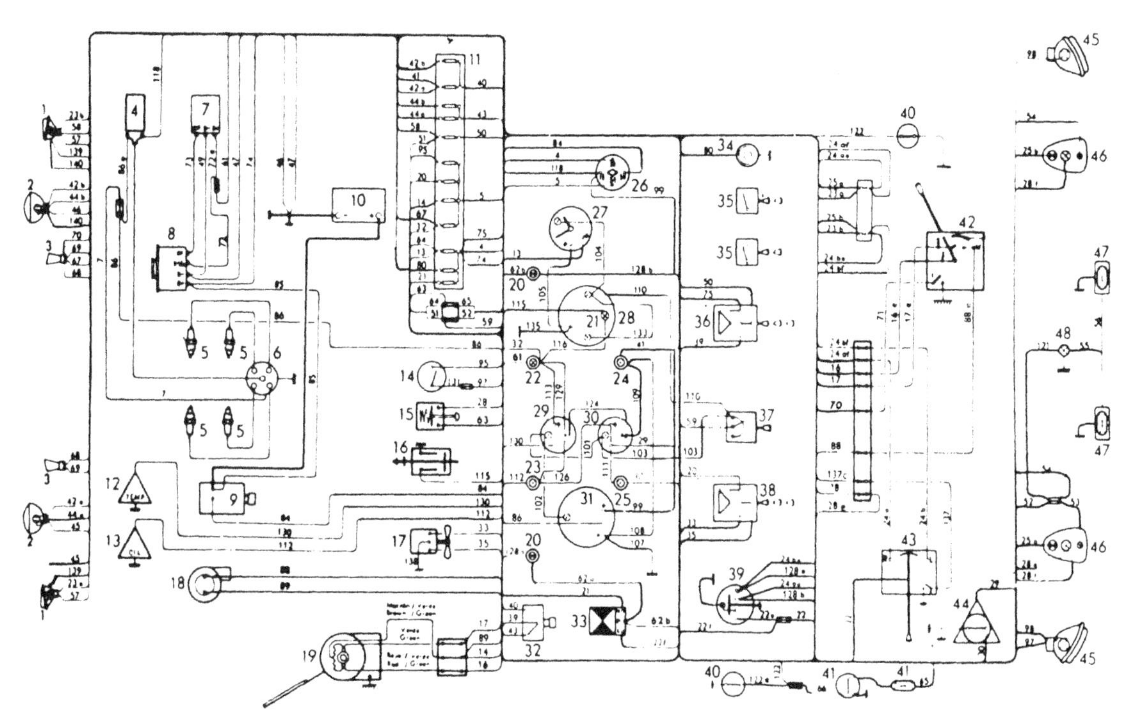

## Wiring diagram De Luxe USA model 1969

*The range of the electrical system is shown by the wiring system below. To simplify the identification, the wires have been covered with insulation of different shades, as shown under 'Cable numbers'*

**Key to numbers in the figure**

1 *Parking light and direction indicators*
2 *Headlights*
3 *Horn*
4 *Ignition coil*
5 *Spark plugs*
6 *Distributor*
7 *Voltage regulator*
8 *Alternator*
9 *Starter*
10 *Battery*
11 *Fuse box*
12 *Temperature transmitter*
13 *Oil pressure switch*
14 *Back-up light switch*
15 *Stop light switch*
16 *Brake warning contact*
17 *Heater fan motor*
18 *Windshield washer pump*
19 *Windshield wiper motor*
20 *Direction indicator repeater light*
21 *Brake warning light*
22 *Charge indicator light*
23 *Oil pressure warning light*
24 *High beam indicator light*
25 *Indicator light, fuel*
26 *Ignition and starter switch*
27 *Electric clock*
28 *Speedometer, odometer and trip meter*
29 *Temperature gauge*
30 *Fuel gauge*
31 *Tachometer*
32 *Flasher unit*
33 *Dimmer relay*
34 *Cigarette lighter*
35 *Switches for extra equipment*
36 *Headlight switch*
37 *Instrument illumination rheostat*
38 *Heater fan switch*
39 *Warning flasher switch*
40 *Courtesy light switch*
41 *Courtesy light with switch*
42 *Switch for windshield wiper, washer and signal horn*
43 *Direction indicator switch with headlight flasher and dimmer switch*
44 *Fuel transmitter*
45 *Back-up lights*
46 *Stop lights, direction indicators and tail lights*
47 *Number plate light*
48 *Trunk light*

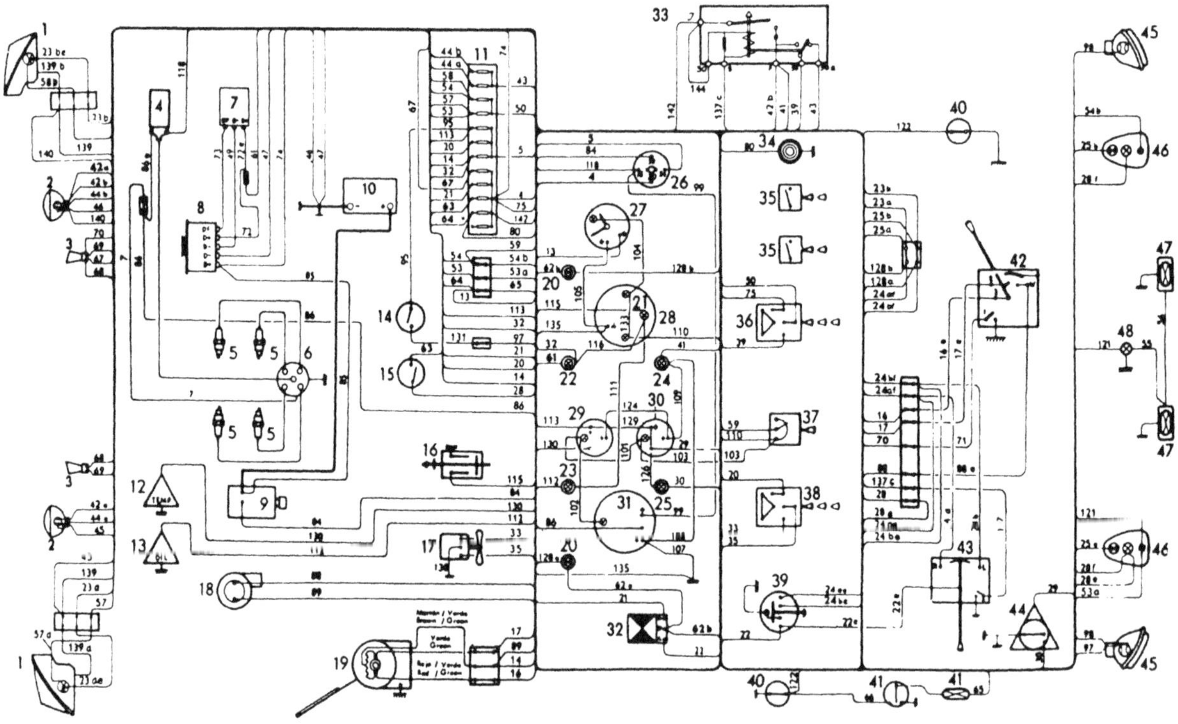

**Cable numbers**

| No | Colour | Area mm² | No | Colour | Area mm² | No | Colour | Area mm² |
|---|---|---|---|---|---|---|---|---|
| 4 | grey | 1,5 | 45 | black | 1,5 | 89 | brown | 0,75 |
| 5 | red | 1,5 | 46 | black | 2,5 | 95 | white | 1,5 |
| 7 | black | 1,5 | 47 | black | 4,0 | 97 | white | 1,5 |
| 13 | blue | 0,75 | 49 | black | 1,0 | 98 | white | 1,0 |
| 14 | brown | 1,0 | 50 | green | 1,0 | 99 | white | 1,0 |
| 16 | grey | 1,0 | 53 | blue | 0,75 | 101 | green | 0,75 |
| 16e | grey | 1,0 | 53a | blue | 0,75 | 102 | green | 0,75 |
| 17 | blue | 1,0 | 54 | green | 0,75 | 103 | green | 0,75 |
| 17e | blue | 1,0 | 54b | green | 0,75 | 104 | green | 0,75 |
| 20 | white | 1,0 | 55 | green | 0,75 | 105 | black | 0,75 |
| 21 | red | 1,0 | 56 | green | 0,75 | 107 | black | 0,75 |
| 22 | green | 1,0 | 57 | blue | 0,75 | 108 | black | 0,75 |
| 22e | green | 1,0 | 57a | blue | 0,75 | 109 | black | 0,75 |
| 23a | yellow | 1,0 | 58 | green | 0,75 | 110 | green | 0,75 |
| 23ae | yellow | 1,0 | 58b | green | 0,75 | 111 | red | 0,75 |
| 23b | white | 1,0 | 59 | green | 0,75 | 112 | blue | 1,0 |
| 23be | white | 1,0 | 61 | red | 0,75 | 113 | white | 0,75 |
| 24a | yellow | 0,75 | 62a | grey | 0,75 | 115 | yellow | 0,75 |
| 24ae | yellow | 0,75 | 62b | grey | 0,75 | 116 | red | 0,75 |
| 24af | yellow | 1,0 | 63 | red | 1,0 | 118 | white | 1,0 |
| 24b | white | 0,75 | 64 | grey | 0,75 | 121 | green | 0,75 |
| 24be | white | 0,75 | 65 | red | 0,75 | 122 | white | 0,75 |
| 24bf | white | 1,0 | 66 | white | 0,75 | 124 | black | 0,75 |
| 25a | blue | 1,0 | 67 | red | 1,5 | 126 | white | 0,75 |
| 25b | grey | 1,0 | 68 | red | 1,0 | 128a | white | 0,75 |
| 28 | red | 1,0 | 69 | black | 1,0 | 128b | yellow | 0,75 |
| 28e | red | 1,0 | 70 | black | 1,5 | 129 | white | 0,75 |
| 28f | red | 0,75 | 71 | black | 1,5 | 130 | brown | 1,0 |
| 29 | grey | 0,75 | 72 | red | 1,0 | 131 | white | 1,5 |
| 30 | brown | 0,75 | 72e | red | 1,0 | 133 | green | 0,75 |
| 32 | red | 0,75 | 73 | yellow | 1,0 | 135 | black | 0,75 |
| 33 | yellow | 1,0 | 74 | grey | 4,0 | 137 | brown | 0,75 |
| 35 | grey | 1,0 | 75 | grey | 2,5 | 137c | brown | 0,75 |
| 39 | red | 2,5 | 80 | black | 1,5 | 138 | black | 1,0 |
| 41 | blue | 0,75 | 84 | yellow | 1,5 | 139 | black | 1,0 |
| 42a | blue | 1,5 | 85 | grey | 4,0 | 139a | black | 1,0 |
| 42b | white | 2,5 | 86 | red | 1,0 | 139b | black | 1,0 |
| 43 | yellow | 2,5 | 86e | red | 1,0 | 140 | black | 1,5 |
| 44a | grey | 1,5 | 88 | black | 0,75 | 142 | grey | 1,5 |
| 44b | yellow | 1,5 | 88e | black | 0,75 | 144 | grey | 0,75 |

## Wiring diagram SAAB Sedan USA model 1967

*The range of the electrical system is shown by the wiring system below. To simplify the identification, the wires have been covered with insulation of different shades, as follows:*

| | |
|---|---|
| *Black* | *7, 18, 19, 45, 46, 47, 49, 71, 80, 105, 109, 125, 135, 136, 138, 139, 140* |
| *Red* | *5, 21, 28, 28e, 28f, 32, 39, 61, 63, 65, 67, 68, 72, 111, 113, 126, 129* |
| *Green* | *16, 22, 22e, 22f, 50, 51, 52, 53, 54, 55, 56, 57, 58, 60, 101, 104, 110, 121, 133* |
| *Grey* | *4, 25b, 29, 35, 44a, 62a, 62b, 64, 69, 70, 74, 75, 85* |
| *White* | *20, 23b, 24b, 24be, 24bf, 40, 42b, 66, 95, 97, 98, 118, 122, 122e, 128a, 131* |
| *Yellow* | *17, 23a, 24a, 24af, 33, 43, 44b, 73, 84, 128b* |
| *Brown* | *14, 30, 130, 137* |
| *Blue* | *13, 25a, 41, 42a, 112* |

### Key to numbers in the figure

1 *Parking and direction indicator lights*
2 *Headlights*
3 *Horns*
4 *Ignition coil*
5 *Spark plugs*
6 *Distributor*
7 *Voltage regulator*
8 *Alternator*
9 *Starter motor*
10 *Battery*
11 *Fuse box*
12 *Temperature gauge, sending unit*
13 *Oil pressure switch*
14 *Back-up light switch*
15 *Stop light switch*
16 *Heater motor*
17 *Windshield wiper motor*
18 *Direction indicator warning lights*
19 *Charge indicator light*
20 *High beam indicator light*
21 *Oil pressure warning light*
22 *Electric clock*
23 *Temperature gauge*
24 *Speedometer with odometer*
25 *Fuel gauge*
26 *Foot dimmer switch*
27 *Flasher*
28 *Cigarette lighter*
29 *Ignition and starter switch*
30 *Headlight and parking light switch with instrument illumination rheostat*
31 *Warning flasher switch with control light*
32 *Heater switch*
33 *Windshield wiper switch*
34 *Automatic door switch for dome light*
35 *Dome light with switch*
36 *Horn ring*
37 *Direction indicator switch*
38 *Fuel tank sending unit*
39 *Back-up lights*
40 *Stop lights, direction indicator and tail lights*
41 *License lights*
42 *Trunk light*

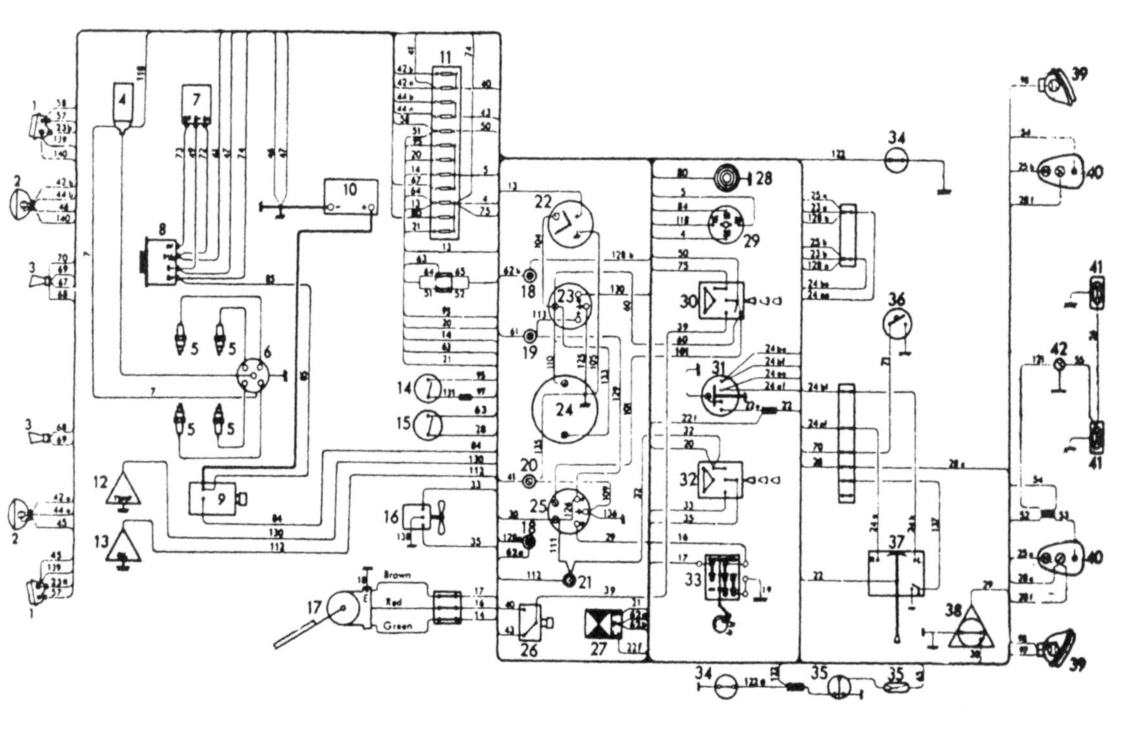

**Wiring diagram SAAB Sedan USA model 1968**

*The range of the electrical system is shown by the wiring system below. To simplify the identification, the wires have been covered with insulation of different shades, as follows:*

| | |
|---|---|
| *Black* | *7, 45, 46, 47, 69, 70, 71, 88, 88e, 109, 124, 125, 135, 136, 138, 139, 140* |
| *Red* | *5, 21, 28, 28e, 28f, 32, 39, 61, 63, 65, 67, 68, 72, 72e, 111, 113, 116, 126, 129* |
| *Green* | *22, 22e, 22f, 50, 51, 52, 53, 54, 55, 56, 57, 58, 59, 60, 101, 110, 121, 133* |
| *Grey* | *4, 16, 16e, 25b, 29, 35, 44a, 62, 64, 74, 75, 85* |
| *White* | *20, 23b, 24b, 24be, 24bf, 40, 42b, 66, 95, 97, 98, 118, 122, 122e, 131* |
| *Yellow* | *23a, 24a, 24ae, 24af, 33, 43, 44b, 73, 84, 115* |
| *Brown* | *14, 30, 89, 130, 137* |
| *Blue* | *17, 17e, 25a, 41, 42a, 112* |

**Key to numbers in the figure**

*1 Direction indicators and side lights*
*2 Headlights*
*3 Horn*
*4 Ignition coil*
*5 Spark plugs*
*6 Distributor*
*7 Voltage regulator*
*8 Alternator*
*9 Starter*
*10 Battery*
*11 Fuse box*
*12 Temperature gauge, sending unit*
*13 Oil pressure switch*
*14 Back-up light switch*
*15 Stop light switch*
*16 Brake warning contact*
*17 Heater fan motor*
*18 Windshield washer pump*
*19 Wiper motor*
*20 Charge indicator light*
*21 Direction indicator repeater light*
*22 Brake warning light*
*23 High beam indicator light*
*24 Oil pressure warning light*
*25 Temperature gauge*
*26 Speedometer with odometer*
*27 Fuel gauge*
*28 Dimmer switch*
*29 Flasher*
*30 Ignition and starter switch*
*31 Headlight switch*
*32 Instrument illumination rheostat*
*33 Heater fan switch*
*34 Warning flasher switch*
*35 Courtesy light switch*
*36 Courtesy light with switch*
*37 Switch for windshield wiper, washer and signal horn*
*38 Direction indicator switch with headlight flasher*
*39 Fuel tank gauge*
*40 Back-up light*
*41 Stop lights, direction indicators and tail lights*
*42 Number plate light*
*43 Trunk light*

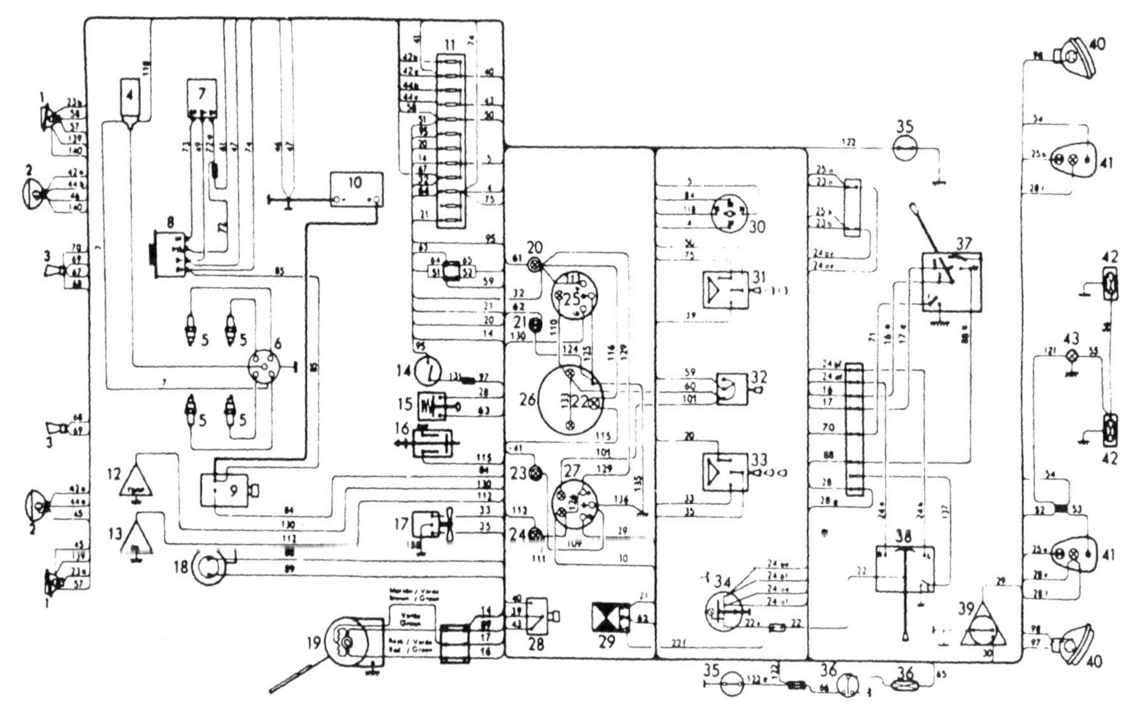

## Wiring diagram SAAB Sedan USA model 1969

*The range of the electrical system is shown by the wiring system below. To simplify the identification, the wires have been covered with insulation of different shades, as shown under 'Cable numbers'*

**Key to numbers in the figure**

1 Parking light and direction indicators
2 Headlights
3 Horn
4 Ignition coil
5 Spark plugs
6 Distributor
7 Voltage regulator
8 Alternator
9 Starter
10 Battery
11 Fuse box
12 Temperature transmitter
13 Oil pressure switch
14 Stop light switch
15 Back-up light switch
16 Brake warning contact
17 Heater fan motor
18 Windshield washer pump
19 Windshield wiper motor
20 Charge indicator light
21 Direction indicator repeater light
22 Brake warning light
23 High beam indicator light
24 Oil pressure warning light
25 Electric clock (extra equipment)
26 Temperature gauge
27 Speedometer with odometer
28 Fuel gauge
29 Flasher unit
30 Dimmer relay
31 Ignition and starter switch
32 Headlight switch
33 Instrument illumination rheostat
34 Heater fan switch
35 Warning flasher switch
36 Courtesy light switch
37 Courtesy light with switch
38 Switch for windshield wiper, washer and signal horn
39 Direction indicator switch with headlight flasher and dimmer switch
40 Fuel transmitter
41 Back-up lights
42 Stop lights, direction indicators and tail light
43 Number plate light
44 Trunk light

**Code numbers**

| No | Colour | Area mm$^2$ | No | Colour | Area mm$^2$ | No | Colour | Area mm$^2$ |
|---|---|---|---|---|---|---|---|---|
| 4 | grey | 1,5 | 44b | yellow | 1,5 | 88e | black | 0,75 |
| 5 | red | 1,5 | 45 | black | 1,5 | 89 | brown | 0,75 |
| 7 | black | 1,5 | 46 | black | 2,5 | 95 | white | 1,5 |
| 13 | blue | 0,75 | 47 | black | 4,0 | 97 | white | 1,5 |
| 14 | brown | 1,0 | 49 | black | 1,0 | 98 | white | 1,0 |
| 16 | grey | 1,0 | 50 | green | 1,0 | 101 | green | 0,75 |
| 16e | grey | 1,0 | 53 | blue | 0,75 | 104 | green | 0,75 |
| 17 | blue | 1,0 | 53a | blue | 0,75 | 105 | black | 0,75 |
| 17e | blue | 1,0 | 54 | green | 0,75 | 109 | black | 0,75 |
| 20 | white | 1,0 | 54b | green | 0,75 | 110 | green | 0,75 |
| 21 | red | 1,0 | 55 | green | 0,75 | 111 | red | 0,75 |
| 22 | green | 1,0 | 56 | green | 0,75 | 112 | blue | 1,0 |
| 22e | green | 1,0 | 57 | blue | 0,75 | 113 | white | 0,75 |
| 23a | yellow | 1,0 | 57a | blue | 0,75 | 115 | yellow | 0,75 |
| 23ae | yellow | 1,0 | 58 | green | 0,75 | 116 | red | 0,75 |
| 23b | white | 1,0 | 58b | green | 0,75 | 118 | white | 1,0 |
| 23be | white | 1,0 | 59 | green | 0,75 | 121 | green | 0,75 |
| 24a | yellow | 0,75 | 60 | green | 0,75 | 122 | white | 0,75 |
| 24ae | yellow | 0,75 | 61 | red | 0,75 | 124 | black | 0,75 |
| 24b | white | 0,75 | 62 | grey | 0,75 | 125 | black | 0,75 |
| 24be | white | 0,75 | 63 | red | 0,75 | 126 | white | 0,75 |
| 25a | blue | 1,0 | 64 | grey | 0,75 | 129 | white | 0,75 |
| 25b | grey | 1,0 | 65 | red | 0,75 | 130 | brown | 1,0 |
| 28 | red | 1,0 | 66 | white | 0,75 | 131 | white | 1,5 |
| 28e | red | 1,0 | 67 | red | 1,5 | 133 | green | 0,75 |
| 28f | red | 0,75 | 68 | red | 1,0 | 135 | black | 0,75 |
| 29 | grey | 0,75 | 69 | black | 1,0 | 136 | black | 0,75 |
| 30 | brown | 0,75 | 70 | black | 1,5 | 137 | brown | 0,75 |
| 32 | red | 0,75 | 71 | black | 1,5 | 137c | brown | 0,75 |
| 33 | yellow | 1,0 | 72 | red | 1,0 | 138 | black | 1,0 |
| 35 | grey | 1,0 | 72e | red | 1,0 | 139 | black | 1,0 |
| 39 | red | 2,5 | 73 | yellow | 1,0 | 139a | black | 1,0 |
| 41 | blue | 0,75 | 74 | grey | 4,0 | 139b | black | 1,0 |
| 42a | blue | 1,5 | 75 | grey | 2,5 | 140 | black | 1,5 |
| 42b | white | 2,5 | 84 | yellow | 1,5 | 142 | grey | 1,5 |
| 43 | yellow | 2,5 | 85 | grey | 4,0 | 144 | grey | 0,75 |
| 44a | grey | 1,5 | 88 | black | 0,75 | | | |

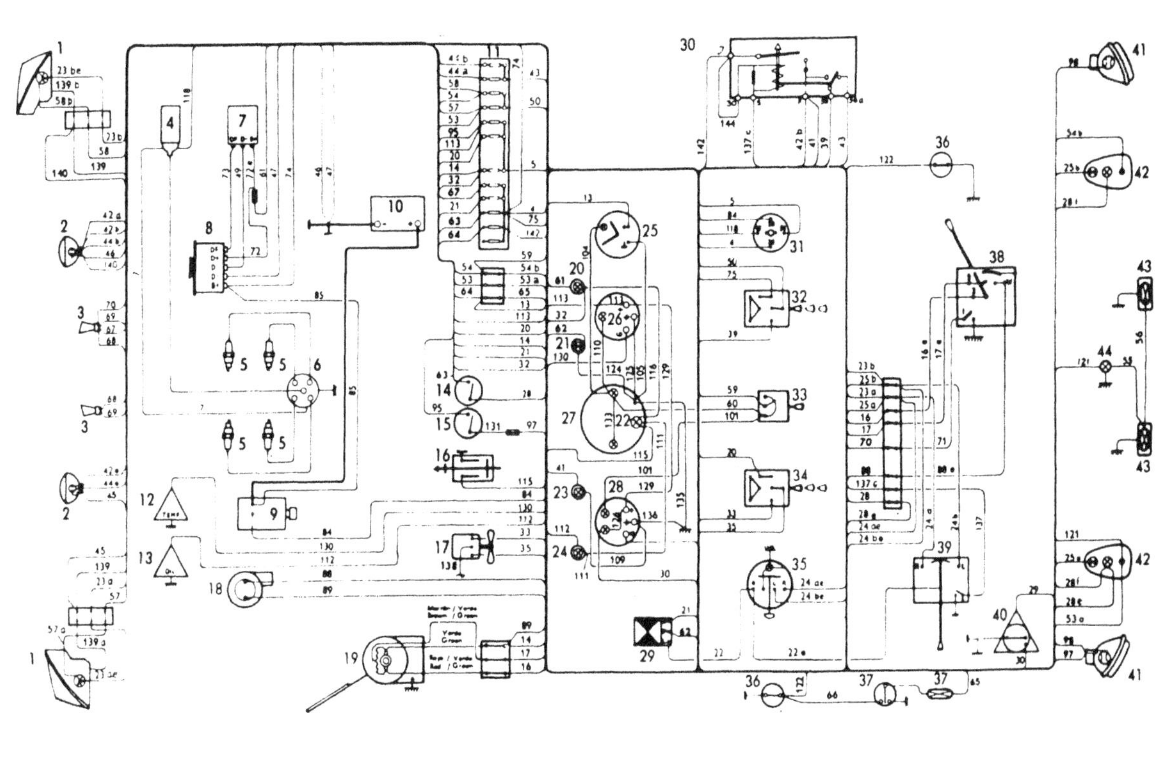

## Wiring diagram SAAB Sedan USA model 1970

*The range of the electrical system is shown by the wiring system below. To simplify the identification the wires have been covered with insulation of different shades, as shown under 'Cable numbers'*

**Key to numbers in the figure**

1 Parking light and direction indicators
2 Headlights
3 Horn
4 Ignition coil
5 Spark plugs
6 Distributor
7 Voltage regulator
8 Alternator
9 Starter
10 Battery
11 Fuse box
12 Temperature transmitter
13 Oil pressure switch
14 Back-up light switch
15 Stop light switch
16 Brake warning contact
17 Heater fan motor
18 Windshield washer pump
19 Windshield wiper motor
20 Cigarette lighter
21 Contact for warning buzzer
22 Buzzer
23 Clock
24 Speedometer with odometer
25 High beam indicator light
26 Direction indicator repeater light
27 Brake warning light
28 Temperature and fuel gauges
29 Indicator light, fuel amount
30 Oil pressure warning light
31 Charge indicator light
32 Flasher unit
33 Dimmer relay
34 Ignition and starter switch
35 Hazard warning flasher switch
36 Instrument illumination rheostat
37 Headlight switch
38 Heater fan switch
39 Dome lamp switch
40 Dome lamp with switch
41 Switch for windshield wiper and washer
42 Signal horn contact
43 Direction indicator switch with headlight flasher and dimmer switch
44 Fuel transmitter
45 Back-up light
46 Stop lights, direction indicators and tail light
47 Number plate light
48 Trunk light

**Cable numbers**

| No | Colour | Area $mm^2$ | No | Colour | Area $mm^2$ | No | Colour | Area $mm^2$ |
|---|---|---|---|---|---|---|---|---|
| 4 | grey | 1,5 | 39 | yellow | 0,75 | 74 | grey | 4,0 |
| 5 | red | 1,5 | 41 | blue | 0,75 | 75 | red | 1,0 |
| 7 | green | 1,5 | 42a | blue | 1,5 | 76 | grey | 1,0 |
| 13 | blue | 0,75 | 42b | white | 2,5 | 80 | black | 1,0 |
| 14 | brown | 1,0 | 43 | yellow | 2,5 | 84 | yellow | 1,5 |
| 14e | brown | 1,0 | 44a | grey | 1,5 | 85 | grey | 4,0 |
| 14f | brown | 1,0 | 44b | yellow | 1,5 | 88 | black | 0,75 |
| 15 | red | 1,0 | 45 | black | 1,5 | 88e | black | 0,75 |
| 15e | red | 1,0 | 46 | black | 2,5 | 89 | brown | 0,75 |
| 16 | grey | 1,0 | 47 | black | 4,0 | 95 | white | 1,5 |
| 16e | grey | 1,0 | 49 | black | 1,0 | 97 | white | 1,5 |
| 17 | blue | 1,0 | 50 | green | 1,0 | 98 | white | 1,0 |
| 17e | blue | 1,0 | 53 | blue | 0,75 | 101 | green | 0,75 |
| 18 | black | 1,0 | 53a | blue | 0,75 | 104 | green | 0,75 |
| 20 | white | 1,0 | 54 | green | 0,75 | 105 | black | 0,75 |
| 21 | red | 1,0 | 54b | green | 0,75 | 109 | black | 0,75 |
| 22 | green | 1,0 | 55 | green | 0,75 | 110 | green | 0,75 |
| 22e | green | 1,0 | 56 | black | 0,75 | 111 | red | 0,75 |
| 23a | yellow | 1,0 | 57 | blue | 0,75 | 112 | blue | 1,0 |
| 23ae | yellow | 1,0 | 57a | blue | 0,75 | 115 | yellow | 0,75 |
| 23b | white | 1,0 | 58 | green | 0,75 | 118 | white | 1,0 |
| 23be | white | 1,0 | 58b | green | 0,75 | 121 | green | 0,75 |
| 24a | yellow | 1,0 | 59 | green | 0,75 | 122 | white | 0,75 |
| 24ae | yellow | 1,0 | 60 | green | 0,75 | 130 | brown | 1,0 |
| 24b | white | 1,0 | 61 | red | 0,75 | 131 | white | 1,5 |
| 24be | white | 1,0 | 62 | grey | 0,75 | 136 | black | 1,0 |
| 25a | blue | 1,0 | 63 | red | 1,0 | 138 | black | 1,0 |
| 25b | grey | 1,0 | 64 | grey | 0,75 | 139 | black | 1,5 |
| 28 | red | 1,0 | 65 | red | 0,75 | 139a | black | 1,0 |
| 28e | red | 1,0 | 66 | white | 0,75 | 139b | black | 1,0 |
| 28f | red | 0,75 | 67 | red | 1,5 | 140 | black | 1,5 |
| 29 | grey | 0,75 | 68 | red | 1,0 | 141 | brown | 0,75 |
| 29e | green | 0,75 | 69 | black | 1,0 | 141e | brown | 0,75 |
| 30 | brown | 0,75 | 70 | black | 1,5 | 142 | grey | 2,5 |
| 30e | brown | 0,75 | 71 | black | 1,5 | 147 | black | 0,75 |
| 32 | red | 0,75 | 72 | red | 1,0 | 190 | yellow | 0,75 |
| 33 | yellow | 1,0 | 72e | red | 1,0 | 191 | grey | 0,75 |
| 35 | grey | 1,0 | 73 | yellow | 1,0 | 192 | black | 0,75 |

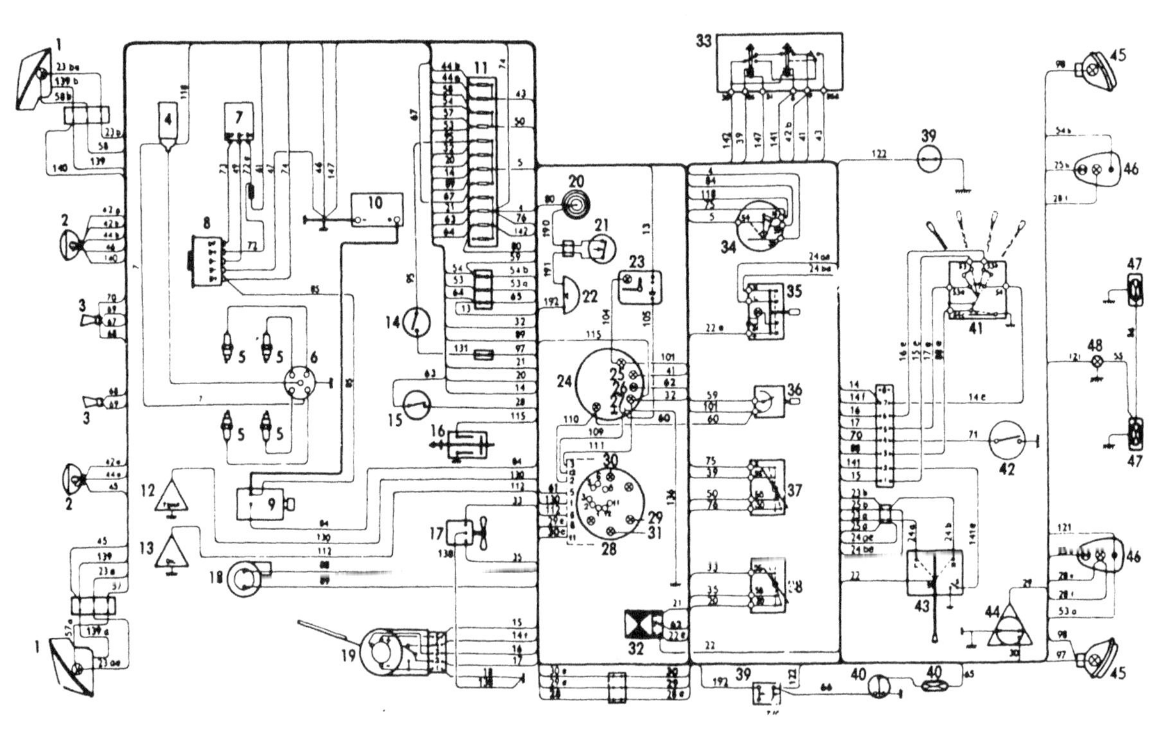

## Wiring diagram SAAB Sedan USA model 1971

*The range of the electrical system is shown by the wiring system below. To simplify the identification the wires have been covered with insulation of different shades, as shown under 'Cable numbers'*

### Key to numbers in figure

1 Parking light and direction indicators
2 Headlights
3 Horn
4 Ignition coil
5 Spark plugs
6 Distributor
7 Voltage regulator
8 Alternator
9 Starter
10 Battery
11 Fuse box
12 Temperature transmitter
13 Oil pressure switch
14 Back-up light switch
15 Stop light switch
16 Brake warning contact
17 Heater fan motor
18 Windshield washer pump
19 Windshield wiper motor
20 Cigarette lighter
21 Contact for warning buzzer
22 Buzzer
23 Clock
24 Speedometer with odometer
25 High beam indicator light
26 Direction indicator repeater light
27 Brake warning light
28 Temperature and fuel gauges
29 Indicator light, fuel amount
30 Oil pressure warning light
31 Charge indicator light
32 Flasher unit
33 Dimmer relay
34 Ignition and starter switch
35 Hazard warning flasher switch
36 Instrument illumination rheostat
37 Headlight switch
38 Heater fan switch
39 Dome lamp switch
40 Dome lamp with switch
41 Switch for windshield wiper and washer
42 Signal horn contact
43 Direction indicator switch with headlight flasher and dimmer switch
44 Fuel transmitter
45 Back-up light
46 Stop lights, direction indicators and tail light
47 Number plate light
48 Trunk light

### Cable numbers

| No | Colour | Area $mm^2$ | No | Colour | Area $mm^2$ | No | Colour | Area $mm^2$ |
|---|---|---|---|---|---|---|---|---|
| 4 | grey | 1,5 | 39 | yellow | 0,75 | 74 | grey | 4,0 |
| 5 | red | 1,5 | 41 | blue | 0,75 | 75 | red | 1,0 |
| 7 | green | 1,5 | 42a | blue | 1,5 | 76 | grey | 1,0 |
| 13 | blue | 0,75 | 42b | white | 2,5 | 80 | black | 1,0 |
| 14 | brown | 1,0 | 43 | yellow | 2,5 | 84 | yellow | 1,5 |
| 14e | brown | 1,0 | 44a | grey | 1,5 | 85 | grey | 4,0 |
| 14f | brown | 1,0 | 44b | yellow | 1,5 | 88 | black | 0,75 |
| 15 | red | 1,0 | 45 | black | 1,5 | 88e | black | 0,75 |
| 15e | red | 1,0 | 46 | black | 2,5 | 89 | brown | 0,75 |
| 16 | grey | 1,0 | 47 | black | 4,0 | 95 | white | 1,5 |
| 16e | grey | 1,0 | 49 | black | 1,0 | 97 | white | 1,5 |
| 17 | blue | 1,0 | 50 | green | 1,0 | 98 | white | 1,0 |
| 17e | blue | 1,0 | 53 | blue | 0,75 | 101 | green | 0,75 |
| 18 | black | 1,0 | 53a | blue | 0,75 | 104 | green | 0,75 |
| 20 | white | 1,0 | 54 | green | 0,75 | 105 | black | 0,75 |
| 21 | red | 1,0 | 54b | green | 0,75 | 109 | black | 0,75 |
| 22 | green | 1,0 | 55 | green | 0,75 | 110 | green | 0,75 |
| 22e | green | 1,0 | 56 | black | 0,75 | 111 | red | 0,75 |
| 23a | yellow | 1,0 | 57 | blue | 0,75 | 112 | blue | 1,0 |
| 23ae | yellow | 1,0 | 57a | blue | 0,75 | 115 | yellow | 0,75 |
| 23b | white | 1,0 | 58 | green | 0,75 | 118 | white | 1,0 |
| 23be | white | 1,0 | 58b | green | 0,75 | 121 | green | 0,75 |
| 24a | yellow | 1,0 | 59 | green | 0,75 | 122 | white | 0,75 |
| 24ae | yellow | 1,0 | 60 | green | 0,75 | 130 | brown | 1,0 |
| 24b | white | 1,0 | 61 | red | 0,75 | 131 | white | 1,5 |
| 24be | white | 1,0 | 62 | grey | 0,75 | 136 | black | 1,0 |
| 25a | blue | 1,0 | 63 | red | 1,0 | 138 | black | 1,0 |
| 25b | grey | 1,0 | 64 | grey | 0,75 | 139 | black | 1,5 |
| 28 | red | 1,0 | 65 | red | 0,75 | 139a | black | 1,0 |
| 28e | red | 1,0 | 66 | white | 0,75 | 139b | black | 1,0 |
| 28f | red | 0,75 | 67 | red | 1,5 | 140 | black | 1,5 |
| 29 | grey | 0,75 | 68 | red | 1,0 | 141 | brown | 0,75 |
| 29e | green | 0,75 | 69 | black | 1,0 | 141e | brown | 0,75 |
| 30 | brown | 0,75 | 70 | black | 1,5 | 142 | grey | 2,5 |
| 30e | brown | 0,75 | 71 | black | 1,5 | 147 | black | 0,75 |
| 32 | red | 0,75 | 72 | red | 1,0 | 190 | yellow | 0,75 |
| 33 | yellow | 1,0 | 72e | red | 1,0 | 191 | grey | 0,75 |
| 35 | grey | 1,0 | 73 | yellow | 1,0 | 192 | black | 0,75 |

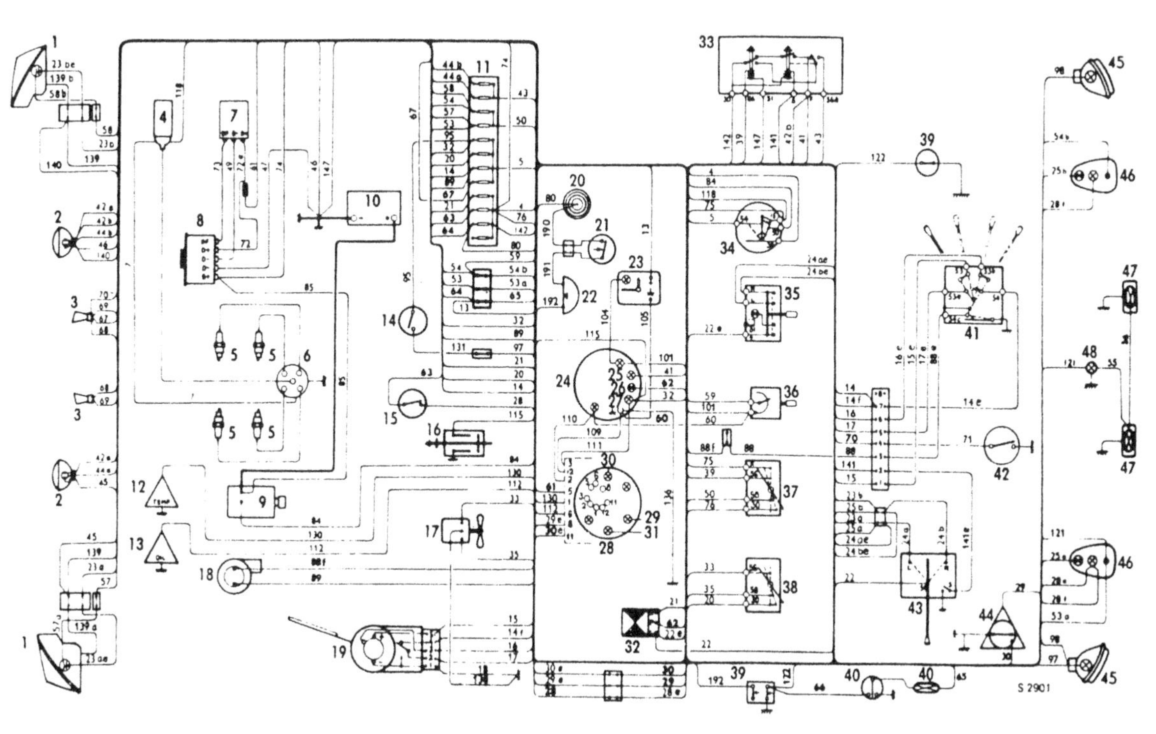

**Wiring diagram SAAB Sedan USA and detail of wiring diagram SAAB Station Wagon USA model 1972 on**

*The tange of the electrical system is shown by the wiring system on the next page*

1 Battery
2 Alternator
3 Voltage regulator
4 Starter motor
5 Ignition coil
6 Ignition distributor
7 Lighting relay
8 Headlight dimmer/flasher switch
9 Light switch
10 High beam
11 Dimmed beam
12 Front parking light
13 Tail light
14 Licence plate light
15 Resistance switch, instrument panel illumination
16 Ignition switch
17 Fuse box
18 Direction indicator flasher unit
19 Direction indicator switch
20 Hazard warning signal switch
21 Hazard warning signal repeater
22 Direction indicator lights, L
23 Direction indicator lights, R
24 Stop light contact
25 Stop lights
26 Ventilator fan switch
27 Ventilator fan motor
28 Horn
29 Horn contact
30 Brake warning contact
31 Oil warning contact
32 Temperature transmitter
33 Fuel level transmitter
34 Combination instrument: fuel gauge, fuel warning light, temperature gauge, oil warning light, ignition light, instrument panel illumination
35 Speedometer
36 Brake warning light
37 High beam indicator light
38 Direction indicator repeater light
39 Instrument panel illumination
40 Dome light
41 Door contact, interior lighting
42 Trunk light
43 Trunk light contact
44 Wiper system switch
45 2-speed windshield wiper
46 Washer motor
50 Seat heating element with thermostat
51 8-pin connector
52 3-pin connector
53 2-pin connector
54 1-pin connector
75 Back-up light contact
76 Back-up lights
77 Cigarette lighter
78 Key contact (buzzer)
79 Buzzer
80 2-pin door contact
81 Clock

**Colour code**

| | |
|---|---|
| BL | Blue |
| BR | Brown |
| GL | Yellow |
| GN | Green |
| RD | Red |
| SV | Black |
| VT | White |

4 GR 1,5

Cable cross-section, mm²

Colour of cable

Cable ref no

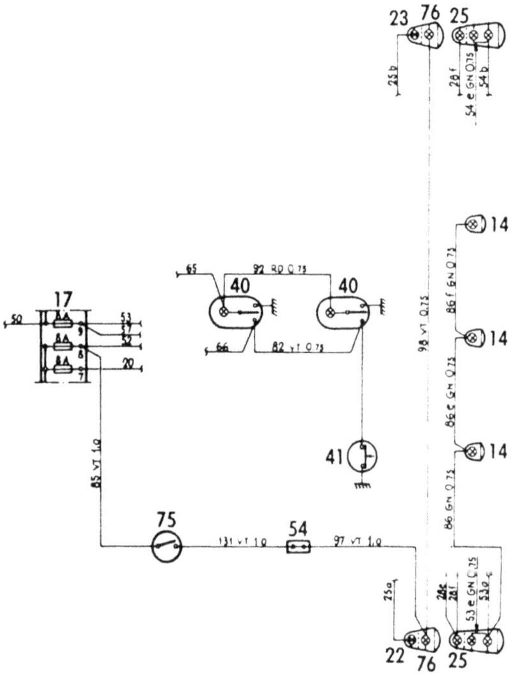

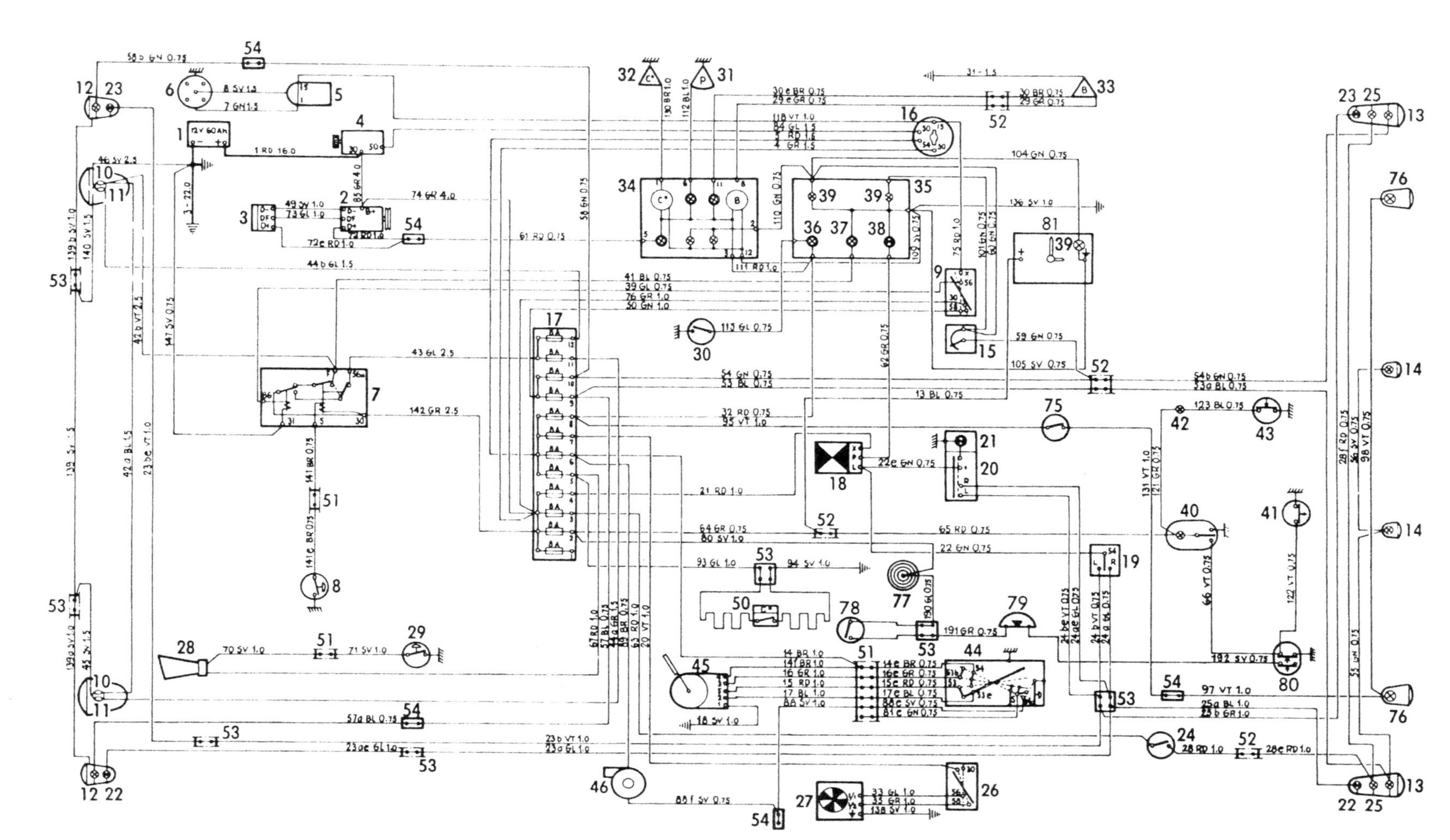

Wiring diagram SAAB Sedan USA model 1972 on

**Wiring diagram SAAB Station Wagon USA model 1967**

*The range of the electrical system is shown by the wiring system below. To simplify the identification the wires have been covered with insulation of different shades, as follows:*

| | |
|---|---|
| *Black* | *7, 18, 19, 45, 46, 47, 49, 71, 80, 105, 109, 125, 135, 136, 138, 139, 140* |
| *Red* | *5, 21, 28, 28e, 28f, 28g, 32, 39, 61, 63, 67, 68, 72, 92, 111, 113, 126, 129* |
| *Green* | *16, 22, 22e, 22f, 50, 51, 53, 54, 55, 57, 58, 60, 86, 87, 88, 101, 104, 110, 133* |
| *Grey* | *4, 25b, 29, 35, 44a, 62a, 62b, 64, 69, 70, 74, 75, 85, 93* |
| *White* | *20, 23b, 24b, 24be, 24bf, 40, 42b, 66, 82, 83, 118, 122, 122e, 128a* |
| *Yellow* | *17, 23a, 24a, 24ae, 24af, 33, 43, 44b, 73, 84, 128b* |
| *Brown* | *14, 30, 130, 137* |
| *Blue* | *13, 25a, 41, 42a, 112* |

**Key to numbers in the figure**

*1 Parking and direction indicator lights*
*2 Headlights*
*3 Horns*
*4 Ignition coil*
*5 Spark plugs*
*6 Distributor*
*7 Voltage regulator*
*8 Alternator*
*9 Starter motor*
*10 Battery*
*11 Fuse box*
*12 Temperature gauge sending unit*
*13 Oil pressure switch*
*14 Stop light switch*
*15 Heater motor*
*16 Windshield wiper motor*
*17 Direction indicator warning lights*
*18 Charge indicator light*
*19 High beam indicator light*
*20 Oil pressure warning light*
*21 Electric clock*
*22 Temperature gauge*
*23 Speedometer with odometer*
*24 Fuel gauge*
*25 Foot dimmer switch*
*26 Flasher*
*27 Cigarette lighter*
*28 Ignition and starter switch*
*29 Headlight and parking light switch with instrument illumination rheostat*
*30 Warning flasher switch with control light*
*31 Heater switch*
*32 Windshield wiper switch*
*33 Automatic door switch for dome light*
*34 Dome light with switch*
*35 Horn ring*
*36 Direction indicator switch*
*37 Fuel tank sending unit*
*38 Stop light and direction indicator light*
*39 Tail lights*
*40 Licence lights*

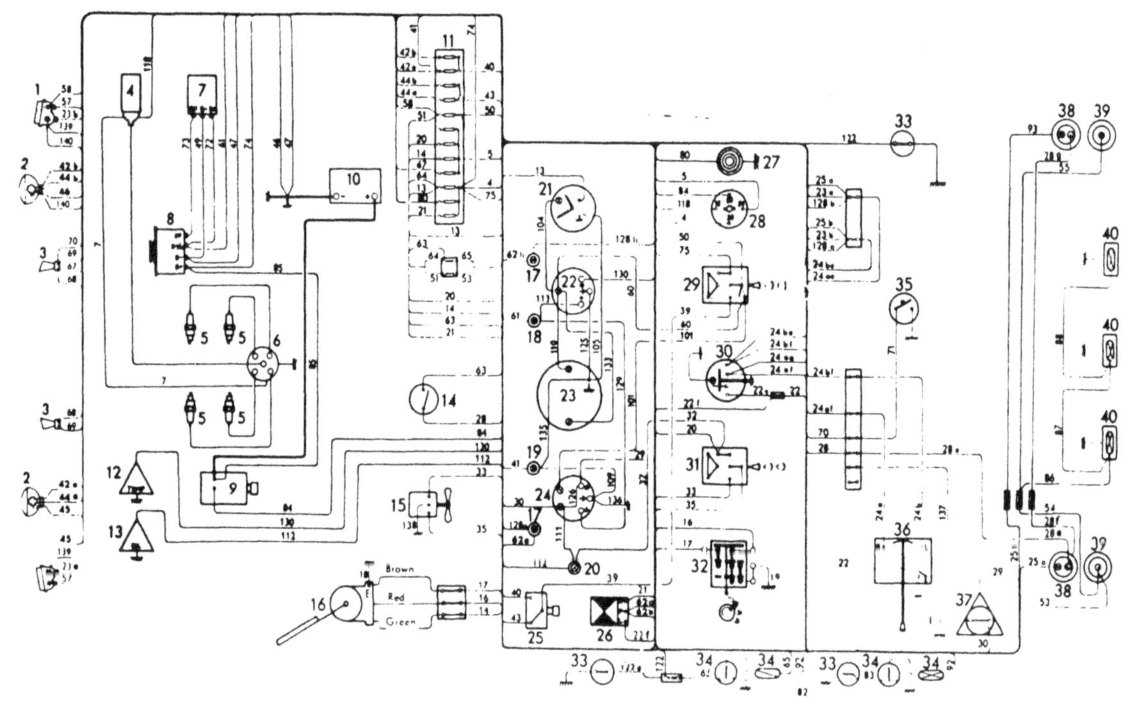

**Wiring diagram SAAB Station Wagon USA model 1968**

*The range of the electrical system is shown by the wiring system below. To simplify the identification, the wires have been covered with insulation of different shades, as follows:*

| | |
|---|---|
| *Black* | *7, 45, 46, 47, 49, 69, 70, 88, 88e, 109, 124, 125, 135, 136, 138, 139, 140* |
| *Red* | *5, 21, 28, 28e, 28f, 28g, 32, 39, 61, 63, 65, 67, 68, 72, 72e, 92, 111, 113, 116, 126, 129* |
| *Green* | *22, 22e, 22f, 50, 51, 53, 54, 55, 57, 58, 59, 60, 86, 86e, 86f, 101, 110* |
| *Grey* | *4, 16, 16e, 25b, 29, 35, 44a, 62, 64, 74, 75, 85, 93* |
| *White* | *20, 23b, 24b, 24be, 24bf, 40, 40c, 42b, 66, 82, 83, 95, 97, 97ae, 98, 118, 112, 122e, 131* |
| *Yellow* | *23a, 24a, 24ae, 24af, 33, 43, 44b, 73, 84, 115* |
| *Brown* | *14, 15, 30, 89, 130, 137* |
| *Blue* | *17, 17e, 25a, 41, 42a, 112* |

**Key to numbers in the figure**

1 *Direction indicators and side lights*
2 *Headlights*
3 *Horn*
4 *Ignition coil*
5 *Spark plugs*
6 *Distributor*
7 *Voltage regulator*
8 *Alternator*
9 *Starter*
10 *Battery*
11 *Fuse box*
12 *Temperature gauge, sending unit*
13 *Oil pressure switch*
14 *Back-up light switch*
15 *Stop light switch*
16 *Brake warning contact*
17 *Heater fan motor*
18 *Windshield washer pump*
19 *Wiper motor*
20 *Charge indicator light*
21 *Direction indicator repeater light*
22 *Brake warning light*
23 *High beam indicator light*
24 *Oil pressure warning light*
25 *Temperature gauge*
26 *Speedometer with odometer*
27 *Fuel gauge*
28 *Dimmer switch*
29 *Flasher*
30 *Ignition and starter switch*
31 *Headlight switch*
32 *Instrument illumination rheostat*
33 *Heater fan switch*
34 *Warning flasher switch*
35 *Courtesy light switch*
36 *Courtesy light with switch*
37 *Switch for windshield wiper, washer and signal horn*
38 *Direction indicator switch with headlight flasher*
39 *Fuel tank gauge*
40 *Stop lights and direction indicators*
41 *Tail lights*
42 *Back-up lights*
43 *Number plate light*

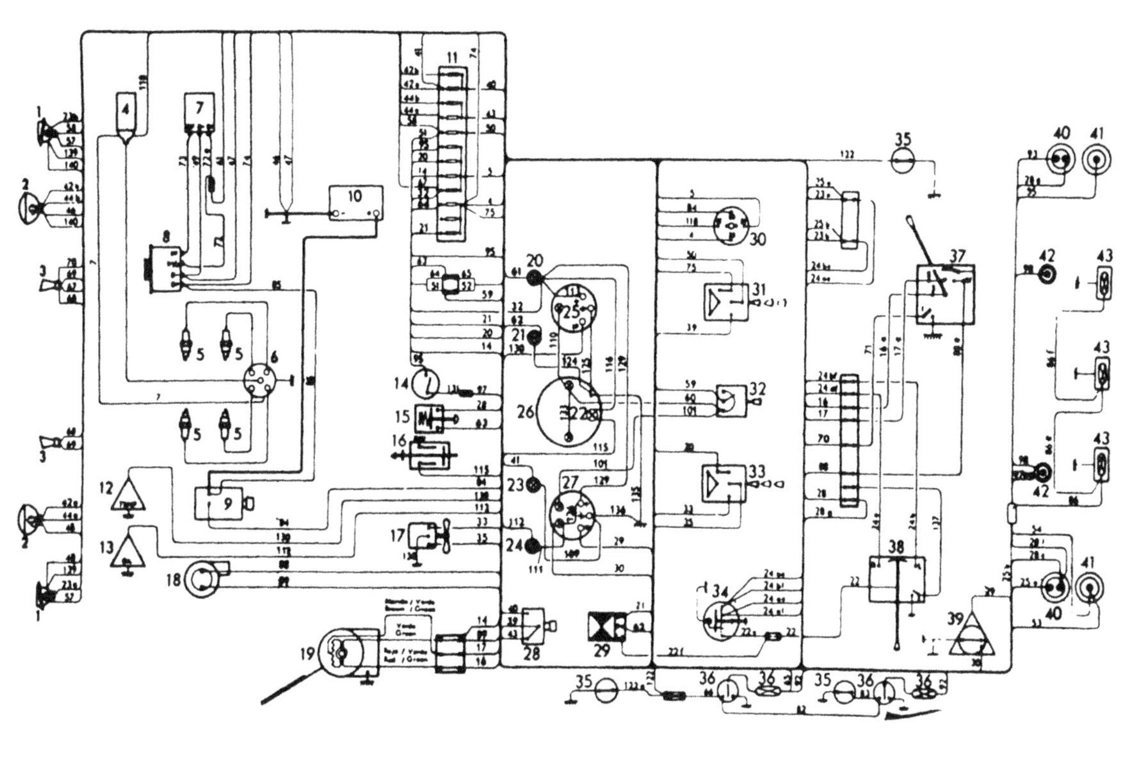

## Wiring diagram SAAB Station Wagon USA model 1969

*The range of the electrical system is shown by the wiring system below. To simplify the identification, the wires have been covered with insulation of different shades, as shown under 'Cable numbers'*

**Key to numbers in the figure**

1 *Parking light and direction indicators*
2 *Headlights*
3 *Horn*
4 *Ignition coil*
5 *Spark plugs*
6 *Distributor*
7 *Voltage regulator*
8 *Alternator*
9 *Starter*
10 *Battery*
11 *Fuse box*
12 *Temperature transmitter*
13 *Oil pressure switch*
14 *Back-up light switch*
15 *Stop light switch*
16 *Brake warning contact*
17 *Heater fan motor*
18 *Windshield washer pump*
19 *Windshield wiper motor*
20 *Charge indicator light*
21 *Direction indicator repeater light*
22 *Brake warning light*
23 *High beam indicator light*
24 *Oil pressure warning light*
25 *Electric clock (extra equipment)*
26 *Temperature gauge*
27 *Speedometer and odometer*
28 *Fuel gauge*
29 *Flasher unit*
30 *Dimmer relay*
31 *Ignition and starter switch*
32 *Headlight switch*
33 *Instrument illumination rheostat*
34 *Heater fan switch*
35 *Warning flasher switch*
36 *Courtesy light switch*
37 *Courtesy light with switch*
38 *Switch for windshield wiper, washer and signal horn*
39 *Direction indicator switch with headlight flasher and dimmer switch*
40 *Fuel transmitter*
41 *Back-up light and direction indicators*
42 *Tail light and stop light*
43 *Number plate light*

**Cable numbers**

| *No* | *Colour* | *Area mm²* | *No* | *Colour* | *Area mm²* | *No* | *Colour* | *Area mm²* |
|---|---|---|---|---|---|---|---|---|
| 4 | grey | 1,5 | 46 | black | 2,5 | 88 | black | 0,75 |
| 5 | red | 1,5 | 47 | black | 4,0 | 88e | black | 0,75 |
| 7 | black | 1,5 | 49 | black | 1,0 | 89 | brown | 0,75 |
| 13 | blue | 0,75 | 50 | green | 1,0 | 92 | red | 0,75 |
| 14 | brown | 1,0 | 53 | blue | 0,75 | 95 | white | 1,5 |
| 16 | grey | 1,0 | 53a | blue | 0,75 | 97 | white | 1,5 |
| 16e | grey | 1,0 | 53e | green | 0,75 | 98 | white | 1,0 |
| 17 | blue | 1,0 | 54 | green | 0,75 | 101 | green | 0,75 |
| 17e | blue | 1,0 | 54b | green | 0,75 | 104 | green | 0,75 |
| 20 | white | 1,0 | 54e | green | 0,75 | 105 | black | 0,75 |
| 21 | red | 1,0 | 57 | blue | 0,75 | 109 | black | 0,75 |
| 22 | green | 1,0 | 57a | blue | 0,75 | 110 | green | 0,75 |
| 22e | green | 1,0 | 58 | green | 0,75 | 111 | red | 0,75 |
| 23a | yellow | 1,0 | 58b | green | 0,75 | 112 | blue | 1,0 |
| 23ae | yellow | 1,0 | 59 | green | 0,75 | 113 | white | 0,75 |
| 23b | white | 1,0 | 60 | green | 0,75 | 115 | yellow | 0,75 |
| 23be | white | 1,0 | 61 | red | 0,75 | 116 | red | 0,75 |
| 24a | yellow | 0,75 | 62 | grey | 0,75 | 118 | white | 1,0 |
| 24ae | yellow | 0,75 | 63 | red | 0,75 | 122 | white | 0,75 |
| 24b | white | 0,75 | 64 | grey | 0,75 | 124 | black | 0,75 |
| 24be | white | 0,75 | 65 | red | 0,75 | 125 | black | 0,75 |
| 25a | blue | 1,0 | 66 | white | 0,75 | 126 | white | 0,75 |
| 25b | grey | 1,0 | 67 | red | 1,5 | 129 | white | 0,75 |
| 28 | red | 1,0 | 68 | red | 1,0 | 130 | brown | 1,0 |
| 28e | red | 1,0 | 69 | black | 1,0 | 131 | white | 1,5 |
| 28f | red | 0,75 | 70 | black | 1,5 | 133 | green | 0,75 |
| 29 | grey | 0,75 | 71 | black | 1,5 | 135 | black | 0,75 |
| 30 | brown | 0,75 | 72 | red | 1,0 | 136 | black | 0,75 |
| 32 | red | 0,75 | 72e | red | 1,0 | 137 | brown | 0,75 |
| 33 | yellow | 1,0 | 73 | yellow | 1,0 | 137c | brown | 0,75 |
| 35 | grey | 1,0 | 74 | grey | 4,0 | 138 | black | 1,0 |
| 39 | red | 2,5 | 75 | grey | 2,5 | 139 | black | 1,0 |
| 41 | blue | 0,75 | 82 | white | 0,75 | 139a | black | 1,0 |
| 42a | blue | 1,5 | 83 | white | 0,75 | 139b | black | 1,0 |
| 42b | white | 2,5 | 84 | yellow | 1,5 | 140 | black | 1,5 |
| 43 | yellow | 2,5 | 85 | grey | 4,0 | 142 | grey | 1,5 |
| 44a | grey | 1,5 | 86 | green | 0,75 | 144 | grey | 0,75 |
| 44b | yellow | 1,5 | 86e | green | 0,75 | | | |
| 45 | black | 1,5 | 86f | green | 0,75 | | | |

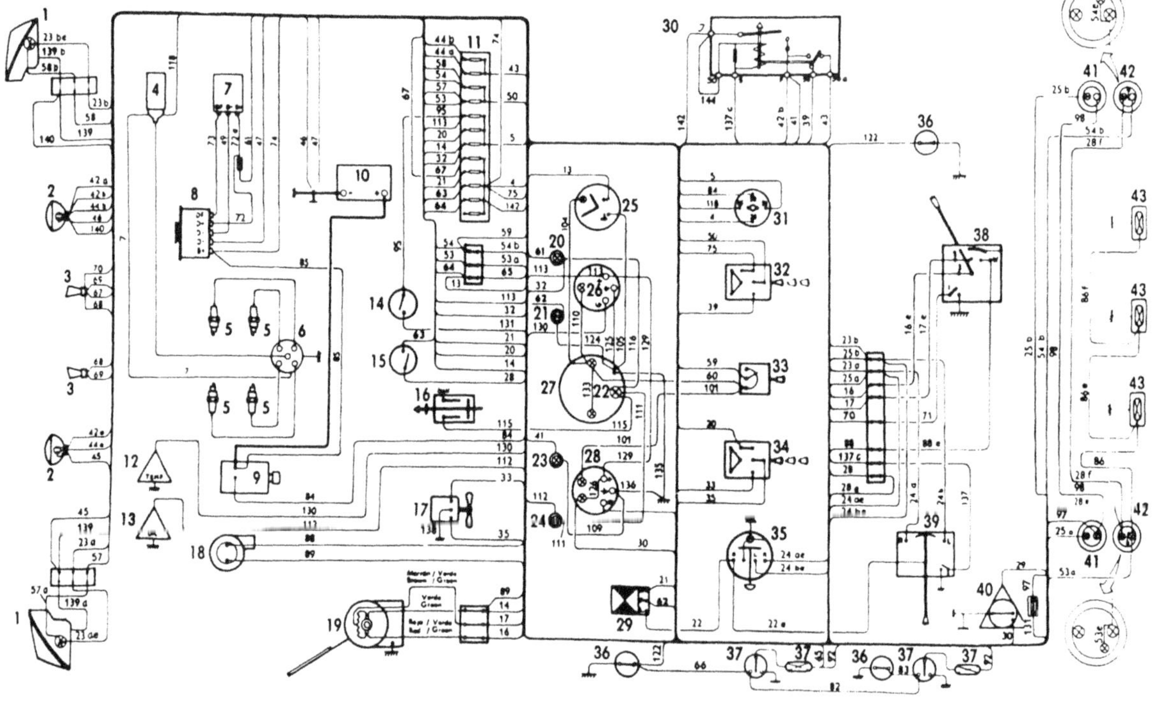

## Wiring diagram SAAB Station Wagon USA model 1970

*The range of the electrical system is shown by the wiring system below. To simplify the identification, the wires have been covered with insulation of different shades, as shown under 'Cable numbers'*

### Key to numbers in the figure

1 Parking light and direction indicators
2 Headlights
3 Horn
4 Ignition coil
5 Spark plugs
6 Distributor
7 Voltage regulator
8 Alternator
9 Starter
10 Battery
11 Fuse box
12 Temperature transmitter
13 Oil pressure switch
14 Back-up light switch
15 Stop light switch
16 Brake warning contact
17 Heater fan motor
18 Windshield washer pump
19 Windshield wiper motor
20 Cigarette lighter
21 Contact for warning buzzer
22 Buzzer
23 Clock
24 Speedometer and odometer
25 High beam indicator light
26 Direction indicator repeater light
27 Brake warning light
28 Temperature and fuel gauges
29 Indicator light, fuel amount
30 Oil pressure warning light
31 Charge indicator light
32 Flasher unit
33 Dimmer relay
34 Ignition and starter switch
35 Hazard warning flasher switch
36 Instrument illumination rheostat
37 Headlight switch
38 Heater fan switch
39 Dome lamp switch
40 Dome lamp with switch
41 Switch for windshield wiper and washer
42 Signal horn contact
43 Direction indicator switch with headlight flasher and dimmer switch
44 Fuel transmitter
45 Back-up light and direction indicators
46 Tail light and stop light
47 Number plate light

### Cable numbers

| No | Colour | Area mm² | No | Colour | Area mm² | No | Colour | Area mm² |
|---|---|---|---|---|---|---|---|---|
| 4 | grey | 1,5 | 42a | blue | 1,5 | 82 | white | 0,75 |
| 5 | red | 1,5 | 42b | white | 2,5 | 83 | white | 0,75 |
| 7 | green | 1,5 | 43 | yellow | 2,5 | 84 | yellow | 1,5 |
| 13 | blue | 0,75 | 44a | grey | 1,5 | 85 | grey | 4,0 |
| 14 | brown | 1,0 | 44b | yellow | 1,5 | 86 | green | 0,75 |
| 14e | brown | 1,0 | 45 | black | 1,5 | 86e | green | 0,75 |
| 14f | brown | 1,0 | 46 | black | 2,5 | 86f | green | 0,75 |
| 15 | red | 1,0 | 47 | black | 4,0 | 88 | black | 0,75 |
| 15e | red | 1,0 | 49 | black | 1,0 | 88e | black | 0,75 |
| 16 | grey | 1,0 | 50 | green | 1,0 | 89 | brown | 0,75 |
| 16e | grey | 1,0 | 53 | blue | 0,75 | 92 | red | 0,75 |
| 17 | blue | 1,0 | 53a | blue | 0,75 | 95 | white | 1,5 |
| 17e | blue | 1,0 | 53e | green | 0,75 | 97 | white | 1,5 |
| 18 | black | 1,0 | 54 | green | 0,75 | 98 | white | 1,0 |
| 20 | white | 1,0 | 54b | green | 0,75 | 101 | green | 0,75 |
| 21 | red | 1,0 | 54e | green | 0,75 | 104 | green | 0,75 |
| 22 | green | 1,0 | 57 | blue | 0,75 | 105 | black | 0,75 |
| 22e | green | 1,0 | 57a | blue | 0,75 | 109 | black | 0,75 |
| 23a | yellow | 1,0 | 58 | green | 0,75 | 110 | green | 0,75 |
| 23ae | yellow | 1,0 | 58b | green | 0,75 | 111 | red | 0,75 |
| 23b | white | 1,0 | 59 | green | 0,75 | 112 | blue | 1,0 |
| 23be | white | 1,0 | 60 | green | 0,75 | 115 | yellow | 0,75 |
| 24a | yellow | 1,0 | 61 | red | 0,75 | 118 | white | 1,0 |
| 24ae | yellow | 1,0 | 62 | grey | 0,75 | 122 | white | 0,75 |
| 24b | white | 1,0 | 63 | red | 1,0 | 130 | brown | 1,0 |
| 24be | white | 1,0 | 64 | grey | 0,75 | 131 | white | 1,5 |
| 25a | blue | 1,0 | 65 | red | 0,75 | 136 | black | 1,0 |
| 25b | grey | 1,0 | 66 | white | 0,75 | 138 | black | 1,0 |
| 28 | red | 1,0 | 67 | red | 1,5 | 139 | black | 1,5 |
| 28e | red | 1,0 | 68 | red | 1,0 | 139a | black | 1,0 |
| 28f | red | 0,75 | 69 | black | 1,0 | 139b | black | 1,0 |
| 29 | grey | 0,75 | 70 | black | 1,5 | 140 | black | 1,5 |
| 39e | green | 0,75 | 71 | black | 1,5 | 141 | brown | 0,75 |
| 30 | brown | 0,75 | 72 | red | 1,0 | 141e | brown | 0,75 |
| 30e | brown | 0,75 | 72e | red | 1,0 | 142 | grey | 2,5 |
| 32 | red | 0,75 | 73 | yellow | 1,0 | 147 | black | 0,75 |
| 33 | yellow | 1,0 | 74 | grey | 4,0 | 190 | yellow | 0,75 |
| 35 | grey | 1,0 | 75 | red | 1,0 | 191 | grey | 0,75 |
| 39 | yellow | 0,75 | 76 | grey | 1,0 | 192 | black | 0,75 |
| 41 | blue | 0,75 | 80 | black | 1,0 | | | |

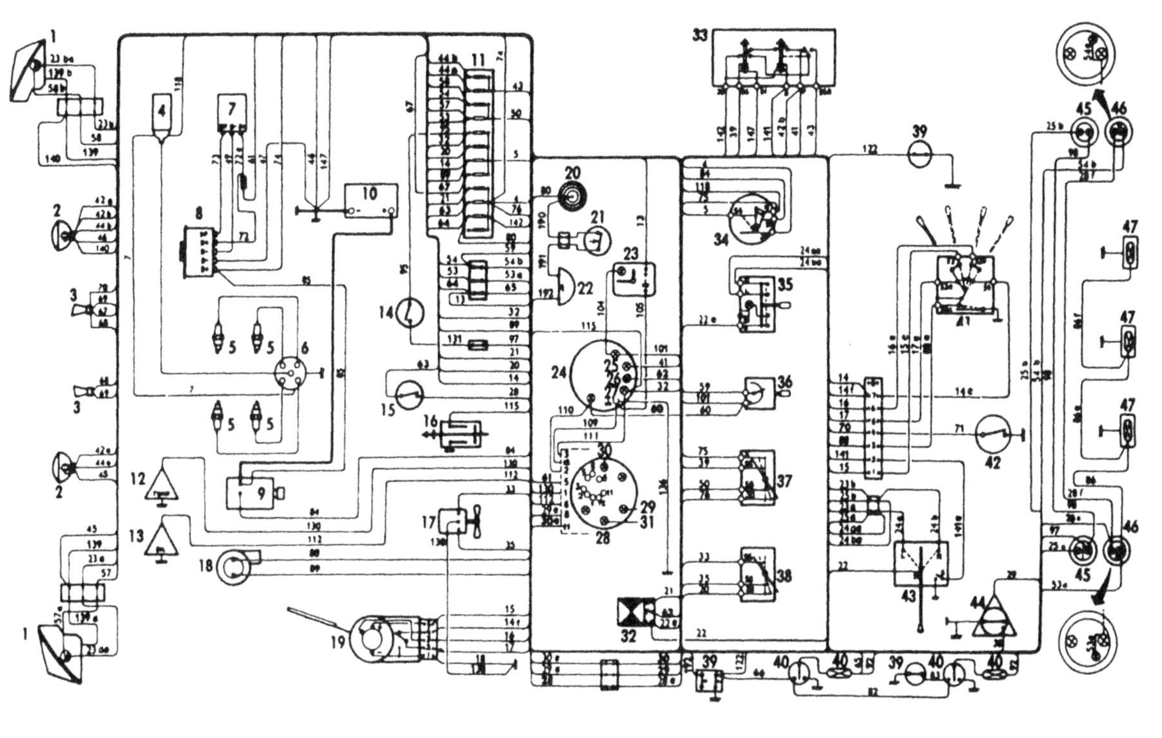

## Wiring diagram SAAB Station Wagon USA model 1971

*The range of the electrical system is shown by the wiring system below. To simplify the identification, the wires have been covered with insulation of different shades, as shown under 'Cable numbers'*

### Key to numbers in figure

1 Parking light and direction indicators
2 Headlights
3 Horn
4 Ignition coil
5 Spark plugs
6 Distributor
7 Voltage regulator
8 Alternator
9 Starter
10 Battery
11 Fuse box
12 Temperature transmitter
13 Oil pressure switch
14 Back-up light switch
15 Stop light switch
16 Brake warning contact
17 Heater fan motor
18 Windshield washer pump
19 Windshield wiper motor
20 Cigarette lighter
21 Contact for warning buzzer
22 Buzzer
23 Clock
24 Speedometer and odometer
25 High beam indicator light
26 Direction indicator repeater light
27 Brake warning light
28 Temperature and fuel gauges
29 Indicator light, fuel amount
30 Oil pressure warning light
31 Charge indicator light
32 Flasher unit
33 Dimmer relay
34 Ignition and starter switch
35 Hazard warning flasher switch
36 Instrument illumination theostat
37 Headlight switch
38 Heater fan switch
39 Dome lamp switch
40 Dome lamp with switch
41 Switch for windshield wiper and washer
42 Signal horn contact
43 Direction indicator switch with headlight flasher and dimmer switch
44 Fuel transmitter
45 Back-up light and direction indicators
46 Tail light and stop light
47 Number plate light

### Cable numbers

| No | Colour | Area mm² | No | Colour | Area mm² | No | Colour | Area mm² |
|---|---|---|---|---|---|---|---|---|
| 4 | grey | 1,5 | 42a | blue | 1,5 | 82 | white | 0,75 |
| 5 | red | 1,5 | 42b | white | 2,5 | 83 | white | 0,75 |
| 7 | green | 1,5 | 43 | yellow | 2,5 | 84 | yellow | 1,5 |
| 13 | blue | 0,75 | 44a | grey | 1,5 | 85 | grey | 4,0 |
| 14 | brown | 1,0 | 44b | yellow | 1,5 | 86 | green | 0,75 |
| 14e | brown | 1,0 | 45 | black | 1,5 | 86e | green | 0,75 |
| 14f | brown | 1,0 | 46 | black | 2,5 | 86f | green | 0,75 |
| 15 | red | 1,0 | 47 | black | 4,0 | 88 | black | 0,75 |
| 15e | red | 1,0 | 49 | black | 1,0 | 88e | black | 0,75 |
| 16 | grey | 1,0 | 50 | green | 1,0 | 89 | brown | 0,75 |
| 16e | grey | 1,0 | 53 | blue | 0,75 | 92 | red | 0,75 |
| 17 | blue | 1,0 | 53a | blue | 0,75 | 95 | white | 1,5 |
| 17e | blue | 1,0 | 53e | green | 0,75 | 97 | white | 1,5 |
| 18 | black | 1,0 | 54 | green | 0,75 | 98 | white | 1,0 |
| 20 | white | 1,0 | 54b | green | 0,75 | 101 | green | 0,75 |
| 21 | red | 1,0 | 54e | green | 0,75 | 104 | green | 0,75 |
| 22 | green | 1,0 | 57 | blue | 0,75 | 105 | black | 0,75 |
| 22e | green | 1,0 | 57a | blue | 0,75 | 109 | black | 0,75 |
| 23a | yellow | 1,0 | 58 | green | 0,75 | 110 | green | 0,75 |
| 23ae | yellow | 1,0 | 58b | green | 0,75 | 111 | red | 0,75 |
| 23b | white | 1,0 | 59 | green | 0,75 | 112 | blue | 1,0 |
| 23be | white | 1,0 | 60 | green | 0,75 | 115 | yellow | 0,75 |
| 24a | yellow | 1,0 | 61 | red | 0,75 | 118 | white | 1,0 |
| 24ae | yellow | 1,0 | 62 | grey | 0,75 | 122 | white | 0,75 |
| 24b | white | 1,0 | 63 | red | 1,0 | 130 | brown | 1,0 |
| 24be | white | 1,0 | 64 | grey | 0,75 | 131 | white | 1,5 |
| 25a | blue | 1,0 | 65 | red | 0,75 | 136 | black | 1,0 |
| 25b | grey | 1,0 | 66 | white | 0,75 | 138 | black | 1,0 |
| 28 | red | 1,0 | 67 | red | 1,5 | 139 | black | 1,5 |
| 28e | red | 1,0 | 68 | red | 1,0 | 139a | black | 1,0 |
| 28f | red | 0,75 | 69 | black | 1,0 | 139b | black | 1,0 |
| 29 | grey | 0,75 | 70 | black | 1,5 | 140 | black | 1,5 |
| 29e | green | 0,75 | 71 | black | 1,5 | 141 | brown | 0,75 |
| 30 | brown | 0,75 | 72 | red | 1,0 | 141e | brown | 0,75 |
| 30e | brown | 0,75 | 72e | red | 1,0 | 142 | grey | 2,5 |
| 32 | red | 0,75 | 73 | yellow | 1,0 | 147 | black | 0,75 |
| 33 | yellow | 1,0 | 74 | grey | 4,0 | 190 | yellow | 0,75 |
| 35 | grey | 1,0 | 75 | red | 1,0 | 191 | grey | 0,75 |
| 39 | yellow | 0,75 | 76 | grey | 1,0 | 192 | black | 0,75 |
| 41 | blue | 0,75 | 80 | black | 1,0 | | | |

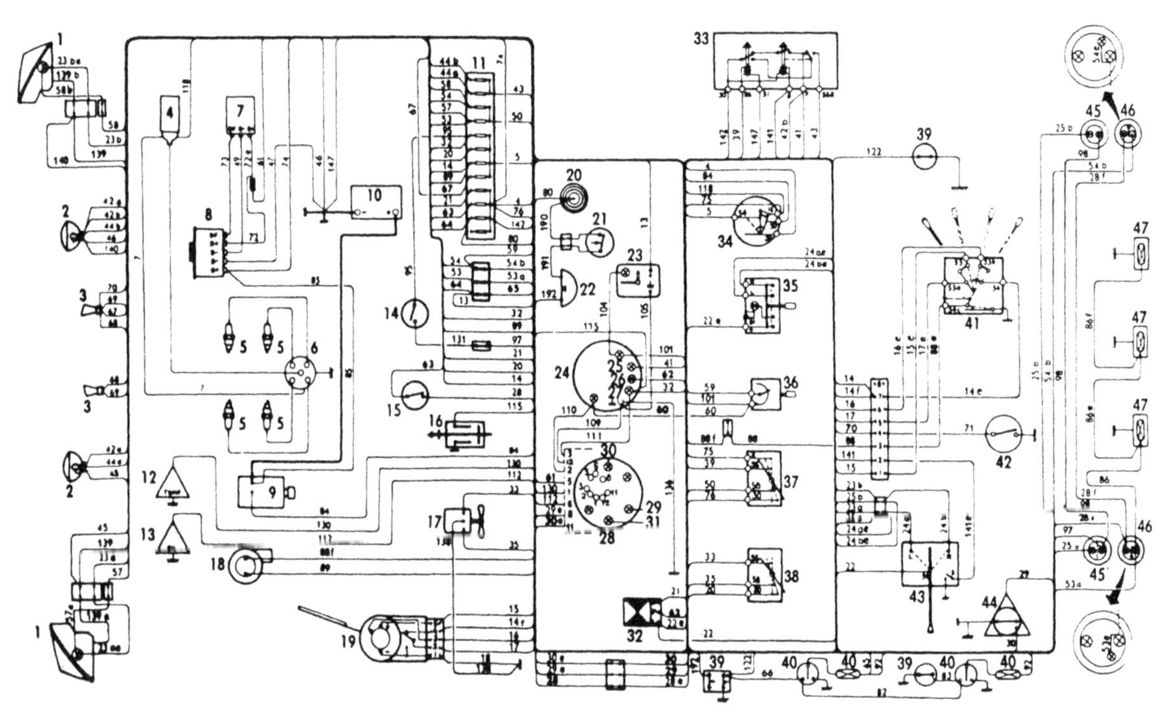

**Wiring diagram SAAB sedan rhd model 1967**

*The range of the electrical system is shown by the wiring system on the next page. To simplify the identification, the wires have been covered with insulation of different shades, as follows:*

| | |
|---|---|
| *Black* | *7, 18, 19, 45, 46, 47, 49, 71, 105, 109, 125, 135, 136, 138, 139, 140* |
| *Red* | *5, 21, 28, 28e, 28f, 32, 39, 61, 63, 65, 67, 68, 72, 111, 113, 126, 129* |
| *Green* | *16, 22, 50, 51, 52, 53, 54, 55, 56, 57, 58, 60, 101, 104, 110, 121, 133, 143* |
| *Grey* | *4, 25b, 25be, 29, 29e, 35, 44a, 62a, 62b, 64, 69, 70, 74, 75, 85, 142, 144* |
| *White* | *20, 23b, 24b, 40, 42b, 66, 118, 122, 122e, 128a* |
| *Yellow* | *17, 23a, 24a, 43 44b, 73, 84, 128b* |
| *Brown* | *14, 30, 30e, 130, 137, 141* |
| *Blue* | *13, 25a, 25ae, 41, 42a, 112, 145* |

**Key to numbers in the figure**

*1 Direction indicator lights and side lights*
*2 Headlights*
*3 HOrns*
*4 Ignition coil*
*5 Spark plugs*
*6 Distributor*
*7 Voltage regulator*
*8 Generator*
*9 Starter motor*
*10 Battery*
*11 Fuse box*
*12 Temperature sender*
*13 Oil pressure switch*
*14 Stop light switch*
*15 Heater motor*
*16 Windshield wiper motor*
*17 Direction indicator warning lights*
*18 High beam warning light*
*19 Generator warning light*
*20 Oil pressure warning light*
*21 Fuel gauge*
*22 Speedometer with odometer*
*23 Temperature gauge*
*24 Electric clock*
*25 Flasher*
*26 Headlamp control relay*
*27 Dimmer relay*
*28 Ignition and starter switch*
*29 Headlights and side lights switch with instrument illumination rheostat*
*30 Heater switch*
*31 Windshield wiper switch*
*32 Courtesy light switches*
*33 Interior light with switch*
*34 Horn ring*
*35 Direction indicators switch with headlight flasher and dimmer switch*
*36 Fuel tank gauge*
*37 Stop lights, direction indicator and rear lights*
*38 Number plate lights*
*39 Trunk lights*

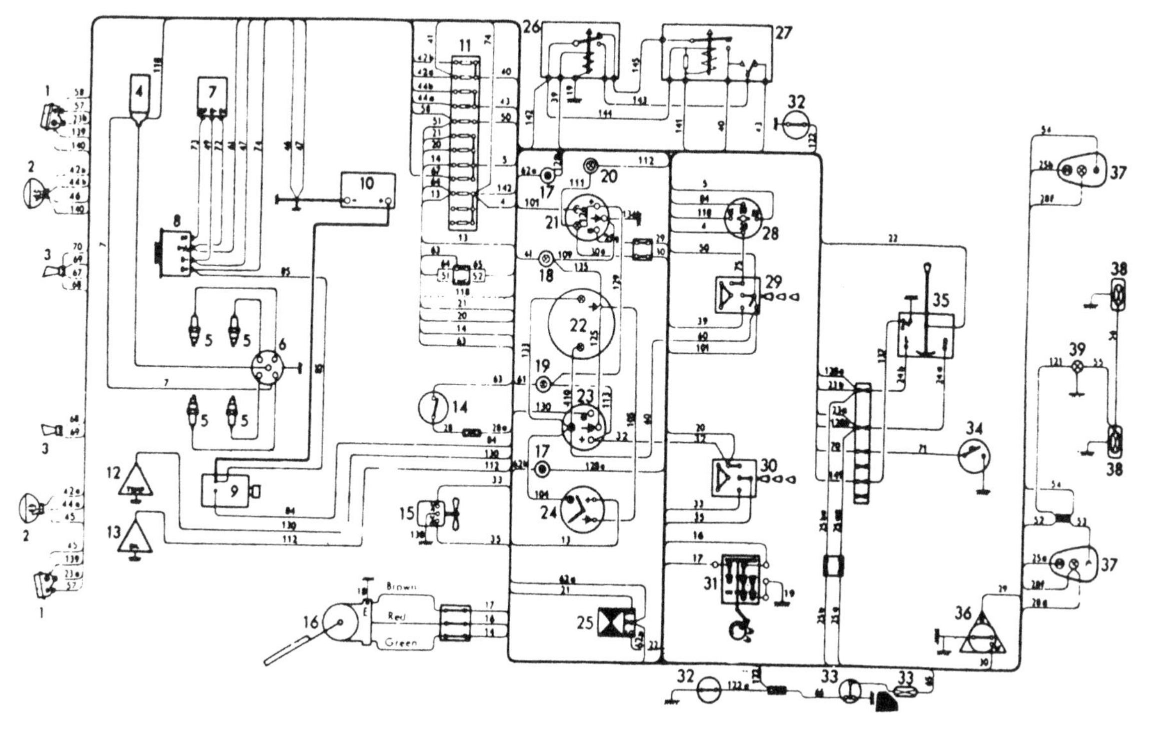

**Wiring diagram SAAB sedan rhd model 1968**

*The range of the electrical system is shown by the wiring system on the next page. To simplify the identification, the wires have been covered with insulation of different shades, as follows:*

| | |
|---|---|
| *Black* | *7, 19, 45, 47, 49, 71, 88, 88e, 105, 109, 124, 125, 135, 136, 138, 139, 140* |
| *Red* | *5, 21, 28, 28e, 28f, 32, 39, 61, 63, 65, 67, 68, 72, 72e, 111, 113, 116, 126, 129* |
| *Green* | *22, 50, 51, 52, 53, 54, 55, 56, 57, 58, 59, 60, 101, 104, 110, 121, 133, 143* |
| *Grey* | *4, 16, 16e, 25b, 25be, 29, 29e, 35, 44a, 62b, 64, 69, 70, 74, 75, 85, 142, 144* |
| *White* | *20, 23b, 24b, 40, 40c, 42b, 66, 118, 122, 122e* |
| *Yellow* | *23a, 24a, 33, 43, 44b, 73, 84, 115* |
| *Brown* | *14, 30, 30e, 89, 130, 137, 141* |
| *Blue* | *13, 17, 17e, 25a, 25ae, 41, 42a, 112, 145* |

**Key to numbers in the figure**

*1 Direction indicators and side lights*
*2 Headlights*
*3 Horn*
*4 Ignition coil*
*5 Spark plugs*
*6 Distributor*
*7 Voltage regulator*
*8 Alternator*
*9 Starter*
*10 Battery*
*11 Fuse box*
*12 Temperature gauge, sending unit*
*13 Oil pressure switch*
*14 Stop light switch*
*15 Brake warning contact*
*16 Heater fan motor*
*17 Windshield washer pump*
*18 Wiper motor*
*19 Chrage indicator light*
*20 Direction indicator repeater light*
*21 Brake warning light*
*22 High beam indicator light*
*23 Oil pressure warning light*
*24 Fuel gauge*
*25 Speedometer with odometer*
*26 Temperature gauge*
*27 Electric clock (extra equipment)*
*28 Flasher*
*29 Manoeuvre relay, light*
*30 Dimmer relay*
*31 Ignition and starter switch*
*32 Headlight switch*
*33 Instrument illumination rheostat*
*34 Heater fan switch*
*35 Courtesy light switch*
*36 Courtesy light with switch*
*37 Direction indicator switch with headlight flasher and dimmer switch*
*38 Fuel tank gauge*
*39 Switch for windshield wiper, washer and signal horn*
*40 Stop lights, direction indicators and tail lights*
*41 Number plate light*
*42 Trunk light*

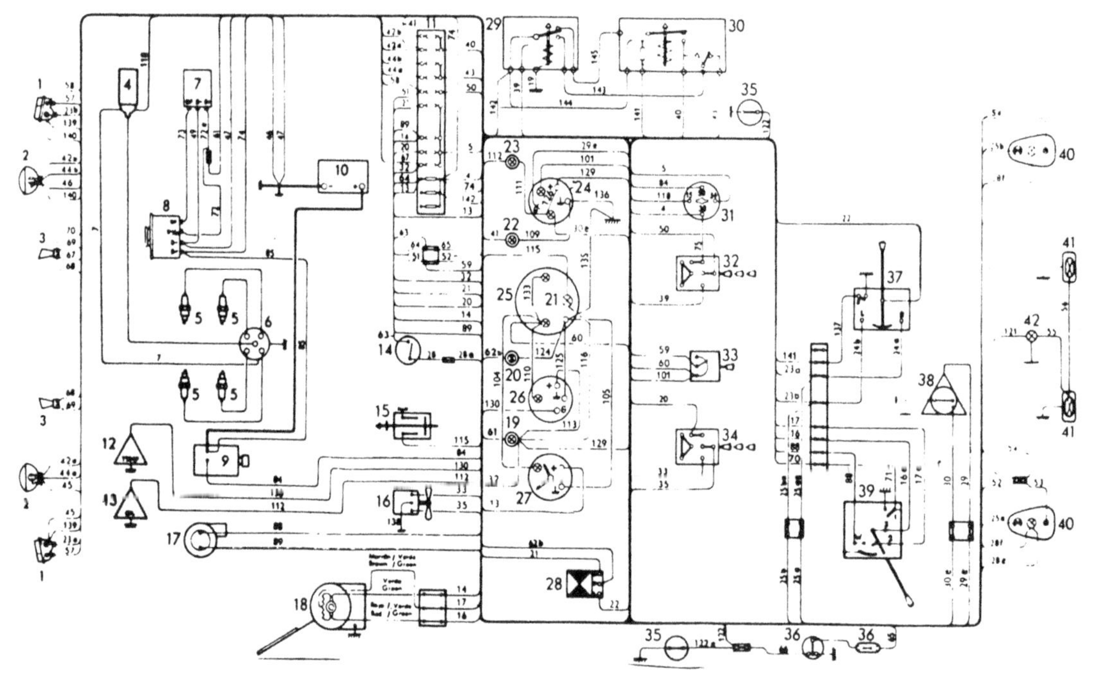

## Wiring diagram SAAB Sedan rhd model 1969

*The range of the electrical system is shown by the wiring system below. To simplify the identification, the wires have been covered with insulation of different shades, as shown under 'Cable numbers'*

### Key to numbers in the figure

1 Parking light and direction indicators
2 Headlights
3 Horn
4 Ignition coil
5 Spark plugs
6 Distributor
7 Voltage regulator
8 Alternator
9 Starter
10 Battery
11 Fuse box
12 Temperature transmitter
13 Oil pressure switch
14 Stop light switch
15 Brake warning contact
16 Heater fan motor
17 Windshield washer pump
18 Windshield wiper motor
19 Charge indicator light
20 Direction indicator repeater light
21 Brake warning light
22 High beam indicator light
23 Oil pressure warning light
24 Fuel gauge
25 Speedometer with odometer
26 Temperature gauge (coolant)
27 Electric clock (De Luxe only)
28 Flasher unit
29 Dimmer relay
30 Ignition and starter switch
31 Headlight switch
32 Instrument illumination rheostat
33 Heater fan switch
34 Warning flasher switch
35 Courtesy light switch
36 Courtesy light with switch
37 Direction indicator switch with headlight flasher and dimmer switch
38 Fuel transmitter
39 Switch for windshield wiper, washer and signal horn
40 Stop lights, direction indicators and tail light
41 Number plate light
42 Trunk light

### Cable numbers

| No | Colour | Area mm$^2$ | No | Colour | Area mm$^2$ | No | Colour | Area mm$^2$ |
|---|---|---|---|---|---|---|---|---|
| 4 | grey | 1,5 | 42a | blue | 1,5 | 75 | grey | 2,5 |
| 5 | red | 1,5 | 42b | white | 2,5 | 84 | yellow | 1,5 |
| 7 | black | 1,5 | 43 | yellow | 2,5 | 85 | grey | 4,0 |
| 13 | blue | 0,75 | 44a | grey | 1,5 | 8 | black | 0,75 |
| 14 | brown | 1,0 | 44b | yellow | 1,5 | 88e | black | 0,75 |
| 16 | grey | 1,0 | 45 | black | 1,5 | 89 | brown | 0,75 |
| 16e | grey | 1,0 | 46 | black | 2,5 | 101 | green | 0,75 |
| 17 | blue | 1,0 | 47 | black | 4,0 | 104 | green | 0,75 |
| 17e | blue | 1,0 | 49 | black | 1,0 | 105 | black | 0,75 |
| 20 | white | 1,0 | 50 | green | 1,0 | 109 | black | 0,75 |
| 21 | red | 1,0 | 53 | blue | 0,75 | 110 | green | 0,75 |
| 22 | green | 1,0 | 53a | blue | 0,75 | 111 | red | 0,75 |
| 22e | green | 1,0 | 54 | green | 0,75 | 112 | blue | 1,0 |
| 23a | yellow | 1,0 | 54b | green | 0,75 | 113 | white | 0,75 |
| 23ae | yellow | 1,0 | 55 | green | 0,75 | 115 | yellow | 0,75 |
| 23b | white | 1,0 | 56 | green | 0,75 | 116 | red | 0,75 |
| 23be | white | 1,0 | 57 | blue | 0,75 | 118 | white | 1,0 |
| 24a | yellow | 0,75 | 57a | blue | 0,75 | 121 | green | 0,75 |
| 24ae | yellow | 0,75 | 58 | green | 0,75 | 122 | white | 0,75 |
| 24b | white | 0,75 | 58b | green | 0,75 | 124 | black | 0,75 |
| 24be | white | 0,75 | 59 | green | 0,75 | 125 | black | 0,75 |
| 25a | blue | 1,0 | 60 | green | 0,75 | 126 | white | 0,75 |
| 25ae | blue | 1,0 | 61 | red | 0,75 | 129 | white | 0,75 |
| 25b | grey | 1,0 | 62 | grey | 0,75 | 130 | brown | 1,0 |
| 25b3 | grey | 1,0 | 63 | red | 0,75 | 133 | green | 0,75 |
| 28 | red | 1,0 | 64 | grey | 0,75 | 135 | black | 0,75 |
| 28e | red | 1,0 | 65 | red | 0,75 | 136 | black | 0,75 |
| 28f | red | 0,75 | 66 | white | 0,75 | 137 | brown | 0,75 |
| 29 | grey | 0,75 | 67 | red | 1,5 | 137c | brown | 0,75 |
| 29e | grey | 0,75 | 68 | red | 1,0 | 138 | black | 1,0 |
| 30 | brown | 0,75 | 69 | black | 1,0 | 139 | black | 1,0 |
| 30e | brown | 0,75 | 70 | black | 1,5 | 139a | black | 1,0 |
| 32 | red | 0,75 | 71 | black | 1,5 | 139b | black | 1,0 |
| 33 | yellow | 1,0 | 72 | red | 1,0 | 140 | black | 1,5 |
| 35 | grey | 1,0 | 72e | red | 1,0 | 142 | grey | 1,5 |
| 39 | red | 2,5 | 73 | yellow | 1,0 | 144 | grey | 0,75 |
| 41 | blue | 0,75 | 74 | grey | 4,0 | | | |

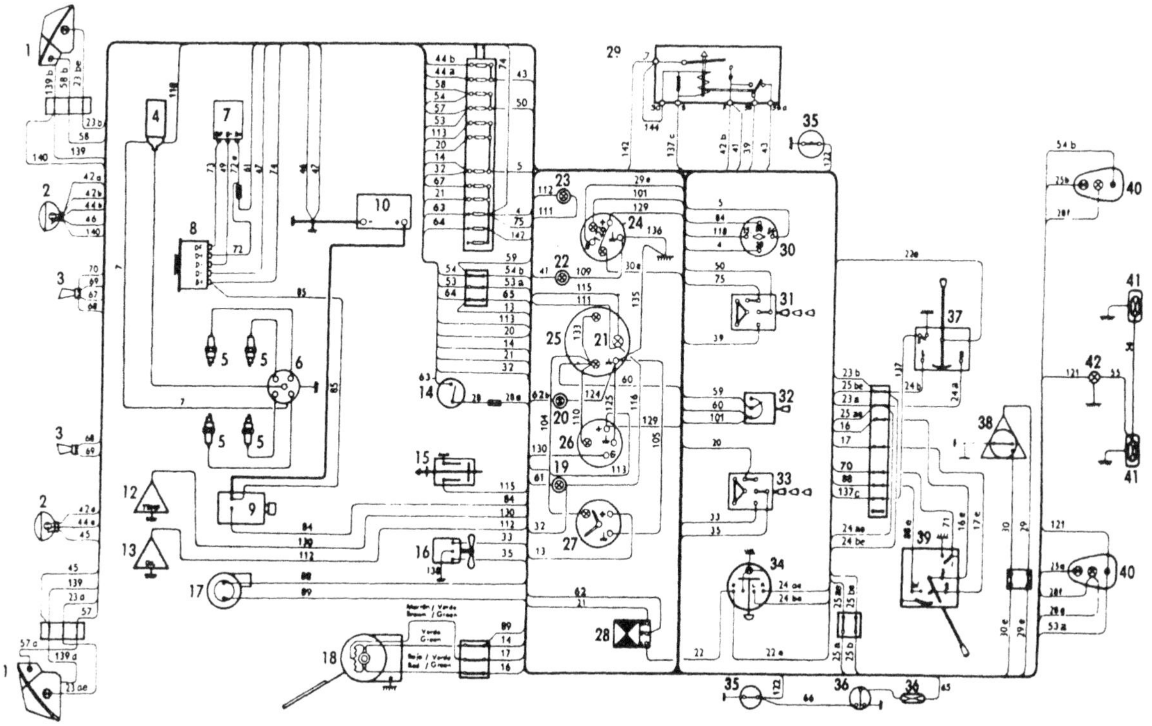

## Wiring diagram SAAB Sedan rhd model 1970

*The range of the electrical system is shown by the wiring system below. To simplify the identification, the wires have been covered with insulation of different shades, as shown under 'Cable numbers'*

**Key to numbers in the figure**

1 Parking light and direction indicators
2 Headlights
3 Horn
4 Ignition coil
5 Spark plugs
6 Distributor
7 Voltage regulator
8 Alternator
9 Starter
10 Battery
11 Fuse box
12 Temperature transmitter
13 Oil pressure switch
14 Stop light switch
15 Brake warning contact
16 Heater fan motor
17 Windshield washer pump
18 Windshield wiper motor
19 Speedometer with odometer
20 High beam indicator light
21 Direction indicator repeater light
22 Brake warning light
23 Temperature and fuel gauges
24 Indicator light, fuel amount
25 Oil pressure warning light
26 Charge indicator light
27 Flasher unit
28 Dimmer relay
29 Ignition and starter switch
30 Hazard warning flasher switch
31 Instrument illumination rheostat
32 Headlight switch
33 Heater fan switch
34 Courtesy light switch
35 Courtesy light with switch
36 Switch for windshield wiper and washer
37 Signal horn contact
38 Direction indicator switch with headlight flasher and dimmer switch
39 Fuel transmitter
40 Stop lights, direction indicators and tail light
41 Number plate light
42 Trunk light

**Cable numbers**

| No | Colour | Area mm$^2$ | No | Colour | Area mm$^2$ | No | Colour | Area mm$^2$ |
|---|---|---|---|---|---|---|---|---|
| 4 | grey | 1,5 | 30 | brown | 0,75 | 67 | red | 1,5 |
| 5 | red | 1,5 | 30e | brown | 0,75 | 68 | red | 1,0 |
| 7 | green | 1,5 | 30f | brown | 0,75 | 69 | black | 1,0 |
| 13 | blue | 0,75 | 32 | red | 0,75 | 70 | black | 1,5 |
| 14 | brown | 1,0 | 33 | yellow | 1,0 | 71 | black | 1,5 |
| 14e | brown | 1,0 | 35 | grey | 1,0 | 72 | red | 1,0 |
| 14f | brown | 1,0 | 39 | yellow | 0,75 | 72e | red | 1,0 |
| 15 | red | 1,0 | 41 | blue | 0,75 | 73 | yellow | 1,0 |
| 15e | red | 1,0 | 42a | blue | 1,5 | 74 | grey | 4,0 |
| 16 | grey | 1,0 | 42b | white | 2,5 | 75 | red | 1,0 |
| 16e | grey | 1,0 | 43 | yellow | 2,5 | 76 | grey | 1,0 |
| 17 | blue | 1,0 | 44a | grey | 1,5 | 84 | yellow | 1,5 |
| 17e | blue | 1,0 | 44b | yellow | 1,5 | 85 | grey | 4,0 |
| 18 | black | 1,0 | 45 | black | 1,5 | 88 | black | 0,75 |
| 20 | white | 1,0 | 46 | black | 2,5 | 88e | black | 0,75 |
| 21 | red | 1,0 | 47 | black | 4,0 | 89 | brown | 0,75 |
| 22 | green | 1,0 | 49 | black | 1,0 | 101 | green | 0,75 |
| 22e | green | 1,0 | 50 | green | 1,0 | 109 | black | 0,75 |
| 23a | yellow | 1,0 | 53 | blue | 0,75 | 110 | green | 0,75 |
| 23ae | yellow | 1,0 | 53a | blue | 0,75 | 111 | red | 0,75 |
| 23b | white | 1,0 | 54 | green | 0,75 | 112 | blue | 1,0 |
| 23be | white | 1,0 | 54b | green | 0,75 | 115 | yellow | 0,75 |
| 24a | yellow | 1,0 | 55 | green | 0,75 | 118 | white | 1,0 |
| 24ae | yellow | 1,0 | 56 | black | 0,75 | 121 | green | 0,75 |
| 24b | white | 1,0 | 57 | blue | 0,75 | 122 | white | 0,75 |
| 24be | white | 1,0 | 57a | blue | 0,75 | 130 | brown | 1,0 |
| 25a | blue | 1,0 | 58 | green | 0,75 | 136 | black | 1,0 |
| 25ae | blue | 1,0 | 58b | green | 0,75 | 138 | black | 1,0 |
| 25b | grey | 1,0 | 59 | green | 0,75 | 139 | black | 1,5 |
| 25be | grey | 1,0 | 60 | green | 0,75 | 139a | black | 1,0 |
| 28 | red | 1,0 | 61 | red | 0,75 | 139b | black | 1,0 |
| 28e | red | 1,0 | 62 | grey | 0,75 | 140 | black | 1,5 |
| 28f | red | 0,75 | 63 | red | 1,0 | 141 | brown | 0,75 |
| 29 | grey | 0,75 | 64 | grey | 0,75 | 141e | brown | 0,75 |
| 29e | grey | 0,75 | 65 | red | 0,75 | 142 | grey | 2,5 |
| 29f | grey | 0,75 | 66 | white | 0,75 | 147 | black | 0,75 |

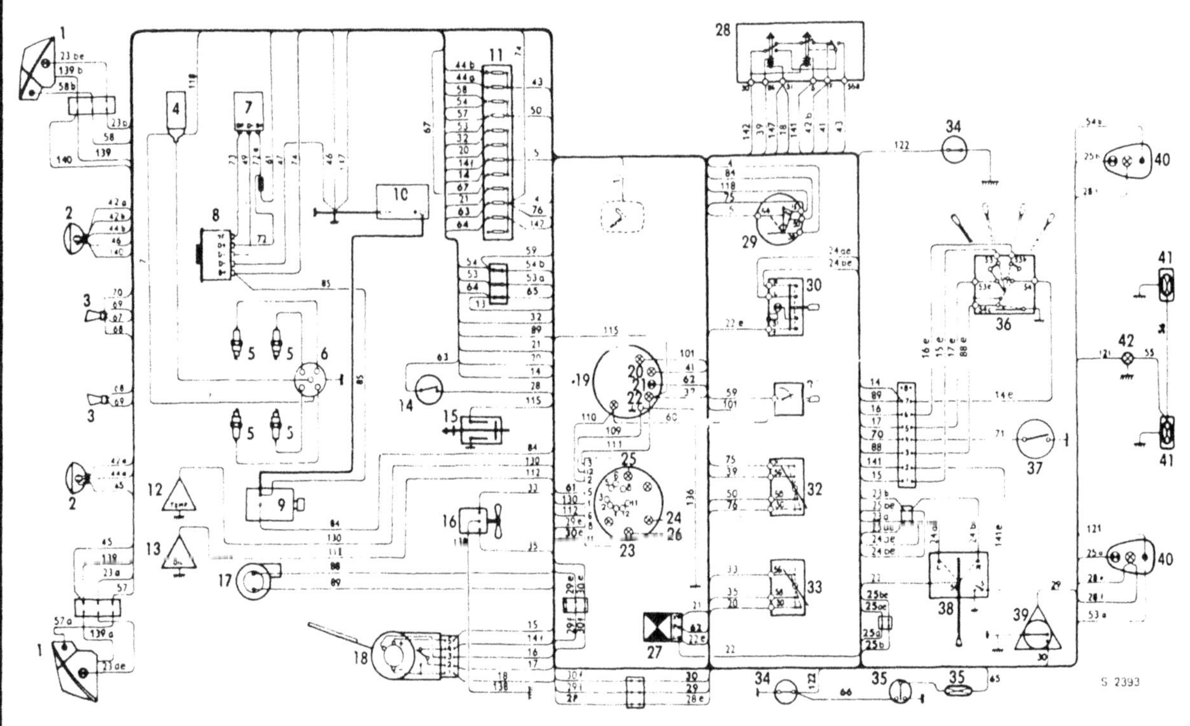

## Wiring diagram SAAB Sedan rhd model 1971

*The range of the electrical system is shown by the wiring system below. To simplify the identification, the wires have been covered with insulation of different shades, as shown under 'Cable numbers'*

### Key to numbers in figure

1 Parking light and direction indicators
2 Headlights
3 Horn
4 Headlight wiper motor
5 Ignition coil
6 Spark plugs
7 Distributor
8 Voltage regulator
9 Alternator
10 Starter
11 Relay, headlight wiper
12 Fuse for headlight wiper
13 Battery
14 Fuse box
15 Temperature transmitter
16 Oil pressure switch
17 Back-up light switch
18 Stop light switch
19 Brake warning contact
20 Heater fan motor
21 Windshield washer pump
22 Headlight washer pump
23 Windshield wiper motor
24 Manoeuvre relay, headlight wiper
25 Speedometer with odometer
26 High beam indicator light
27 Direction indicator repeater light
28 Brake warning light
29 Temperature and fuel gauges
30 Indicator light, fuel amount
31 Oil pressure warning light
32 Charge indicator light
33 Flasher unit
34 Dimmer relay
35 Ignition and starter switch
36 Hazard warning flasher switch
37 Diode
38 Instrument illumination rheostat
39 Headlight switch
40 Heater fan switch
41 Courtesy light switch
42 Courtesy light with switch
43 Trunk light with contact
44 Switch for windshield wiper, headlight wiper and washer
45 Signal horn contact
46 Direction indicator switch with headlight flasher and dimmer switch
47 Fuel transmitter
48 Stop lights, direction indicators and tail light
49 Back-up light
50 Number plate light

### Cable numbers

| No | Colour | Area mm$^2$ | No | Colour | Area mm$^2$ | No | Colour | Area mm$^2$ |
|---|---|---|---|---|---|---|---|---|
| 4 | grey | 1,5 | 41 | blue | 0,75 | 77f | red | 0,75 |
| 5 | red | 1,5 | 42a | blue | 1,5 | 78 | brown | 0,75 |
| 7 | green | 1,5 | 42b | white | 2,5 | 79 | green | 0,75 |
| 13 | blue | 0,75 | 43 | yellow | 2,5 | 81 | grey | 0,75 |
| 14 | brown | 1,0 | 44a | grey | 1,5 | 81e | blue | 0,75 |
| 14e | brown | 1,0 | 44b | yellow | 1,5 | 82 | yellow | 0,75 |
| 14f | brown | 1,0 | 45 | black | 1,5 | 82e | black | 0,75 |
| 15 | red | 1,0 | 46 | black | 2,5 | 83 | black | 0,75 |
| 15e | red | 1,0 | 49 | black | 1,0 | 83e | black | 0,75 |
| 16 | grey | 1,0 | 50 | green | 1,0 | 84 | yellow | 1,5 |
| 16e | grey | 1,0 | 53 | blue | 0,75 | 85 | grey | 4,0 |
| 17 | blue | 1,0 | 53a | blue | 0,75 | 88 | black | 0,75 |
| 17e | blue | 1,0 | 54 | green | 0,75 | 88e | black | 0,75 |
| 18 | black | 1,0 | 54b | green | 0,75 | 88f | black | 0,75 |
| 20 | white | 1,0 | 55 | green | 0,75 | 88g | black | 0,75 |
| 21 | red | 1,0 | 56 | black | 0,75 | 89 | brown | 0,75 |
| 22 | green | 1,0 | 57 | blue | 0,75 | 89f | yellow | 0,75 |
| 22e | green | 1,0 | 57a | blue | 0,75 | 95 | white | 1,0 |
| 23a | yellow | 1,0 | 58 | green | 0,75 | 97 | white | 1,0 |
| 23ae | yellow | 1,0 | 58b | green | 0,75 | 98 | white | 0,75 |
| 23b | white | 1,0 | 59 | green | 0,75 | 101 | green | 0,75 |
| 23be | white | 1,0 | 60 | green | 0,75 | 109 | black | 0,75 |
| 24a | yellow | 1,0 | 61 | red | 0,75 | 110 | green | 0,75 |
| 24ae | yellow | 1,0 | 62 | grey | 0,75 | 111 | red | 0,75 |
| 24b | white | 1,0 | 63 | red | 1,0 | 112 | blue | 1,0 |
| 24be | white | 1,0 | 64 | grey | 0,75 | 115 | yellow | 0,75 |
| 25a | blue | 1,0 | 65 | red | 0,75 | 118 | white | 1,0 |
| 25ae | blue | 1,0 | 66 | white | 0,75 | 121 | green | 0,75 |
| 25b | grey | 1,0 | 67 | red | 1,5 | 122 | white | 0,75 |
| 25be | grey | 1,0 | 68 | red | 1,0 | 123 | blue | 0,75 |
| 28 | red | 1,0 | 69 | black | 1,0 | 130 | brown | 1,0 |
| 28e | red | 1,0 | 70 | black | 1,5 | 131 | white | 1,0 |
| 28f | red | 0,75 | 71 | black | 1,5 | 136 | black | 1,0 |
| 29 | grey | 0,75 | 72 | red | 1,0 | 138 | black | 1,0 |
| 29e | grey | 0,75 | 72e | red | 1,0 | 139 | black | 1,5 |
| 29f | grey | 0,75 | 73 | yellow | 1,0 | 139a | black | 1,0 |
| 30 | brown | 0,75 | 74 | grey | 4,0 | 139b | black | 1,0 |
| 30e | brown | 0,75 | 75 | red | 1,0 | 140 | black | 1,5 |
| 30f | brown | 0,75 | 76 | grey | 1,0 | 141 | brown | 0,75 |
| 32 | red | 0,75 | 77 | red | 0,75 | 141e | brown | 0,75 |
| 33 | yellow | 1,0 | 77a | red | 0,75 | 142 | grey | 2,5 |
| 35 | grey | 1,0 | 77e | red | 0,75 | 147 | black | 0,75 |
| 39 | yellow | 0,75 | | | | | | |

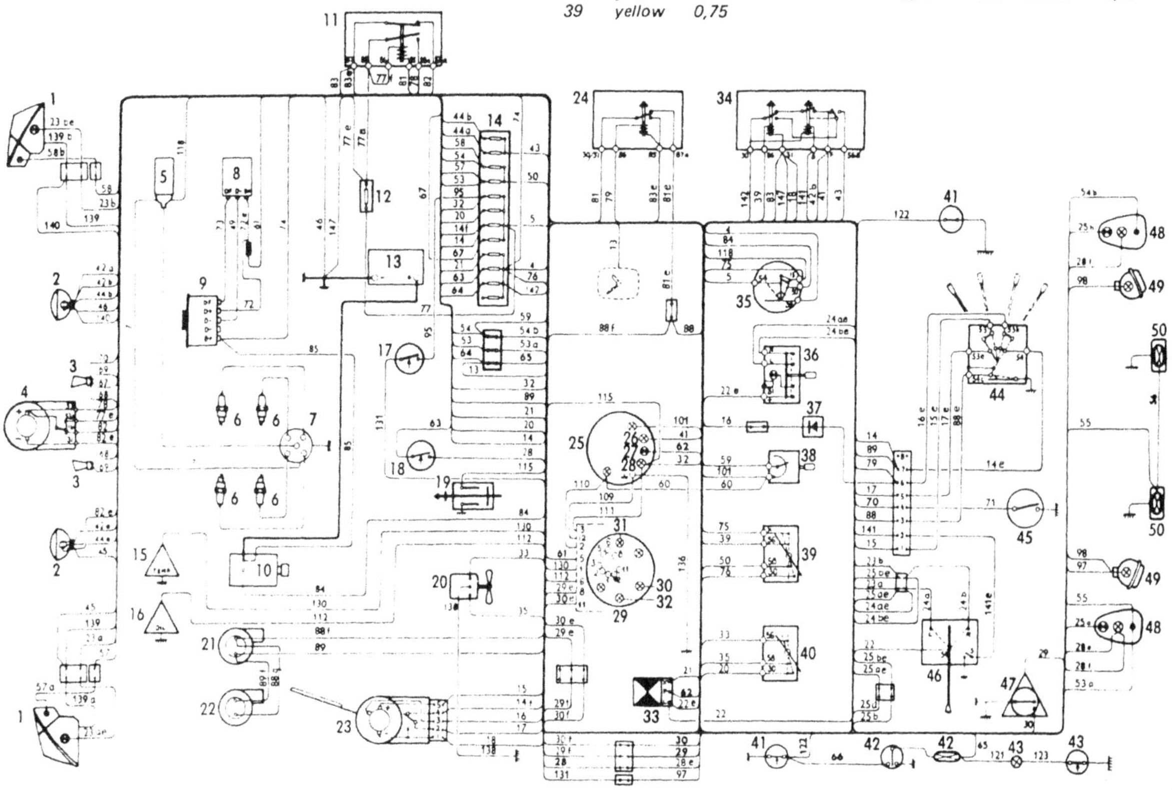

**Wiring diagram SAAB sedan rhd and detail of wiring diagram SAAB station wagon rhd model 1972 on**

*The range of the electrical system is shown by the wiring system on the next page*

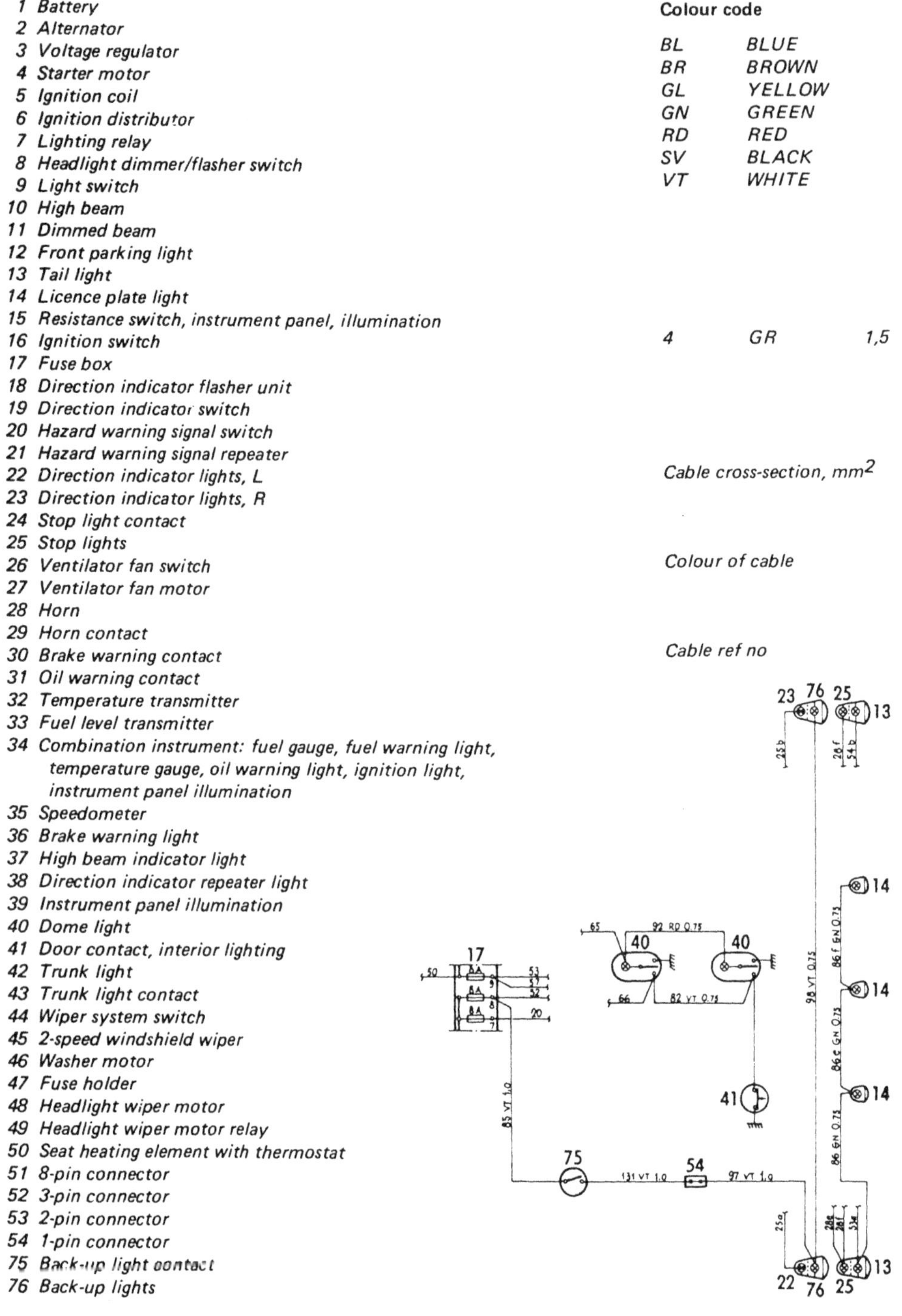

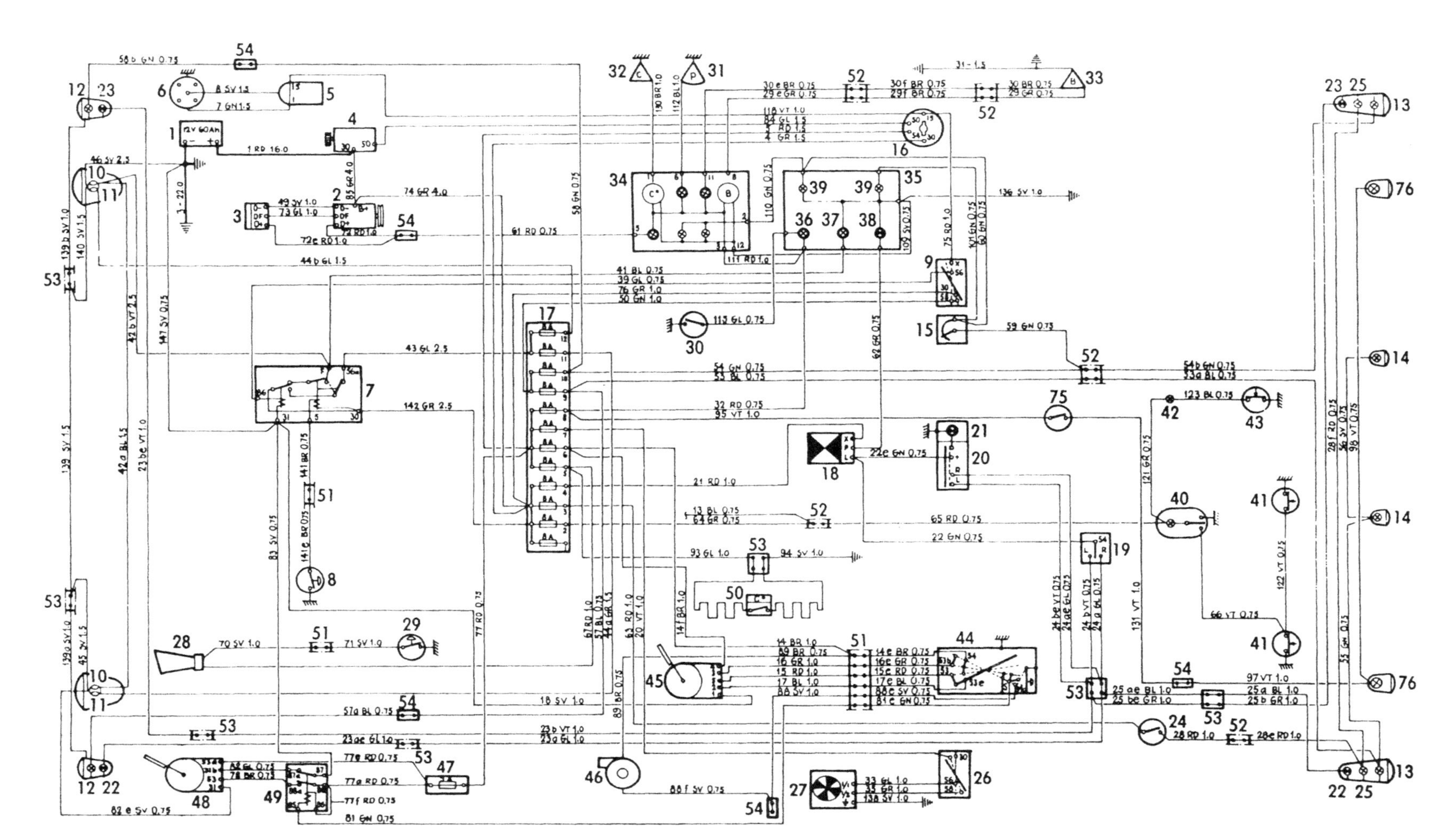


Wiring diagram SAAB Sedan r.h.d. model 1972 on

**Wiring diagram SAAB station wagon rhd model 1967**

*The range of the electrical system is shown by the wiring system below. To simplify the identification, the wires have been covered with insulation of different shades, as follows:*

| | |
|---|---|
| *Black* | *7, 7b, 18, 19, 45, 46, 47, 49, 71, 105, 109, 125, 135, 136, 138, 139, 140* |
| *Red* | *5, 21, 28, 28e, 28f, 28g, 32, 39, 61, 63, 65, 67, 68, 72, 92, 111, 113, 126, 129* |
| *Green* | *16, 22, 50, 51, 53, 54, 55, 57, 58, 60, 86, 87, 88, 101, 104, 110, 133, 143* |
| *Grey* | *4, 25b, 25be, 29, 29e, 35, 44a, 62a, 62b, 64, 69, 70, 74, 75, 85, 93, 142, 144* |
| *White* | *20, 23b, 24b, 40, 42b, 66, 82, 83, 118, 122, 122e, 128a* |
| *Yellow* | *17, 23a, 24a, 33, 43, 44b, 73, 84, 128b* |
| *Brown* | *14, 30, 30e, 130, 137, 141* |
| *Blue* | *13, 25a, 25ae, 41, 42a, 112, 145* |

**Key to numbers in the figure**

1 *Direction indicator lights and side lights*
2 *Headlights*
3 *Horns*
4 *Ignition coil*
5 *Spark plugs*
6 *Distributor*
7 *Voltage regulator*
8 *Alternator*
9 *Starter motor*
10 *Battery*
11 *Fuse box*
12 *Temperature sender*
13 *Oil pressure switch*
14 *Stop light switch*
15 *Heater motor*
16 *Windshield wiper motor*
17 *Direction indicator warning lights*
18 *High beam warning light*
19 *Generator warning light*
20 *Oil pressure warning light*
21 *Fuel gauge*
22 *Speedometer with odometer*
23 *Temperature gauge*
24 *Electric clock*
25 *Flasher*
26 *Headlight control relay*
27 *Dimmer relay*
28 *Ignition and starter switch*
29 *Headlight and side light switch with instrument illumination rheostat*
30 *Heater switch*
31 *Windshield wiper switch*
32 *Courtesy light switches*
33 *Interior light with switch*
34 *Horn ring*
35 *Direction indicators switch with headlight flasher and dimmer switch*
36 *Fuel tank gauge*
37 *Stop lights and direction lights*
38 *Rear lights*
39 *Number plate light*

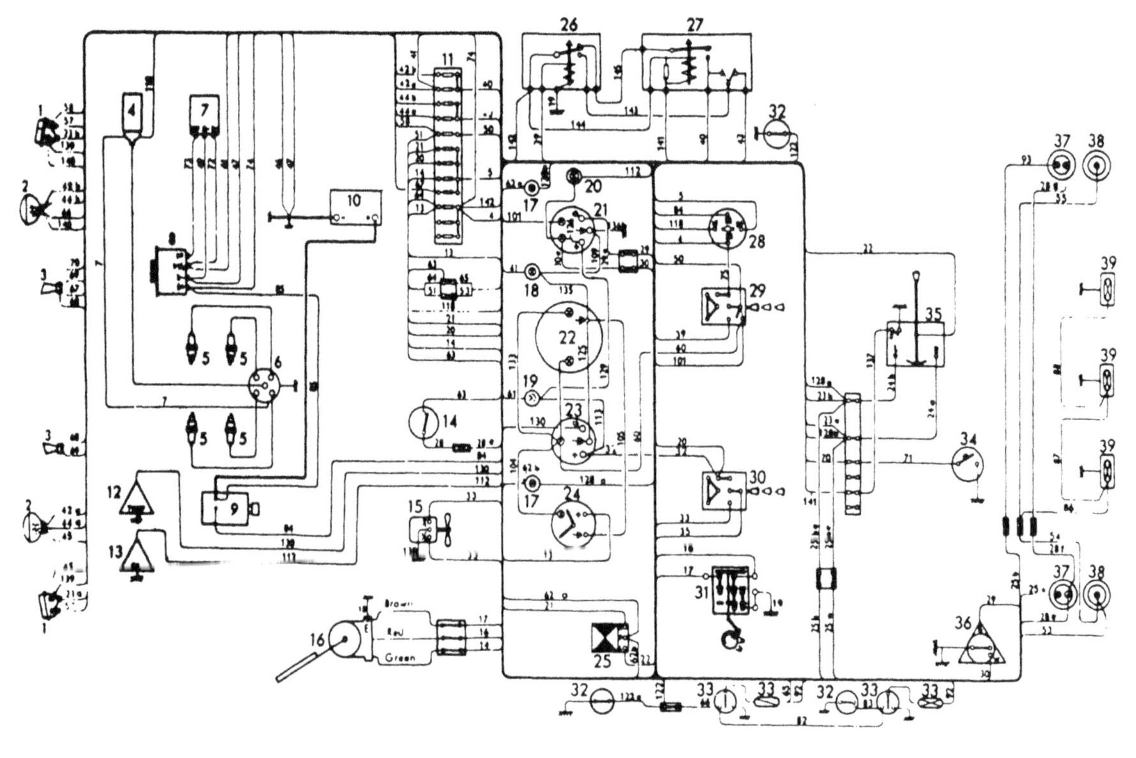

Wiring diagram SAAB station wagon rhd model 1968

*The range of the electrical system is shown by the wiring system below. To simplify the identification, the wires have been covered with insulation of different shades, as follows:*

| | |
|---|---|
| *Black* | *7, 19, 45, 46, 47, 49, 71, 88, 88e, 105, 109, 124, 125, 135, 136, 138, 139, 140* |
| *Red* | *5, 21, 28, 28e, 28f, 28g, 32, 39, 61, 63, 65, 67, 68, 72, 72e, 92, 111, 113, 116, 126, 129* |
| *Green* | *22, 50, 51, 53, 54, 55, 57, 58, 59, 60, 86, 86e, 86f, 101, 104, 110, 143* |
| *Grey* | *4, 16, 16e, 25b, 29, 35, 44a, 62b, 64, 69, 70, 74, 75, 85, 93, 142, 144* |
| *White* | *20, 23b, 24b, 40, 40c, 42b, 66, 82, 83, 118, 122, 122e* |
| *Yellow* | *23a, 24a, 33, 43, 44b, 73, 84, 115* |
| *Brown* | *14, 30, 30e, 89, 130, 137, 141* |
| *Blue* | *13, 17, 17e, 25a, 15ae, 41, 42a, 112, 145* |

Key to numbers in the figure

1 *Direction indicators and side lights*
2 *Headlights*
3 *Horn*
4 *Ignition coil*
5 *Spark plugs*
6 *Distributor*
7 *Voltage regulator*
8 *Alternator*
9 *Starter*
10 *Battery*
11 *Fuse box*
12 *Temperature gauge, sending unit*
13 *Oil pressure switch*
14 *Stop light switch*
15 *Brake warning contact*
16 *Heater fan motor*
17 *Windshield washer pump*
18 *Wiper motor*
19 *Charge indicator light*
20 *Direction indicator repeater light*
21 *Brake warning light*
22 *High beam indicator light*
23 *Oil pressure warning light*
24 *Fuel gauge*
25 *Speedometer with odometer*
26 *Temperature gauge*
27 *Electric clock (extra equipment)*
28 *Flasher*
29 *Manoeuvre relay, light*
30 *Dimmer relay*
31 *Ignition and starter switch*
32 *Headlight switch*
33 *Instrument illumination rheostat*
34 *Heater fan switch*
35 *Courtesy light switch*
36 *Courtesy light with switch*
37 *Direction indicator switch with headlight flasher and dimmer switch*
38 *Fuel tank gauge*
39 *Switch for windshield wiper, washer and signal horn*
40 *Stop lights and direction indicators*
41 *Tail lights*
42 *Number plate light*

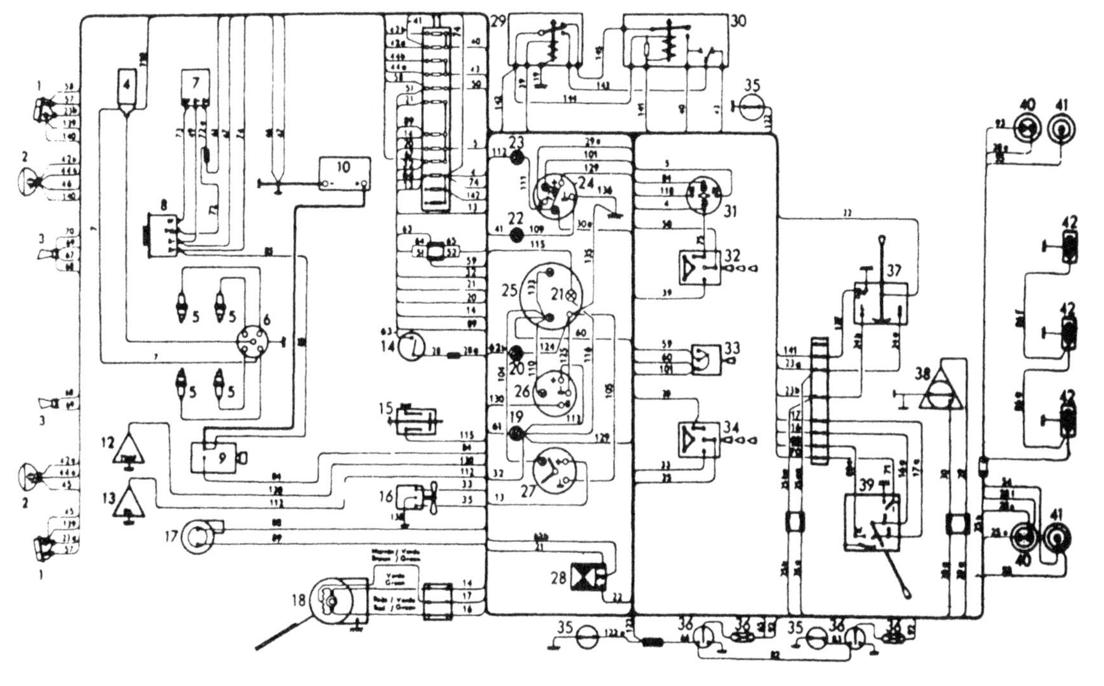

## Wiring diagram SAAB Station Wagon rhd model 1969

*The range of the electrical system is shown by the wiring system below. To simplify the identification, the wires have been covered with insulation of different shades, as shown under 'Cable numbers'*

### Cable numbers

| No | Colour | Area mm2 | No | Colour | Area mm2 | No | Colour | Area mm2 |
|---|---|---|---|---|---|---|---|---|
| 4 | grey | 1,5 | 43 | yellow | 2,5 | 86e | green | 0,75 |
| 5 | red | 1,5 | 44a | grey | 1,5 | 86f | green | 0,75 |
| 7 | black | 1,5 | 44b | yellow | 1,5 | 88 | black | 0,75 |
| 13 | blue | 0,75 | 45 | black | 1,5 | 88e | black | 0,75 |
| 14 | brown | 1,0 | 46 | black | 2,5 | 89 | brown | 0,75 |
| 16 | grey | 1,0 | 47 | black | 4,0 | 92 | red | 0,75 |
| 16e | grey | 1,0 | 49 | black | 1,0 | 95 | white | 1,5 |
| 17 | blue | 1,0 | 50 | green | 1,0 | 97 | white | 1,5 |
| 17e | blue | 1,0 | 53 | blue | 0,75 | 98 | white | 1,0 |
| 20 | white | 1,0 | 53a | blue | 0,75 | 101 | green | 0,75 |
| 21 | red | 1,0 | 54 | green | 0,75 | 104 | green | 0,75 |
| 22 | green | 1,0 | 54b | green | 0,75 | 105 | black | 0,75 |
| 22e | green | 1,0 | 57 | blue | 0,75 | 109 | black | 0,75 |
| 23a | yellow | 1,0 | 57a | blue | 0,75 | 110 | green | 0,75 |
| 23ae | yellow | 1,0 | 58 | green | 0,75 | 111 | red | 0,75 |
| 23b | white | 1,0 | 58b | green | 0,75 | 112 | blue | 1,0 |
| 23be | white | 1,0 | 59 | green | 0,75 | 113 | white | 0,75 |
| 24a | yellow | 0,75 | 60 | green | 0,75 | 115 | yellow | 0,75 |
| 24ae | yellow | 0,75 | 61 | red | 0,75 | 116 | red | 0,75 |
| 24b | white | 0,75 | 62 | grey | 0,75 | 118 | white | 1,0 |
| 24be | white | 0,75 | 63 | red | 0,75 | 122 | white | 0,75 |
| 25a | blue | 1,0 | 64 | grey | 0,75 | 124 | black | 0,75 |
| 25ae | blue | 1,0 | 65 | red | 0,75 | 125 | black | 0,75 |
| 25b | grey | 1,0 | 66 | white | 0,75 | 126 | white | 0,75 |
| 25be | grey | 1,0 | 67 | red | 1,5 | 129 | white | 0,75 |
| 28 | red | 1,0 | 68 | red | 1,0 | 130 | brown | 1,0 |
| 28e | red | 1,0 | 69 | black | 1,0 | 131 | white | 1,5 |
| 28f | red | 0,75 | 70 | black | 1,5 | 133 | green | 0,75 |
| 29 | grey | 0,75 | 71 | black | 1,5 | 135 | black | 0,75 |
| 29e | grey | 0,75 | 72 | red | 1,0 | 136 | black | 0,75 |
| 30 | brown | 0,75 | 72e | red | 1,0 | 137 | brown | 0,75 |
| 30e | brown | 0,75 | 73 | yellow | 1,0 | 137c | brown | 0,75 |
| 32 | red | 0,75 | 74 | grey | 4,0 | 138 | black | 1,0 |
| 33 | yellow | 1,0 | 75 | grey | 2,5 | 139 | black | 1,0 |
| 35 | grey | 1,0 | 82 | white | 0,75 | 139a | black | 1,0 |
| 39 | red | 2,5 | 83 | white | 0,75 | 139b | black | 1,0 |
| 41 | blue | 0,75 | 84 | yellow | 1,5 | 140 | black | 1,5 |
| 42a | blue | 1,5 | 85 | grey | 4,0 | 142 | grey | 1,5 |
| 42b | white | 2,5 | 86 | green | 0,75 | 144 | grey | 0,75 |

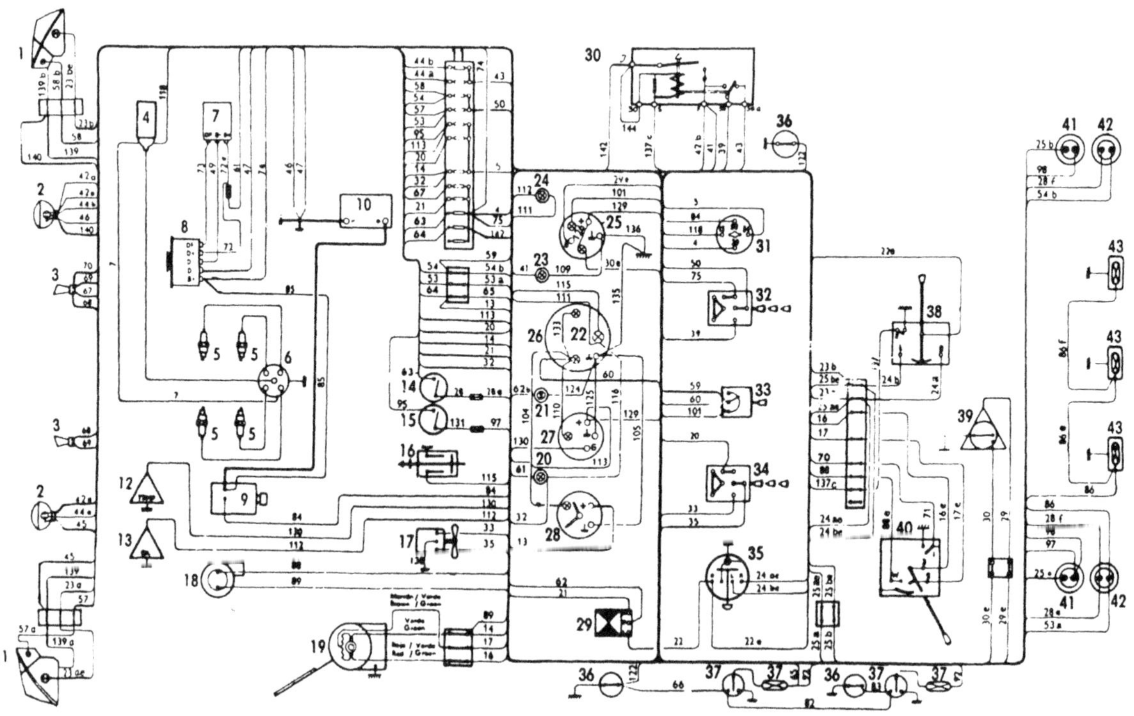

### Key to numbers in the figure

*1 Parking light and direction indicators*
*2 Headlights*
*3 Horn*
*4 Ignition coil*
*5 Spark plugs*
*6 Distributor*
*7 Voltage regulator*
*8 Alternator*
*9 Starter*
*10 Battery*
*11 Fuse box*
*12 Temperature transmitter*
*13 Oil pressure switch*
*14 Stop light switch*
*15 Back-up light switch*
*16 Brake warning contact*
*17 Heater fan motor*
*18 Windshield washer pump*
*19 Windshield wiper motor*
*20 Charge indicator light*
*21 Direction indicator repeater light*
*22 Brake warning light*
*23 High beam indicator light*
*24 Oil pressure warning light*
*25 Fuel gauge*
*26 Speedometer and odometer*
*27 Temperature gauge (coolant)*
*28 Electric clock (De Luxe only)*
*29 Flasher unit*
*30 Dimmer relay*
*31 Ignition and starter switch*
*32 Headlight switch*
*33 Instrument illumination rheostat*
*34 Heater fan switch*
*35 Warning flasher switch*
*36 Courtesy light switch*
*37 Courtesy light with switch*
*38 Direction indicator switch with headlight flasher and dimmer switch*
*39 Fuel transmitter*
*40 Switch for windshield wiper, washer and signal horn*
*41 Back-up light and direction indicators*
*42 Tail light and stop light*
*43 Number plate light*

## Wiring diagram SAAB Station Wagon rhd model 1970

*The range of the electrical system is shown by the wiring system below. To simplify the identification, the wires have been covered with insulation of different shades, as shown under 'Cable numbers'*

### Key to numbers in the figure

1 *Parking light and direction indicators*
2 *Headlights*
3 *Horn*
4 *Ignition coil*
5 *Spark plugs*
6 *Distributor*
7 *Voltage regulator*
8 *Alternator*
9 *Starter*
10 *Battery*
11 *Fuse box*
12 *Temperature transmitter*
13 *Oil pressure switch*
14 *Back-up light switch*
15 *Stop light switch*
16 *Brake warning contact*
17 *Heater fan motor*
18 *Windshield washer pump*
19 *Windshield wiper motor*
20 *Speedometer and odometer*
21 *High beam indicator light*
22 *Direction indicator repeater light*
23 *Brake warning light*
24 *Temperature and fuel gauges*
25 *Indicator light, fuel amount*
26 *Oil pressure warning light*
27 *Charge indicator light*
28 *Flasher unit*
29 *Dimmer relay*
30 *Ignition and starter switch*
31 *Hazard warning flasher switch*
32 *Instrument illumination rheostat*
33 *Headlight switch*
34 *Heater fan switch*
35 *Courtesy light switch*
36 *Courtesy light with switch*
37 *Switch for windshield wiper and washer*
38 *Signal horn contact*
39 *Direction indicator switch with headlight flasher and dimmer switch*
40 *Fuel transmitter*
41 *Back-up light and direction indicators*
42 *Tail light and stop light*
43 *Number plate light*

### Cable numbers

| No | Colour | Area mm$^2$ | No | Colour | Area mm$^2$ | No | Colour | Area mm$^2$ |
|---|---|---|---|---|---|---|---|---|
| 4 | grey | 1,5 | 32 | red | 0,75 | 74 | grey | 4,0 |
| 5 | red | 1,5 | 33 | yellow | 1,0 | 75 | red | 1,0 |
| 7 | green | 1,5 | 35 | grey | 1,0 | 76 | grey | 1,0 |
| 13 | blue | 0,75 | 39 | yellow | 0,75 | 82 | white | 0,75 |
| 14 | brown | 1,0 | 41 | blue | 0,75 | 83 | white | 0,75 |
| 14e | brown | 1,0 | 42a | blue | 1,5 | 84 | yellow | 1,5 |
| 14f | brown | 1,0 | 42b | white | 2,5 | 85 | grey | 4,0 |
| 15 | red | 1,0 | 43 | yellow | 2,5 | 86 | green | 0,75 |
| 15e | red | 1,0 | 44a | grey | 1,5 | 86e | green | 0,75 |
| 16 | grey | 1,0 | 44b | yellow | 1,5 | 86f | green | 0,75 |
| 16e | grey | 1,0 | 45 | black | 1,5 | 88 | black | 0,75 |
| 17 | blue | 1,0 | 46 | black | 2,5 | 88e | black | 0,75 |
| 17e | blue | 1,0 | 47 | black | 4,0 | 89 | brown | 0,75 |
| 18 | black | 1,0 | 49 | black | 1,0 | 92 | red | 0,75 |
| 20 | white | 1,0 | 50 | green | 1,0 | 95 | white | 1,5 |
| 21 | red | 1,0 | 53 | blue | 0,75 | 97 | white | 1,5 |
| 22 | green | 1,0 | 53a | blue | 0,75 | 98 | white | 1,0 |
| 22e | green | 1,0 | 54 | green | 0,75 | 101 | green | 0,75 |
| 23a | yellow | 1,0 | 54b | green | 0,75 | 109 | black | 0,75 |
| 23ae | yellow | 1,0 | 57 | blue | 0,75 | 110 | green | 0,75 |
| 23b | white | 1,0 | 57a | blue | 0,75 | 111 | red | 0,75 |
| 23be | white | 1,0 | 58 | green | 0,75 | 112 | blue | 1,0 |
| 24a | yellow | 1,0 | 58b | green | 0,75 | 115 | yellow | 0,75 |
| 24ae | yellow | 1,0 | 59 | green | 0,75 | 118 | white | 1,0 |
| 24b | white | 1,0 | 60 | green | 0,75 | 122 | white | 0,75 |
| 24be | white | 1,0 | 61 | red | 0,75 | 130 | brown | 1,0 |
| 25a | blue | 1,0 | 62 | grey | 0,75 | 131 | white | 1,5 |
| 25ae | blue | 1,0 | 63 | red | 1,0 | 136 | black | 1,0 |
| 25b | grey | 1,0 | 64 | grey | 0,75 | 138 | black | 1,0 |
| 25be | grey | 1,0 | 65 | red | 0,75 | 139 | black | 1,5 |
| 28 | red | 1,0 | 66 | white | 0,75 | 139a | black | 1,0 |
| 28a | red | 1,0 | 67 | red | 1,5 | 139b | black | 1,0 |
| 28f | red | 0,75 | 68 | red | 1,0 | 140 | black | 1,5 |
| 29 | grey | 0,75 | 69 | black | 1,0 | 141 | brown | 0,75 |
| 29e | green | 0,75 | 70 | black | 1,5 | 141e | brown | 0,75 |
| 29f | grey | 0,75 | 71 | black | 1,5 | 142 | grey | 2,5 |
| 30 | brown | 0,75 | 72 | red | 1,0 | 147 | black | 0,75 |
| 30e | brown | 0,75 | 72e | red | 1,0 | | | |
| 30f | brown | 0,75 | 73 | yellow | 1,0 | | | |

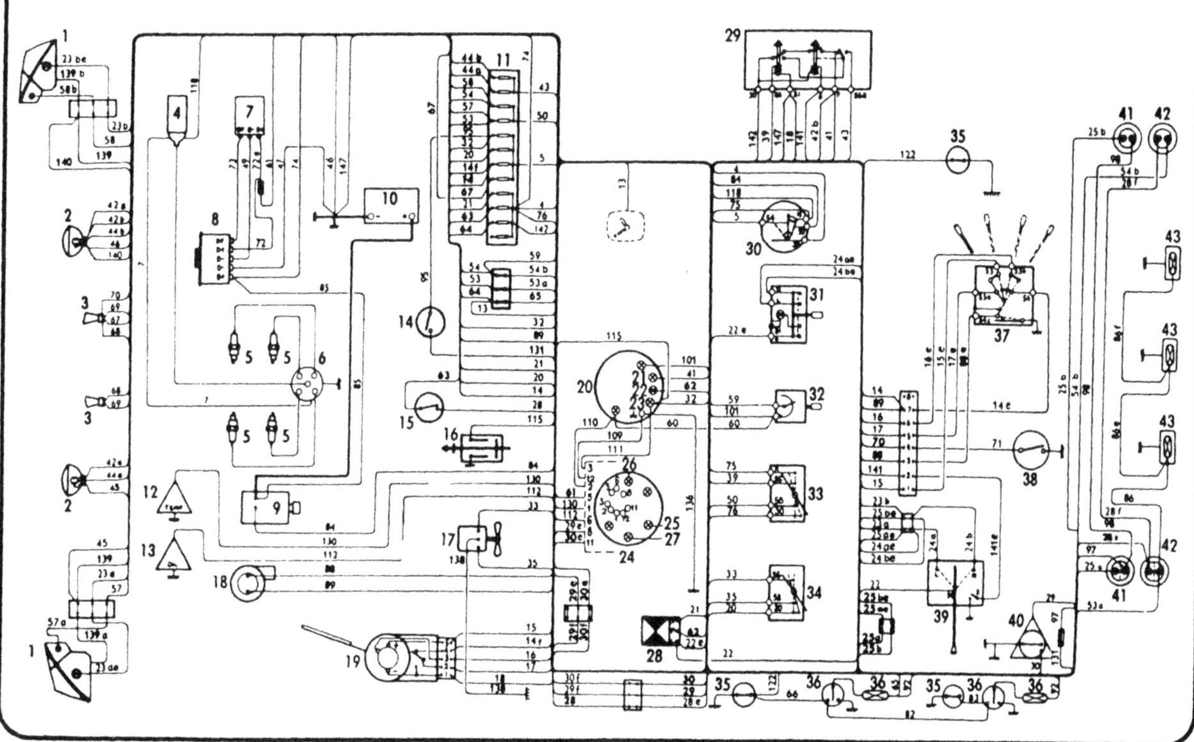

## Wiring diagram SAAB Station Wagon rhd model 1971

*The range of the electrical system is shown by the wiring system below. To simplify the identification, the wires have been covered with insulation of different shades, as shown under 'Cable numbers'*

**Key to numbers in figure**

1 Parking light and direction indicators
2 Headlights
3 Horn
4 Headlight wiper motor
5 Ignition coil
6 Spark plugs
7 Distributor
8 Voltage regulator
9 Alternator
10 Starter
11 Relay, headlight wiper
12 Fuse for headlight wiper
13 Battery
14 Fuse box
15 Temperature transmitter
16 Oil pressure switch
17 Back-up light switch
18 Stop light switch
19 Brake warning contact
20 Heater fan motor
21 Windshield washer pump
22 Headlight washer pump
23 Windshield wiper motor
24 Manoeuvre relay, headlight wiper
25 Speedometer and odometer
26 High beam indicator light
27 Direction indicator repeater light
28 Brake warning light
29 Temperature and fuel gauges
30 Indicator light, fuel amount
31 Oil pressure warning light
32 Charge indicator light
33 Flasher unit
34 Dimmer relay
35 Ignition and starter switch
36 Hazard warning flasher switch
37 Diode
38 Instrument illumination rheostat
39 Headlight switch
40 Heater fan switch
41 Courtesy light switch
42 Courtesy light with switch
43 Switch for windshield wiper, headlight wiper and washer
44 Signal horn contact
45 Direction indicator switch with headlight flasher and dimmer switch
46 Fuel transmitter
47 Back-up light and direction indicators
48 Tail light and stop light
49 Number plate light

**Cable numbers**

| No | Colour | Area $mm^2$ | No | Colour | Area $mm^2$ | No | Colour | Area $mm^2$ |
|---|---|---|---|---|---|---|---|---|
| 4 | grey | 1,5 | 41 | blue | 0,75 | 81 | grey | 0,75 |
| 5 | red | 1,5 | 42a | blue | 1,5 | 81e | blue | 0,75 |
| 7 | green | 1,5 | 42b | white | 2,5 | 82 | white | 0,75 |
| 13 | blue | 0,75 | 43 | yellow | 2,5 | 82 | yellow | 0,75 |
| 14 | brown | 1,0 | 44a | grey | 1,5 | 82e | black | 0,75 |
| 14e | brown | 1,0 | 44b | yellow | 1,5 | 83 | white | 0,75 |
| 14f | brown | 1,0 | 45 | black | 1,5 | 83 | black | 0,75 |
| 15 | red | 1,0 | 46 | black | 2,5 | 83e | black | 0,75 |
| 15e | red | 1,0 | 49 | black | 1,0 | 84 | yellow | 1,5 |
| 16 | grey | 1,0 | 50 | green | 1,0 | 85 | grey | 4,0 |
| 16e | grey | 1,0 | 53 | blue | 0,75 | 86 | green | 0,75 |
| 17 | blue | 1,0 | 53a | blue | 0,75 | 86e | green | 0,75 |
| 17e | blue | 1,0 | 54 | green | 0,75 | 86f | green | 0,75 |
| 18 | black | 1,0 | 54b | green | 0,75 | 88 | black | 0,75 |
| 20 | white | 1,0 | 57 | blue | 0,75 | 88e | black | 0,75 |
| 21 | red | 1,0 | 57a | blue | 0,75 | 88f | black | 0,75 |
| 22 | green | 1,0 | 58 | green | 0,75 | 88g | black | 0,75 |
| 22e | green | 1,0 | 58b | green | 0,75 | 89 | brown | 0,75 |
| 23a | yellow | 1,0 | 59 | green | 0,75 | 89f | yellow | 0,75 |
| 23ae | yellow | 1,0 | 60 | green | 0,75 | 92 | red | 0,75 |
| 23b | white | 1,0 | 61 | red | 0,75 | 95 | white | 1,5 |
| 23be | white | 1,0 | 62 | grey | 0,75 | 97 | white | 1,5 |
| 24a | yellow | 1,0 | 63 | red | 1,0 | 98 | white | 1,0 |
| 24ae | yellow | 1,0 | 64 | grey | 0,75 | 101 | green | 0,75 |
| 24b | white | 1,0 | 65 | red | 0,75 | 109 | black | 0,75 |
| 24be | white | 1,0 | 66 | white | 0,75 | 110 | green | 0,75 |
| 25a | blue | 1,0 | 67 | red | 1,5 | 111 | red | 0,75 |
| 25ae | blue | 1,0 | 68 | red | 1,0 | 112 | blue | 1,0 |
| 25b | grey | 1,0 | 69 | black | 1,0 | 115 | yellow | 0,75 |
| 25be | grey | 1,0 | 70 | black | 1,5 | 118 | white | 1,0 |
| 28 | red | 1,0 | 71 | black | 1,5 | 122 | white | 0,75 |
| 28e | red | 1,0 | 72 | red | 1,0 | 130 | brown | 0,75 |
| 28f | red | 0,75 | 72e | red | 1,0 | 131 | white | 1,5 |
| 29 | grey | 0,75 | 73 | yellow | 1,0 | 136 | black | 1,0 |
| 29e | grey | 0,75 | 74 | grey | 4,0 | 138 | black | 1,0 |
| 29f | grey | 0,75 | 75 | red | 1,0 | 139 | black | 1,5 |
| 30 | brown | 0,75 | 76 | grey | 1,0 | 139a | black | 1,0 |
| 30e | brown | 0,75 | 77 | red | 0,75 | 139b | black | 1,0 |
| 30f | brown | 0,75 | 77a | red | 0,75 | 140 | black | 1,5 |
| 32 | red | 0,75 | 77e | red | 0,75 | 141 | brown | 0,75 |
| 33 | yellow | 1,0 | 77f | red | 0,75 | 141e | brown | 0,75 |
| 35 | grey | 1,0 | 78 | brown | 0,75 | 142 | grey | 2,5 |
| 39 | yellow | 0,75 | 79 | green | 0,75 | 147 | black | 0,75 |

# Chapter 12 Body and fittings

**Contents**



**Specifications**

### 1967 to 1968 models

| | Saab 95 | Saab 96 and Monte Carlo |
|---|---|---|
| Overall length | 14 ft (4.27 m) | 13 ft 8 in (4.17 m) |
| Overall width | 5 ft 2 in (1.58 m) | 5 ft 2 in (1.58 m) |
| Ground clearance (2 people) | 5.1 in (130.0 mm) | 5.1 in (130.0 mm) |
| Track | 4 ft (1.22 m) | 4 ft (1.22 m) |
| Wheelbase | 8 ft 2 in (2.50 m) | 8 ft 2 in (2.50 m) |
| Weight (ready for road) | 2080 lb (945 kg) | 1940 lb (880 kg) Saab 96<br>2000 lb (910 kg) Monte Carlo |

### 1969 model

| | Saab 95 | Saab 96 |
|---|---|---|
| Overall length | 14 ft 1 in (4.30 m) | 13 ft 9 in (4.20 m) |
| Overall width | 5 ft 2 in (1.58 m) | 5 ft 2 in (1.58 m) |
| Ground clearance (2 people) | 5.1 in (130.0 mm) | 5.1 in (130.0 mm) |
| Track | 4 ft (1.22 m) | 4 ft (1.22 m) |
| Wheelbase | 8 ft 2 in (2.50 m) | 8 ft 2 in (2.50 m) |
| Weight (ready for road) | 2160 lb (980 kg) | 2000 lb (910 kg) |

### 1970 model

| | Saab 95 | Saab 96 |
|---|---|---|
| Specifications as 1969 model except for: | | |
| Weight (ready for road) | 2150 lb (975 kg) | 2000 lb (905 kg) |

### 1971 model (onwards)

| | Saab 95 | Saab 96 |
|---|---|---|
| Specifications as 1969 model except for: | | |
| Weight (ready for road) | 2200 lb (1000 kg) | 2000 lb (920 kg) |

## 1 General description

The SAAB 95, 96 and Monte Carlo have a combined bodyshell and frame of welded all steel construction. Although built on the principle of unitary construction, the front and rear wings, the doors, the bonnet and boot lids, can all be unbolted in the event of damage and new components fitted. This offers an economy over components which are normally welded into position.

Should an electric welder be used to repair bodywork damage, make sure that all battery and alternator cables are first disconnected, otherwise the alternator will be seriously damaged.

A fresh air type of heater is installed which uses water from the engine cooling system. On vehicles built from 1971 onwards, hot air ducts are installed to provide warmth to the rear passenger compartment.

## 2 Maintenance - bodywork and underframe

1 The condition of your car's bodywork is of considerable importance as it is on this that the second hand value of the car will mainly depend. It is much more difficult to repair neglected bodywork than to renew mechanical assemblies. The hidden portions of the body, such as the wheel arches, the underframe and the engine compartment are equally important, although obviously not requiring such frequent attention as the immediately visible paintwork.

2 Once a year or every 12,000 miles (20,000 km) it is a sound scheme to visit your local main agent and have the underside of the body steam cleaned. All traces of dirt and oil will be

removed and the underside can then be inspected carefully for rust, damaged hydraulic pipes, frayed electrical wiring and similar maladies.

3 At the same time the engine compartment should be cleaned in a similar manner. If steam cleaning facilities are not available then brush 'Gunk' or a similar cleanser over the whole engine and engine compartment with a stiff paint brush, working it well in where there is an accumulation of oil and dirt. Do not paint the ignition system, and protect it with oily rags when the 'Gunk' is washed off. As the 'Gunk' is washed away it will take with it all traces of oil and dirt, leaving the engine looking clean and bright.

4 The wheel arches should be given particular attention as under sealing can easily come away here and stones and dirt thrown up from the road wheels can soon cause the paint to chip and flake, and so allow rust to set in. If rust is found, clean down to the bare metal with wet and dry paper and an anti-corrosive coating such as Kurust, or if preferred, red lead, and renew the paintwork and undercoating.

5 The bodywork should be washed once a week or when dirty. Thoroughly wet the car to soften the dirt and then wash the car down with a soft sponge and plenty of clean water. If the surplus dirt is not washed off very gently, in time it will wear paint down as surely as wet and dry paper. It is best to use a hose if this is available. Give the car a final wash down and then dry with a soft chamois leather to prevent the formation of spots.

6 Spots of tar and grease thrown up from the road can be removed by a rag dampened with petrol.

7 Once every six months, or every three months if wished, give the bodywork and chromium trim a thoroughly good wax polish. If a chromium cleaner is used to remove rust on any of the car's plated parts remember that the cleaner also removes part of the chromium so use sparingly.

## 3 Maintenance - upholstery and carpets

1 Remove the carpets or mats, and thoroughly vacuum clean the interior of the car every three months, or more frequently if necessary.

2 Beat out the carpets and vacuum clean them if they are very dirty. If the upholstery is soiled apply an upholstery cleaner with a damp sponge and wipe off with a clean dry cloth.

## 4 Minor body damage - repair

*See illustrations on pages 195, 196 and 197.*

### Repair of minor scratches in the car's bodywork

If the scratch is very superficial, and does not penetrate to the metal of the bodywork repair is very simple. Lightly rub the area of the scratch with a paintwork renovator (eg 'Top-Cut'), or a very fine cutting paste, to remove loose paint from the scratch and to clear the surrounding bodywork of wax polish. Rinse the area with clean water.

Apply touch-up paint to the scratch using a thin paint brush; continue to apply thin layers of paint until the surface of the paint in the scratch is level with surrounding paintwork. Allow the new paint at least two weeks to harden; then, blend it into the surrounding paintwork by rubbing the paintwork in the scratch area with a paintwork renovator (eg. 'Top-Cut'), or a very fine cutting paste. Finally apply wax polish.

An alternative to painting over the scratch is to use Holts 'Scratch-Patch'. Use the same preparation for the affected area; then simply, pick a patch of a suitable size to cover the scratch completely. Hold the patch against the scratch and burnish its backing paper; the patch will adhere to the paintwork, freeing itself from the backing paper at the same time. Polish the affected area to blend the patch into the surrounding paintwork.

Where a scratch has penetrated, right through to the metal of the bodywork, causing the metal to rust, a different repair technique is required. Remove any loose rust from the bottom of the scratch with a penknife, then apply rust inhibiting paint (eg. 'Kurust') to prevent the formation of rust in the future. Using a rubber or nylon applicator fill the scratch with body-stopper paste. If required, this paste can be mixed with cellulose thinners to provide a very thin paste which is ideal for filling narrow scratches. Before the stopper-paste in the scratch hardens, wrap a piece of smooth cotton rag around the tip of a finger. Dip the finger in cellulose thinners and then quickly sweep it across the surface of the stopper-paste in the scratch; this will ensure that the surface of the stopper-paste is slightly hollowed. The scratch can now be painted over as described earlier in this Section.

### Repair of dents in the car's bodywork

When deep denting of the car's bodywork has taken place, the first task is to pull the dent out, until the affected bodywork almost attains its original shape. There is little point in trying to restore the original shape completely, as the metal in the damaged area will have stretched on impact and cannot be reshaped fully to its original contour. It is better to bring the level of the dent up to a point which is about 1/8 inch (3 mm) below the level of the surrounding bodywork. In cases where the dent is very shallow anyway, it is not worth trying to pull it out at all.

If the underside of the dent is accessible, it can be hammered out gently from behind, using a mallet with a wooden or plastic head. Whilst doing this, hold a suitable block of wood firmly against the outside of the dent. This block will absorb the impact from the hammer blows and thus prevent a large area of bodywork from being 'belled-out'.

Should the dent be in a section of the bodywork which has a double skin or some other factor making it inaccessible from behind, a different technique is called for. Drill several small holes through the metal inside the dent area - particularly in the deeper sections. Then screw long self-tapping screws into the holes just sufficiently for them to gain a good purchase in the metal. Now the dent can be pulled out by pulling on the protruding heads of the screws with a pair of pliers.

The next stage of the repair is the removal of the paint from the damaged area, and from an inch or so of the surrounding 'sound' bodywork. This is accomplished most easily by using a wire brush or abrasive pad on a power drill, although it can be done just as effectively by hand using sheets of abrasive paper. To complete the preparations for filling, score the surface of the bare metal with a screwdriver or the tang of a file, or alternatively, drill small holes in the affected area. This will provide a really good 'key' for the filler paste.

To complete the repair see the Section on filling and re-spraying.

### Repair of rust holes or gashes in the car's bodywork

Remove all paint from the affected area and from an inch or so of the surrounding 'sound' bodywork, using an abrasive pad or a wire brush on a power drill. If these are not available a few sheets of abrasive paper will do the job just as effectively. With the paint removed you will be able to gauge the severity of the corrosion and therefore decide whether to replace the whole panel (if this is possible) or to repair the affected area. Replacement body panels are not as expensive as most people think and it is often quicker and more satisfactory to fit a new panel than to attempt to repair large areas of corrosion.

Remove all fittings from the affected area, except those which will act as a guide to the original shape of the damaged bodywork (eg. headlamp shells etc.,). Then, using tin snips or a hacksaw blade, remove all loose metal and any other metal badly affected by corrosion. Hammer the edges of the hole inwards in order to create a slight depression for the filler paste.

Wire brush the affected area to remove the powdery rust from the surface of the remaining metal. Paint the affected area with rust inhibiting paint (eg. 'Kurust'); if the back of the rusted area is accessible treat this also.

Before filling can take place it will be necessary to block the hole in some way. This can be achieved by the use of one of the following materials: Zinc gauze, Aluminium tape or

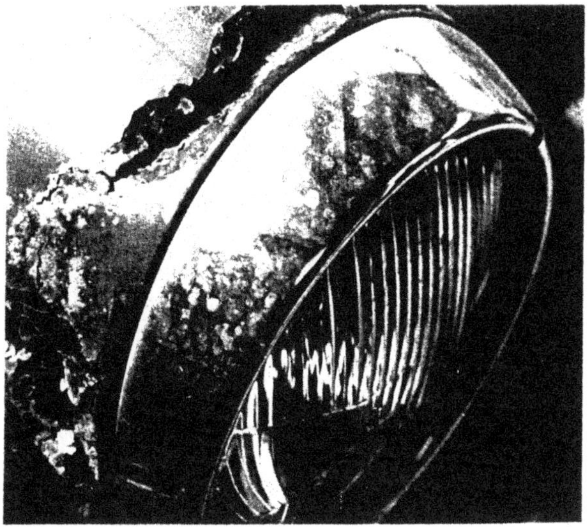

**Preparation for filling**
Typical example of rust damage to a body panel. Before starting ensure that you have all of the materials required to hand. The first task is to ...

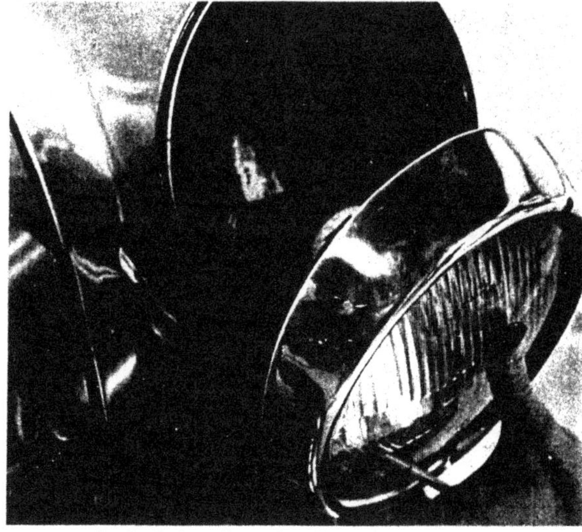

... remove body fittings from the affected area, except those which can act as a guide to the original shape of the damaged bodywork - the headlamp shell in this case.

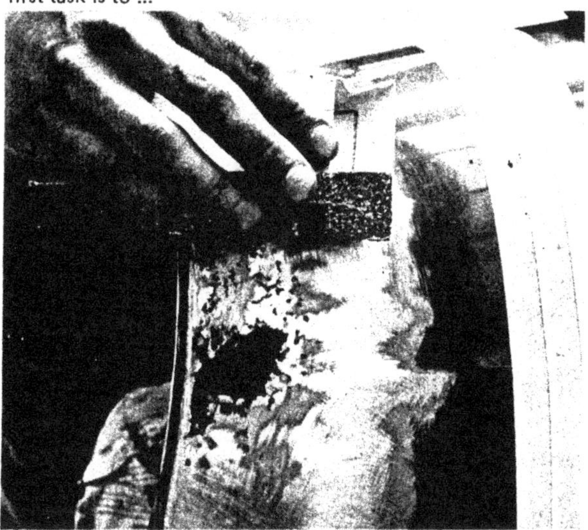

Remove all paint from the rusted area and from an inch or so of the adjoining 'sound' bodywork - use coarse abrasive paper or a power drill fitted with a wire brush or abrasive pad. Gently hammer in the edges of the hole to provide a hollow for the filler.

Before filling, the larger holes must be blocked off. Adhesive aluminium tape is one method; cut the tape to the required shape and size, peel off the backing strip (where used), position the tape over the hole and burnish to ensure adhesion.

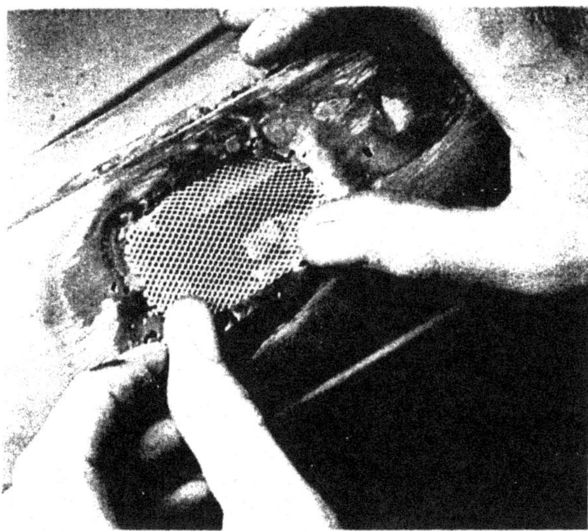

Alternatively, zinc gauze can be used. Cut a piece of the gauze to the required shape and size; position it in the hole below the level of the surrounding bodywork; then ...

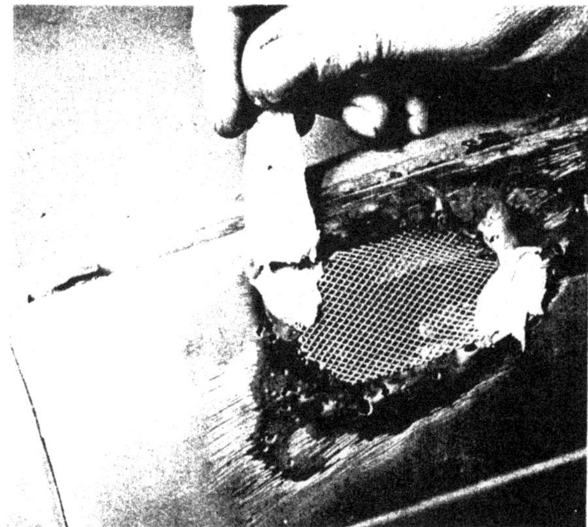

... secure in position by placing a few blobs of filler paste around its periphery. Alternatively, pop rivets or self-tapping screws can be used. Preparation for filling is now complete.

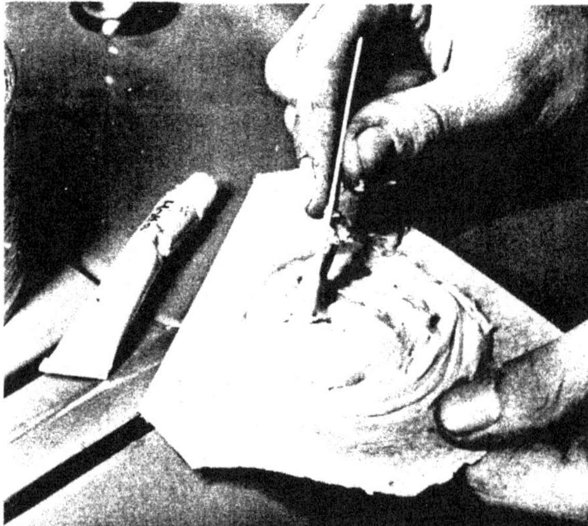

**Filling and shaping**
Mix filler and hardener according to manufacturer's instructions - avoid using too much hardener otherwise the filler will harden before you have a chance to work it.

Apply the filler to the affected area with a flexible applicator - this will ensure a smooth finish. Apply thin layers of filler at 20 minute intervals, until the surface of the filler is just 'proud' of the surrounding bodywork. Then ...

... remove excess filler and start shaping with a Surform plane or a dreadnought file. Once an approximate contour has been obtained and the surface is relatively smooth, start using ...

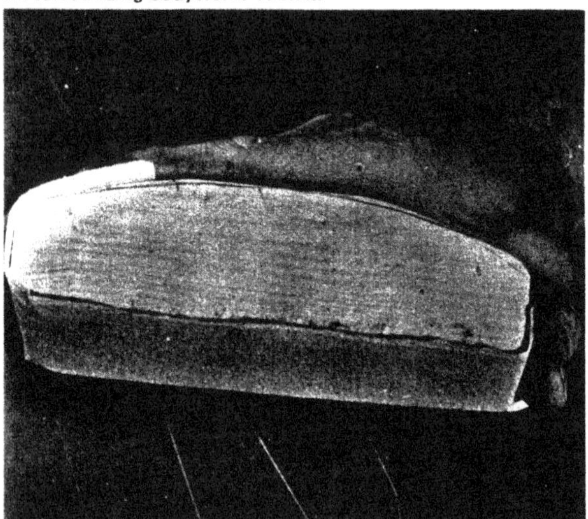

... abrasive paper. The paper should be wrapped around a flat wood, cork or rubber block - this will ensure that it imparts a smooth surface to the filler.

40 grit production paper is best to start with, then use progressively finer abrasive paper, finishing with 400 grade 'wet-and-dry'. When using 'wet-and-dry' paper, periodically rinse it in water ensuring also, that the work area is kept wet continuously.

Rubbing-down is complete when the surface of the filler is really smooth and flat, and the edges of the surrounding paintwork are finely 'feathered'. Wash the area thoroughly with clean water and allow to dry before commencing re-spray.

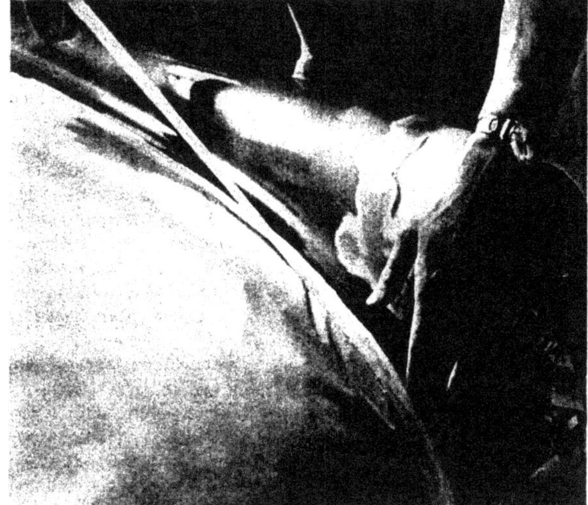

**Masking and spraying**
Firstly, mask off all adjoining panels and the fittings in the spray area. Ensure that the area to be sprayed is completely free of dust. Practice using an aerosol on a piece of waste metal sheet until the technique is mastered.

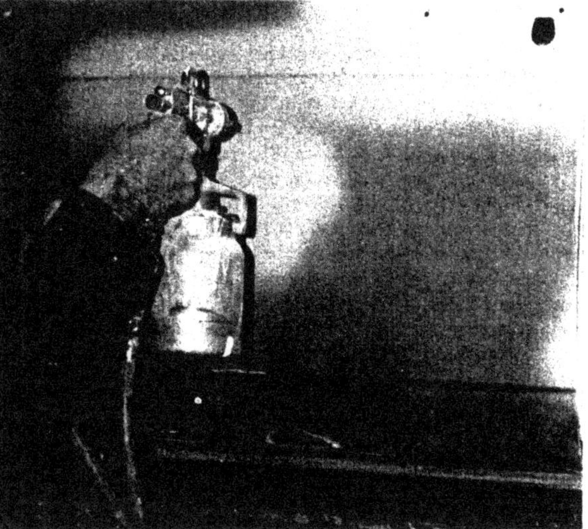

Spray the affected area with primer - apply several thin coats rather than one thick one. Start spraying in the centre of the repair area and then work outwards using a circular motion - in this way the paint will be evenly distributed.

When the primer has dried inspect its surface for imperfections. Holes can be filled with filler paste or body-stopper, and lumps can be sanded smooth. Apply a further coat of primer, then 'flat' its surface with 400 grade 'wet-and-dry' paper.

Spray on the top coat, again building up the thickness with several thin coats of paint. Overspray onto the surrounding original paintwork to a depth of about five inches, applying a very thin coat at the outer edges.

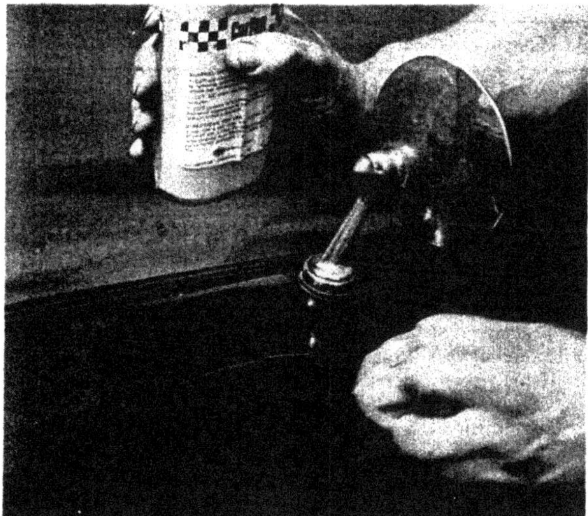

Allow the new paint two weeks, at least, to harden fully, then blend it into the surrounding original paintwork with a paint restorative compound or very fine cutting paste. Use wax polish to finish off.

The finished job should look like this. Remember, the quality of the completed work is directly proportional to the amount of time and effort expended at each stage of the preparation.

Polyurethane foam.

Zinc gauze is probably the best material to use for a large hole. Cut a piece to the approximate size and shape of the hole to be filled, then position it in the hole so that its edges are below the level of the surrounding bodywork. It can be retained in position by several blobs of filler paste around its periphery.

Aluminium tape should be used for small or very narrow holes. Pull a piece off the roll and trim it to the approximate size and shape required, then pull off the backing paper (if used) and stick the tape over the hole; it can be overlapped if the thickness of one piece is insufficient. Burnish down the edges of the tape with the handle of a screwdriver or similar, to ensure that the tape is securely attached to the metal underneath.

Polyurethane foam is best used where the holes are situated in a section of bodywork of complex shape, backed by a small box section (eg. where the sill panel meets the rear wheel arch - most cars). The usual mixing procedure for this foam is as follows: Put equal amounts of fluid from each of the two cans provided in the kit, into one container. Stir until the mixture begins to thicken, then quickly pour this mixture into the hole, and hold a piece of cardboard over the larger apertures. Almost immediately the polyurethane will begin to expand, gushing frantically out of any small holes left unblocked. When the foam hardens it can be cut back to just below the level of the surrounding bodywork with a hacksaw blade.

## Bodywork repairs - filling and re-spraying

Before using this Section, see the Sections on dent, deep scratch, rust hole, and gash repairs.

Many types of bodyfiller are available, but generally speaking those proprietary kits which contain a tin of filler paste and a tube of resin hardener (eg. "Holts Cataloy") are best for this type of repair. A wide, flexible plastic or nylon applicator will be found invaluable for imparting a smooth and well contoured finish to the surface of the filler.

Mix up a little filler on a clean piece of card or board - use the hardener sparingly (follow the maker's instructions on the packet), otherwise the filler will set very rapidly.

Using the applicator, apply the filler paste to the prepared area; draw the applicator across the surface of the filler to achieve the correct contour and to level the filler surface. As soon as a contour that approximates the correct one is achieved, stop working the paste. If you carry on too long the paste will become sticky and begin to 'pick-up' on the applicator. Continue to add thin layers of filler paste at twenty-minute intervals until the level of the filler is just 'proud' of the surrounding bodywork.

Once the filler has hardened, excess can be removed using a Surform plane or Dreadnought file. From then on, progressively finer grades of abrasive paper should be used, starting with a 40 grade production paper and finishing with 400 grade 'wet-and-dry' paper. Always wrap the abrasive paper around a flat rubber, cork, or wooden block - otherwise the surface of the filler will not be completely flat. During the smoothing of the filler surface the 'wet-and-dry' paper should be periodically rinsed in water; this will ensure that a very smooth finish is imparted to the filler at the final stage.

At this stage the 'dent' should be surrounded by a ring of bare metal, which in turn should be encircled by the finely 'feathered' edge of the good paintwork. Rinse the repair area with clean water, until all of the dust produced by the rubbing-down operation is gone.

Spray the whole repair area with a light coat of grey primer - this will show up any imperfections in the surface of the filler. Repair these imperfections with fresh filler paste or bodystopper, and once more smooth the surface with abrasive paper. If bodystopper is used, it can be mixed with cellulose thinners to form a really thin paste which is ideal for filling small holes. Repeat this spray and repair procedure until you are satisfied that the surface of the filler, and the feathered edge of the paintwork are perfect. Clean the repair area with clean water and allow to dry fully.

The repair area is now ready for spraying. Paint spraying must be carried out in a warm, dry, windless and dust free atmosphere. This condition can be created artifically if you have access to a large indoor working area, but if you are forced to work in the open, you will have to pick your day very carefully. If you are working indoors, dousing the floor in the work area with water will 'lay' the dust which would otherwise be in the atmosphere. If the repair area is confined to one body panel, mask off the surrounding panels; this will help to minimise the effect of a slight mis-match in paint colours. Bodywork fittings (eg chrome strips, door handles etc) will also need to be masked off. Use genuine masking tape and several thicknesses of newspaper for the masking operation.

Before commencing to spray, agitate the aerosol can thoroughly, then spray a test area (an old tin, or similar) until the technique is mastered. Cover the repair area with a thick coat of primer; the thickness should be built up using several thin layers of paint rather than one thick one. Using 400 grade 'wet-and-dry' paper, rub down the surface of the primer until it is really smooth. While doing this, the work area should be thoroughly doused with water, and the wet-and-dry paper periodically rinsed in water. Allow to dry before spraying on more paint.

Spray on the top coat, again building up the thickness by using several thin layers of paint. Start spraying in the centre of the repair area and then, using a circular motion, work outwards until the whole repair area and about 2 inches of the surrounding original paintwork is covered. Remove all masking material 10 to 15 minutes after spraying on the final coat of paint.

Allow the new paint at least 2 weeks to harden fully; then, using a paintwork renovator (eg "Top-Cut") or a very fine cutting paste, blend the edges of the new paint into the existing paintwork. Finally, apply wax polish.

## 5 Major body damage - repair

1 Because the body is built on the unitary principle and is integral with the underframe, major damage must be repaired by competent mechanics with the necessary welding and hdyraulic straightening equipment.

2 If the damage has been serious it is vital that the body is checked for correct alignment as otherwise the handling of the car will suffer and many other faults such as excessive tyre wear and wear in the transmission and steering may occur.

3 There is a special body jig which most large body repair shops have and to ensure that all is correct it is important that this jig be used for all major repair work.

## 6 Maintenance - hinges and locks

Periodically apply a few drops of engine oil to all hinges and locks and smear a little grease on the door striker plates.

## 7 Door rattles - tracing and rectification

1 The most common cause of door rattles is a misaligned, loose or worn striker plate but other causes may be:
Loose door handles, window winder handles or door hinges;
Loose, worn or misaligned door lock components;
Loose or worn remote control mechanism;
or a combination of these.

2 If the striker catch is worn as a result of door rattles renew it and adjust as described later in this Chapter.

3 Should the hinges be badly worn then they must be renewed.

## 8 Wings - removal and refitting

1 Jack-up the appropriate side of the vehicle and remove the

roadwheel.

2 Unscrew and remove each of the retaining screws, commencing with the two lower ones (C and D). It will probably be necessary to remove the undersealing from the screw heads and apply freeing fluid to facilitate their removal (Fig. 12.1).

3 Disconnect any electrical leads as necessary and then unscrew and remove the upper screws (B).

4 Withdraw the wing and its sealing strip.

5 In the case of the left-hand rear wing, the fuel filler pipe will have to be disconnected. Plug the tank opening to prevent the entry of dirt. After 1970 the position of the filler entry on the wing was altered and only the new type wing is supplied as a replacement. If a new wing is being fitted to a pre 1970 vehicle then a new filler assembly will also have to be installed in the following manner. Remove the fuel filler tube and connecting hose. Let the vent tube connecting hose remain in position on the vent tube of the fuel tank. Blank the small vent of the new filler tube supplied, with the plastic plug. Connect the filler tube flexible hose between the fuel tank and the filler tube and install the hose clips. Install the vent and connecting tubes.

6 Installation of the wing is a reversal of removal but use a new sealing strip and ensure that the body mounting flange is clean.

7 Fit the wing securing screws finger tight initially so that the alignment of the wing can be checked. Finally tighten the screws, apply underseal, fit the roadwheel and lower the jack.

8 Where a modified fuel filler assembly has been fitted, apply sealant between the wing and the filler tube mounting flange and screw in the four self-tapping screws to secure the flange. The original cap must be used which has a vent hole.

9 Painting the exterior surface of the wing may either be carried out professionally or by application of primer and matching body colour from aerosol cans.

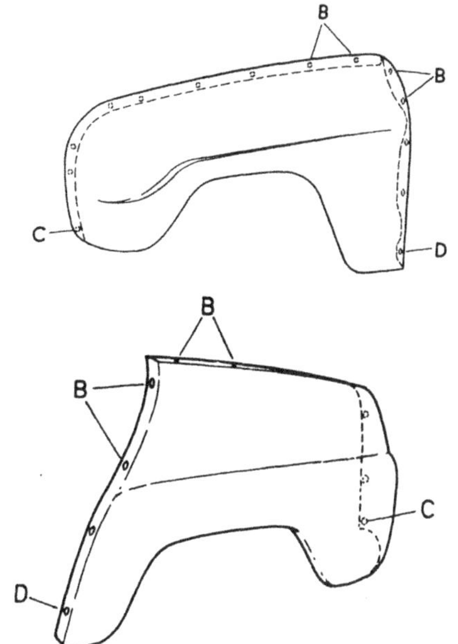


**Fig 12.1 Front and rear wing assembly (for key, refer to text)**

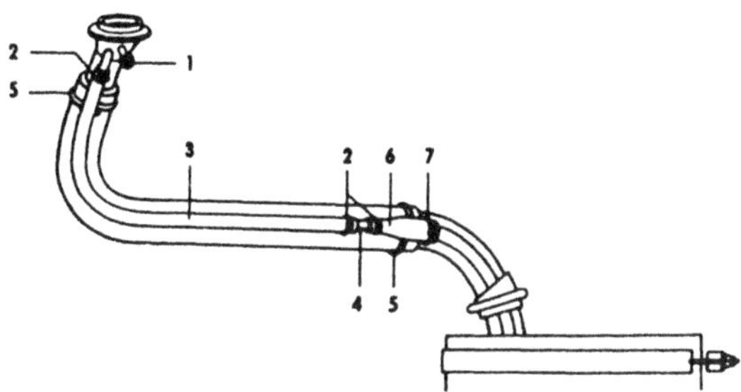


**Fig 12.2 Modified fuel filler required if pre-1970 wing replaced with redesigned type**

*1 Plastic plug*
*2 Hose clamp*
*3 Vent hose*
*4 Connecting tube*
*5 Clip*
*6 Connecting hose*
*7 Clip*

## 9 Windscreen glass - removal and refitting

1 The windscreen may be of toughened or laminated type. If of the former then the screen will probably be renewed because it has broken, in which case the crystals should be knocked from the frame. Take care to cover the defroster slots and the bonnet surface to prevent damage by glass crystals and remove the wiper arms. If the screen is of laminated type or an unbroken toughened type then prise the lip of one corner of the rubber surround over the edge of the body aperture and push the glass from the inside outwards. The help of an assistant will greatly facilitate this operation.

2 With the glass and its surround removed, clean all traces of sealing compound from the edges of the body aperture.

3 Separate the bright moulding from the rubber surround and discard the latter.

4 Fit a new rubber surround to the new windscreen glass so that the joint is at the centre of the lower edge.

5 Press the bright trim securely into the groove in the rubber surround and fit the two joint covering clips.

6 Insert a length of cord into the channel in the rubber surround so that the two ends of the cord are crossed over and hang out at the centre of the top edge.

7 Rub some soapy water solution round the lip of the rubber and then engage the top edge of the surround with the body flange. Check that the two ends of the cord hang down inside the vehicle.

8 With an assistant pressing firmly but evenly on the outside of the glass, pull the two ends of the cord so that the rubber lip engages all the way round with the body flange. The cord can be extracted at the moment when the windscreen snaps into its final position.

9 Using a tube of black sealing compound fitted with a nozzle, insert a bead of compound between the rubber surround and the glass and between the interior rubber lip and the body flange. Wipe away excess sealant using a piece of rag soaked in paraffin.

10 Check that the bright moulding is firmly in position and adjust the cover clips if necessary.

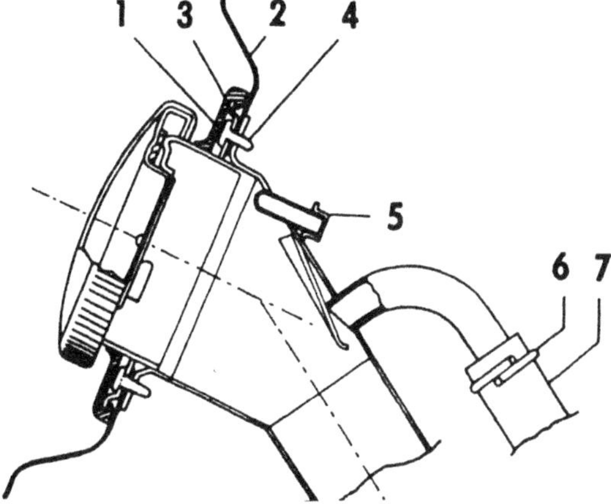


**Fig 12.3 Sectional view of modified filler cap and tube**

*1 Sealing collar*
*2 Wing*
*3 Retainer*
*4 Self-tapping screw*
*5 Plastic plug*
*6 Hose clip*
*7 Vent hose*

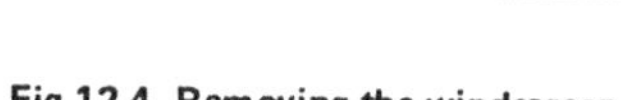

Fig 12.4 Removing the windscreen

Fig 12.5 Fitting the windscreen

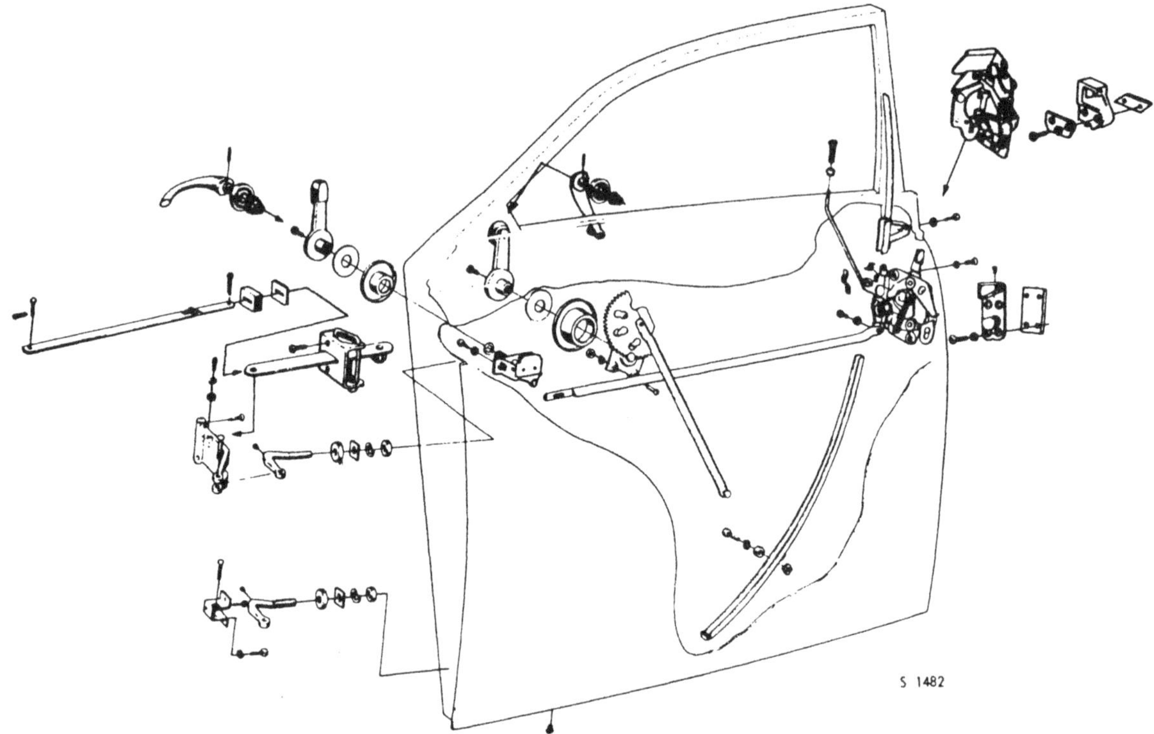


Fig 12.6 Door lock and window regulator components (1968 onwards) – early model components arrowed

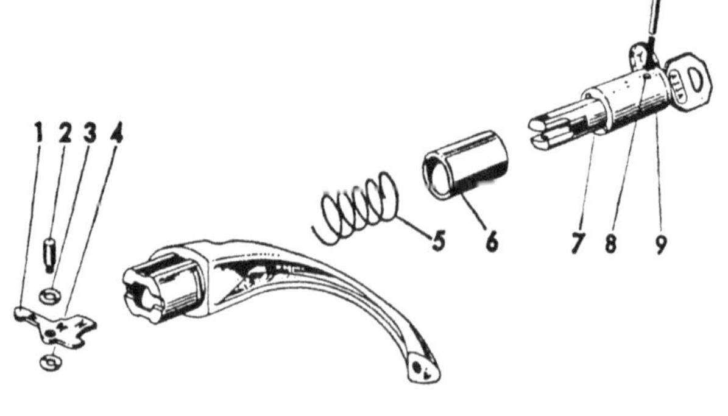


Fig 12.7 Exploded view of pushbutton door lock

*1 Arm*
*2 Pin*
*3 Washer*
*4 Washer*
*5 Spring*
*6 Sleeve*
*7 Pushbutton*
*8 Catch pin*
*9 Cylinder*

## 10 Rear window glass - removal and refitting

1 The procedure is similar to that described for the windscreen in the preceding Section except that the shelf above the luggage boot must first be removed.

## 11 Opening quarterlight window glass - renewal

1 On vehicles fitted with opening rear (quarterlight) windows, the glass is supplied complete with frame.
2 Remove the toggle catch and then open the window far enough to permit removal of the hinges.
3 Refitting is a reversal of removal.

## 12 Door lock - removal, refitting and adjustment

1 Wind up the window to its fully closed position.
2 Press the interior door handle escutcheon in and drive out the retaining pin (pre-1968 models). Remove the window regulator in a similar manner. On vehicles built after 1968, these handles are retained by screws.
3 Prise the trim panel from the door frame. This is best carried out by inserting the fingers or a rule between the trim panel and the door frame and levering the spring retaining clips from their holes. Work progressively round the panel without distorting or tearing it.
4 Unscrew the door interior locking knob from its rod and then remove the seven screws which secure the lock to the door frame (three on the interior panel and four on the edge).
5 Withdraw the lock complete with remote control rod from the door cavity.
6 If required, the door exterior handle may be removed after unscrewing the two screws (one within the door cavity and one on the door edge).
7 Refitting is a reversal of removal but grease the moving parts.
8 When the lock has been installed, check the door closure and adjust the position of the striker plate if necessary by loosening the screws. When correctly positioned, the door should close smoothly and be flush with the adjacent body panels without the striker plate forcing it up or down during closure.

## 13 Door lock cylinder - removal and refitting

1 The exterior handle should be removed by unscrewing the two retaining screws (one within the door cavity and one on the door edge) after the door trim has been withdrawn (see Section 12).
2 Depress the push-button and then drive out the pin and remove the arm and two washers (note different diameter holes). (Fig. 12.7)
3 Remove the push-button and the spring.
4 Press the push-button from its sleeve.
5 Insert and turn the key approximately 35$^{o}$ in a clockwise direction and then drive in the retaining pin.
6 The cylinder can then be extracted from the push-button.
7 Should the key have been lost, the pin will have to be driven in with force which will of course, ruin the cylinder.
8 Insert the new cylinder into the push-button and drive in the catch pin. The rest of the reassembly procedure is a reversal of dismantling.

## 14 Door window glass and regulator - removal and refitting

1 Remove the door interior trim as described in Section 12.
2 Temporarily refit the window regulator handle and wind down the window until the highest point of its top edge is just below the weather seal.
3 Unscrew the two screws from the hinge at the front end of the glass retainer channel.
4 Turn the glass so that its rear edge starts to move upwards and disconnect the regulator arm from the retainer channel.
5 Continue to turn the glass and withdraw it from the door cavity past the weather seal. It may be necessary to detach the retainer channel from the glass to allow the glass to be withdrawn.
6 The window regulator mechanism can be removed after unscrewing and removing the securing screws (accessible through the gear segment) and withdrawing it through the aperture in the door inner panel. The regulator mechanism can be removed without first removing the glass by unscrewing the retaining screws and turning the mechanism to disengage its operating arm from the glass retainer channel.
7 Refitting is a reversal of removal but check that the window can be raised and lowered smoothly and adjust the retainer channel by moving the hinge slightly before finally tightening the hinge screws.

## 15 Doors - removal, refitting and adjustment

1 Remove the door interior trim (Section 12).
2 Drive out the pin at the upper hinge to release the check strap. Take care that the door, now unchecked, does not damage the front wing.
3 Support the bottom edge of the door on jacks or blocks using cloth pads as insulators to prevent damage to the paintwork.
4 Bend back the locking tabs from the external nuts of the hinge support threaded rods and then unscrew and remove the two internal nuts which are accessible from within the door cavity.
5 Remove the door by drawing it straight off the hinge support rods.
6 The hinge plates may be removed from the body by unscrewing the securing bolts.
7 Installation is a reversal of removal but with the door adequately supported, the door must be aligned within the body frame to provide an even gap all round. This is carried out by adjusting the positions of the two nuts on the hinge support rods and by moving the hinge plates up or down within the scope of the elongated holes.

## 16 Luggage boot lid (SAAB 96 and Monte Carlo) - removal and refitting

1 Raise the lid and remove the support stay.
2 Disconnect the leads to the number plate and boot lamps.
3 Mark the outline of the hinge plates and then unscrew the hinge bolts and with the help of an assistant, lift the boot lid from the vehicle.
4 Refitting is a reversal of removal; check for satisfactory

**Fig 12.8 Removing door hinge retaining nuts**

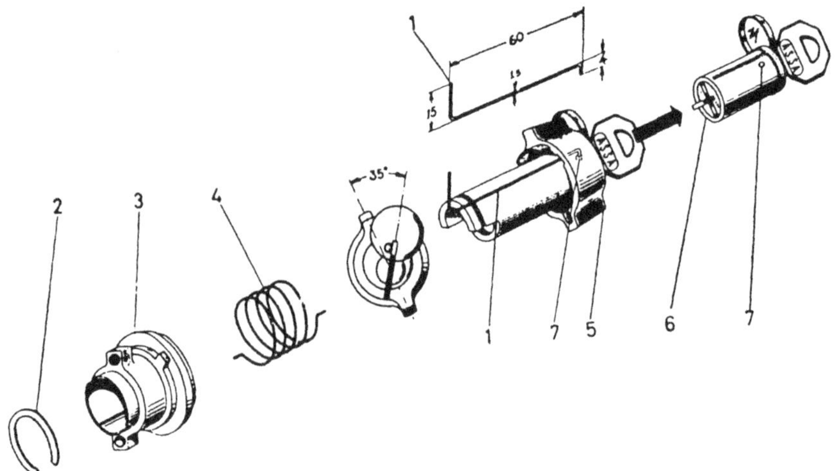


Fig 12.9 Luggage boot lid lock

*1 Wire pro*
*2 Circlip*
*3 Housing*
*4 Spring*
*5 Sleeve*
*6 Cylinder*
*7 Catch pin*

alignment and closure and adjust the lock striker plate if necessary.

**17 Luggage boot lock (SAAB 96 and Monte Carlo) - dismantling and reassembly**

1 Unbolt and remove the lock.
2 Remove the circlip (2), draw off the housing (3) and the spring (4) (Fig. 12.9).
3 Turn the key, after inserting it, about 35° clockwise and insert a piece of wire having a right-angled end (1) so that it will depress the locking pin (7) in towards the lock cylinder.
4 The cylinder can now be withdrawn from the lock sleeve (5).
5 Reassembly is a reversal of dismantling.

**18 Tailgate (SAAB 95) - removal, installation and adjustment**

1 Open the tailgate fully.

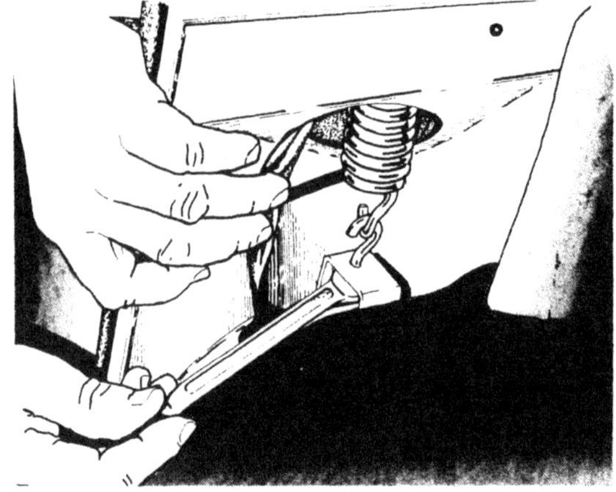

Fig 12.10 Tailgate counter balance spring - adjustment of tension

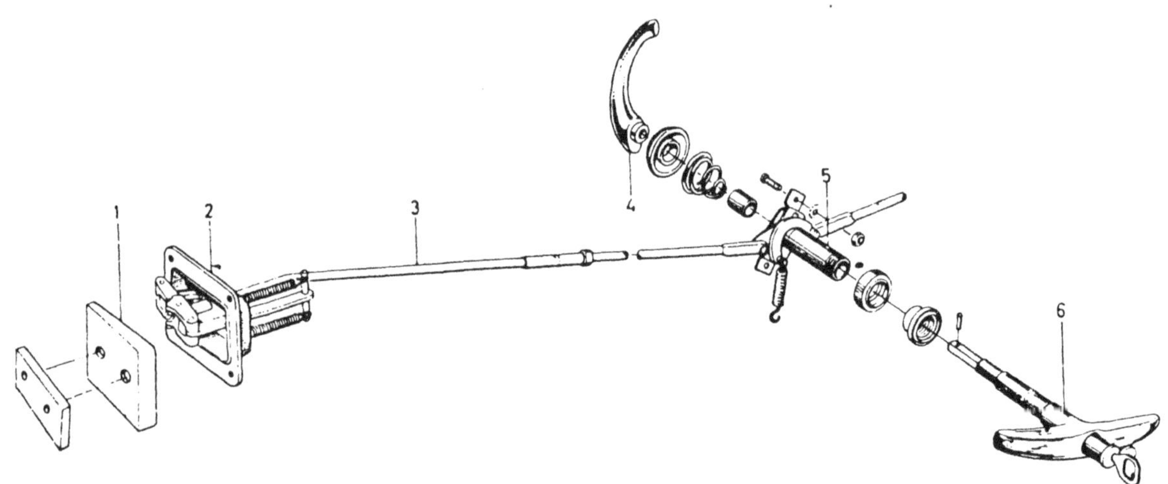


Fig 12.11 Exploded view of tailgate lock

*1 Lockplate*
*2 Lock assembly*
*3 Adjustable control rod*
*4 Interior handle*
*5 Latch*
*6 Exterior handle*

2 Remove the sealing strip which is located between the tailgate and the body by unscrewing and removing the self-tapping screws.
3 Remove the hinge retaining bolts which are accessible with the tailgate in the fully open position.
4 Unscrew and remove the nuts from the counterbalance lever. This must be done carefully and progressively as the lever is spring loaded and under tension.
5 Close the tailgate and remove the remaining hinge bolts.
6 The tailgate can now be lifted away with the help of an assistant.
7 Installation is a reversal of removal but the counterbalance action of the tailgate may need adjustment. To do this, remove the trim between the tailgate and the quarter window. Adjust the tension of the springs by turning the nut on the retaining hook until the tailgate will remain in any position to which it is opened.

## 19 Tailgate door lock - removal, dismantling, reassembly and refitting

1 Remove the interior trim from the tailgate. This and the interior lock handle are removed in a similar manner to that described for the front doors (Section 12), the handle being retained by a pin.
2 The control rods are adjustable for length and should be adjusted in accordance with the movable striker plates to provide smooth and positive closure of the tailgate.
3 The lock cylinder may be removed from the exterior handle in a similar manner to that described in Section 17.
4 Reassembly and refitting are reversals of removal and dismantling.

## 20 Instrument panel - removal and refitting

1 Although the instruments can be removed individually (see Chapter 11), the complete instrument panel assembly can be removed if required.
2 Remove the fairings at each end of the instrument panel by unscrewing the self-tapping screws.
3 Release the instrument panel centre support from its connection to the body.
4 Unscrew and remove the two panel securing screws located at each end and retain the washers and rubber insulators.
5 Withdraw the instrument panel far enough to permit disconnection of all leads, the speedometer cable and the windscreen washer hoses, and the demister tubes.
6 Refitting is a reversal of removal.

## 21 Heater blower - removal and refitting

1 Disconnect the three electrical leads from the heater blower motor and mark them so that they can be correctly refitted.
2 Unscrew and remove the six screws which secure the front cover of the heater blower housing.
3 Extract the cover complete with motor.
4 The motor/fan assembly may be detached from the cover after unscrewing the nuts. If the motor or fan is faulty, exchange the complete assembly, which is balanced during manufacture, for a reconditioned unit.
5 Installation is a reversal of removal.

## 22 Heater matrix - removal and refitting

1 Drain the cooling system as described in Chapter 2.
2 Disconnect the two heater hoses from the heater matrix.
3 Disconnect the three leads from the heater blower motor.
4 Unscrew and remove the six screws which secure the front cover of the heater blower housing. Extract the cover and motor.

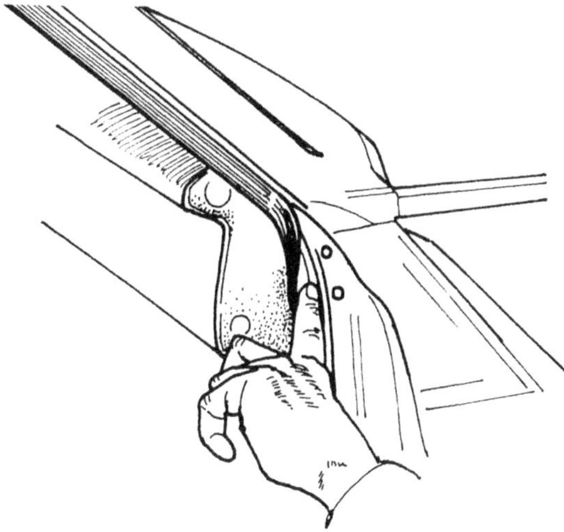

Fig 12.12 Instrument panel retaining screws at each end

Fig 12.13 Removing the heater blower motor

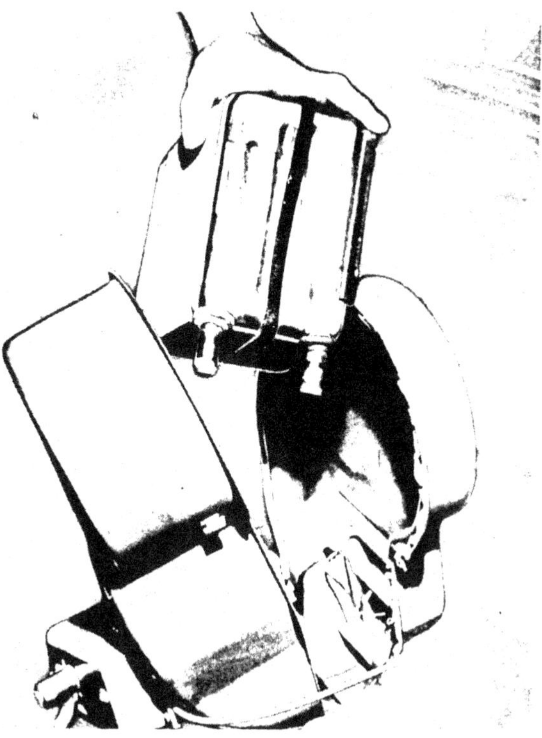

Fig 12.14 Removing the heater matrix

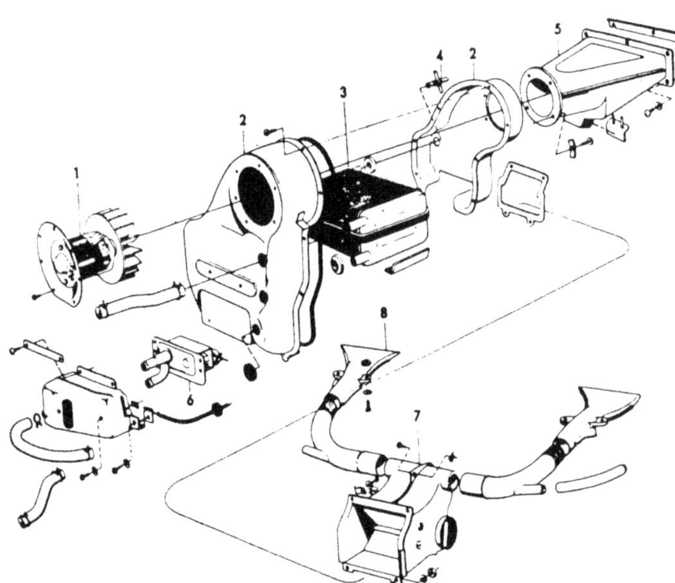

**Fig 12.15 Exploded view of the heater assembly**

*1 Motor/fan assembly*
*2 Heater casings*
*3 Matrix*
*4 Bleed nipple*
*5 Air intake*
*6 Thermostatic valve*
*7 Control flap*
*8 Demister nozzle*

5 Unscrew the bolts which secure the two halves of the heater blower casing together. Eight of these bolts are accessible from within the engine compartment and two nuts from within the vehicle after the rubber floor mat has been pushed back, the free wheel control handle unscrewed and the two trim clips removed.
6 The front half of the casing can be pulled forward to enable the heater matrix to be withdrawn but take care not to damage the thermostatic bulb.
7 Installation of the matrix is a reversal of removal but ensure that each of the sealing rings on the two water pipe stubs is correctly located.
8 Refill the cooling system using the heater bleed screw as described in Chapter 2.

## 23 Heater thermostatic valve - removal and refitting

1 Drain the cooling system (Chapter 2) and disconnect the heater hoses from the heater matrix and the thermostatic valve.
2 Disconnect the throttle linkage at its flexible joint and then withdraw the throttle shaft from the thermostatic valve housing.
3 Unscrew and remove the four screws which secure the thermostatic valve housing to the blower motor casing.
4 Remove the heater matrix as described in the preceding Section.
5 Disconnect the thermostat coil by bending back the securing tabs on the inside of the heater casing. (Fig. 12.16)

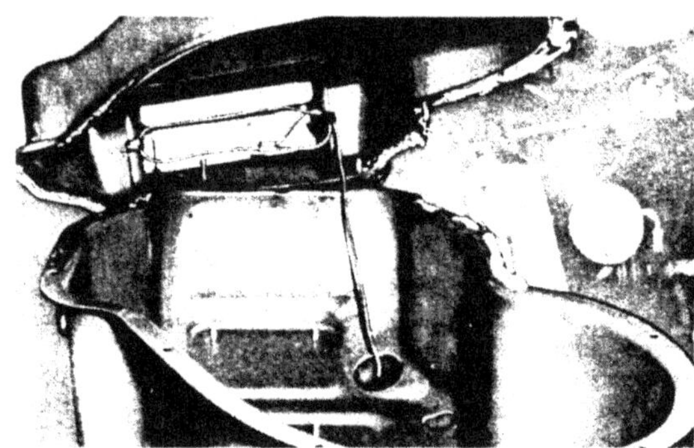

**Fig 12.16 Location of thermostatic valve coil**

6 The valve control and protective casing (two screws) can be withdrawn followed by the valve itself.
7 Installation is a reversal of removal. Refill and bleed the cooling system on completion.

# General repair procedures

Whenever servicing, repair or overhaul work is carried out on the car or its components, it is necessary to observe the following procedures and instructions. This will assist in carrying out the operation efficiently and to a professional standard of workmanship.

## *Joint mating faces and gaskets*

Where a gasket is used between the mating faces of two components, ensure that it is renewed on reassembly, and fit it dry unless otherwise stated in the repair procedure. Make sure that the mating faces are clean and dry with all traces of old gasket removed. When cleaning a joint face, use a tool which is not likely to score or damage the face, and remove any burrs or nicks with an oilstone or fine file.

Make sure that tapped holes are cleaned with a pipe cleaner, and keep them free of jointing compound if this is being used unless specifically instructed otherwise.

Ensure that all orifices, channels or pipes are clear and blow through them, preferably using compressed air.

## *Oil seals*

Whenever an oil seal is removed from its working location, either individually or as part of an assembly, it should be renewed.

The very fine sealing lip of the seal is easily damaged and will not seal if the surface it contacts is not completely clean and free from scratches, nicks or grooves. If the original sealing surface of the component cannot be restored, the component should be renewed.

Protect the lips of the seal from any surface which may damage them in the course of fitting. Use tape or a conical sleeve where possible. Lubricate the seal lips with oil before fitting and, on dual lipped seals, fill the space between the lips with grease.

Unless otherwise stated, oil seals must be fitted with their sealing lips toward the lubricant to be sealed.

Use a tubular drift or block of wood of the appropriate size to install the seal and, if the seal housing is shouldered, drive the seal down to the shoulder. If the seal housing is unshouldered, the seal should be fitted with its face flush with the housing top face.

## *Screw threads and fastenings*

Always ensure that a blind tapped hole is completely free from oil, grease, water or other fluid before installing the bolt or stud. Failure to do this could cause the housing to crack due to the hydraulic action of the bolt or stud as it is screwed in.

When tightening a castellated nut to accept a split pin, tighten the nut to the specified torque, where applicable, and then tighten further to the next split pin hole. Never slacken the nut to align a split pin hole unless stated in the repair procedure.

When checking or retightening a nut or bolt to a specified torque setting, slacken the nut or bolt by a quarter of a turn, and then retighten to the specified setting.

## *Locknuts, locktabs and washers*

Any fastening which will rotate against a component or housing in the course of tightening should always have a washer between it and the relevant component or housing.

Spring or split washers should always be renewed when they are used to lock a critical component such as a big-end bearing retaining nut or bolt.

Locktabs which are folded over to retain a nut or bolt should always be renewed.

Self-locking nuts can be reused in non-critical areas, providing resistance can be felt when the locking portion passes over the bolt or stud thread.

Split pins must always be replaced with new ones of the correct size for the hole.

## *Special tools*

Some repair procedures in this manual entail the use of special tools such as a press, two or three-legged pullers, spring compressors etc. Wherever possible, suitable readily available alternatives to the manufacturer's special tools are described, and are shown in use. In some instances, where no alternative is possible, it has been necessary to resort to the use of a manufacturer's tool and this has been done for reasons of safety as well as the efficient completion of the repair operation. Unless you are highly skilled and have a thorough understanding of the procedure described, never attempt to bypass the use of any special tool when the procedure described specifies its use. Not only is there a very great risk of personal injury, but expensive damage could be caused to the components involved.

# Safety first!

Professional motor mechanics are trained in safe working procedures. However enthusiastic you may be about getting on with the job in hand, do take the time to ensure that your safety is not put at risk. A moment's lack of attention can result in an accident, as can failure to observe certain elementary precautions.

There will always be new ways of having accidents, and the following points do not pretend to be a comprehensive list of all dangers; they are intended rather to make you aware of the risks and to encourage a safety-conscious approach to all work you carry out on your vehicle.

## *Essential DOs and DON'Ts*

**DON'T** start the engine without first ascertaining that the transmission is in neutral.

**DON'T** suddenly remove the filler cap from a hot cooling system – cover it with a cloth and release the pressure gradually first, or you may get scalded by escaping coolant.

**DON'T** attempt to drain oil until you are sure it has cooled sufficiently to avoid scalding you.

**DON'T** grasp any part of the engine, exhaust or silencer without first ascertaining that it is sufficiently cool to avoid burning you.

**DON'T** allow brake fluid or antifreeze to contact the machine's paintwork or plastic components.

**DON'T** syphon toxic liquids such as fuel, brake fluid or antifreeze by mouth, or allow them to remain on your skin.

**DON'T** inhale dust – it may be injurious to health (see *Asbestos* heading).

**DON'T** allow any spilt oil or grease to remain on the floor – wipe it up straight away, before someone slips on it.

**DON'T** use ill-fitting spanners or other tools which may slip and cause injury.

**DON'T** attempt to lift a heavy component which may be beyond your capability – get assistance.

**DON'T** rush to finish a job, or take unverified short cuts.

**DON'T** allow children or animals in or around an unattended vehicle.

**DON'T** inflate a tyre to a pressure above the recommended maximum. Apart from overstressing the carcase and wheel rim, in extreme cases the tyre may blow off forcibly.

**DO** ensure that the machine is supported securely at all times. This is especially important when the machine is blocked up to aid wheel or fork removal.

**DO** take care when attempting to slacken a stubborn nut or bolt. It is generally better to pull on a spanner, rather than push, so that if slippage occurs you fall away from the machine rather than on to it.

**DO** wear eye protection when using power tools such as drill, sander, bench grinder etc.

**DO** use a barrier cream on your hands prior to undertaking dirty jobs – it will protect your skin from infection as well as making the dirt easier to remove afterwards; but make sure your hands aren't left slippery. Note that long-term contact with used engine oil can be a health hazard.

**DO** keep loose clothing (cuffs, tie etc) and long hair well out of the way of moving mechanical parts.

**DO** remove rings, wristwatch etc, before working on the vehicle – especially the electrical system.

**DO** keep your work area tidy – it is only too easy to fall over articles left lying around.

**DO** exercise caution when compressing springs for removal or installation. Ensure that the tension is applied and released in a controlled manner, using suitable tools which preclude the possibility of the spring escaping violently.

**DO** ensure that any lifting tackle used has a safe working load rating adequate for the job.

**DO** get someone to check periodically that all is well, when working alone on the vehicle.

**DO** carry out work in a logical sequence and check that everything is correctly assembled and tightened afterwards.

**DO** remember that your vehicle's safety affects that of yourself and others. If in doubt on any point, get specialist advice.

**IF**, in spite of following these precautions, you are unfortunate enough to injure yourself, seek medical attention as soon as possible.

## *Asbestos*

Certain friction, insulating, sealing, and other products – such as brake linings, clutch linings, gaskets, etc – contain asbestos. *Extreme care must be taken to avoid inhalation of dust from such products since it is hazardous to health.* If in doubt, assume that they *do* contain asbestos.

## *Fire*

Remember at all times that petrol (gasoline) is highly flammable. Never smoke, or have any kind of naked flame around, when working on the vehicle. But the risk does not end there – a spark caused by an electrical short-circuit, by two metal surfaces contacting each other, by careless use of tools, or even by static electricity built up in your body under certain conditions, can ignite petrol vapour, which in a confined space is highly explosive.

Always disconnect the battery earth (ground) terminal before working on any part of the fuel or electrical system, and never risk spilling fuel on to a hot engine or exhaust.

It is recommended that a fire extinguisher of a type suitable for fuel and electrical fires is kept handy in the garage or workplace at all times. Never try to extinguish a fuel or electrical fire with water.

## *Fumes*

Certain fumes are highly toxic and can quickly cause unconsciousness and even death if inhaled to any extent. Petrol (gasoline) vapour comes into this category, as do the vapours from certain solvents such as trichloroethylene. Any draining or pouring of such volatile fluids should be done in a well ventilated area.

When using cleaning fluids and solvents, read the instructions carefully. Never use materials from unmarked containers – they may give off poisonous vapours.

Never run the engine of a motor vehicle in an enclosed space such as a garage. Exhaust fumes contain carbon monoxide which is extremely poisonous; if you need to run the engine, always do so in the open air or at least have the rear of the vehicle outside the workplace.

## *The battery*

Never cause a spark, or allow a naked light, near the vehicle's battery. It will normally be giving off a certain amount of hydrogen gas, which is highly explosive.

Always disconnect the battery earth (ground) terminal before working on the fuel or electrical systems.

If possible, loosen the filler plugs or cover when charging the battery from an external source. Do not charge at an excessive rate or the battery may burst.

Take care when topping up and when carrying the battery. The acid electrolyte, even when diluted, is very corrosive and should not be allowed to contact the eyes or skin.

If you ever need to prepare electrolyte yourself, always add the acid slowly to the water, and never the other way round. Protect against splashes by wearing rubber gloves and goggles.

## *Mains electricity*

When using an electric power tool, inspection light etc which works from the mains, always ensure that the appliance is correctly connected to its plug and that, where necessary, it is properly earthed (grounded). Do not use such appliances in damp conditions and, again, beware of creating a spark or applying excessive heat in the vicinity of fuel or fuel vapour.

## *Ignition HT voltage*

A severe electric shock can result from touching certain parts of the ignition system, such as the HT leads, when the engine is running or being cranked, particularly if components are damp or the insulation is defective. Where an electronic ignition system is fitted, the HT voltage is much higher and could prove fatal.

# Conversion factors

### *Length (distance)*

| | | | | | | |
|---|---|---|---|---|---|---|
| Inches (in) | X | 25.4 | = Millimetres (mm) | X | 0.0394 | = Inches (in) |
| Feet (ft) | X | 0.305 | = Metres (m) | X | 3.281 | = Feet (ft) |
| Miles | X | 1.609 | = Kilometres (km) | X | 0.621 | = Miles |

### *Volume (capacity)*

| | | | | | | |
|---|---|---|---|---|---|---|
| Cubic inches (cu in; $in^3$) | X | 16.387 | = Cubic centimetres (cc; $cm^3$) | X | 0.061 | = Cubic inches (cu in; $in^3$) |
| Imperial pints (Imp pt) | X | 0.568 | = Litres (l) | X | 1.76 | = Imperial pints (Imp pt) |
| Imperial quarts (Imp qt) | X | 1.137 | = Litres (l) | X | 0.88 | = Imperial quarts (Imp qt) |
| Imperial quarts (Imp qt) | X | 1.201 | = US quarts (US qt) | X | 0.833 | = Imperial quarts (Imp qt) |
| US quarts (US qt) | X | 0.946 | = Litres (l) | X | 1.057 | = US quarts (US qt) |
| Imperial gallons (Imp gal) | X | 4.546 | = Litres (l) | X | 0.22 | = Imperial gallons (Imp gal) |
| Imperial gallons (Imp gal) | X | 1.201 | = US gallons (US gal) | X | 0.833 | = Imperial gallons (Imp gal) |
| US gallons (US gal) | X | 3.785 | = Litres (l) | X | 0.264 | = US gallons (US gal) |

### *Mass (weight)*

| | | | | | | |
|---|---|---|---|---|---|---|
| Ounces (oz) | X | 28.35 | = Grams (g) | X | 0.035 | = Ounces (oz) |
| Pounds (lb) | X | 0.454 | = Kilograms (kg) | X | 2.205 | = Pounds (lb) |

### *Force*

| | | | | | | |
|---|---|---|---|---|---|---|
| Ounces-force (ozf; oz) | X | 0.278 | = Newtons (N) | X | 3.6 | = Ounces-force (ozf; oz) |
| Pounds-force (lbf; lb) | X | 4.448 | = Newtons (N) | X | 0.225 | = Pounds-force (lbf; lb) |
| Newtons (N) | X | 0.1 | = Kilograms-force (kgf; kg) | X | 9.81 | = Newtons (N) |

### *Pressure*

| | | | | | | |
|---|---|---|---|---|---|---|
| Pounds-force per square inch (psi; $lbf/in^2$; $lb/in^2$) | X | 0.070 | = Kilograms-force per square centimetre ($kgf/cm^2$; $kg/cm^2$) | X | 14.223 | = Pounds-force per square inch (psi; $lbf/in^2$; $lb/in^2$) |
| Pounds-force per square inch (psi; $lbf/in^2$; $lb/in^2$) | X | 0.068 | = Atmospheres (atm) | X | 14.696 | = Pounds-force per square inch (psi; $lbf/in^2$; $lb/in^2$) |
| Pounds-force per square inch (psi; $lbf/in^2$; $lb/in^2$) | X | 0.069 | = Bars | X | 14.5 | = Pounds-force per square inch (psi; $lbf/in^2$; $lb/in^2$) |
| Pounds-force per square inch (psi; $lbf/in^2$; $lb/in^2$) | X | 6.895 | = Kilopascals (kPa) | X | 0.145 | = Pounds-force per square inch (psi; $lbf/in^2$; $lb/in^2$) |
| Kilopascals (kPa) | X | 0.01 | = Kilograms-force per square centimetre ($kgf/cm^2$; $kg/cm^2$) | X | 98.1 | = Kilopascals (kPa) |
| Millibar (mbar) | X | 100 | = Pascals (Pa) | X | 0.01 | = Millibar (mbar) |
| Millibar (mbar) | X | 0.0145 | = Pounds-force per square inch (psi; $lbf/in^2$, $lb/in^2$) | X | 68.947 | = Millibar (mbar) |
| Millibar (mbar) | X | 0.75 | = Millimetres of mercury (mmHg) | X | 1.333 | = Millibar (mbar) |
| Millibar (mbar) | X | 1.40 | = Inches of water ($inH_2O$) | X | 0.714 | = Millibar (mbar) |
| Millimetres of mercury (mmHg) | X | 1.868 | = Inches of water ($inH_2O$) | X | 0.535 | = Millimetres of mercury (mmHg) |
| Inches of water ($inH_2O$) | X | 27.68 | = Pounds-force per square inch (psi, $lbf/in^2$, $lb/in^2$) | X | 0.036 | = Inches of water ($inH_2O$) |

### *Torque (moment of force)*

| | | | | | | |
|---|---|---|---|---|---|---|
| Pounds-force inches (lbf in; lb in) | X | 1.152 | = Kilograms-force centimetre (kgf cm; kg cm) | X | 0.868 | = Pounds-force inches (lbf in; lb in) |
| Pounds-force inches (lbf in; lb in) | X | 0.113 | = Newton metres (Nm) | X | 8.85 | = Pounds-force inches (lbf in; lb in) |
| Pounds-force inches (lbf in; lb in) | X | 0.083 | = Pounds-force feet (lbf ft; lb ft) | X | 12 | = Pounds-force inches (lbf in; lb in) |
| Pounds-force feet (lbf ft; lb ft) | X | 0.138 | = Kilograms-force metres (kgf m; kg m) | X | 7.233 | = Pounds-force feet (lbf ft; lb ft) |
| Pounds-force feet (lbf ft; lb ft) | X | 1.356 | = Newton metres (Nm) | X | 0.738 | = Pounds-force feet (lbf ft; lb ft) |
| Newton metres (Nm) | X | 0.102 | = Kilograms-force metres (kgf m; kg m) | X | 9.804 | = Newton metres (Nm) |

### *Power*

| | | | | | | |
|---|---|---|---|---|---|---|
| Horsepower (hp) | X | 745.7 | = Watts (W) | X | 0.0013 | = Horsepower (hp) |

### *Velocity (speed)*

| | | | | | | |
|---|---|---|---|---|---|---|
| Miles per hour (miles/hr; mph) | X | 1.609 | = Kilometres per hour (km/hr; kph) | X | 0.621 | = Miles per hour (miles/hr; mph) |

### *Fuel consumption**

| | | | | | | |
|---|---|---|---|---|---|---|
| Miles per gallon, Imperial (mpg) | X | 0.354 | = Kilometres per litre (km/l) | X | 2.825 | = Miles per gallon, Imperial (mpg) |
| Miles per gallon, US (mpg) | X | 0.425 | = Kilometres per litre (km/l) | X | 2.352 | = Miles per gallon, US (mpg) |

### *Temperature*

Degrees Fahrenheit = (°C x 1.8) + 32

Degrees Celsius (Degrees Centigrade; °C) = (°F - 32) x 0.56

**It is common practice to convert from miles per gallon (mpg) to litres/100 kilometres (l/100km), where mpg (Imperial) x l/100 km = 282 and mpg (US) x l/100 km = 235*

# Index